FRANKLIN D. ROOSEVELT

A Rendezvous with Destiny

Also by Frank Freidel

FRANKLIN D. ROOSEVELT
The Apprenticeship

FRANKLIN D. ROOSEVELT
The Ordeal

FRANKLIN D. ROOSEVELT
The Triumph

FRANKLIN D. ROOSEVELT
Launching the New Deal

FRANCIS LIEBER
Nineteenth-Century Liberal

THE SPLENDID LITTLE WAR

THE GOLDEN AGE OF AMERICAN HISTORY
(editor)

AMERICA IN THE TWENTIETH CENTURY

OVER THERE

F.D.R. AND THE SOUTH

THE PRESIDENTS OF THE UNITED STATES

OUR COUNTRY'S PRESIDENTS

UNION PAMPHLETS OF THE CIVIL WAR
(editor)

HARVARD GUIDE TO AMERICAN HISTORY
(co-editor)

Franklin Roosevelt

A Rendezvous With Destiny

By

FRANK FREIDEL

Published by American Political Biography Press

Newtown, CT

Published by
AMERICAN POLITICAL BIOGRAPHY PRESS

Library of Congress Control Number 2005934851
ISBN Number 978-0-945707-38-7

The dust jacket photo is from the Library of Congress
(Number USZ62-26759)

39 Boggs Hill,
Newtown, CT
06470-1971
Tel: (203) 270-9777 ✧ Fax: (203) 270-0091
E-Mail: APBPress@EarthLink.Net
www.apbpress.com

All publications of
AMERICAN POLITICAL BIOGRAPHY PRESS
Are dedicated to my wife
Ellen and our two children
Katherine and William II

This particular book is
Dedicated to:

Stephen & Barbara Pearlman
and
Col. Jack (Ret.) & Renay Bassi

Frank Freidel
dedicated his book

For
Madeleine
and for
Christine and Irene

CONTENTS

1 The Upbringing of a Genteel Reformer 3
2 A Progressive Apprenticeship 16
3 Years of Testing 33
4 The Political Comeback: Governor of New York 49
5 Winning the Presidency 63
6 The Interregnum Crisis 79
7 The Hundred Days 92
8 A Tightrope Foreign Policy 106
9 Installing the New Deal Programs 119
10 The Failure of Bootstrap Recovery 130
11 A New Deal for the Dispossessed 142
12 A Low-Key Interlude 152
13 The Fight for the Reform Program 160
14 Seeking Security Short of War 171
15 Threats from Left and Right 185
16 The People Approve 195
17 The Good Neighbor Promotes Hemispheric Defense 209
18 The Struggle to Transform the Supreme Court 221
19 New Dealer with Brakes On 240
20 Quarantine or Appeasement 258
21 Administrative Reform and Attempted Party Purge 273
22 A Powerless Witness to Munich 289
23 Girding for Hitler's Onslaught 305
24 The German Blitz and American Peril 321
25 The Third Term Campaign in Time of Crisis 341
26 Arsenal of Democracy 358

27 Escalating Pressure on Japan and Germany 377
28 To the Brink of War 391
29 A Day of Infamy: The Shift to Action 404
30 Final Arbiter over War Production 417
31 The Struggle to Contain Inflation 429
32 Striking Back amid Disasters 441
33 Into North Africa 453
34 Victories — and the Shadow of Stalin 465
35 The Conference at Tehran 477
36 Doctor Win-the-War 494
37 Declining Health and Escalating Politics 507
38 A Roosevelt-Truman Ticket 525
39 To the Pacific and Quebec 539
40 A Fourth Term 556
41 Yalta 577
42 Roosevelt's Triumph and Tragedy 593
Abbreviations and Short Titles 609
Chapter Notes 611
Bibliographical Note 663
Acknowledgments 665
Index 667

FRANKLIN D. ROOSEVELT

A Rendezvous with Destiny

Chapter 1

THE UPBRINGING OF A GENTEEL REFORMER

IF, as Franklin D. Roosevelt's parents had wished, he had grown up to become another Hudson River Valley aristocrat, managing the family estates, meeting civic and charitable obligations, and serving as vestryman of his church, there would have seemed nothing memorable in his rearing. It would have been of no wider interest than that of his older half-brother, James Roosevelt Roosevelt, an estimable socialite. Indeed, Franklin Roosevelt did mature to fill all the expected functions, to become, as one of his most ascerbic critics called him, a country squire, but with a difference.

Roosevelt came of age with firm roots in both the reform movements of the progressive era and the genteel Grover Cleveland conservatism of the late nineteenth century. He was in the tradition of both the social justice movement and the mugwumps. His wife, Eleanor Roosevelt, impatient for the quick righting of wrongs, was well aware of the conservative side of her husband. Once during World War II when the Roosevelts were bidding farewell to Prime Minister Winston Churchill, Roosevelt commented as they waved that Churchill was hopelessly Victorian. Mrs. Roosevelt thought to herself, "You too, Franklin, are much in the nineteenth century."[1]

Eleanor Roosevelt was correct; in some ways Roosevelt was a nineteenth-century figure like Disraeli and the Tory aristocrats in Victorian England, so certain of themselves that they dared undertake reforms. He was indeed anchored in the attitudes and traditions of the Roosevelts and the Delanos during the years of his upbringing, the last two decades of the nineteenth century. These views, with an emphasis upon the obligations of the well-born to aid those less fortunate than themselves, served as a base of belief. In his case they also gave him the self-assurance to innovate daringly on the premise that he was thus implementing the fundamentals he had learned at home and in his schooling.

Roosevelt, optimistic by nature, never doubted the mission of the American people and their great destiny. American history was so immediate and personal to him that he frequently illustrated it with stories of his forebears. They were patricians living on a comfortable estate at Hyde Park, New York. Together with their numerous relatives and friends they were the Hudson River counterpart to the landed gentry of England, secure in the financial means and social standing that had been theirs for generations. Roosevelt grew up with a strong sense of their lasting role in the community and the nation.

The Roosevelts early became established as successful merchants in New York City. The first of them, Claes Martenszen Van Rosenvelt, who arrived from the Netherlands in the seventeenth century, was, together with his son Nicholas, the common ancestor of Franklin Roosevelt and of Theodore Roosevelt and his niece Eleanor. The Hyde Park line began with the third generation, Jacobus Roosevelt, upon whose Dutch Bible Franklin D. Roosevelt took his oath of office as president.[2]

Because the original spelling of the name was Van Rosenvelt (from the rose field), questions arose in both friendly and anti-Semitic circles whether the family was originally Jewish. In 1935, Roosevelt replied in response to one query, "In the dim distant past they may have been Jews or Catholics or Protestants — what I am more interested in is whether they were good citizens and believers in God — I hope they were both."[3]

By the time of the American Revolution the Roosevelts were prosperous sugar refiners. Roosevelt, in 1939 when accused of being pro-British and pro-French, resorted to family tradition to try to prove otherwise, "that the Roosevelt family, in the West Indian sugar business was compelled to contend many years against the British and French interests in those Islands — and that is what made them revolutionists rather than Tories in 1776." So far as the French were concerned, Roosevelt was not being accurate — which again makes the story typical of his intermingling of family and history.[4]

Roosevelt was rightly proud of the most notable of his ancestors, Isaac Roosevelt (1726–1794), who was one of the first New York State senators, responsible for the issuance of the state's paper money, president of the Bank of New York, and a Federalist who served in the convention that ratified the Constitution. A fine Gilbert Stuart portrait of Isaac hung in the living room at Hyde Park. Still, Roosevelt would have liked Isaac to have been a bit less conservative. In his last days, while working on a Jefferson Day address, he tried in vain to find a link between Isaac and Thomas Jefferson.[5]

Although Roosevelt was well aware that his ancestry was predominantly English, more so than that of Theodore Roosevelt, he liked to emphasize his Dutchness. It was good politics. Being Dutch implied economic enterprise, resourcefulness, good citizenship, and democracy. It also stood for stubbornness, which Roosevelt possessed aplenty, and led him in time to refer to himself in private as an "old Dutchman." He was active in the Holland Society and the Netherlands-America Foundation, and was responsible for a renaissance of Dutch Colonial architecture in Hyde Park and its vicinity. On his last day of campaigning in 1944, speaking in Kingston, New York, he once more expressed pride in his descent from one of the original settlers who had served in the local militia.[6]

In the nineteenth century, the Roosevelts moved to lands on the Hudson River about Poughkeepsie, where they assumed the role of country gentlemen. It was also the pattern of life of Warren Delano, who resided across the river near Newburgh and whose daughter Sara married James Roosevelt. Both Warren Delano and James Roosevelt maintained a serene, well-ordered existence within their families. Whether they were at home or traveling abroad, they seemed insulated against the pressures and unpleasantness of the everyday world.

Nevertheless, that world did absorb Warren Delano and James Roosevelt. Both were engaged in large enterprises. Delano won, lost, and rewon fortunes in the China trade, dealing in opium, and then became a heavy investor in Appalachian coal mines. James Roosevelt also invested in coal, but was primarily involved in railroads, serving for years as the vice president of the Delaware and Hudson, one of the coal routes. He too undertook daring business ventures, but less successfully than Delano. After the Civil War he became president of the first American holding company, which combined a number of lines south of Washington into what became the Southern Railway. It was a victim of the depression of the 1870s. Another of James Roosevelt's speculations was a company seeking to build a canal across Nicaragua, a project that involved much lobbying in Washington. It too failed, but even during the depression years of the 1890s the Roosevelt family still had adequate money; their life went on with no discernible change or outside intrusions.

Nor did the social status of the Roosevelts depend upon the size of their fortune. James Roosevelt's estate at the time of his death was about $300,000, while Cornelius Vanderbilt, who sat with him on the board of the Delaware and Hudson, left $72,500,000, yet the Roosevelts felt in no way socially inferior to the Vanderbilts. On the other hand, the contrast between the Roosevelt home with its rather simple comfort, and the nearby Vanderbilt mansion, as ostentatiously elegant as a royal chateau on the Loire, helps explain why Franklin D. Roosevelt never thought of himself as wealthy.[7]

Into this setting Franklin D. Roosevelt was born, January 30, 1882. He was a healthy, happy youngster, the focus of his parents' attention. Sara Delano Roosevelt, twenty-six years younger than her husband, concentrated her considerable maternal energies upon this lone child of hers. Although there were servants and a nursemaid, she herself bathed and dressed her baby, and breast-fed him for almost a year. He was eight years old before he was permitted to take a bath alone. Until he was in his twenties, she kept the most minute diary record of his activities. His upbringing absorbed her, as indeed later she was to lavish her maternal warmth upon her grandchildren and great-grandchildren. But she did not smother him. Franklin did not grow up a momma's boy. In part this may have been because his parents were from time to time gone on long trips, when he was under the care of his nurse or his governess. Even more it may have been because, strong-minded and vital though she was, Sara expected the men around her to be strong also. She deferred in all matters to her husband, and James Roosevelt played a considerable part in the upbringing of his son.

James Roosevelt, middle-aged, and devoting only a minor part of his time to his profession, often spent his afternoons with Franklin, taking him sledding, fishing, and sailing. Franklin also accompanied his father on the rounds of the estate, learning about the management of land and the nurture of trees. These were to be lifelong interests. Also, from time to time Franklin traveled with his parents in the Roosevelt private railroad car, rolling along slowly on inspection trips. It was the mode of land transportation he was always to prefer.

Until he was fourteen, Franklin D. Roosevelt lived a life of well-ordered routine, spending most of his time with his parents. He rose at seven, ate breakfast at eight, had lessons in the morning and afternoon, and enjoyed prescribed periods of recreation. From one governess he began to learn German when he was only six; from another he obtained a grounding in French that remained with him all of his life.

It was a sequestered life, in which his playmates were almost always countless cousins and the children from neighboring estates. It was also a highly routine existence, even in summers at Campobello Island, New Brunswick. Only once did Roosevelt ask for release from his routine, and when he returned from the day of freedom his parents permitted, he made no comment. Whatever loneliness or rebelliousness he may have occasionally felt he kept to himself, but that was in the family pattern. Twice in his teens when he suffered painful accidents, a gash in the head and the loss of a tooth, he tried to conceal them in order not to alarm his ailing father. The habit of being private about both his illnesses and his thoughts became embedded and lifelong. From his boyhood on, he wrote ingratiating letters to his parents, actually primarily to his mother, telling her what he knew she wanted to hear. While Sara Roosevelt more and more built her life around her son, he early learned to preserve some degree of independence.

Outwardly it was a happy, privileged existence. He had a passion for sailing, and became an accomplished skipper of the 51-foot *Half Moon;* in the winter there was iceboating on the Hudson. On his eleventh birthday he received a gun and began the large collection of birds that stands inside the entrance to the Hyde Park house. He read widely, and he added to the stamp collection that his mother had started as a girl.

Nine times, the first when he was three, there were interludes in Europe. He was taken to the English manors of friends and relatives, to the French Riviera, where he saw the exiled emperor of Brazil, and frequently to German watering places where his father took the cure. The summer he was nine his parents enrolled him for six weeks in a *Volksschule* at Bad Nauheim in the hope of improving his German. He was particularly impressed with the course in military geography that the new kaiser had introduced in German schools. During World War II he would reminisce that he had witnessed the growth of German militarism, but of course at his age had no awareness of the tensions and arms race that quarrels over empire were generating. He wrote a friend that he was in school "with a lot of little mickies . . . and I like it very much." The Europe he knew was that of the elite and seemed so placid and secure, he remembered, that visitors needed no passports and his father could meet any eventuality with a handful of gold coins he kept in the bottom of his trunk in case of an emergency.

The Roosevelts kept their son equally sheltered from the upheavals and excitement of the depression wracking the United States in the 1890s — the populist revolt sweeping the prairie wheat fields and the cotton South, Coxey's Army of unemployed marching to Washington to demand work relief, and the smashing of the Pullman strike. In the summer of 1896, while William Jennings Bryan was campaigning for silver inflation to aid the farmers, young Roosevelt, accompanied by a tutor, was on a bicycle tour of Germany.

Thus until the age of fourteen Roosevelt was reared in the sheltered world of the novels of Edith Wharton and Henry James. If there was something of the themes of Frank Norris in the careers of his grandfather and father in the China trade, railroading, and development of coalfields, he was not aware of it. He was so little in touch with the main flow of American life that he spoke English with a trace of foreign accent, and could not pronounce correctly the name of a city some miles to the north, Schenectady.[8]

In the fall of 1896 a change came. Roosevelt began his education — at Groton School and in time Harvard University. While he continued to live the life of a patrician youth, remote from even middle-class America, he did become aware of the great issues being debated in the United States, and of the stirrings of reform that soon culminated in progressivism.

If President Roosevelt in some ways resembled the Tory reformers of Victorian England, it was the impress upon him of Rector Endicott Peabody of Groton School. He always credited Peabody with being one of the major influences of his life, leading him toward Christian service to the nation and those less fortunate than himself. Peabody, the son of a wealthy financier, had himself been educated in England, and in the 1880s tried to re-create in New England the equivalent of Thomas Arnold's Rugby to educate boys from leading families. He established an Episcopal school in which he combined a classical curriculum with Spartan living and strenuous sports. His emphasis was upon physical and moral vigor in the pursuit of religious and civic responsibilities. Peabody's ideal was Charles Kingsley, one of the founders of the Christian Socialist movement in England, and a model Tory social reformer. Peabody sought similar goals at Groton through his own exhortations, those of his staff, and even, on occasion, those of his glamorous friend Theodore Roosevelt. Peabody declared in 1894, "If some Groton boys do not enter political life and do something for our land it won't be because they have not been urged."

Despite Peabody's exhortations, wearers of the old school tie, whether from Groton or its several Episcopal counterparts, did not take over the government of the United States as had the graduates of elite English public schools that of Britain. By the mid-thirties only ten of the one thousand Groton alumni listed government as their occupation, but those ten included Bronson Cutting, Francis Biddle, Joseph Grew, Sumner Welles, Averell Harriman, Dean Acheson, and above all, Franklin Roosevelt.

At the time Roosevelt was a student at Groton, there was scant indication that he would become the most famous exemplar of Peabody's teachings. He was undistinguished, and indeed until his last year rather inconspicuous. Since he had entered two years late, friendships had already been formed among his classmates, who tended to look with some suspicion on this new boy with his strange accent, whose parents sent him *Punch* and the *Spectator*. Roosevelt concentrated upon staying out of trouble with his classmates in order to avoid their ferocious hazing. He soon acquired their accent with its broad "a" and inaudible "r," and retained it for life. Conforming to the Spartan routine and rigorous schedule of studies caused him no problem. He was a model in deportment as he had been at home, until he realized the other students suspected him of deficiency in school spirit. Thereafter he cautiously acquired a respectable number of "black marks." Sports were the only acceptable route to success, but Roosevelt, who suffered cuts and bruises, was too light to excel in football. Golf and tennis, in which he was outstanding, did not count. To have been conspicuous in academic work also could have brought the disapproval of peers, but Roosevelt did win the Latin prize and during his four years at Groton completed the first year of his college courses. Although he was not very popular, he managed to avoid trouble, overcame his shyness, and participated vigorously in student activities. He learned how to get along with his peers.

By his last year in the school, he had made some good friends and achieved sufficient standing among his classmates to be more relaxed. One classmate remembered, "He developed an independent, cocky manner and at times became very argumentative and sarcastic. In an argument he always liked to take the side opposite to that maintained by those with whom he was talking. This irritated the other boys considerably." On the other hand, the artist George Biddle, several years younger, recalled, "He was gray-eyed, cool, self-possessed, intelligent, and had the warmest, most friendly and understanding smile."

Few of Roosevelt's classmates could have realized how deeply Peabody and the masters impressed him with their advocacy of strenuous Christianity. Roosevelt attended Peabody's confirmation class. He accompanied one of the masters, the Reverend Sherrard Billings, to neighboring towns where Billings preached or paid charitable visits, and he joined the Missionary Society, which helped underprivileged boys at a summer camp and a club in Boston. One winter it was his responsibility to help care for an old black woman, bringing her provisions and fuel. Roosevelt's religion, like that of Peabody, was simple and unquestioning, rather than based upon complex theological argument. As president, he was to hold private church services before his inauguration and on other momentous occasions. Whenever possible he obtained Peabody to conduct the services.

While Roosevelt was at Groton he also first fell under the spell of his remote cousin Theodore Roosevelt. While Peabody's exhortations to service carried religious overtones, those of TR gave promise of excitement. "After supper tonight Cousin Theodore gave us a splendid talk on his adventures when he was on the Police Board." Franklin was so dazzled that he accepted Theodore's invitation to spend the Fourth of July at Oyster Bay, although he knew his mother would probably not approve.

Young Franklin would have liked to seek adventure and public service through a career in the navy. He loved ships and the sea. As a boy he had pored over old whaling logbooks in the Delano family attic at Fairhaven, Massachusetts, and was fascinated by his grandfather's adventures in the China trade. By the 1890s, an imperialist age, the modernized navy offered more challenges. Already he was reading Alfred T. Mahan's books extolling sea power, and cited them in a debate at Groton. When the Spanish-American War broke out, he plotted with friends to run away to Boston and enlist in the navy, but an attack of scarlet fever ended his dream. His parents frustrated his wish to attend Annapolis and become a naval officer. They decreed that he should go to Harvard and then law school to prepare to manage the family affairs. Already Roosevelt's plans for his future went much further. The Reverend Billings, writing in an era before inflation of recommendations, informed the Harvard admissions officer: "F. D. Roosevelt is a fellow of *exceptional ability* and *high character*. . . . He hopes to go into public life, and will shape his work at Cambridge with that end in view."[9]

While Groton gave Roosevelt an impetus toward public service, Harvard provided him with some of the ideas he would bring to it. As was true of the young socialites in that era of the gentlemanly C grade, scholarship was near the bottom of priorities. Nevertheless, Roosevelt enrolled in substantial courses, many of them in economics and history, in which he was exposed to the new progressive concepts of the role of government in regulating the economy. He became a personal friend of Abram Piatt Andrew, one of the economics professors, who was later assistant secretary of the Treasury in the Taft administration.

Yet it would be easy to exaggerate the influence of the brilliant Harvard faculty upon Roosevelt. The few samples of his undergraduate writing that have survived are mediocre and uncritical. Extracurricular activities and social life were so much more important to Roosevelt that the wonder is his receiving passing grades, not his failure to dazzle his professors as did Walter Lippmann a few years later. The influence of Frederick Jackson Turner, exponent of the role of the frontier in American history, could not have been very marked even though Roosevelt did enroll in his famous course. For the first six weeks, Roosevelt was on a cruise of the Caribbean with his mother.

A greater ideological influence than Harvard was Theodore Roosevelt. The Hyde Park Roosevelts had put aside their traditional Democratic allegiance to cheer for TR when he ran for governor of New York in the fall of 1896. In 1900, when TR ran for vice president with William McKinley, Franklin joined the Harvard Republican Club and marched eight miles in a torchlight procession. In 1904, he cast his first ballot in a presidential election for Theodore Roosevelt.

What Franklin D. Roosevelt learned at Harvard that would be of later use in politics came less from the classroom than from extracurricular activities. He made friends more rapidly than at Groton, and while he still accepted the Groton standards, made a far wider circle of acquaintances than most of his social peers. A single disappointment rankled him; he failed to win election to the Porcellian, the most prestigious club, probably because of the scandalous behavior of his nephew, a Harvard student who married a dance-hall girl from the New York Tenderloin district. Eleanor Roosevelt thought the disappointment impelled him to be more democratic.

Whatever Roosevelt's deficiencies in sports, he began to emerge as a student leader, winning offices with regularity. His major undergraduate achievement was to become president for a semester of the *Harvard Crimson*. He wrote all the editorials, and for some years liked to describe himself as a former newspaperman, who through his editorials had fought for reforms at Harvard. That was a romantic exaggeration, typical of Roosevelt. Rather, he had drawn unfavorable comment for the extremity of his editorial demands upon the football team, and had sought no reform more drastic than the laying of boards on the muddy paths between Harvard buildings. There was no need for Roosevelt to enhance reality; he had functioned creditably as a college editor of that era. Shortly afterward, while in law school, Roosevelt modestly wrote that the major achievement of his editorship was a "signal triumph over the business end," cutting its share of the profits from a third to a fifth. He was competitive, eager to be a leader, and like many future politicians had begun to practice some of the fundamentals. In his geniality in dealing with the *Crimson* printers, a classmate recalled, he displayed "a kind of frictionless command."[10]

Roosevelt marshaled all of his charm in 1904 to win the hand of his distant cousin Eleanor Roosevelt. It was the sort of romance Sara Roosevelt's old friend Edith Wharton might have written about. Roosevelt had always had girls around him in the incessant round of parties and social functions of his growing up, and at Harvard had even for a while been serious about a North Shore girl, Alice Sohier. Gradually, beginning in 1902, he saw more and more of the daughter of his godfather, Elliott Roosevelt, who was also the niece of his idol, Theodore Roosevelt.

Eleanor Roosevelt was a serious, high-minded teenager. She had been orphaned at ten and then had lived with a neurotic aunt and alcoholic uncle in the household of a stern grandmother. It was a most unhappy upbringing. She thought of herself as an ugly duckling, when in fact she was a willowy, animated beauty. At school in England she had been a devoted student and a leader among her classmates. At eighteen in New York City she was already committed to the social justice movement, teaching at the Rivington Street Settlement House and investigating women's working conditions for the Consumers' League. Late in her final illness, she recounted with pride to friends how she had arranged for Franklin to meet her first at one, then another tenement on the lower East Side, thus causing him to witness conditions that he said he had never known existed.[11]

Part of the attraction between Eleanor and Franklin Roosevelt was their noble aspirations. Part was desire for a different life from what they had known growing up. Franklin, an only child, had frightened off Alice Sohier, whom he had earlier courted, by telling her he wanted six children. Eleanor hoped for the stability she had lacked in her family and had not found since returning from school in England. In tears she had lamented to Corinne Roosevelt Robinson, "Auntie, I have no home." The Roosevelts both had firm goals in life and already were showing signs of the qualities of intelligence and leadership that would make some of the goals attainable. Eleanor Roosevelt would have preferred to return to Allenwood School in England, where she was the favorite of the headmistress, Mlle. Marie Souvestre, to prepare for teaching or social service. Since that was impossible, she was willing to subordinate her career aspirations to become a wife and mother. At that time in her circles to have undertaken otherwise would have been almost unthinkable.[12]

These hopes and dreams must have come into the earnest discourse between the Roosevelts when, while visiting Groton one Sunday afternoon in the fall of 1903, they plighted their troth. Franklin noted in his diary in a simple cipher, "After lunch I have a never to be forgotten walk to the river with my darling." All Eleanor could recall much later was his telling her that with her help he could achieve something someday. She replied, "Why me? I am plain. I have little to bring you." Certainly she dreamed of the eternal love that had not come to her unhappy parents. She quoted to him from a poem of Elizabeth Barrett Browning:

Unless you can swear, "For life, for death!"
Oh fear to call it loving!

Several days later, Eleanor commented to Franklin in a letter: "I wondered if it meant 'for life, for death' to you at first but I know it does now. . . . I can only wait & long for Sunday when I shall tell you all I feel I cannot write."[13]

In the politics of reform, the Roosevelts were to achieve all, and more, than they could have dreamed. In personal relationships there were to be the problems that remain when romance gives way to reality. Franklin, a strong, stubborn, secretive person, met his match in Eleanor, equally strong and stubborn but forthright. For all their high ideals they were to have difficulty in communicating with each other, especially concerning Franklin's mother.

Sara Delano Roosevelt, single-minded in her maternal devotion, did not take well to the news of the engagement. She had lost her husband in 1900, and had spent the next two winters in Boston to be near Franklin. She had hoped Franklin would follow the example of her father, who had not married until he was thirty-three and had made his mark. Franklin was adamant, and in the end she capitulated, taking in Eleanor as though she were an additional child to protect.

Franklin and Eleanor Roosevelt were married on St. Patrick's Day, 1905, in New York City. Theodore Roosevelt gave away the bride, and immediately after the ceremony became the center of all attention, including that of the newlyweds, as he held forth on his exciting exploits as president. Eleanor continued to feel put in a shadow by her new mother-in-law. Sara's wedding present was a New York town house opening into one of hers, for which she selected all the furnishings. A few weeks after they moved in, Eleanor wept as she sat at the dressing table Sara had selected. "When my bewildered young husband asked me what on earth was the matter with me, I said I did not like to live in a house which was not in any way mine, one that I had done nothing about and which did not represent the way I wanted to live."[14]

The house at Hyde Park was no different, except that by the time Eleanor saw it, Sara had turned the entrance room into a sort of shrine to Franklin, displaying his splendid collection of stuffed birds and a three-quarter-length seated statue of young Franklin that she had commissioned a popular sculptor, Prince Paul Troubetzkoy, to execute. Roosevelt explained to guests during World War II that Troubetzkoy had "for some odd reason stopped just below the knees." The guests thought this curious truncation symbolic and sadly prophetic. The house held no charm for Eleanor. Sara, who always presided, assigned no fixed place for Eleanor at the dining table or in the living room. Upstairs, in later years, it was Sara's bedroom, not Eleanor's, which was next to Franklin's. The house never contained anything that Eleanor considered her own.[15]

Seeking love, Eleanor was submissive, acting the part of a dutiful daughter-in-law, but suffering acutely. By the 1930s her feelings were erupting in bitter words that she wrote, then did not publish, about her mother-in-law: "She determined to bend the marriage to the way she wanted it to be. What she wanted was to hold on to Franklin and his children; she wanted them to grow as she wished. As it turned out, Franklin's children were more my mother-in-law's children than they were mine."[16]

Sara Roosevelt, as her descendants and nephews and nieces attest, was warm and caring with the younger members of the family, though sometimes generous to a fault and disruptive of their parents' discipline.

Franklin seemed oblivious to Eleanor's discomfort. It baffled him, but he did not seem to give it much thought. The remarkable sensitivity that he came to develop in the field of politics remained atrophied within his own household.

For some years Eleanor was a withdrawn housewife, occupied with the routines of household and social activities, bearing baby after baby. A daughter, Anna, arrived in 1906, and five sons between 1907 and 1916: James, a first Franklin, Jr., who died of pneumonia when he was eighteen months old, then Elliott, Franklin, Jr., and John. Eleanor found little opportunity to pursue her dreams of social justice.

Franklin also, for several years, seemed destined for little other than a quite ordinary career as a socialite corporation lawyer. He had entered Columbia University Law School in the fall of 1904, squeezing classwork into a full social calendar with less than happy results. Although the law faculty was one of the most distinguished in the nation, the professors elicited little response from Roosevelt. When in the spring of his third year he passed his bar examinations, he did not bother to finish his courses and take his LL.B. degree.

The following three years were fallow ones for Roosevelt. He worked without much enthusiasm as a clerk in one of the leading Wall Street firms of corporation lawyers: Carter, Ledyard and Milburn, counsel for Standard Oil and American Tobacco in the antitrust suits against them. Despite his worship of TR, the supposed trust-buster, Franklin D. Roosevelt seemed undisturbed, and indeed toyed with the idea of writing a sympathetic novel about a self-made Chicago businessman, rather like William Dean Howells' *The Rise of Silas Lapham*.

What captured Roosevelt's interest were not the major corporate suits but the petty cases involving claims in municipal courts. He became managing clerk in charge of cases of this kind. Roosevelt not only enjoyed the give-and-take of matching wits with opponents in the small courts, but also demonstrated compassion as he learned first-hand about the problems of poverty. Later, with some embellishment of the facts he said that at Harvard he had through social service work "learned enough about the poorer classes, the people who are having a desperately hard time making a living, so that I knew their language and their way of thinking," and that this "helped me a lot in my first law job . . . [when I] had to appear in two-by-four cases in the municipal courts."

There was no future in handling these small cases, but they did help Roosevelt to learn how to get along with the common man, a knowledge vital to success in politics. He decided to turn toward the excitement of politics rather than the dullness and security of a career in corporate law. The urgings of Theodore Roosevelt, whom the young Roosevelts had seen at the White House from time to time, with his repeated emphasis upon public service, had much to do with the decision. One day, sitting at his rolltop desk, Franklin D. Roosevelt began speculating aloud about his future. One of his fellow clerks, Grenville Clark, later recalled: "I remember him saying with engaging frankness that he wasn't going to practice law forever, that he intended to run for office at the first opportunity, and that he wanted to be and thought he had a very real chance to be President."[17]

Chapter 2

A PROGRESSIVE APPRENTICESHIP

ROOSEVELT SERVED a long and varied political apprenticeship in the culminating years of the Progressive Era and in the First World War. His first enthusiasm had been for Theodore Roosevelt; his early years of notable service were in the administration of Woodrow Wilson. Both these strong presidents in their personalities, their ideologies, and their political strategies made an enduring impression upon him. He was to incorporate in the New Deal much of TR's New Nationalism and more of Wilson's New Freedom. It is even possible that at heart he always remained more a Progressive than a New Dealer.

The social and political ideas that Roosevelt brought to politics from his upbringing were a further ingredient in his thinking. Some traces of Victorian conservatism persisted. In its American version it was more puritanical than in England, involving a strict social code among the elite, and, as emphasized at Rector Peabody's Groton School, a strenuous Christian effort to do good. In American politics that effort embodied the reform drive in the Democratic party, the Mugwump movement of the 1880s with its emphasis upon states' rights and small government, the purging of corruption, and the maintenance of a laissez-faire economy. The ideal leader of the Mugwumps and reform Democrats of the 1880s and 1890s was Grover Cleveland. As a young man, Roosevelt liked to tell audiences how when he was a small boy his father had taken him to see Cleveland at the White House. The sad, worn president told the lad he hoped he would not have the misfortune to grow up to become president.

In contrast there was the positive, optimistic approach of the Progressives. Theodore Roosevelt believed in using to the utmost the constitutional power of the president to restrain foreign threats, regulate powerful monopolies, preserve natural resources, and bring social justice to those suffering from exploitation, poverty, and disease. This strong use of government was for the most part appealing to Franklin, especially when its exponent was the figure he now called "Uncle Ted." After describing his encounter with the dolorous Cleveland, Franklin told an audience in 1914 how in contrast at the White House he had heard someone ask Theodore Roosevelt how he liked being president. Imitating the "Teddy" grimace, Franklin gave the answer, "Ripping, simply ripping!"[1]

There was no question which presidential style appealed to young Franklin Roosevelt. Entering politics in a Democratic party only uncertainly moving toward progressivism, he seemed for some years to be rather hazy in his ideology, but he was firm in his enthusiasm for energetic leadership.

Roosevelt's political education owed little to the classroom and much to his trial-and-error practice. As president, in 1941 he looked back and commented to a group of teachers that he wished his schooling had been more practical. He had become a full-fledged lawyer without ever having stepped into a courtroom or a county clerk's office. He was rather skeptical of theory, remarking to the teachers that he had always claimed that there was no such thing as a proven system of economics: "I took economics courses in college for four years, and everything that I was taught was wrong. The economics of the beginning of this century are completely out of date. Why? Experience. . . . We are groping."[2]

In the beginning, Roosevelt's interest in politics was applied. Although he probably never read John Dewey, he was a strong advocate of learning through doing. Just as he felt he had begun his practice of the law by entering a courtroom, so his career in politics began by attending a picnic held by the Dutchess County Democrats. "On that joyous occasion of clams and sauerkraut and real beer I made my first speech," he once recalled. It was probably not much of a speech, but the politicians liked him. He was so eager to run for office that he accepted the 1910 nomination for the state senate, although he was warned he had no better than one chance in five of winning.[3]

Roosevelt entered politics as a Democrat because his branch of the family had always been Democrats, and for the more compelling reason that it was the Democratic party which nominated him. He was fearful only that he might offend Theodore Roosevelt, who was heavily involved that fall in New York politics, and through an intermediary obtained TR's approval. TR thought Franklin a fine fellow, but wished he were a Republican.[4]

Actually, Theodore Roosevelt's intervention in New York politics made

1910 a far from hopeless year for Franklin D. Roosevelt, although he was running for a state senate seat that had been won only once by the Democrats since the emergence of the Republican party. Farmers and Progressives within the Republican party were becoming increasingly restless over the policies of President William Howard Taft and the Old Guard Republicans in Washington, and of the Republican boss in New York State. Theodore Roosevelt and his followers succeeded in obtaining the nomination of the progressive Henry L. Stimson for governor of New York; the Republican boss and his followers reciprocated by doing little to prevent a Democratic victory in November.[5]

Franklin D. Roosevelt spent four weeks campaigning strenuously, breaking precedent by touring the district in an automobile, a red Maxwell touring car. At first he was rather wooden in his gestures and hesitating in his remarks. When the Republican newspaper in Poughkeepsie gibed at him for his "high talk," Roosevelt drafted a letter of protest that he tried to find some Republican to sign and send to the paper. The letter indicated how sensitive he was to such criticism: "What he says is always simple and to the point, and he is the last person in the world to be called condescending. He is less like a snob than any one I know."[6]

At the outset of one speech Roosevelt remarked, "I'm not Teddy." He said a little boy told him he knew he wasn't because he didn't show his teeth. It was a more acute remark than he realized; far from showing his teeth, Franklin confined himself to being ingratiating. He stood "squarely on the issue of honesty and economy and efficiency in our State Senate." That was sufficient in 1910. There was a national Democratic groundswell, which carried Woodrow Wilson by a respectable plurality, well ahead of the Democratic ticket.[7]

In January, 1911, Roosevelt, about to turn twenty-nine, entered the New York State Senate. From the outset he won newspaper attention because of his name. Within a few weeks he was one of the most conspicuous members of the legislature because of his dramatic actions. In his campaign he had stood above all for clean government and opposition to the bosses, as had his Democratic father and his friends in their earlier support of Samuel J. Tilden and Cleveland. It was the clean government issue that won him notice in Albany. New York still elected United States senators through the legislature, and voters had scarcely realized that in electing a Democratic legislature in 1910 they were mandating a Democratic senator. By the time Roosevelt arrived in Albany, it had become clear that the boss of New York City's Tammany Hall, Charles F. Murphy, would use the dominant Tammany block of votes to pay a political debt to a Buffalo traction magnate, "Blue-eyed Billy" Sheehan. A group of twenty upstate Democratic legislators refused to enter the Democratic caucus or be bound by it. Through roll call after roll call they blocked the election of Sheehan. They chose Roosevelt to be their leader and met daily at the large house he had rented in Albany.[8]

As the senatorial contest dragged on from January into March, Roosevelt gained attention throughout the state and even beyond its borders. By advocating the direct election of senators — a dramatic national issue — Roosevelt advanced toward the forefront of the young progressives. He seemed to possess the same knack for acquiring publicity that had distinguished Theodore Roosevelt years earlier in the state legislature. From TR and his Groton masters came congratulations on his strenuous courage in fighting for a just cause.

Behind the scenes Roosevelt engaged in maneuvers that, had they become widely known, would have damaged his reputation as a progressive. He became involved with some old-line conservative clean-government Democrats who encouraged him to block not only Sheehan, but also, apparently, Samuel Untermyer. Nominally a member of Tammany, Untermyer was notable for his struggles on behalf of insurance company stockholders and against J. P. Morgan and the trusts. Roosevelt's conservative advisers tried to push him further and induce him to lead the insurgents in preventing New York ratification of the income-tax amendment, but Roosevelt would have no part of that scheme. Soon he was pulling away from the conservatives and moving toward the progressives.[9]

In the deadlock over the senatorial election, Roosevelt and the insurgents possessed only a negative power. They were able to force the withdrawal of Sheehan but could not elect a candidate of their own and finally had to agree to a substitute. Tammany threatened, if Roosevelt did not accept its candidate, to publicize his earlier opposition to Untermyer. Roosevelt joined the demoralized insurgents in accepting a candidate more pleasing to Boss Murphy than Sheehan would have been, a conservative former Tammany Grand Sachem, James A. O'Gorman. As political commentators pointed out at the time, it was a sorry end to the insurgents, but Roosevelt immediately proclaimed victory and later boasted of the "Tammany surrender." Voters, remembering the valiant fight better than they did the inglorious outcome, became widely aware of the emergent new political personality bearing the magic name Roosevelt.[10]

As Roosevelt set about consolidating his position in Democratic politics, he concentrated at first upon harassing the Tammany machine and fighting for the interests of his farmer constituents. He fought various Tammany measures before the state senate, including a Tammany-sponsored charter for New York City even though it provided equal pay for woman schoolteachers. Several times he was outmaneuvered and badly defeated, but after the 1911 election went against the Democrats, he asserted: "C. F. Murphy and his kind must, like the noxious weed, be plucked out." Further, "From the ruins of the political machines we will reconstruct something more nearly conforming to a democratic conception of government." Tammanyites regarded Roosevelt as anti-Irish and anti-Catholic and ridiculed him as a toplofty snob. For several years newspapers ran a photograph of him that was almost a caricature — pince-nez perched on his nose, his head tilted high. Roosevelt protested that it made him look "like an English Duke."[11]

For Roosevelt it was a painful seasoning, comparable to what he had undergone after entering Groton School. Still malleable, as at Groton, he quietly altered his appearance and attitudes. It was a genuine change. Slowly he came to appreciate some of the Tammany leaders in the legislature, both for their political astuteness and for the zeal with which they sought to improve the living and working conditions of the city dwellers. When Roosevelt entered the state senate, Robert F. Wagner, at thirty-three, became its president pro tempore, and Al Smith, at thirty-seven, became majority leader of the assembly. These two surprised the state, said Roosevelt some years later, by their support for progressive legislation. "Mixed up with the usual run of wholly partisan measures were proposals for sound steps in social reform — factory laws, workmen's compensation, the protection of women and children in industry." Boss Murphy had come to favor some social justice legislation because it was popular with his constituents, and the frightful fire at the Triangle Shirtwaist factory on Washington Square shocked even conservatives into accepting safety legislation.[12]

To the disappointment of a young social worker, Frances Perkins, Roosevelt was less energetic on behalf of factory reforms than were some of the Tammany leaders. More concerned with the interests of the farmers and middle-class voters in his own district, he concentrated at first on the promotion of agriculture and conservation. Gradually he began to look beyond his district, to statewide and even national issues. On the troublesome question of prohibition, popular upstate but detested in the city, he hedged by proposing local option. He was also cautious at first concerning woman suffrage, despite pressure from his Vassar College constituents. Toward organized labor he was friendly, but like many progressives he favored paternalistic legislation rather than guarantees of collective bargaining. He was slow to support a bill that would limit to fifty-four hours a week the work of boys from sixteen to twenty-one, and would regulate the work of children in canning sheds. Years later Louis Howe, who was Roosevelt's most ardent promoter, apparently invented the story that when the bill lacked only a single vote to pass the senate, Roosevelt filibustered, talking about birds, until that vote could be found. Tammany's "Big Tim" Sullivan, who was brought back from the boat he was to take to New York, did provide that vote — whether or not Roosevelt had been filibustering.[13]

On the other hand, Tammany did not as yet accept conservation bills, which were Roosevelt's keenest interest. With the advice of a forestry expert, Gifford Pinchot, he introduced a bill for the "Protection of Lands, Forest, and Public Parks." It passed the senate after the deletion of a section that prohibited the cutting of trees below a certain girth even on private lands. In the assembly, Tammany cooperated with Republicans to turn the measure into one favoring the private power interest. Roosevelt succeeded in killing his mangled bill when it came back to the senate.[14]

Primarily, Roosevelt was the proponent of government intervention on behalf of agriculture. At the beginning of 1913 he introduced a comprehensive series of bills, which he had drafted with the aid of the State Grange and a famous agricultural expert, Liberty Hyde Bailey, head of the college of agriculture at Cornell University. The intent of these bills was to protect New York farmers from exploitation by commission merchants, to aid them in cooperative marketing, and to extend to them low-cost farm improvement loans through agricultural credit banks. The powerful Grange lobby managed to counter the massive lobbying of the commission merchants and the bills went through. Roosevelt never let the farmers forget what he had done for them.[15]

By that time, in the spring of 1913, Roosevelt was also zealous on behalf of social justice legislation to aid city dwellers. While he had not helped shape the bills that resulted from the aftermath of the Triangle fire, at the request of the chief counsel of the Factory Investigating Commission, he testified at a hearing on behalf of all thirty-two of the Tammany-sponsored bills.[16]

On specifics, Roosevelt's progressivism was clear-cut. Overall he was somewhat vague in articulating his philosophy. In one rather confused speech in 1912 he declared that competition was useful up to a certain point, but then cooperation became essential. He termed cooperation the "struggle for liberty of the community rather than liberty of the individual." It was "what the founders of the republic were groping for."[17]

While Roosevelt could not expound a consistent ideology, day-by-day politics transformed him into an energetic young progressive. During his first two years in the New York Senate he became one of the best-known progressive Democratic leaders in the state, a prime mover among the upstate anti-Tammany Democrats. Already he was looking ahead. Chances for advancement in New York were poor, even though he was occasionally suggested as a gubernatorial possibility. Against the strong opposition of both Tammany and the powerful Republican party, he would be fortunate to survive in the state senate.[18]

An attractive alternative was open to Roosevelt, and he speedily took advantage of it. Before the end of 1911 he went to New Jersey to confer with Governor Woodrow Wilson and align himself with Wilson's presidential campaign. He could do little within the New York Democratic party to break the Tammany hold on the delegates to the nominating convention, but he did work with other reformers to organize upstate Democrats into the New York State Wilson Conference. It was a minor claque at the Democratic convention, but Wilson won the nomination, and Roosevelt established himself as a Wilson man. He returned to New York to build a new Wilson organization, the Empire State Democracy. It was ineffective, it ran out of funds, and Roosevelt himself came down with typhoid fever.[19]

The illness made the odds against Roosevelt's reelection to the state senate seem unsurmountable. At this point a remarkable figure came to Roosevelt's rescue and became thenceforth his alter ego. This was Louis McHenry Howe, a resourceful, cynical newspaperman who concealed a vaulting ambition within a personal facade so wizened and rumpled that a political career seemed impossible for him. Like Roosevelt he was rather uncertain in his progressive ideology, but was already tied politically to progressive Democrats. Further, Howe was a firm believer in the role of the great man in history. When Roosevelt, bedridden for the duration of the campaign, turned to him, Howe responded with enthusiasm, attaching his aspirations to the future of the handsome, charming young man.[20]

Howe was a skilled political tactician, brilliant in the arts of publicity and public relations. In 1912 he displayed his talents through the concocting of letters, handbills, and press handouts so effective that Roosevelt won reelection without campaigning in person. From the beginning, Howe demonstrated total faith in and loyalty to Roosevelt. Even during the campaign of 1912 he jokingly addressed a note to him as "Beloved and Revered Future President."[21]

Roosevelt turned toward opportunities that might open in Washington when Woodrow Wilson took office in the spring of 1913. Wilson had easily defeated both the Progressive party candidate, Theodore Roosevelt, and the Republican William Howard Taft. In January, Roosevelt talked to Wilson about patronage matters, and may have mentioned his own ambitions. In any event, at the time of the inauguration he declined offers, including that of collector of the Port of New York, which would have given him influence in New York politics. Rather, he succeeded in obtaining the appointment that best reflected his own interests and assured him the most publicity; he became assistant secretary of the navy. It was, he let no one forget, the position from which Theodore Roosevelt had catapulted himself to fame at the time of the Spanish-American War crisis. TR had secretly ordered Commodore George Dewey's squadron to take Manila in case of hostilities. Although Franklin D. Roosevelt was never able to act so spectacularly during his seven years as assistant secretary of the navy, he did manage greatly to advance his political education and his standing as a promising Democratic figure.[22]

The move to Washington brought Roosevelt under the influence of Woodrow Wilson, the second of the progressive presidents who made a deep impression upon him. Theodore Roosevelt had been a flamboyant relative, beckoning young Franklin to an exciting life of political strenuosity; Wilson was an austere, revered schoolmaster, like Peabody of Groton, teaching the uses and responsibilities of power. There was never any free give-and-take between the president and the youthful assistant secretary, but there were numerous discussions of policy problems. Official Washington was still so small that Roosevelt as the only assistant secretary of the navy was a figure of some consequence, and even the subcabinet members had fairly easy access to the president. Either as assistant secretary or as acting secretary when his superior, Josephus Daniels, was away, Roosevelt took occasional matters to the president.

Some of Wilson's remarks made such a lasting impression upon Roosevelt that years later when he himself was in the White House he liked to repeat them. In one early discussion, Roosevelt remembered, Wilson remarked, "It is only once in a generation that a people can be lifted above material things. That is why conservative government is in the saddle two-thirds of the time." As president, Roosevelt compared TR and Wilson in a way that suggested what he had learned from each of them: "Theodore Roosevelt lacked Woodrow Wilson's appeal to the fundamental and failed to stir, as Wilson did, the truly profound moral and social convictions. Wilson, on the other hand, failed where Theodore Roosevelt succeeded in stirring people to enthusiasm over specific individual events."

Roosevelt long underrated his "Chief," Secretary Josephus Daniels, an old-fashioned southern progressive editor and politician, pacifist in inclinations, a zealous foe of both alcohol and the monopolies, and a longtime disciple of William Jennings Bryan. Daniels was concerned with increasing efficiency in the navy and in bettering the lot of enlisted men through education. He was the butt of naval officers' jokes, and young Roosevelt, who spent much of his time with the officers, was known for his imitations of Daniels. In time Roosevelt came to appreciate Daniels' outstanding qualities, his warmth, generosity, integrity, and firm progressivism. He found, too, after he had come out second-best in several encounters with congressional figures, that there was much to learn from Daniels' astute approach to them. Indeed, Daniels was one of the most effective proponents of Wilson's progressive proposals, the New Freedom program, on Capitol Hill.[23]

Roosevelt was not so deeply involved with the issues of President Wilson's New Freedom as he had been with progressive questions in Albany. During his Washington years, his focus was upon the navy, in which he took an absorbing pride, and upon politics, both national and in New York. It was as part of that politics that he was an ardent exponent of the New Freedom, a states' rights, limited government version of progressivism. He forged lasting relationships with many of the Democratic leaders, and was a member of a luncheon group of twenty younger progressives, the Common Counsel Club. Yet he had no direct part either in obtaining passage of Wilson's domestic measures or in implementing them. In his speeches during these years he hailed the New Freedom but demonstrated no mastery of its intricacies or overall significance. Yet its fundamentals, with the emphasis upon regulation and state action, made a lasting impression upon him.

Roosevelt never cut his ties with Theodore Roosevelt or repudiated the ideology of the New Nationalism with its greater emphasis upon federal regulation. In his social life during the Washington years, he and Eleanor Roosevelt were welcome at the homes of Theodore Roosevelt's friends, Henry Adams, Oliver Wendell Holmes, Henry Cabot Lodge, and numerous others who had no sympathy for Wilson. Somehow, Roosevelt could spend frequent evenings with them, yet remain basically a believer in Wilsonian principles. The effect of his association with Republicans and those who had left the Republican party for Theodore Roosevelt's Progressive party may have been responsible for his later feeling that there was nothing irreconcilable about the two movements, the New Nationalism and the New Freedom. While the New Freedom became fundamental in his thinking, he was ready to add to it significant segments of the New Nationalism, as indeed did Wilson himself in 1916.

Like any practical politician, Roosevelt was interested in increasing the influence of his party and enhancing his own standing in it. During the rapid decline of the Progressive party after the 1912 election, he was thus involved in trying to bring Progressives into the Democratic party, either nationally or in New York State. He also tried to arrange "fusion" tickets of the two parties in upstate New York, but in the end failed to persuade his progressive neighbor Hamilton Fish to join the Democrats. Fish later became a Republican congressman and bitter opponent of Roosevelt.[24]

Obviously in joining the Wilson administration, Roosevelt was increasing his power in New York politics through his involvement in patronage. Through the proper dispensing of jobs he would have liked to build a strong upstate pro-Wilson and anti-Tammany organization, and he devoted a large amount of time and effort to this undertaking. He and Louis Howe, whom he had brought to the Navy Department, fought especially doggedly for postmasterships in upstate Republican congressional districts. Wilson for his part was concerned with obtaining the rapid passage of his New Freedom program, and gave much of the most important New York patronage to the conservative Senator O'Gorman. Despite his Tammany ties, O'Gorman had favored Wilson at the 1912 convention, and more important still, was persuaded to give his powerful support to the Federal Reserve bill.[25]

Roosevelt, undaunted by his failure to obtain more than a share of patronage, continued his vigorous attacks upon Tammany and in the summer of 1914 quixotically engaged in a test of strength. Direct election of senators had been attained, and he entered the New York primary senatorial race, probably at the urging of Secretary of the Treasury William Gibbs McAdoo. The campaign was a fiasco. Boss Murphy of Tammany put up an opposing candidate, James W. Gerard, ambassador to Germany, who without returning to the United States severely trounced Roosevelt. The lesson was not lost upon Roosevelt; he could not win New York primaries without Tammany support. But there was a lesson for Tammany too in the November election, where Gerard and the Democratic ticket lost badly; it needed the upstate Democrats.[26]

After the 1914 fiasco, Roosevelt entered slowly into a more cautious relationship with Tammany and its allies. He became most cooperative in helping find Brooklyn Navy Yard jobs for the powerful congressman John J. Fitzgerald, with whom he had previously battled over patronage. It was not difficult for him to be a vigorous supporter of the younger

Tammany progressives, Al Smith and Robert Wagner, since he had no conflict with them over issues. Indeed by 1918 he was an advocate of Smith for governor. Murphy, for his part, was considering Roosevelt for the candidacy, and on July 4, 1917, brought him to New York City to be the principal speaker at the Society of St. Tammany Celebration. For both men it was an uneasy but useful alliance.[27]

In the Navy Department, Roosevelt gradually became adept in the politics of administration. Secretary Daniels saw to it that Roosevelt was not the real power in the department. Senator Elihu Root had warned Daniels, "Whenever a Roosevelt rides, he wishes to ride in front." Daniels was too able and strong to allow Roosevelt much rope, but treated him with affection as a most promising protégé. Roosevelt's duties involved whatever Daniels assigned, but primarily he was in charge of all civilian workers, including those in the navy yards, and of contracts that did not involve policy decisions.[28]

The handling of labor relations involving fifty to a hundred thousand civilian employees was an invaluable experience. Under the tutelage of Howe, who became Roosevelt's assistant, he personally participated in wage hearings and became adept in day-by-day negotiations with labor leaders. Howe quietly acted as a troubleshooter, hastening wherever strikes threatened, and usually managing to obtain settlements satisfactory to the workers. He saw to it that the credit went to Roosevelt, who by the end of the Wilson years had built a reputation for being a strong friend of labor.[29]

Roosevelt, again working with Howe, tried to bring about more competitive bidding for contracts, to lower costs, and to attain greater efficiency in the navy yards. Some of the efforts to prevent collusive bidding were amateurish and unsuccessful, especially in the procuring of high-quality soft coal for the coal-burning ships, and after World War I when the navy was switching to oil, in trying to bring down its price.[30]

Despite angry protests from defenders of the status quo, Roosevelt and Howe could point to numerous achievements. Most of these came, however, after an effective and innovative paymaster general, Samuel McGowan, and his subordinate Christian J. Peoples took over direction of the Bureau of Supplies and Accounts. Roosevelt called them the "Heavenly Twins," and along with Daniels delightedly took credit for their substantial savings. He would have liked to go further and bring about a more businesslike organization of the overlapping jurisdictions of the bureaus and the operation of the navy yards, but was not notably successful. He became keenly aware, like so many young progressive administrators, of the need for greater efficiency in government, and it was to become a major theme in his political speeches.[31]

Conflicting with the efficiency theme was the local pressure on behalf of each of the navy's many yards scattered around the periphery of the continent. One of Roosevelt's perquisites was to visit these yards on inspection trips. Not only did he enjoy the pomp and circumstance, but he made the most of the opportunity to make local headlines and political friends by predicting an enlarged future for each of these establishments. He was particularly imaginative in thinking up ways in which the closed yards at Pensacola and New Orleans could be opened and made of service. He sent marines to Pensacola, and in January, 1914, began moving in naval aviators who in time made it an air training center. Roosevelt's trips were arduous, involving rounds of inspections and entertainment that left little time for sleep. Eleanor Roosevelt, who accompanied him on several of the tours, remembered them as feats of endurance through which one built strength. She was referring to personal strength. For her husband they were a start toward developing a national political following.[32]

While politics had become Roosevelt's vocation, the sea and the navy had long been his avocation. This would-be admiral gloried in his new status, receiving a salute of seventeen guns and a ruffle when he stepped aboard a naval vessel, four more guns than a rear admiral. Since both the president and the secretary had their own flags, he designed an assistant secretary's flag to be flown when he was aboard a ship. He gloried in naval reviews, and took full advantage of the opportunity to summon a battleship to Campobello waters and to take over the wheel of a destroyer. These were enthusiasms that never faded. His skill at the helm and his knowledge of navy lore helped make him an easy companion of naval officers. In time he became a keen judge of their capacities, making use of this knowledge when he was president.[33]

Naval and foreign policy were of absorbing interest to him, and in these areas, too, he served an apprenticeship for presidential undertakings. He was known as a big navy man when he arrived at the department; the pacifist editor Oswald Garrison Villard wrote, "Battleship man — or mad! — though you be I am truly glad of your appointment to Washington. May it lead straight onward for you as it did for TR — but *not* by means of that barbarism known as war."[34]

From the outset, Roosevelt, to the delight of the admirals, acted in the spirit of TR, seeking the enlargement of the navy and urging militancy in every crisis. The 1913 U.S. Navy and Marine Corps numbered 65,000 officers and men, and operated on a budget of

$143,497,000. It was inferior to those of Great Britain and Germany, and before many months Roosevelt's was one of the first voices bold enough to declare it should be second to none.[35]

In the serious crisis with Japan that opened the Wilson administration, Roosevelt sided with the admirals. Wilson soon brought the difficulties to a quiet end, but thereafter Roosevelt from time to time speculated, as he had during the crisis, on the concrete steps the navy should take in case of hostilities. When President Wilson ordered the occupation of Vera Cruz, Mexico, Roosevelt was on a western tour. In his excitement he told reporters that the meaning of the crisis was "war, and we're ready." Almost instantly Wilson accepted mediation, ending the excitement and leaving Roosevelt deflated.[36]

In common with so many of his contemporaries, Roosevelt looked upon Wilson's efforts to bring order in Mexico as an extension of progressivism beyond American borders. He was particularly enthusiastic about the marine occupation of Haiti, a nation that had been disease-ridden and revolution-wracked. At the beginning of 1917 he went on an inspection trip to Haiti, and congratulated the marine commandant, Smedley Butler, upon the imposition of order, sanitation, and a road system, despite the fierce opposition of so-called bandit bands. One aspect of the marine occupation was the ratification of a new constitution, which permitted alien ownership of land. In the 1920 campaign, Roosevelt was so ill advised as to exaggerate that he himself had written the Haitian constitution. It was a bit of boasting he was to rue and repudiate. His political enemies long made capital of it.[37]

When war broke out in Europe in August, 1914, Roosevelt became a leading advocate of preparedness within the Wilson administration. He became the proponent of the admirals' proposals for action, and was rather scornful of Daniels. "I am *running* the real work; although Josephus is here!" he wrote his wife. "He is bewildered by it all, very sweet but very sad!" From the time of the outbreak of hostilities, Roosevelt's sympathies were totally with the Allies, and he hoped they would dictate peace in Berlin.

In the fall of 1914, Roosevelt embarked upon a politically perilous course; at least by implication he was critical of the neutral inaction for which President Wilson so firmly stood, and which Secretary Daniels determinedly implemented in the Navy Department. Within the administration, Roosevelt was the one civilian already strongly advocating preparedness. Moreover, he quietly fed navy information to Wilson's foes in Congress, Senator Henry Cabot Lodge and Lodge's son-in-law, Representative Augustus P. Gardner. When he testified before the House

Naval Affairs Committee on the deficiencies of the navy, he received far more newspaper attention than ever before. Gardner declared, "I admire the courage of Franklin Roosevelt."[38]

In the fall of 1915, when President Wilson began to formulate a preparedness program, Roosevelt enthusiastically cooperated, and was one of those who pressed him to establish a Council of National Defense. Yet he continued openly to advocate policies more militant than those of the administration and to consort with Wilson's critics. During the campaign of 1916, when Wilson ran for reelection, Roosevelt supported him most strongly on his domestic policies; by this time he was making no secret of his feeling that the United States must enter the war. At the beginning of January, 1917, he was so bold as to send Wilson an original memorandum of James Monroe's justifying the "appeal to the sword" in 1812 after frustrating years of neutrality.[39]

Then came the startling challenge from the German military command, the announcement that on February 1, 1917, they would begin unrestricted submarine warfare. They were taking the calculated risk that they could starve out Britain and overrun France before American intervention could shift the balance against them.

In the critical weeks that followed, Roosevelt was in a frenzy of impatience over the deliberate course that Wilson set and that Daniels followed. It was he who directed the ferreting out of old legislation under which Wilson could authorize the arming of merchant vessels without fresh congressional action. Finally, after a Senate filibuster blocked legislation, Wilson used the old law Roosevelt had located. It was Roosevelt who went to see the president to urge that the fleet be moved and made ready for action. Wilson firmly said "No." Then, as Roosevelt was about to leave, he called him back to explain why. The words he used then were ones that Roosevelt recalled accurately and cited years later, when he was in a similar position and reluctant to take the final steps to bring the nation into war. As Roosevelt told it in 1919, Wilson said: "I want history to show not only that we have tried every diplomatic means to keep out of the war; to show that war has been forced upon us deliberately by Germany; but also that we have come into the court of history with clean hands."[40]

When, in April, 1917, Wilson called for a declaration of war, Roosevelt plunged into a new struggle to make the naval participation in the war as large and vital as possible. Immediately after the war Roosevelt would try to give the impression that, in order to bring speedy mobilization, he had broken enough regulations to land in jail for a hundred years. He would also boast that almost every naval achievement originated with him, as he repeatedly circumvented the lethargy and conservatism of Secretary Daniels and the senior officers.

The facts are considerably less dramatic, although interesting enough. Roosevelt dearly loved a semblance of insubordination, and, as during the neutrality years, was more cautious than he liked to appear. Daniels was secure in Wilson's confidence in him, and was firmly in control of major navy policies. His affection for Roosevelt outweighed his indignation over the rather petty offenses.[41]

Too, Daniels and Wilson may have felt that Roosevelt could cause them less trouble within the Navy Department than without. Despite the accolades that Roosevelt received from all the most vociferous critics of the war administration, Wilson and Daniels insisted he should remain in Washington rather than enter the armed services. Roosevelt wanted to get into uniform and was under pressure from Theodore Roosevelt to do so, but had no opportunity until the last weeks of the war, when President Wilson informed him it was too late. He suffered a lasting feeling of frustration.[42]

With his superabundant energy and ample powers of persuasion, Roosevelt did in fact achieve much in wartime Washington. He had a hand in the rapid construction of training centers, the speeding of contracts, and above all in the laying of a North Sea mine barrage to contain German submarines. On the other hand, his passion for small boats led him to obtain quantities of wooden harbor patrol boats (forerunners of the PT boats of World War II), which were not of much use.[43]

Finally, to Roosevelt's delight, in the summer of 1918 he was able to go to Europe on an official visit. He engaged in troubleshooting, minor diplomatic negotiations, and succeeded in getting so close to the front that several times he was under fire. His adventures made up to some degree for his frustrations, and in later years, even toward the close of World War II, he recounted them with imaginative elaboration. His uneventful destroyer trips were transformed into dramatic encounters with submarines; a shot he fired from a French 155-millimeter cannon came to land on a German-held railway junction. He did also see enough blood and destruction to warrant his later assertion that he hated war. He visited Belleau Wood only a few weeks after the battle and wrote in his diary:

> We had to thread our way up the steep slope over outcropping rocks, overturned boulders, down[ed] trees, hastily improvised shelter pits, rusty bayonets, broken guns, emergency ration tins, hand grenades, discarded overcoats, rain-stained love letters, crawling

> lines of ants and many little mounds, some wholly unmarked, some with a rifle stuck bayonet down in the earth, some with a helmet, and some, too, with a whittled cross with a tag of wood or wrapping paper hung over it and in a pencil scrawl an American name.[44]

In retrospect, Roosevelt remembered the horror of the battlefields, and so did Eleanor Roosevelt, who saw them the following winter. At the time, there was the excitement of being under fire, of reporting on the bad condition of seaplane components arriving from the United States, and the pomp and circumstance lavished upon him as a visiting dignitary in London, Paris, and Rome. He chatted with King George, Lloyd George, and Clemenceau, and, though it did not impress him at the time, Winston Churchill. On behalf of the Admiralty he went to Italy to try to stir the Italian Navy into greater action, and to persuade them to accept what amounted to British command. In this instance, Roosevelt was acting on the assumption he had Daniels' approval, but the French expressed their irritation to President Wilson, who conveyed his to Daniels.[45]

Nevertheless, after the Armistice Roosevelt had an even more exhilarating taste of diplomacy when he returned to Europe with Mrs. Roosevelt to supervise the disposal of naval property, although he was only on the fringes of the Versailles conference. On his way back to the United States, President Wilson summoned him one day to his cabin on the *George Washington* to discuss the proposed covenant of the League of Nations. The United States must go in, he said at a luncheon with the Roosevelts, or it would break the heart of the world. Roosevelt was profoundly impressed and thereafter an ardent advocate of the League of Nations. Earlier, during the campaign of 1916, he had supported, privately as well as publicly, Wilson's domestic policy. Thenceforth he was also a Wilsonian in foreign policy.[46]

Altogether Roosevelt received a remarkably broad political education in his thirties. He had made a name for himself as an exponent of progressive legislation and a crusader against a political machine, but had learned that the alternative to defeat must be a tenuous alliance with the bosses. In Washington, he had been a big navy man and an imperialist, but at the end of the war was a conspicuous proponent of the League of Nations. Further, he had an outstanding reputation as an administrator. "See young Roosevelt about it," reported *Time* several years later, was "a by-word in Washington." He was also charming, handsome, and affable — such a pleasant party-goer that his critics did not take him seriously. It was certainly true that he was impressionable, that he had been learning through experience, and that as circumstances altered so did his views. Many of his experiences through these years affected his later course of action. It was also true that he was widely regarded as one of the most able and ambitious of the young progressive Democrats, a man with a future.[47]

Chapter 3

YEARS OF TESTING

ROOSEVELT EMERGED from World War I as one of the outstanding young men among the Wilsonian progressives. The possibility that in a few years he might be a contender for the presidency was already more than a daydream. Yet that might be said also of a number of his contemporaries, and several, like Newton D. Baker, Wilson's secretary of war, were decidedly more prestigious. Roosevelt still appeared to many of his associates and social acquaintances to be too young and handsome, too superficial and full of haphazard energy to be taken very seriously. He had been an apt learner in politics and statecraft, but as yet had undertaken little real testing of his political and personal courage. Nor had he acquired the aura of authority. Challenges, both personal and political, soon came. Roosevelt surmounted them one by one, maturing politically with such success that ten years after the Armistice he was elected governor of New York, and four years later, president.

A personal crisis in the fall of 1918 raised the possibility of a divorce, which would have put an end to Roosevelt's presidential ambitions. It must have been painful for him; it was crushing for his wife. After his return from his first European trip while he was convalescing from influenza, Eleanor Roosevelt was helping him handle some of his correspondence. To her dismay she came upon a packet of love letters from her social secretary, Lucy Mercer. She felt shattered and betrayed, confronted Franklin with the evidence, and offered him a divorce. Late in life, she told a friend, Raymond Corry, that her husband had replied, "Don't be a goose!" And, she continued, "I was a goose." She was long despondent and never entirely recovered from the shock. One of Franklin's relatives declared years later that there had been a great family confrontation at which Sara threatened to end her financial aid to Franklin unless he gave up Lucy. The evidence, the relative said, was in Sara's diary. Whatever the merit of the story, there is no mention of it in the diary of the discreet Sara.[1]

What is certain was Eleanor's ultimatum, that if she were to remain married to Franklin she would not share his bed, and he must promise never again to see Lucy. He agreed.

From the time of their wedding there had been differences between the Roosevelts, growing out of their backgrounds and temperaments. Both had been brought up within the rigid personal code of their social class. Eleanor had felt frowned upon if she even received a letter from a young man; to have been kissed before engagement would have been unthinkable. Franklin had once been forward enough to earn a sharp slap from Alice Sohier, but was probably not much better prepared than Eleanor for physical intimacy. Eleanor once remarked to her daughter that sex was a burden, and sometimes implied to close friends that she could not let herself go. Some of her children were of the impression that after the birth of her sixth child, John, in March, 1916, she felt the family was large enough and as a means of birth control moved to a separate bedroom.[2]

The personality differences between the young Roosevelts led to continuing irritations, which Eleanor in her widowed years discussed freely. Franklin contributed little to resolving problems over the rearing of the children; he was loath to engage in serious discussion of them. It bothered her that he was no disciplinarian, and that while he insisted the children go to church on Sunday mornings, he himself might head to a golf course.

Franklin, lighthearted and secure, continued to function as he did when growing up, at times romping with the children. Or, as his father had done with him, he would place his oldest, Anna, in front of him on his saddle, and talk to her about the trees he was growing. These activities pleased Eleanor, but his frivolity could bother her. He liked to party sometimes until late at night, drinking with friends, laughing, joking, and acting silly. He had grown up a tease and never abandoned the habit; his sons also became incorrigible teases.

Eleanor could not stand being teased, and sometimes broke into tears and left the table during a meal. Or she would retreat into stoicism, assuming, as she later said, a "patient Griselda" facade. In after years she was quite severe with herself in relating these characteristics. In itself this was another difference from Franklin, who avoided confrontations and introspection and did not share her intense seriousness.[3]

After Franklin became involved in politics in 1910, Eleanor gradually became more and more interested and helpful. It could draw them together, but also pull them apart. Mrs. Roosevelt could, when need be, prod her husband firmly, giving an impression of moral superiority. In 1915 when the Roosevelts were sharing a hotel suite in San Francisco with Assistant Secretary of State William Phillips, who was a personal friend, Phillips observed her watchful interest. Over coffee one morning she asked Franklin if he had received a certain letter. He had. Had he answered it? No. Should he not? Yes. Should he not answer it right away? He agreed that he should, and immediately wrote a reply.[4]

While the Roosevelts were in Washington, Franklin, handsome, dashing, and fun-loving, was highly attractive to women. One, serving as a yeomanette in the navy during World War I, remembered that they used to stop on the street to watch him stride by. At parties, he was a center of gaiety, frequently mentioned in the socialites' gossip sheet. In the aftermath of one dance came a sad tale, confided by Eleanor, that circulated around Washington. When the time came to go home she looked for her husband, and not finding him returned alone to their house on R Street. She did not have a key, and not wanting to awake the servants, sat on the floor of the vestibule and dozed. Much later her husband arrived and let her in. From their house guests that evening, Franklin's cousin Warren Delano Robbins and his wife, came a varying version. Eleanor, on the plea that she hated dancing, left them quite early. When the others finally arrived, she explained, "I knew you were all having such a glorious time and I didn't want to spoil the fun."[5]

This episode took place when Roosevelt's romance with his wife's social secretary, Lucy Mercer, although over, was continuing to cast a deep shadow. In the love affair, Franklin D. Roosevelt, in his mid-thirties, had found escape from some of the frustrations and tensions of his marriage. By all accounts Lucy, in her early twenties, was most attractive. She came from a socially prominent Maryland family, but had suffered financial misfortune. It was easy for Franklin to include her in his circle of friends while Eleanor was at Campobello, and to list her, disarmingly, in a letter to his wife, among those with whom he had gone down the Potomac over the weekend. He was quite open in being with her. Earlier when Eleanor's cousin Alice Roosevelt Longworth commented to Franklin that she had seen them together in an open car, he replied, "Isn't she lovely?" Mrs. Longworth, who had one of the sharpest tongues in Washington, never regarded it as an adulterous relationship. Some others took a differing view. What outsiders saw was a pleasant, carefree friendship of the sort Franklin had always enjoyed with female friends and relatives — and always was to enjoy in the future. In 1920, when he was a candidate for vice president, a newspaper carried a picture of him at a baseball game with a pretty woman cousin, who was misidentified as Mrs. Roosevelt. The editor had cropped out Eleanor Roosevelt, who was sitting behind her husband.[6]

There were serious obstacles to marriage with Lucy Mercer, even if that had been what Roosevelt wished. It would certainly have made the presidency impossible, and might have blocked any political advancement. It would have been equally unthinkable for Lucy, a Roman Catholic. For Franklin it would have been an acute breach of the propriety in which he had been reared. Some years later he was censorious and cut off relations with one of his closest and most convivial friends, scandalized in part by his unpleasant divorce.

Outwardly Roosevelt accepted his agreement with his wife; inwardly he did not conform. He saw to it that Lucy, who had become Mrs. Winthrop Rutherford, was present, but not seen, on each of the four occasions when he was inaugurated president.[7]

For her part, Eleanor Roosevelt felt betrayed and the scars remained with her permanently. She could forgive her alcoholic father his misdeeds, but never her husband for breaking his marital vow. Yet she was disposed to remain married, perhaps because she too had been raised in a society that abhorred divorce. Once, in speaking of the younger generation, she remarked, "I was taught when I was young that when you made your bed you had to lie in it." At times she was depressed, and in the decades that followed, craving love and intimacy, she formed relationships with both men and women that were intense, but never seemed to go beyond hugging and showers of affectionate letters.[8]

The adjustments the Roosevelts made were not very satisfactory, but they were tolerable. The two continued to be deeply involved with each other, and despite annoyances, to manifest at least familial affection for each other. It was not the all-consuming tenderness they had dreamed of during their engagement, but they became closely associated politically, and in the years ahead through active partnership they achieved more than they ever could have earlier dreamed. It was an irony if indeed, as Eleanor allegedly thought, what held their marriage together was Franklin's knowledge that to sever it would be politically ruinous. Whatever the deficiencies in their intimate relationships, they became the greatest husband-and-wife political partners in American history.

The crisis speeded the transformation Eleanor Roosevelt had already begun from a submissive wife and daughter-in-law into a woman with an active life of her own outside of the household. During World War I she had worked as much as sixteen hours a day in the cook shack of a Washington Red Cross canteen. In the winter of 1920–1921, she studied shorthand, typing, and cooking; in later years she became part owner of the Todhunter School, a girls' school in New York City, and of a furniture factory in Hyde Park.[9]

So far as Roosevelt's career was concerned, the two years after the Armistice seemed a rather duller continuation of patterns already set. Progressivism showed signs of disintegrating in the Democratic party as it had in the Republican, and he established himself as one of the outstanding young spokesmen for the movement. His major theme in both congressional hearings and public addresses, in keeping with the postwar spirit, was on the need for more efficient government. He delighted an audience of Harvard students by telling them that four different departments were responsible for various species of bears in Alaska. More seriously, he pointed out to them that four different navies were being operated outside of the Navy Department. In a businessmen's era, he became a spokesman for efficiency and cutbacks in government spending, even on the navy.[10]

In the aftermath of the war, as Republicans in control of Congress began investigations of the Democratic administration, Roosevelt out of self-defense shifted away from the naval officers he had so long revered. Admiral William S. Sims launched a widely publicized attack upon the department for its lack of preparedness in 1917. Roosevelt's first response was to deliver an unfortunate address corroborating some of Sims's charges. Soon it became apparent that he would be tarred along with Daniels if charges of maladministration were proven, and he backtracked. Thenceforth he stalwartly fought shoulder to shoulder with his chief.

Further, Roosevelt became the target of additional serious charges, potentially ruinous, which Sims was secretly encouraging. Roosevelt had lavished admiration upon Sims, but it soon became apparent that Sims's response was contempt. One set of accusations focused upon the naval prison at Portsmouth, which Roosevelt and Daniels had transformed from a grim, punitive place where guards outnumbered prisoners into a model center for rehabilitation, under Roosevelt's friend Thomas Mott Osborne, former warden of Sing Sing. One charge, quite possibly true, was that life in the prison had been more pleasant than that on fleet duty — certainly aboard destroyers in the wintry seas of the North Atlantic. The crux was that Roosevelt, over the strong protests of personnel officers, had favored returning to active duty rehabilitated men guilty only of military offenses. Two thirds of the six thousand men who had passed through Portsmouth during the war had gone back to duty. What was dangerous to Roosevelt was the charge that he had returned as many as a hundred homosexuals. He flatly denied the charge and made his denial stick.

A related charge hung over Roosevelt for many months, that in trying to clean up unsavory conditions at the Newport, Rhode Island, navy base, involving bootlegging, drugs, and immorality, he had condoned the use of decoys to trap homosexuals. He denied being aware of the method, and asked for a congressional investigation to exonerate him. Through 1920, the Senate Naval Affairs Committee was focusing upon Daniels, and failed to act. Roosevelt thus far had come through these unpleasant encounters shaken but relatively unscathed politically.[11]

As the campaign of 1920 approached and with it the end of the Wilson administration, Roosevelt was uncertain whether to try to run for the United States Senate. The thought of being a senator did not appeal to him. Rather, he would have liked the Democratic nomination for governor, but Al Smith was already governor. Therefore, his friends sought at least to call attention to him by quietly promoting him for the vice presidential nomination.

At the Democratic convention Roosevelt once again appeared to advantage, by scuffling with Tammany men who tried to prevent him from carrying the New York standard into a demonstration for President Wilson. Yet he made a seconding speech on behalf of New York's favorite son, Governor Smith. When ultimately Governor James Cox of Ohio was nominated, to balance the ticket, the Cox managers with Murphy's consent chose Roosevelt, aged thirty-eight, as the vice presidential nominee.[12]

It was a forlorn year for the Democrats. The Republicans, capitalizing upon the reaction against wartime regimentation and postwar inflation and unrest, were running Senator Warren G. Harding, who promised to return the nation to "normalcy." That might imply also returning to traditional isolation and refusing to enter the League of Nations. Twice the Senate had failed to ratify the Versailles Treaty without reservations. Wilson, a physically shattered figure in the White House since his serious stroke the previous September, wanted the election to be a solemn referendum on league membership. Cox and Roosevelt visited the ailing Wilson and announced they would indeed make entrance into the league the focal campaign issue.

The appalling appearance of Wilson indelibly impressed Roosevelt. During World War II he reminisced to the writer and diplomat Claude

Bowers: "As we came in sight of the [White House] portico we saw the President in a wheel chair, his left shoulder covered with a shawl which concealed his left arm which was paralyzed. . . . Wilson looked up [at Cox] and in a very low, weak voice said, 'Thank you for coming. . . .' His utter weakness was startling and I noticed tears in the eyes of Cox."[13]

For Roosevelt, the opportunity to run for vice president, even in a year when there was no prospect of victory, was an exhilarating one. No one would hold him responsible for the imminent defeat, and he gained the valuable experience of campaigning throughout the nation. It was exciting to tour in a private railroad car, making new acquaintances among politicians from coast to coast. Roosevelt spoke an average of seven times a day, from as early as seven in the morning until as late as midnight. Into each speech he fitted the local references that his advance man, a newspaperman, Stephen Early, sent him. He talked widely and not always consistently on a number of topics. Fortunately for him, he was not yet widely reported; the Associated Press did not assign a man to cover him. Even his boast that he had written the constitution of Haiti attracted only brief attention, but it gave Harding the opportunity to declare that when he became president, "I will not empower an Assistant Secretary of the Navy to draft a constitution for helpless neighbors in the West Indies and jam it down their throats at the point of bayonets borne by United States Marines."[14]

Roosevelt, as he had promised Wilson, concentrated upon the league issue. In his acceptance address he declared that the United States must prepare to live in isolation behind a barricade of heavy armaments, or accept the fact that "modern civilization has become so complex and the lives of civilized men so interwoven with the lives of other men in other countries as to make it impossible to be in this world and not of it." The next two decades proved Roosevelt right, but in 1920 it was impossible to interest the electorate in the league. The issue changed few votes. Many voters could not fathom the intricacies of the League Covenant, but were generally in favor of it. On the other hand, as Roosevelt's advance man wrote from Sioux Falls, South Dakota, "The bitterness toward Wilson is evident everywhere and deeply rooted. He hasn't a friend." There was resentment over postwar shortages and escalating prices, anger over strikes, and fear that Bolshevism was spreading in America. Those with loyalties to Germany or Ireland were angry over Wilson's failure to support them at Versailles. One of Roosevelt's friends circulating through audiences told him that people liked him and his speeches, but would not vote for "Mr. Wilson's League." Many pro-league voters accepted the assurance of thirty-one eminent Republicans that a vote for Harding was a vote for the league. The campaign sputtered out and Harding won by a landslide.[15]

Roosevelt gained politically from the 1920 campaign. He learned much about public speaking, and especially the need for caution. When Frank Knox was the Republican candidate for vice president in 1936, he made stinging attacks upon Roosevelt. In 1939, the president, courting him, assured Knox, "I, too, was inexperienced in national campaigns in 1920 and later regretted many of the things I said at that time!" It was in 1920 that for the first time Roosevelt attracted national attention, and throughout the country began to build a network of political friends for the future.[16]

After the election, Roosevelt returned to private life. He accepted the vice presidency of a surety bonding firm, Fidelity and Deposit, and made use of his political connections to help double the business of the New York office by 1928. At first as a partner with Grenville T. Emmet and Langdon Marvin, both good friends, he gave little attention to the practice of the law, admitting that "estates, wills, etc. . . . bore me to death." He founded a new firm with the energetic D. Basil O'Connor, a lasting arrangement. He also dabbled in a variety of small enterprises, often speculative. Some, like placing advertising in taxicabs and marketing merchandise through vending machines, were ahead of their time. They were indicative of his boredom with ordinary business and law practice, and were comparable to the imaginative innovations he brought to the poker table. Later some of his enterprises, especially his successful speculation in German marks during the postwar European inflation, brought him political criticism.[17]

One enterprise, involving no business investment, was of more serious consequence. This was the effort of Roosevelt to try to bring order and smooth out cycles of boom and bust in the building trades through the American Construction Council, a trade association. As president of the council he cooperated with his wartime friend Secretary of Commerce Herbert Hoover, who was interested in trade associations as a force for stabilization and promotion of efficiency. But the council had no funds, could not obtain government aid through Hoover, and was totally ineffectual. The lesson was not lost upon Roosevelt.[18]

Although Roosevelt was primarily a lawyer and businessman and was engaged in a number of philanthropic activities, his keenest interest was still politics. In the normal course of events, he quite possibly would have been elected to the United States Senate in 1922. But a dangerous illness intervened, which would have finished the career of almost anyone else.

At the end of July, 1921, Roosevelt was hot, exhausted, and dispirited. In vain he had dashed to Washington to try to prevent the Republican majority on a Senate subcommittee from issuing a scurrilous report blaming him for the Newport affair. The report was so partisan and unfair that it did Roosevelt's reputation little damage, but it caused him much pain. Roosevelt seemed to regain his equilibrium quickly, but privately he agonized. He hoped his maligners would reap their reward in the next life.[19]

Outwardly skylarking, but emotionally and physically exhausted, Roosevelt went with a group of notables to visit a Boy Scout camp at Palisades Interstate Park, the last time newspapers would ever picture him walking unaided.[20] He sailed to Campobello Island aboard a yacht. For the next several days he did not feel well. On August 10, he noticed a sensitivity in his legs, but continued a strenuous regimen, fighting a forest fire and cooling off with a long dip in the cold waters of the Bay of Fundy. "I didn't feel the usual reaction, the glow I'd expected," recalled Roosevelt. "I sat reading for a while, too tired even to dress. I'd never felt quite that way before. . . . The next morning when I swung out of bed my left leg lagged but I managed to move about and to shave. I tried to persuade myself that the trouble with my leg was muscular, that it would disappear as I used it. But presently it refused to work, and then the other."[21]

When his daughter, Anna, entered the bedroom, Roosevelt greeted her with a smile and a wisecrack, but his temperature was 102°. A Lubec, Maine, doctor diagnosed the illness as no more than a cold, but by the next morning Roosevelt could not stand up. By evening his legs were numb but very sensitive to touch and he could not move them. He ached all over and was at least partially paralyzed from the waist down. For the first few days, he once admitted to Frances Perkins, he was in deep despair, feeling God had abandoned him. After a week his temperature dropped and his spirits rose. His buoyancy and strong religious faith reasserted themselves, and he felt he must have been shattered and spared for a purpose beyond his knowledge. Mrs. Roosevelt wrote at the time, "I think he's getting back his grip and a better mental attitude though he had of course times of great disappointment."[22]

Two weeks after the attack began, a Boston specialist, Dr. Robert W. Lovett, visited Roosevelt, diagnosed him as suffering from poliomyelitis, stopped the painful massages, and prescribed hot baths. He gave a further boost to Roosevelt's morale by assuring him that the attack was mild, that he might recover completely. To Dr. George Draper in New

York City, who was to take prime responsibility for the case, Lovett sent his prognosis:

> It seems to me that it was a mild case within the range of possible complete recovery. I told them very frankly that no one could tell where they stood . . . that complete recovery or partial recovery to any point was possible, that disability was not to be feared, and that the only [doubt] about it was the long continued character of the treatment. . . . it looked to me as if some of the important muscles might be on the edge where they could be influenced either way — toward recovery, or turn into completely paralyzed muscles.[23]

Thus began Roosevelt's trial by the ordeal of polio. Roosevelt had been so fearful his children might contract polio during the dangerous epidemic of 1916 that he had brought them back to Hyde Park from Campobello Island on a destroyer, but he had thought of it as a child's disease, not a danger for a man in his fortieth year. The crisis brought out the best in both of the Roosevelts. They hid their inner anguish behind a facade of optimism and jollity. Roosevelt entered a hospital in New York City, suffered acute pain for many weeks, and for a while there was a question whether he would again be able to sit up. Sara Roosevelt, wishing to do what was best for her son, wanted him to retire to Hyde Park and live in leisure, a country gentleman like his father. Eleanor Roosevelt and Louis Howe insisted rather upon sustaining Roosevelt's morale by keeping him active in politics. As for Roosevelt himself, he never gave the impression that he could consider any course but a continuation of his career, to be delayed only briefly while he regained the use of his legs. He came to this decision, Mrs. Roosevelt would say, at a time when he was flat on his back in bed, spending hours trying to wiggle a big toe.[24]

There was literally no break during his weeks of peril and agony and his continued participation in Democratic politics through letters and statements. Since to be a seeker of high office from a wheelchair seemed impossible at that time, he never let the impression circulate that he was other than lame, rapidly progressing toward recovery. "Thanks to a severe chill which I lay to the vagaries of the Bay of Fundy climate," he wrote in the first week of his illness, "I am . . . under the stern eye of a doctor who refuses to allow me to more than look at my mail and sign a few letters each day." As late as the following March he balked at going for a ride from his New York City home because he did not want people to see him being lifted into his car: his therapist tried to persuade him to go at night; he said that was a good idea, but for the time being did not go. Gradually Roosevelt became less sensitive about his appearance, and when he went sprawling while entering his Wall Street offices several years later, grinned cheerfully as he was helped to his feet.[25]

Not that Roosevelt's optimism was merely a political screen against a damaging reality. He was determined to conquer the adversity that had befallen him. For seven years, except for a few lapses into despair, he devoted his agile intelligence and indomitable will to the fight to regain the use of his legs. It was not entirely a successful enterprise.

It was a long discouraging fall in 1921, for Dr. Lovett's prognosis (which his New York physician, Dr. Draper, had accepted before seeing Roosevelt) was far too favorable. For weeks he showed little or no improvement, at times running a high temperature, and was agonizingly sensitive if someone even touched the sheet on his bed. While Roosevelt was determined to leave the hospital in two or three weeks, Dr. Draper feared he might not ever be able to sit upright without support.

Gradually Roosevelt began to make progress, regaining the strength in his arms and back, learning to pull himself up with a strap, and in time swinging into a wheelchair. "He is a wonderful patient," reported his chief physical therapist, Mrs. Kathleen Lake, "very cheerful, & works awfully hard, & tries every suggestion one makes to help him." Roosevelt hoped he would soon be on crutches. "The doctors say that there is no question but that by the Spring I will be walking without any limp."[26]

By February, 1922, Roosevelt was indeed on crutches, but it was through wearing fourteen pounds of painful steel braces and swinging his hips. He had no power or balance in his legs, and began gentle exercises to try to restore his leg muscles. Although his braces hurt and he was enduring additional pain from wedges to straighten his left leg, he outwardly maintained a semblance of well-being.[27]

So did everyone else in the household on 65th Street, while under the veneer tensions became almost intolerable. Roosevelt would romp on the floor with his children, but they did not always understand they must be gentle not to hurt him. Louis Howe and Mrs. Roosevelt were keeping Roosevelt involved in politics, while his mother was still campaigning doggedly for him to retire to Hyde Park. The children did not like having Howe in the household and Sara encouraged them in their resentment. Even Eleanor's remarkable reserve finally gave way one spring day, and while reading to her two youngest sons, she broke down and cried for hours.[28]

Yet Roosevelt doggedly worked on at his exercises, addressing himself to the problem of recovery as wholeheartedly as he had to naval administration and politics. His physical therapist, Mrs. Lake, reported in March, "He has all sorts of new ideas about developing his muscles, & I have to discourage him periodically as tactfully as possible, otherwise he does more harm than good." At the same time he worried about expenses, and wanted to economize in the summer by having his wife take over the duties of the two therapists. Dr. Draper commented to Dr. Lovett, "Mrs. R. is pretty much at the end of her tether with the long hard strain she has been through, and I feel that if she had to take on this activity, that the whole situation would collapse." At the same time, by spring Roosevelt's physical therapists felt he had become too dependent upon them. Mrs. Lake recommended, "He should certainly lead a much more normal life, & cut out a good deal of this sick room atmosphere." Dr. Draper commented to Dr. Lovett that during the winter he had not seen much of Roosevelt because nothing could be gained during such a slow-moving recovery process. "Furthermore, I was able to see with a better perspective the intense and devastating influence of the interplay of these high voltage personalities one upon another."[29]

The next phase, during the summer, was also typical of Roosevelt. Ingratiating toward those handling his case, he gave them repeatedly the impression that he was quite satisfied with his progress. At the same time, making little improvement, he focused his energies upon his business, politics, and social life to such a degree that he appeared tired. After seeing Mrs. Roosevelt in August, Dr. Lovett prodded him "to do all the walking that you can within your limit of fatigue," and wrote that he should practice getting up and down stairs. It was well over a month before Roosevelt replied, and then:

> . . . to report that I have faithfully followed out the walking and am really getting so that both legs take it quite naturally, and I can stay on my feet for an hour without feeling tired. I think the balance is coming back also, and though I can negotiate stairs if I have a hand rail I cannot get up steps with only the crutches, and I doubt if this feat can be accomplished for a long time.[30]

Despite these brave words, Roosevelt continued to slacken his efforts. Therapist Edna Rockey reported, "All this lovely fall has gone with only a few minutes devoted to walking, not every day. . . . Several days ago he was compelled to walk about one quarter of a mile which completely took him off his feet for about four days. . . . The corset was quite a relief during this period." Roosevelt complained to Dr. Lovett that his new braces, which he returned, were causing trouble with his walking; the corset, so far as walking was concerned, was "a distinct help." He added, "It almost cuts me in two, however, when I sit down. I am more glad than ever that I do not belong to the other sex!"

Miss Rockey blamed Roosevelt's avoidance of walking on his mother's desire for him to take advantage of being in the country and the fact that he was very busy and showing signs of nervousness.[31]

The ups and downs continued. At the end of February, 1923, Roosevelt chartered a houseboat, the *Weona II*, and spent several happy weeks cruising in Florida. The swimming in warm water improved his legs so notably that he hoped he would be able to rid them of straight braces and go up and down stairs. "Except for the braces I have never been in better health in my life," he wrote Senator Carter Glass of Virginia.[32]

Again, he was innovative, sending Dr. Lovett a five-point memorandum that might be useful for other recuperating polio patients living on a houseboat:

> I was much worried by the problem of getting up and down stairs. This I solved by sitting down on the third step from the bottom and placing my hands on the steps lifting myself up (or down) one step at a time. A handrail on one side only was of great assistance. . . .
>
> I managed to catch a number of large fish, some running as high as 40 pounds. At first I tied a strap around my chest and around the back of the revolving fishing chair. This gave the necessary purchase. After a little practice I was able to discard the strap and was able to hold heavy fish on a large rod without much difficulty.[33]

Upon his return there came the usual slight setback. Mrs. Lake reported he came back much improved, looking ten years younger, able with slight assistance to sit from a lying position. But with "people in to dinner every night . . . came down with a bad cold . . . & practically lost everything he had gained. . . . If only his wife could be persuaded that he does not need urging on all day & entertaining all evening, I think he would not be tired & would do better physically."[34]

The Florida experiment was so successful that Roosevelt bought a houseboat jointly with a friend, John S. Lawrence, dubbed it the *Larooco* (Lawrence, Roosevelt, and Company), and spent part of three winters on it in 1924–1926. It was a relaxed existence that brought some improvement to Roosevelt, and some surcease to Mrs. Roosevelt, who, focusing upon the Todhunter school and other enterprises, seldom visited. However, a number of friends did. Roosevelt's almost constant companion on the houseboats was Marguerite ("Missy") LeHand. She was an attractive, intelligent young woman, who had worked in the New York Roosevelt headquarters in 1920 and become his personal secretary the next year. She was absolutely discreet and totally devoted to Roosevelt, serving him as secretary, confidant, companion, and frequently as hostess for the rest of her career.[35] Life on the houseboats afforded little privacy, as "Admiral" Roosevelt recorded in his humorous log, with everyone lolling around "in pyjamas, nighties, and bathing suits":

When they first come on board they think it's so nice —
With staterooms and bathtubs and comforts sans price —
Till they suddenly realize that every partition
Sounds intimate echoes of each guest's condition
Of mind and of body — . . . .
No secrets or thoughts between husband and wife
Can safely be had in Community Life. . . .[36]

Mrs. Roosevelt seldom visited either the houseboat or later Warm Springs, with its comparable intimate living and lack of privacy. She could not easily maintain her separate way of life under these conditions. In some accommodations Missy LeHand had to go through Roosevelt's bedroom to use the bathroom. Yet Mrs. Roosevelt never indicated any suspicion or jealousy toward Missy, perhaps because Missy was of a different social class, and certainly because her attendance upon Franklin freed Eleanor to serve her husband as his political surrogate and adviser, a role she preferred.

Houseboating in Florida turned out to bring, despite its heavy expenses, only limited recovery and rather a greater degree of boredom than treatment elsewhere. Nevertheless warm water seemed to be the best therapy. At this point, fortuitously, Roosevelt discovered Warm Springs, Georgia, which was to be a focal point in his physical well-being and personal interests for the rest of his life. Buoyant spring water from Pine Mountain poured out into a pool at a temperature of 88°. After a few weeks, in the fall of 1924 he began to feel life in his toes and could walk around in water only four feet deep without braces or crutches.[37]

Roosevelt undertook to transform Warm Springs into a major treatment center for polio victims. Reporters wrote about his success there and patients began to arrive before there were any facilities to treat them. Roosevelt had a physician give them a general checkup: "Then I undertook to be doctor and physio-therapist, all rolled into one." In addition he undertook to modernize the area: "I am consulting architect and landscape engineer for the Warm Springs Co. — am giving free advice on the moving of buildings, the building of roads, setting out of trees and remodelling the hotel."[38]

In 1927, Roosevelt established the Warm Springs Foundation to take over the property and transform it into a renowned national center for the treatment of polio. Two thirds of his personal fortune went into the enterprise. He bought a 1,750-acre farm on nearby Pine Mountain, constructed a five-mile scenic road along the crest, and tried to demonstrate to Georgia farmers how they could diversify and improve their crops. Ultimately because of operating losses he had to sell the farm. Altogether, though, the Warm Springs enterprises brought Roosevelt an outlet for his organizing and promotional skills and sent his morale soaring.[39]

By September, 1928, seven years after his polio attack, Roosevelt still had not regained the use of his legs, but had come to terms with his adversity and was turning it to his advantage. He had advanced only to the point of taking a few hesitant steps unaided, wearing braces. There was no more than the slightest possibility he would make significant further progress. Yet he was again enjoying life thoroughly, having devised ways around his handicap. He found a means of appearing in public apparently merely lame, rather than crippled, through a variation of the "tripod system" for bearing his weight that therapists had taught him. With his legs firm in locked braces he would hold a cane in one hand and take a tight grip on the arm of a son with the other, advancing slowly without crutches. In addition he and the ever-watchful Howe had persuaded press photographers and newsreel cameramen not to snap him in a wheelchair or while locking his braces before he emerged from an automobile. "No movies of me getting out the machine, boys," he would ask. Roosevelt had perfected so effective an illusion that most Americans did not realize until after his death that he was a paraplegic.[40]

In his personal life, Roosevelt with his powerful arms and shoulders had learned how to cope comfortably, swinging from his armless wheelchair to a desk chair or sofa. A year or two after the polio attack he amazed friends at evening parties by demonstrating how he could drag himself around on the floor. Yet he was aware of the hazards of being immobile and had an abiding fear of fire, an important reason why he always wanted people with him or nearby.

There were two exhilarating escapes from the wheelchair and crutches. One was the water, where, like a seal, after being slow and ungainly on land, he became a graceful, dynamic leader in water polo and frolics. The other, of great political value as well as personal satisfaction, was his instant equality once he got into an automobile. A later polio victim, Charles McLaughlin, comments: "I discovered that the only way . . . to have other people react normally was to drive a car. All of a sudden I was back with the human race, to be honked at and shouted at out of windows." Both at Warm Springs and at Hyde Park, Roosevelt owned cars with hand controls with which he could go zipping over country roads, stopping here and there to talk to his Georgia and Dutchess County neighbors, enjoying the mobility and satisfying his interest in everyone and everything. During World War II, Roosevelt demonstrated this exuberant side of himself to a startled Winston Churchill, who months earlier had arranged for him to be carried to the top of a tower in Marrakesh to enjoy the sunset view. Upon Churchill's arrival at Hyde Park, Roosevelt reversed the earlier role, taking him on a breathtaking dash around the estate, braking to a sharp halt at the edge of a promontory so that the startled, nervous Churchill could gaze upon the vista of the Hudson River.[41]

Chapter 4

THE POLITICAL COMEBACK: GOVERNOR OF NEW YORK

WHILE ROOSEVELT for seven years was concentrating his efforts upon trying to walk again unaided, he was also working toward an equally difficult goal, ultimately to win high office. During the first discouraging year or more it must have seemed like chasing a will-o'-the-wisp, serving little purpose but to bolster Roosevelt's morale. Louis Howe was so successful at the outset in downplaying the illness that Roosevelt received a note in the fall of 1921 asking him to attend a meeting of the Democratic Executive Committee. Howe scribbled in the margin that the sender should "wake up & hear the birdies!" The invitation was an indication of how well Roosevelt was creating the impression that he was only temporarily ill. During the long struggle for recovery, Roosevelt through the aid of his wife and Howe succeeded in remaining a prominent political figure.[1]

Howe and Mrs. Roosevelt skillfully divided their responsibilities. Howe was prime strategist for Roosevelt, devising schemes to gain publicity, and engaging in state and national correspondence in Roosevelt's name to keep him in the front of Democratic politics. Since Howe operated best behind a desk, Mrs. Roosevelt learned to speak for her husband and to act as his eyes and ears at political meetings. She forced herself to make political speeches, and under the tutelage of Howe, who would sit in the rear of the audience, learned to suppress her shyness and nervous giggle. Rapidly she became one of the most effective woman Democratic leaders during the 1920s, when women for the first time were becoming a factor of consequence in New York and national politics. Roosevelt was well aware of the added strength that women could bring to the Democratic party. He not only made important use of his wife, he encouraged her development as a political figure in her own right, and took seriously the new Democratic women. To Mrs. Roosevelt's friend Caroline O'Day, head of the New York women's division, he sent advice on how to enlarge the Democratic minority in Republican upstate New York:

"Get the right kind of women in every election district in the various rural counties. . . . There are thousands of election districts upstate where it is not only unfashionable to be a Democrat, but even where Democrats are rather looked down upon. . . . Democratic women . . . should let the world and their neighbors know that they take great pride in their Party."[2]

For her part, Mrs. Roosevelt enlarged her husband's knowledge of issues. She began a practice, which she continued through the White House years, of placing books she thought would be of value to him beside her husband's bed. After he had read a book she would bring the author to dinner. She also brought to Hyde Park or their New York residence people like Rose Schneiderman of the Women's Trade Union League, with whom he talked for hours, heightening his concern for the plight of the underprivileged, becoming informed in areas of deep concern to his wife, and enlarging his future political agenda.

On his own Roosevelt sought information with keen curiosity. Bertie Hamlin, a friend since he was ten, visited him at Marion, Massachusetts, while he was undergoing polio therapy, and met a young man hurrying to return to New York City:

> After he had gone — Franklin told me that he was an east side Jew — a tailor — from New York. He had come over on the boat the previous night and had been over once before to spend the day. Franklin said he had a chance in this way to learn a great deal about conditions in [the man's] life — his clubs and other organizations — at first hand. He felt he got to the bottom of situations that could and should be remedied — the scandalous housing conditions — labor — schools — churches and the family life. He [commented on] the patience of people under unbearable tenement living — the lack of decent provisions for sanitary purposes — sometimes one water faucet for a whole house.[3]

Roosevelt's concern with Democratic party policies increased during the 1920s, and gradually many of his ideas underwent modification. He became something of a spokesman on foreign policy, favoring a new international agency to replace the League of Nations, one in which there could be no possible impairment of national sovereignty. He abandoned his big navy views and criticized President Coolidge's recommendations to enlarge the fleet. The only possible naval foe was Japan, and "there is no fundamental reason why our relations with Japan should not be on a permanent and cordial basis." In 1927, during the protracted Marine Corps intervention in Nicaragua, he pointed to "this present . . . mess" as "a further reason for dislike of the United States by every Central and South American nation." While he lauded the efficient work of the marines, he lamented that they were enforcing "an agreement which has never had the sanction of Congress." The occupations with which he had been involved in the Wilson administration now seemed to him unwise, and he moved toward what he was later to call the Good Neighbor policy.

By the campaign of 1928, Roosevelt was assuming the role of foreign policy spokesman for the Democratic party. He gathered memoranda from Norman H. Davis, Sumner Welles, and other foreign policy experts and prepared an article on the Democratic views for *Foreign Affairs*.[4]

Roosevelt profited politically from being disabled during the years of Republican prosperity when no Democrat could possibly win the presidency. It removed him temporarily from contention for office and allayed the suspicions of potential rivals. He was acceptable in his role as a conciliator among Democratic factions. Nationally he could appear as a Wilsonian progressive and a Georgia farmer, equally sympathetic and adroit at speaking the language of those on both sides of the great rift within the party during the years of Prohibition and the Ku Klux Klan, the urban Catholic wets and the rural Protestant dries.

As the Democratic national convention of 1924 approached, Governor Al Smith, who was the hero of the urban Democrats and who enjoyed a good working relationship with Roosevelt, appointed him head of his campaign, to appeal to the southern and western dry, Protestant wing of the party. In 1922, Roosevelt had issued the call for Smith to leave private life to run again for governor. Smith and his advisers underestimated Roosevelt, regarding him as a rather superficial bit of window dressing who had a national reputation. Roosevelt, for his part, was firmly loyal to the Smith candidacy, shrewd and able in working for it. In New York City, Roosevelt finally expunged the suspicion that he was anti-Catholic, prevalent since his crusade against Tammany's 1911 candidate for the Senate, "Blue-eyed Billy" Sheehan. He worked hard to try to divert the Democrats from the issues dividing them disastrously, liquor and creed.

At the convention, Roosevelt's appearance on crutches to nominate

Smith was a personal triumph; he was wildly acclaimed. It was a standard nominating speech, enumerating Smith's achievements as a great progressive governor. It also contained an appeal for unity quite lost on the delegates, who deadlocked bitterly until, after fourteen days and 102 ballots, they nominated John W. Davis, a conservative Democrat and renowned constitutional lawyer. The convention made the quarreling Democrats look ludicrous. As one delegate pointed out to Roosevelt, "The crepe was hung on the door before the election instead of after." No matter. With the nation prosperous, and Robert M. La Follette running on a Progressive ticket, the Democrats would have lost badly no matter whom they had nominated. It was the national consensus to "Keep Cool with Coolidge."[5]

Despite the Republican landslide, Roosevelt looked upon the future with equanimity, writing an acquaintance:

> In 1920 after the poke we got that year, I remarked . . . that I did not think the nation would elect a Democrat again until the Republicans had led us into a serious period of depression and unemployment. I still [believe] that forecast holds true . . . the people will not turn out the Republicans while wages are good and the markets are booming. Every war brings after it a period of materialism and conservatism; people tire quickly of ideals and we are now but repeating history.[6]

For several more years because of his physical handicap Roosevelt continued to reap publicity as a premature "elder statesman" trying to bring harmony among quarreling Democrats. He thus avoided being the target of jealousy. Twice, in 1922 and 1926, he fended off Democratic movements to nominate him for a seat in the Senate, an office which he probably would have won, but which would have sidetracked him from his long-range plans. Nor did he wish any other nomination in the boom year 1928, when again there would be no hope for the Democrats. Occasionally Roosevelt was mentioned for president, but usually for ulterior political motives. He must have been too shrewd to think he could run successfully without having first held some additional important office. The one in his mind was governor of New York, and according to remarks Howe dropped later, the year was to be 1932, in the expectation that there would be a depression in the early 1930s and that in 1936 the nation would turn to a Democrat for president.[7]

In consequence, as 1928 approached, Roosevelt was still maneuvering carefully, building his political reputation, but devoting himself once more to the candidacy of Al Smith. He tried, and failed, to persuade

Smith to speak throughout the nation. Smith felt the nomination must seek him. So it did, in a year when unprecedented prosperity was sure to sweep in the Republican candidate, Herbert Hoover. Even southern Democrats were disposed to let Smith run, some of them with the expectation he would be defeated and eliminated as a major contender. Roosevelt was even more active for Smith than four years previously, concerning himself with issues. At the Houston convention, Roosevelt again was floor manager for Smith, and created the impression of being no more than lame when he appeared in the aisles of the sweltering convention hall. The crutches were gone, and he maneuvered with a cane, grasping the arm of his son Elliott.

Roosevelt, aware of the political potential of the new national radio networks, aimed his nominating speech less at the delegates than at the enormous audience throughout the country. The *New York Times* editorially heralded it as "A High-Bred Speech" — "the address of a fair minded and cultivated man." Smith sent the editorial to Roosevelt, writing in the margin, "This must be right because it brought tears in the [Executive] Mansion when you spoke it." Smith gained more than the requisite two-thirds votes of the delegates and was nominated on the first ballot. Roosevelt afterward joked that the only memorable remark made in Houston was that of Will Rogers, the humorist, who said that in trying to wipe his brow in the jammed lobby of the Rice Hotel he wiped that of three other people.[8]

In order to strengthen the Democratic ticket in New York State, Smith at the end of the summer brought irresistible pressure to bear upon Roosevelt to run for governor. Roosevelt, his wife, and Howe had all firmly agreed before Roosevelt left in September for Warm Springs that the timing was wrong, that he must refuse in order to run in a later year when the economic cycle turned down.

While Roosevelt's first answer to Smith was an unequivocal no, the lure of political adventure led him to weigh the potential assets and he stalled. When his daughter, Anna, wired, "GO AHEAD AND TAKE IT," his reply indicated the turn his thinking was taking: "YOU OUGHT TO BE SPANKED." As in past years, Roosevelt argued that he needed more time to improve the use of his legs. Howe warned, "THERE IS NO ANSWER TO THE HEALTH PLEA BUT ANY OTHER REASON WILL BE OVERRULED BY THE GOVERNOR HIMSELF." Roosevelt ignored this message and did add another reason, his financial worry. His funds were deeply committed in loans to Warm Springs and his income would drop if he became governor. Smith's campaign manager, the wealthy conservative John J. Raskob of Du Pont and General Motors, promised financial aid and did become a major donor to Warm Springs. In the end, when Smith finally got Roosevelt on the phone and asked him what he would do if nominated, Roosevelt responded he did not know. The New York convention nominated Roosevelt by acclamation.[9]

"MESS IS NO NAME FOR IT," Howe, dismayed and fearing a debacle, wired Roosevelt. Mrs. Roosevelt was more comforting: "REGRET THAT YOU HAD TO ACCEPT BUT KNOW THAT YOU FELT IT OBLIGATORY." On his own, against the advice of others, Roosevelt, at perhaps the most critical point in his political career, took a bold gamble. He might not have been able to win the gubernatorial nomination later, and although he was often mentioned among potential presidential nominees, he badly needed the governorship if he were to be a major contender.[10]

When Roosevelt returned to New York there were only four remaining weeks in which he could campaign for the governorship, and prospects seemed dismal for the Democrats. Roosevelt was back doing what he liked best and with a new authority and attractiveness. At first, even Republican papers lauded Roosevelt's idealism, but others prodded the most vulnerable point. "There is something both pathetic and pitiless in the 'drafting' of Franklin D. Roosevelt," asserted the *New York Post*, ". . . even [Roosevelt's] own friends, out of love for him, will hesitate to vote for him now." Smith did much to deflate the issue by remarking, "A Governor does not have to be an acrobat."[11]

Roosevelt himself removed remaining doubts by the optimistic dynamism with which he threw himself into the campaign. On his initial campaign trip by automobile through the Republican towns in southwestern New York, at each stop he snapped his braces, rose to his feet in the back of the automobile, and spoke strongly on behalf of Smith. Then he would ask if he looked like a sick man, and the crowd would laugh appreciatively. After four days of what Democratic headquarters feared was a quixotic campaign for Smith, Roosevelt abruptly shifted to state issues. From Buffalo through Rochester and into the Mohawk Valley, in each speech he talked vividly about one of the vital state issues, from agricultural problems through support of labor and advocacy of the Democratic humanitarian program. On prohibition he skillfully straddled Smith's wet position and the upstate dry credo. At the end of the campaign when he joined Smith in New York City, he was enthusiastically acclaimed. His vigor continued undiminished, laying to rest the health issue. In Yorkville, he had to be carried up a fire escape and in a back window, something he detested, but he appeared grinning, unruffled.[12]

By a slim margin of only 25,000 votes out of four and a quarter million, Roosevelt breasted the Republican tide and was elected. In private he joked that he was the "one half of one per cent governor." Smith suffered a landslide defeat, losing to Hoover even in New York by 100,000 votes. He was shocked and depressed. Roosevelt had won such a singular victory amidst the debacle that he immediately received a flurry of attention as a potential nominee for president in 1932. But if prosperity and Hoover's popularity continued, the nomination would be an empty honor. In any event, Roosevelt still had to surmount national doubts about his legs. "Were it not for his precarious health, the party might find a new national leader in . . . Roosevelt," stated the Republican *Los Angeles Times*, "but his physical condition seems to eliminate him."[13]

The immediate and substantial task confronting Roosevelt was to emerge from the shadow of Smith, one of the most notable governors of the twentieth century, renowned for his modernization of the New York government. Smith had persuaded Roosevelt to become a candidate because of the appeal of his name to the voters. He seems to have regarded Roosevelt with a bit of condescension and to have expected that Roosevelt would spend much of his time at Warm Springs and that Smith's own capable lieutenants, Mrs. Belle Moscowitz and Secretary of State Robert Moses, would set policy in Albany. When young Sam Rosenman, a talented lawyer devoted to Smith, was assigned to write speeches for Roosevelt, he too shared this patronizing view; during the campaign it evaporated. "I had heard stories of his being something of a playboy and idler, of his weakness and ineffectiveness," Rosenman recalled years later. "But the broad jaw and upthrust chin, the piercing, flashing eyes, the firm hands — they did not fit the description." Nor did Roosevelt's subsequent actions.[14]

The key decision Roosevelt had to make was whether or not he would be his own man as governor. Eleanor Roosevelt urged her husband to face the issue squarely. Would he, as Smith wished, retain Mrs. Moscowitz and Robert Moses? Roosevelt still had, and never lost, the tendency to mull over and procrastinate in coming to difficult decisions. In this instance if he had postponed action until he arrived in Albany in January, Smith's lieutenants would have been firmly entrenched in his office. Roosevelt immediately took his wife's advice and dropped them, even though it meant an inevitable estrangement from Smith. There had been no love lost between these two brilliant political operators and the Roosevelts. Mrs. Moscowitz, one of the shrewdest and most effective politicians of her generation, had blocked Roosevelt's access to Smith during the campaign summer. Moses, already notable as the builder of parks and parkways on Long Island, had clashed unpleasantly with Roosevelt, who as chairman of another commission was trying to construct the Taconic Parkway up into Dutchess County.[15]

Roosevelt felt no such animus toward other of Smith's able department heads and kept most of them. He came especially to recognize the qualities of Frances Perkins, chairman of the Industrial Board, whom he promoted to be industrial commissioner. Miss Perkins, who became one of the most loyal and effective of Roosevelt's subordinates in Albany, nevertheless remained also devoted to Smith. Roosevelt, well aware of the growing political importance of recognizing women, boasted to Miss Perkins that he had "more nerve about women and their status . . . than Al has." Miss Perkins retorted, "But it was more of a victory for Al to bring himself to appoint a woman, never appointed before . . . than it is for you [after] I had made a record."[16]

As Roosevelt took over the governorship and began to fashion it toward his own ends, tension began to develop with Smith that gradually curdled into rancor. It was inevitable between two leaders with strong egos. Both men were wounded, Roosevelt so much so that a decade later he dictated an account less than fair and put it into his files for posterity:

> I think [Smith] was sincere when he told me over the telephone at Warm Springs that if I were elected Governor, I could be sworn in and then go South for January and February, leaving the Governorship to [Lieutenant Governor] Herbert Lehman in the meantime, and returning a few days before the close of the Legislative Session.
>
> In line with this he planned . . . to stay in Albany at the De Witt Clinton Hotel for several weeks after January 1, 1929 to help me. . . .
>
> About a week before Christmas, 1928, Al came to see me and told me that Mrs. Moscowitz was preparing my Inaugural Address and Message to the Legislature. Honestly I think he did this in complete good faith . . . but at the same time with the rather definite thought that he himself would continue to run the Governorship. His first bad shock came when I told him that I had already prepared my Inaugural Address and that my Message to the Legislature was nearly finished.[17]

The inauguration, on January 1, 1929, set the stage for both the Roosevelt administration and the break with Smith. Although Roosevelt was considerate, and altered the inaugural ceremonies so that Smith could deliver a valedictory enumerating his achievements, the proceedings had something of the atmosphere of a wake for Smith. Roosevelt delivered an inaugural address setting forth the progressive principles upon which he would base his administration. "It had become pretty evident I was going to be my own Governor," reminisced Roosevelt in 1938. "You know, too, the politics in any Capitol. . . . The crowd . . . began to flock around their new Governor. Thus without any premeditation or action on my part, Al, I think, got the impression that to hang around Albany would be a grave mistake."[18]

During his first two-year term, Roosevelt focused on politics and issues within the state of New York. His task within the Democratic party was to build support for himself among political leaders, for the most part fanatically loyal to Smith, and to do so without alienating Tammany. Smith had depended largely upon the New York City organization to sweep him to victory over the preponderantly Republican upstate vote. His issues and legislative proposals had been mainly urban ones, which, with the support of reformers throughout the state, he had forced through the Republican legislature. Roosevelt concentrated upon upstate agricultural issues and the building of Democratic strength north of the Bronx. He depended upon a number of experts in developing his program, and upon James A. Farley, secretary and later chairman of the state Democratic Committee, to build the party. Farley, the son of Irish immigrants, began his political career as town clerk of Grassy Point, on the Hudson River. He shared Roosevelt's view that it was imperative to bring the moribund Democratic party back to life in upstate New York, and functioned as a politician's politician, a gifted, energetic traveling salesman organizing for the governor. Roosevelt felt that the program and the organization were closely interrelated, that both must be strong and effective in order to win elections. He kept firm control over both his administration and the party organization; his were the ultimate decisions.[19]

Through the issues, Roosevelt in his first two years established himself as a progressive governor. Again, as when he was state senator, he championed the upstate farmers, developing legislation with the aid of the state Grange, agricultural specialists, and his Dutchess County friend Henry Morgenthau, Jr., editor of the *American Agriculturalist*. Most of this legislation helped farmers through giving them tax relief. It brought national attention to Roosevelt as a friend of the farmers, suffering from low prices for their produce, without committing him prematurely to one or another of the controversial national crop-control programs that the desperate wheat and cotton producers were seeking.[20]

Through his advocacy of cheap electric power, Roosevelt appealed effectively to middle-class consumers not only in New York but throughout the nation. Power was a key issue among progressives in the 1920s. He contrasted the rates in Buffalo, New York, with the far cheaper ones across the Niagara River in Canada, and tried to obtain serious reductions. An average family electric bill was $17.50 in Manhattan, $7.80 in Buffalo, and $3.00 in Ontario. He favored not only large-scale public production of power, as did Smith and Hoover, but was ready to go further and fight for public transmission if need be. He also engaged in a struggle with the Public Service Commission, which he insisted should act on behalf of consumers rather than as an arbiter between the utilities and their consumers. Utility rates were too high, he said, and the commission must force them down. Roosevelt attracted a good deal of attention through his demands for lower power rates and for development of cheap St. Lawrence River power. His achievements fell short of his objectives; he succeeded only in persuading the legislature to create a state power authority.[21]

Much of Roosevelt's most substantial work as governor was in less spectacular areas of primary interest in the state. Through the 1920s he had been concerned about crime and had expended considerable effort in improving the judicial system, the prisons, and parole programs. His efforts to overhaul the antiquated structure of county governments failed, but he won some limited gains in banking reform and continued the liberal labor program he had inherited from Smith.[22]

After his first year as governor, Roosevelt became as effective as Smith had been in pressuring constructive measures out of the legislature despite Republican majorities in both houses. On the Mondays when the legislature was meeting, he assembled Democratic leaders, who came to be called the "cold turkey cabinet," for lunches where he primed them for the evening's session. He brought pressure upon the constituencies of the legislators through press releases to local newspapers. Since most of these papers were Republican and some would not print his releases, he made use of radio to appeal directly to the people. It was a medium that most politicians did not as yet take seriously. Once a month the state Democratic Committee bought radio time so that he could speak to the people of the state. He developed to perfection a simple, conversational way of talking, in happy contrast to conventional political oratory. When he became president he continued these talks as the "Fireside Chats."[23]

As an administrator, Roosevelt was also effective. He appointed numbers of able subordinates and kept in touch with their work. In addition he drew upon specialists in whatever areas concerned him, whether agriculture, public power, or prison reform. It was as an expert on crime that Raymond Moley, a Barnard College professor, first began to work for Roosevelt, writing a speech for him advocating reform of the administration of justice, and then serving as a member of an informal committee on parole problems. Thence Moley went on to larger and larger assignments. Roosevelt was receptive to the recommendations of such specialists and eloquently transformed them into political issues.[24]

Only slowly did Roosevelt manage to establish so well organized a system. In his first months as a fledgling governor he was not so impressive, but undaunted was working to build support. When the legislature adjourned in the spring of 1929, it left Roosevelt with almost nothing of his agenda enacted. Indeed, it was so conservative that it had blocked almost all of the parallel Republican program with which the party had appealed to middle-class voters. In the summer, Roosevelt combined politicking with vacationing as he toured upstate New York on a state-owned boat, which at six or seven miles an hour took Roosevelt on an inspection trip along the state's barge canal, following the route of the old Erie Canal. He visited amiably with numerous newspapermen and political figures, more of them Republican than Democratic, winning friends and building for the future.[25]

Outside of the state, Roosevelt rather cautiously was calling attention to himself, wanting to be in the limelight but firm in his denial that he was thinking beyond his duties as governor. In April he appeared at the newspapermen's Gridiron Dinner in Washington, along with President Hoover and Chief Justice William Howard Taft. When he arose to speak the correspondents serenaded him:

Oh, Franklin, Franklin Roosevelt,
Is there something in a name?
When you tire of being Governor
Will you look for bigger game?[26]

During the commencement season he received four honorary degrees and two honorary Phi Beta Kappa memberships, including one of each from Harvard. There, participating in the twenty-fifth reunion of the class of 1904, he was Phi Beta Kappa orator and chief marshal at commencement. He and Mrs. Roosevelt stayed for five days with his classmates and families in one of the old dormitories where he had never been willing to live as an undergraduate. Afterward he confused the jewelry firm that supplied the Phi Beta Kappa keys by ordering two of them, one of which he frequently wore. It was not the one from Harvard, but that from Hobart College, which was larger.[27]

Already Roosevelt was attracting national attention and demonstrating that he was an energetic governor, but with Hoover, "the great engineer," in the White House, the possibility that Roosevelt might become president seemed remote indeed.

The stock market crash in October, 1929, changed that. While Roosevelt had expected a future depression, he had no idea in the summer of 1929 that an economic crackup was impending. He was aware of the continuing distress of the farmers, but did not attach significance to the fact that construction had been down for three years and freight-car loadings declining, nor did he know that some insiders like Bernard Baruch, who had been one of the nation's most successful investors, were quietly liquidating their holdings in the great bull stock market. Nor, when the crash came, did Roosevelt at first grasp its significance. From Warm Springs he wired a New York newspaper, the morning after Black Thursday, his firm belief "that industrial and trade conditions are sound." Several days later he lectured a churchmen's group on the theme that the crash was a punishment unscrupulous speculators had brought upon themselves. A month later, when President Hoover urged all governors to engage in the "energetic yet prudent pursuit of public works," Roosevelt's emphasis was upon prudence, promising a program "limited only by the estimated receipts from revenues without increasing taxes."[28]

Through the first stages of the economic decline when conditions were not too bad, Roosevelt continued to be slow in sensing its implications or proposing means to combat it. For a year his approach was that of a cautious progressive. He favored only limited assistance to the unemployed through some expansion of public works.

On the other hand, he took seriously the growing difficulties, and sought to learn all he could about developments. Miss Perkins was supplying him with weekly state employment figures on dwindling payrolls and with employment figures that she was obtaining from industry. Roosevelt would telephone her to obtain data even more often. She was indignant when President Hoover announced at the end of January that, according to United States Employment Service data, employment was rising. Her New York figures indicated the opposite, and the USES figures were based only upon placements and job applications. Without consulting the governor, she issued a press statement contradicting the president. Roosevelt was delighted. Already he was trying to measure his actions at the state level against those of Hoover nationally.[29]

It took little nudging from Miss Perkins for Roosevelt to begin studying the employment problems in depth with such specialists as Professor

Paul Douglas of the University of Chicago. Political expediency had something to do with his receptivity, but his humanitarianism and fascination with innovation were paramount. He was far in advance of most other governors in advocating long-range reforms to ease future depressions. By 1931 he was proposing that industries revise their production schedules to eliminate seasonal fluctuations in employment, and that the state explore programs in unemployment insurance and old-age benefits.

There were echoes of progressivism in Roosevelt's speeches analyzing the causes of the depression. He attacked the concentration of corporate wealth, and at the 1930 Governors Conference criticized the Hoover administration for abandoning laissez-faire to advocate "a wholly new economic theory that high wages and high pressure selling could guarantee prosperity at all times regardless of supply and demand." He was fearful that if public works spending, which Hoover was recommending as a means of combating unemployment, was to become too substantial the result might be dangerous deficits.[30]

As the depression became catastrophic, Governor Roosevelt abandoned his conservative stance and advanced beyond President Hoover to become one of the most emphatic proponents of vigorous government action to restore prosperity. In a special message to the legislature in March, 1931, he asked for a commission to investigate unemployment insurance. He obtained such a commission but during his years as governor no insurance program; it would have helped only in the future anyway. At the 1931 Governors Conference he declared, "More and more, those who are victims of dislocations and defects of our social and economic life are beginning to ask . . . why government can not and should not act to protect its citizens from disaster."[31]

Within New York Roosevelt extended as strong protection as he could. The state and federal governments in the complex industrial society of the 1930s were totally unprepared to cope with cataclysmic depression. Most states were still functioning on the basis of poor-relief legislation devised in the reign of Queen Elizabeth I, which often provided little except to relegate the destitute to poorhouses or workhouses. New York was not much further advanced. In August, 1931, Roosevelt obtained legislation to establish the Temporary Emergency Relief Administration (TERA), and appointed to administer it a man he had not known except for a casual handshake in the 1928 campaign. That was Harry L. Hopkins, intense, shrewd, and highly capable, who had been executive director of the New York Tuberculosis and Health Association. Hopkins' role was almost entirely nonpolitical as he built a smooth-running agency, which was to be the prototype for subsequent New Deal relief programs, and he had little direct involvement with the governor.[32]

Circumstances continued to push Roosevelt's thinking toward new conclusions. At first he tried to run the TERA on a pay-as-you-go basis through increased taxes, but by the winter of 1931–1932 was forced to resort to heavy state borrowing and to seek federal aid. TERA was providing relief to nearly 10 percent of New York families, giving them an average of $23 per month, enough to prevent starvation at a time when the city of Rochester, through arrangements with wholesalers, could feed people for 15 cents a day. The New York program was munificent compared with that in some areas; Detroit could allow only 5 cents a day per person.[33]

Roosevelt, who had begun with the belief that relief must be a private and local matter, had come to realize that in the Great Depression only massive federal intervention would suffice.

Chapter 5

WINNING THE PRESIDENCY

WITH THE COLLAPSE of prosperity, Roosevelt's political fortunes began to rise. Republicans, who had taken credit for the boom, were blamed for the depression. Democrats, who had been so badly split into urban and rural factions, began to reconcile their differences as the economic crisis rather than prohibition became the prime issue. When he ran again for governor in 1930, Roosevelt adroitly sidetracked the waning debate over prohibition by asserting, as he had in the Progressive Era, that he favored state and local option on the sale of alcoholic beverages. One of the old prohibitionist slogans served his new purpose; the real problem, he said, was "bread not booze."[1]

Obviously Roosevelt could expect reelection — the odds were three to one in his favor by the end of September — but a comfortable victory would not be enough. With politicians and newspapermen throughout the country watching him, the degree of his success in 1930 would have a direct bearing upon his chances for the presidential nomination in 1932. It was equally important for the Republicans to stop him. The election of 1930 in New York seemed to center more on national than state issues and it was even something of a test run against the Hoover administration. The president sent three members of his cabinet, Secretary of State Henry L. Stimson, Secretary of the Treasury Ogden Mills, and Secretary of War Patrick Hurley, into New York to campaign against the governor. It was attention Roosevelt relished.[2]

Republicans tried during the campaign to divert attention from the depression by building a case that Roosevelt had failed to clean up the corruption of the Tammany machine in New York City, hoping they could drive a wedge between him and his largest block of sure votes.

Since Roosevelt was clinging to the narrow constitutional opinion that he was responsible solely for the government of the state, not of the city, the opponents seemed to have an opportunity to picture him as less than a crusader.

Through their pressure upon Roosevelt, the Republicans drove the Tammany leaders into the governor's camp; registration went up 17 percent in New York City, compared with 5 percent upstate. But they damaged Roosevelt seriously among those fighting for clean government. As Roosevelt alternated an occasional publicized crackdown with long spells of shilly-shallying, reformers became increasingly irritated over his failure to follow up his most forceful blow, a demand that officials should waive immunity and testify as to their official acts. Roosevelt lost stature among thousands of well-educated, well-informed people, such as the publicist Walter Lippmann, writing in the *New York World.* They deemed him a weak governor. The Olympian Stimson, after blasting Roosevelt in a radio talk, informed Lippmann that the *World* had been his prime source. As for Roosevelt, he campaigned as if the corruption issue did not exist.[3]

Again the health issue worried Roosevelt, and he took a dramatic step to try to forestall both decorous editorials and at least one indecent anonymous circular alleging that his physical problem was syphilis. A group of physicians on behalf of insurance companies examined him and publicly pronounced him in fine physical shape. He could expand his chest five and a half inches compared with the average person's three and one half. The insurance companies issued him $560,000 in policies at normal rates, with Georgia Warm Springs Foundation to be the beneficiary.[4]

The newly strengthened Democratic organizations were also of importance to Roosevelt. Jim Farley had helped revitalize upstate Democrats and was fond of pointing out how cumulatively helpful it would be if workers could turn out ten more voters in each of the 9,000 precincts. Mary (Molly) Dewson, a hearty bundle of energy, took charge of women's activities, campaigning on issues appealing to housewives. Roosevelt again singled out the high cost of electricity and commissioned a handbill comparing the cost of operating stoves, irons, and other appliances in New York and Canadian cities. Miss Dewson kept three stenographers busy writing letters to Democratic woman workers, enlisting their help in making use of the handbill. It worked so well that some women later referred to the 1930 election as the "waffle-iron campaign."[5]

Beginning with the peroration of his acceptance address, Roosevelt throughout the campaign focused upon the depression, and threw down the gauntlet to Hoover: "Lack of leadership in Washington has brought our country face to face with serious questions of unemployment and financial depression." In subsequent speeches he faulted the Republicans for not having curbed speculation in 1928–1929, for their falsely optimistic statements after the crash, and for their failure to take swift action — "nothing happened but words."[6]

Roosevelt won by a landslide, even carrying upstate New York, thanks to the defection of drys, who switched from the wet Republican candidate to the Prohibitionist. Tammany in New York City had turned out nine voters out of every ten. In addition, Roosevelt proved himself a formidable vote getter. North of New York City he had received a larger vote than the Democratic party registration, proof positive that he could win Republican votes. The margin for Roosevelt was 725,000 votes, almost double that of Smith in his best year.[7]

"The Democrats nominated their President yesterday, Franklin D. Roosevelt," wrote Will Rogers, the cowboy humorist, the day after the election. It was not a wisecrack. Numerous newspapers predicted his likely nomination, as 1932 showed signs of being a Democratic year and a Roosevelt year. Already the 1930 election had brought the Democrats control of the House of Representatives and near control of the Senate, and the 1932 nomination had become a valuable prize. Since Roosevelt was so conspicuous, his best strategy seemed to be to move rapidly to obtain pledges of delegates so that he would stay in front. Consequently, Farley after the election, without consulting the governor, at once announced, "I do not see how Mr. Roosevelt can escape becoming the next presidential nominee of his party." Roosevelt, as was expected of him, expressed his surprise and insisted that he was totally occupied with his duties as governor.[8]

Even though Roosevelt enjoyed considerable national popularity, the task of obtaining the requisite two thirds of the delegates to win the nomination at the 1932 convention was a formidable one. The rule, which had existed since the presidency of Jackson, was a reassurance to the "Solid South" that it could block candidates not to its taste.

An effective Roosevelt organization went to work. Behind the scenes in New York City, Howe increased the output of the letter-writing team, who wrote thousands of stock replies to correspondence from all over the nation, to which they signed Roosevelt's name. Roosevelt himself wrote extensively to Democratic leaders, both large and small. Farley became the "political drummer," swinging around the nation to sound out politicians and obtain commitments. Others who had been associated with Roosevelt in the Wilson era labored in Washington on his behalf.[9]

Since Roosevelt believed that his campaign must center on issues, early in 1932 he enlarged his group of advisers, bringing in several academic figures from Columbia University under the leadership of Moley to work on special problems and help draft speeches. Roosevelt came naturally to the idea. Smith had done so in the campaign of 1928, and Roosevelt depended upon professors in developing almost all of his key policies as governor. Moley was tried and trusted, sympathetic to Roosevelt's quest for change. He had come out of the Ohio of the dynamic progressive reformers Tom Johnson and Newton D. Baker, and had studied with Charles A. Beard, the renowned progressive historian. Moley proposed others of differing backgrounds to serve as advisers. On agriculture, he suggested Rexford G. Tugwell, an economist trained at the Wharton School, who proposed drastically remodeling the economic system. Tugwell was to become a major theoretician of the New Deal. Moley has reminisced, "Rex was like a cocktail. His conversation picked you up and made your brain race along." On credit and corporations, Moley chose Adolf A. Berle, Jr., of the Columbia Law School, who during the summer of 1932 published with Gardiner C. Means a landmark analysis, *The Modern Corporation and Private Property*. Many others were on the periphery.[10]

Moley and Sam Rosenman took these scholars and other candidates for what newspapermen were to call the "brain trust" to Albany, one or two at a time. After dinner, Roosevelt would pick their brains and make the final selection. According to Moley:

> The Governor was at once a student, a cross-examiner, and a judge. He would listen with rapt attention for a few minutes and then break in with a question whose sharpness was characteristically blurred with an anecdotal introduction or an air of sympathetic agreement with the speaker. . . . The questions . . . would become meatier, more informed — the infallible index to the amount [Roosevelt] was picking up in the evening's course.
>
> By midnight . . . the visitor . . . would look a trifle wilted; and the Governor . . . would be making vigorous pronouncements on the subject we had been discussing, waving his cigarette holder to emphasize his points.[11]

All this was essential to Roosevelt's education, since he must be able in the months ahead to extemporize quickly and correctly on many issues. Tugwell became especially skillful in briefing Roosevelt, whom he discovered lacking in knowledge of economics. Tugwell would reduce what he had to say to simple graphic terms, compressed to five minutes. Usually, he had the satisfaction within a few additional minutes of hearing his gifted pupil expound to someone else with emphasis and feeling what he had just acquired.[12]

The most complex problem facing Roosevelt was, ironically, that of Tammany and Al Smith. While he was refusing on constitutional grounds to give in to the goading of the Republican legislature and intervene in New York City to clean up corruption, he was also facing keen competition from Smith for the presidential nomination. Smith, feeling hurt that Roosevelt did not stand aside, rallied the urban machines and eastern conservative Democrats. Roosevelt aligned himself with southern and western leaders, who saw in him their best opportunity to thwart Smith and the urban wing of the party. There were several sharp contests in the meetings of the Democratic National Committee, which the Roosevelt forces won. Yet at the same time, numerous reformers within the Democratic party, and others without, like the Socialist Norman Thomas, were belaboring Roosevelt for not being more vigorous in the policing of Tammany. For his part, Roosevelt knew from painful experience that he would have trouble winning the presidential nomination if he were to alienate the urban Democrats. Moreover, as a member of the minority party he would badly need the urban machine votes if he were to win the election.[13]

With so many traps along the route to the nomination, Roosevelt had to proceed gingerly. He sought to avoid any animus that might make negotiations impossible at the convention or create a split in the party that would throw the election to President Hoover. Issues were intruding. Roosevelt had clear-cut programs as governor in the areas of agriculture, conservation, power development, social welfare, and unemployment relief. With some success he had followed a firm policy of declining to address issues in domestic or international affairs on the rather improbable grounds that it would be improper for him as governor to do so. The only area of his administration where his position was seriously equivocal was on Tammany corruption in New York City. From without, the League of Nations issue was to give him trouble.[14]

For well-informed citizens, especially intellectuals, Roosevelt's hedging was intolerable, and Lippmann, the most prestigious publicist of the era, fed their indignation. The game of gathering delegates first and defining policies later was ignoble, he asserted. "Governor Roosevelt belongs to the new postwar school of politicians who do not believe in stating their views unless and until there is no avoiding it." In a *New York Herald-Tribune* column on January 8, 1932, he protested that the governor was trying to straddle the whole country. Roosevelt, Lippmann warned, "is a highly impressionable person, without a firm grasp of public affairs, and without very strong convictions. . . . an amiable man with many philanthropic impulses, but he is not the dangerous enemy of anything. He is too eager to please." In total, charged Lippmann: "Franklin D. Roosevelt is no crusader. He is no tribune of the people. He is no enemy of entrenched privilege. He is a pleasant man who, without any important qualifications for the office, would very much like to be President."[15]

Lippmann's was the most penetrating attack upon Roosevelt in all the months leading up to the convention. It appeared in newspapers from coast to coast, and was reprinted and circulated as a telling analysis of Roosevelt's weakness. Through this and other columns ran a thread of praise for Newton D. Baker, but it was the "Friends of Smith" who capitalized most upon the critique. By January, 1932, Baker was clearing his way to be the compromise candidate should Roosevelt and Smith block each other. Lippmann's criticisms, although too harsh, came close to the mark; Roosevelt was too shrewd to reveal his hand except to gain vital support.[16]

In order to avoid future disaster, Roosevelt early in 1932 set forth his position on the League of Nations, although it was likely to cost him defections. It was a painful maneuver and he did it with caution. The powerful publisher William Randolph Hearst, with his national chain of newspapers, forced Roosevelt's hand. On New Year's Day, 1932, Hearst nominated Speaker John Nance Garner of Texas, urging the nation to reject the Wilsonian internationalists and elect a president whose slogan would be "America First." Hearst's attacks upon Roosevelt as being pro-league began to rally old isolationists against the governor. Roosevelt had to act. In an address to the New York State Grange, he granted that he had worked for the league in 1920, but said that the league of 1932 was not the one Wilson had conceived. Its members had focused upon European difficulties in which the United States should have no part; they had not diverted the huge sums spent on armaments to the balancing of budgets and payment of obligations — war debts owed the United States. "American participation . . . would not serve the highest purpose of the prevention of war and a settlement of international difficulties. . . . Therefore I do not favor American participation."[17]

The disavowal of the league was not particularly inconsistent with Roosevelt's views at the time or for some years to come, but did involve a mixture of political cynicism and desperation. Had Hearst pressed Roosevelt, he would have also turned against the World Court, which even Coolidge had favored entering. Colonel Edward M. House, who had been Wilson's closest adviser, lamented that Roosevelt had "created something akin to panic among the devoted Wilson followers." Bertie Hamlin wrote tartly, "I am devoted to Franklin but he ought to be spanked." However, the statement served its political purpose; without it Roosevelt probably would not have won the nomination.[18]

There was no such easy solution to the equivocation on Tammany corruption. Had Roosevelt been too vigorous in trying to clean up New York City, he would have jeopardized not only the block of 96 New York votes at the convention but also the machine votes of Illinois, Indiana, and New Jersey. As with the isolationist supporters of Garner, Roosevelt wanted their votes if possible, and at least not their unswerving opposition. Nor did Roosevelt have any illusions about the popular playboy mayor of New York City, Jimmy Walker. As early as March, 1931, he commented, "our little Mayor can save much trouble in the future by getting on the job, cleaning his own house and stopping wisecracks."[19]

The Jimmy Walker problem would not go away. In the spring of 1931, Roosevelt would not accede to the demands of two reformers, the Reverend John Haynes Holmes and Rabbi Stephen S. Wise, that he remove Walker, as was within his power as governor. He did, however, sign a bill authorizing a legislative investigation of New York City corruption. It got under way in June, 1931, with the energetic Samuel Seabury as chief counsel. The Seabury investigation gathered an enormous amount of evidence, some of it appalling. Roosevelt did act against Sheriff Thomas M. Farley of New York County, who despite a salary and legitimate income of only $87,000 in a seven-year period, made bank deposits of $396,000. Roosevelt in February, 1932, ordered Farley removed. He balked, though, when Holmes and Wise asked him to remove two other officeholders. In May, 1932, Walker had to take the stand, and evaded serious questions Seabury put to him. How had a bookkeeper in his old law firm been able to deposit $961,000 in the bank and pay many of Walker's bills out of it? Roosevelt met the clamor for action by declaring, "It is time to stop talking and do something." Seabury did act, sending Roosevelt a transcript of the hearings and fifteen accusations against Walker. It put Roosevelt in a moral as well as political predicament, as Lippmann pointed out, "For to try James J. Walker before a man who stands to profit enormously by convicting him is a revolting spectacle."[20]

Roosevelt did the one thing possible: on June 21, six days before the Democratic convention met, he sent Seabury's charges to Walker and reqested a reply. Walker declared he would respond after the convention was over. Consequently, Roosevelt was forced to fight for the nomination with the Walker problem unsettled.[21]

Through the preceding months Roosevelt had been competing for delegates, moving beyond the old-fashioned belief that the nomination should seek the candidate, but staying short of the activism of later generations. He delivered a few long talks and made a radio broadcast or two, each with a strong, but not too specific, progressive approach. The most notable, on April 7, was a broadcast in which he asserted that the depression was a graver emergency than World War I, but that the Hoover administration, far from mobilizing the nation, had ignored or overlooked the "forgotten men." By these, Roosevelt meant both the middle and lower class. He advocated raising the purchasing power of the farmer, since "no nation can endure half bankrupt." The government must do more than loan money at the top; it must help farmers and homeowners with their mortgages. These mild generalizations offended conservatives, and so antagonized Smith that in a Jefferson Day address he declared, "I will . . . fight to the end against any candidate who persists in any demagogic appeal to the masses of the working people of this country . . . by setting class against class and rich against poor." Later, at Oglethorpe University in Georgia, Roosevelt again laid himself open to charges of radicalism by declaring, "The country needs, and unless I mistake its temper, the country demands bold, persistent experimentation."[22]

Ideologically Roosevelt was in step with the dominant public mood and made an early and impressive start in winning delegates. Although he was an eastern governor, he especially aimed his public statements toward the South and West and there he was most successful. Throughout the South he worked with the regular party leaders and tied up the delegations of all but four of the sixteen southern and border states. From the Middle West to the Pacific Coast he also did well. Yet there were setbacks. He botched Massachusetts, where he had been maneuvered into cooperating with the minority faction of Mayor James Michael Curley of Boston, and Smith won three to one. In California, Smith's entrance changed a predicted walkaway for Roosevelt into a Garner victory. There were further disappointments but no more spectacular mishaps.[23]

By the end of June the outcome at the Chicago convention was still in some doubt. Smith and the "Stop Roosevelt" forces had demonstrated strength in the East; Garner had behind him the large delegations of Texas and California. Roosevelt had acquired more than a majority of the delegates, but had failed by some eighty votes to acquire the two thirds necessary to nominate on the first ballot.

Additional problems awaited in Chicago. One was the prospect that Jouett Shouse, chairman of the Democratic National Committee and closely tied to Al Smith and John Raskob, who had been Smith's campaign manager, might become permanent chairman of the convention. His rulings could have been damaging, even fatal — as subsequently when the Minnesota delegation sought a ruling to permit delegates to vote their individual preferences rather than be bound as a solid unit. Roosevelt devised a compromise on the permanent chairmanship. The arrangements committee was to commend rather than recommend Shouse, and "commend," Roosevelt made clear, was to be no more than a nonbinding gesture of goodwill. Shouse, of course, dropped the distinction between the two words, and claimed he had been promised the permanent chairmanship. At the convention, when Roosevelt forces chose Senator Thomas J. Walsh of Montana, Shouse and the Smith forces charged bad faith.[24]

Further dispute broke out over the rule requiring two thirds of the delegates' votes in order to nominate, which had led to the long and bitter deadlock at the 1924 convention. Had Roosevelt leaders suddenly popped a proposal to repeal it to the assembled convention, they probably would have won, but Huey Long, the Louisiana "Kingfish," prematurely offered a resolution to abolish the rule. It led to such vehement protests of bad sportsmanship from Smith and the noncandidate Baker that Roosevelt and Farley wisely dropped the issue. The Allies, as the "Stop Roosevelt" forces called themselves, began to believe they could win.[25] Farley has pointed out that the Allies saw nothing unsporting in their efforts to block a candidate with well over a majority of the delegates. (Neither had Roosevelt in 1924, when it was McAdoo who for endless ballots commanded a majority.)

The "Stop Roosevelt" movement almost succeeded. Had it done so, the beneficiary would not have been Smith, who keenly sought the vindication of the nomination and presidency after his humiliating defeat in 1928. Nor would it have been the Texan John Nance Garner, who at the time seemed to have a touch of populism about him. Rather, it would have been Baker, a former Wilsonian progressive, who had refused to abandon his faith in the League of Nations. In recent years he had been legal counsel for electric utility companies and the Van Sweringen railroad interests. Democratic conservatives had good reason to rally around him. The Allies were, consequently, an unstable coalition, bound only by their wish to defeat Roosevelt. Farley and numerous of the Roosevelt leaders ceaselessly negotiated to try to gain one or another block of delegates committed to favorite sons or Garner. Conversely, the Allies worked hard on every wavering Roosevelt delegate and found weaknesses in Mississippi and were pressing Iowa, Michigan, and Maine. Smith kept predicting Roosevelt's support would disintegrate after the first ballot, and the sardonic commentator Henry L. Mencken, hostile to Roosevelt, reported, "His followers here are as silent as if they were up to something unpalatable to the police." On the contrary, the Roosevelt delegates were loud, but sometimes had trouble making themselves heard over the Smith claque, with which Mayor Anton Cermak's Chicago machine had packed the galleries.[26]

Through the nervous night, when names of candidates were being put in nomination, Roosevelt in Albany, chain-smoking, was closely following the proceedings. It was dawn before the nominating process ended. Roosevelt ordered an immediate ballot; to act otherwise would have been a sign of weakness. He received 666¼ votes, 89 more than a majority, and 464½ ahead of the nearest rival, but 104 short of two thirds. For two more ballots, as Farley squeezed out a few reserve votes to bring Roosevelt slightly up, the Allies stood firm. Roosevelt was still 87 votes short. Finally at 9:15 in the morning the delegates staggered back to their hotel rooms, feeling that Roosevelt had been stopped and the convention deadlocked.[27]

Through the day the Roosevelt supporters negotiated, knowing that unless they succeeded immediately, Roosevelt probably was through. The Mississippi delegation was about to switch. Farley and Howe agreed to stake everything on Texas, and Farley had a quick conversation with Garner's manager, Sam Rayburn. "We'll see what can be done," said Rayburn. Others, including Joseph P. Kennedy, a financier involved in Democratic politics, tried to persuade Hearst, who hated Smith and feared Baker, to swing the California delegation. Only Garner could do that. Garner refused to accept a phone call from Smith; he heard from Hearst only indirectly.

Garner himself played the decisive role in guaranteeing the nomination to Roosevelt. He feared that a stalemate in Chicago would hurt public confidence and that a compromise candidate — he too thought it would be Baker — was not likely to win. Furthermore, Roosevelt was closer to his views than Smith or Baker. He called Rayburn to tell him he thought the time had come to end the balloting. Rayburn later reported California would switch, but not Texas, unless Garner would be vice presidential nominee. Garner disliked leaving the powerful position of Speaker, but said, "Hell, I'll do anything to see the Democrats win one more national election."

On the fourth ballot that night, when California was called, McAdoo announced the switch to Roosevelt. The galleries rocked with hisses and boos; Roosevelt delegates went wild with joy. Texas went along. Thus Roosevelt received the nomination.[28]

The tight squeeze at the convention had been too short for bitterness to develop. Except for a few die-hard Smith supporters, the Democrats united quickly behind Roosevelt. One disgruntled Texas delegate grumbled on the way home that the Roosevelt-Garner slate was a kangaroo ticket, stronger in the hind end than the front. No matter. Old-line Texas agrarians and ward heelers in the eastern machines, sensing victory in the fall, buried their differences.[29]

Instantly Roosevelt dramatized to the American people in their depression plight his willingness to break with tradition. As part of political ritual all previous nominees had waited some weeks before receiving notification of their nomination and delivering acceptance speeches; none as candidate had flown in an airplane. As he had planned for weeks, Roosevelt early the next morning boarded a plane, although he did not relish flying, and flew to Chicago to address the waiting delegates. Since World War I Roosevelt had not trusted airplanes, and the flight against head winds was particularly slow and bumpy. Unperturbed, he worked over his acceptance speech with Rosenman and even napped. Amidst the cheering throng at the airport, the passengers finally disembarked, first Mrs. Roosevelt, Elliott, and John, who was airsick. Then Roosevelt, nonchalant and beaming. "I was a good sailor," he remarked to Mayor Cermak, who had come to greet him. He rode through the streets, waving to the cheering throngs and riffling through another draft acceptance speech that Howe handed him.

At the convention hall, amid thunderous applause, Roosevelt began delivering his speech. Moley, in the rear, followed Roosevelt on his copy of the address, and was puzzled by the unfamiliar words. Then in a couple of minutes the phrases fell into line. Roosevelt, not wishing to disappoint Howe in his hour of triumph, had substituted the first page of Howe's draft for the one he brought with him, and then swung into his prepared speech.[30]

In outline, Roosevelt set forth the positions he had been advocating through the spring: government economy, prohibition repeal, regulation of securities sales, self-sustaining public works, reforestation, a lower tariff, a voluntary crop control program, refinancing of farm and home mortgages, and federal relief. In his peroration there was a note of progressive zeal:

"I pledge you, I pledge myself, to a new deal for the American people. . . . Give me your help, not to win votes alone, but to win in this crusade to restore America to its own people."[31]

The words "new deal" stuck. There was nothing new about them, and nothing consciously slogan-making in their insertion in the speech. They were so widely in use that no one noticed when several hours before, John McDuffie of Alabama had declared in nominating Garner for vice president: "There is a demand for a new deal. . . ." The appearance of the phrase in Roosevelt's peroration caused it to catch the imagination of newspapermen. The next day a Rollin Kirby cartoon appeared depicting a farmer gazing skyward at an airplane. On it was the legend "New Deal."[32]

Roosevelt, as full of verve and energy as though he had just returned from vacation, plunged into his campaign work before applause died down, shaking hands with delegates as he left the platform and for hours afterward. At dinner with the Democratic National Committee, he lavished praise upon "my very good and old friend John Raskob" and "my old friend Jouett Shouse," his bitter adversaries of the day before. After midnight in his hotel room, alone with Moley, he talked for an hour and a half about his plans, while Moley jotted pages and pages of notes on trips, speeches, and even on speech content.[33]

Roosevelt waged a shrewd, unspectacular campaign. Since less than a third of the registered voters were Democrats, in order to win he had to attract large numbers of normally Republican voters. He reasoned that the depression was the overriding issue and that disillusioned voters would be turning against Hoover. In late August at Columbus, Ohio, Roosevelt enlivened his first major campaign speech with an *Alice in Wonderland* parody of Republican policies of the 1920s, which incidentally throws light on Roosevelt's own views:

> A puzzled, somewhat skeptical Alice asked the Republican leadership some simple questions: . . .
>
> "What if we produce a surplus?"
>
> "Oh, we can sell it to foreign consumers."
>
> "How can the foreigners pay for it?"
>
> "Why, we will lend them the money."
>
> "I see," said little Alice, "they will buy our surplus with our money. Of course, these foreigners will pay us back by selling us their goods?"
>
> "Oh, not at all," said Humpty Dumpty. "We set up a high wall called the tariff."
>
> "And," said Alice at last, "how will the foreigners pay off these loans?"
>
> "That is easy," said Humpty Dumpty, "did you ever hear of moratorium?"[34]

Republicans attacked the speech as a monumental folly, another sign of Roosevelt's weakness. For some time President Hoover had felt blue, Secretary of State Stimson noted in his diary, because he and his advisers "were awake to the full power which Roosevelt will produce in the field to the radical elements of the West and the South." Their consolation was that they considered Roosevelt not a strong character and expected he would lose the confidence of eastern businessmen.[35]

The one real Republican hope was that a sudden, spectacular return of prosperity might save their ticket. There were indeed some signs of improvement. The *New York Times* "Weekly Index of Business Activity," including car loadings and production of steel, electric power, automobiles, and lumber, rose from about two thirds of normal on August 6, 1932, to three fourths of normal by January 7, 1933. Hoover in later years regarded this as the beginning of true recovery, destroyed by the politicking of Roosevelt and the Democrats. Claude Bowers, an ardently Democratic historian, wrote Roosevelt his suspicions that the Republicans were manipulating the market. "You are right about the Republican game —" Roosevelt replied, "their strategy is now perfectly plain."[36]

Any economic upswing was not reaching the average voter, especially farmers. Prices had not gone up since spring, when one of Roosevelt's angry constituents sent him a voucher indicating she had received 39 cents net for the sale of a four-week-old calf. The ugly encampment of the Bonus Army in Washington was further evidence of national desperation. Some eleven thousand veterans were encamped, many in a shantytown by the Anacostia River, trying to pressure Congress into paying them the bonus it had earlier voted for service in World War I. As disorder increased, the president instructed the army to evict the bonus marchers. Newsreels showed tanks rumbling through the streets and soldiers equipped with gas masks and fixed bayonets advancing on the jeering veterans. Refugees carrying their possessions rushed from their burning hovels as the soldiers charged, throwing tear gas ahead of them. From coast to coast, theater audiences hissed and booed as they viewed the shocking scenes. It may have been a necessary move, but it was bad politics, underscoring as it did the desperation of masses of Americans and adding to the personal unpopularity of Hoover.[37]

As for Roosevelt, there was indeed danger during the summer of 1932 that, in confining himself to middle-of-the-road generalities in order not to offend differing components of the Democratic coalition, he would appear weak not merely in his economic thinking but in his personal decisiveness. It was at this point that he rose to the challenge of the postponed problem over the Tammany mayor, Jimmy Walker. From

Chicago, that erstwhile Bull Moose Republican Harold L. Ickes warned, "While many independents and Republicans are favorably inclined toward you at this time I find that they are not prepared to make up their minds finally until you have passed upon the case of Mayor Walker."[38]

On August 11, 1932, Roosevelt opened the Walker hearings. Flanked by his brilliant counsel Martin Conboy, he began an acute and merciless questioning of Walker. The hearing dragged on and Roosevelt stepped up the pace with additional sessions from eight to eleven in the evening. As Roosevelt fired questions, many who had doubted the depth and capacity of the governor began to regard him with a new respect. Throughout, Walker gave no better answers than he had to Seabury. Roosevelt expected to be exceedingly careful in coming to a decision; he had invited Felix Frankfurter of Harvard Law School to come to Albany to advise him on ethical and legal points. Observers wondered if Roosevelt would merely censure Walker. One day Roosevelt mused to Moley, "What if I gave the little mayor hell and then let him off?" Roosevelt never had to decide, for Walker on September 1 resigned as mayor.[39]

Roosevelt and his advisers were relieved, for now they could concentrate entirely upon the campaign. Robert W. Bingham of the *Louisville Courier-Journal* expressed the consensus that "you gave a host of people throughout the country an opportunity to know you. It was a grand job, fearlessly, fairly, nobly done." Tammanyites were resentful, but Smith at the state Democratic convention closed the rift with Roosevelt and campaigned for him.[40]

Professionals, still having some qualms about Roosevelt's health, urged him to play it safe and limit himself to a few national radio speeches. On the other hand, Senator Thomas Walsh of Montana told him what he wanted to hear, that a trip to the Pacific Coast would dispel any remaining whispers. He loved to barnstorm, and so enjoyed himself on a western swing that subsequently he campaigned through the South, although in the entire area not an electoral vote was in question. There was another justification. Both in the West and South he spent time with the congressional leaders upon whom he would depend for the enactment of his program. More than merely seeking election, he was already selling his program in its rudiments.[41]

On these trips Roosevelt perfected a routine, which he seemed to relish as much as his audiences did. At each whistle-stop the engineer would pull the train in for only about a minute. As soon as it came to a dead stop, Roosevelt would step out onto the back of the last car, his hand tightly grasping the arm of his tall, prematurely bald, eldest son,

James. Roosevelt would grin and remark, "It's nice to be back in so-and-so. I am just out here to look, learn and listen." He would introduce his daughter, Anna, and his daughter-in-law, James's wife, Betsy Cushing Roosevelt, and finally turn to his son. "And this is my little boy James. I have more hair than he has." The crowd would roar, but Moley observed that after about a score of these performances James grew rather depressed. Evenings after his speeches Roosevelt held open house to all comers in his rooms. He would shake hands and exchange pleasantries until after midnight, yet the next day be fresh and vigorous, making his appearances, conferring with local politicians, and polishing speeches.[42]

In the major addresses, Roosevelt framed his positive recommendations in such broad generalities that those seeking specific remedies would think they had found them and others would not be offended. His farm speech at Topeka, Kansas, was a prime example. He pledged himself in murky terms, using code words, to what farmers would know to be a crop reduction program, and each of several rival farm factions could assume to be its specific program. At the same time he did not frighten urban and suburban America, since he also pledged the program should not cost the taxpayers.[43]

Altogether, there were in Roosevelt's campaign speeches, if one read them properly, promises of a full array of progressive measures. A memorandum Moley drafted in May, 1932, foreshadowed almost all of the early New Deal legislation except the National Industrial Recovery Act. Roosevelt said nothing to indicate he was considering the politically hazardous course of inflating the currency. On public development of hydroelectric power, he was, to the delight of its great exponent, Senator George Norris, firm and specific. In calling for a drastic cut in government expenditures to balance the budget, he was also emphatic, to the delight of conservatives, and more than that, he was sincere. In the most frequently quoted of his campaign speeches, before the Commonwealth Club in San Francisco, he declared that the nation had reached the frontiers of its economic development. Thereafter the government must regulate the economy so that everyone could "possess himself of a portion of that plenty sufficient for his needs, through his own work."[44]

Some intellectuals found little to choose between Roosevelt's bland promises and the grim speeches in which Hoover contended that without his remedial measures the nation would be in a much worse plight. Yet to Hoover, the New Deal seemed to threaten the American way of life. "This campaign is more than a contest between two parties," he declared. "It is a contest between two philosophies of government."[45]

Nothing of shocking dimensions divided the two candidates, but there were basic differences. President Hoover had seen the depression as being worldwide in origin and development; Roosevelt chose to view it as a domestic calamity and, capitalizing upon the popular tendency to make the president the scapegoat, blamed it upon the Republican party. The concept of the depression as domestic marked also the direction in which Roosevelt was ready to take the New Deal. Since he had scuttled the tariff issue and beaten the League of Nations dead horse, he was free to move in the direction of economic nationalism. Through his speeches, too, there had run the theme of social and economic planning for the general welfare. Although this ran counter to the reiterated pledges of economy and a balanced budget, it was clearly the stronger of the two themes, and Roosevelt never worried when two of his policies were contradictory. This outline was not clear to most voters, but is significant as representing the great strides Roosevelt himself had taken in self-education before and during the campaign.

On election eve, Roosevelt must have been thinking about these things. Moley remembers him sitting quietly in front of an open fire at the home in Hyde Park talking "of the campaign, of the gathering economic storm clouds — the tumbling prices, the mounting unemployment." He would be assuming a gargantuan task and an awesome responsibility.[46]

When the final vote was in, Roosevelt had carried 42 states, and Hoover only 6. The electoral vote was 472 to 59. He received 57.4 percent of the popular vote, and Hoover 39.7 percent. The responsibility was falling upon Roosevelt.

Chapter 6

THE INTERREGNUM CRISIS

AMID THE ACUTE ECONOMIC DETERIORATION during the winter of 1932–1933, the nation had to wait four months before Roosevelt could take office and inaugurate his promised program to combat the depression. The somewhat encouraging signs of the summer had vanished with the autumn leaves, and the American people had to endure rising unemployment, falling business index figures, and farm prices dropping to catastrophic levels. From Chicago, where Edmund Wilson witnessed hungry women scavenging on garbage heaps for scraps of food, Jane Addams of Hull House noted to a friend, "One has a sense of at least 'standing by' if only to hear the stories of the unemployed. It has been like a disaster or flood, fire or earthquake, this universal wiping out of resources." The climax came with runs on banks during the last weeks and days before President Hoover left office.[1]

Throughout the industrial nations of the world, economic conditions were desperate, from Japan, resorting to imperialist ventures on the Asiatic mainland, to Germany, where the Nazi fanatic Adolf Hitler was coming into power. Some frightened observers worried not only whether the American economic system could survive, but even whether democratic institutions could weather the economic storm. All Americans waited for Roosevelt, and without too much hope.

Roosevelt for his part allowed the impression to grow through these months that he would be little more than a weak, albeit optimistic, facade for the conservative Democratic leaders in Congress. To judge by newspaper accounts, his chief concern was the same as theirs, indeed that of the most respected pundits of both parties: to make drastic cuts in government services and, if need be, to raise taxes in order to balance the budget. Like that of an eighteenth-century physician, the prescription for the depressed economy, which was bleeding acutely through deflation, seemed to be more bleeding. It was not a heartening prospect, and may have caused economic as well as psychological damage.

Roosevelt did have a grand design for both domestic and foreign policy, but he did not announce more than a few details and did not allow it to become a focal point of newspaper speculation. His dream was that relatively minor readjustments in the governmental and economic systems would bring a rapid and lasting return to prosperity. Like Hoover he believed in only limited governmental action to stimulate an economy that he regarded as basically self-regulating, but the limits he was ready to set upon the role of the government even during the interregnum were far less stringent than Hoover's. The first step would be emergency measures to stimulate recovery, perhaps in a matter of months, and the second, long-range reforms to forestall future depressions and to guarantee greater security to all of the American people. He hoped, too, to bring the United States into the forefront in underwriting world security from both depression and military aggression.

Readers would have searched in vain through most journals of the period for indications of Roosevelt's overall plans. True, in *Liberty* magazine he reiterated his campaign promises in generalities encompassing almost every aspect of the subsequent legislation of the first hundred days in office, but only insiders knew what the generalities might mean. In private, he tried to quell the fears of progressive supporters through assurances that he was not repudiating his earlier positions.[2]

There were compelling reasons for Roosevelt to give an impression of weak conservatism. He had not yet worked out the details of many of his more innovative schemes, nor did he know when it would be advantageous to submit them to Congress. To discuss them in advance would destroy the dramatic effect of surprise messages to Congress. More important, it would give the conservatives of both parties time to muster strength against the proposals. It would cost Roosevelt in advance the support of many people of differing views who had coalesced behind him because they wanted to be rid of Hoover, not because they wished bold action. Specifics would have given President Hoover, who embarked upon an intense power struggle with Roosevelt, significant leverage against the president-elect.

To a later generation, the idea seems incredible that such a mild program could appear, as it did to leaders of both parties and to most better-educated citizens, as a daring, dangerous break with the past. It embodied nothing more than a limited enlistment of federal power on behalf of economic planning and regulation, but would indeed be a departure from the economic fundamentalism of the era. In February the Senate Finance Committee held hearings, hailed by the press as a "depression clinic," to provide guidelines for the president-elect. For weeks the nation's most prestigious financiers, industrialists, bankers, brokers, economists, and statesmen testified before it, giving advice they hoped would be binding. With a few exceptions their consensus was that the new president must cut federal spending drastically and impose new taxes in order to balance the budget. They recommended piling new deflationary measures upon those of Hoover, who had already increased taxes by nearly a third. That was the received wisdom of the day. Roosevelt seemed to accept it wholeheartedly. He concealed what he intended to do in addition. With a few exceptions he did not announce his plans until he possessed the power and prestige of the presidency with which to sell them to the electorate and Congress. The American people, nurtured upon the doctrines of laissez-faire and limited government, could easily be frightened. Al Smith, a year before, tried unsuccessfully to demolish Roosevelt as a radical before swinging back to denunciation of him as a political lightweight. It was less damaging to Roosevelt during the interregnum to be considered a weakling than a dangerous man.[3]

Meanwhile, through his charm and amiability, Roosevelt lulled the Democratic leadership in Congress and preserved the broad coalition that had elected him. He also made himself less vulnerable to President Hoover's efforts to abort the New Deal before it could come into being.

Hoover, continuing in office for months after his defeat, sought resourcefully to save the nation from what he felt was its fatal error at the polls in electing Roosevelt. The fact that Senator George Norris' "lame-duck" amendment, advancing Inauguration Day from March 4 to January 20, had not yet gone into effect gave him additional weeks to work upon the president-elect. Hoover became ever firmer in his view that his program was correct and that whatever Roosevelt might be projecting threatened disaster.

The interregnum thus developed into a power struggle between Hoover and Roosevelt. Congress was already rather completely under Hoover's negative control. Although the Democrats, thanks to progressive Republican aid in the Senate, could command a majority, they were fragmented into several views. Whatever legislation they enacted that went contrary to the specific judgment of President Hoover faced certain veto. As economic conditions worsened, Hoover blamed Roosevelt for their decline and tightened pressure upon him to relinquish his plans for the New Deal.

The struggle between the two men was the more painful because they had enjoyed a pleasant social relationship when both served under Wilson during World War I. Roosevelt had so admired Hoover that he had hoped Hoover would be the Democratic candidate for president in 1920. But Hoover was a Republican. Still, that did not dampen their cordiality, which continued for some years. Then, after Hoover was president, he became incensed upon seeing a letter of Roosevelt's widely distributed in the 1928 campaign urging voters to fulfill the ideals of Wilson by putting Al Smith in the White House rather than Hoover because of his "materialistic and self-seeking advisors." That hurt Hoover to the quick. On the Roosevelt side of the split, the incident was equally trivial and untoward. In the spring of 1932 when the governors had come to the White House, Hoover kept them waiting for perhaps a half hour. It was a hot day, Roosevelt was wearing his steel braces, and he stood with perspiration running down his face, refusing to take a chair. Rumors were still circulating that he was a cripple without the physical stamina to be president. He was convinced, and so was Mrs. Roosevelt, accompanying him, that Hoover's action was deliberate. It was over these pathetic unintended slights on each side that the relationship became so bitter, and cooperation during the interregnum so difficult.[4]

The futile interchange between the outgoing and incoming presidents began when, several days after the election, Hoover wired Roosevelt inviting him to confer on three interrelated questions, the European payment of war debts owed to the United States, the role of the United States in the disarmament conference at Geneva, and plans for a world economic conference. Hoover hoped to convert Roosevelt to his view on all these matters. On disarmament there was no conflict, but on war debts and the economic conference there was.

At the heart of the matter was Hoover's firm conviction that the depression was of world origin, and that a vital step to recovery was maintenance of the gold standard among the great powers. Hoover hoped that through trading concessions on war debt payments he could persuade the British to return to the gold standard. It was a forlorn hope, since the British had no intention of making more than token payments on the war debts, or of returning to the gold standard. Further, since reports had come to Hoover during the campaign that Roosevelt was thinking of abandoning the gold standard, he seems thus to have hoped to maneuver Roosevelt into committing himself to gold.

The conference at the White House was dismal. Hoover, well informed, was nervous. Roosevelt, vague about specifics, was so outwardly affable that he seemed to be agreeing to Hoover's proposal for establishment of a commission on war debts when in fact he was not. A second meeting some weeks later went little better. The meetings served only to heighten misunderstanding between the two men. Hoover felt he had acted as a man of goodwill who wished to prevent a dangerous delay in international negotiations and wanted to help Roosevelt with his own program. What Hoover overlooked was that he was willing to aid only if Roosevelt totally conformed to his views; he would not accept even minor differences. When the two men conferred privately for a few minutes, Roosevelt asked support on a farm measure; Hoover, believing in a somewhat different formula, refused. As for Roosevelt, from the beginning to the end of the interregnum he insisted that he would not assume responsibility through joint action with the president when as the president-elect he still lacked power.[5]

Nevertheless out of these initial interchanges Roosevelt did begin to attain power over foreign policy. He met with the outgoing secretary of state, Henry L. Stimson, and readily agreed to continue the "Stimson doctrine" of refusing to recognize the Japanese conquests in Manchuria. The public avowal was of some consequence, coming as the member nations of the league were about to vote whether or not to censure Japan. Moreover, Roosevelt, acting through Secretary Stimson, became directly involved in war debt discussions and undertook his own planning for the world economic conference.[6]

With far more ease Roosevelt husbanded his goodwill in Congress during these preparatory months. At first he seemed to hope that two of his key recovery measures, those balancing the budget and providing aid to farmers, could go through the lame-duck session. In consequence, while he gave private assurances to both Democratic and Republican progressives that he was not abandoning them, he courted the more conservative Democratic leaders. He was so deferential that Senator Cordell Hull of Tennessee thought of establishing a congressional advisory system to act almost as a regency for the incoming president. The cautious Hull, who favored only tariff reductions and farm relief, became so fearful of Roosevelt's apparent conservatism that he sent an intermediary to exhort him toward progressivism.[7]

Any hope Roosevelt may have had of obtaining legislation before March 4 soon became obviously futile. There was both disunity in Congress and the certainty that President Hoover would veto whatever did not measure up to his precise specifications. Yet the false impression of weakness did not in the end seem to have harmed Roosevelt with either the public or Congress. The nation regarded Congress as too divided to act, and even many members of Congress felt the need for strong presidential leadership. Senator Josiah Bailey of North Carolina, later to be one of Roosevelt's most persistent critics, wrote in January, 1933:

"Dictatorships act upon reason and democracies act upon necessity. It is not difficult to get one man to decide on the course but it is very difficult to get five hundred men to decide on anything, and this is especially true in the present state of the public mind."[8]

Simultaneously Roosevelt was planning programs involving both international and national approaches to economic recovery. As yet he did not seem to feel the need to choose between the two, although to his competing groups of advisers, they were incompatible. The onetime Wilsonian diplomatists like Colonel Edward M. House and Norman Davis, and some influential young men like James Warburg of the international banking family and Representative Lewis Douglas of Arizona, urged him toward international monetary stabilization and economic cooperation to bring recovery. Senator Cordell Hull sought above all to reduce trade barriers. On the other side, Roosevelt's principal advisers, most notably Raymond Moley and Rexford Tugwell of Columbia University, were earnestly advocating the development of a national recovery program behind tariff walls. Further, they profoundly feared that Roosevelt's tentative ventures toward collective security would bring involvement in war. Roosevelt listened encouragingly to the proposals of each side. The development of a domestic recovery program, especially in the area of agriculture, began slowly to pull him into commitments to economic nationalism.

Roosevelt went about planning the recovery program in a systematic way. Moley presided over a group of experts, most of whom had been members of the speech-writing "brain trust" during the campaign, and assigned each a specific problem or problems. In characteristic fashion, Roosevelt also turned for advice to numerous others outside of this group, sometimes setting them to work on parallel or at times even contrary projects. Thus individuals or teams planned legislation and action in areas ranging from the rehabilitation of agriculture and railroads through regulation of securities offerings and the balancing of the budget. Moley was aware of most of what was going on, but from time to time discovered additional persons at work under mandates from Roosevelt. Only he in the final analysis knew in total what the overall program was and who was working upon it. Whether or not Roosevelt always acted intentionally, in this fashion he kept control over policy. His approach to the New Deal was experimental, and he gave frequent encouragement to members of his circle proposing novel solutions to problems. In the end he could weigh the competing plans, and move from his initial enthusiasm for what was fresh or even bizarre to a more conservative choice of what might be acceptable to Congress. Or, as often was the case, when he confronted strong pressures among lobbies and within Congress for competing alternatives, he would synthesize them all into a single bulging parcel. He thus held at least temporarily the support of numerous influential figures of fundamentally differing views. It was vital for Roosevelt to build a broad consensus for the forthcoming New Deal.

The New Deal, as Roosevelt planned it, was to be economic regulation through a concert of the major interests. If this be treason, he had responded to conservative challengers in April, 1932, "make the most of it." On that occasion he had lauded Andrew Jackson for having declared, "The spirit of equity requires that the great interests of agriculture, commerce, and manufactures should be equally treated."[9]

Of all the programs, agriculture was foremost in Roosevelt's thinking and planning. He regarded it as the key to overall recovery; if the buying power of the farmers could be restored, their purchases would stimulate industrial, urban recovery. He felt that the lean years of agriculture in the 1920s, curtailing the purchasing power of the 22 percent of the people living on farms, had in time dragged down the entire economy. Gross farm income had dropped from $17 billion in 1919 to $12 billion in 1929, while middle-class city dwellers were enjoying Coolidge prosperity — and by the depression year 1932 it had fallen to $5 billion. During his campaign, Roosevelt, paraphrasing Lincoln, had declared, "This Nation cannot endure if it is half 'boom' and half 'broke.' " The immediate necessity, Roosevelt emphasized, was to raise farm prices.

For the long range, Roosevelt was keenly interested in rural planning and conservation, and in romantic Jeffersonian terms talked of the necessity to move millions of permanently unemployed city dwellers back onto the land, where they could produce their own food on small plots and work at least part-time in local, decentralized factories. That would be for the future.

The immediate necessity in the winter of 1932–1933 was to devise legislation to reduce production and increase the prices of the basic commodities. Grains were selling for so little that farmers on the prairies and Great Plains were burning corn and wheat to keep warm; cotton prices were a disaster. While food was rotting in some areas, in others even farmers were going hungry. Some farmers in a vigilante spirit went to foreclosure sales with guns and hangman's nooses to frighten away outside bidders and to bid back for the victim his horses, cows, and machinery at a pittance.

In this crisis of agrarian desperation, Roosevelt demonstrated his adeptness in publicizing and steering the planning for the farm program. While he asserted frequently that the agriculture bill should be whatever the farmers wished, he put quiet pressure upon the farm organizations to reconcile their differences and draft a single program. In turn, their unified pressure upon the conservative chairmen of the House and Senate agricultural committees would help in time to bring action. Finally, since almost all the competing proposals involved limitation of production, it was essential to act fast before the wheat-planting and hog-farrowing seasons arrived.

Without making clear who was in charge, Roosevelt assigned several of his top advisers to cooperate with the leaders of the farm organizations in devising a program. Tugwell, who along with Moley was closest to Roosevelt among the brain trusters, found himself sometimes acting at cross-purposes to Roosevelt's intimate friend of many years Henry Morgenthau, Jr. Soon Roosevelt asked Henry A. Wallace, a midwestern farm editor, to work with Tugwell; the two of them formed a compatible and successful team. But Morgenthau independently of the others also made contributions of consequence. He drafted the section of the farm bill dealing with agricultural credit, and prepared the way with the prime minister of Canada for an international agreement limiting wheat production.

While the scheme for agricultural recovery was in theory to be whatever the farm organizations wanted, both Roosevelt and the most powerful of these groups, the Farm Bureau Federation, were predisposed toward the "domestic allotment" plan. It would pay farmers to reduce production of key commodities and obtain funds for the payment through a "processing tax" on the commodities. In the negotiations both before and after Roosevelt took office, New Deal advisers and farm leaders agreed to include authorization for several other schemes in the basic legislation in order to bring more support to it.[10]

Conservative leaders in Congress easily blocked the legislative proposals during the lame-duck session of the winter of 1933. Also, farm supporters like the Republican Senator Charles L. McNary saw little reason to exert themselves for a farm bill that President Hoover manifestly would veto. Yet Roosevelt had gained substantially. He succeeded in developing the fundamentals of his farm program while keeping behind him most of the diverse farm groups and even winning some approval from Walter Lippmann and other eastern molders of opinion.

All was ready for Roosevelt once he had taken office and could marshal his forces against the opposition.

Roosevelt's one other public departure from conservatism was spectacular yet politically safe, the proposal of what became the Tennessee Valley Authority. He journeyed to Wilson Dam at Muscle Shoals on the Tennessee River, taking with him Senator Norris and a group of key southern senators and representatives. All through the twenties, private utilities and Republican presidents had thwarted Norris' proposals for public use of the power. As Roosevelt stood by the roaring spillways, almost within sight of farmhouses still lit with kerosene lamps, he avowed he would put the wasted power to work as part of a program to develop the entire Tennessee Valley. Later, speaking from the portico of the Alabama capitol in Montgomery, where Jefferson Davis had taken his oath of office as president of the Confederacy, he extemporaneously made a bold proposal that the Tennessee Valley program serve as an example of planning "for generations to come, tying in industry and agriculture and forestry and flood prevention, tying them all into a unified whole over a distance of a thousand miles so that we can afford better opportunities and better places for millions of yet unborn to live in the days to come."[11]

Despite their states' rights heritage, the southern leaders were delighted at the prospect of a Tennessee Valley project; it promised so much for their region. Roosevelt's announcement tied them more closely to him. Norris, with tears in his eyes, told Roosevelt at Muscle Shoals that he saw his dreams coming true; progressives also were more closely cemented to the president-elect. There was scant objection, since the private power companies in the aftermath of the recent collapse of the Insull utility empire were in no position to muster a major protest. Throughout most of the nation, the Tennessee Valley proposal received favorable editorial comment but commanded fewer headlines than did the intensifying economic distress.[12]

Several days later, in mid-February, there came a new national shock when Roosevelt narrowly missed assassination. He had just finished a brief speech in a Miami park when Joseph Zangara jumped onto a bench and, drawing an eight-dollar revolver, from a distance of little more than ten yards fired five shots at Roosevelt. Fortunately a woman tugged at Zangara's arm, spoiling his aim. Roosevelt was not hit, but Mayor Anton Cermak of Chicago was fatally wounded. Immediately, Roosevelt with rapid, self-assured action demonstrated his fearlessness. He countermanded a Secret Service order to leave, put Cermak into the car, and rushed him to the hospital. As a means of reassuring the nation, Moley, an expert in criminology, interviewed Zangara at the Miami jail later that evening, and told the press that the incident was not part of a radical plot. Zangara, suffering from stomach pains, said he hated all presidents and the rich. Neither, despite richly elaborated legends that have developed over the years, was Zangara deliberately gunning for Cermak. Some weeks later Cermak died; Zangara was tried, convicted, and executed.

As for Roosevelt, he expressed his solicitousness for Cermak and four others wounded. Later that evening when he was alone with intimates, he showed no sign of shock. "Roosevelt was simply himself — easy, confident, poised, to all appearances unmoved," Moley has reminisced. Several others, their nerves frayed, stayed up talking, but Roosevelt after a tumbler of whiskey slept soundly. His view of the incident was fatalistic and he would not allow any tightening of the security around him, not even the construction of a high wire fence around the Warm Springs cottage. *Time* reported, "People seemed to feel that their faith in the future was also the assassin's target." Roosevelt had been spared, and that fact together with his courage and quick thinking under stress buoyed national morale.[13]

Public confidence in Roosevelt remained high during the frightening two weeks of crisis that followed as banks began to succumb to the economic stress. Roosevelt during the intensifying runs on the banks remained calm and optimistic, perhaps too much so, and declined to take affirmative action to bring the panic to an end. In part Roosevelt was miscalculating the grievous economic damage the bank runs and closings were inflicting, and in part he was reacting to President Hoover's major effort to force him to alter his future course of action.

While Roosevelt was attending a reporters' banquet in New York City on the evening of February 18, a Secret Service man quietly delivered to him a ten-page handwritten letter, which Hoover had written under such stress that he misspelled Roosevelt's name. In the letter, Hoover set forth once again his belief that recovery had been on the way in the summer of 1932, and that the crisis of the winter was due to fears that Roosevelt and the Democratic Congress would abandon a conservative economic course. Hoover urged Roosevelt to guarantee a balanced budget, even if it necessitated new taxes; Roosevelt had repeatedly pledged a balanced budget, although not new taxes. There was a further demand at the crux of the conflict; Hoover urged "prompt assurance that there will be no tampering or inflation of the currency." Hoover had been fearful since the previous summer when an economist involved in the Democratic campaign had warned him that Roosevelt was thinking of abandoning the gold standard. Roosevelt was indeed thinking of taking the United States off gold, and had no intention of giving up his option to do so. He carefully wrote on Hoover's envelope the time and place of receipt, discussed the contents with his advisers far into the night — and made no reply.[14]

A gold drain from the United States was undoubtedly, as Hoover and Secretary of the Treasury Ogden Mills contended, a factor in the banking crisis. It was largely the handiwork of European economic interests and speculators acting in anticipation that the United States would abandon the gold standard. Surprisingly few Americans engaged in gold buying. A year earlier the Treasury had met a heavy run on gold by providing all that speculators wished, and had saved the gold standard, but at the cost of augmenting the already serious deflation. Had Roosevelt promised to keep the nation on gold, he would have lost what seemed to him a prime weapon to combat deflation. Further, the United States had already lost heavily in world trade through remaining on the gold standard when Great Britain had abandoned it. Pounds with which to purchase British goods were a better bargain than dollars. While world trade had declined by a quarter, United States trade with other nations was down by a half. Correctly, Hoover looked upon the international gold standard as a means of promoting economic stability, and thus moving toward recovery. Incorrectly, he thought he could lure the British back onto gold. In consequence, the United States would continue at a disadvantage if it remained on the gold standard. The difference between the outgoing and incoming presidents was irreconcilable, since Hoover's insistence upon joint action went no further than to urge that Roosevelt guarantee the gold standard.

There was far more than the question of gold to the banking crisis. Basically it came about because innumerable small depositors, aware of the pressure banks had been under for years, when they read that banks elsewhere were collapsing stood in long queues to withdraw their savings. They desperately needed the money. The crisis began in acutely depressed Michigan and spread to state after state. Nor could banks, fundamentally sound, but with a large part of their assets frozen in depressed obligations, withstand the strain. The one point over which Hoover was rightfully indignant with Roosevelt and the congressional Democrats was that Congress had voted to publish lists of the banks that the Reconstruction Finance Corporation had supported with loans. Roosevelt did not ask Congress to stop publishing the lists until after he had taken office. On the other hand had Roosevelt complied with Hoover's prime request and promised a continued gold standard, it is doubtful that the pledge would have stemmed the banking panic.

Beginning in Michigan, several governors ended the runs on banks by declaring bank holidays, either closing all banks in their states or drastically limiting their services. Roosevelt, acutely underestimating the need for banking services, seemed to feel that people could continue their day-to-day life by substituting script or IOUs for money. Further, out of his frustrations with bankers when he was governor of New York, he seemed to feel they were receiving appropriate punishment for the excesses they had committed during the prosperity decade. While sitting in his pew in St. James Episcopal Church in Hyde Park, he conceived a pledge he wrote into his inaugural address, to drive the money changers from the temple. A Morgan partner, Thomas Lamont, tried in vain to persuade Roosevelt to ask Congress to put Reconstruction Finance Corporation guarantees behind banks. "It is impossible to contemplate the extent of the human suffering, and the social consequences of a denial of currency and credit to our urban populations," Lamont warned. Roosevelt, in a punitive and conservative mood, was unmoved. He regarded Lamont's proposal as impractical.[15]

The crisis worsened, and a second letter came from President Hoover on March 1. Roosevelt sent hurried replies to both it and the previous letter, pretending the belated reply was due to a secretary's error. His expectation by then, only three days before taking office, was to handle the matter himself as president, calling the new Congress into special session. He continued in a bitter impasse with Hoover, but privately was checking to see if he possessed legal power dating from the First World War to regulate gold and currency.[16]

By this point, banking throughout the nation was in a state of either chaos or paralysis. Treasury and Federal Reserve officials, Moley, Roosevelt's incoming Secretary of the Treasury William Woodin, and President Hoover himself were all negotiating day and night to try to bring the crisis to an end. After Roosevelt arrived in Washington on March 2, Hoover made several efforts to persuade him to participate in joint action or give his approval to Hoover's action declaring a banking moratorium. Roosevelt declined, asserting to the end that Hoover had ample power to act alone. The night before the inauguration, Roosevelt's advisers and the Treasury officials worked into the early morning pressuring governors to issue proclamations. By inauguration morning, all the banks and the New York Stock Exchange were closed.

The United States was suffering acutely from the depression and the banking crisis, but was far from the brink of economic collapse. The dollar was strong, and during the last days of the runs on banks, the stock market in contrast to banks was rising in anticipation of the New Deal. The *Wall Street Journal* on Inauguration Day hailed the change in administrations. "A common adversity has much subdued the recalcitrance of groups bent upon self-interest," it declared editorially. "All of us the country over are now ready to make sacrifices to a common necessity and to accept realities as we would not have done three months ago."[17]

Chapter 7

THE HUNDRED DAYS

THE ROOSEVELT LEGEND began dramatically the day he took office, March 4, 1933. It was a time of acute national privation and foreboding that the closing of the banks reinforced. Roosevelt instantly countered the pessimism with a bold, reassuring inaugural address that shifted the national spirit from gloom toward optimism. From an ambiguous figure seeming to possess more charm than backbone, Roosevelt emerged amazingly as a confident, commanding president. The nation was eager to entrust its destiny to this new, powerful leader. The years of deepening depression and the months of marking time since the November election, culminating in the shock of the banking crisis, had shattered the confidence of the electorate and of much of Congress. For a brief period the popular demand for immediate positive action swept aside the ordinarily powerful negative check of Congress.

In the spring of 1933, Roosevelt possessed a mandate to shift dramatically the course of American policy comparable to that of Lincoln taking office as the Federal Union disintegrated. The depression crisis was not of the magnitude of the secession crisis, but the entire nation was unified behind Roosevelt as passionately as the northern half had been briefly behind Lincoln. Roosevelt did not think of the Civil War precedent but was well aware of the fleeting nature of the massive support. He possessed for the moment power to innovate such as few presidents ever enjoy, and he made the most of it. He immediately speeded his rather deliberate schedule and during his first hundred days in office rushed through Congress an array of legislation in the areas of recovery, relief, and reform unparalleled in American history.

The inauguration ceremony was dramatic. Roosevelt, in taking the oath of office, discarded earlier tradition to create a new one, in a strong, clear voice reciting the oath after Chief Justice Charles Evans Hughes. In the same solemn, affirmative fashion he read his brief inaugural address, remembered best for the assurance that "the only thing we have to fear is fear itself." He backed this assertion with the promise of "a leadership of frankness and vigor."[1]

In that era of growing totalitarianism, with Mussolini entrenched in Italy and Hitler beginning to consolidate power in Germany, there was a chilling analogy to war in Roosevelt's address. He spoke of assuming leadership of "this great army of our people." While he paid tribute to "the normal balance of Executive and legislative authority," he warned that if Congress did not enact recovery measures, he would then ask it "for the one remaining instrument to meet the crisis — broad Executive power to wage a war against the emergency, as great as the power that would be given to me if we were in fact invaded by a foreign foe."[2]

There was no need for apprehension. Roosevelt meant what he said when he avowed his trust in "the future of essential democracy." He expected only to carry out his popular mandate from the people for "direct vigorous action . . . discipline and direction under leadership," regarding himself as "the present instrument of their wishes." Once during this period, when Mrs. Roosevelt lamented that the nation lacked a benevolent dictator to force through reforms, he replied skeptically that one could not count on a dictator continuing to be benevolent. It was not the European dictators who inspired Roosevelt's reference to power comparable to that in time of war, but the vast marshaling of economic controls in the Wilson administration during World War I.[3]

For millions of American farmers and workers, and for a large part of the businessmen, the massive federal intervention in the economy, the planning and rationalization, and the controls over production, prices, and wages during World War I had seemed benign. Those measures had operated more through financial incentives than stern legal restrictions. Indeed, the philosopher John Dewey and quite a few other intellectuals had looked upon Wilson's wartime administration as the prototype for the ideal American society. When economic distress had hit first railroad workers, then farmers, then after 1930 the businessmen, each group looked back to the war agencies as containing the key to their salvation. Roosevelt himself had been one of the most dynamic and imaginative of the young war administrators. It is not surprising that both in the New Deal agencies and among the personnel that ran them there was a picking up where the Wilson administration had ended after the Armistice.

Behind the analogy to war was the vital fact that in the United States, the greatest industrial nation in the world, only the federal government had the massive economic power to borrow, tax, spend, and regulate that might be brought to bear to stimulate economic recovery. It was only during the First World War that the federal government had exercised that power. Previously, in the Progressive Era, and in the Republican twenties, there had been only mild use, little beyond the police power. Throughout the 1920s federal budgets had remained fairly steady at about $3.3 billion, while the total of the Gross National Product soared. There was the potential in federal resources during the 1930s to bring both recovery and a greater degree of security for all of the American people.

The reform thread also ran through Roosevelt's inaugural address, as it was to run through the New Deal years. In words reminiscent of the progressive fervor of 1912, Roosevelt declared: "The money changers have fled from their high seats in the temple of our civilization. We may now restore that temple to the ancient truths. The measure of restoration lies in the extent to which we apply social values more noble than mere monetary profit."

Beginning with his inaugural address, Franklin D. Roosevelt made the presidency, as had Theodore Roosevelt, "a bully pulpit" for the expounding of moral values. "The presidency . . . ," he had remarked while preparing to take office, "is not merely an administrative office. . . . It is predominantly a place of moral leadership."[4] Both Franklin and Eleanor Roosevelt fundamentally took a moral rather than an economic view of the great problems facing the nation, but Franklin Roosevelt tempered his moral fervor with political realism that sometimes to his wife seemed to be overcaution. "You'll never be a good politician," she remembered her husband once told her. "You are too impatient." One had to wait, he believed, until the electorate had been educated to support a change.[5]

The Great Depression and the banking crisis had brought the electorate to a point where it was eager, in the spring of 1933, to accept changes well beyond the conservative perceived wisdom that had dominated both business and political thinking.

Yet, for the first few days of the new administration, Roosevelt himself failed to advance beyond the perceived wisdom. First, he resolved the banking crisis in a decidedly conservative way. On the morning of Inauguration Day, before leaving to deliver his address heaping scorn on the money changers, he agreed to summon leading bankers to Washington to participate in the solution. His quarrel with them had been over their speculative recklessness; he wanted them to be more cautious. As a remedy he accepted a plan that Hoover's Treasury officials had developed. He proclaimed a national banking holiday to prevent any further runs on banks or withdrawals of gold, and summoned Congress to meet in special session. To Congress he submitted the Emergency Banking bill, which permitted sound banks to reopen and authorized the issue of Federal Reserve bank notes to meet future runs. The long-range provision of greatest consequence was that banks could issue preferred stock, and on the basis of this security the Reconstruction Finance Corporation (RFC) could loan them funds to buoy them in the future. Another device, the federal insurance of deposits, to restore public confidence in banks still seemed too dangerous to Roosevelt. In June, 1933, it was forced upon him, and came to be listed as one of his notable achievements.

Congress acted within several hours, almost unanimously enacting the banking bill without even reading it. A year or two later there were lamentations that Roosevelt had not nationalized the banking system, that he could have done so with the greatest of ease. Not only was that far from his thoughts, but there is no indication that even the most progressive members of Congress favored anything more drastic than enlarged federal regulation. Banking reform was to come later; Roosevelt remarked at the time that it was impossible to write a permanent banking act in three days.

Sound banks reopened, and through guarantees coming through RFC purchase of their preferred stock and the Federal Deposit Insurance Corporation, remained open. It was ironic that the remedies Roosevelt had rejected before his inauguration as too costly were in the end the solution. In the fall of 1933, with Roosevelt's encouragement, Jesse Jones, the administrator of the RFC, provided a billion dollars of capital to six thousand banks to ensure the working of the deposit insurance program. The cost to the RFC was nil. Unfortunately many banks that in normal times would have been sound were liquidated, creating further economic havoc in their areas. When the Federal Reserve tried to prevent the reopening of the Bank of America with its 410 branches in California, Roosevelt refused to intervene. On the basis of figures, Secretary of the Treasury William Woodin did act. A disaster for the West Coast was averted, and Roosevelt received the credit. The emergency had been resolved, but the crisis and its overcautious solution drove economic indices still lower during ensuing weeks. Yet it was Roosevelt's solution that convinced the American public he was a courageous, innovative president worthy of their trust.[6]

For the next several days Roosevelt continued on his conservative course, on March 10, 1933, sending Congress an economy bill that would give him the power to reduce government salaries as much as 15 percent and to reduce or even eliminate veterans' pensions. Roosevelt wished to cut government salaries by $100 million and veterans' pensions by $400 million, in total reducing the 1934 federal budget by nearly 13 percent. At the same time, through making use of authorization he had persuaded Democrats to vote during the lame-duck session of Congress, he hoped to bring about extensive reorganization of the government. Partly he wanted to reorganize to obtain additional savings; even more, he sought greater efficiency.

The economy program was not a minor aberration of the spring of 1933, or a hypocritical concession to delighted conservatives. Rather it was an integral part of Roosevelt's overall New Deal, and a key aspect of his thinking both then and later. As a first step he wished to economize drastically; as a second he wished through self-financing bootstrap measures to attain quick recovery. Throughout the thirties he seldom wavered in his firm commitment to economy.[7]

The prime responsibility for developing the economy program fell upon a brilliant young Arizonan, Lewis Douglas, whom Roosevelt appointed director of the budget. The prime roadblock was the American Legion, resourceful guardians of veterans' benefits. Douglas as a congressman had withstood the wrath of the veterans' lobby. Once again the Legion mobilized, but even many Legionnaires gave way before Roosevelt's insistence upon solvency. The specter of the runaway inflation that had wiped out the German mark only a decade earlier was still well remembered and frightening. In his message Roosevelt declared, "Too often in recent history liberal governments have been wrecked on the rocks of loose fiscal policy." Lippmann and almost every other respected commentator applauded.[8]

The economy bill was rushed through the House. When there seemed danger that it might run afoul of unlimited debate in the Senate, Roosevelt resorted to a stratagem to avoid delay. "I think this would be a good time for beer," he told friends, and introduced a proposal for a highly popular measure to legalize weak beer. He also arranged that the Senate should not have an opportunity to vote through the beer bill until it had approved the economy bill. There was some opposition to the economy bill in the Senate, but even Senator William E. Borah's amendment to exempt from salary cuts federal employees receiving a pathetic $1,000 per year or less was voted down. Roosevelt's logic was that prices had decreased and that salaries should also. Congress voted him blanket authorization to make reductions. It also voted for beer of 3.2 percent alcoholic content (and supposedly therefore nonintoxicating), a makeshift until the end of 1933 when the repeal amendment, which Congress passed just before Roosevelt took office, and which the states speedily ratified, went into effect.[9]

Roosevelt obtained blanket authorization to cut salaries and veterans' benefits by telling congressional leaders that he would serve as their whipping boy, that the veterans' lobby could turn its wrath upon him. By June, when it turned out that even veterans with war disabilities had suffered pension cuts far beyond the expected 25 percent, Congress, facing the 1934 elections, forced Roosevelt to restore $100 million of the cuts. Nevertheless expenditures on veterans' services dropped more than 40 percent between the 1932 and 1934 fiscal years.[10]

Under the aegis of Roosevelt, Budget Director Douglas not only cut salaries but reduced the number of personnel throughout the federal bureaucracy. Roosevelt eliminated some minor agencies and consolidated others, but did not attempt major reorganization of the administration until 1937. At a time when the federal services were a slight fraction of what they have been since, Roosevelt like many conservatives was disturbed because government services were so enormous compared with those of his youth. Like most progressives he was critical of the aid that Republican administrations had provided to business. He curtailed drastically the scientific and statistical work of the government; the National Bureau of Standards did not regain its 1931 budget level until 1940. There was no New Deal for science until World War II. Roosevelt even cut the defense budget from $752 million in fiscal 1932 to $531 million in fiscal 1934, but later allocated some emergency money to both the navy and the army. Through these devices, Roosevelt was able to boast that he had indeed kept his campaign pledge of drastic economy. He not only cut back the regular expenditures of the government but kept them reduced through the 1930s.

The blanket authorizations that Congress bestowed upon Roosevelt led from the very beginning to a few cries of "dictator," even in the Senate. General John J. Pershing responded that, on the contrary, because the machinery of Congress was by nature deliberate, the only way to obtain speedy, decisive action in time of emergency was to concentrate general authority in the chief executive. It was, said Pershing, "democracy's own method of acting quickly in time of crisis." Less felicitously it was conducive to slipshod action. Members of Congress could most easily reconcile differences among themselves through bundling a variety of conflicting authorizations into a compromise omnibus measure, leaving it to Roosevelt to decide which he wished to utilize. While indeed the device did not represent a tendency to dictatorship, it did begin a great augmentation of presidential power. Whether Roosevelt sought it or not, power accrued to him.[11]

Even in the euphoric spring of 1933, when Congress, the press, and the public overwhelmingly praised the new president, there were powerful moderating forces at work. There was Roosevelt's own caution, and that of most of his advisers. His political upbringing had been in the nineteenth-century-style Jeffersonian democracy with Wilsonian modifications; he subscribed vigorously to the Jeffersonian and Jacksonian concern for the individual, and was also something of a states' righter with suspicion of the big government toward which he was inevitably moving. This side of Roosevelt was manifest in the banking and economy measures, and, as he moved rapidly toward other components of the New Deal, in his unwillingness to wield much of the optional power that Congress was to bestow upon him. Too, there were his advisers, representing diverse points of view and often countering each other in their arguments. There was also the restraining influence upon him of all the disparate interest groups that in the aggregate formed the national polity. Roosevelt paid some heed to all of these and tried somehow to reconcile their conflicting objectives into a national consensus. He did indeed regard himself, as he had declared in his inaugural address, as the president of all the American people, "the present instrument of their wishes." In that time of acute economic need, he sought impartially to provide for each what it most needed to attain recovery.

Above all, during the Hundred Days as later, Congress exercised a powerful influence upon Roosevelt. After the passage of the first two emergency measures, it operated by no means, as a few Republicans claimed, like a "rubber stamp." Some of its leaders, especially Senators George Norris and Robert Wagner and Representative Sam Rayburn, provided the impetus and concepts for key pieces of legislation. Others in Congress did much to shape and sometimes improve the bills before them.

There was much give-and-take between the president and Congress. Roosevelt had to marshal his political skills and rally the overwhelming public sentiment behind him to obtain passage of his program. He capitalized upon the party loyalty of the leaders and flatteringly consulted them. A reorganization of the House made it especially pliable at that time, so that he could focus upon the Senate. Its progressive Republican members, especially George Norris and Hiram Johnson, who might provide the margin of victory in close contests, enjoyed a welcome at the White House unknown to them in the Republican twenties. Especially, Roosevelt made effective use of patronage, desperately sought in those times of unemployment, by the simple expedient of withholding it until the special session was over.

Indirectly Roosevelt kept the pressure upon Congress through the media. He began a new sort of press conference routine, allowing a limited number of reporters to crowd into the Oval Office. There he cheerfully exchanged banter with them, and gave them earnest expositions of his proposals that made them feel as though they were inside participants. Most of what he said was for background use only, or off the record, but it brought him enthusiastic coverage in the newspapers.

In addition, Roosevelt went directly to the people through the device he had perfected as governor of New York, the radio Fireside Chats, which he kept low-key and informal. Roosevelt used to imagine he was engaged in explaining a policy to his tenant farmer at Hyde Park. They were notably effective, in part because Roosevelt shrewdly made rare use of them.

Despite Roosevelt's political aptitude and phenomenal popularity, on some points he had to accept compromise or even defeat. Congress contributed much, both negatively and positively, and the legislation of the spring of 1933 is a monument to it as well as to Roosevelt.

The program took shape between March and June. Although Roosevelt was eager to obtain a balanced budget, he worried about the basically deflationary effects of his economy measures. He worried too about the plight of the millions of unemployed to whom state and local governments and private charity could scarcely provide the most meager subsistence. It was imperative to provide aid immediately, and the overwhelming public sentiment behind Roosevelt made it possible. Herbert Feis, economist in the State Department, reported from Washington to Stimson, "The outside public seems to behave as if Angel Gabriel had come to earth." Congressmen, acutely aware of this sentiment, put aside for the moment their traditional caution. Roosevelt remarked to Moley that the "thing to do was to strike while Congress was hot." The national needs were too great and the ephemeral psychological advantage was too precious for Roosevelt to let his opportunity slip. He had been planning to let Congress recess for a few weeks while he drafted further legislation, but only two weeks after he had taken office, on March 17, he announced that he and the congressional leaders had agreed to continue.[12]

Dramatically, in helter-skelter fashion, Roosevelt every few days sent Congress a new proposal. Even James Byrnes, who was laboring as a

Roosevelt leader in the Senate, had to confess that he did not know all that was on the agenda or how long the process would continue. On March 15, the president asked for farm legislation; on March 21, he called for unemployment relief, which came to include a Civilian Conservation Corps, Federal Emergency Relief Administration, and Public Works Administration; on March 29, he recommended federal securities regulation; on April 3, legislation to save farm mortgages from foreclosure; on April 10, the Tennessee Valley Authority. And so it continued, climaxing on May 17 when Roosevelt requested Congress to enact a national industrial recovery bill.

It all seemed rather haphazard, the result of day-by-day improvisations, but behind the program had been much planning, going back as far as the previous spring. Within it was a response to the requests of each of the principal interest groups. The measures embodied several lines of economic thought, but Roosevelt considered them by no means incompatible. In any event, his approach to the New Deal was more consistent politically than economically.

During the first two weeks Roosevelt was in office, he had seemed to be dispensing aid to bankers and favoring those of conservative laissez-faire views. He was worried because this phase was deflationary, and he wished to shift quickly, as he had long since planned, to mildly inflationary measures even though they would cost him some conservative support. Economic indices were lagging well behind those for the same weeks in 1932. Mild inflation would bring these indices up at least temporarily. Further, Roosevelt and his advisers were particularly worried because, while prices and values in general had dropped spectacularly, since 1929 the debt structure had remained high. Roosevelt wrote a few months later:

> Two courses were open: to cut down the debts through bankruptcies and foreclosures to such a point that they would be below property values; or else, to increase property values until they were greater than the debts.
>
> Obviously, the latter course was the only legitimate method of putting the country back on its feet without destroying human values.[13]

Gradually Roosevelt had abandoned his fears that inflation might get out of hand and had come to accept the view that controlled inflation without the danger of repetition of the German fiasco was possible. He had long flirted with the scheme that George F. Warren, a Cornell agricultural economist, was pressing upon him, to abandon the gold standard and let gold, like any other commodity, rise in value. In its rise, Warren argued, gold would bring up with it the prices of wheat, cotton, and other agricultural staples. A silver subsidy, which western senators insistently sought, would supplement the program. There was the advantage in the gold and silver schemes that Roosevelt could count upon much western and agricultural support for them. Some conservative and international bankers also favored this form of inflation, feeling that through this sole minor palliative and no other measures it would be possible to attain recovery. There was the safeguard that inflation through manipulating gold and silver could not advance very far.[14]

The confluence of international and domestic crises led Roosevelt to act in April, 1933. He was forced to retaliate when, after he tentatively lifted the embargo on the export of gold, European speculators drained away $100 million of the United States gold reserves. At the same time Congress, debating the agriculture bill, was coming more and more under the influence of western inflationary forces. Some wished unlimited printing-press money, and perhaps as much as a majority in the Senate favored, in the populist tradition, the issuing of silver currency at an overvalued ratio to gold.

Roosevelt used the European raid on gold and the inflationary sentiment in Congress to justify his own predetermined course. On the evening of April 18, he summoned his advisers to the White House and shocked them by telling them the United States was off the gold standard. Further, he told them he intended to accept the inflationary amendment to the agriculture bill that Senator Elmer Thomas of Oklahoma had drafted. The banker James Warburg and Budget Director Douglas were so horrified that one or the other of them lamented the decision as marking the end of western civilization. Nonetheless, Roosevelt persuaded them to work through the night watering down and inserting safeguards in the Thomas amendment. It its final form it authorized, but did not require, the president to stimulate inflation in six different ways. Subsequently, Roosevelt argued in defense of his moves that had he not acted, Congress would have forced more drastic inflation upon him. In fact, none of the inflationary proposals gaining supporters in Congress had been mandatory.

To reporters, Roosevelt explained that he wanted to raise commodity prices at home by a moderate amount. Through allowing the dollar to drop from its artificially high gold-standard level to one equitable with other currencies, he hoped to increase the pressure upon other nations to "get the world as a whole back on some form of gold standard."[15]

Internationally the United States seemed to gain some advantage preliminary to anticipated currency stabilization at the forthcoming world economic conference. The dollar did indeed decline in relation to the pound, to the outrage of the City of London, which for eighteen months had enjoyed the advantages of sterling devaluation. J. P. Morgan, the leading international banker, hailed the move as a means of countering deflation. Delegations from European nations coming to Washington to confer with Roosevelt concerning war debts questions and the economic conference were not especially disturbed, since they gained the impression Roosevelt favored future stabilization.

Many conservatives within the United States were irreconcilably alienated, either because of their undying faith in the gold standard or because of Roosevelt's subsequent signing, in June, 1933, of legislation abrogating the gold clause in public and private contracts. They could no longer cash in government bonds for gold and enjoy substantial gains. Roosevelt was not dismayed; he had prophesied privately before taking office that conservatives would not support him for long.

At this relatively low cost, Roosevelt wrought a major change in federal economic policy, abandoning the rigidity of the gold standard for the flexibility of a managed currency. Monetarism became a key component of the New Deal mix. Further, he was following the lead of other industrial powers in moving toward a policy of economic nationalism, even though he was hoping for international economic cooperation in overcoming the depression. His immediate gains were to stem the congressional pressures for substantial inflation and to launch the economic indices on an upward course. While the dollar fell 12 percent on international markets, the prices of farm commodities and metals rose moderately until mid-July. It was a temporary panacea that gave the nation a taste of recovery while Roosevelt was maneuvering his program through Congress.[16]

Roosevelt had to act fast and use every stratagem of persuasiveness at his command. As signs of recovery began to multiply, the public pressure for legislation dwindled and Congress became more disposed to return to the old economic fundamentalism. Conservatives then and later came to feel that the first economy phase of the New Deal had been all that was needed; the president had restored confidence, which had been all that was lacking, and should have stopped at that point.

The pressures that Roosevelt and his cohorts in Congress managed to apply brought the enactment, despite conservative forces, of almost the entire New Deal program. The process varied from bill to bill. Some, like the measure to establish the Civilian Conservation Corps, went through quickly and early with little change. The Securities Act, to require full financial disclosure relating to new securities issues, involved a rewriting and reconciliation of competing proposals within the administration and Congress — and had to be followed in 1934 with stronger legislation, establishing the Securities and Exchange Commission. Roosevelt intended the Emergency Railroad Transportation Act to provide drastic reorganization and coordination of the depression-stricken railroads, but as economic conditions improved in May and June, railroad executives lost interest, and Congress weakened the measure.

The farm bill, which Roosevelt considered the key to recovery, illustrates the relationship between president and Congress. It began on March 16 when he sent a brief message asking for immediate farm legislation, since "the spring crops will soon be planted and if we wait for another month or six weeks the effect on the prices of this year's crops will be wholly lost." Although he had thoroughly prepared the way before he took office, the bill became the object of much pulling and hauling, and of considerable delay.[17]

In the brief House debate on the farm bill, opponents brought up most of the arguments that were to be characteristic of anti–New Deal attacks. Joseph Martin of Massachusetts, ultimately to become Republican Speaker of the House, warned it would put America on the road to Moscow, and then more seriously questioned the billion-dollar burden its processing tax would levy upon consumers. Others plastered a red label on Roosevelt's agricultural experts, or denounced them as professors who had no knowledge of farm realities. They ignored the fact that while M. L. Wilson, who had developed the domestic allotment idea, did indeed teach at Montana State, he was also running a Montana wheat ranch. Both Secretary of Agriculture Wallace and Assistant Secretary Tugwell, incessantly derided as dreamers, had earlier roots in agricultural business. Within the Senate, Roosevelt's gestures toward inflation helped prevent plains states extremists from rebelling. He placated conservatives by announcing in advance that he would appoint Bernard Baruch's lieutenant George Peek to be head of the new Agricultural Adjustment Administration (AAA).

Lobbyists representing farm organizations bested those of the food and fiber processors, and the omnibus Farm Relief Act, combining bills establishing the AAA and emergency farm mortgage relief, became law on May 12, 1933. It included not only the inflationary Thomas amendment but also one that in the future helped in overseas marketing of crops. Roosevelt had compromised seriously in promising to appoint Peek, a notable opponent of crop restriction, to head a crop restriction program, but he had obtained legislation that as recently as February had seemed by no means a certainty. The AAA immediately started the machinery to persuade producers of wheat, cotton, corn, and hogs to reduce output in return for subsidies to be financed by taxes at the point of processing. The nation had embarked upon what was to be an enduring program of national planning in agriculture.[18]

Not until fairly late in the spring of 1933 did Roosevelt propose to Congress a business counterpart to the farm recovery program. He seems for weeks not to have thought it necessary, believing that a rise in farm prices together with mild inflation and a prudent amount of public works would suffice to bring recovery. It is an incongruity that he should have favored firm regulation and planning for agriculture and railroads but not industry. Moley and Tugwell both urged him to explore possible industrial recovery schemes; Tugwell wanted him to act more in the tradition of Theodore Roosevelt and the New Nationalism and less in that of Wilson and the New Freedom. And so in time he did, under pressure from his economic advisers, numerous business leaders, and as powerful a Senate figure as Robert Wagner. More imperative pressure came from the growing popularity of Senator Hugo Black's proposal to limit the work week to thirty hours and thus share the work. If Roosevelt were to forestall the Black bill, he had to come forth with a positive program.

The amalgamated product of three interacting bill-drafting groups was the National Industrial Recovery bill, incorporating most of the recovery schemes. Business would obtain what it had long sought, government backing of trade association codes of fair practice to prevent price cutting, and labor would obtain guarantees of minimum wages and maximum hours and the right to engage in collective bargaining. There was even supposed to be protection of consumer interests. One aspect of keen interest to Roosevelt was the "prevention of foolish overproduction," the wastage of bituminous coal and petroleum resources. And tied to the measure was the substantial public works appropriation that progressives in Congress had so long sought. Roosevelt, still seeking to avoid heavy budget deficits, and skeptical of public spending, countered when Senator Wagner proposed $5 billion by suggesting $1 billion. He compromised on $3.3 billion. A new agency, the Public Works Administration, was to supervise the expenditure.[19]

In advocating the National Industrial Recovery bill, Roosevelt seemed to be forsaking trust-busting for a partnership between government and business. He seemed also to be choosing economic nationalism over international economic cooperation and lowering of trade barriers. He was aware of what he was undertaking; Moley painstakingly reviewed the alternatives with him. Yet he did not wish to make choices, feeling that all these contradictory courses of action were to some extent interrelated and worthy of experimentation.

Into June, Roosevelt had to struggle hard with Congress to obtain passage of remaining segments of his program, especially the industrial recovery bill. It seemed less urgent since the stock market had gone up more than 60 percent since April 1. He had driven Congress so hard for so long that its members, especially in the Senate, were beginning to balk. It was hot; they were tired, susceptible to lobbyists, and beginning to reassert their old convictions. Hiram Johnson, who had been enthusiastic in his support of Roosevelt, wrote his sons, "Men have followed him upstairs without question or criticism. . . . These men have about reached the limit of their endurance." In the end they forced Roosevelt to accept bank deposit insurance and a restoration of some cuts in veterans' pensions, but did enact the recovery bill unscathed.[20]

During the weeks that Roosevelt was pressuring Congress on behalf of his measures, he had to make concessions to gain votes and in the process gradually narrowed his alternatives. He became increasingly committed to the planning involved in the agricultural and industrial recovery programs. He gave them priority over his ambitious international schemes. In order to retain the support of congressional isolationists for his domestic measures, he postponed his efforts to obtain several pieces of legislation authorizing him, if he wished, to embargo arms, renegotiate war debt payments, and lower tariffs. In his swing toward economic nationalism, Roosevelt abandoned even his general commitment to currency stabilization.[21]

In the summer of 1933, Roosevelt faced the task of implementing an unparalleled array of new legislation, embracing the agricultural and industrial recovery experiments, mortgage relief, welfare and public works, and reform ranging from securities regulation to the establishment of the TVA. All these required immediate and energetic administration if Roosevelt were to achieve his goals of a lasting recovery and a more secure America. The path ahead was full of hazards.

Chapter 8

A TIGHTROPE FOREIGN POLICY

AT THE TIME of the 1933 London Economic Conference, Owen D. Young described the Roosevelt foreign policy as an "exercise in tight-rope walking, which so far has been highly successful and might continue to be if he doesn't fall off." Indeed, Roosevelt seemed to maintain a precarious balance between nationalism and internationalism, between the demands of domestic politics and the requirements of diplomacy. For some years he made only a hesitant and wobbly advance toward his constant goal, world security.[1]

As the head of a fundamentally isolationist nation, Roosevelt sought somehow to attain collective security — to build a formidable barrier against aggressors — without committing the nation to war. He was a nationalist in the sense that never at any time during his presidency did he fail to put the interests of the United States first; he was an internationalist in that he believed that the well-being of the American nation was dependent upon the political and economic security of other nations. A large part of the American populace and its leadership was not so sure.

Within this national limitation, Roosevelt by trial and error slowly built his foreign and defense policies. They went through several phases and involved such a variety of techniques that on the surface they seemed to lack direction.

During the interregnum and his first months in office, he tried to assume world leadership so as to combat the depression and counter the distant threat from Japanese military leaders and the new fuehrer of Germany, Adolf Hitler. Not many Americans took the threat very seriously. They were shocked to see newsreels of Japanese legions smashing across North China, and Nazis holding anti-Semitic rallies in Germany, but these events seemed far away. Roosevelt, acutely aware of the Senate's humiliation of Wilson and rejection of the League of Nations, never discounted the force of isolationism within the nation. The developing New Deal program created further limitations as he built his structure for recovery upon a foundation of economic nationalism, yet for years he hoped to pursue in economic matters both a nationalist and internationalist course, and in some respects succeeded. Overall, he hoped to preserve the peace without violating the nation's isolationist tradition, pursuing contradictory courses of action and trying to make them compatible through moral suasion. To a certain extent that balance had been the thrust of Republican foreign policy since Harding had taken office.

Roosevelt was ready to develop his international policies, as he did the New Deal domestic programs, on the structure he inherited from the Hoover administration, but to lengths that Hoover would find abhorrent. There was greater continuity in foreign policy, largely because of the influence of Hoover's secretary of state, Henry L. Stimson, and the strong career foreign service officers both within the State Department and overseas. Roosevelt had threatened before he took office to remove some of the senior diplomats who he felt were out of touch with American developments, and throughout his years in office he grumbled occasionally about the career foreign service. Nevertheless, he depended upon it, and even those who had been close to Hoover, like the diplomat Hugh Gibson, did not suffer disfavor long under Roosevelt. Joseph Grew, who had served on the *Harvard Crimson* with Roosevelt, remained the ambassador to Japan, and J. Pierrepont Moffat, his brilliant son-in-law, continued in charge of western European affairs in the State Department. Career diplomats headed half of the missions; political appointees, some of them of distinction, headed the rest. To London, Roosevelt sent Secretary Hull's good friend Robert Bingham of the *Louisville Courier–Journal,* who was especially effective in his relations with upper-class British leaders. To Berlin, after much pondering, he dispatched Professor William E. Dodd, who was never close to the new Nazi hierarchy but sent long, eloquent warnings back to the president.

Within the State Department, Secretary Cordell Hull soon became respected, presiding carefully over its intricate machinery, and gathering gradually a national reputation second only to that of the president. He got along well with Under Secretary William Phillips, another old friend of Roosevelt's, but detested Assistant Secretary Moley, who had unfortunately been attached to the State Department while his duties at the White House were overwhelming. The power of Secretary Hull and the State Department machinery should not be underestimated, since they carried out the routine small matters that in large total could lead to consequential results. Yet on many significant policy questions, Hull, who was given to long, dull declamations on free trade, found himself bypassed. His first target of resentment was Moley, and in later years he became furious with Sumner Welles, because both seemed to have an access to the White House he lacked. At times, though, no one in the State Department knew Roosevelt's thinking or was even aware of his actions. Before the end of the Hundred Days, Hull was already complaining, with his slight lisp, about "that man across the street who never tells me anything." Ultimately, Roosevelt had to make his peace with Hull by inviting him regularly to lunch at the White House, and Hull came to exercise a restraining effect, warning Roosevelt against schemes that would bring strong protest in the Senate. In the Hoover administration, an active secretary had prodded the cautious president; under Roosevelt, the reverse was the case.[2]

Roosevelt had every intention of operating in the grand tradition of Theodore Roosevelt and Wilson as his own secretary of state. He thought in terms of global schemes and brilliant maneuvers, shocking his auditors by trying out new ideas to which he had obviously given little or no consideration. Often he would never allude to them again. On the other hand, as in domestic matters, he could launch proposals of great significance that as yet had little popular support, and refer to them again and again until he had built sufficient support to act upon them. Despite his occasional spectacular suggestions to visitors, he usually came to decisions only after long and thoughtful consideration, and was usually, though not always, prudent.

Roosevelt had a boundless interest in foreign affairs, and as with concerns at home kept informed through both official channels and countless personal contacts. He habitually suggested to outgoing envoys that they write to him; quite correctly he considered them as his ambassadors. Frequently he had significant discussions with foreign diplomats or officials. What was troublesome for the State Department was his failure often to keep it informed. He almost never wrote an *aide-mémoire* after a conversation.

The Roosevelt style shook the State Department. Moffat wrote in April, 1933:

> You have no idea of the White House control over foreign affairs now. To do so you must go back to the regime of the great Theodore. Not only are there personal negotiations between the Presi-

> dent and Ambassadors, but telegrams go over by the score and return with notations in the President's handwriting. . . . The system has its advantages and disadvantages. It gives a distinct finality and I think a degree of consistency to our policy that will bear fruit. On the other hand, it is extremely difficult to know what has gone before and this doubt of knowing background extends even in high circles.[3]

Although the style was startling, the conclusions might be conventional. Thus, concerning Japan, Roosevelt was disposed at least privately to engage in speculation ranging beyond Stimson's militancy, yet he settled until 1937 upon policies almost indistinguishable from Hoover's. His bias, as he freely illustrated with reminiscences, was toward the Chinese. After all, the Delanos had been in the China trade, and his mother had sailed to Hong Kong aboard the famous Yankee clipper *Surprise* during the Civil War. Yet for many years China reaped precious little from that bias.

The question facing Roosevelt was how to counter further Japanese aggression on the East Asian mainland. President Hoover had cautiously announced the "Stimson doctrine," that the United States would not recognize the Japanese conquest of Manchuria. Secretary Stimson, whose views were most attractive to Roosevelt, would have liked to proceed to economic sanctions. Roosevelt had no wish to involve the United States in war, and in the treacherous years ahead tried to avoid it; yet, thanks to his years in the Navy Department, from time to time he speculated on the possibility. In January, 1933, he frightened two of his advisers, Moley and Tugwell, by commenting that it might be better to have war now rather than later; at his first cabinet meeting he warned that war with Japan was a possibility.

Japan gave some reason for Roosevelt's speculations. The Japanese Army was sweeping toward the Great Wall of China, and the reaction of Japan's government to league censure and the Stimson doctrine was to withdraw from the league and direct much of its resentment toward the United States. Japanese publications hypothecated attacks upon the Philippines and Hawaii. Naval Intelligence in 1934 sent Roosevelt a Japanese comic book that opened with an attack upon Pearl Harbor and ended with the dictating of peace in the White House.

Throughout the spring of 1933, Roosevelt tried cautiously and quietly to cope with Japan without alarming the public. He was disposed to embargo war supplies, and obtained passage in the House of a resolution empowering him to impose a discretionary embargo. In the

Senate he faced opposition from isolationists on the Foreign Relations Committee, and he was eager not to lose their votes on vital New Deal legislation still pending. In addition, by the end of May the Japanese generals, only thirteen miles from Peking, had advanced as far as they wished and negotiated a truce with the Chinese government. Since Roosevelt seemed to have no urgent need for an arms embargo, he agreed reluctantly to Hiram Johnson's amendment taking away from him the right to discriminate between an aggressor and a victim. Roosevelt decided to wait until the next January, but thereafter he was not able to obtain discretionary embargo legislation and had to accept the mandatory legislation that isolationists favored.

In Roosevelt's eyes, this first minor crisis with Japan seemed to have passed satisfactorily. He accepted the analysis of the influential expert in the State Department, Stanley Hornbeck, that the Japanese armies, overextended, were a "paper dragon" that would have to pull back. The seeds of conflict were sprouting in East Asia, but so slowly that Roosevelt gave far more attention to Europe with its immediate dangers.[4]

There was little menace but much irritation in the questions of World War I debts and reparations, which he had been debating with Hoover. Roosevelt's concern seemed to be less with obtaining full payments than in dunning the defaulting nations sufficiently to placate an electorate and Congress, many of whom felt, like Coolidge, "They hired the money, didn't they?" Therefore they should repay it. Personally Roosevelt was more sophisticated and favored leniency on the debts, but acted cautiously. Token payments would have eased the political pressure upon him. He set forth his views by indirection in his conversations with envoys, telling the French ambassador, "A great people never default."

What became irritating to Roosevelt was the amount of time during his first year in office that he had to spend in fruitless debts discussion, and his difficulties in obtaining even token payments or any related economic concessions. The debts debate began to make him feel that relations with the British and French involved much take on their part and little give.[5]

The goals of world recovery and the preservation of peace were of far more consequence to Roosevelt. Early in his administration he invited all of the debtor nations to send representatives to hold discussions with him in Washington on the debts, preparatory to the world economic conference to open in London in June, but what was most on his mind was to use the question of the debts to seek economic recovery and peace through disarmament. At the end of January, 1933, at Warm Springs, he had set forth his overall foreign policy views to the British ambassador, Sir Ronald Lindsay, who throughout the thirties looked upon Roosevelt with condescension. It was a characteristic exposition, ranging from the fundamental to the frivolous. Lindsay reported to the Foreign Office that Roosevelt proposed tariff concessions to increase international trade, international limitation of wheat production, an increased valuation of silver, and perhaps currency stabilization. To keep the peace, he sought disarmament and a European settlement. The disarmament conference at Geneva had been floundering since 1931, but as had Hoover, Roosevelt wished to limit offensive land armaments. Like the chief of staff, Douglas MacArthur, he would have banned all military planes and aircraft carriers. To reduce European tensions he favored returning to Germany the Polish Corridor linking that inland country to the Baltic, in return for a guarantee to Poland of railway transit.[6]

In this conversation as in many subsequent ones, Roosevelt was firm in his basic premises although vague or ignorant concerning some specifics. He was less weak on economic questions than wary of losing his options. The suggestion to eliminate the Polish Corridor may have seemed a wild scheme — but it was there that World War II began. Overall, Roosevelt was presenting a world view based on the aftermath of World War I and the depression crisis.

Ambassador Lindsay was typical of the British and French in being little interested in Roosevelt's proposals, and focusing upon cancellation of the war debts they felt morally they should not owe. Neither placed much value on cordial relations with the United States. Indeed, to the French it seemed of little concern. Among the small staff of the French foreign office responsible for all of the Americas, only one spoke English and none had visited the United States.[7]

The advent of Hitler rendered obsolete much of the thinking on world problems on both sides of the Atlantic. On the day following Roosevelt's exposition of his foreign policy views to the British ambassador, Hitler became chancellor of the German Reich. Within the week, Hitler told his army chiefs that first he wanted to attain full political power within Germany, then turn outward, probably "to conquer new living space in the East and Germanize it ruthlessly." The day after Roosevelt took office, Chancellor Hitler won a rigged election in Germany, and the Nazis wiped out all other political parties, gained economic control, and marshaled military and paramilitary forces. Within weeks the possibility of a war to absorb Austria or regain the Polish Corridor seemed far from an evil dream.[8]

An immediate problem for Roosevelt in March, 1933, was how he should respond to the atrocious Nazi treatment of Jews. The Nazis suspended civil and property rights, and gangs of uniformed Nazis raided, picketed, and boycotted Jewish stores and, brandishing steel springs with balls on the end, thrashed hundreds of Jewish victims. The Nazis were evicting Jews from the government, professions, business, education, and the arts.

Within the United States, most people were shocked, and some non-Jewish leaders like Al Smith joined Jews under the leadership of Rabbi Stephen Wise in leading protest meetings. The indignant Nazis responded by announcing a boycott of all Jewish business establishments; Rabbi Wise planned a retaliatory boycott.

Roosevelt, under strong pressure from the State Department, remained publicly silent. The United States, Secretary Hull and his subordinates insisted, must not interfere with the internal affairs of another nation. Their assumption, and that of many European leaders, was one Hitler cleverly encouraged, that the violent anti-Semitism in Germany was no more than the excess enthusiasm of young followers whom Hitler would soon restrain. After all, anti-Semitism was an old malady in Europe; State Department officials compared it to that in Romania a few years before. The remedy they sought was to calm the excitement in both Germany and the United States.

Among Americans there was enough latent anti-Semitism, extending even into the State Department, to cause Jewish organizations throughout the 1930s to be cautious for fear of a backlash. The Roosevelts had long since outgrown much of the anti-Semitism with which those of their background had been brought up. The president would have liked to aid the Jews, but never found a successful way to do so. He was more open and resourceful, though no more successful, in trying to thwart German militarism.[9]

Optimistic words, reiterated reassurances that Hitler would soon settle down, were the predominant west European response to the Nazi arms buildup. They were exactly what Hitler had hoped for. The British prime minister, Ramsay MacDonald, suggested making concessions to Hitler "not at the point of a bayonet but at the point of reason." It was the beginning of what became known as appeasement, the view that, if the inequities liberals saw in the Versailles Treaty were eliminated, Hitler would be reasonable. In time, because concessions failed, appeasement became a notorious concept, but for a long time after the Nazis came into power the hope lingered that Hitler, like Mussolini in Italy, beneath the bellicosity was a moderate leader. It was an illusion that Hitler astutely nurtured.

Although Roosevelt seems from the beginning to have had few illusions, he was disposed first to test Hitler to see if he would respond to peaceable overtures. If not, Roosevelt would then move as best he could toward more drastic security measures. He sought to assume leadership along with the British and French in a plea to the Germans not to rearm; in return other nations would reduce their armaments to a bare defense level.

In working toward the proposal, Roosevelt wanted first to confer with Prime Minister MacDonald and a French emissary, Eduard Herriot. The bait to bring them to Washington was economic; they would also discuss war debts and the question of currency stabilization. Roosevelt did not even let Secretary Hull know what was really on his mind, and used the economic questions as a screen for his real purpose. Further, he announced his willingness to discuss these matters with other nations, so that for several weeks envoys came to the White House for hurried conferences. The optimistic communiqués with which each visit ended built false hopes that the economic conference in London that June would bring a spectacular world effort for recovery.

So far as the main point of the meeting with the British and French was concerned — to counter the Nazi military threat — Roosevelt was not too hopeful. The words with which he invited the French to a meeting were blunt enough. He told the ambassador:

"The situation is alarming. Hitler is a madman and his counsellors, some of whom I personally know, are even madder than he is.

"*France cannot disarm now and nobody will ask her to.*"[10]

The discussions gave Roosevelt his first taste of personal diplomacy, and he found it delightful. He was a charming host, exchanging intimate thoughts at informal luncheons and on Potomac cruises aboard the *Sequoia*. He and his guests learned much about each other's views, so in this sense the conversations were useful. On the other hand, Roosevelt, overwhelmed with his first legislative program, was not well prepared or entirely certain concerning some policies. His politician's affability misled negotiators into thinking he was more favorable to their viewpoints than was sometimes the case.

By mid-May, 1933, the Nazis had brought western Europe to a state of alarm almost comparable to that of 1914. Hitler had sent as his envoy to the Geneva disarmament conference Dr. Alfred Rosenberg, who had once declared, "On every telegraph pole from Munich to Berlin the head of a prominent Jew must be stuck." The fuehrer summoned the Reichstag to meet in special session on May 17 to hear a statement on armaments and foreign policy.

In hurried anticipation of Hitler, Roosevelt issued a letter to the heads of each of the fifty-four nations attending the disarmament conference. Again he called for disarmament, to begin with the British plan. Meanwhile he proposed that all nations pledge their intention to disarm, sign a nonaggression pact, and affirm that they would send no armed force across their frontiers. To Congress, Roosevelt explained more succinctly, "The way to disarm is to disarm. The way to prevent invasion is to make it impossible."

The challenge was to Hitler, who was well prepared for it. Baron Konstantin von Neurath, his foreign minister, showed him how he could appear receptive without deviating seriously from the plans that in five years would equip Germany for war. Hitler delivered an unspectacular and conciliatory speech to the Reichstag. Roosevelt, sitting in the White House at his radio, caught some of the key phrases and translated them to Howe and Moley: "Germany is ready to join a solemn non-aggression pact. . . . Germany would be ready to dissolve its whole military establishment if . . ." Germany was ready immediately to endorse "the American President's magnanimous proposal to put up the powerful United States as a guarantor of peace."[11]

For the moment at least, Roosevelt seemed to have forestalled the Nazis. He had feared that Hitler would deliver a bellicose message, and exclaimed to Morgenthau, "I think I have averted a war." The French were disappointed that the message had not contained a security guarantee, and within a week Roosevelt issued a guarantee, directing Norman Davis to embody one in an address to the Geneva conference. For 1933, it was bold: the United States would be willing to consult with other states in case of a threat to peace and, if it concurred in the judgment that a nation was violating its international obligations, would do nothing to interfere with the collective effort to restore peace. This negative role was so sufficient a departure from isolationism that Roosevelt hoped it would be as august and effective as the Monroe Doctrine. The British foreign secretary, Sir John Simon, told the House of Commons, "The American people are prepared to abandon a tradition which they have most jealously guarded and have made a fundamental change in their country's position." The *San Francisco Chronicle*, a Republican newspaper, declared, "President Roosevelt has taken a great and dramatic step to return America to the world and the world to sanity."[12]

From this point of euphoria there was almost immediate retreat. Powerful isolationists in Congress expressed their alarm, and Roosevelt, worrying about enactment of the industrial recovery bill and several other measures, issued an immediate weakening statement. In case of a violation of agreements, the United States was committed only to consult with other nations. There was, he insisted, "no change from the long-standing and existing policy." Simultaneously the Senate Foreign Relations Committee denied Roosevelt the authorization to declare an arms embargo against an aggressor.

Roosevelt, having tried in vain to lead threatened nations in a scheme for mutual protection, retreated temporarily to positions more politically acceptable within the United States. An economic retreat also followed. By the end of June he faced the reality that for the time being he would have to choose between national and international economic policies, and opted for nationalism. The decision came over the question of currency stabilization at the London Economic Conference.

During the weeks before the economic conference opened, Roosevelt became discouraged over the failure of his plea for disarmament, less intrigued about negotiating with foreign embassies, and sobered by the slim prospects for international economic agreements to aid recovery. He had liked MacDonald and Herriot, but their governments would not back them. The British and French cabinets accepted all the concessions that Roosevelt was willing to proffer, and then were ready (as the wearying discussions over June 15 war debt payments indicated) to ask for still more. Roosevelt tartly told Morgenthau that the foreign officials were "a bunch of bastards."[13]

The pressures at home, from both Congress and his advisers, were toward economic as well as political isolation. In response Roosevelt dropped temporarily the one proposal to Congress that Hull sought above all, the authorization for a reciprocal trade program. Rather, as Wallace and others wished, Roosevelt would try to attain recovery behind tariff walls so high that they would keep out competing farm products and manufactured goods. Hull left quite depressed for London. The general expectation was that despite the hopes Roosevelt had stimulated in the spring, the conference would be a failure.

As for Roosevelt, he continued to insist that there was no need to choose between the domestic recovery program and international economic cooperation. Having obtained his final recovery measures by the end of the exhausting session of Congress, he headed off on vacation. During the crucial opening days of the conference he was yachting up the New England coast on the *Amberjack II*, in touch with developments only through ill-coordinated State Department and naval communications.

In London, Hull and his delegation, armed with Roosevelt's eloquent exhortations on behalf of international economic cooperation, possessed almost no concrete authority. Had Roosevelt focused upon the conference and kept in continuous touch, it is barely possible he might have obtained some of what most interested him, international agreements to limit production and increase the prices on commodities ranging from wheat through sugar to copper. Had he succeeded, then the tariff agreements Hull wanted and the currency stabilization upon which the French were insisting would not have been harmful to the United States. Without Roosevelt's strong direction and intricate maneuvering they were foredoomed, since other nations had only a secondary interest at best in these goals.

The opening weeks of the London conference centered around the question of temporary currency stabilization, a complex issue upon which Roosevelt had yet to commit himself. At first Roosevelt was disposed to bargain, and from Nantucket on June 19 sent a proposal that the delegates offer to keep the pound from going above $4.25 for the duration of the conference. Moley, opposed to stabilization, on his own initiative visited Roosevelt on the *Amberjack II* the next day, and left with him an antistabilization memorandum. Roosevelt insisted Moley go to London, scoffing at Moley's protestations that newspapers would sensationalize the trip, and still sending instructions to seek temporary stabilization at a ratio that would leave the dollar a good bargain in foreign markets.[14]

While Roosevelt sailed on up the coast, Moley, although acting only as a liaison for him, embarked for London amid rumors that he was coming with a plan to save the conference. When Moley arrived in London, all attention focused upon him, and Hull felt more than ever like a figurehead. Actually, Roosevelt had no intention of giving authority to either of them; he wished as always to be in command. He received some optimistic reports that led him to believe that no temporary stabilization was necessary, and ignored warnings that the drop of the dollar to 76.3 cents in gold made stabilization imperative. Moley and the delegation did not receive Roosevelt's instructions embodying these views and worked out what seemed to be in keeping with earlier instructions (and Moley's own opposition to any firm stabilization), "some sort of innocuous, non-binding compromise." It called for the central banks of signatory powers voluntarily to cooperate with each other in limiting speculation. This they cabled to Roosevelt for approval.[15]

As Moley and the American delegation in London waited with growing tension, Roosevelt decided upon a reply. The messages from London and Washington reached him at Campobello Island, where he was with Howe, Morgenthau, and Mrs. Roosevelt.

On the night of June 30, the stabilization proposal finally reached

Roosevelt. He was away from the usual restraining counsels and was on edge. Mrs. Roosevelt had lashed out at him that evening as though he were a small boy because he had served their teen-age son Franklin, Jr., a cocktail and they were late to supper. Roosevelt retorted, "You can't scold me this way." Some of his feelings may have carried over into his actions as head of state.[16]

The next afternoon Roosevelt, sitting in the captain's cabin of the cruiser *Indianapolis*, wrote a dispatch to London so vigorous that it became known as the bombshell message. In it he expressed his indignation that the economic conference should be diverted from its large purposes through concern with temporary monetary stabilization, affecting only a few nations.

Altogether, Roosevelt indulged in psychological overkill, quite uncharacteristic of him. He seemed scarcely to have noted the mild, almost meaningless compromise Moley had cabled him, and to be responding to a range of pent-up irritations. The message blew up the already dying conference. The British and the French placed the blame on Roosevelt. Both contrasted his firm stand in the message with his promises of the spring.

Fundamentally, the president did not want stabilization because it would cost the United States some of its gold reserve, which could be a political, even if not an economic, disaster. Further, it would interfere with his plans for a managed currency. Herbert Feis a generation later concluded that Roosevelt had averted the peril of a drain of a half billion dollars in gold.

Roosevelt's bombshell message brought nationalistic cheers within the United States, and both accolades and chidings in Europe. The British economist John Maynard Keynes and Winston Churchill were supportive; the *Journal de Genève* in Switzerland went so far as to assert that the collapse of international confidence was due to two individuals — Hitler, who had paralyzed the disarmament conference, and Roosevelt, through his egoistic and incoherent policies wrecking the economic conference.[17]

Altogether, Roosevelt's first Hundred Days in foreign affairs were far from a success. He had seized world leadership, only to have Hitler and Congress deflate his bold stand for collective security and disarmament. He had thrown away much of what remained through his blow to the moribund economic conference. In both instances he had created false expectations upon which he could or would not make good. Yet he did not abandon fully his international goals. By mid-July, when the dollar dropped to a ratio of $4.86 to the pound, Roosevelt became fearful of a fresh British devaluation and resorted to the unilateral stabilization he had kept in reserve as a weapon. As for collective security, at the end of 1934 he told Morgenthau that if the Nazis' inhuman aggressions should extend to England he believed that the United States would of course go in and help England.[18]

Until conditions became more propitious, Roosevelt focused upon problems at home and in the western hemisphere, biding his time and trying step-by-step to educate the electorate to meet the challenges of a menacing future. An analyst in the British Foreign Office noted, "Mr. Roosevelt is giving up hope in the old world and is turning to the new."[19]

Chapter 9

INSTALLING THE NEW DEAL PROGRAMS

IN THE SUMMER of 1933, the euphoria of the Hundred Days dissipated and Roosevelt had to focus upon installing and conducting a long-range recovery program. The spectacular improvement in the economy, which had led Roosevelt and the nation to hope for "crash recovery," came to a sudden end within a matter of months.

It had been an encouraging start toward recovery while it lasted. Industrial production had risen to the 1923–1925 level and the stock market had soared. The hoped-for end to the depression seemed to become an almost instant reality, but Roosevelt in June was worried. The indices, except for employment, were rising so rapidly that he was fearful of a repetition of the boom and crash of 1928–1929.

In mid-July the boomlet collapsed, and Roosevelt thought his misgivings had been borne out. He had warned in May, "I do not want the people to take the foolish course of letting this improvement come back on another speculative wave. . . . Such a course may bring us immediate and false prosperity but it will be the kind of prosperity that will lead us into another tailspin." Throughout the New Deal he continued fearful of another "great crash," a fear that the fiasco of July, 1933, may have reinforced.[1]

The setback must have been painful to Roosevelt, but he showed no sign of dismay, nor did he accept any blame. Rather, he analyzed the collapse as a logical and reprehensible result of speculation. As early as August 9, he made up his mind what had gone wrong: "Everybody got to speculating and things went too fast; that got a perfectly natural corrective." A few months later he commented that a good many manufacturers, especially those of steel and textiles, had overproduced, trying to build inventories with low-paid labor before the National Recovery Administration (NRA) codes would go into effect, forcing them to pay higher wages. Wheat also, he declared, had gone up too fast, to $1.25 per bushel. He interpreted the July drop in prices consequently as "a perfectly natural one . . . a perfectly healthy thing."[2]

These vicissitudes and more to follow tarnished the public image of Roosevelt as an infallible worker of miracles. He had been wary of that image during the spring, nor had he expected it to last. "I have no expectation of making a hit every time I come to bat," he had warned. "What I seek is the highest possible batting average, not only for myself but for the team." For a large part of the American people then and later the fact that Roosevelt was trying to help them, that he cared, was sufficient to retain their support. But his popularity was dented and disillusion and opposition began to spread. By the end of 1933, conservative protests once again received a respectful hearing. Under these less auspicious circumstances, he undertook the long and complex struggle toward recovery and reform.[3]

In putting his program into effect, Roosevelt drew from an arsenal of new legislation and agencies at his disposal. He commanded more funds and more executive power than any previous president in peacetime. Congress had adjourned until January, 1934, and with little interference he could concentrate upon the task of administering the New Deal. His hope was to bring immediate relief and steady, substantial recovery through a dozen or more new agencies that Congress had authorized.

The New Deal program with its many ramifications headed in several directions at once, and so too did the sprawling administration Roosevelt built to run it. As an administrator, he was unconventional, but the government was still small enough that he could keep an eye on most operations. The White House staff was minuscule compared with that of later presidents, and during the first years did not erect a bureaucratic wall around him. Four secretaries, all of whom he had known for many years, served him well. In addition, a few experts assisted him and wrote speeches, like Moley, Tugwell, and two talented young lawyers, Thomas Corcoran and Benjamin Cohen. All the experts were either elsewhere on the federal payroll or volunteered their services.

Roosevelt loved to experiment; new ideas always intrigued him. If they failed to gain political support or in practice did not work out, he was ready to modify or abandon them. So it was with people, too. In planning new agencies or an administrative reorganization, he liked to sketch organization charts with neat boxes and lines of authority. Yet in practice his agencies and his administrators frequently overlapped, leading sometimes to healthy rivalry and at other times to bitter quarrels and inaction.

Many of Roosevelt's administrators were able, and of strong, often quite differing views. Sometimes, like the old Bull Mooser Harold L. Ickes, the secretary of the interior, or the conservative Texas Democrat Jesse H. Jones, head of the Reconstruction Finance Corporation (RFC), they commanded considerable and useful political support. Their varying policies, mirroring diverse constituencies, ranged from the old-time laissez-faire Cleveland Democratic dogma among those like Jones to the heresies of the iconoclastic young planners and regulators like Tugwell.

In the lesser positions, young talent flooded into Washington or enlisted in New Deal enterprises throughout the country. Those who in the prosperous twenties might have joined law, banking, engineering, or business firms or staffed universities often found their greatest opportunities in the New Deal and brought it their youthful enthusiasm and energy. A good many of the excellent lawyers, coming under the auspices of Felix Frankfurter of Harvard Law School, were disciples of Justice Louis D. Brandeis, perpetuating his emphasis upon decentralization and small enterprise. One of these, Charles Wyzanski, Jr., who at twenty-eight became solicitor in the Department of Labor, long afterward looked back at himself as having been a pretty conservative fellow. But by and large these young administrators provided a powerful forward thrust to the New Deal well in advance of Roosevelt. In comparison, as Anne O'Hare McCormick of the *New York Times* noted in 1934, the president sounded like a Jeffersonian upholding the older verities. There were perhaps 15,000 of these New Dealers in Washington by the summer of 1934, and 250,000 throughout the country. Roosevelt considered them the leaders of the next generation, and so in time many of them were to be, in government and a wide array of other fields.

The New Dealers, staffing the numerous new agencies, with few exceptions gave Roosevelt their zealous support. He had been eager to avoid an appearance of politics in appointing them, and often remarked that he had chosen them without thought to their being Democrats or Republicans. A good many of them were of Republican background, and a few of these in relief agencies operating in the states did cause political trouble. Most of the appointees in the end had to be acceptable to James A. Farley, postmaster general and head of the Democratic National Committee, who, under pressure from Democratic politicians throughout the country, was much more orthodox about appointments than Roosevelt. In appointments as elsewhere, the president was continually seeking to transcend the Democratic party, a minority party, and to rally behind him a far larger coalition.[4]

Within the president's own household, Eleanor Roosevelt, acting in concert with Molly Dewson of the Democratic National Committee and Secretary of Labor Frances Perkins, the first woman cabinet member, brought effective pressure upon Roosevelt and Farley for the appointment of women. In the first years of the New Deal they succeeded in obtaining a sprinkling of women in fairly significant positions, far more than ever before. But it was both popular dogma and government policy during the depression years that a woman should not receive a government job if her husband held one. After the first two years, traditional Democratic politicians again had the upper hand, and the role of women in government declined.[5]

Roosevelt appointed sufficient blacks to form what some of them referred to as a black subcabinet. They made more progress than in the 1920s, but not enough to gain many jobs except at the lowest-paying levels.

The New Deal agencies, thus staffed, were far more responsive to Roosevelt than the regular departments would likely have been. Within the departments most of the personnel were Republicans with civil service protection. Bureau chiefs, stinging from the cutbacks they had suffered in the spring of 1933, possessed direct ties to congressional appropriations committees, and hence had little reason to be beholden to the president. Roosevelt had no desire to add to their numbers; at first he made few appointments from the civil service lists, which were old and mostly made up of Republicans. By 1935, when conditions had changed and it was Democrats who would be frozen in if civil service were invoked, like many a predecessor he returned to his earlier enthusiasm for civil service. In giving support to the merit system only later in his administration, when it would protect loyal supporters, he was following the traditional course of presidents since the enactment of civil-service reform legislation in the 1880s.

At first, the New Deal agencies were expected to be only temporary, and after two years Roosevelt had to use some of his influence to secure their continuance from Congress. His appointees did not always manage to set policy to his satisfaction. As the new triumvirate he appointed to head the Tennessee Valley Authority discovered, he was habitually hazy in his instructions. In effect he was challenging the administrators to make the most of their opportunities. It was up to them to succeed as best they could and to avoid as far as possible troubles that would embarrass Roosevelt or force him to intervene.

Some of the new agencies, especially the Agricultural Adjustment Administration (AAA), started with an advantage because rudimentary prototypes had come into existence during the Hoover presidency. Experts like Mordecai Ezekiel, involved with the Hoover Farm Board or the Department of Agriculture, made possible the surprising speed of the crash program in the summer of 1933. The RFC was already in full operation with Jones as chairman. Several of the more prominent New Dealers, most notably Corcoran of the RFC and William O. Douglas, later head of the Securities and Exchange Commission, had already served as experts for the Hoover administration. This is not to suggest that Hoover deserves credit for devising the New Deal administrative agencies. He would have vehemently disavowed them. Rather, Roosevelt and the New Dealers took the existing machinery in the fields of farm relief, government loans, work relief, and public works, remodeled it, and put it to uses that Hoover soon viewed with alarm and even outrage.[6]

In public, Hoover held his tongue for some months, but in private, as early as March, 1933, he was protesting that even the conservative banking act, though framed by his own Treasury expert, would "raise the most appalling difficulties." He warned, "Our fight is going to be to stop this move to gigantic socialism."[7]

Within the White House, Roosevelt moved into the administrative routines that he had found comfortable and effective when he was governor. At their heart were his trusted secretary Missy LeHand, and the asthmatic Louis Howe, in increasingly bad physical condition. Howe, glorying in the title "Colonel," lived in the White House, but was too ill and out of touch to be a powerful adviser like Wilson's Colonel House. Howe collaborated most often with Mrs. Roosevelt in her projects to improve living conditions of impoverished West Virginia rural folk.

Eleanor Roosevelt herself, with her own entourage, served much of the time, as she had in New York State, as her husband's eyes and ears. She was also his conscience, prodding him on social justice matters such as the need to help black people in their plight. She had much influence upon him, and also developed into something of an independent political force in her own right.

In the White House offices there were Marvin McIntyre, the appointments secretary, and Stephen Early, the press secretary, both southerners. As newspapermen covering the Navy Department during World War I, they had aided Roosevelt in the 1920 campaign. Both were devoted to Roosevelt and edged him toward caution in his dealings with blacks, for fear of inflaming southern white prejudices. Black newspapermen were barred from press conferences, and leaders like Walter White of the National Association for the Advancement of Colored People could seldom obtain access to the president except through Mrs. Roosevelt.

Then there were all the cabinet members, administrators, various members of both houses of Congress, diplomats, and private citizens seeking Roosevelt's ear and being called upon to aid in various projects. Which individuals were close to him depended upon both their personalities and his own priorities at any given time. The order of importance sometimes became apparent the first thing in the morning.

After breakfasting and reading the papers in bed, Roosevelt while he shaved and dressed often conferred with several of his advisers. The competition to be with the president in his bedroom carried amusing overtones of the rivalry among courtiers at the eighteenth-century Versailles palace. Roosevelt was not trying to be regal (or imperial). Rather, he was enjoying the relative mobility and relaxation of his bedroom before he put on his braces and began the long hours in the Oval Office, where he was not able to move from his desk except by wheelchair. He conducted much business in his pajamas out of necessity rather than to flout convention; when he received the French ambassador in his bedroom he created no stir, as had Jefferson in offending the British envoy.

The competition among the advisers was useful for Roosevelt, who listened to their often conflicting recommendations and kept for himself the power of ultimate decision. With the pressures of the Hundred Days over, and Moley relegated to the role of occasional adviser and speechwriter commuting from Columbia University, Roosevelt operated as his own chief of staff. Not until the pressures of the defense crisis after the outbreak of World War II accelerated the rise of Harry Hopkins did any single adviser enjoy the scope and authority Moley had possessed. Usually Roosevelt called upon numerous administrators for aid on specific problems. The influence of various of them waxed and ebbed, sometimes, as in the case of Hopkins, going through repeated cycles. Even the influence of Eleanor Roosevelt, who was so vital to him overall, had its ups and downs. Several advisers at one time or another basked in his favor only to return to relative obscurity, but few were fired. Roosevelt hated to fire people.

From these advisers and a multitude of other sources, Roosevelt gathered information and impressions. He liked, when he could, to get out of the White House and directly in touch with the people. It is interesting that the handful of ordinary people who thus occasionally caught his ear were for the most part living in small-town or rural New York or Georgia. He still relaxed in Hyde Park and Warm Springs.

In conversation with both the eminent and the obscure, Roosevelt usually had so much to say, both on the subject and anecdotally far afield, that it is surprising how much he listened. He basically grasped issues by ear. When he was garrulous it was sometimes because he did not want to hear what someone had come to the Oval Office to tell him. Often he tested ideas by trying out on a visitor what a previous one had suggested. Sometimes even with Eleanor Roosevelt he played devil's advocate, arguing a course of action that it turned out was quite opposite to what he really favored.

Roosevelt was a fast reader, and also learned much that way. In his scanning of the newspapers, he was sensitive, indeed hypersensitive, to the criticisms of editorial writers and columnists, and quick to protest whatever seemed to him inaccurate reporting. There was a huge correspondence, and there were great stacks of reports. The reports had to begin with brief striking summaries if they were to catch his eye, and many he altogether avoided. But he was master of important materials, and some influenced him deeply. Whatever the sources of his information, Roosevelt demonstrated a remarkable breadth and detail of knowledge concerning the ramifications of both his administrative and political domains. Both at press conferences and meetings of his administrative councils, his range was often startling.

After a lengthy lunch at the president's desk in late March, 1933, Stimson expressed his admiration to a former colleague, who noted:

> Time and again they were interrupted by people coming in on urgent matters, and he said that the versatility of the President and his ability to reach the kernel of a problem was astounding. His mind is not that of a lawyer or scholar, and he rarely is familiar with past history or detail, but nonetheless he showed that he could grasp the essentials, reach a decision and complete action with speed and clarity.[8]

Two new councils helped Roosevelt to stay abreast of New Deal developments and sometimes to coordinate overlapping programs. In the summer of 1933 he created first the Executive Council, a sort of oversized emergency cabinet, and then the smaller National Emergency Council. They were so similar that before the end of 1934 they were merged. Both bodies served the same basic function, to gather full information on the organization and function of new agencies. As in World War I, it was vital to have fresh, full, and accurate economic data. As a component of the Executive Council, Roosevelt established a Central Statistical Board and appointed a distinguished statistician, Winfield W. Riefler, to head it. Riefler condensed both general economic data and agency progress reports into a brief weekly digest, and predicted trends. In the early New Deal, Roosevelt met with the councils and on the basis of statistics and discussion set policies. The device was in some respects a forerunner of the Council of Economic Advisors.[9]

During July and August, Roosevelt seemed fairly well satisfied with the way that the recovery and relief programs were going into operation. He dismissed the stock market collapse with much the same view he had taken of the great crash in 1929. "If there are enough silly people in the world to go ahead and bid up stocks too far above their value, those people are very apt to lose their money," he remarked at a press conference.[10]

By this time Roosevelt was looking toward a fairly slow, steady recovery. "We are a little bit like the old railroad train that has to travel up a long grade," he remarked extemporaneously. "We have got the train started and it is running, let us say, twenty miles an hour. We must get that train to go forty miles an hour and then there is an assurance that it will go over the top."[11]

The twin engines of recovery, the triple-A and the NRA, started amid much fanfare, but by the end of the summer both were wheezing. The difficulties of the NRA did not so readily engage Roosevelt's attention as did those of the AAA. The NRA codes, which businessmen had sought, were to establish standards of fair practices, but supposedly not price-fixing. In practice, the code quality controls could lead to tacitly established higher prices, and thus give promise of restored profits. In return the businessmen were expected to accept wages and hours guarantees for workers and protection for consumers, but these would threaten profits. In reality, businessmen were to dominate the code making and the subsequent operation of the NRA. Like the earlier War Industries Board, and, a decade later, the War Production Board, it brought into government service businessmen to regulate businessmen.

Despite the hyperbole with which Roosevelt had hailed the enactment of the industrial recovery program, and the exuberance with which he explained it in a Fireside Chat at the end of July, he gave little personal attention to the code-making process. The onus fell upon the administrator, General Hugh Johnson, who had accurately predicted that it would be red fire at first and dead cats afterward.

To Roosevelt the launching of the NRA was another campaign for social justice, rather akin to American entrance into the First World War. He brought to it his moralistic view of the American economic system. There was to be something for everybody in the NRA, for businessmen, workers, and consumers, and linked with them in the AAA, the farmers. And there was, in return, to be something exacted from everybody. The NRA postage stamp issued that summer illustrated his view of the program, depicting, as the delighted Roosevelt wrote Farley, "the honest farmer, who looks like me; the honest businessman . . . the honest blacksmith . . . [and] what a girl!" They were all marching together toward recovery, as were innumerable Americans in NRA parades, flying Blue Eagle flags bearing the inscription "We Do Our Part." Since specific code making went on too slowly, Roosevelt persuaded most Americans, whether businessmen or consumers, to subscribe individually to a blanket code and to pledge to do business only with those displaying the insignia. Only a few businessmen, like Henry Ford, resisted the movement.[12]

By the late summer, Roosevelt seemed to think his experiment in democratic self-discipline in industry was working. He had already acclaimed the cotton textile code because it abolished child labor. In August, he was talking about the deeper purposes of the NRA in building up wages that were at the starvation level and in slashing hours that were too long, resulting in "a greater distribution of income and wages" and consequently an increase in employment and in "the purchasing power of the average American citizen and, therefore, of the Nation as a whole."[13]

Roosevelt was hoping that the NRA and AAA schemes would work through this redistribution of income and assurance of greater buying power for all Americans. Then the surge of demand would lead businesses to invest their funds in new enterprise.[14]

Roosevelt was aware that redistribution of income was not by itself enough, but persisted in feeling that the injection of public works money into the economy must be slow and prudent. He and the Democrats had lambasted President Hoover for granting RFC loans to large corporations, saying that the idea that the benefits would trickle down to the needy was specious. Yet Roosevelt himself, determined to keep government costs at a minimum as he had pledged during his campaign, sanctioned little expenditure upon public works. Part of the problem was that it took much time and work for engineers, architects, and lawyers to prepare acceptable proposals. Only late in the New Deal did quantities of projects come before Roosevelt for approval. Still, he was innately cautious about heavy federal construction projects. He once suggested to Ickes that perhaps the buildings of failed banks might be bought to serve as post offices. Generally he insisted upon self-liquidating projects that Republicans could not criticize. The political factor motivated him less than his own moral certainty that only projects that could pay for themselves were justifiable. By the end of 1933 he had allocated most of the $3.3 billion public works appropriation, but was spreading the money out over three years. It did not serve as a quick, massive stimulus to the economy.[15]

Nor did the AAA, as it went into operation in 1933, seem to promise more than to shift income from urban consumers by increasing some farm prices. The theory was, of course, that in the end these consumers would benefit, since increased agricultural purchasing power would result in renewed prosperity for businessmen and workers. Here again Roosevelt seemed to be relying upon a trickle process, a lateral one of seepage from farmers to city dwellers.

Roosevelt's course, viewed from a post-Keynesian perspective, seems far more conservative than it appeared at the time. Among all the economists of diverging views, there were almost none willing to advocate deliberate deficit spending. Even those progressives seeking a public works program much larger than Roosevelt's clung to their faith in the balanced budget, and favored heavy taxation to fund the program.

The progressives sought redistribution of the wealth. So did Roosevelt. On the one hand, Roosevelt wanted his program to be politically acceptable, to contain something for everybody. On the other, he seemed to favor exacting more from the wealthy, and giving more to the underprivileged. He was desperately anxious to turn his minority party into one of an overwhelming majority, and he wanted the support of Republicans as well as Democrats, of businessmen, bankers, and professional people as well as workers and farmers. Nevertheless he frequently gave expression to attitudes characteristic of the most advanced progressives, that the wealthy must bear a larger part of the social burdens. It was his view during his relatively placid first year in office and became accentuated by 1935. He tried to give the impression that his view had always been an integral part of the American political tradition. "Many years ago," he declared in an informal talk in August, 1933, the nation had accepted graduated income taxes "because of a simple principle that very large profits were made at the expense of neighbors and, therefore, should at least to some extent be used through taxes for the benefit of the neighbors."[16]

In a variation on the same point, in March, 1934, he urged Speaker Henry Rainey to oppose a bill that would raise the ceiling on the federal guarantee of bank deposits from $2,500 to $10,000, on the grounds that it "would aid only the three per cent of rich depositors who have more than twenty-five hundred in any one bank." (Congress compromised at $5,000, and raised the ceiling in 1935 to $10,000.) He added to Rainey, perhaps not altogether facetiously, "The bill as passed by the Senate takes care of the other ninety-seven percent who are people like you and me." Behind Roosevelt's patrician facade there occasionally flickered the shadow of a populist.[17]

In actuality not much redistribution of wealth took place during the New Deal, as New Left critics were bitterly to point out. Had redistribution occurred, there is no valid reason to think that it would have brought rapid recovery from the depression of the 1930s.

Chapter 10

THE FAILURE OF BOOTSTRAP RECOVERY

THROUGH THE REMAINDER of 1933 and 1934, Roosevelt continued to place his faith in a recovery program that in theory at least would be of no cost to the taxpayers — operating on the premise that the nation could lift itself out of the depression by its bootstraps. It was a scheme in keeping with Roosevelt's ardent and long-continuing belief in a balanced budget. The business recovery program, the NRA, was to operate on a self-policing basis at minimum cost, and that of agriculture, the AAA, was to be financed by a processing tax on cotton, wheat, and pork, to pay farmers to limit their production of them. In theory, but only in theory, the processing tax paid at the cotton gin or flour mill was not to be passed on to the consumer. Other self-financing recovery schemes aimed at raising commodity prices through devaluing the dollar on international markets.

Intertwined with these cautious approaches was another that Roosevelt regarded with some misgivings and was ready to use only with care. That was pump priming, the stimulus of the economy with borrowed money, which worried him because it was contrary to the orthodox dogma that the budget must be balanced and the national debt not increased. Relief spending could have the same effect but was not at that time looked upon as pump priming. A few days after the Los Angeles earthquake in the spring of 1933, at a press conference he set forth a clever rationale: supposing Manhattan were leveled by an earthquake, would it not be essential to rebuild it at once? A large nonrecurring expenditure of that sort should be considered as a response to an emergency and allocated separately. With this rationale he established an "emergency budget," recording the deficit expenditures for national rehabilitation, and separately maintained the regular budget, which he sought assiduously to keep balanced.[1]

As winter approached in 1933, bootstrap recovery was lagging. Since economic indices were up from the low point of the spring, Roosevelt could issue occasional optimistic statements, but neither lagging farm prices nor continuing massive unemployment gave much reason for them. The *New York Times* business index stood at 72 in October compared with 60 in March, but in June it had stood at 99. The price of wheat had soared from 44 cents to $1.25 per bushel, then had fallen back.

At first Roosevelt did not appear dismayed; he felt the July break in prices was a healthy reaction to speculation. The achievement of recovery, it was becoming clear, must be a slow process. By October, industrial production and farm prices were continuing to decline, and while Roosevelt expressed no public alarm, he became privately worried.

The prime component in Roosevelt's quest for recovery, the AAA, was not functioning well in its first year. It began operating too late in the spring to limit the planting of crops and breeding of sows. At its inception it had offered farmers substantial benefit payments to reduce the yield of basic commodities — a hundred million dollars to cotton farmers for plowing under a quarter of their cotton. The carryover was so enormous that not an extra bale would have been needed in 1933 to supply the world market. In exchange for benefits, corn-hogs farmers of the Middle West shipped millions of surplus breeding sows and small pigs to the stockyards. This kind of program went diametrically opposite to the course that Roosevelt and Secretary of Agriculture Henry A. Wallace sought, to move toward an economy of abundance, but they felt it was essential as a first step. They must lower production, they reasoned; when recovery came, expansion would follow.

The reduction was not sufficiently drastic to prevent a fresh collapse of commodity prices during the summer. By fall cotton farmers were demanding stricter controls; through intensive cultivation they had grown more cotton than on their full acreage the year before. Midwest farmers were rallying around Milo Reno of the Farmer's Holiday Association and his drastic "cost of production" scheme to raise commodity prices far higher.[2]

The president took interim actions. He did not need to call Congress back into session but utilized blanket authorizations and broad appropriations that he had obtained in the spring. As a first step, both to bolster prices and to relieve suffering, Roosevelt initiated a program through the AAA to purchase surplus foods and distribute them to the unemployed. During the summer of 1933 there had been much lamentation among Republican politicos and the press over the slaughter of baby pigs to bring pork prices up. It was one of the first criticisms of the New Deal to capture the public imagination. The lamentations were to continue through the campaign of 1936, as though the baby pigs had been wasted. All had been utilized, those of edible size for food, those too small, for fertilizer. The initial allocation to the needy through state relief administrations was 100 million pounds of cured pork. Those on relief were receiving inadequate amounts of food and clothing; their inability to purchase a normal amount was contributing to the glut of meats, grains, and cotton. Roosevelt wanted to release quantities of stored cotton for the manufacture of clothing for destitute people. He had been touched by a story that Lorena A. Hickok, an intimate of Mrs. Roosevelt and investigator for Harry Hopkins, head of the relief program, had brought from the mining towns of southeast Kentucky. Roosevelt related:

> She got into one of those mining towns and came around a corner of an alley and started to walk up the alley. There was a group of miners sitting in front of the shacks, and they pulled down their caps over their faces. As soon as she caught sight of that she walked up and said, "What is the matter? What are you pulling your caps down for?" They said, "Oh, it is all right." "Why pull your caps down?" They said, "It is a sort of custom to pull caps down because so many of the women have not enough clothes to cover them."[3]

Roosevelt hailed the program to utilize surplus cotton and foodstuffs as "one of the most direct blows at the economic paradox which has choked farms with an abundance of farm products while many of the unemployed have gone hungry."[4]

The surplus food program began, as Roosevelt planned, with an initial allocation of $75 million. It was to endure, and before the end of the 1930s was to be modified into a system operating through supplying food stamps to the needy. It had the double advantage of aiding those in want and providing additional income for farmers, but was beginning on a scale too small to generate a marked stimulus on the national economy.

Rather, Roosevelt resorted to two more powerful tools to raise farm prices. He gave in to the pressures from John Bankhead of Alabama and other powerful cotton state senators, chairmen of several committees through which New Deal legislation must pass, and announced a program for cotton producers more sweeping than he would have liked but less than they sought. It provided an immediate loan of 10 cents a pound on the 1933 cotton crop, a little higher than the current price (and not the 15 cents Bankhead had sought). He thus established a price floor. The loan was to go only to cotton growers who accepted a 40 percent restriction of their 1934 acreage.

In addition Roosevelt established the Commodity Credit Corporation, authorized to borrow from the Reconstruction Finance Corporation, as the machinery through which the government could support the price not only of cotton but also of other basic farm produce. Here again was a device outside of the "bootstrap" AAA processing-tax scheme. The cotton program was basically conservative, like the ill-fated, ineffectual efforts of President Hoover's Farm Board. It could do no more than prevent price collapse. In mid-October, Roosevelt, acting more positively, began open market purchases of wheat and sometimes corn for Harry Hopkins' relief distribution.[5]

Neither of these devices sufficed to stem falling prices and rising rural discontent. Consequently, Roosevelt, still viewing gold as a commodity, which if it rose in price would bring up the prices of all other commodities along with it, resorted, under authorization from the Thomas Amendment to the AAA legislation, to purchase of gold at a price above that prevailing on the gold market. Correspondingly, the value of the dollar should drop, making it easier for other nations to purchase American goods. Among most farmers and some others the scheme was popular, but some of Roosevelt's most important financial advisers broke with him over it. At the height of the controversy, Roosevelt dismissed his under secretary of the treasury, Dean Acheson. Secretary William Woodin was terminally ill, and Henry Morgenthau, Jr., governor of the Farm Credit Administration, who cooperated with Roosevelt in the gold buying, became first acting, then full secretary of the treasury.

There was a clamor of disapproval from financiers, economists, and politicians. Al Smith called the "commodity dollar" the "baloney dollar." John Maynard Keynes, in an open letter to Roosevelt that appeared in the *New York Times* at the end of the year, scoffed at the scheme as puerile. Day by day Roosevelt was setting a different buying figure for gold, sending it inching upward and the dollar downward. Keynes irreverently remarked that the fluctuations seemed more like "a gold standard on booze than the ideal managed currency of my dreams." Roosevelt in defense of his policies argued among his advisers that without the manipulations there would have been serious trouble. He pointed to Milo Reno's not very successful farm strike, by this time under way, and remarked that were it not for his purchases of gold and agricultural commodities there would have been an agrarian revolution in the country.[6]

Despite the protests, Roosevelt continued his gold buying into January, 1934. The results were disappointing, bearing out neither Roosevelt's expectations nor those of his critics. The "commodity dollar" theory did not prove to be correct. While Roosevelt drove the price of gold up 17 percent, and the average value of a group of key industrial stocks kept pace, cotton lagged, up 14 percent. The index of all farm products actually slipped during the gold-buying months. But Roosevelt was able to stabilize wheat, which had fallen to 60 cents a bushel, at 85 cents through both gold and wheat purchases.

In January Roosevelt was ready, as he had stated in advance, to stabilize a devalued dollar. He obtained the Gold Reserve Act from Congress, and under its provisions set the value of the dollar at 59.06 percent of its pre–New Deal value, which pegged gold at $35 an ounce. There the price of gold was to remain for a generation. To Roosevelt, the dollar seemed to be at an equitable exchange value with previously devalued currencies like that of Great Britain, and thereafter the United States helped fight off a raid on the franc.

Most economists at the time scoffed at the "commodity dollar," and many historians since have been critical of Roosevelt's maneuver. Yet viewed politically, it contributed to the sputtering out of Reno's farm strike by late November, and took the pressure out of demands for more drastic inflation. From Roosevelt's viewpoint of economic morality, it brought severely deflated prices more in line with the high prices prevailing when farmers and others had contracted mortgages and other debts. The new prices were in Roosevelt's eyes more equitable; repayment would be a little easier. His management of the currency helped stave off what seemed to be an impending second economic collapse. "A continuation of the fall of the price level," Roosevelt wrote Colonel House, "would have brought the whole Recovery Program toppling about our ears." The decline in economic indices came to a halt, and slowly they turned upward.[7]

What probably hastened the upturn more than the gold and price support experiments was a program in the winter of 1933–1934 conceived out of compassion. With reemployment lagging and relief programs, even with federal aid, inadequate in many states, millions seemed likely to suffer. Harry Hopkins convinced Roosevelt to create a temporary work program on an unprecedented scale to carry unemployed workers through the winter. They were to receive regular wages for a limited number of working hours per week, and to perform a wide variety of blue-collar and white-collar projects for states and localities. Speed, not the merit of the projects, was essential, and between early November, when Roosevelt first announced the program, and mid-December, the Civil Works Administration (CWA) put four million people to work at whatever projects were locally proposed. None of the careful deliberation of the Public Works Administration (PWA) went into the venture. They repaired buildings wrecked in the Los Angeles earthquake, labored on public works, taught school, performed in the arts — or, where projects had been ill conceived, did no more than rake leaves. The made work was often conspicuous — the term "boondoggling" came to be applied to it — and politics, both Democratic and Republican, were involved. Overall, nonetheless, the CWA was highly popular and in a brief span of time accomplished much.

From the outset both Roosevelt and Hopkins thought of the CWA as an expedient to endure only through the cold months. As early as mid-December, Roosevelt was announcing a schedule for tapering off, first in the South and then northward with the advancing spring. Later in the winter he spoke sharply against proposals to prolong the program. "We must not take the position that we are going to have permanent depression in this country," he told the National Emergency Council. He expected that in the spring the PWA would be in full operation and employ some of the CWA workers, and that the normal increase in outdoor jobs would take care of the rest. "Nobody is going to starve during the warm weather."[8]

By the spring of 1934, the portents seemed favorable. The CWA had put an infusion of money into the economy and the *New York Times* business index was up to 86 by May. Roosevelt had obtained the money for the CWA through combining funds that states and Hopkins' Federal Emergency Relief Administration (FERA) had already been spending (some of it on work relief), with a large dollop of 30 percent from Ickes' PWA kitty. In total, in a few months the CWA poured a billion dollars into the economy, making possible not only a minimum living standard but even some Christmas purchases for millions of heads of families receiving $15 a week paychecks. The money thus put into circulation had a multiplier effect as it passed through the economy.

Unfortunately, neither the public works program nor private employment took up much of the slack after the CWA came to an end in the late spring. Large numbers of those who had been on the CWA had to take a humiliating "means test" to seek work relief from the FERA. It took over many of the CWA projects, but paid less than half as much, only $6.50 per week. Spending had slackened, and while there was no real threat of recession, recovery seemed stalled. Economic indices varied little from the figures of May, which had brought a premature promise of improvement. The bootstrap route to recovery through the AAA and the NRA was not working very well. The AAA was a modest success, in part because machinery was already in place within the Department of Agriculture to put it into motion in the spring of 1933, and more so because drought on the Great Plains reduced grain production and brought an infusion of federal relief funds.

In contrast the NRA was a fiasco. It had indeed, as General Hugh Johnson, its administrator, predicted, been red fire at first, with the excitement during the summer of 1933 of great NRA parades and sign-up campaigns comparable to the Liberty Loan drives of World War I. Then there had been the lengthy, complicated code-making process. Instead of a handful of codes of fair practice with a few simple provisions applying to the nation's major industries, there was a plethora of them, ranging down to codes for the mopstick and feather-duster industries. Most often the codes were complex, putting the force of federal law behind the previous regulations of trade associations — to give a single example, to forbid the packaging of egg noodles in yellow cellophane, which would make them appear richer than they really were. Often the larger, more powerful companies in an industry dominated the code making, obtaining provisions expensive if not ruinous for smaller firms to comply with. Above all, the objective of the businessmen drafting the codes was to set floors on prices, to prevent "chiselers" from selling for less or from marketing substandard merchandise.

Throughout the whole code-making process and later in operation of the NRA, Johnson for all his appearance of toughness did little to control the business leaders. In practice, the codes were as difficult to police as prohibition had been, and there was little enforcement machinery. Unlike the AAA, there were no administrators already in place to run the NRA; a staff had to be recruited and gain experience. Although Johnson made protestations against price fixing, the codes inevitably operated in that direction, and were onerous for small businessmen. By the beginning of 1934, complaints were so pervasive and pressure upon Congress so strong that Roosevelt appointed the National Recovery Review Board to investigate monopolistic tendencies in the NRA, and Johnson agreed to having his old friend Clarence Darrow as the chairman. The Darrow Report, as could be expected from an old Progressive of socialist leanings, damned the NRA. Dead cats had replaced the red fire, and Johnson was the recipient.

As for Roosevelt, after his exaggerated praise for the NRA concept in the summer of 1933, he was singularly silent about it in press conferences. He did at the end of December, 1933, express his fear that the codes might benefit big business at the expense of small enterprise and that some industries might be under the misapprehension that the legislation had abolished the Sherman Anti-Trust Act. In the spring, when the spectacular Darrow Report came out, he managed for weeks to sidestep public comment. Not until late in the summer, when Johnson's troubles with the NRA, compounded by heavy drinking, became too acute to be any longer ignored, did Roosevelt finally act. It was not until his second session with Johnson in September, 1934, that he obtained Johnson's resignation and turned the NRA over to Donald Richberg, who was even more sympathetic toward business.

In 1935 Roosevelt would have to seek a fresh congressional authorization, and for some months before he dismissed Johnson he had been planning a more simplified structure. He had long worried about the continued high price of steel, so that at one point he speculated to financial writers that he might seek to examine the books of the four producers of steel rails "to find out whether they are making 75% or 3%" profit. As always his sympathies were with smaller manufacturers outside of urban areas; shortly after he established the Darrow board he was expressing his concern over an issue that was at the crux of small-business complaints against the NRA, that in rural communities where living costs were decidedly lower, employers were having to pay the same standard wages as in industrial areas. He cited specifically a knitting mill in Troy, New York, employing thirty people, which claimed it had been put out of business.[9] That was part of Roosevelt's persistent feeling that the future health of American enterprise depended upon moving much of industrial productivity away from the large cities.

Even though a preponderant part of the litigation over the NRA focused upon violations of other code regulations, employers objected above all to its regulation of wages and hours and the hiring of children, and to Section 7-a of the legislation guaranteeing the right to collective bargaining. These to Roosevelt were the heart of the NRA, which he was determined to perpetuate. In the spring of 1934, when he met a delegation from the National Association of Manufacturers, he pointed out to them that they had never come out in favor of any of these reforms, or of workmen's compensation and unemployment insurance. He still seemed hopeful he could win them over. "It is a great bunch," he told the Emergency Council, "but you have to 'talk turkey' to them."[10]

From the beginning of the NRA, strikes were one of its by-products, as workers sought to attain its specified wages and hours, or began to organize under 7-a. Newspapers gave them large headlines, and middle-class readers, seldom favorable to organized labor, shuddered. By April, 1934, Roosevelt was not only still firm in his basic commitment to collective bargaining, but was agreeing in substance with the proposal of Senator Robert Wagner of New York for new, more effective legislation. His reason, he told reporters informally, was that he wanted some stronger, more permanent labor board to settle labor disputes. He had just spent a week acting as mediator for the United Automobile Workers, and did not savor the role. "I would be doing nothing else but arbitration," he remarked, "if I took cognizance and jurisdiction over all" of the disputes.[11]

Off the record, Roosevelt pointed out in late May: "In any period of this kind you are bound to have, with a return of prosperity and a return of reemployment and an increase in values, more strikes. I look for a great many strikes in the course of this summer." His prophecy was correct, but he had the good fortune to be cruising in the Pacific on the USS *Houston* when a longshoremen's strike in San Francisco escalated into a general strike, stirring national alarm. By the time Roosevelt returned it had long since failed. When finally in September he commented upon it, he blamed on the one hand "hot-headed young leaders" lacking experience, who did not realize that a general strike always fails, and on the other "the old, conservative crowd," including West Coast publishers, who would profit politically from the failure.[12]

No matter how evenhanded Roosevelt might try to be in his assessments of labor problems, they were bringing him a good deal of hostility from business. The reference to "the old conservative crowd," which Roosevelt allowed reporters to use in indirect discourse, was an indication of his reaction to the increasing barrage of criticism that businessmen were directing at him. Not only were they blaming him for labor disputes (and the resulting increases in wages), but also for the devaluation of the dollar and consequent lowering of the return they could obtain from gold bonds. Especially they viewed as catastrophic the sums Roosevelt was allocating for relief and public works. In contrast, many economists of later generations have regarded the amounts as seriously inadequate.

On public spending, too, Roosevelt was trying to attain equilibrium between immediate budget balancing and expenditures adequate to aid the farmers and unemployed. In December, 1933, he remarked facetiously to reporters that somewhere between Budget Director Douglas' "efforts to spend nothing . . . and the point of view of the people who want to spend ten billions additional on public works, we will get somewhere."[13]

Both humanitarian and political considerations, plus Roosevelt's zest for positive, innovative action, drove him further and further away from budget-balancing conservatism. Moreover, Roosevelt's 1934 legislative program was not at all to the liking of most businessmen.

Politics led to the silver program. Roosevelt had already accepted a silver purchase measure, beneficial primarily to copper companies producing silver as a by-product. In the spring of 1934 he had to compromise with Senators Key Pittman of Nevada and Burton K. Wheeler of Montana and a bloc of western senators, because their votes were essential to him, and in addition he agreed to more massive buying of silver. Since the measure was mildly inflationary, like the gold purchases, it pleased agrarian inflationists, but it undercut the silver-based currencies of China and Peru, and gave the corporate mining interests of the West a bigger subsidy than that going to all of the nation's farmers. It also failed as an inflationary device. Eastern creditors shuddered.[14]

The least controversial of Roosevelt's actions involving brokers and bankers was to obtain the Federal Housing Act, guaranteeing low-interest loans to stimulate housing repairs and construction. Roosevelt hoped it would release parts of the large amounts of capital that bankers were cautiously refusing to lend except on very substantial security.

The Roosevelt program also moved more firmly toward regulation. Congress extended the securities regulation of 1933 to cover the exchanges and established a new body, the Securities and Exchange Commission. In a typical move, Roosevelt chose one of the most successful of the Wall Street operators, Joseph P. Kennedy, to be its first chairman. Investment houses were not reassured. In addition, Congress created the Federal Communications Commission to unify regulation of services relying upon "wires, cables or radio as a medium of transmission." Roosevelt created a furor by canceling all commercial contracts for carrying airmail on the grounds that they were not competitive. Ten army pilots, inexperienced in flying the routes, were killed carrying the mails. Roosevelt then obtained legislation placing firm safeguards on contracts and returned the carrying of airmail to commercial airlines.[15]

As the congressional election of 1934 approached, Roosevelt had little success in mollifying conservatives. On the grounds that he was relying upon both Democrats and Republicans to engage in a nonpartisan effort to attain recovery, he declined to address a Democratic celebration of Jefferson Day in the spring of 1934. A little later, he confided to Colonel House that while Congress was acting upon his legislative proposals, "I am purposely avoiding the use of the air because to use it at the controversial stage of a controversial legislative body spells more controversy!"

If Roosevelt hoped through these tactics to lull the conservatives into thinking that the New Deal was now complete, he failed. He already had indicated that the following year he would seek the social security program, which had been in the planning stage since he took office. Moreover, at the same time he told Colonel House he was staying off the air, he promised that the summer would bring "many new manifestations of the New Deal, even though the orthodox protest and heathen roar!" He explained, "We must keep the sheer momentum from slacking up too much and I have no intention of relinquishing the offensive in favor of defensive tactics." In June he gave notice to Congress that for its next session he would propose programs for social insurance and the utilization of land and water resources. No sooner had Congress adjourned than through executive orders he established a National Labor Relations Board to oversee collective bargaining, and a National Resources Board to plan development of land, water, and other resources.[16]

For many Democrats who had supported Roosevelt during the early stages of the New Deal, he had gone too far. Lewis Douglas, despairing over Roosevelt's failure to move closer to a balanced budget, resigned in August, 1934. That same month a number of the most conservative Democrats who in 1932 had opposed Roosevelt's nomination, under the aegis of the Du Ponts, formed the American Liberty League. The leaders, utilizing some of the organizational framework they had used in the fight for the repeal of prohibition, felt they were continuing a struggle for personal liberty — against government interference with their freedom to make money. "All the big guns have started shooting — Al Smith, John W. Davis, James W. Wadsworth, du Pont, Shouse, etc.," Roosevelt commented in correspondence. "Their organization has already been labeled the I CAN'T TAKE IT CLUB."[17]

The Republican Hoover would not join a Democratic organization like the Liberty League, but in his book *Challenge to Liberty* he voiced parallel themes. Nor did Republican campaigners in the fall of 1934 often suggest alternatives to the voters other than a return to the old order of the 1920s. Publishers of some of the nation's largest newspapers, such as Colonel R. R. McCormick of the *Chicago Tribune*, thundered similar denunciations.

Republican press attacks made Roosevelt appear far more radical than he was in reality. Judged by the enemies he had made, he seemed to be the champion of the common man. In the fall of 1934, the Republicans offered voters who were still in want little alternative to the New Deal.

Nor at the polls was there much alternative on the left. The exception, in California, was the flamboyant onetime muckraker and Socialist Upton Sinclair, who had won the Democratic nomination for governor with a scheme for state-sponsored producers' cooperatives that would barter goods and services among their members. Roosevelt toyed with endorsing Sinclair, and then backed away, letting him slip to defeat. A formidable potential challenge from the left was already in the early stages of development, centering around Senator Huey Long, Father Charles Coughlin, and Dr. Francis Townsend, but that was a threat for 1936. Some midwest farmers, unhappy with all manifestations of the New Deal except agricultural benefits, were able to vote for Republican candidates for Congress who promised them exactly that split in policies. But disillusioned workers, who had assailed the NRA as the "National Run-Around," still preferred supporters of Roosevelt to his opponents.[18]

Roosevelt gave his serious answer both to Liberty League Democrats and to Republicans rallying behind Hoover's theme that the New Deal was a "challenge to liberty," in a Fireside Chat at the end of September, 1934. Except for a subsequent call upon bankers to join "an alliance of all forces bent upon the business of recovery," it was almost his only manifesto in the congressional campaign. He declared:

> In our efforts for recovery we have avoided, on the one hand, the theory that business should and must be taken over into an all-embracing Government. We have avoided, on the other hand, the equally untenable theory that it is an interference with liberty to offer reasonable help when private enterprise is in need of help.[19]

The popular response to the New Deal in November, 1934, was surprising. Contrary to the usual decline in midterm elections, the Democrats gained thirteen new seats in the House and nine in the Senate, giving them more than a two-thirds majority in both houses. The historian Charles A. Beard gauged the election results to be "thunder on the left." Harry Hopkins on election night regarded it as creating the prime opportunity to obtain everything he had been wanting, "a works program, social security, wages and hours, everything — now or never." Roosevelt, who in the election had put down the challenge from the right, was ready to act as Hopkins hoped, in response to the thunder on the left.[20]

Chapter 11

A NEW DEAL FOR THE DISPOSSESSED

As 1935 OPENED, Roosevelt faced critical challenges from both the right and the left. His ultimate response was what most analysts have referred to as a "second New Deal." Roosevelt, they point out, swung from a program emphasizing national planning in the Theodore Roosevelt tradition and reverted to a Wilsonian policing of economic enterprise. In economic affairs at least, some of them argue, he was shifting toward the right. Something of this change is discernible, but far more vital factors were involved.

By the late summer of 1934, with the unemployment rate still at 17 percent, Roosevelt became convinced that he must undertake a drastic new program to alleviate distress, bring recovery, and guarantee the future security of the American people. He began, therefore, two months before the 1934 congressional election, the planning of what became the Works Progress Administration and linked with it the long-projected social security program.

Through extensive public works, Roosevelt sought to provide employment to millions and pour large sums into the economy to stimulate recovery. Through social security he would assure a minimum income during future dips in the economy, and thus create built-in stabilizers to prevent those dips from plummeting into depressions. Here was to be the basic social and economic program of the New Deal.

Through this reordering of priorities, Roosevelt moved cautiously from a program dependent upon the cooperation of the business community to one aimed primarily at bettering the lot of the dispossessed. Basically his shift was a political reaction to pressures from both the right and the left, but it was also a reflection of his fundamental humanitarianism.

Two years had elapsed since the Hundred Days. The sense of emergency had long since evaporated and with it the almost total consensus behind Roosevelt. The crisis atmosphere had given way to a continuing malaise; the analogy to war and appeals to sacrifice could no longer unify the electorate to support the drawn-out recovery effort. Emergency legislation, including that establishing the NRA, had given Roosevelt a two-year mandate, and was about to expire. His momentum had slowed, and indeed by early 1935 seemed to have come to a complete halt.

The feelings of the people toward Roosevelt were polarizing. While a substantial part still unquestioningly, even ardently, supported him, far larger numbers were bringing pressure from the left. A more conspicuous but smaller number were vehemently opposing him from the right.

In response to the polarization, Roosevelt remained, at least in appearance, doggedly in the center, seeking to command a broad coalition extending well beyond the Democratic party. He had changed less in his basic policies and politics than had much of the electorate, and modified his positions only slowly in response to their pressures. Gradually he was becoming more concerned over the plight of the underprivileged, and irritated by the failure of business to meet its responsibilities. As the rhetoric of others began to sharpen, so did that of Roosevelt—although those who wished him to advance more boldly lamented that his words were more electric than his actions.

Roosevelt continued to court businessmen and bankers, trying to incorporate as many of them as possible in his New Deal alliance. He had, after all, in his earlier programs achieved more for them than for farmers or workers. Economic indices in 1935 indicated that, while employment was seriously lagging, both industrial production and profits were improving. But no statistics could convince much of the business community that he was other than its archenemy. Most businessmen had never accepted the reform goals of the NRA. They were especially angered over their difficulties with their workers, which they blamed upon the wages and hours and collective bargaining provisions of the NRA. Further, with new government regulations had come quantities of new forms to be filled out. Some smaller businessmen felt Washington was burying them under paper.

The alienation of the businessmen was having an important impact upon New Deal programs and politics. It made the NRA scheme almost impossible to operate, since that depended upon business cooperation.

The policing of the codes was scantier than that of prohibition had been; in practice there had to be largely voluntary compliance. In contrast, the regulatory programs that New Deal disciples of Brandeis were advocating did not require business support.

Business hostility seemed unjustified to Roosevelt and irritated him. He was basically no more antibusiness than Wilson had been and was demanding little more than that employers play fair with each other, their workers, and the consumers. Their animus hurt, since they were pouring campaign contributions into the coffers of the Republican party in the North, and those of the Democratic congressional leaders in the South. It meant, too, that many of the most influential newspapers were attacking Roosevelt.

Not only businessmen but almost all of the conservatives had become bitter opponents of Roosevelt and the New Deal. The right included most well-to-do people together with some of the poor, especially in small towns, who clung to the nineteenth-century precepts of the Grand Old Party and Grover Cleveland. In total they represented the center and right of the Republicans and the right of the Democrats. The progressive wing of the Republican party was divided; some of its most influential spokesmen still supported the president. He offended the right as little as possible and made intermittent overtures to the progressives.

At the polls the right as yet posed little serious threat to the New Deal. Although its leaders were vehement in their denunciations of Roosevelt, they could rally no more than a fraction of the electorate. Their assaults pricked his pride but did not alarm him.

The Supreme Court invalidation of New Deal measures on the grounds that they went beyond constitutional limits was another matter. Two years later, Roosevelt subtitled the 1935 volume of his public papers *The Court Disapproves*. He might appropriately have called it "The Right Disapproves," for the court was reflecting the growing anger of the business and financial community. What the right could not achieve at the polls it might gain through adverse Supreme Court decisions.

The critical threat to Roosevelt was nevertheless from the left, not the right. There was a disquieting restlessness among poor farmers and workers, the unemployed and underemployed, all those who had given such a top-heavy margin to the Democrats in the congressional elections just past. If they were to coalesce they might topple Roosevelt and the Democratic party. In 1934 they demonstrated their power as the key elements in the New Deal political coalition. Roosevelt's imperative task was to consolidate them firmly behind him. In the process, he was to change decidedly the overall thrust of his administration and to solidify a political alliance that held firm for decades to come.

Diagnoses of the shortcomings of the New Deal in meeting the needs of those in distress were coming from liberal as well as radical intellectuals. They pointed with disenchantment to the failure of the NRA to give substantial benefits to either small businessmen or workers and to the malfunctioning of the AAA, which throughout the South was benefiting larger cotton farmers at the expense of their sharecroppers, whom they often evicted from their fields. Within the AAA, Jerome Frank, Gardner Jackson, and others tried to interpret the cotton contracts to protect the sharecroppers, and for their pains lost their jobs.[1]

Roosevelt's responses to liberal complaints against New Deal shortcomings were irritating, yet somehow sufficed. When Norman Thomas, perennial Socialist candidate for president, tried to protest against the maltreatment of sharecroppers, Roosevelt broke in, saying, "Oh, Norman, I'm a damned sight better politician than you are." Then Roosevelt mollified Thomas by adding, "I know the South and there is arising a new generation of leaders . . . we've got to be patient." It was the typical Roosevelt touch, the sort that kept most intellectuals voting for him despite their reservations. While Roosevelt offered them visions of a greatly improved future, he was forever embracing a less pleasant status quo on the grounds of political realism. Thus, off the record, in blaming Thomas for a southern textile strike, he remarked to reporters in September, 1934, "He is an idealist, but, when it comes down to practical things, he is not there at all." Liberals were rankled but not totally alienated. A witty commentator, Leo C. Rosten, spoke for many of them when he defined the New Deal as "the wedding of good intentions to bad economics."[2]

In total, the number of harsh intellectual critics from the left was so small that they might prod Roosevelt but were no threat. The serious peril to which Roosevelt gave close heed came from a trio commanding a large, rather nebulous, and shifting following throughout the nation.

There was the unlikely leader of the old-age pension movement, a wispy retired physician from Long Beach, California, Dr. Francis Townsend, who proposed what was at that time a princely sum, $200 per month, for every retired person over sixty. It would have diverted 40 percent of the national income to 9 percent of the people. Townsendites argued that the elderly through retiring would provide jobs for the young, and through spending their pension checks return the nation to boom times. Regardless of the economic merits of the Townsend movement it gained so many millions of adherents, most of them from among otherwise conservative people, that politicians throughout the country became wary or even compliant toward this new untested political force.[3]

The following of the Reverend Charles E. Coughlin was somewhat more diffuse; it numbered many millions and was concentrated among the Catholic poor of the northern cities. Coughlin, broadcasting from a suburb of Detroit, combined the liberal social doctrines of Pope Leo XIII with populist attacks upon bankers. At first he supported Roosevelt, but as his advocacy of a silver panacea for the depression became more shrill, he moved toward opposition. By 1935, Coughlin was expounding a program for social justice not unlike the fascism of Mussolini's Italy, and containing hints of anti-Semitism, which gradually became a dominant theme.[4]

The leader with the largest following, presenting the most serious challenge to Roosevelt, was Huey Long, the Louisiana senator whose Share Our Wealth program was winning converts far beyond the borders of his state. Long, who frightened most educated liberals as well as conservatives by the dictatorial way he ran Louisiana, for all his demagogic devices operated in the progressive-populist traditions. In the Senate, he had a coterie of well-wishers of similar background, like Burton K. Wheeler of Montana. His easily understandable program, providing something for everyone, and the trenchant, sometimes humorous, fashion in which he presented it made him an effective vote getter. He had attracted large audiences campaigning for Roosevelt in 1932, but soon moved into the opposition, and became disruptive in 1935. Long once dramatized his antagonism toward Roosevelt by keeping his hat on while he talked to the president in the Oval Office. Roosevelt, poker-faced, gave no sign that he noticed. In all-out war with Long, Roosevelt ordered administrators to employ no one working for Long, and he gave inducements to new senators to answer Long whenever he spoke on the floor of the Senate.[5]

Roosevelt took seriously the danger to his reelection in 1936. A poll that Farley commissioned indicated Long strength throughout the country; even in New Hampshire there seemed to be a few thousand potential Long votes, enough to tip the balance of the state to the Republicans. A strong, positive legislative program in 1935, therefore, could be seen as Roosevelt's effort to undercut the forces to the left. Since Roosevelt usually had many and complex motives for his political maneuvers, no doubt he was only in part responding to these forces. It is even possible that, in the same way Theodore Roosevelt used fear of socialism as a club to obtain moderate railroad legislation, Roosevelt capitalized upon fear of Long, Coughlin, and Townsend to obtain his 1935 program. Conservatives, especially among the southern Democrats in Congress, would reluctantly support Roosevelt rather than chance fueling the Long movement.[6]

The challenge from the right seemed fairly easy to contain, provided the left could be kept from massive defection. Roosevelt talked frequently about 85 percent of the press being opposed to him. It was a mythic figure and one he used for his own political advantage, making himself look like an underdog when in fact he could dominate the media at will. Hostile headlines in right-wing newspapers were probably more service to him than menace, since they could help convince the dispossessed that Roosevelt was indeed championing their cause.

Since Roosevelt was well aware that the achievement of recovery was going to be a slow, complex task taking several years, he sought more lasting legislation to supplement earlier measures. He still hoped to attain recovery through a combination of national planning, regulation, perhaps monetarism, and as ever his goal was a balanced budget, but the new focus was to be on massive spending.

The two great agencies with their emphasis upon planning in agriculture and business, the AAA and the NRA, were still mainstays of Roosevelt's recovery program. Late in 1934, he remarked to his administrators, "It is perfectly clear to me that the present policy of crop control is working, and it will be continued." As for the NRA, he recognized the serious flaws in it, but decided to seek improvements to force down the price of steel and other durable goods, which he was convinced had remained too high. The NRA was not a Little Orphan Annie, he asserted, but a means of attaining a more equitable economy.[7]

Regulation also should advance another step. The Securities and Exchange Commission was coming into operation, and what Roosevelt wanted next was to obtain legislation strengthening the Tennessee Valley Authority and the Federal Reserve system. What was most innovative and would cause the most vehement reaction from business was his feeling that something must be done to stop the proliferation of public utility holding companies. The collapse of the midwest empire of Samuel Insull, with consequent losses to large numbers of small stockholders, had resulted in widespread public awareness of the problem. In 1929, sixteen holding-company groups had controlled 92 percent of private electric power production, and were charging far more than comparable public power authorities in Canada. The question of holding companies was a consumer issue. In the summer of 1934, Roosevelt appointed a National Power Policy Committee; in November at Warm Springs he informed it that regulation of holding companies would not be effective and hence they must be eliminated. What form holding-company reform should take was not at first clear to Roosevelt. He thought the companies at the top, provided they operated as investment trusts, might be preserved, but he was determined to eliminate the intermediate tiers of operating companies.[8]

In addition there were two pieces of legislation from which Roosevelt would be pleased to extract all possible credit but which could occasion right-wing attacks. He did not endorse them openly or place them on his agenda but let congressional sponsors advance them as best they could. One was the National Labor Relations bill. Once again there was the prickly problem of strengthening the unions in their relations with employers. Unions were now strong enough to provide formidable support for the bill, but powerful business lobbyists were equally opposed. Roosevelt long kept silent and let Senator Wagner, the staunch defender of unions, advance his bill as best he could. The antilynching bill that Senator Edward P. Costigan and Wagner sought was also one upon which he would take no special position. Enactment was impossible, and the proponents were considerate enough toward Roosevelt to bring it to the floor of the Senate at the end of March, prompting the inevitable southern filibuster at a time when it would not endanger the presidential program. By sanctioning a debate, Roosevelt gave at least tacit, token support to a black grievance.

The administration agenda was a lengthy one. There would need to be modifications of the AAA, the TVA, and the Federal Reserve system. All these matters at the outset were subordinate to Roosevelt's major security program. It would provide the immediate material necessities through massive work relief and give protection in the future through comprehensive social security. Roosevelt would have liked to put both work relief and social security in a single bill, but his new budget director, Daniel Bell, convinced him that it would be unworkable.

In the fall of 1934, Roosevelt met frequently with Hopkins, Ickes, Morgenthau, and others trying to devise an effective work relief bill that would both give immediate aid to the unemployed on relief and stimulate recovery. Hopkins, as he repeatedly said in meetings that fall, was obtaining gloomy reports from relief supervisors. Those on relief were not getting adequate food, shelter, or clothing. If they could not look forward to jobs within the next eighteen months, they might well take desperate action. Tugwell suggested that unemployment insurance could be deferred for several years until reserves accumulated to pay for it. It later followed that unemployment insurance should be funded out of a payroll tax; only an immediate work program should require federal financing. In the end Roosevelt accepted this view of unemployment insurance and ordering of priorities, and with enthusiasm undertook what to him was one of his special pleasures, the planning of a new program.[9]

From the outset Roosevelt accepted the fundamental premise that the work relief bill was to take all employable people off the relief rolls and provide them with public employment. The only direct relief should be for unemployables, and it should be the responsibility of local governmental units.

A basic question was the magnitude of the program. Hopkins on Labor Day, 1934, proposed $5 billion a year for five years, which, given the extent of unemployment and the size of the economic stimulus needed to restore prosperity, was not unreasonable. There were of course both budgetary and political considerations. Roosevelt did not fully face them at the outset, and at the opening meeting proposed a three-year program, costing $5 billion in the first year, $4 billion in the second, and $3 billion in the third. He hoped spending of this magnitude would so stimulate private industry that by the fourth year everyone would be absorbed into private employment.[10]

The proposal to spend such huge sums was sure to bring sharp opposition. There were not only the objections of financiers and the Treasury Department, but more important, the problem of getting appropriations through congressional committees. Roosevelt began shaving figures lower and lower. By the time he sent his proposal to Congress it was down to $4 billion of new money plus the reallocation of $880 million previously appropriated. Unfortunately, too, it was no longer nearly of a size to give a job to everyone in need.[11]

Roosevelt, clinging to his usual hope that he could develop a program that ultimately would be of no cost to taxpayers, eagerly grasped suggestions for self-liquidating works. He settled on a large-scale program of slum clearance, the construction of low-priced houses and apartments, the elimination of railroad grade crossings, and the improvement of rivers and harbors and water transportation. The trouble was that all of these were likely to be extensions of Ickes' existing Public Works Administration. As Roosevelt pointed out to the cabinet in December, Ickes had had to start cold with the PWA and it had been a target for criticism because it had functioned so slowly. Ickes, Morgenthau once recalled, "was so anxious to keep graft and politics out of the public works program that he practically spent money through a medicine dropper." Also, most of the unemployed were semiskilled or unskilled people and some were white-collar workers. Only a segment were skilled construction workers of the sort Ickes' projects could absorb.[12]

Yet Roosevelt did not want to return to the Civil Works Administration model. "The country was not satisfied with it," he had reminded the cabinet. Ickes noted: "It had made a bad impression on taxpayers to see men raking leaves or mowing grass along the roadside. He was for a program of real public works, which at the same time would give work to practically all idle employables." Further, there was a bitter and unpleasant struggle between Ickes and Hopkins for Roosevelt's favor. Each wanted desperately to control the program.

The president succeeded in drafting a scheme that left ambiguous whether Hopkins, Ickes, or both were to be in charge. Their contentiousness wore upon him, and together with the problems he faced in drawing up his budget and planning a social security program, left him weary.[13]

The social security bill was the handiwork of a number of outstanding specialists in the various areas it covered, but it also bore Roosevelt's firm views. During his years as governor of New York he had learned much through the tutelage of Frances Perkins and the specialists she had brought to Albany. He promised Miss Perkins a social security program when he offered her a cabinet position. In 1934, Roosevelt appointed the Committee on Economic Security, chaired by Miss Perkins, with a strong, effective staff under Edwin E. Witte of the University of Wisconsin. Work began under rather foreboding circumstances. Roosevelt in early August reiterated his faith in social security as creating "a wider opportunity for the average man," and the stock market in reaction dropped several points. Roosevelt's more conservative counselors, especially those in the Treasury, urged muting the discussion of economic security. Witte convinced the president at the outset that the "cradle to grave" approach that he wanted was not realistic and must be scaled down.[14]

Upon one point Roosevelt was insistent from start to finish. That was the placing of a tax for unemployment and old-age benefits on both employers and employees. In 1941, Luther Gulick, a public administration expert, suggested to Roosevelt that it might have been a mistake to levy these deflationary taxes during the depression. Roosevelt replied, according to Gulick:

> I guess you're right on the economics, but those taxes were never a problem of economics. They are politics all the way through. We put those payroll contributions there so as to give the contributors a legal, moral, and political right to collect their pensions and their unemployment benefits. With those taxes in there, no damn politician can ever scrap my social security program.[15]

Further, said Roosevelt, the contributions had the important psychological effect of destroying the "relief attitude." He never liked people to receive something for nothing.

The annual message to Congress in January, 1935, launched the work relief bill. Roosevelt stated: "Continued dependence upon relief induces a spiritual and moral disintegration fundamentally destructive to the national fiber. . . . It is in violation of the traditions of America. . . . Work must be found for able-bodied but destitute workers."[16]

Immediately the president called upon Congress to implement his work relief proposal. A few days later he sent the long-awaited social security message, then in February called for extension of the NRA and in March for the regulation of holding companies.

By openly making the holding-company legislation part of his administrative program, Roosevelt further widened the growing rift with the business community. It was a belligerent message, in which he said he had been watching the fight against the legislation, "the use of investor's money to make the investor believe that the efforts of the Government to protect him are designed to defraud him," and asserted he sought the "necessary reorganization of the holding company with safeguards which will in fact protect the investor."[17]

When an old professor complained that Roosevelt would destroy stable and efficient holding companies, he retorted, citing one company that contained 246 corporate entities, "If you could see the organization chart of, for example, the Associated Gas and Electric Company, I know you would realize the need for the dissolution of that type of organized banditry!" But he made no such vigorous comments publicly at that time.[18]

Chapter 12

A LOW-KEY INTERLUDE

ALTHOUGH CRITICS from both right and left were assailing Roosevelt, he remained singularly quiet as Congress deliberated upon the new and controversial "second New Deal" program. A century earlier the Whigs in their attack upon Andrew Jackson, whom they caricatured as dressed in ermine and sitting on a throne, asserted that the role of a president was solely to administer, that it was up to Congress to determine policies. For the first five months of 1935, Roosevelt chose to appear an old-fashioned Whig or Republican president. In his messages he set forth general proposals, and then, in the tradition not of TR or Wilson but of William Howard Taft, left it to Congress to work out the details and advance the legislation. The national impression was that Roosevelt was faltering in response to the powerful challenges against him. Vice President Garner complained in private that the president was accomplishing little and losing ground.

Yet Roosevelt operated through these months with outward self-confidence. Undoubtedly he had not decided upon numerous details. Perhaps they were not entirely vital to him, and he was politically quite content to allow the heavy New Deal majority in Congress to battle over them with the old-line Democratic minority, powerful in its seniority. Leaving much of the content of bills to Congress deflected charges that he was acting in a dictatorial fashion, and put the onus on the legislators.

The controlling factor with Roosevelt was the timing. The presidential election the following year had something to do with his caution and the image he presented to the public. He firmly believed that the electorate could not be kept at a fever pitch for any lengthy period, and he wanted the excitement to come during the campaign of 1936.

Roosevelt was well positioned to influence Congress, although he was giving the impression that it had the upper hand. Conservative or liberal, the Democratic leadership was not much more rebellious in 1935 than it had been in 1933, although by the end of the session it was much closer to breaking with Roosevelt.

In the House the fairly weak, not entirely liberal leadership created additional difficulties for the president. The new Speaker, Joseph Byrns of Tennessee, was amiable but a lax disciplinarian. The able majority leader, William Bankhead of Alabama (brother of Senator John Bankhead), went to the hospital the day he was elected, leaving the management of legislation throughout the session to the aged, cautious, acting majority leader, Edward T. Taylor of Colorado, who did not believe in Roosevelt's program and was more interested in preserving his own health than in leading a vigorous fight.

In the Senate, the majority leader, Joseph Robinson, like Pat Harrison, the chairman of the Finance Committee, was conservative but still did Roosevelt's bidding. When Robinson grumbled that serving Roosevelt was hell, someone suggested that the number of appointments he had controlled was so phenomenal — about two thousand — that clearly the road to hell was lined with post offices. When need be, Roosevelt was adroit in pacifying conservative Democrats with patronage, public works projects, and flattering recognition.

Overall, the Senate was a bit more liberal in makeup than in 1933. Some of its members, like Senators Robert Wagner and Robert M. La Follette together with younger, newly elected rank and file, were not only ready to accept Roosevelt's proposals but to push him to the left. They went further than in 1933–1934 in shaping New Deal legislation.

There was discussion then and later of the unwieldy nature of the top-heavy Democratic majority; some scholars have argued that Roosevelt would have been better off had there been more nearly a balance with the Republicans. Undoubtedly stronger leadership, especially in the House, committed to Roosevelt's program as well as operating out of traditional party loyalty, would have been a help. Much of the problem of numbers was, as James T. Patterson points out, that quite a few of the Democrats who had been elected to either the Senate or the House in the 1934 landslide were by no means New Dealers. They were members of well-entrenched state and local organizations that changed little in ideology during these years.[1]

Well into the spring months Roosevelt presented a tranquil facade. He commented to Wilson's biographer, Ray Stannard Baker, that Theodore Roosevelt had erred politically in being so continuously frenetic that he wearied his followers:

> The public psychology . . . cannot . . . be attuned for long periods of time to a constant repetition of the highest note in the scale. . . . People tire of seeing the same name day after day in the important headlines of the papers, and the same voice night after night over the radio. For example, if since last November I had tried to keep up the pace of 1933 and 1934, the inevitable histrionics of the new actors, Long and Coughlin . . . would have turned the eyes of the audience away from the main drama itself![2]

Not everything was going well. Foreign policy took much of Roosevelt's attention and complicated his relations with Congress. Mussolini was threatening to invade Ethiopia, and Hitler was becoming so aggressive that a new war in Europe seemed possible. Roosevelt placed his prestige behind a Senate resolution to bring the United States into the World Court and was defeated. Congress voted Roosevelt neutrality legislation far short of what he had requested.[3]

Within his administration, Roosevelt seemed for some weeks not only preoccupied but weary, as he devoted himself to planning the many ramifications of his pending work relief program. He had to moderate the intense rivalry between Ickes and Hopkins and a quarrel involving Ickes and Farley. In newspapers and on the air there were increasingly strident criticisms. Roosevelt's spring of silence was not a happy time for him and he was at times irritable, but there is no indication that he was worried.

It was a bad few months also for advanced New Dealers and progressives, even though Roosevelt was moving in their direction. He had given only limited support to Republican progressive senators running in 1934, and as a result of the election was less in need of their votes in 1935. Liberal publicists and politicians expressed their exasperation because Roosevelt sided, at least tacitly, with the powerful farm organizations and congressmen when Secretary Wallace removed the reformers from the AAA.[4]

The evidence is clear that Roosevelt, as during the interregnum, was following a deliberate policy. While he seemed to be courting the right more than the left, he had called for a large agenda of basically liberal legislation. The work relief and social security proposals were of crucial importance to him. For their enactment in both houses of Congress he was dependent upon the goodwill of leaders mostly from the South, who possessed the power to delay, modify, or even defeat the measures. Their effective sabotage that spring of a third measure of consequence to Roosevelt, the extension of the NRA, was an indication of their strength.

In February, Roosevelt began to act deferentially toward Congress. He sought to pacify a delegation from the House, irritated, among other things, over hostile appointments, especially in Harry Hopkins' domain. In its aftermath, he told the National Emergency Council that "proposed legislation . . . is being pretty well received up on the Hill," but added that he wanted bills to originate with Congress: "We do not want to be in the position in this particular year — because we are not in the middle of a crisis as in 1933 — . . . that we are sending things up there that they must pass. They understand that now and the feeling in that respect is much better. They are getting cooperation instead of orders and are very happy about it."[5]

Congress proceeded with deliberate speed, paying little heed to the White House compared to 1933. Roosevelt noted to Josephus Daniels, whom he had appointed ambassador to Mexico, "I am saying very little, keeping my temper and letting them literally stew in their own juice. I think it is the best policy for a while, and, incidentally, I hope that the Longs and others will stub their toes!"[6]

In a quiet fashion, Roosevelt continued to be involved when it suited his interests, more often than not in the direction of moderation. Advanced New Dealers in Congress were as discouraged with Roosevelt as were those in his administration. Senator Wagner and his allies had to carry much of the burden of battling for what became the second New Deal program, and part of the time they were fighting Roosevelt.[7]

The first struggle was over the work relief bill, the dazzling proposal to vote $4 billion (plus $880 million in previously authorized money), an appropriation half again as large as the staggering one of 1933, to put 3.5 million men to work for a year. The emphasis was upon jobs, the taking of the federal government out of the relief business, and giving to the economy a stimulus that would bring full recovery. Regular Republicans were aghast; Republican progressives under the leadership of La Follette thought the appropriation should be doubled. Correctly, the progressives thought it fell seriously short of what would be needed to put to work all the able unemployed. Both groups failed to muster sufficient votes to modify the bill. In April, Congress passed the final measure and Roosevelt for weeks lavished much of his attention upon this massive new program that was to bring immediate added sustenance to millions.

While the work relief bill had been under the aegis of Senator Wagner, Roosevelt's social security program was dependent for enactment upon two southerners of great power and influence. Fortunately for Roosevelt, Robert Lee Doughton of North Carolina, chairman of the

House Ways and Means Committee, was as politically loyal to the president as he was old-fashioned in his thinking. He preferred to be known as "Farmer Bob," but the nickname that stuck was "Muley." The chairman of the Senate Finance Committee, Pat Harrison of Mississippi, fundamentally even more conservative, was expert in making deals and drawing upon friendships to maneuver legislation through the Senate. He too was loyal to Roosevelt, but as time would tell, for him there was a breaking point. Roosevelt was wise in the spring of 1935 to make Congress feel it had freedom to legislate, if for no other reason than to retain the talents of these proud leaders.

Since Roosevelt wanted the social security bill enacted speedily, both houses began hearings simultaneously before the end of January. The hearings turned quickly into a confrontation between the committee members and Dr. Townsend and his supporters, who wished to substitute their plan for Roosevelt's program. Almost all congressmen had disliked the economically unfeasible Townsend plan, but had received such heavy mail in favor of it that they had not dared oppose it openly. The hearings exposed so many deficiencies in the plan that numerous congressmen became emboldened to express their opposition to it. Nevertheless, the Townsendites, mostly elderly and Republican, helped create complications for the social security bill, since they combined with conservatives in opposing it. President William Green of the American Federation of Labor (AFL) was so critical that he was thought at first to be an opponent. In traditional union fashion, he was more interested in collective bargaining legislation.

The social security program in consequence seemed vulnerable in both the House and Senate committees, where a considerable proportion of the members were far from friendly. Roosevelt tried not to involve himself during the lengthy and difficult executive sessions of the House Ways and Means Committee. When members asked him which provisions he regarded as essential, he told them he wanted all of them but refused to specify details. During Roosevelt's weeks of inaction, opposition to the bill began to increase. Numerous congressmen, receiving quantities of unfavorable mail from both Townsendites and businessmen fearful of new taxes, concluded that the bill had little real support. Doughton was running executive sessions in so democratic a fashion that he was making little headway with the measure. It seemed to be heading toward decimation or defeat.

Late in March, the House leaders on the committee again went to the White House to tell Roosevelt that old-age insurance could not be enacted. He informed them that it was the heart of the bill and that he wanted it, and indeed all the other basic provisions. At the same time, Miss Perkins and others began to campaign to bring popular pressure upon Congress. Edwin Witte later felt that only Roosevelt's belated intervention saved old-age insurance and perhaps unemployment insurance. In any event, Doughton through his personal popularity got the bill through committee. House leaders then were surprisingly successful in defeating amendments and obtaining passage of the measure unimpaired.

The Senate Finance Committee did not take up the social security bill until it had finished with several other pieces of legislation. While it was considering the measure, the Supreme Court gave ammunition to opponents by holding the Railroad Retirement Act unconstitutional. Several on the committee centered their attacks upon the question of the constitutionality of the old-age program. At a critical point when defeat seemed likely, Witte was called upon to give the arguments in favor of old-age insurance. He granted that there were defects but pointed out that the alternative would probably be a modified Townsend plan.

In the end it was the skill of Senator Harrison that carried the social security legislation basically intact through the committee, the Senate, and then the conference committee between the two houses. Finally, on August 14, 1935, Roosevelt signed into law the Social Security Act.[8]

Through the spring of 1935, while Roosevelt firmly sought social security legislation, he was less ready to give his support to legislation Senator Wagner pursued in behalf of organized labor to strengthen their power in collective bargaining. In the progressive tradition, Roosevelt was more interested in providing wages and hours protection and social insurance programs for workers than in giving them power to wrest greater benefits from employers. He was counting upon a two-year extension of a modified NRA and the enactment of his social security program to achieve these ends. Roosevelt wanted to get rid of the unworkable and monopolistic aspects of the NRA, much of the unenforceable accretion that had come from the burden of placing federal enforcement behind technical trade-association regulations. There were important economic roles that Roosevelt wanted the NRA to continue to fill — bringing order in a chaotic industry like bituminous coal, and perhaps price-fixing to shelter small businessmen, especially retailers, from cutthroat competition. At the end of April, in talking publicly about the extension of NRA, his emphasis was upon better working conditions: "No reasonable person wants to abandon our present gains — we must continue to protect children, to enforce minimum wages, to prevent excessive hours, to safeguard, define, and enforce collective bargaining."[9]

Organized labor in the spring of 1935 had been more interested in the Wagner bill as the means of obtaining what was of paramount interest to them, a strengthening of federal guarantees of collective bargaining. In the tradition of Samuel Gompers they wanted workers to look to the unions rather than to government for economic security. They were lukewarm toward wages and hours guarantees just as Roosevelt was toward greater protection of the unions. During the 1934 session of Congress, Roosevelt had not let Wagner bring his collective-bargaining bill to a vote in the Senate, but in 1935 he remained neutral. He was willing to see how far Wagner could get with it. Surprisingly, Wagner began to gather strong support despite thunderous business opposition. Union labor with its growing strength was offsetting business pressures.

In early April when Roosevelt returned tanned and looking fit from a fishing trip off the Bahamas, a reporter asked, "Did you return just as tough as you did last year?" "Oh yes," Roosevelt replied, "tougher."[10]

There was need for him to be tough, and before the end of the month he was. Both Congress and the country seemed to be getting out of hand, and Roosevelt again began to show himself as a firm and decisive president. On April 28, he delivered his first Fireside Chat of 1935, the longest yet, explaining how the new Works Progress Administration (WPA) would work and strongly supporting social security, at that point bogged down in Congress.

During the next several months both the electorate and Congress did hear from the president more frequently, as circumstances forced him to make a vigorous stand against the right. Both the National Association of Manufacturers and the United States Chamber of Commerce issued statements opposing Roosevelt's legislative proposals, warning that they were preventing recovery.

At a press conference, he charged that in the past, chambers of commerce and manufacturers' associations had spent large sums trying to block legislation like fire safety laws and workman's compensation, even though most businessmen, bankers, and manufacturers were sympathetic toward the reforms. The reception Roosevelt's remarks received was an indication of how far polarization had progressed. *Time* pontificated that he was beginning to suffer from the disease of presidents, "a growing impatience and resentment of criticism." On the contrary, Senator Norris directed his disgust toward "the selfish and greedy man of great wealth . . . who had been helped by the federal government . . . so oblivious to the suffering going on all around him."[11]

Business was making its voice heard effectively in the Senate on the question of NRA extension and was winning the support even of some of Norris' progressive colleagues. Norris himself, though steadfastly loyal to Roosevelt, felt that "a fair trial of the National Recovery Act has demonstrated that in its operation it has been injurious to the small businesses and had given preference to the big fellows." Yet the U.S. Chamber of Commerce, which had so strongly promoted the NRA idea in 1933, was joining with the National Association of Manufacturers in lobbying against extension. Too, there was apparently some trading of votes in the Senate between foes of the NRA and friends of the Wagner bill. The Senate voted to give Roosevelt only a ten-month extension of a watered-down NRA. That, he told newspapermen, was not acceptable.[12]

In late May, Roosevelt gave at least casual endorsement to Senator Wagner's National Labor Relations bill. There is no indication that he did so in anticipation of having to abandon the NRA, even though there had been ominous signs when the Supreme Court heard arguments in the Schechter case challenging the NRA codes. Rather, almost in the same breath at a press conference, Roosevelt spoke up both for extension of the NRA and for the labor bill with some amendment. When he was told that President Green of the AFL had left his office saying he thought Roosevelt was in sympathy with and friendly to the purposes of the Wagner bill, Roosevelt remarked, "Well, I think that is a fair statement." In this almost offhand way, without the slightest expenditure of his lobbying strength upon Congress, Roosevelt linked himself with a measure that cemented the New Deal alliance with organized labor.[13]

The National Labor Relations Act, which Roosevelt signed in July, 1935, forbade a number of "unfair practices" through which management had kept unions weak, and created as an enforcement body a National Labor Relations Board far more powerful than its predecessors. Militant organizers gained the federal protection they needed to move into the previously open-shop mass-production industries. As unions grew in strength and membership expanded, Roosevelt became the beneficiary of the labor vote, but also the target of outrage among those opposed to unions. The Wagner Act was one of the most momentous pieces of legislation during the New Deal years. Ironically, in the light of his gingerly approach, it was one most closely associated with him and of greatest consequence to his political fortunes.[14]

Chapter 13

THE FIGHT FOR THE REFORM PROGRAM

ON "BLACK MONDAY" for the New Deal, May 27, 1935, only three days after Roosevelt had endorsed the Wagner labor relations bill, the Supreme Court invalidated the National Recovery Act program and electrified the president into action. He responded strongly to the court challenge to federal economic regulation, and once more asserted leadership over Congress.

Chief Justice Charles Evans Hughes, speaking for a unanimous court in the Schechter decision, startled the nation by holding the NRA code system to be unconstitutional. The so-called sick-chicken case involved charges against wholesale live poultry dealers in Brooklyn, New York, that they were violating wages and hours and other regulations, including the sale of diseased poultry.

Solicitor General Stanley Reed argued in vain that the commerce clause of the Constitution covered the code regulations, since 96 percent of the live poultry came from outside New York State, and the prices set in the metropolitan area market largely determined prices elsewhere. The most shocking evidence in the case was that the Schechters had sold thousands of pounds of diseased poultry at 4 to 6 cents a pound below the market price. This contributed to the depressing of national poultry prices, and sometimes transmitted tuberculosis to the purchasers, predominantly poor blacks.

As for constitutional precedents, Reed pointed out that only a year earlier the Supreme Court had held in a case involving racketeering that live poultry coming into New York was in interstate commerce. Hughes was known to object to congressional delegation of power to the president, but Reed cited the delegation of authority that the court had upheld in cases involving the tariff and the Federal Trade Commission.

The court had never held delegation of authority to be unconstitutional. These factors are germane to Roosevelt's subsequent comments upon the decision.

Chief Justice Hughes was devastating. He held that Roosevelt's code-making authority was indeed "unconstitutional delegation of legislative power." The Schechters, in any event, were not subject to federal regulation, according to Hughes. Once the poultry arrived in New York City it was out of interstate commerce and hence the commerce clause of the Constitution did not apply. In consequence of the decision, both the NRA code system and the collective-bargaining provision (Section 7-a) of the industrial recovery act were dead. Adding to the ominous nature of the occasion was the fact that not only the right and center of the court but also its progressive wing, Justices Harlan F. Stone, Benjamin Cardozo, and Louis D. Brandeis, had joined in the decision.[1]

The Schechter decision, together with two lesser ones announced at the same time, wrought even further destruction. They cast doubt as to the constitutionality of other major New Deal measures, both present and pending. Immediately after the court rendered the opinions, Justice Brandeis summoned Benjamin V. Cohen and Thomas G. Corcoran to his chambers, and urged them to bring Frankfurter to Washington immediately to explain to Roosevelt what had happened. "You have heard three decisions," he told them in agitated fashion. "They change everything. The Court was unanimous. . . . The President has been living in a fools paradise."[2]

Those opposed to the New Deal, whether from the left or right, were jubilant. "The Constitution is re-established," asserted that unpredictable old progressive, Senator William Borah. "Tyranny is overthrown," declared the firmly conservative *New York Herald-Tribune*. There were voices of dismay as well. The NRA, declared the *Christian Science Monitor*, "did accomplish much to put a bottom under sweat-shop wages, to abolish child labor, and bring a semblance of fair competition into demoralized trade." These factors caused mixed feelings among many editors, who praised the achievements of the NRA, and among some businessmen who had benefited from the setting of floors on prices.

Retailers instantly resumed price wars with loss leaders, especially cartons of cigarettes, which they reduced to little more than the cost of tax. To recoup the losses they lengthened the hours and cut the wages of their clerks. Within two weeks most grocery clerks were again working 65 to 72 hours per week rather than the NRA limit of 48 hours. In the first two weeks, according to the American Federation of Labor, a million workers were affected by the end of the codes.

For several days the furor increased. Thousands of people sent telegrams or letters to the White House, and waited expectantly for the president's reaction. He bided his time. For months he had remained silent as the Supreme Court showed signs of placing impediments in the path of the New Deal. In January, 1935, in the "hot oil" decision it had invalidated legislation aimed at preventing wasteful, competitive production in the oil fields. Congress passed new legislation intended to meet the court's constitutional specifications. In March Roosevelt had a narrow squeak when the court found the repudiation of the gold clause in government bonds unconstitutional, but five to four had held that bondholders could not sue. Justice James McReynolds in his dissent asserted that the Constitution was gone and the nation shamed. If the gold decision had gone against the government, Roosevelt would have circumvented it with a proclamation. Early in May the Supreme Court invalidated the Railroad Retirement Act, casting doubt on the social security legislation. On none of these cases had the president made comments in press conferences.

At the first press conference after the Schechter decision, Roosevelt made only a few mild remarks. "The real spot news," he suggested, "is what is happening . . . in every industry and in every community in America. . . . Are there any of the garment trade people in the City of New York who cut their wages from twelve dollars [per week] minimum to eight dollars today?"[3]

Two days later he was ready. Frankfurter had hastened to Washington and had advised him to bide his time before clashing with the Supreme Court: let more adverse decisions accumulate and then propose a constitutional amendment. Roosevelt ignored the advice and set forth upon his own course of action.

Rather than making a direct appeal through a Fireside Chat, Roosevelt chose to reach the people through the newspapers, although under press conference rules they could not quote him directly. At his press conference on May 31, he held forth for an hour and twenty-five minutes in a remarkable extemporaneous discourse. On his desk was a pile of telegrams and an open copy of the Schechter decision. When the inevitable question about the NRA came, he launched into his remarks. First he read a score of telegrams from small businessmen, mostly retailers, imploring protection: "Chiselers already at our throats and have begun choking us. Need immediate action."

Next Roosevelt analyzed the Schechter decision, reading passages and giving a commentary that ranged back to the Founding Fathers. "The implications of this decision," he asserted, "are much more important than any decision probably since the Dred Scott case." He did not worry about Hughes's stricture on unconstitutional delegation of power to the executive; Congress could easily remedy that problem. Rather, it was the narrow interpretation of the power of the federal government to regulate commerce, limiting it apparently to what was in transit among the states, that threatened the entire economic recovery program. Regulation of commerce was a different matter in the simple economy of the fledgling republic than in the complex interdependent economy of the 1930s, yet the Supreme Court seemed to be taking the traditional view. The national issue, said Roosevelt, was:

> Are the people of this country going to decide that their Federal Government shall in the future have no right under any implied power or any court-approved power to enter into a national economic problem . . . ?
>
> Shall we view our social problems — and in that I bring employment of all kinds — . . . that the Federal Government has no right under this or following opinions to take any part in trying to better national social conditions? . . .
>
> If we accept [that] point of view . . . we will go back to a government of 48 states and see what happens.
>
> Or we can go ahead with every possible effort to make a national decision based on the fact that 48 sovereignties cannot, in our belief, agree quickly enough or practically enough on any solution for a national economic problem or a national social problem.

Roosevelt concluded, "We are the only nation in the world that has not solved that problem. We thought we were solving it, and now it has been thrown right straight in our faces and we have been relegated to the horse-and-buggy definition of interstate commerce."[4]

"HORSE AND BUGGY LAW BACK — ROOSEVELT," read a headline cited in *Time*, which concluded dramatically that Roosevelt had sought to provoke a reaction against not the court but the Constitution. The performance, *Time* asserted, was a trial balloon for a constitutional amendment, and the constitutional issue would be the fulcrum of the 1936 campaign. The *New York Times* chided the president for his display of pique.

From Roosevelt's standpoint, the emotion was not pique but outrage. His target was not the Constitution but rather the outmoded Supreme Court interpretation of it. That interpretation had backed him into a position where he had to acknowledge the conflict that had developed between him and the corporate and financial interests and their legal conservators. Through his exposition he had identified the issues sharply and had picked up the gauntlet. The point of open struggle was overdue. Roosevelt was wily in engaging his opponents and, although he was now committing himself, still was trying to preserve as much of a following as possible among small businessmen.

The threat of the Supreme Court to the New Deal was more long-range than immediate. It was the possibility that decision after decision would strictly construe the federal powers of economic regulation and thus thwart Roosevelt. For the time being, Roosevelt could go ahead with his legislative program and from the wreckage of the NRA salvage those parts that had been of use and persuade Congress to reenact them. Then in the future, if the court continued to hand down adverse decisions, he could choose a plan of action from among his options. To that extent he was to follow Frankfurter's suggestion.

In response to the intensifying blows from the right, Roosevelt went more vigorously upon the offensive than ever before, and in the process did something to undercut the opposition on the left. Unexpectedly on June 19 he sent a tax message to Congress. It was a day the Senate made bleak enough for conservatives through passing both the social security and Wagner bills. Roosevelt's message came as an added outrage, endorsing "the very sound public policy of encouraging a wider distribution of wealth" through levying graduated taxes upon rich individuals and large corporations in proportion to their ability to pay. In words reminiscent of the Theodore Roosevelt in the Progressive Era, but no less chilling to those still possessing large fortunes during the Great Depression, Roosevelt declared:

> Social unrest and a deepening sense of unfairness are dangers to our national life which we must minimize by rigorous methods. People know that vast personal incomes come not only through the effort or ability or luck of those who receive them, but also because of the opportunities for advantage which Government itself contributes. Therefore, the duty rests upon the Government to restrict such incomes by very high taxes.[5]

The only specific tax rates Roosevelt proposed were those hitting business. Once again he tried to court small enterprises while smiting the large and powerful. He proposed changing the corporate income tax from a flat 13¾ percent to a graduated levy with a minimum of 10¾ percent rising to 16¾ percent for the largest corporations. He also recommended higher personal income taxes and the imposing of new estate taxes on vast inheritances. As if in mockery of wealthy people who had been demanding a lowering of the national debt, he proposed that these new levies be segregated and applied to that end.

The wielders of great economic power had, of course, proposed a drastic curtailing of New Deal expenditures, not imposition of new taxes. The president of the National Association of Manufacturers damned the program as an "uncertain element which can only act as a new artificial barrier to recovery." Editorial comments in conservative newspapers were equally predictable, in calling, as did the *Boston Transcript*, for "an aroused opposition to this purely socialistic experiment." Surprisingly few suggested that the heavier taxes would, as the Boise, Idaho, *Statesman* declared, "keep capital sealed up in its hole and . . . prevent the return of prosperity," although that would have been the economic consensus of later generations.[6]

Roosevelt also seemed to be mocking his enemy to the left, Huey Long, by threatening to undercut the Share Our Wealth program. While the message was being read in the Senate, Long walked around grinning and pointing at his chest; at the conclusion, he said, "Amen." Will Rogers pictured Roosevelt as crawling into bed with Long, but a better simile was one Long himself had provided the Senate during a debate in February. He compared Roosevelt to a "scrootch owl" in a chicken house. "A scrootch owl slips into the roost and scrootches up to the hen and talks softly to her," Long declaimed. "And the hen just falls in love with him, and the next thing you know there ain't no hen."[7]

While Long was conspicuously proclaiming victory for his Share Our Wealth principles, he was obviously aware that the scrootch owl was at work among his none-too-stable national following. He sent a public letter to the president aimed at demonstrating how mild and ineffective the proposals were, but headlines denouncing the "soak the rich" taxes gave people of small means a quite different impression.

The appeal of Roosevelt's crusade against wealth and privilege extended far beyond the followers of Long and Coughlin. "The dislike of exceptionally large inheritances is almost universal, except perhaps among those who benefit by them," observed a columnist in *Today*, who reported that many Washington journalists and politicians regarded it as the president's master political maneuver, it "struck so close to the heart of the thought of the overwhelming majority of American citizens."[8]

In Congress, the tax message served to recement Roosevelt's rather shaky alliance with progressives by giving concrete backing to his assurances of several days earlier. Under the leadership of La Follette, who had had no inkling that Roosevelt planned a tax proposal, the progressive senators of both parties went into action. Twenty-two of them signed a round robin declaring that they were willing to keep the Senate in session until the new taxes became law. Long did not sign the manifesto. The progressives were determined that the tax message was to be more than a gesture of defiance toward big business; it was to lead to legislation at once, even though Washington was hot and the agenda was already crowded.

The prospect was appalling to many of the regular Democratic leaders, as Roosevelt knew it would be. "Pat Harrison's going to . . . have kittens on the spot," Roosevelt remarked as he worked on the draft message from the Treasury Department. As for Harrison, when it fell upon him to guide the tax program through the Senate, he was too suave to betray his feelings to reporters and loyally undertook to do the president's bidding. A good many of the Democratic members of each house conceded the popularity of the proposal but were uncomfortable. Their reasons were fundamentally political. "They were embarrassed," the columnist in *Today* pointed out, "because they have received or expect to receive favors from men who will be affected by the tax program."[9]

A large part of Congress for the same vital reason was less than enthusiastic about Roosevelt's "death sentence" for holding companies. Scattered throughout the country, countless utilities had contributed to their campaign funds in the past, and if displeased might in the future switch to their foes. Associated Gas and Electric Company, unable to pay a dividend to stockholders in the past four years, nonetheless in this emergency found $700,000 with which to combat the bill. Other opponents, most notably Wendell Willkie, the young president of Commonwealth and Southern, were eloquent and persuasive. When Roosevelt sought to prohibit utilities from taking tax deductions for their charitable donations, the president of Georgia Power recalled wryly his company's past generosity to Roosevelt's Warm Springs Foundation and pointed out how little it had received in return.

In the "soak the rich" tax bill and the holding-company "death sentence," Roosevelt was developing two issues widely appealing to the electorate, which would strengthen his position in the 1936 election. But he was placing the congressional Democrats, especially those from the one-party "Solid South," in a bind between constituents and contributors.

The result was an unpleasant summer for both Roosevelt and Congress. He reverted to open leadership like that of 1933, but there was no longer the public sense of emergency or as much patronage with which to prod and lure the reluctant. Roosevelt made use of his own blandishments, taking many disaffected leaders on cruises down the Potomac aboard the *Sequoia*.[10]

Despite difficulties, Roosevelt sought enactment of his entire agenda. There was some problem with the Guffey bill to reenact the NRA bituminous coal code, which had the support both of John L. Lewis' United Mine Workers and of mine operators, who wanted the fixed prices the bill would permit. Roosevelt created a stir when, in recommending its passage, he urged that Congress not let doubts of constitutionality stand in their way. Although Republicans attacked the Guffey bill it passed in the final rush of legislation.

There were also difficulties with the bill to bring the Federal Reserve system under public control. Since spring, Roosevelt had engaged in intricate maneuvering with Senator Carter Glass, who considered the Federal Reserve his personal domain. Roosevelt had not wanted to risk the sabotage of legislation to continue the Federal Deposit Insurance Corporation, and tried to give the impression that the bill was no more than the handiwork of Marriner Eccles, whom Roosevelt had appointed head of the Federal Reserve Board. After much conflict and considerable compromise, Roosevelt and Morgenthau obtained a somewhat strengthened board.[11]

The sound and fury through the summer centered on the holding-company and tax bills. On taxation, Roosevelt was as elusive as on the banking bill, shifting back and forth in response to conflicting demands; then, under pressure from La Follette and his colleagues, at the end of June he called for immediate action. In the end, Roosevelt did not obtain an inheritance tax; it was removed in Harrison's committee.

The Revenue Act of 1935 increased gift and estate taxes, raised the top income tax rates from 59 to 75 percent, and imposed a corporate income tax. It by no means brought marked redistribution of wealth; it was at the most something of a counterbalance to the regressive new social security taxes and the proliferation of state sales taxes on consumers. Since April, 1932, twenty-one states had imposed sales taxes.[12]

In the bitter battle over the holding-company "death sentence," Roosevelt drew firmer lines and for weeks was stubbornly unwilling to compromise. In explaining the measure to the press in June, Roosevelt, using the Associated Gas and Electric Company as an example, demonstrated how much of the profit was drained off by the chain of subordinate holding companies and never reached the stockholders.[13] Senator Hugo Black ably abetted him with widely publicized hearings exposing the machinations of the utility lobbyists, and the manipulations of the holding companies. The $60,000 salary of one of the Associated Company vice presidents was paid by one of its holding companies, which in turn assessed other holding companies a total of $150,000 for their shares of it.[14]

In opposition to the holding-company bill, from early July into August the House membership, for the first time since the New Deal began, vigorously resisted the president. Neither his arguments nor the later findings of Black's investigation made much impression upon them. A heretofore obscure Alabama congressman, George Huddleston, insisting that Commonwealth and Southern should not be dismantled in his state, fired the House into open revolt against White House pressure for the "death sentence." On the very day that Roosevelt was denouncing utility company propaganda, Huddleston asserted in the House: "Whether it be propaganda from one source or another . . . or whether it be to oppose the Chief Executive of this nation, I will do what I think right, and all hell cannot stop me."[15]

House members rose to give Huddleston a standing ovation for several minutes. Congressmen from northeastern industrial states dependent upon private power were ready to desert Sam Rayburn of Texas and those from the South and West looking to the federal government for power development. On July 2, they stood firm against the Senate bill, 258–147, and then passed the more conservative House version, 323–81.

Through the next month, the members of the House fought off White House pressure. The prospects of plums for their districts from the $4.8 billion relief bill made little impression upon them. A Republican, Representative Ralph Owen Brewster of Maine, made headlines by asserting that Thomas Corcoran, who was acting for the White House on the Hill, had pressured him by threatening to cut off funds for the harnessing of Bay of Fundy tidal power at Passamaquoddy. It was a ridiculous charge, since Passamaquoddy was Roosevelt's pet project and already funded, but the accusation was indicative of the virulent partisanship developing in the House. Again on August 1 it voted against the "death sentence."

The progressive Democrat Burton K. Wheeler of Montana, handling the bill in the Senate, was equally firm in favor of the "death penalty" and for weeks let the stalemate continue. Outwardly there seemed no enormous difference between the House and Senate bills. Consequently the drawn-out struggle gave the impression of being not so much substantive as a matter of prestige, a symbolic test of strength. Within the conference committee more was involved, as Frankfurter, who was acting for Roosevelt at the Capitol, reported. The House bill would allow one tier of holding companies as normal, and Huddleston and his two Republican cohorts on the conference committee were determined to water it down still further. Rayburn, eager to obtain some sort of bill, was ready to accept two tiers, a compromise at which Roosevelt balked. The two largest utilities, one of them Willkie's Commonwealth and Southern, were two-tier companies.[16]

Roosevelt's strategy was to demonstrate that he could outlast all opposition by holding the weary Congress in Washington where, in an era before air conditioning had become commonplace, the heat was punishment itself. Perhaps he would let the holding-company death sentence wait, but he was determined to get a tax bill.[17]

It was well into August before opponents to the tax and holding-company bills were ready for compromise. By this time, too, Roosevelt, about to leave on a western trip, wanted Congress to go home. On August 15, the tax bill finally passed. A few days later, Roosevelt accepted a compromise version of the holding-company bill that Frankfurter and Senator Alben Barkley had devised. Holding companies were to be limited to no more than one operating company and one subsidiary, except where the SEC found that the system could not stand alone or that it was not so large that it would impair "the advantages of localized management, efficient operation and the effectiveness of regulation." The compromise measure passed both houses on August 25. Roosevelt in authorizing it wrote Rayburn that it represented a greater recession from the Senate bill than he should like to see made, but when he signed the Public Utility Holding Act he hailed it as his greatest legislative triumph. The holding companies regarded it as a defeat, filing suits in the courts against the measure; two years later, two thirds of them were still refusing to register with the SEC as the law specified.[18]

On August 26, the session came to an agonizing and exhausting end. It had been, acting House Majority Leader Taylor wrote, "a gruelling, nervewracking and strenuous session." There had been ructions and rebellions enough in the defiant Congress to lead the press to hail a Republican resurgence and predict that Roosevelt would have difficulties in the 1936 election. What became apparent only over time was that Roosevelt, in pushing the Democrats in Congress as hard as he had, particularly on the holding-company and tax bills, had built such keen resentment among conservative Democrats that they were joining repeatedly with the Republicans against him. From his study of congressional voting patterns, James T. Patterson has concluded that in the 1935 session a conservative coalition against Roosevelt was already taking form. At the end of the session, Walter Lippmann termed it the "closing days of a period in American history," stating that the emergency was over, "that personal government, that sudden announcements and hasty legislation are no longer necessary and are now to be put aside." His wish for a turn to the right was to come true, but it was to come from Congress, not the president.[19]

The 1935 session was the high point of New Deal domestic legislation. Few Congresses in American history have wrought such a basic change as the enactment of the social security program. "If the Senate and the House of Representatives . . . had done nothing more than pass this Bill," said Roosevelt at the ceremony when he signed it, "the session would be regarded as historic for all time." There were also the National Labor Relations Act, the work relief program, and the tax, public utilities, and banking legislation to make the session memorable. The first New Deal in response to the depression emergency was, as Lippmann wished, over. Roosevelt was bringing into being a second New Deal, establishing new responsibilities for the welfare of the American people.[20]

The customary view of the events of 1935 has pictured a lethargic, confused Roosevelt finally in May stunned into positive action by the Supreme Court decision destroying the NRA codes. The evidence supports the contrary notion that he kept the ship of state well under control through considerable buffeting from both port and starboard, modifying his course as need be as he doggedly made his way toward his destination. Once again he tacked, veteran political yachtsman that he was, and this time obtained measures that have left their mark upon the nation for generations.

Chapter 14

SEEKING SECURITY SHORT OF WAR

FOR SOME months and years after the spring of 1933, Roosevelt, focusing upon domestic matters, contributed few tangibles to the conduct of world politics. His foreign policy seemed to be in a mundane, minor phase as from the sidelines he monitored the threat from Germany and Japan. Yet it was during this period that he began to fabricate a formula for collective security compatible with isolation — policies that would aid nations threatened by aggressors, but not plunge the United States into war. Slowly over the next two years schemes for boycotts and blockades took shape in Roosevelt's mind.

Not wanting to alarm Congress, Roosevelt appeared to stay within the bounds of political isolationism. In 1933 he did not dare ask Congress to postpone war debt installments. He tried to wheedle token payments, but obtained only a pittance from the British, $10 million in silver at an inflated valuation. Fortunately for Roosevelt, not only his interest but that of the public had greatly diminished. Then came a mercy blow from Senator Hiram Johnson, who in 1934 obtained passage of the Johnson Act. It contained a provision that by 1941 was of serious consequence, forbidding loans to nations in default on their debts. Since it banned token payments, all payments stopped, except for those from Finland, which continued to pay in full. The debt question had finally faded away.[1]

Even isolationists favored policies that might improve foreign trade and thus strengthen the economy. Roosevelt took advantage of the latitude he enjoyed to recognize the Soviet Union, which since the Bolshevik Revolution of 1917 had had no diplomatic relations with the United States. What seemed to Congress and at first to the president as a recovery measure came to be a collective security diplomatic move, an apparent alignment of the United States with the Soviet Union at a time when it was under serious pressure from Japan. It was also an instructive introduction to relationships with the Soviet Union.[2]

Americans, unrealistically hoping for large overseas markets, put aside their fears of Communist subversion within the United States and their repugnance toward Soviet atheism. The Soviet armed forces had a poor reputation and seemed in no way a military threat in America or elsewhere. Chief of Staff Douglas MacArthur, upon his return from Europe, had informed Henry L. Stimson that the Russian army equipment was mediocre and the generals incompetent. Since no one was afraid of the Soviet Union, even some cautious isolationists pressed for recognition. Senator Johnson deemed nonrecognition idiocy when "there are billions of dollars worth of future orders in Russia for American workers to fill." Roosevelt, after checking public sentiment in several areas early in 1933, through the informal personal diplomacy he so relished, extended feelers to the Russians.[3]

The Soviets, fearful that the Japanese might attack them, responded favorably. Roosevelt, bypassing the State Department, operated through Henry Morgenthau, Jr., at that time head of the Farm Credit Administration. Perhaps Roosevelt was ready to proffer credits and de facto recognition through Amtorg, the Russian trading agency. The Russians, rather, sought full de jure recognition and the exchange of envoys, hoping that the United States would serve as a counterweight to the Japanese.

Impatient with the slow negotiations, Roosevelt by September was ready to bring "this whole Russian question into our front parlor instead of back in the kitchen." He gave principal responsibility to William C. Bullitt, who had felt out the Russians in 1932 and had become a special assistant to the secretary of state. Bullitt, who had gone on a fact-finding mission to the Soviet Union for President Wilson and Colonel House in 1919, strongly favored the recognition of Russia.

Secretary Cordell Hull and State Department officials were more cautious, fearing to upset public opinion, insistent that before recognition there be a firm settlement of questions involving both Communist activity and the Russian debt to the United States. Overall, Hull favored recognition, telling Roosevelt that Russia could be a great help in stabilizing dangerous conditions in Europe and Asia.

"I agree entirely," Roosevelt told Hull. Indeed, what had started in Roosevelt's mind as a venture to improve trade seemed to have shifted in focus, to serve as a counterweight against Germany and Japan. Under the cloak of trade, Roosevelt might augment security.

If Roosevelt had followed the advice of Secretary Hull and the State Department, he would have allowed them to engage in lengthy negotiations, cautiously working out firm agreements on each of the serious points of difference between the Russians and the United States. Roosevelt was aware of the importance of firm agreements to disarm political opposition within the United States. Father Edmund A. Walsh of Georgetown University, who had long fought against recognition, was ready to support it on economic grounds, but it was important to reassure him and all Catholics that they would be free to worship in the Soviet Union. A few others, like Roosevelt's congressman, the conservative Hamilton Fish, Jr., were warning that recognition would establish the Communist Internationale (the Comintern) under diplomatic immunity in the nation's industrial cities and among blacks of the South. Recognition, said Fish, would save the USSR from its imminent collapse.[4]

There was also the danger of pitfalls in negotiating with the Russians. The chief of the Division of Eastern European Affairs, Robert F. Kelley, prepared a memorandum for Roosevelt emphasizing that, as other nations had learned, the time to drive hard bargains was in advance of recognition. Kelley was correct in his recommendation, and late 1933 was an unusually fortuitous time to negotiate. Joseph Stalin, overestimating the benefits he might obtain from the United States, was eager for recognition. He thought the danger of a Japanese attack was imminent, and the advent of the Nazis to power, promising future peril, had ended the warm informal relations between Russia and Germany.[5]

Roosevelt let his advantage slip in his eagerness to engage once more in personal diplomacy to win a quick coup. He ignored Hull's advice to reach agreement on basic issues at a lower diplomatic level before inviting a Soviet envoy to the United States. Moreover, he bundled Hull off to the Inter-American Conference in Montevideo, conceding only that Hull could delay his sailing in order to be present for the first few days of negotiations.

Bullitt was to be the prime negotiator. He was a brilliant, articulate figure, one who had shared the dream of the young American journalist John Reed that a new and finer order would come through the Bolshevik Revolution. He had broken with President Wilson over the Versailles Treaty, which with remarkable foresight he had feared could lead to German irredentism and Japanese imperialism. Yet for all his insights he remained a gifted, wealthy amateur, happiest as a luminary in the scintillating Parisian society between the wars. With his patrician ways, wide acquaintanceship, and mastery of both trends and gossip, he was fascinating to that other amateur diplomatist, Roosevelt. Both believed that a gentleman's word was his bond. There was much for them to learn from Stalin and the representative he sent to Washington, Maxim Litvinov, Commissar of Foreign Affairs.[6]

Litvinov was also articulate and affable, married to an Englishwoman, yet an Old Bolshevik and a shrewd practitioner of diplomacy under first Lenin, then Stalin. Like Stalin he was a cold realist, who could drop revolutionary rhetoric in favor of warm reassurances whenever it was to the advantage of the Soviet Union. Roosevelt and Bullitt both seriously misgauged him.

Upon his arrival in Washington on November 7, 1933, Litvinov began conversations with Secretary Hull and Bullitt. Roosevelt and the State Department officials thought they were well prepared. Nevertheless, after two days of negotiations, Litvinov would agree to nothing. Roosevelt with his own skilled touch took a personal hand with Litvinov. According to Under Secretary of State William Phillips:

> Somehow the President succeeded in changing the whole atmosphere. . . . Mr. Litvinov agreed to consider the proposition on propaganda . . . which he had previously refused to consider. He agreed substantially to our proposition of religious liberty for Americans in Russia, but, of course, we got down to no details or phraseology. . . . After Mr. Litvinov left the room the President said he was somewhat frightened at the idea of a man-to-man conversation on so many points on which he was not fully versed and I recommended that Bullitt be present. The President readily accepted.[7]

From this point on Roosevelt and Bullitt personally carried on the negotiations. "Everything is coming along splendidly," Roosevelt assured Farley after he had spent three hours alone with Litvinov on the evening of November 10. "Of course, Litvinov wanted me to recognize Russia and then work out the conditions. He's a great trader, but I wasn't going to let him get away with that. I made it clear that everything must be cleared up first."[8]

On the contrary, Roosevelt failed to attain an agreement that the Soviets could not construe contrary to American intent. One aim had been to obtain a pledge that the Russians would not allow on their soil any organization aiming to overthrow the political or social order in the United States, as did the Comintern. The State Department did not mention the Comintern in its draft, since then the Soviets could have set up a similar organization with a different name. Under pressure from Bullitt, Litvinov finally signed. Yet in 1935, the Comintern met in Moscow with American delegates participating, as though there had been no agreement.

The question of debt settlement was no more successful. After much bargaining, Roosevelt reached what he considered a gentleman's agreement with Litvinov and he told his cabinet that the United States would be receiving $150 million. It never received anything, since Litvinov subsequently interpreted the word "loan," which Roosevelt had hastily written into the agreement, as meaning a sum that could be spent anywhere in the world, although Roosevelt had declared it would probably be a credit that could be used only for American purchases. Oral interpretations meant nothing to the Soviets. They made no debt repayments, and the United States extended no credit.

A promise that Americans in the Soviet Union should enjoy freedom of religion was of crucial political importance to Roosevelt, especially because of Catholic concern. He obtained Litvinov's agreement to respect the religious rights of American citizens. Out of the negotiations came one of Roosevelt's favorite anecdotes, which he related in 1937 to Archbishop Francis Spellman. He said he had told Litvinov:

"You have a perfect right to be an Atheist if you want to be, but you ought to permit the same measure of liberty to others. . . . Now Mr. Litvinoff — . . . before you die you will think of your father and mother and the religion they taught you. Mr. Litvinoff . . . (and Roosevelt pointed his finger at Spellman) before you die, you will believe in God!"[9]

Roosevelt may well have misgauged Litvinov, but not the religious Americans to whom he told the story. He pointed out to them with pride that now it would be possible for them to attend church services in the Soviet Union, and indeed an American Catholic priest was allowed in Moscow. That seemed to be the only assurance they sought. A few days later, members of a Catholic club cheered a speaker when he declared, "Roosevelt has put God back into Russia."[10]

Recognition took place on November 17, 1933, amid an aura of expectations that encompassed the Kremlin as well as the White House. When Bullitt, Roosevelt's first ambassador to the Soviet Union, arrived in Moscow, Russian officialdom, including even Stalin, greeted him with unprecedented acclaim. In consequence, Bullitt, convinced that everything Russian was at his command, in his search for a site for an embassy, settled upon "a bluff covered with beautiful woods containing a lake overlooking the river and the whole city of Moscow in the center of the great city park." Litvinov told him the site would be impossible, but at a dinner in the Kremlin, Stalin told Bullitt, "You shall have it." It was rather as if Roosevelt had assured the Russians they could build an embassy in Rock Creek Park.[11]

Scarcely concealed behind the generosity and gaiety of the Soviet leaders at the dinner was their concern over Japan. The host, Marshall Kliment E. Voroshilov, urged Bullitt to bring army, naval, and air attachés to the American mission, and Stalin asked if the United States could sell 250,000 tons of steel rails to complete the second line of the railroad to Vladivostok. Bullitt said he would be glad to help. Stalin replied, "Without these rails we shall beat the Japanese, but if we have the rails it will be easier." So it went for several weeks.[12]

Within a few months, the United States demonstrated that it had no intention of becoming involved in serious cooperative arrangements with the Soviet Union, since it wanted to attain tranquil relations with Japan. Soon, too, the Japanese threat against Russia faded to insignificance. Sharp differences developed between Litvinov's interpretation of the "gentleman's agreement" on debt settlement and Bullitt's recollections. The Moscow Soviet in March, 1934, not surprisingly refused to cede fifteen acres of parkland to the United States, and the Kremlin would not overrule it.

By Easter, 1934, Bullitt informed Roosevelt, the honeymoon atmosphere had evaporated completely. At first Roosevelt did not seem to take Bullitt's difficulties very seriously. Subsequently, after reports of innumerable indignities, he advised, "I think we should match every Soviet annoyance by a similar annoyance here against them."[13]

As for the agreements Roosevelt and Litvinov had signed, the Soviets either ignored or misconstrued them as suited their purposes. In December, 1934, came the assassination of a top Soviet official, Sergei Kirov, the beginning of Stalin's frightful purge extending from 1935 to 1939. A by-product was intensified xenophobia. Bullitt's sympathetic enthusiasm for the Bolshevik experiment changed by the spring of 1935 into a hard realism, which his talented staff shared. He predicted to Roosevelt that Russia, like France, would seek close relations with Germany. Roosevelt replied: "I hope you are not being ostracized by the 'information givers' at Moscow, though I gather that no European Capital in the present confusion cares a continental damn what the United States thinks or does. They are very unwise in this attitude."[14]

By this point, Roosevelt seemed to care little what the Soviets thought of the United States. He treated Bullitt with familiar affection, bringing him back to the United States to work on foreign policy speeches and the campaign preparations, then, in August, 1936, dispatching him to be ambassador to France. Roosevelt demonstrated his relative indifference toward the Soviet Union by sending as Bullitt's replacement an amiable, credulous Wilsonian politician, Joseph E. Davies. Roosevelt did want whatever Soviet weight there might be in the balance against Germany, so he instructed Davies to win the confidence of Stalin. Davies' technique was to gloss over differences and to demonstrate the enthusiasm characteristic of those who took Intourist-sponsored summer junkets. The night Davies arrived, George Kennan and others of the young Soviet specialists on the staff gathered to debate whether to resign as a body in protest. Happily they remained, for it was they (and Charles Bohlen, another specialist, by this time in Washington) who were to fabricate the policy toward Russia in the 1940s. It was above all their presence in Moscow, gathering information and growing in experience, that made Roosevelt's recognition of Russia worthwhile.[15]

Roosevelt and the State Department have been criticized because they did not draw up airtight agreements with the Soviet Union before they granted recognition. Yet, as the staff of Russian experts in Moscow soon came to realize, the only advantage would have been a legal one, to be able to point to firm agreements being ignored or violated. Within the Soviet Union, the foreign office could seldom dictate policy. The provisions Roosevelt signed were, Kennan has suggested, of political value in the United States. His characteristic fashion of making general arrangements that later he could expand to his advantage was valueless in negotiating with the Soviets. The only surprising thing, considering the disappointments through the 1930s, was that Roosevelt in the 1940s was ready to negotiate afresh with the Russians as if his earlier experiences had never taken place. Fortunately Kennan, Bohlen, and others knew better and were effective in day-by-day operations.[16]

With European foreign offices not seeming to give a damn, as Roosevelt noted in 1935, Americans, on the other hand, became increasingly apprehensive that they would be drawn into the dangerous confrontations outside the hemisphere. Public opinion demanded of Roosevelt policies so cautious that there was no need for Germany, Italy, or Japan to consider the United States as a deterrent to their long-range plans. All he could do was to continue to press for disarmament, and to hope for embargo legislation that could be utilized to bolster collective security.

As late as 1935, Roosevelt, listening to Norman Davis and some other of his advisers, was hopeful that disarmament might yet be achieved. Some of the most prestigious British and French observers kept expecting, like Davis, that Hitler would be reasonable and that therefore disarmament would be practical. For his part, Hitler did intermittently make benign assurances, emphasizing to Davis on one occasion that Germany wanted disarmament and peace. "I think," Davis declared privately in mid-September, 1933, "that Hitler is a *good* man — stupid and uneducated but still a good man."[17]

In the treacherous waters of onrushing realities, Roosevelt's disarmament scheme foundered. Before the end of 1933, Hitler withdrew from the league and rapidly built the armed forces and paramilitary units. A horrified American diplomat in Berlin reported that his small daughter at school had to practice throwing dummy hand grenades.[18]

Roosevelt, except on a few occasions when he came under the direct influence of Davis, feared that Hitler would launch a war when he was militarily ready, which might not be far in the future. In September, 1934, after lunching with Pierre Flandin, the French minister of public works, he passed on to reporters "entirely off the record" the table talk about the massive German production of guns and airplanes and the digging of bomb shelters.[19]

Germany constituted a present and growing menace. The problem was not a failure of awareness among Americans but rather their fear of being involved. That fear put Roosevelt in an unheroic and uncomfortable position, so hamstrung that there was nothing significant he could do. He kept thoroughly informed, tried through minor quiet efforts to counter the threat, and as it escalated, sought to build public support for collective security. It was an unspectacular policy that carried not much weight at home, less with Britain and France, and none with Germany.

The martial nationalism and racism of Hitler was in appalling contrast to Roosevelt's aspiration to be good neighbor to the world. Then and later there have been comparisons of Roosevelt and the New Deal with Hitler and the Third Reich. There is some validity to the comparisons insofar as they involve the establishment of government agencies to rationalize the economy and put people back to work. Both German and American agencies were based upon antecedents developed during World War I. There the resemblance stopped, for Roosevelt's agencies existed solely to speed recovery and Hitler's to marshal the people and economy for war. There was similarity, too, in some of Hitler's techniques as a leader. He too might be hazy about immediate details in his plans, ready to improvise or to retreat if he ran into difficulties and then thrust forward again at a propitious time, always working toward basic long-range ends.[20]

The difference was that Hitler's ends were monstrous — so repugnant to American readers of *Mein Kampf*, which he had written in the early 1920s, that they discounted them as the rantings of a rabble-rouser seeking power. Yet he drove firmly toward the ultimate purposes he had set forth in *Mein Kampf*: The Germans were the superior people of the world. They must guarantee that superiority through eliminating the alien Jewish element within the Reich, and then through obtaining *lebensraum* — living space — in eastern Europe. The people in that area were to be evicted or killed so that the superior Germans could populate it and develop its resources. This program would entail two wars, first against France, then against the Soviet Union. Roosevelt, on the basis of information coming to him from the Third Reich, took *Mein Kampf* quite seriously, but hoped that Hitler through either inducements or the erection of formidable barriers against him could be persuaded to keep the peace.

Hitler, by the time he came into power, looked upon the depression-wracked United States as populated by a mongrel race incapable of causing him much trouble. It seemed no impediment to Hitler's schemes and he had little interest in it. At the proper time, he felt, it would fall into the German empire.[21]

The contrast was interesting — Hitler rapidly developing military power, paying little heed to Roosevelt, and the hamstrung president monitoring Hitler's rise with growing dismay. Hitler's actions were not to Germany's long-range advantage. Through ignoring the United States, Hitler helped bring about the gradual change in American opinion so vital to Roosevelt before he could assume an open collective security policy. Hitler, not caring what the United States thought of Germany and scornful of its feeble military power, blatantly built his war machine and did nothing to stop the beating of Jews, including several American citizens.

The threat Roosevelt saw to the United States was more long-range than immediate, unlike that to Germany's neighbors. During his first term and much of the second, he placed his reliance upon the navy, which he favored modernizing and strengthening, but only slowly, in order to keep down budget deficits. Roosevelt diverted $238 million from the first emergency public works appropriation of 1933 to construct thirty-two new ships. The following year he signed the Vinson-Trammell Act, which by 1942 would bring the navy to the strength the treaties of 1922 and 1930 permitted. Pacifists were appalled that Roosevelt was committing a billion dollars to naval construction. Yet Roosevelt, much as he loved the navy and firm though he was in considering it the safeguard of future security, kept it lean. In June, 1933, when he addressed the graduating class at Annapolis, the occasion was not entirely festive. In order to economize, the Navy Department gave commissions to little more than half the graduating class of 432 midshipmen.[22]

Roosevelt cut the army far more severely, despite the fact that its budget was only $229 million. The regular army numbered only 140,000 men (including 6,500 Philippine Scouts) and was so little mechanized that it possessed only 6,000 trucks, of which 4,000 were World War I leftovers. The cavalry still functioned; young Ronald Reagan obtained a reserve commission in it because he liked to ride horseback. Roosevelt reduced the complement of 12,000 army officers by transferring 3,000 of them to command Civilian Conservation Corps camps. Chief of Staff MacArthur was so upset that he warned the president that the United States would lose the next war:

> When a dying American boy spat out his last curse, "I wanted the name not to be MacArthur, but Roosevelt."
>
> The President grew livid. "You must not talk that way to the President!" he roared. He was, of course, right. . . . I said that I was sorry and apologized. . . . I told him he had my resignation as Chief of Staff. As I reached the door his voice came with that cool detachment which so reflected his extraordinary self-control, "Don't be foolish, Douglas; you and the budget must get together on this."[23]

MacArthur's histrionics had little lasting impact upon Roosevelt, who wanted to neutralize the officer he considered potentially dangerous. More important, the time when Roosevelt would feel the need for a large army was still years away. The navy was the force that could back Britain and France if need be, and more immediately could serve as a possible warning to Japan.

Prospects of peace in East Asia were gradually growing dimmer, although Roosevelt, Hull, and Ambassador Joseph Grew tried to cultivate better relations with Japan. They hoped that moderate civilians in the government could gain the upper hand. In February, 1934, Roosevelt enthusiastically greeted a distinguished Japanese leader, Otohiko Matsukata, who had been at Harvard with him and whom many years earlier he had entertained at Hyde Park. Matsukata assured Roosevelt that Japan was gradually regaining normality, and that since Roosevelt had become president national sentiment toward the United States had signally improved.[24]

Yet overall, Roosevelt sought a strong naval presence in the Pacific. Japan did not seem to be overly bothered by the building of vessels that would not be ready for service for several years. While construction slowly went on, Roosevelt tried, through continued naval limitations negotiations, to forestall a naval race. The Japanese were adamant that they must receive parity with the United States, and when they failed at the London Naval Conference of 1935 to break the earlier 5:5:3 ratio with the British and Americans, they withdrew. Still, Roosevelt did not resort to large-scale construction.

If relations with Japan did not markedly improve, neither did they reach a point of crisis. The forces threatening ultimate conflict were building, as Japanese militants continued to be dominant and consolidated their hold on Manchuria and North China. Roosevelt was marshaling naval strength but threatening no confrontation, and the State Department made only mild protests. With basic policy set and East Asian problems no longer urgent, Roosevelt diverted his attention elsewhere and allowed Stanley Hornbeck, no friend of Japan, to gather power through his day-by-day direction of State Department policy.[25]

Although the American people were dismayed by the expansionist threats of the Japanese and of European dictators, they were determined that the United States should not again become involved in foreign wars. Roosevelt was finding these views attractive, and expressed his enthusiasm for the 1935 Nye Committee investigation into wartime profits of the munitions manufacturers and international bankers. To his old chief, Josephus Daniels, he lamented in 1934 that if the peace-minded William Jennings Bryan had stayed on as secretary of state in 1915, "the country would have been better off." Sentiment was veering toward the belief that the United States could stay out of future wars only if it abandoned the traditional neutral rights that Wilson had defended. A distinguished international lawyer, Charles Warren, asserted, "It is better that our citizens should run the risk of commercial loss than the country should be involved in a war to protect their alleged commercial rights." These sentiments appealed even to Roosevelt, who instructed the State Department to draft legislation embodying his principles — belligerents could not send armed vessels or aircraft into American territory, and United States citizens could not travel on belligerent ships. Warren recommended a mandatory arms embargo; Roosevelt and the State Department wanted a discretionary one.[26]

In the antiwar excitement of 1935, even some of the State Department officials were wavering, and Roosevelt suddenly abandoned the cause of a discretionary arms embargo. Hitler was massively rearming Germany, and the Italians were pouring troops into Africa in preparation for an assault on Ethiopia — events that seemed to bear an ominous parallel to those of the summer of 1914. In January, Roosevelt had learned how effectively public sentiment could stampede the Senate. After careful preparation, he had made good on his 1932 campaign promise and recommended to the Senate that it approve American membership in the World Court — a step so conservative that even President Coolidge had advocated it. Father Coughlin on the airwaves and William Randolph Hearst in his newspapers called for telegrams of protest to the Senate, and they had come in vast numbers. The vote on January 29, 1935, was seven short of a two-thirds majority.[27]

Roosevelt was furious. He sent his thanks through Senate Majority Leader Robinson to the fifty-three who voted for adherence, and as for the rest, he wrote in words that he toned down before sending: "I am inclined to think that . . . if they ever get to Heaven . . . they will be doing a lot of apologizing . . . that is if God is against war — and I think He is."[28]

The voice of the people was clear to Roosevelt in the spring of 1935. If he were to obtain from Congress the fundamental reforms he was seeking, and were to be a strong candidate for reelection the following year, it was logical that he should avoid a congressional fight that he might well lose over a discretionary embargo. There is no indication that he changed his fundamental belief in collective security. Rather, he frequently trimmed his sails in response to political gusts.

When Roosevelt met with the Nye Committee, which was investigating World War I profits, he expressed his enthusiastic approval of committee schemes to take the profits out of war, and suggested that the legislation should cover periods of neutrality as well as war. Senator Gerald P. Nye was startled since he had considered the schemes radical.

For some months, while public interest in neutrality legislation became more intense, the Nye Committee and the Foreign Relations Committee jousted with each other over neutrality proposals. The State Department tried to soothe ruffled feelings and Roosevelt kept quiet. With Italy poised to invade Ethiopia, Roosevelt on August 19, 1935, finally sent Chairman Key Pittman of the Senate Foreign Relations Committee a bill providing for a discretionary embargo. Pittman, long irate because of Roosevelt's flirtation with "that fool Munitions Committee," telephoned Steve Early at the White House that only three members of the Foreign Relations committee had voted for the bill. "I tell you Steve," Pittman warned, "the President is riding for a fall if he insists on designating the aggressor. . . . He had better have nothing than to get licked, and I assure you that is what he is facing."[29]

Roosevelt would have been content with nothing, but the Nye Committee threatened a filibuster to kill several domestic measures still before Congress unless the Senate took up a neutrality bill. In order not to lose his "second New Deal" program, Roosevelt withdrew his request for a discretionary embargo. The Senate voted for a mandatory embargo, but the House leaders stood firmly behind Roosevelt's real choice, a discretionary one. That enabled Roosevelt to negotiate a compromise. The House voted mandatory legislation that would expire at the end of the following February. He made the most of what he could obtain — an embargo against Italy that would not in reality harm Ethiopia since it would not be able to import arms anyway through the Italian-controlled ports. In his statement when he signed the measure, he praised its purpose and said it represented "the fixed desire of the government and people of the United States to avoid any action which will involve us in war." But he criticized the "inflexible provisions [which] might drag us into war instead of keeping us out." He continued to want to aid victims of aggression and hoped gradually to win support for his view.

Mussolini, ignoring the league and refusing a settlement with Emperor Haile Selassie that would have given Italy the opportunity to exploit Ethiopia economically, on October 2, 1935, gave the word to advance. Italian bombers dropped their missiles on defenseless mud villages, and one of Mussolini's sons boasted how beautiful it was to see the bursts of flame and wreckage. Americans shuddered. Roosevelt issued the expected neutrality proclamation, and speaking at San Diego, expressed the American concern that despite the danger that some nations might repeat the folly of twenty years earlier and imperil civilization, the United States, as the Founding Fathers had prayed, should remain "unentangled and free." Yet he concluded by invoking the "gospel of the good neighbor."[30]

As a good neighbor — or good Samaritan — Roosevelt through the spring had been seeking some means of aiding victims of aggressors without being blocked by Congress. Like the British and the French he was more concerned with Hitler's open renunciation in March, 1935, of the disarmament clauses of the Versailles Treaty than with Mussolini's African adventure. Indeed, the French, British, and Italians agreed to meet at Stresa in Italy the next month to plan joint action against Nazi expansionism. Roosevelt devised a scheme to remain separate yet cooperate, if only the potential victims of Nazism should decide upon a blockade. To Colonel House he wrote on April 10, 1935:

> I am, of course, greatly disturbed by events on the other side — perhaps more than I should be. I have thought over two or three

> different methods by which the weight of America could be thrown into the scale of peace and of stopping the armament race. I rejected each in turn for the principal reason that I fear any suggestion on our part would meet with the same kind of chilly, half-contemptuous reception on the other side as an appeal would have met in July or August, 1914.

His first impulse, then and later, was to seek a top-level international conference, which he was quite correct in thinking would have met a "half-contemptuous" response. The course he suggested to Colonel House grew out of rumors he had heard that at the Stresa conference, France, Britain, and Italy might decide to join with the "Little Entente" neighbors to the east of Germany to impose an effective blockade entirely around the country. If they did so, he could aid by recognizing it and not trying to breach it:

> This, after all, is not a boycott nor an economic sanction, but in effect it is the same thing. A boycott or sanction could not be recognized by us without Congressional action but a blockade would fall under the Executive's power after establishment of the fact.[31]

Colonel House responded favorably to the suggestion, but Under Secretary Phillips thought Roosevelt "for once, was completely off the straight road." In any event no such concrete act came out of Stresa to give Roosevelt an opportunity to put his scheme into operation. Rather, the three powers agreed only to take common cause in the future. The Italian conquest of Ethiopia, complete by May, 1936, ended any likelihood of cooperation. Mussolini withdrew from the league, and in October, 1936, joined Hitler in establishing a new Rome–Berlin axis. Hitler meanwhile had militarized the Rhineland with retaliatory action from France. The dictators seemed to be rushing toward war, and collective security, whether through the league or united resistance, seemed impotent.

Nevertheless, Roosevelt returned several times to the idea of a blockade, perhaps against Germany, maybe against Japan. He began too to conceive of the isolation of the United States as confining its actions not to the shorelines but to the bounds of the hemisphere, both to east and west.[32]

Chapter 15

THREATS FROM LEFT AND RIGHT

AT THE CLOSE of the memorable session of Congress that enacted Roosevelt's second major agenda of legislation, political prognosticators were by no means sure he would win reelection in 1936. Republicans, taking heart, were boasting that they would regain the federal administration; the bitterness of the struggles in Congress indicated that many traditional Democrats were far from enthusiastic about him. Huey Long was planning to organize a third party with the avowed purpose of drawing enough votes away from Roosevelt to throw the election to the Republicans. Then, with an ineffectual Republican president in the White House, Long expected to win in 1940.[1]

A new political tool, the device of sampling public opinion, suggested that Roosevelt had reason to be cautious. Emil Hurja took a poll for Farley that indicated Long could perhaps indeed draw enough votes to elect a Republican. In the latter part of 1935, both Elmo Roper and George Gallup began publishing polls. The first Gallup poll on Roosevelt indicated that while a majority continued to favor him except in the New England and Middle Atlantic states, his popularity had declined except in the Rocky Mountain area.[2]

With many vital matters pressing upon him, Roosevelt at the end of the 1935 session of Congress was in a state of fatigue. On some days he suffered headaches and was irritable. Months later, Roosevelt, making amends to Morgenthau, whom he had harassed, conceded, "I was so tired that I would have enjoyed seeing you cry or would have gotten pleasure out of sticking pins into people and hurting them."[3]

Nonetheless, early in September, 1935, it seemed to Morgenthau that reelection was Roosevelt's prime concern, and planning it helped refresh him. If he worried about the bad omens, he gave no sign. Morgenthau did worry. The president continued to stand simultaneously for heavy spending and strict economy. Both had a marked appeal to him; both had ardent supporters within his administration. Morgenthau stood for fiscal conservatism and was almost at the point of resigning when Roosevelt suggested they work out some way to dispose of the veterans' bonus, a serious political liability. Roosevelt was inclined to construct his policies out of compromise.[4]

Roosevelt also toyed with the idea of making a deal with Huey Long. For some time the Department of Justice had been investigating the Long machine, and on two occasions Long had approached Attorney General Homer Cummings to find out how he could avoid being charged with corruption. The president never had to decide whether to make Long an offer. On September 8 came the shocking news that an assassin had shot Long in the lobby of the Louisiana state capitol. The death of Long, deplorable to Roosevelt, who understandably had a dread of assassination, did remove one of the potential obstacles from the 1936 campaign. Long had indeed been *sui generis*, as he said of himself. His unique ability to rally a coalition against Roosevelt was a legacy that the rabble-rousing Gerald L. K. Smith tried in vain to claim. Most of Long's ardent followers had also been attracted to Roosevelt. Nor did the Louisiana politicians, split into factions, have any stomach to continue to defy the president. Almost immediately the Long organization offered Roosevelt its support if he would restore patronage. The investigations stopped and Louisiana returned to the New Deal; Roosevelt made what some cynics called "the second Louisiana Purchase."[5]

In September Roosevelt also had to come to decisions on the politically sensitive priorities in his new work relief program; choosing between Harry Hopkins and relief and Harold L. Ickes and public works. The quarrel between the two men had become so vehement and public that Roosevelt summoned them to his Hyde Park home and sat with them and their staffs around the big table in the library. The figures supported Hopkins. To put 3,500,000 people on relief to work even at a cost of no more than $850 per person per year would leave less money than Ickes wished for the Public Works Administration (PWA).[6]

Ickes, disgruntled, viewed the decision darkly as the triumph of boondoggling over worthy public works. Hopkins and the Works Progress Administration (WPA) seemed to him the greatest threat to the New Deal at the polls in 1936. Even Roosevelt was slightly suspect to Ickes, still a nominal Republican. He told a *Washington Star* editorial writer that he favored the president's reelection provided he adhered to progressive ideas, but Ickes considered victory by no means certain.

For his part, Hopkins put no strings on his loyalty to Roosevelt and was finding himself being drawn more and more into politics. He had struggled to keep the Federal Emergency Relief Administration (FERA) out of it, insisting that state directors must be appointed on the basis of professional ability, not party loyalty. Politics had long since crept into work relief (the WPA). While Republicans protested against the FERA serving purposes of Democratic patronage, James Farley received even more vehement complaints from areas where Republicans were in control. Congress had been well aware of the patronage and pork barrel potentialities of the new relief program. They tried, without much success, to allocate funds accordingly, and did manage to write into the law an amendment Senator Pat McCarran of Nevada had proposed, subjecting any appointee receiving a salary of $5,000 or more to Senate confirmation. Inevitably, therefore, many of the state directors were political appointees. Hopkins continued to struggle for professional standards, but his prime concern was to support the president.

The political assets of the work relief program were obvious to Roosevelt and he made full use of them. Upon occasion he paid political debts by suggesting possible staff members. More significantly, he at times awarded projects so that political leaders loyal to him throughout the country could gain credit from their constituents — and conversely so that the disloyal suffered punishment. These uses of the program would become more apparent in the future. In the fall of 1935 there was an appearance of nonpartisanship, with something for each county in the United States except for a few where Hopkins certified that no one was on relief.

Although Ickes groused because he did not receive more, Roosevelt did sanction substantial grants to the PWA. When Ickes went to the White House with a large book listing three thousand projects, the president was in good spirits and approved them without modification. In later years he would pore over the large ledger listing public works projects, personally initialing each one he favored. These projects funded throughout the land were visible evidence of his interest in every locality in every state, and his detailed knowledge of the worthiness of Democratic lieutenants throughout the nation.[7]

During the year before the election the public works of Hopkins' WPA were also under way everywhere. Most of them were small; in countless communities there are still sidewalks bearing the indented imprint WPA. Through dividing a few large undertakings like the La Guardia and Newark airports into a number of $25,000 segments, WPA took over construction that Ickes felt rightfully belonged in his domain.

The work of artists, musicians, and writers became conspicuous. They were especially hard hit by the depression, and sought refuge on WPA rolls. From the outset of his relief programs, Roosevelt had been willing to accept the maxim that artists too must eat, even though his own criteria for art were whether or not the subject was a nautical one and, if so, how faithful it was to the ship being portrayed. Art, most often of a nationalist realism sort, began to flourish, especially in murals; copyists and draftsmen recorded folk art; architects drew the plans of historic edifices. Musicians performed symphonies, operas, and chamber music; actors produced plays and created a "Living Newspaper." Writers collected the oral histories of ex-slaves and laboring people; they also produced guides to each of the states.

There was much in the WPA that angered conservatives. They were irritated with the public works because the projects such as the installation of sewers often left streets torn up for many months. To Roosevelt, the basic purpose was to provide employment for those who would otherwise be on relief; he was determined to channel no more money than necessary into machinery and material. As in Asia, throngs of workers with shovels lined the thoroughfares, and they seemed to be torn up interminably. Many a hapless salesman or shipping clerk found himself digging ditches or doing other heavy labor for which he was ill suited. At any given time, numbers of WPA workers were conspicuously resting on their shovels, giving ammunition to the Republicans. It may be argued that the use of conventional ditch-digging and earth-moving machinery might well have brought much more substantial benefits, both economic and political. As for the cultural projects, they too came under attack for being both a waste of taxpayers' money and a haven for radicals.

Politicking in relief affairs inevitably became a viable Republican campaign issue. Soon opponents of Roosevelt had a number of specifics to cite. Yet Hopkins, acting under Roosevelt's orders, was as circumspect as possible. In consequence, during 1935–1936, while politics did indeed govern administrative appointments, there were relatively few flagrant instances in which they extended to the placement of the unemployed on WPA rolls. In addition, neither Roosevelt nor Hopkins condoned political assessments against the workers. In December, 1935, Governor Gifford Pinchot of Pennsylvania wrote a public letter to Roosevelt charging that Joseph Guffey, a "notorious spoilsman," was holding Pennsylvania work relief in "political bondage." Roosevelt responded personally, assuring Pinchot he was investigating the one concrete instance Pinchot cited. As for the generalities that made up most of the letter, Roosevelt dismissed them as "merely a tirade against persons whom you conceive to be your political enemies."[8]

Overall, it is possible that WPA seemed to Roosevelt a political liability. Once during his fall campaign trip, relaxing over cocktails with Judge Samuel I. Rosenman, still one of his speech-writers, he mused that it would be fun to be running against Roosevelt:

> I would say: "I am for social security, work relief, etc., etc. But the Democrats cannot be entrusted with the administration of these fine ideals." I would cite chapter and verse on WPA inefficiency — and there's plenty of it — as there is bound to be in such a vast, emergency program.
>
> You know . . . the more I think about it, the more I think I could lick myself.[9]

In this instance, Roosevelt was being more whimsical than analytic, for his opponent was to make just such arguments and they fell short with the electorate. As for the WPA, it brought Roosevelt strength in 1936 and was an important factor in building Democratic organizations in the cities. Through work relief patronage, the Pittsburgh Democratic machine grew in power while the anti–New Deal mayor futilely protested, "Who is going against Santa Claus?" Even among Democrats, 55 percent in a sample queried by Gallup thought politics played a part in handling relief in their localities; only 25 percent thought it did not.[10]

The perception carried over into presidential politics. When late in September, 1935, Roosevelt departed on a three-thousand-mile trip westward and took along both Hopkins and Ickes, *Time* suggested one reason was so that "the President could use his two prime Relievers to make his tour a happy one by promising Federal gold at strategic points en route."

The trip to the West was of the sort Roosevelt liked best, traveling on a ten-car train, together with Mrs. Roosevelt, a dozen of the White House staff, and three carloads of reporters and photographers. In theory the trip was nonpolitical, but Roosevelt appeared on the rear platform through Ohio and Indiana and westward, and brought Democratic leaders aboard to talk with him as the train proceeded at a leisurely pace from one stop to the next. In brief extemporaneous remarks at station after station he honed the theme that was to serve him best a year later: times were far better than in 1932 and the people could judge who was responsible.[11]

A major purpose of the trip was to extoll federal public works through dedication of the great dam on the Colorado River, known in earlier and later times as Hoover Dam, but to which Ickes with Roosevelt's blessing had affixed the name Boulder Dam. Farley issued a commemorative postage stamp upon the occasion bearing the legend "Boulder

Dam." It was an awesome sight and the most spectacular example of a self-liquidating public works project. While Roosevelt hailed the number of people employed and the great benefits that would come from its electric power and irrigation water, Boulder Dam gave him an opportunity to point to the value of all the projected public works whatever their size.[12]

While in Nevada, Roosevelt had a nervous few minutes on a mountainside. Senator Key Pittman suggested he drive up a narrow, steep gravel road that the Civilian Conservation Corps had constructed on Mount Charleston. Ten miles up the road, when the driver tried to turn the car around with Roosevelt in it, the wheels slid to within a foot of the edge. The frail White House appointments secretary, Marvin McIntyre, pushed against the side of the car, trying to keep it from going over the precipice. It was a special kind of peril that Roosevelt as a paraplegic had to endure.[13]

Smiling, fresh, and relaxed, Roosevelt appeared in Los Angeles the next day. His task, a difficult one, was to try to mend rifts in the California Democratic party. They were so serious that Roosevelt's adviser on California politics, Comptroller of the Currency J. F. T. O'Connor, had suggested that Roosevelt not appear at a luncheon in order to avoid offending politicians who might not get invitations.

In his discussions with O'Connor, Roosevelt demonstrated a surprisingly detailed knowledge of California politicians. On the whole he did well with them during his visit, but one San Diego Democratic congressman embarrassed him. Subsequently, he instructed O'Connor to make sure that the congressman was not reelected; the offender did not even run again. In 1936, Roosevelt went over a proposed slate of California delegates to the Democratic convention with O'Connor, making additions and deletions name by name. He struck from the list outright enemies including one of McAdoo's law partners, William E. Neblett. When McAdoo protested that Neblett was loyal, Roosevelt replied he had newspaper accounts to the contrary.[14]

What was most remarkable about Roosevelt's intricate knowledge of Democratic politics and his personal intervention in California was that he was equally informed and involved in numerous other states.

At the end of Roosevelt's western visit, an ominous new theme entered his final speech, on October 2, 1935, at the San Diego Exposition — the peril from incipient war overseas. Mussolini gave vital meaning to the warning, when, just a few hours earlier, he issued his long-anticipated order for Italian troops to advance into Ethiopia. Roosevelt called the menace of war a "potent danger at this moment to the future of civilization," and pledged that the United States "shall and must remain . . . unentangled and free."[15]

The corollary, that the United States must maintain powerful defense forces, was one that Roosevelt dramatized the next day when, aboard the USS *Houston* off San Diego, he witnessed the largest single tactical naval exercise that had ever been held. No president had ever watched naval maneuvers before. At their conclusion, Roosevelt wired his congratulations, expressing his interest in the "timing and precision of attacks." He signed himself "Roosevelt, Commander-in-Chief."[16]

Roosevelt was seriously concerned about the war, but refused to give up his vacation cruise because of it.

When he returned to Washington, Roosevelt focused upon economizing in response to increasing Republican accusations that he was trying to buy the election and was bringing the nation to the brink of bankruptcy. In his planning for the next budget he was cutting his estimate for relief to a billion dollars and for public works to 500 million, plus a carryover of a billion dollars from the spring appropriation. Much of the cutting was at the expense of the dispossessed. The figures shifted over the months that followed, but Roosevelt continued to be determined to trim spending, even though he had been well aware since September that his estimate of 3,500,000 employables to put on work relief was a full million short of the actual number. In consequence, even before the massive work program came fully into operation, Roosevelt was paring away at it. The prime election issue among Republicans, Gallup had reported in April, was government extravagance. Roosevelt took strong defensive measures.[17]

The 1937 budget, which would go into effect on July 1, 1936, was a triumph of fiscal conservatism. Again, as in the past two years, he declared that the regular budget was balanced. For the 1937 fiscal year the only deficit would be for work relief, and that he proposed holding below $2.1 billion in new funds. What was impressive, as an indication of a growing recovery, was a steady increase in revenues.[18]

The Supreme Court threw Roosevelt's fiscal calculations into disarray as soon as he announced them, and within weeks Congress dealt an added blow. On January 6, 1936, at the exact time that clerks were reading Roosevelt's budget message to Congress, Justice Owen J. Roberts was delivering the Supreme Court opinion in *United States v. Butler,* a test case against a New England textile mill, the Hoosac Mills Corporation, destroying the basis of the AAA crop control program. Taxation, said Roberts, was constitutional only if it were for the purpose of raising revenue, or to regulate in an area where Congress already had the power to regulate. The processing tax, he concluded, was "but means to an unconstitutional end." The decision was six to three against the AAA. In vigorous dissent, Justice Harlan F. Stone suggested the wisdom of judicial self-restraint.[19]

Roosevelt faced the prospect of a sharp decline in farm prices, something that could be fatal to him in the election. Several weeks earlier at Warm Springs, the influential Bernard Baruch had impressed him by remarking that if he could keep commodity prices up that would do more than anything else to reelect him. The basic question was what form the new farm program should take. He adopted a relatively simple device, to modify a little-noticed piece of existing legislation, the Soil Conservation Act, passed the previous year. Under its authorization, the AAA achieved the same ends of reducing overproduction by contracting with farmers to take part of their acreage out of the major crops, ostensibly to improve the fertility of the soil. It was an effective scheme, and one in keeping with Roosevelt's fundamental interest in conservation.[20]

A second blow fell on Roosevelt when Congress quickly enacted the veterans' bonus bill over his veto, requiring the payment of perhaps $2 billion. Politically the finale of the bonus issue was advantageous, but he did not want the onus of an increased deficit. He saw to it that the payments to veterans fell into the next fiscal year. Checks and baby bonds did not start to go out until June 15, 1936. Also Roosevelt once again tightened his overall 1936 budget, shunting unexpended funds into relief rather than seeking additional monies. These bits of legerdemain alone would not suffice. There had to be a new tax bill.[21]

Again, as in the summer of 1935, Roosevelt underwent the travail of sustained negotiations with Congress over a tax measure. Finally, in June, 1936, he obtained a corporate income tax and also a nominal tax on undistributed corporate profits that had some tangible value, stimulating an increase in corporate dividends that raised consumer purchasing power about $500 million per year. The veterans' bonus Roosevelt had so long opposed pumped an additional $2 billion into the economy in the months before the election, even more than the substantial WPA outlay of 1936.

The added stock dividends and the bonus helped stimulate recovery, some Keynesians have asserted in retrospect. The expenditures helped counteract the otherwise regressive nature of total federal, state, and local taxation in the 1930s. The windfalls in considerable part went to those who could afford to spend them on durable goods such as new automobiles or improvements to their homes, and in consequence contributed more than the subsistence payments to the unemployed in stimulating the decided economic upswing of 1936–1937.

Judged by his record, Roosevelt during the first six months of 1936 was a fiscal conservative, striving to keep federal expenditures down and the deficit to a minimum, yet he placed little restriction upon Congress, letting it whoop through the $2 billion bonus for veterans, for which he received the political and economic benefits without assuming the responsibility. Through insisting upon at least a mild undistributed profits tax, he gave reassurance to old progressives that there was a bit more than rhetoric to his sorties against the bastions of economic power.[22]

In one respect, Roosevelt was erring politically. Perhaps because he was becoming increasingly preoccupied with both foreign problems and the presidential campaign, he saw relatively little of the congressional leaders. Perhaps boredom was the reason. In earlier sessions they had spent much time at the White House or cruising down the Potomac with him, basking in the prestige of the presidential presence and beaming in response to his soothing inquiries about their opinions. Roosevelt may have tired of building their egos. As Eleanor Roosevelt has pointed out, his span of interest was relatively short. Certainly he was weary of their cautious advice. In 1936 his remoteness from them was of little consequence, but the following year would be different.

In terms of the election issues of 1936, Roosevelt's strategy was hard to fault. The two most startling charges that the Republicans could bring to bear against him were that he was spending the nation into bankruptcy and that he aspired to be a dictator. His relations with Congress and his almost complete silence toward the Supreme Court belied both accusations.

The smoldering issue of the campaign was the court. The implication of the AAA decision was that very little of the New Deal economic program could escape invalidation. There was a slight respite from the onslaught in February, when the judges upheld the Tennessee Valley Authority; Roosevelt refused to comment. In May, the court ruled against the Guffey Act, enacted to preserve stability in the coal industry after the court had invalidated the NRA codes. Roosevelt confined himself to remarking that the decision was of educational value. It seemed to confirm what Congress and the administration had inferred from the AAA decision, that economic regulation could come only at the state level. As a means of complying with the decision, they had provided in the new soil conservation legislation that the secretary of agriculture, once each state had passed enabling legislation, could create "48 little AAA's." Then on June 2, the court seemed to foreclose even that alternative when it invalidated a New York minimum wage law. Several hours later Roosevelt was ready with an immediate, succinct comment: "The 'no-man's-land' where no government can function is being more clearly defined." Neither the federal nor the state government, according to a majority on the court, could act.[23]

Roosevelt refused to comment further yet there was need to do so. In private, he had long since been mulling possibilities. In the fall of 1935, he had been so indiscreet as to suggest at a luncheon with Paul Block, publisher of several newspapers, that if need be he would pack the Supreme Court. As an illustration he recalled how Lord Asquith had forced the balking House of Lords to pass a health and unemployment insurance program in 1911. Asquith had threatened to create sufficient new peers to carry the measure. When Block recounted the conversation to the Toledo Bar Association "off the record," Roosevelt's press secretary, Steve Early, called him firmly to heel.[24]

Roosevelt made no such slips thereafter. His cabinet also remained silent; Henry Wallace postponed the publication of *Whose Constitution?* until after the election. So far as the Democrats were concerned, the Supreme Court was the tacit issue of the campaign. It was all too apparent what was likely to happen to the New Deal program — employers were already openly violating the National Labor Relations Act and scoffing at the social security program, they were so certain the Supreme Court would invalidate them.

Chapter 16

THE PEOPLE APPROVE

IN 1936 earlier forebodings evaporated and the electorate swept Roosevelt back into office by a landslide. The next year he would entitle the 1936 volume of his public papers *The People Approve.*

The campaign began informally in the fall of 1935, as Roosevelt on his transcontinental trip tested issues and rhetoric, and the loyalty of state and local political supporters. Thereafter, to the irritation of Republicans, he campaigned effectively while claiming blandly that he was only undertaking his duties as chief executive.

In January, 1936, Roosevelt transformed the usually dull occasion of the State of the Union message into a national spectacle. He appeared in person before Congress to deliver it in the evening. What is standard in the television age seemed sensational then, and to the Republican politicians, sacrilege. "Why this departure from our former dignified practice?" protested the House Minority leader. Only once before had a president addressed Congress at night, and that had been when Wilson called for a declaration of war against Germany. No previous president had so utilized radio as did Roosevelt, and in the pretelevision era, newsreels. For forty-five minutes before six hundred senators and representatives, he faced klieg lights and twenty-six microphones.

There was an implied parallel to Wilson's evening message in the opening of his speech, a grave warning of the threat of a new world conflict. "Peace is threatened by those who seek selfish power," he asserted. The American response must be a well-ordered neutrality, adequate defense, and all legitimate encouragement to other nations to return to ways of peace. These were comforting words. Turning to domestic matters, Roosevelt suggested a comparable threat: "We have earned the hatred of entrenched greed." The money changers had been driven from the temple, but now "they seek the restoration of their selfish power."

The occasion took on the air of a political rally, with the Democratic congressmen giving so many hearty cheers that they even applauded mistakenly when he remarked that the money changers were trying to make a comeback. Roosevelt, startled, lost his place in his speech, skipping a line. Later, when he said he was nearing the end, the Republicans hooted derisively.[1]

Within the next few days, Roosevelt sounded two notes of political counterpoint, making overtures to both businessmen and Republican progressives. At the dedication of the Theodore Roosevelt Memorial at the American Museum of Natural History in New York, he quoted his predecessor on social justice and conservation, and then added, "You and I still remember how those he denounced with righteous wrath winced under the stigma of such fighting epithets as 'malefactors of great wealth' . . . and the 'lunatic fringe.' " Of all the Oyster Bay Roosevelts present, only Theodore Roosevelt, Jr., protested, quietly remarking that when his father was alive, he and FDR were not on the same side of the political fence.[2]

From this point in late January on, Roosevelt was too cunning to make overtly political speeches. At a much heralded Liberty League dinner, Al Smith answered Roosevelt's attack upon "entrenched greed" with even more exaggerated hyperbole: "There can be only one capital, Washington or Moscow." Roosevelt made no reply. Rather he assigned Smith's running mate of 1928, the conservative Senator Robinson, to go on the air and mourn that Smith had exchanged his brown derby for a top hat.[3]

Roosevelt had no intention of giving his challengers an advantage through engaging in political debate, or of wearing out the novelty and excitement that he intended to reserve for his speeches of the fall. As a matter of fact, almost all samplings of public opinion early in 1936 indicated that Roosevelt was well in front of any potential opposition. The straw poll, at which the Republicans were already grasping, was that of the *Literary Digest*, a mailing of nearly a million ballots to telephone subscribers and automobile owners. It was a quite unreliable sampling in time of depression, as the new professional pollsters immediately pointed out. When a reporter in January confronted Roosevelt with the final *Literary Digest* results, 62 percent opposed, his only response was a confident grin.[4]

The prime task was to guarantee that well-wishers went to the polls. Organizing political campaigns was a favorite enterprise of Roosevelt's, and with enthusiasm he made plans to open the throttle of the Democratic machine. Thanks to Farley's constant ministrations it was already highly efficient compared to that of the Republicans, but Roosevelt wanted a large and intricate expansion in 1936.

Amid the exhilaration of preparing for the campaign, there was one poignant transition. For the first time since Roosevelt had run for reelection to the state senate in 1912, Louis Howe was no longer the behind-the-scenes chief of staff. Pulmonary ailments brought his collapse in March, 1935, and he barely clung to life in his room in the White House. Roosevelt frequently came to cheer him up, arriving in high spirits and departing with loud laughter. Later when Howe was moved to the Naval Hospital, Roosevelt still came every few days to see him. By early spring, Howe, so ill that even he gave up hope, remarked, "Franklin's on his own now."

In April, Howe died. Roosevelt, expressing his grief to Farley, admitted it was a blessing in disguise since Howe had declined to the point of giving orders that could cause trouble. It was a measure of Roosevelt's faithfulness that during an important conference he had accepted a phone call from Howe, who wanted no more than to have a White House chauffeur drive a young navy medical corpsman to the bedside of the man's sick mother. Roosevelt had agreed to do so and returned to the conference.[5]

Some of Roosevelt's detractors suggested that the president had lost his balance wheel. The notion has long persisted. Had Franklin not been on his own, the legend runs, there would not have been the spectacular mishaps of the second term. The fact was that, while Roosevelt's debt was boundless, he had long since absorbed Howe's lessons. In the White House, Howe had continued as a useful tactician, handling many errands involving Congress, and at times acting firmly as the head of the White House secretariat. He could indeed strongly say "no" to Roosevelt, but seldom if ever did Roosevelt involve him in major decisions where he could raise his voice.

For much of the troubleshooting that Howe previously had undertaken, Roosevelt turned to his wife. In July, at his request she inestigated the functioning at the Democratic headquarters and made numerous specific suggestions.

Roosevelt himself became deeply involved in campaign matters. To several ambassadors he wrote requesting that they resign and return to work in the campaign. After the election, he promised, they would rejoin his administration. Thus he obtained their services as speakers, and was able relatively painlessly to redistribute diplomatic patronage. To

Farley he sent suggestions for the organizing of speech-writing, pamphleteering, and publicity through the press and radio.

The image Roosevelt gave the public was of a busy president. There was no need for him to undertake much more until after the Democratic convention. He faced no challenge whatever in state primaries and conventions, and could be a relaxed observer of the Republican contest for the nomination. He would have preferred someone as conservative as Senator Arthur Vandenberg of Michigan, rather than the progressive Governor Alf M. Landon of Kansas, but it made little difference. In any event he would campaign against Hoover and the Republican right.[6]

Much of Roosevelt's most effective campaigning would be ostensibly not campaigning at all. He planned to spend part of the summer inspecting PWA projects and viewing areas suffering from drought. "Of course," he remarked to Farley with a wink and a laugh, "there won't be anything political about . . . inspection trips."[7]

In June, while the Republicans were holding their convention in Cleveland, Roosevelt was off on the first of his "nonpolitical" tours, traveling as far west as Texas. In advance he told reporters who referred to it as the first campaign trip that they were wrong, that his speeches were to be historical. So they were, as Roosevelt associated himself with past American heroes, and placed the New Deal in the mainstream of American tradition. At each stop he also put in a word for Democratic candidates running for reelection, from Senator Robinson in Little Rock to Congressman Maury Maverick in San Antonio. At the battlefield of San Jacinto he shook hands with the ninety-year-old son of Sam Houston and told how his own father had met old Senator Houston garbed in nightcap and nightgown, sitting up in bed in a Washington hotel. In Arkansas, part of the Louisiana Purchase, he paid tribute to Robert Livingston (an ancestor of Eleanor Roosevelt) for having negotiated the bargain, and turned the Federalist opposition to the purchase into a parable for the present. By the time Roosevelt returned, he had also invoked the spirit of George Rogers Clark at Vincennes, had dedicated a statue to Robert E. Lee, and had visited the birthplace of Abraham Lincoln.[8]

As counterpoint to Roosevelt's identification with Lincoln, Republican orators at Cleveland painted him as a destroyer of the American dream, and the New Deal as a calamity. The keynoter, Senator Frederick Steiwer, shaped his speech into a continuing attack upon Roosevelt's three years of heavy spending and taxation, leading to much versification to the tune of "Three Blind Mice":

Three long years! . . .
Full of grief and tears
Roosevelt gave us to understand
If we would lend a helping hand
He'd lead us all to the promised land
For three long years! . . .
When we got to the promised land
We found it nothing but shifting sand,
And he left us stripped like Sally Rand
For three long years!

There was no levity like this in former President Hoover's stern admonitions to the Republicans to regain their heritage from Roosevelt and the New Dealers. The delegates roared their approval, demonstrating so wildly for a half hour that they paid no heed even when the chairman tried to introduce the widow of President Benjamin Harrison.[9]

While emotionally the delegates in their acclaim for Hoover seemed to want to take the nation back to Harrison, the spirit of the man they nominated, Alf Landon, was quite modern. Landon's roots were as solidly in the progressive tradition as those of Roosevelt. As a young oil man in 1912, he entered Kansas politics to work for Theodore Roosevelt's new Bull Moose party. In the 1920s he was a rising member of the progressive faction in the Kansas Republican party, and despite the Hoover debacle in 1932, was elected governor.

By the election of 1934, Landon had built such a solid record as an able, moderate administrator that he won reelection against the New Deal landslide that year. By doing so he became a potential Republican nominee, but scarcely a front-runner. He had balanced his budget, but his opponents charged he had done so only through use of New Deal grants. Gradually Landon acquired powerful supporters, including Hearst. He was a man of remarkable fairness toward his political opponents. He never became as emotional in his opposition of Roosevelt as did his progressive Kansas backer William Allen White, who despite his avowed friendship for the president, in campaign years could launch vehement attacks. Landon was a firm constitutionalist fearful that Roosevelt would tamper with the Supreme Court, and an ardent believer in the balanced budget. Yet, like the American voters, he was ready to accept most of the changes in social and economic services that the New Deal had brought. He gave promises of efficient, frugal administration in Washington, but how he would reconcile preservation of New Deal programs with the balancing of the budget was little clearer in his case than in that of Roosevelt. Subsequently, conservatives attributed his defeat to his moderation. It is easier to make a case that the Republicans nominated their strongest candidate in 1936. He was so attractive that public opinion polls after the convention gave promise of a fairly close race.[10]

Roosevelt himself was symbolically the issue in the 1936 campaign, as he well knew and as many commentators pointed out; Landon was the counterissue. Several months before the campaign Arthur Krock, prestigious *New York Times* columnist, pointing out that voters cast their ballots for candidates as they personify issues rather than voting upon the issues themselves, aptly set forth the contrast between the Republican and Democratic view of Roosevelt:

> The Republicans say officially that the President is an impulsive, uninformed opportunist, lacking policy or stability, wasteful, reckless, unreliable in act and contract. . . . Mr. Roosevelt seeks to supervene the constitutional processes of government, dominate Congress and the Supreme Court by illegal means and regiment the country to his shifting and current ideas — a perilous egomaniac.
>
> The Democrats say officially that the President is the greatest practical humanitarian who ever averted social upheaval, the wisest economic mechanician who ever modernized a government . . . savior and protector of the American way — including the capitalist system — and rebuilder of the nation. . . . Mr. Roosevelt has constructed, with daring and fortitude, a sound bridge from the perilous past to the secure future.
>
> He is not wholly either, and he is certainly something of both. In the opinion of this writer he is much more of the latter than the former.[11]

Krock's balancing of pros and cons was probably typical of the less New Dealish majority of the Democratic leadership in 1936. He was an intimate both of southern congressional leaders and of some northern conservatives like Joseph P. Kennedy, and doubtless was speaking for them. Only a handful of elder statesmen with nothing remaining at stake bolted to Landon. At the Democratic convention when it met in Philadelphia in late June, professional Democrats kept misgivings to themselves and orated only what Krock called the official view.

There were no tense moments for Roosevelt as there had been at the convention of 1932; he and Farley were able to orchestrate it carefully in advance. This time, he easily eliminated the stumbling block that had given near veto power to the southern minority of delegates since the first party convention in the Jacksonian era, the rule requiring a two-thirds vote to nominate a president. It could have been a possible impediment to Roosevelt's domination of the 1940 convention.

The renomination of Roosevelt was an elaborate and wearying ceremony, significant only for the way in which he managed to give an unprecedented number of Democratic leaders a sense of participation. When finally at 12:42 A.M. the tide of encomiums ceased, the convention nominated Roosevelt by acclamation. The next morning they wearily nominated Garner for vice president, then slept until evening, awaiting the climax of the convention, Roosevelt's address of acceptance.

Once again Roosevelt had undertaken a spread-eagle approach, setting two separate teams of writers to work drafting his address. He had assigned the task to his new favorites, Sam Rosenman and Stanley High, and in addition to Raymond Moley and Thomas Corcoran. Neither team initially knew of the existence of the other. Rosenman in retrospect thought that Roosevelt did so because he was irritated by Moley's growing independence and frequent right-wing criticisms in the magazine Moley edited, *Today*, yet did not want to tell Moley he wished to have others draft speeches. Roosevelt was indeed irritated, as became apparent three days before he was to deliver the speech, when he angrily reproached Moley. By this time the two pairs of speech-writers knew of each other's efforts; Roosevelt assigned Rosenman and High to incorporate Moley's and Corcoran's conciliatory words into their militant defense of the New Deal.[12]

Roosevelt made amends to Moley the next day, but their relationship was over. There was no sharp break, but rather a drifting away. Thereafter Moley became an increasingly energetic critic of the New Deal, and in time a Republican columnist and speech-writer. Yet whenever he dreamed of Roosevelt, he remarked years later, he dreamed that they were making up.[13]

Through the four years of their association there had been personality differences between Roosevelt and Moley, but not sufficient ideological incompatibility to require Moley's departure. Rather, Roosevelt was commissioning two speech drafts to give comfort to the cautious middle-of-the-roaders and businessmen yet evoke enthusiasm among the advanced New Dealers. In his speech at Franklin Field, Philadelphia, he succeeded admirably in achieving both goals.

The acceptance ceremony was one of the dramatic episodes of Roosevelt's political career, and part of the drama was not apparent to most of the audience that night. As Roosevelt slowly made his way toward the platform, firmly grasping the arm of his son James, someone jostled James against his father so heavily that one of Roosevelt's leg braces unsnapped. Roosevelt went sprawling and his speech manuscript went slithering onto the floor. The Secret Service men managed to break the fall and relock the brace. Shaken, Roosevelt ordered them to clean him up and retrieve the scattered pages before someone stepped on them. "I was the damnedest, maddest white man at that moment you ever saw," he remarked to one of his secretaries, Grace Tully, later that night.[14]

Roosevelt presented himself to the throng poised as though nothing had happened and delivered the acceptance address in a strong, confident fashion. The first few pages were the "fighting speech" that High and Rosenman had drafted. Once more he invoked history, recalling the struggle in the Philadelphia of 1776 for the political rights of the American people, endangered by the "tyranny of a political autocracy . . . the eighteenth century royalists who held special privileges from the crown." Then came an analogy straight from the Progressive Era. Inventive genius had brought technological wonders, mass production, and a new problem:

> For out of this modern civilization economic royalists carved new dynasties. New kingdoms were built upon concentration of control over material things. . . .
>
> There was no place among this royalty for our many thousands of small businessmen and merchants who sought to make a worthy use of the American system of initiative and profit. . . .
>
> Against economic tyranny such as this, the American citizen could appeal only to the organized power of Government. . . .
>
> These economic royalists complain that we seek to overthrow the institutions of America. What they really complain of is that we seek to take away their power. . . . In vain they seek to hide behind the Flag and the Constitution.

Then Roosevelt shifted to the more conciliatory themes that he had summoned Moley and Corcoran to the White House to draft. At his instruction they had prepared passages on the biblical virtues of hope, faith, and charity (charity meaning love). These he set forth, applying the concept of Christian charity to his own administration.

Tucked in just before the peroration were what became some of the most famous of Roosevelt's words:

> There is a mysterious cycle in human events. To some generations much is given. Of other generations much is expected. This generation of Americans has a rendezvous with destiny.

That destiny, Roosevelt suggested, lay in the great and successful struggle against want and for the survival of democracy. It transcended American shores, and might hearten those in other lands who had yielded their democracy. "We are fighting to save a great and precious form of government for ourselves and for the world."

When Roosevelt reached the words, "I accept the commission you have tendered me," the crowd began to applaud thunderously. They continued to cheer when, a few minutes later, in an open car, he twice circled the field within the stadium. Without specifics, he had effectively set the theme of his campaign. It was to be a war upon entrenched privilege.[15]

A few days later at Topeka, Landon in his acceptance address set forth the shortcomings of the New Deal in failing to achieve full recovery and employment, and promised a more efficient, frugal administration, though not at the expense of those on relief. It was, like the candidate himself, a careful, moderate, businesslike speech, in both rhetoric and delivery a sharp contrast to Roosevelt's. The president had worried that perhaps his delivery was too dramatic, too oratorical; Landon hoped that the electorate would perceive Roosevelt that way, and in contrast prefer his flat, unsensational way of reading a speech. Landon joked years later that there may have been some merit to the antithesis but he feared he had overdone it.[16]

Roosevelt nevertheless found several reasons for worry. One was that Landon basked in the editorial praise of a preponderance of the newspapers. The president complained endlessly, even though most reporters, unlike editorial writers, wrote sympathetically. He was also concerned over his relative lack of campaign funds. Wealthy Republicans and Liberty Leaguers opened their coffers to Landon, raising some $14 million, much of which the party frittered away. The Democrats found many of their sources of 1932 dried up; major contributions from bankers and brokers declined from 24 to 4 percent.

The main contributors to Roosevelt's 1936 campaign were John L. Lewis's United Mine Workers and other unions. The president was eager for their money but did not wish to give the Republicans the opportunity to make political capital of it. When Lewis, accompanied by a photographer, brought a draft for $250,000 to the White House, Roosevelt parried, "Just keep it and I'll call on you, if and when any small need arises." Lewis wound up receiving less publicity and giving more money than he had calculated. Small needs arose so incessantly that in the end the United Mine Workers and a campaign organization of the unions, Labor's Non-Partisan League, contributed close to a half million dollars. Altogether, the Democrats raised only a little over $9 million, but spent it more effectively than the Republicans. Their organizations were in fine working order, and had to achieve much with carefully rationed funds.[17]

Those around the president became uneasy during the summer of 1936, Landon's campaign went so well while Roosevelt was inspecting and vacationing. The threat came from Landon's appeal, combined with that of a new third party, which Father Coughlin, Dr. Townsend, and the political heirs to Huey Long fabricated that summer. They called it the Union party, and chose as the presidential candidate Representative William Lemke of North Dakota, an exponent of prairie radicalism who had been a leader of the Non-Partisan League. The concern was needless, since the Lemke ticket created scarcely a ripple among the electorate. A simple quip made the rounds concerning "Liberty Bell" Lemke: "Cracked."

Not that Roosevelt, deliberately keeping rather quiet as part of his strategy of political timing, was indulging in false complacency. Rather, he was weighing each of Landon's statements and deciding who should answer them. He was also watching every detail of the multiplicity of campaign organizations, and concerning himself with weaknesses in strategic states. He brought great pressure upon Herbert Lehman of New York to rescind his announcement that he would not run for another term as governor in order to seek a seat in the Senate. The Democratic party was so splintered in the state that Lehman was needed to unify it. Loyal politician that he was, Lehman in the end gave way, but years later still regretted that he had not been able to enter the Senate earlier and build seniority. Further, to bring into the fold New York City voters leaning toward socialism and disliking Tammany, Roosevelt encouraged formation of the American Labor party. As for Michigan, where Democrats were weak, Roosevelt gave Frank Murphy, the governor of the Philippines, no choice but to leave his luxurious life in Manila and run for governor. Returned ambassadors found themselves assigned to speak to ethnic groups from countries where they had been serving. All the campaign apparatus by the end of the summer was functioning; all the Democratic orators had their instructions.

In August, Roosevelt forestalled what might have become a troublesome foreign policy issue. The fear that the United States might again be involved in a European war was intensified with the outbreak of the Spanish Civil War in July. Landon, at the suggestion of William Allen White, drafted a campaign speech declaring his abhorrence of war and pledging to avoid involvement in overseas conflict. Landon hesitated, and before he could give it, Roosevelt set forth similar views forcefully at Chautauqua:

> We shun political commitments which might entangle us in foreign wars. . . .
>
> I have seen war. I have seen war on land and sea. I have seen blood running from the wounded. . . . I have seen the dead in the mud. . . . I hate war.
>
> I have spent unnumbered hours, I shall pass unnumbered hours, thinking and planning how war may be kept from this Nation.[18]

Roosevelt's emphatic statements made a profound impression upon the nation. A few days later the *New York Times* reported that Roosevelt was hoping to assemble European leaders, including Mussolini, Hitler, and Stalin, in a conference to avoid a general war. Arthur Krock apparently learned of the plan from the British ambassador, who disapproved, and then checked with Roosevelt's secretary, Missy LeHand, who said the president would not repudiate the story. Roosevelt appeared committed actively to the maintenance of peace, and foreign policy did not become important in the campaign.

By the time Roosevelt formally opened his campaign at the New York State Democratic convention of September 29, leading polls, except for that of *Literary Digest*, showed him comfortably in front of Landon. In consequence, Roosevelt was able to run on his policies of the previous three years, giving only a few indications of what a second term might bring.

Roosevelt opened his campaign with humor, gibing at the attacks of the wealthy upon him. He himself made up a little parable and inserted it in the speech:

> In the summer of 1933, a nice old gentleman wearing a silk hat fell off the end of a pier. He was unable to swim. A friend ran down the pier, dived overboard and pulled him out; but the silk hat floated off with the tide. After the old gentleman had been revived, he was effusive in his thanks. He praised his friend for saving his life. Today, three years later, the old gentleman is berating his friend because his silk hat was lost.

The retort came from Hoover — that in the first place someone had pushed the old gentleman off the pier.[19]

On economic policies, Roosevelt emphasized the need to improve the income of farmers and to alleviate rural poverty. He emphasized, as he had four years before, the interdependence of the countryside and the cities. He did cite some specifics on agriculture that would appeal to commercial farmers. At one point he announced, just ahead of Landon, some benefits for farmers that Landon too favored. Landon had to issue a press release anticipating some of the points in his own big farm speech.

In the cities, Roosevelt's appeal was both to labor and to small businessmen. A notable speech in a ballpark in Pittsburgh was his response to the assertions that he was recklessly spending the nation toward bankruptcy. He took the view that his policies had only increased the national debt by $8 billion in nonrecoverable costs, and that that expenditure had brought many times more billions in additional income to the American people. In simplified form it became a component of his numerous whistle-stop speeches, and it worked. Month after month economic conditions had been improving, and as they did Roosevelt's political fortunes waxed with them.

The attacks by Republicans upon Roosevelt became increasingly bitter and extreme, even as their campaign became less likely to succeed. Landon's campaign manager, John D. M. Hamilton, and his running mate, Colonel Frank Knox, campaigned well to the right of him, making little appeal to moderate voters and, to Landon's chagrin, none to labor. In the later stages of the campaign, even Landon became more vigorous in his criticisms. In one speech he warned that Roosevelt was on his way toward becoming a dictator.[20]

A more serious matter than these vague allegations was Landon's futile attempt to smoke out Roosevelt on his intentions toward the Supreme Court; Paul Block had told Landon of Roosevelt's luncheon remarks the previous year. But there was no political need for Roosevelt to answer. Landon's rightward turn might have pleased those ardently opposed to Roosevelt, but it brought Landon no fresh support.[21]

Roosevelt accepted much of the antipathy with relative equanimity. In September, speaking before a far-from-sympathetic audience at the Harvard Tercentenary celebration, he pointed out that at the Bicentenary, "many of the alumni of Harvard were sorely troubled concerning the state of the Nation. Andrew Jackson was President. On the two hundred fiftieth anniversary of the founding of Harvard College, alumni again were sorely troubled. Grover Cleveland was President. Now, on the three hundredth anniversary, I am President."[22]

His audience laughed.

By the end of the campaign, Roosevelt was no longer willing to parry political epithets in a gentle manner. There had been an unhappy escalation of rhetoric, as if to try to evoke the "red scare" of the 1920s and reinvigorate its spent hatreds. With numerous variations the theme ran that Roosevelt was taking the nation down the path to a socialist or communist dictatorship. Fortunately the time was not right for a conflagration and all the blowing and puffing did not reignite the embers.

Roosevelt was particularly indignant over Republican efforts to stuff pay envelopes with anti–social security propaganda, alleging that workers would get few benefits for the taxes they paid, indeed that Congress might later divert the funds to other purposes, and failing to point out that employers would pay $2 into social security for every $1 employers contributed. He made angry retorts on several occasions.

In his final address at Madison Square Garden on October 31, Roosevelt for once abandoned the characteristic balance of his addresses and focused his feelings in a stinging attack:

> For twelve years this Nation was afflicted with hear-nothing, see-nothing, do-nothing Government. . . . Powerful influences strive today to restore that kind of government with its doctrine that that Government is best which is most indifferent. . . .
>
> Never before in all our history have these forces been so united against one candidate as they stand today. They are unanimous in their hatred for me — and I welcome their hatred.
>
> I should like to have it said of my first Administration that in it the forces of selfishness and of lust for power met their match. I should like to have it said of my second Administration that in it these forces met their master.[23]

The only serious question seemed to be the breadth of Roosevelt's margin of victory. When the returns began to come in election evening, they were so overwhelmingly Democratic that even Roosevelt could scarcely believe it. At the house in Hyde Park while relatives, friends, and a few of those closest to him in the campaign listened to returns in the large library, he sat in the dining room by the press teletype machines and the telephones, supervising the tally on a large chart. One of the early returns showed him carrying New Haven, in supposedly hostile New England, by 15,000. He was incredulous and had the report checked by telephone. Word came it was true. Rosenman remembered: "He leaned back in his chair, blew a ring of smoke at the ceiling and exclaimed: 'Wow!' He knew it was over and at ten-thirty came down the hall to the library for some sandwiches."[24]

It was one of the greatest election sweeps in American history. Roosevelt received 27,750,000 votes to 16,680,000 for Landon, and carried the electoral college 523 to 8. He won every state but Maine and Vermont. Lemke's Union party received only 890,000 votes.

"I am beginning to come up for air after the baptism by total submersion on Tuesday night last!" Roosevelt wrote Ambassador Josephus Daniels. "The other fellow was the one who nearly drowned! . . .

"We have — all of us — been leaning over backward in taking the general victory calmly."[25]

It was some days before Roosevelt began to feel the full impact and to consider methodically its implications for his second term.

Chapter 17

THE GOOD NEIGHBOR PROMOTES HEMISPHERIC DEFENSE

In the aftermath of the decisive 1936 election, Roosevelt sailed to address in person the Inter-American Conference convening in Buenos Aires. It gave him an occasion to dramatize to the old world, overrun or threatened by totalitarianism, the alternative of the Good Neighbor policy, and to encourage dictators and peoples of Latin America to democratize their nations. Beyond was an even more vital objective, to lay the groundwork for defense of the new world against threats from the old.

By the end of 1936, as a major response to the limitations and frustrations hampering his quest for world security, Roosevelt was disposed to turn inward to the American hemisphere. There, building upon the small beginnings of the Good Neighbor policy, he enjoyed such freedom that he was able to construct politically, economically, and militarily, a pilot plant for an ideal global order.[1]

Compelling reasons directed Roosevelt's attention toward the Good Neighbor policy, which had been only a minor theme during his first three years in office. One was his conviction that the hemisphere would be vulnerable to the future ventures of Hitler — a view that many scoffed at, but that subsequent evidence has borne out. Therefore the expansion of the Good Neighbor program into a hemispheric alliance for defense was prudent and vital. The other reason was the relative ease with which he could convince his critics of the need for hemispheric security. Many of the most ardent isolationists were by no means pacifists. While they might view with apprehension Roosevelt's repeated efforts to impose arms embargoes on aggressors, they cheered his efforts to increase hemispheric armed strength.

Hemispheric defense, proposed as the means to keep out foreign entanglements, served Roosevelt to court pacifists. Many of them were former Wilsonians, believers in the League of Nations and enthusiasts for the toothless Kellogg-Briand peace pact, whose ardor for disarmament continued undimmed. Others, who had not notably been pacifists, nevertheless were distressed over the rapid increase in defense appropriations, from $533 million in 1935 to an estimated $937 million in the 1936 budget — almost as much as in 1916. Yet they perceived no peril comparable to that of 1916, protesting that the arms buildup should be limited to a level adequate to defend American soil and to act the part of the "good neighbor." Among the almost five hundred signatories of an appeal to this effect were President James R. Angell of Yale and the Kansas journalist William Allen White, who in 1940 was to play a quite different role.[2]

President Mary Woolley of Mount Holyoke College, who headed another group, the People's Mandate to End War Committee, had been one of the United States delegates to the Geneva arms conference in 1932, yet seemed little aware of the militancy of dictators since. She proposed to Roosevelt that he work for a "truce of God" similar to those of the Middle Ages to provide five or ten years in which world leaders could sort out their problems. She was also enthusiastic over Roosevelt's Good Neighbor policy and his proposal for a "Parley on Pan-American Peace." Her committee had already obtained a million signatures to a petition against all increases in armaments and hoped to obtain eleven million more.[3]

In March, 1936, Roosevelt saw delegations from each group, explained to them in conciliatory fashion his ominous view of the dictators, and related it to the Good Neighbor policy. The prime problem, said the president, was to get nations to live up to the treaties they signed. He pointed to American efforts to limit armaments and the aggressors' false promises not to arm unless other nations threatened them. Someone asked, "Do you think Europe feels it would be to their interest to attack us?"

Roosevelt replied: "That is a problem we have to think about. Are we going to stand for European nations coming in and attacking independent countries on this hemisphere in order to get raw materials? We cannot permit that. We have had one hundred years of opinion on that."[4]

Thus, with considerable success, Roosevelt by 1936 was expounding the need for defense in hemispheric terms of the good neighbor. He was giving a new and reassuring focus to the earlier Wilsonian aim to make the world safe for democracy. The hemisphere was a politically viable way station.

For Roosevelt, the Good Neighbor policy was more than a political device, it was one of his achievements in which he took the most pride. He saw it as a new partnership among the nations of the western hemisphere. Good neighborliness to him was a practical application of the Golden Rule. In his thinking it had begun with the Hyde Park neighbors he had known since boyhood, extended out to the United States, the western hemisphere, and already in his rhetoric of the mid-thirties, to much of the world.

In practice, of course, there was a good bit to lament as well as much to hail in the way that the Good Neighbor policy worked out, for whatever the president's high-minded intentions and frequent recalling of the genesis and triumphs of the Good Neighbor policy, it evolved and operated amidst confusions and vicissitudes, like most else in this imperfect world.

Roosevelt, only slowly in his thinking and out of his reactions to practical problems, arrived at the concepts that came to be embodied in the Good Neighbor policy. He came to office with overall predispositions and principles, which in the realities of the presidency underwent refinement.

Thus there was a considerable element of chance even in the application of the term "Good Neighbor policy" to inter-American relations. In his First Inaugural Address, Roosevelt had declared: "In the field of world policy I would dedicate this Nation to the policy of the good neighbor — the neighbor who resolutely respects himself and, because he does so, respects the rights of others — the neighbor who respects his obligations and respects the sanctity of his agreements in and with a world of neighbors."[5]

A little over a month later, on April 12, 1933, Roosevelt, speaking on Pan-American Day, repeated these words, and applying them to the American hemisphere, declared, "Never before has the significance of the words 'good neighbor' been so manifest in international relations." The phrase "Good Neighbor" thereafter was applied to Roosevelt's Latin American policy. There was nothing really novel in the use of the term in referring to a nation to the south; it appears in the Treaty of Guadalupe Hidalgo of 1848.[6]

The Good Neighbor policy evolved to mean the substitution of nonintervention and, in theory at least, of partnership for the heavy-handed imperialism and paternalism of earlier decades. There too, as in the evolution of the term "Good Neighbor," the transition was neither so sharp nor so complete as Roosevelt would have liked to think. Yet there were decided modifications that made Roosevelt's Latin American policy both more dramatic and more successful than what went before.

While some experts assert vigorously that President Hoover in Latin American as well as domestic affairs anticipated the Roosevelt program, and that the Roosevelt program differed only in being more dramatic, others disagree. There were indeed tangible and significant differences in the Good Neighbor policy as it came to mature. One of the most apparent was the contrast between the rather formal, almost dour official personality of Hoover and the warm, affable approach of Roosevelt. At the secretary of state level, while the correctness of Stimson had been salutary, the warmth of Secretary of State Hull, a seasoned politician, and even the capacity of the somewhat stiff Welles to make friends, were notably effective. Gradually the Roosevelt administration, thanks largely to the insistence of Secretary Hull, developed novel economic policies attractive to Latin American countries.

Concerning nonintervention, while Hoover's avowals were those of a single administration, Roosevelt's became a government commitment transcending a single presidency. It was especially appealing because Roosevelt emphasized cooperation among partners in place of the unilateral fiat of a superpower. There was more fiction than reality in that approach, but it was a fiction essential to the promotion of friendly relations with Latin America. Ultimately, Roosevelt was able through the Good Neighbor program to organize the American states into an inter-American collective security system. They became an association of democracies united to meet the threat from totalitarian nations overseas.

The Good Neighbor policy differed from the Hoover policies especially in its overall impact. As with domestic programs, Roosevelt utilized the pieces he inherited from Hoover, reshaping them, rather as one would blocks of Dutchess County fieldstone, and constructing them into an edifice that bore his own distinctive design. There were false starts and setbacks, and in the end, rather like Roosevelt's youthful remodeling of his home at Hyde Park, the facade was more imposing than what was to be found within. Yet altogether what he achieved was of enduring significance.

Roosevelt's success to a considerable degree depended upon the strength of those concerned with Latin American policy in the State Department. He frequently, even habitually, bypassed Secretary Hull in most other affairs of state, but Hull was doggedly insistent in fighting for a hemispheric reciprocal trade program and appeared most statesmanlike as well as most cordial in his dealings with the American republics. Hull maintained little better than an uneasy modus vivendi with Sumner Welles, who was first ambassador to Cuba, then an assistant secretary, and later under secretary of state, but did not block Welles's effectiveness as the fount of ideas on Latin American policy. When he was quite young, Welles had returned from his post in the Dominican Republic to write *Naboth's Vineyard,* proposing the abandonment of imperialism. He still had some things to learn early in the Roosevelt administration; during the Cuban crisis of 1933, his erstwhile pupils, Roosevelt and Hull, taught him to take an even stronger stand than he wished against intervention.

More than a few administrations have wallowed in Cuban problems from the days of William McKinley on, and Roosevelt's was one of them. Cuba provided a rather salutary education, or refresher course, for as the historian Irwin Gellman has suggested concerning the initial knowledge of these three architects of the Good Neighbor policy, "Roosevelt's was superficial; Hull's almost nonexistent; and Welles's out of date." Cubans, suffering from the depression, were united in their hatred of their president and of the United States, which totally dominated the island's economy. As ambassador, Welles tried to restore stability, and, failing, as a last resort after the president was overthrown, wanted to call in the marines to protect Americans and their property. Roosevelt and Hull were willing to cooperate to the extent of ringing the island with naval vessels, but insisted that the ships were to be used only to evacuate American citizens if their lives were in danger. Cuba was a protectorate and the United States had a treaty right to intervene, as it had several times in the past, but intervention was unpopular at home and would have caused an uproar throughout Latin America.

On September 6, 1933, at the height of the excitement, Roosevelt took an action of which he was later exceedingly proud. He called in the envoys from Argentina, Brazil, Chile, and Mexico to assure them that the purpose of the warships was to rescue Americans; he was not planning intervention, since he hoped the Cubans could solve their own domestic problems. (Hull explained to the press that while the United States did not wish to intervene, it had a treaty responsibility to assure order in Cuba.) Until World War II Roosevelt again and again reminded listeners of his action, giving it a majestic firmness and wiping away the caveats of the time.

Of course, the United States, through the presence of its naval forces and the activities of Ambassador Welles, was making use of pressure to try to stabilize Cuba. One of the effects ultimately was to bring into power in Cuba a young army sergeant, Fulgencio Batista, and it was to him that Roosevelt once directed his boasts of nonintervention in the form of a toast at a state dinner in 1942.

The incident illustrates both the strength and the weakness of the nonintervention policy as Roosevelt and Hull developed it. The policy did become official, was embodied in treaties, and involved a multilateral approach. In the instance of Cuba, the United States did end the protectorate, abrogating the Platt Amendment treaty of 1902 that gave the United States the right to intervene in time of disorder. On the other hand, in order to maintain stability, Roosevelt did not interfere with existing dictators or stop the rise of strongmen like Batista in Cuba and Somoza in Nicaragua, provided they were friendly to the United States. After Roosevelt in 1934 brought home the last marines from Haiti, which had been occupied since the Wilson administration, Walter White of the NAACP, who had been a critic of the occupation, began protesting in vain against the tyranny of the Haitian president. Roosevelt would not intervene. Ultimately, at the end of the 1950s it was the excesses of the Batista dictatorship that led to Fidel Castro.[7]

The second step in developing an effective Good Neighbor policy came about not through Roosevelt but the doggedness of Cordell Hull in insisting upon a reciprocal trade program. Although reciprocal trade had limitations, it came to serve as the essential economic underpinning. The forum at which Hull set forth his proposals for improving trade among the American republics was the Seventh International Conference of American States, which met in Montevideo in December, 1933.

Despite Roosevelt's and his own early misgivings, Hull transformed the conference from an anticipated fiasco into a personal triumph. It was exclusively Hull's and he sorely needed it after his humiliation at the London Economic Conference. Hull never forgave Roosevelt for not backing him either in London or Montevideo. Roosevelt, for his part, graciously refused to allow his own name to be nominated for the Nobel Peace Prize, and energetically promoted that of Hull, who ultimately received the award in 1945.[8]

In the aftermath of the Montevideo conference, Latin American nations continued to hail the new spirit of the United States manifested in Hull's disavowal of intervention. They ignored his warning that the nation still had treaty rights and responsibilities, which under certain dire circumstances could bring intervention. Roosevelt, in his consultations with Latin American envoys during the Cuban crisis, and in his renegotiation of canal arrangements with Panama, removal of the remaining marines from Haiti, and refusal to collect monies on behalf of American bondholders, and subsequently of oil companies, gave meaning to Hull's pledges.

As for reciprocal trade agreements, Congress in June, 1934, passed enabling legislation that, through extensions in succeeding years, ended the tedious and painful congressional lobbying and logrolling that had brought higher and higher tariffs. It was a worldwide, not solely Latin American, program — Sweden was in the first list of nations with which Roosevelt announced negotiations. Gradually he came around to Hull's viewpoint, speeded realistically by the troubles that George Peek, an advocate of the dumping of farm surpluses, made for him.

In reality the treaties during the New Deal years did little to break down basic protection, but rather expedited the import into the United States of tropical products and raw materials that this nation did not produce, in return for sales to Latin America of American manufactured goods. Limited as it was in its functioning, the reciprocal trade program brought some, by no means spectacular, increase in trade between the United States and its southern neighbors. A sharp jump came only with the European crisis and outbreak of war in 1939.[9]

By 1936, the threats of a totalitarian onslaught in Europe caused Roosevelt to give a far higher priority to the Good Neighbor policy. The special relationship inherent in the traditional Monroe Doctrine provided him a wide latitude for innovation, greater than in East Asia and far greater than in Europe. The resistance of a rival Argentina could be expected, but was not comparable to that of a Hitler. In the Americas, Roosevelt would be free to establish a model program of international economic and cultural cooperation, and of mutual security to prevent wars within the hemisphere and to force the totalitarian powers to keep their distance. He could begin building immediately the ideal international neighborhood that he would like to extend to the entire world.

Roosevelt himself was responsible for the convening in December, 1936, of a special conference in Buenos Aires; no president had ever traveled so far while in office as he did to address the meeting. Not only did he hope to carry the Good Neighbor message to South America, but also, though he expected "little practical or immediate effect in Europe," he hoped knowledge of the trip would "spread down to the masses of the people in Germany and Italy." His most extravagant hope was that it could lead to a comparable conference to settle the problems threatening to engulf Europe in war. He also dreamed of a similar settlement with Japan in the western Pacific. Before departing from Washington, he told the cabinet, according to Ickes:

> . . . if we were successful in reaching some sort of an understanding on peace and disarmament at the Buenos Aires conference, we might later try something of the same sort in the Pacific Ocean. This would be an ambitious program. . . . He suggested a

possible agreement for the disarmament of practically everything in the Pacific except Japan, Australia, New Zealand, and Singapore.[10]

The sea voyage, Roosevelt's favorite form of vacation, also gave him an opportunity to relax. There was the fishing, not good, and the horseplay, which filled him with delight when the crew of the *Indianapolis* convened Neptune's court as they crossed the equator. "Great fun. . . . Marvellous costumes," he wrote his wife with all the enthusiasm with which he had once reported to his mother on doings at Groton. "The Pollywogs were given an intensive initiation lasting two days, but we have all survived and are now full-fledged Shellbacks."[11]

Extravaganzas followed, first in Brazil, then in Argentina, where Roosevelt demonstrated to foreign throngs his magic as a campaigner. He was the central figure in spectacles, beginning with his arrival at Rio, where he embraced President Getúlio Vargas while thousands of schoolchildren assembled on the docks waved American flags. Roosevelt easily entered into the hyperbole of Latin America; he was well aware that Vargas and many other heads of state were far from democratic, but was too shrewd ever to say so. When Vargas remarked that some people thought him a dictator, Roosevelt parried that some people in the United States thought he, Roosevelt, was too. At a banquet he hailed Vargas as the co-inventor of the New Deal. He reported to Eleanor: "There was real enthusiasm in the streets. I really begin to think the moral effect of the Good Neighbor Policy is making itself definitely felt." In Buenos Aires again there was an enormous outpouring of people — "a vast surging throng all the way . . . tossed flowers, cheers . . . balconies filled."[12]

Behind the pageantry there lay the serious purpose Roosevelt emphasized in his address before the opening session of the Inter-American Conference. That was to unite the New World with strong bonds of commerce and cultural exchange, and to commit it to the maintenance of peace. The State Department had worked out detailed proposals for the conference, ranging from collective security against outside threats to the exchange of professors. Roosevelt, according to Adolf Berle, who worked on the speech, was addressing himself more to Europe than America. Ideally the conference could be the forerunner of a European conference working toward peace, but, as Berle was well aware, the odds against success were extreme.[13]

Roosevelt inquired rhetorically in his address, "Can we, the Republics of the New World, help the Old World to avert the catastrophe which impends?" He boldly answered, "Yes. I am confident that we can," citing specifics that he implied were equally applicable in Europe. It was his formula for a new order, which, of necessity, he sought first to put into operation in the Americas. At its heart was the strengthening of the processes of constitutional democratic government, on the premise — based on Wilsonian idealism — that the peoples in democracies would insist upon the preservation of peace. It followed that "thus will democratic government be justified throughout the world." The role of the democracies must be to consult for mutual safety against aggressors, to raise living standards and promote social and political justice at home, and, in their relations with other nations, to exchange both commodities and ideas.

Roosevelt seemed to aim his strictures against economic rivalries directly at Germany and Japan, who within the week had signed the anti-Comintern pact. Ostensibly they aimed the treaty at the Soviet Union, but it was perceived as a threat to weaker nations everywhere. He declared: "Every Nation of the world has felt the evil effects of recent efforts to erect trade barriers of every known kind. . . . It is no accident that the Nations which have carried this process farthest are those which proclaim most loudly that they require war as an instrument of their policy."[14]

Roosevelt's words had little impact outside of the Americas. Even in the United States, reporters emphasized the pageantry of the ceremonies and the popularity of Roosevelt rather than the significance of his proposals. *Time* noted "little world-shaking advice" in his speech, but loud applause and bravos at its conclusion. As a means of igniting world sentiment for a program to avert war and promote democracy and prosperity, Roosevelt's visit to Latin America did indeed fail.

Within Latin America, Roosevelt's dramatic trip was of more consequence. He became a living symbol of the Good Neighbor program. There was one embarrassing moment when, as he rose to speak before the delegates to the conference, someone in the galleries shouted, "Down with imperialism!" It was the son of the president of Argentina, who had recently been deported from Brazil for being an undesirable radical. The lone voice was a reminder of what had been the prevalent Latin American view of the United States. Roosevelt did something to alter it, to emphasize that the Monroe Doctrine no longer meant, as in earlier generations, unilateral United States action, but rather collective consultation among the American nations in fending off outside threats.[15]

A painful personal loss saddened Roosevelt's return voyage. In Buenos

Aires, Roosevelt's bodyguard, Gus Gennerich, suddenly died of a heart attack. Although a member of the New York State Police and later of the Secret Service, Gennerich had done more than protect Roosevelt; he had assisted him in dressing and undressing, and getting in and out of bathtubs, swimming pools, and automobiles. He had been buoyant in spirits and uninhibited in his remarks, a favorite of Roosevelt and the family. Roosevelt was so upset that he immediately called his wife. "My heart sank," she wrote in her column, *My Day*, "for I knew that only something serious would make my rather careful husband telephone from that distance."[16]

Roosevelt's notion that from his rostrum in Buenos Aires he could somehow appeal over the heads of Hitler and Mussolini to the German and Italian populace, and thus bring pressure upon the dictators, was a strange bit of fantasy. It was mildly reminiscent of Wilson misgauging the cheering European throngs in the weeks before the Versailles conference opened.

The acclaim left Roosevelt in an exalted state of mind. "I wish you could have seen those South American crowds," he wrote William E. Dodd, ambassador to Germany. "Their great shout as I passed was 'viva la democracía!' " His hosts explained to him, he later told Ickes, that the people regarded him as the defender of democracy as opposed to fascism or communism, and "that his trip strengthened the democratic sentiment throughout the world."

Nevertheless Roosevelt did not lose sight of realities in Europe, and realized the time was not propitious to try to bring Hitler and Mussolini to a conference. That time never arrived.

Roosevelt did succeed, at least in a limited way, in developing the type of international programs he envisaged within the hemisphere. Out of the Buenos Aires conference came a number of treaties providing for consultation if a nation's security were endangered, for further promotion of trade, and for the establishment of a modest cultural exchange program. When it began, one of the first professors, Charles Griffin, in September, 1940, sailed to Venezuela to teach United States history at the Pedagogical Institute in Caracas.[17]

From the Buenos Aires conference on, the threat of world war and of Nazi and Fascist penetration of the Americas became paramount and shaped the nature of the Good Neighbor program. Cultural exchanges were quite modest, and often more popular than academic. The aim seemed largely to win friends for the United States. The most vital way to retain friends was through economic aid, which soon began and, when war came, became relatively substantial. Roosevelt was concerned also that United States orders for raw materials whenever possible be directed toward Latin America to shore up economies there.

Collective security, of necessity, became the crux of the Good Neighbor policy. Shortly after visiting Buenos Aires, Roosevelt sought to provide destroyers for Brazil, but the threat to Argentina and the danger of starting a new South American arms race prevented the transfer or loan. Later, arms did flow to the south. So, too, did experts from the FBI to train security forces that were ostensibly to ferret out Nazis and Fascists, but obviously came to be used also against any opponents of unpopular regimes. Roosevelt's judgment of these regimes was largely based on their attitude toward the United States. There was some excuse for this policy in time of danger from Europe, but it was a continuation of what had been the traditional Washington attitude, and boded ill for the postwar world.

During the war, the Latin American republics, with the exception of Argentina, cooperated with the United States in the alliance of the United Nations against the Axis, and in return received considerable economic and military aid, and much attention through the auspices of Nelson Rockefeller's Office of Inter-American Affairs. Roosevelt still found time to discuss Latin American problems. When he saw the president of Ecuador in 1942, he told newspapermen they talked in part, as he had with a number of heads of American states, "about the future, about trying to get an economy . . . which will raise their standards . . . without hurting our economy."

In the aftermath, Latin America felt neglected with Roosevelt gone and the cold war shifting the focus and funds of the United States toward Europe and Asia. Some critics felt that little had been achieved, that the wealthy had added to their riches and the poverty-stricken had multiplied in numbers, that American armaments had helped bolster the dictators and promoted tyranny. Much that was unfortunate had indeed occurred.

Roosevelt did not succeed in rebuilding Latin American society in the image of the American dream of affluent neighborliness. Under the most optimal circumstances he could have done little to redress the maladjustments of the centuries. Yet many Latin American nations did during the war move rapidly toward becoming urban, moderate societies. The peacekeeping responsibilities and the economic and cultural interchanges were, on the whole, more successful than in other tropical or less industrialized areas of the world. Above all, the relationship with the United States, although far from euphoric at times, was more cordial and cooperative than in the pre–New Deal era.

There is no more positive proof of the change than the warmth and admiration for Roosevelt throughout Latin America. He is still one of the heroes of the hemisphere.

As Roosevelt wished, there remains a larger significance to the Good Neighbor policy. At a time when he was circumscribed in his actions, he was able to establish a prototype in this hemisphere of the international order that he wished extended to the world. In the years since his death, the collective security machinery, trade and economic aid programs, and cultural arrangements with all their blemishes and strengths have indeed knit together large parts of the world. This is as Roosevelt had hoped. In September, 1943, in reporting to Congress on the progress of the war, he declared, "The policy of the Good Neighbor has shown such success in the hemisphere of the Americas that its extension to the whole world seems to be the logical next step."[18]

Chapter 18

THE STRUGGLE TO TRANSFORM THE SUPREME COURT

SPECTACULAR VICTORY in the 1936 election emboldened Roosevelt to embark upon policies equally spectacular. As a means of strengthening democracy, he sought to modernize both the judicial and the executive branches of the government. At first he suffered painful setbacks but ultimately obtained major changes. Later he added a third objective, which he never attained, to overhaul the Democratic party.

Roosevelt introduced his new proposals like sudden bursts of fireworks, but he had long been planning them. In February, 1936, when Secretary Ickes, Charles E. Merriam, a political scientist, and Frederick A. Delano of the National Resources Committee met with him to discuss a government management study, he brought up both the executive branch and the federal courts, as though they were related aspects of the same problem. Two months later he remarked enigmatically to Morgenthau:

"Wait until next year, Henry, I am going to be really radical. . . . I am going to recommend a lot of radical legislation."

Countered Morgenthau: "You are going to be very careful about money spending?"

"Yes, I am."[1]

Indeed Roosevelt was seeking to attain basic changes without increasing the deficit. Simultaneously with his reform efforts he insisted upon taking advantage of the improvements in the economy to curtail spending. Yet in his quest for new triumphs he was to suffer the disappointments of the court fight and the recession of 1937–1938. Bitter over the way that strategically placed Democratic leaders blocked his enterprises, in time he sought to drive them out of his political party, and that led to still further frustrations. It was an outcome far different from what he had envisaged in the euphoric weeks after his 1936 election victory.

Fantasies in the realm of domestic policy lingered for some months. The combination of the acclaim Roosevelt enjoyed throughout the fall campaign trips, together with his triumphs in South America, subtly misled him. There was no doubt of his phenomenal popularity both at home and abroad. There was no doubt, either, of the size of the Democratic majorities in Congress, for the first time three fourths in each house. There was, in addition, the precedent of the Hundred Days, when public pressure upon Congress was so overwhelming that its members frequently voted for measures they disliked. Could not Roosevelt confidently expect that popular enthusiasm would once again force a great surge of legislation through Congress?

Roosevelt was well aware that he would have a serious struggle in Congress. At the time when his bank account of goodwill with the electorate was at its highest point, his balance with the Democratic leadership was almost exhausted. The congressional sessions from 1933 through 1936 had been increasingly difficult, and now some of the basically conservative members, upon whom he had most depended, were freshly reelected and in an independent mood. The day after his return from South America, according to his own account, Senator Pat Harrison gave him a bad morning. Stretched out in his chair, his feet on Roosevelt's desk, Harrison argued on and on that whatever money Congress appropriated for relief should be distributed according to population. Roosevelt countered that it should go where need was greatest, which meant mainly to the big cities. Harrison's formula would favor rural states like Mississippi. James Byrnes, also on the Appropriations Committee, seemed to Tom Corcoran to have gone sour even before the big struggles began. Ickes noted at the end of January that Byrnes, with a term extending beyond that of the president, "has jumped over the traces and gone conservative."[2]

Roosevelt lacked weapons as effective as his earlier ones to bring these leaders into line. Although times were better, numerous constituents were demanding jobs, and Roosevelt did not have a fraction of the earlier patronage to promise them. He did obtain letters of resignation from all of the political appointees to legations and planned some reshuffling, but that took care of only a few demands. In his drive toward a balanced budget, he was cutting back on public works and WPA expenditures, the major source of jobs. Even before Christmas, 1936, Roosevelt was feeling, to his distaste, the pressure for patronage.

Further, by entering his second and presumably last term, Roosevelt was losing substantial political clout. At the outset he, as well as the Democratic leaders, assumed unhesitatingly that in 1940 someone else would be the Democratic candidate for president.

One means of bringing pressure upon Congress nevertheless, Ickes suggested (reading Roosevelt a letter from Raymond Robbins), would be for the president to serve notice that in 1938 he would seek to elect friends and defeat enemies. Roosevelt was taken with the idea. Early in the new term, he said, he might summon congressional leaders to the White House and warn them of his intentions. There quite possibly was the seed of the 1938 purge attempt, for Roosevelt could nurture grudges as well as warm loyalties. There is no evidence that Roosevelt early in 1937 made advance threats to bludgeon the leaders, but reorganization of the Democratic party did become a prime aim after he suffered frustrations.[3]

Again, as after the 1934 election, there were questions over the loyalty of the top-heavy Democratic majority in Congress. In November, 1936, Roosevelt seemed more worried about the left than the right. Steve Early confided to one of the Washington correspondents that the president was concerned over the number of crackpots who had ridden into Congress with him, fearing they would enact bad legislation and override his vetoes. These views represented a passing mood of Roosevelt's. He foresaw difficult struggles, as in the two previous sessions of Congress, but he expected to win them.[4]

Roosevelt had no notion how tough the fights would be, and operated with an unjustified degree of self-confidence. He looked upon his presumably last term less as meaning a decline in power over Congress than as endowing him with independence, both from Congress and from previous advisers in the White House. From the original brain trust, both Moley and Tugwell had finally made their departure in 1936, but Rosenman still was of vital assistance in writing speeches. Shifts were more in faces than in ideologies. Since the beginning of the New Deal, there had been almost kaleidoscopic changes among those closest to the president; there had been momentary favorites, but almost no one upon whom he was fully dependent for very long. That had also been true in his relationship with congressional advisers. "I owe nothing to anyone," he remarked a few days after the election, felt free from political obligations, and also was more than ever disposed to take only his own political counsels. On his two major proposals, Supreme Court and administrative reform, he sought a narrower range of opinions than was usual for him.[5]

What was more out of character, Roosevelt did not go through the customary preliminary ritual, at which he was so adroit, of flattering, cajoling, and placating key members of Congress to smooth the way for his proposals. He could justify this omission on the grounds that the element of surprise was vital; after the damage had been done, late in March, when something had leaked from congressional leaders, he remarked to reporters, "that shows why it was impossible to talk to them before I announced the Supreme Court thing." Another probable reason, but one impossible to prove, is that Roosevelt, as his wife has pointed out, was becoming bored with the congressional leadership. It was not pleasant to have Pat Harrison slouching in a chair, interminably seeking to thwart what Roosevelt wanted to do, or to have to mollify the conservative Joe Robinson with promises of additional patronage. He had gradually slipped out of the habit of seeing the leaders very often or of keeping them informed. Besides, Roosevelt was rather mercurial in his interests, focusing upon objects of his immediate enthusiasm. The manipulation of the Democratic leaders no longer was one of these. The swaying of crowds, almost in the fashion of Woodrow Wilson, was more exciting.[6]

Showman that Roosevelt was, he continued to delight in surprises, overlooking the fact that recovery had dulled the feeling of urgency, on the part of both Congress and the electorate — an urgency that had done much to push his Hundred Days program to successful enactment. There was no longer an emergency to justify startling, unexpected proposals. Nor did Roosevelt sense the degree of alienation of those upon whom he must depend for legislation. By the beginning of January, 1937, he had made up his mind about what he wanted to do and embarked upon a great test of will with the congressional leadership.

First, he sent Congress a bill to modernize the administrative branch; then he startled Congress with his parallel bill, purportedly to bring efficiency to the judicial system.

Early in 1937, Roosevelt in both his State of the Union and Inaugural Addresses developed the same theme: an emphasis upon democracy, the necessity to make it work on behalf of the social and economic welfare of the American people, and the question whether the nation could reach these goals unless the Supreme Court gave its sanction.

At a press conference earlier, Roosevelt had given a poignant illustration of what he meant: an episode at New Bedford, Massachusetts, during the 1936 campaign, when a young woman in the crowd tried to reach his car to pass him an envelope. Roosevelt asked a Secret Service man to get the note, and quoted it from memory to the reporters:

"Dear Mr. President: I wish you could do something to help us girls. You are the only recourse we have got left. We have been working in a . . . garment factory, and up to a few months ago we were getting our minimum pay of $11 a week. . . . Today the 200 of us girls have been cut down to $4 and $5 and $6 a week. You are the only man that can do anything about it."

Roosevelt commented: "That is something that so many of us found in the Campaign, that these people think that I have the power to restore things like minimum wages and maximum hours and the elimination of child labor . . . and, of course, I haven't got any power to do it."[7]

In his Second Inaugural Address, Roosevelt took a statesmanlike approach. It was a dramatic occasion and he made the most of it. A cold driving rain was soaking the audience, and sweeping into the inaugural pavilion in front of the Capitol. As he stood reading his inaugural message, the raindrops beating on the microphones in front of him, seven of the nine Supreme Court justices, including all the conservatives, were arrayed in the pavilion with him. Once again he addressed his concern to bring through democratic means a more abundant life to the American people, especially those who were economically deprived, and invoked the precedent of the Fathers of the Constitution in establishing a government strong enough to achieve these same objectives, asserting: "The Constitution of 1787 did not make our democracy impotent."

Roosevelt set forth an eloquent bill of particulars on the national needs:

> I see a great nation, upon a great continent, blessed with a great wealth of natural resources. . . . I see a United States which can demonstrate that, under democratic methods of government, national wealth can be translated into a spreading volume of human comforts hitherto unknown, and the lowest standard of living can be raised far above the level of mere subsistence.
>
> But here is the challenge to our democracy: In this nation I see tens of millions of its citizens — a substantial part of its whole population — who at this very moment are denied the greater part of what the very lowest standards of today call the necessities of life. . . .

Specifics followed, then a poignant summation that he himself penned:

> I see one-third of a nation ill-housed, ill-clad, ill-nourished.

Roosevelt said he painted that picture not in despair, but in hope.

> The test of our progress is not whether we add more to the abundance of those who have much; it is whether we provide enough for those who have too little.[8]

These strong words caught the attention of listeners and commentators. The veiled reference to the Supreme Court seemed little noticed.

For the remainder of the day, Roosevelt seemed to be dedicating himself to the common man, sharing the drenching as he rode in an open car with Mrs. Roosevelt. He stood for an hour and a half exposed to more rain, as he reviewed the inaugural parade in a stand modeled on Jackson's home, The Hermitage. Mrs. Roosevelt's new hat was sodden into the form of a bathing cap; Roosevelt went through two silk hats. Then three thousand guests crushed into the White House for tea. When Roosevelt greeted the reporters two days later, he was still buoyant.[9]

Talking about the inaugural ceremonies afterward with Rosenman, Roosevelt remarked: "When the Chief Justice read me the oath and came to the words 'support the Constitution of the United States' I felt like saying: 'Yes, but it's the Constitution as *I* understand it, flexible enough to meet any new problem of democracy — not the kind of Constitution your Court has raised up as a barrier to progress and democracy.' "[10]

With the inauguration past, Roosevelt was ready finally to act on the Supreme Court problem. Since his vigorous response to the invalidation of the NRA in the spring of 1935, he had been pondering alternate solutions, consulting with persons as diverse in background as George Fort Milton, a Tennessee newspaperman, and, at Frankfurter's suggestion, young Charles Wyzanski in the Department of Justice. He kept hoping that the problem would solve itself through vacancies on the Supreme Court, but the justices doggedly remained on the bench. Perhaps there was an economic reason: they risked salary cuts if they retired, such as Holmes had suffered. Certainly there was an ideological one, although they did not state it as firmly as had the ailing Chief Justice Taft, who had tried to survive President Hoover, whom he distrusted: "I must stay on the court in order to prevent the Bolsheviki from getting control."[11]

No matter why the conservative justices were holding out, the effect was the same. The fervor of their anti–New Deal decisions gave credence to Roosevelt's feeling that they were not likely to abandon their seats, and their strict interpretation of the Constitution was serving as a bulwark against change they abhorred. "The Supreme Court," Barry Karl, a historian, has suggested, "forced the issue." It was "the enunciator of the fact that change was taking place and that such change would have to be woven into the traditional fabric of government or dealt with as revolution."[12]

By the time of his reelection, Roosevelt was determined that the changes should become the warp and woof of the traditional fabric of government, that they were by no means revolutionary. His and the Supreme Court's interpretations of the role of government differed as fundamentally (though in strikingly reverse ways) as those of the nationalistic Marshall court and the states' rights Jeffersonian Republicans at the beginning of the nineteenth century.

In his liberal construction of the Constitution, Roosevelt felt that he had behind him an overwhelming proportion of the American public and even a minority of the court itself. He set forth that construction carefully in his public addresses, substantiating it with quotations from some of the tart dissents to the anti–New Deal decisions of 1936.

In consequence, Roosevelt decided that he needed only to transform the liberal minority on the court into a majority. For some time the Department of Justice had been researching various alternatives for him, consulting some outside constitutional authorities. Nothing fit into the overall judicial reorganization bill that Roosevelt wished to send to Congress. Subsequently, Attorney General Cummings suggested, "Why not make the judge's age the principle?"[13]

The device for carrying out the principle appealed to Roosevelt's sense of irony, for its original proponent had been none other than James C. McReynolds, one of the most adamantly conservative of the justices, about to celebrate his seventy-fifth birthday. As attorney general in the Wilson administration, McReynolds had recommended that when any federal judge except those on the Supreme Court failed to retire at the age the law provided, since constitutionally they could not be obliged to retire, the president should be empowered to appoint an additional judge. There was no retirement age for Supreme Court justices. If the judicial reorganization bill set the age at seventy, Roosevelt would be able to appoint six additional justices. It was, he remarked to one of his advisers, "the answer to a maiden's prayer."[14]

There was more cleverness than careful evaluation in Roosevelt's reasoning that he did not have to give advance warning to his allies, the leaders of the progressives, farmers, and labor, since they would be behind him anyway. Nor would he consult the nominally loyal but conservative Democratic leaders in Congress, since they might seek to thwart him. To intensify the popular pressure upon Congress, he would make court reform the priority piece of legislation that it must pass before it took action on agricultural and wages and hours bills. Recovery, which seemed well advanced, was to be hostage to reform in the spring of 1937.

All these decisions were dubious; what followed was a formula for disaster. That was Roosevelt's insistence upon presenting the proposal not in the realistic terms that he had been setting forth to the nation from the aftermath of the NRA decision through his 1937 State of the Union message, but rather in the specious terms that the superannuated justices could not keep up with their work and therefore needed the assistance of additional appointees.

That was a statement which, while not true, was logical in placing the proposal in the larger matrix of a reorganization of the judiciary comparable to that of the executive branch. A judiciary reform bill was needed to provide more judges in lower courts to keep up with the press of litigation. Further, over a hundred federal judges had placed their own roadblocks in Roosevelt's path during 1935–1936 through issuing injunctions restraining the operation of one or another New Deal measure. Roosevelt and Cummings wanted to slow down or stop that practice; out of the whirlwind of the court fight they did reap a measure specifying that the power should be limited to three-judge courts. The setting in which Roosevelt placed the court plan was of little general concern. It was the plan itself and the manner in which Roosevelt presented it that would be the focus of interest.

By the end of January, 1937, Roosevelt, with the aid of Cummings and Solicitor General Stanley Reed, had his court reform plan in its dubious packaging almost in final form. When Donald R. Richberg, who had been chairman of the NRA Board, first became privy to the secret late in January, meeting with Roosevelt, Cummings, and Reed, he immediately protested that Roosevelt should candidly state his reasons for the proposal. Reed firmly concurred. So did Rosenman when he was introduced into the circle. The emphasis even in the final message remained on overworked judges and crowded calendars resulting in delays in justice. So Roosevelt insisted it be, despite warnings of consequences. Near the end of her life, Eleanor Roosevelt still would shake her head and say that she could not imagine what had led her husband to follow such a disastrous course.[15]

On February 5, 1937, Roosevelt exploded the bombshell. He had kept security so tight that he did not show his press secretary, Steve Early, a copy of the message until the afternoon before. When the cabinet members and a handful of congressional leaders assembled, he gave each of them a copy, and made only a few remarks. Those present said little; Roosevelt did not ask for comments. In each house of Congress a few minutes later, as reading clerks delivered the message, the initial reaction was one of surprise. There, embedded in a message and bill ostensibly intended to bring about greater efficiency and modernization of the courts, was a proposal to circumvent the Supreme Court obstruction of the New Deal. Only in a single passage did Roosevelt dwell upon the problem that he had addressed so firmly in his State of the Union message:

"Modern complexities call also for a constant infusion of new blood in the courts, just as it is needed in executive functions of the Government and in private business. Older men, assuming that the scene is the same as it was in the past, cease to explore or inquire into the present or the future."[16]

The immediate congressional response to the proposal was about what Roosevelt must have anticipated. Ardent New Dealers and a few progressives greeted it with enthusiasm. In the House, Maury Maverick of Texas hastily inscribed his name on his mimeographed copy of the bill and rushed to introduce it by dropping it into the hopper. The older, powerful Democratic leaders were far from pleased. In the car riding back from the meeting with Roosevelt, Hatton Sumners, chairman of the House Judiciary Committee, remarked ominously, "Boys, here's where I cash in my chips." His immediate and dogged opposition was a key factor in leading the White House to settle on a strategy of pushing the measure through the Senate first. Most of the leaders, whatever their personal feelings, could be counted upon, professionals that they were, to "stay hitched." While the bill was being read in the Senate chamber, Vice President Garner in the lobby expressed his feelings to a group of senators by holding his nose and gesturing thumbs down. Yet throughout the fight, Garner extended at least his nominal loyalty to the president. Even Senator Henry F. Ashurst, chairman of the Judiciary Committee, who as early as 1933 complained in his diary that the New Deal was transmuting the American way of life into state socialism, after a full day's wait announced that he favored Roosevelt's proposal.

From congressional conservatives there came the vehement protests that the president had expected, but they seemed at first the lamentations of those raising the banner of a lost cause. "Of course I shall oppose it," declared Senator Glass of Virginia. "I shall oppose it with all the strength which remains to me, but I don't imagine for a minute that it'll do any good. Why, if the President asked Congress to commit suicide tomorrow they'd do it."

Throughout the country there was also protest from conservative publicists, organizations, and journals. But since they, like Glass and his beleaguered associates in Congress, had long since been hurling their jeremiads at the White House, there seemed little new or potentially fatal in their thrusts. Roosevelt, confident, was ready to pursue the same strategy that had been successful in 1935, to remain silent, let the opposition exhaust itself pouring out invective, and then push the program through Congress. As Glass had lamented, Roosevelt held huge majorities in each house of Congress, and the leaders, though reluctant, seemed ready to go along with him except for Sumners. Senate Majority Leader Robinson could be counted on to stay loyal, not only through long habit but because he felt Roosevelt had promised him the first vacancy on the Supreme Court.[17]

Roosevelt was basking in false security. In several vital ways the struggle with Congress in 1937 was quite different from that of 1935. The loyalties of a number of the conservative Democratic leaders had already been stretched close to the breaking point — the snapping of Sumners' ties was indicative of how close the southern Democratic leaders were to the edge. Roosevelt's failure to take them into his confidence earlier, to invest them with the prestige of being coplanners, left them irritated. Other legislative proposals of his in 1937 were distasteful, and even without the court fight would have made the session exceedingly difficult for him. These were old factors exacerbated.

What was new was the instant protest of a considerable part of those within Congress and throughout the country who to this point had been supporters of Roosevelt and the New Deal. In 1935, Roosevelt had enjoyed the backing of the center as he struggled against the right and the far left, against the groups he had labeled the "lunatic fringe." Now a weighty part of the liberals and moderates joined the revolt against the court plan.

Indignant though many of them had been over the anti–New Deal decisions, a considerable part of the liberals viewed the court as the bulwark of American liberties. At that very time, when European dictators were stripping populaces of their liberties, they were especially sensitive to the danger that the United States might suffer the same malign fate. Certainly they, unlike the reactionaries, did not fear Roosevelt's intentions, but were wary of what some unscrupulous successor might undertake. What might another Huey Long attempt if he came into power in Washington? In the 1780s the attacks upon the courts by Daniel Shays's followers spurred both men of substance and those of Enlightenment views to fabricate a constitution providing for a strong judiciary. In the 1930s many of those with progressive and liberal ideas aligned themselves with those of property against what they perceived as an ultimate danger greater than the immediate problem. Of those who had sought, through one or another proposed constitutional amendment, to lift the economic restrictions that the court was imposing upon the federal and state governments, many feared the Roosevelt plan as an ominous portent.

One of the unhappier aspects of the proposal was its deviousness. No sophisticated person took Roosevelt seriously when he insisted afterward that what he had wanted was to speed the business of the court through providing additional aid to superannuated justices. That smacked of the trickery of demagogues. Particularly offended were the admirers of Justice Brandeis, one of the oldest justices on the court and one of the most liberal. In the later stages of the controversy, when it was being fought on the clear-cut issue of whether or not the court should invalidate social and economic legislation, the question of the age of the justices did much to becloud the question.

A considerable number of the progressives in the Senate were either staunchly opposed to or at best lukewarm toward Roosevelt's plan. One exception among the Republicans was Robert La Follette of Wisconsin, who took the Roosevelt view that the court was blocking vital economic programs and so stated vigorously both in the Senate and to the nation. The ailing Hiram Johnson of California, already close to deserting Roosevelt, jumped wholeheartedly into the opposition and for the rest of his life was one of the most scathing opponents of Roosevelt. On the Democratic side, there were several progressives who defected, most painfully of all Burton K. Wheeler of Montana, who became the leader of the Democratic opposition in the Senate and expressed eloquently the misgivings that troubled so many liberals.

The opposition mounting in Congress mirrored the voices throughout the nation. National resistance to the court-packing plan gained intensity, and supportive mail flooded in to the congressional conservatives and rebels alike. For the first time, the opposition to Roosevelt had seized upon a cause of widespread popularity. His weeks of silence, rather than leading the opponents to talk themselves out and become isolated, gave them the opportunity to become firmly organized in Congress and to win increasing support from their constituencies.

Roosevelt's confidence led him to react with too little too late. He did not turn over to the congressional leaders the task of organizing firm majorities for the bill. Rather he assigned his own staff, which while competent and experienced, could not call upon longtime loyalties as would Senator Robinson and his inner circle. The onus thus fell firmly upon Roosevelt rather than being shared, as it had been in 1935, with congressional leadership. He and his lieutenants made full use of the assignment of WPA projects and of patronage to try to win waverers or punish opponents. When Wheeler refused the president's blandishments, Roosevelt tried even to deprive him of farm patronage.

By this time, the opposition Democrats had already effectively organized themselves under Wheeler. They also formed a strategy committee that met almost every day. It was a surprising coalition of liberals and conservatives, bringing Wheeler together with senators like Harry Byrd of Virginia and Millard Tydings of Maryland. The Republican minority was solidly united behind Charles L. McNary, William E. Borah, and Arthur Vandenberg, who agreed on the day the bill was introduced to remain silent in the Senate and let Wheeler and his Democratic cohorts carry the brunt of the fight against the bill.

At the end of February, the supporters of the court bill were much weaker than Roosevelt might have expected. The lines were drawn on a question of constitutional separation of powers rather than on that of the desirability of New Deal measures the court had invalidated.

Since the fight was not going well, Roosevelt's strategists persuaded him to abandon his ill-conceived subterfuge in proposing the court bill, and to begin to fight for it with the same candor he had displayed in his "horse-and-buggy" press conference and State of the Union message. In early March, Roosevelt, a month late, set forth clear, powerful reasons for adding new justices to the Supreme Court. The intervening weeks had been punishing ones, since they had left him open to the charge of seeking to augment his power through subterfuge in the style of a would-be dictator rather than a democratic leader. It would have been more effective rhetoric had it accompanied the bill to Congress.[18]

Roosevelt's theme was that the Supreme Court was blocking the New Deal efforts to improve the lot of the American people, and it must not be allowed to do so any longer. He enumerated the effects of the unfavorable Supreme Court decisions, and then warned of the future. Roosevelt made his appeal in terms of the needs of the underprivileged; Senator Wheeler delivered a radio rebuttal on quite a different basis: "Create now a political Court to echo the ideas of the executive and you have created a weapon; a weapon which in the hands of another President could . . . cut down those guarantees of liberty written by the blood of your forefathers."[19]

Both Roosevelt and Wheeler were emphasizing the fear of dictatorships and the need to make democracy effective. Roosevelt addressed his appeal particularly to the underprivileged, and Wheeler his to the middle class — which in this instance was the more receptive and more articulate.

Beyond these logical, ultimate arguments lay a wide range of motivations, some clear and firmly stated, some difficult or impossible to document. Unquestionably those well to the right throughout the nation sought the defeat and humiliation of Roosevelt, a negating of previous New Deal programs, and a blocking of future ventures. Senator Carter Glass best articulated the fears of many southerners in and out of Congress when, in a radio address he delivered in April, he warned that a Roosevelt-dominated court could be a threat to white supremacy, that it might open the way to a new Reconstruction.

Many congressional leaders were more moderate. Senator Pat Harrison was less alarmed over the court plan than concerned with placing limits upon Roosevelt and the New Deal. Harrison's Mississippi constituents rather heavily favored the plan; Harrison was determined to keep New Deal spending within bounds and under congressional rather than presidential control. Consequently, until the bitter end of the fight there was a strong disposition toward compromise among many of the key figures in Congress.

It is tempting to view Roosevelt as having fallen into the same trap as had Wilson earlier, in the struggle over ratification of the Versailles Treaty, when he was so overconfident, so certain that the people were behind him that he refused to make any sort of deal. The analogy is only on the surface. Into March, there seemed no need for Roosevelt to make a deal, even though he was encountering decidedly more opposition in Congress and the country than he had expected.

Subsequent events drastically altered that scenario. Roosevelt then continued to resist compromise, for reasons which, like those of his congressional opponents, seemed to involve political prestige more than legislative substance.

In the first stage, through March, except for the unusual excitement over the Supreme Court issue, events moved much as in past encounters. In February Democratic leaders, in private referring to Roosevelt's proposal as raw, wanted in one way or another to settle the matter quickly before it did too much damage to the party in Congress. Garner led a delegation to the White House to try to persuade Roosevelt to accept two or three justices rather than the six he had requested. Roosevelt was in high spirits, and firm in his rejection of the suggestion. They went ahead with another project of not much interest to him, and pushed through both houses a bill Sumners had introduced that provided full retirement benefits to justices, in the hope that some of the conservatives might take advantage of it. Roosevelt signed the measure, but it seemed of little consequence then.

In March, Senator Ashurst finally began Senate hearings on the court bill and subtly transformed them into a great national forum against the measure, dragging on and on for weeks. Wheeler made use of the forum when he appeared at the hearings and produced a letter signed by Chief Justice Charles Evans Hughes and approved by Justices Louis Brandeis and Willis Van Devanter, undermining the reasoning in Roosevelt's message calling for additional justices. The Supreme Court, Hughes insisted, was able to keep up with its work load.[20]

Already Hughes and his colleagues had prepared a more potent response to the court plan, which in the spring totally changed the nature of the struggle. Whether it was a deliberate response, or only incidental to a following of constitutional precedents, their decisions of late March into May undermined the basic reasons for adding additional justices to the court. During the months before Roosevelt announced his court plan, when it was clear that some measure of constitutional amendment was imminent, Hughes was concerned that the court might suffer a serious loss of prestige, as it had during Reconstruction. He was relieved, therefore, when on a new case involving a state minimum wage Justice Owen J. Roberts decided to vote with Hughes and the three liberal justices, creating a five-to-four majority holding the law constitutional. Hughes reportedly congratulated Roberts, telling him he had saved the court. The vote came at a judicial conference in January before Roosevelt announced his court plan, but Hughes did not deliver the decision until Monday, March 29. He differentiated it from the decision of the previous year, but the effect was to wipe out the judicial no-man's-land, to extend state authority over at least the working conditions of women. Perhaps the decision was no more than an aberration from the prevailing pattern. The expectation continued that on the key decision soon to be announced concerning the National Labor Relations Act, the court would be unfavorable. Monday, April 12, became, then, the crucial day in the court fight, for Chief Justice Hughes read the decision, for a five-to-four majority again including Roberts, upholding the constitutionality of the legislation. The decision was a sensation, validating as it did a major New Deal economic program, the regulation of labor relations, at the very time when furor over the sit-down strikes was at its height.[21]

At the White House, Roosevelt's outward response to the news was jubilation. He told reporters, "Today is a very, very happy day." But when the serious question of his future action arose, he cited to them the remark of one newspaperman that the no-man's-land had been replaced with "Robert's land." He raised immediately the question whether favorable decisions would continue, and within a few days was asking it specifically concerning the Social Security Act, which was also before the Supreme Court that spring.[22]

At the Capitol, the Roosevelt forces were in disarray, and Wheeler was in fine fettle. The recruiting of moderates from this point on would be easy.

Roosevelt had won his great objective, to remove the obstacle of the Supreme Court from his path. The time had come to hold the bill in abeyance, to return to it later only if the Supreme Court failed to validate the Social Security Act or some other major legislation. Left pending, it might serve as a persuader to the justices to continue their new course of voting. Or, if he chose, Roosevelt could gracefully accept a solid compromise. As Byrnes commented in private, "Why run for a train after you've caught it?" Robinson sent word to the president through Joseph Keenan, assistant to the attorney general:

"This bill's raising hell in the Senate . . . but if the President wants to compromise I can get him a couple of extra Justices tomorrow. What he ought to do is say he's won, which he has, agree to compromise, to make the whole thing sure, and wind the whole business up."[23]

Roosevelt firmly insisted upon continuing the struggle; he would not stop while he was ahead. There was the uncertainty over the future course of the Supreme Court. He and his advisers wanted to be sure it would be reliable. If he accepted a bill to appoint two justices, he would still not be sure, since the first appointee (in keeping with a pledge Farley had given two years earlier) would have to be the conservative Robinson.[24]

In his ebullience that spring Roosevelt let the controversy slip into an ugly stage. Increasingly, as reason after reason for the original proposal lapsed, it seemed to become fundamentally a power struggle between the president and the Senate. Who was to be master? It is likely that Roosevelt saw the chance to give the conservatives their comeuppance; it is even more certain that they were rallying around the Supreme Court issue, which increasingly they were in a position to win, as a means of settling their scores with him.

In mid-May, Roosevelt returned from a fishing trip, bringing with him on the train from Texas young Lyndon B. Johnson, who had just won an interim election to the House campaigning on the Supreme Court issue. Roosevelt, in his misgauged optimism, called in Robinson, Bankhead, and Rayburn to tell them that they didn't know what was going on back home, that they must continue the fight. Even if they lost, there was 1938, when he could go to the electorate. And there was, he added, naming a date that startled them, 1940.[25]

Several days later, when Roosevelt was closer in touch with Washington realities, his advisers suggested that he let the bill go over to the next session. He was readier to listen, but just then circumstances intervened. Senator Borah persuaded his friend Justice Van Devanter to submit a letter to Roosevelt requesting retirement from active service, on the same day the Senate Judiciary Committee brought in an adverse report on the bill. That left Roosevelt in the unpalatable position of having only one vacancy to fill, one that if it did not go as promised to the conservative Robinson would create havoc in the Senate. Again, Roosevelt could have attained compromise had he requested it instantly, at the same time that he nominated the popular majority leader. Rather, while the debate continued, he delayed for days, hurting Robinson's feelings. Then came the final blow, on May 24, the court's decision upholding the Social Security Act.[26]

For some days Roosevelt was not clear in his own mind what he wanted to do. He dictated a memorandum concluding:

> He has yet to obtain these two *objectives:*
> (a) insurance of the continuity of . . . liberalism and
> (b) a more perfect judicial mechanism for giving a maximum of justice in a minimum of time.[27]

These remaining objectives became his justification for continuing the struggle in the Senate. On June 3, deciding he would settle for as much as he could get from Congress, he came to terms with Robinson. Both the working out of an acceptable scheme and obtaining its passage became Robinson's responsibility. Robinson was delighted to take command, and such was his eagerness to fulfill his ambition to sit upon the court that, although he was tired and ailing, he plunged into the undertaking with all his remaining energy. The compromise proposed was to appoint one extra justice for each one sitting on the court who had passed the age of seventy-five, but to allow the president only one such appointment per year. The compromise bill fared badly. In early July, Robinson, facing the prospect of a lengthy filibuster, struggled on past the point of his physical capacities, despite chest pains. The drama then came to an abrupt climax. On the morning of July 14, Robinson was found dead in his apartment.[28]

Amid the lengthy funeral ritual, with numbers of congressional leaders accompanying Robinson's body back to Little Rock, the politicking reached a crescendo. Roosevelt wisely did not go with them, although his failure thus to pay tribute to Robinson evoked fresh criticism. What was at stake on the long train ride to and from Arkansas was not the court compromise; that was beyond saving. Rather it was the future of the Senate leadership. Roosevelt had a heavy stake in it, but had to keep sufficient distance to pay obeisance to the fiction that he was allowing the Senate Democrats a free choice.

For some days past, as the familiar arguments for and against a court-packing bill were filling the Senate chamber, the struggle in the lobby for the succession was already under way in anticipation that Robinson was about to be elevated to the Supreme Court. Dissidents opposing Roosevelt's policies in general and the court plan specifically were rallying behind Byrnes of South Carolina, whom Garner had been backing, and Harrison of Mississippi. At the crucial moment, it was rumored, Byrnes would withdraw in favor of Harrison. Roosevelt supporters were aligning themselves in favor of Alben Barkley of Kentucky.

Roosevelt's immediate reaction to the death of Robinson was to throw his weight behind Barkley, the acting majority leader, sending him a letter renewing the call for judicial reform. The letter stirred excitement as a tacit endorsement of Barkley. On the funeral train, a large number of the senators, including some who had favored the court plan, coalesced behind Harrison. The counting of the ballots at the Democratic caucus on July 21 was a tense occasion. With only one vote remaining to be counted, the tally stood at 37 to 37. The final vote went to Barkley.[29]

Many professional politicians, Farley among them, considered the outcome a Pyrrhic victory for Roosevelt. Certainly it was costly, since it gave Harrison and Byrnes political freedom to oppose Roosevelt more vigorously than in the past. It deprived him, too, of a leader who could wrest votes from wavering senators by eliciting their personal loyalties. Barkley could not claim so strong a circle of intimates, and was to be more of a White House errand boy. On the other hand, as long as possible in the court fight, and often before, Roosevelt had treated his congressional leaders like errand boys. One lesson he learned from that struggle was to treat them overall with more consideration. Legislative conferences at the White House would become more regular in the future.

For Roosevelt to have remained genuinely neutral and allowed Harrison to become majority leader would have been costly also. As Roosevelt complained to Farley later, he was seriously at odds with Harrison over spending and taxation legislation. Nor was Harrison's prime loyalty ever to Roosevelt. In the growing swing to the right in the Senate, antedating the court fight and the 1936 election, future difficulties were predictable. They might well have been greater had Harrison been majority leader.

As for the court program, despite Roosevelt's ringing message to Barkley the struggle was at an end. By the time the mourners had returned from Arkansas it was obvious that not even the flimsiest face-saving compromise could win Senate approval. On July 20, Garner visited the Oval Office to give Roosevelt his appraisal. "Do you want it with the bark on or the bark off?" Garner inquired. When Garner explained that "with the bark off" meant the plain truth, Roosevelt laughed, and asked for it. Garner told him he was whipped and he should end the court issue as quickly as he could. Roosevelt shrugged his shoulders and accepted reality. The next day, as soon as Barkley had been elected majority leader, Garner told Wheeler he could write his own ticket, but urged him to be reasonable.

That afternoon, a motion came before the Senate to recommit the court bill to the Judiciary Committee. Hiram Johnson inquired, "The Supreme Court is out of the way?" He was assured it was. Johnson intoned, "Glory be to God!"

A few weeks later, Congress enacted and Roosevelt signed a measure making minor reforms in the lower courts, and expediting the determination of constitutional questions.[30] In the aftermath of the court fight, Roosevelt made one further step toward his ultimate goal. He discomfited his conservative opponents by securing the confirmation of a conspicuous liberal to the seat on the court left vacant through the retirement of Van Devanter. Roosevelt settled upon one whom the Senate could not well reject, and acted with such secrecy that he wrote the nomination in his own hand. Vice President Garner opened the envelope, and read to the Senate the name of Senator Hugo L. Black of Alabama. Everyone was astonished.

Tradition won out over outrage nevertheless. Despite whispers throughout the Senate that early in his career Black had belonged to the Ku Klux Klan, there was no searching investigation at the brief Judiciary Committee hearing and no serious challenge in the Senate debate. Black, refusing to make a public statement, merely told friends that at this time he was not a Klansman. To have said more would have eliminated him from the court and dealt a fresh defeat to Roosevelt. On that basis, Senator Borah assured the Senate that Black did not belong to the Klan. On August 17 he was confirmed by a vote of 63 to 16.

In September, while Black was vacationing in Europe, Scripps Howard newspapers ran a series of investigative articles proving that Black, as a young politician, had indeed belonged to the Klan. Roosevelt and Black were able to weather the furor, which soon subsided as Black began a most distinguished career on the Supreme Court.[31]

The court fight was over. In January, 1938, Justice Sutherland retired and Roosevelt made a second appointment, Stanley Reed. Within two years he appointed three more justices, Felix Frankfurter, William O. Douglas, and Frank Murphy. He had acquired a "Roosevelt Court." No longer was there a serious threat to federal or state programs of economic and social reform. From this standpoint the court fight had brought the great end Roosevelt sought. The end was far more acceptable because he had not attained even a compromise; the legitimation of the New Deal reforms came from a court with the traditional nine justices, and it came fundamentally before even the first Roosevelt appointee took his seat. A momentous turning point had come in constitutional law.

The price was high. Politically, Roosevelt had suffered a staggering setback from a Congress top-heavy with Democrats. He had expended a large part of his political capital on a failed enterprise. He had given a winning cause to conservatives long opposed to him, and had seen former allies, even some of the strongest progressives, join them. What he doubtless intended to be political showmanship, drama to enlist the interest of the electorate, appeared to his opponents and even a considerable part of the public to be a dangerous deviousness, smacking of dictatorial ways. The suspicions the court fight engendered carried over into struggles over other domestic issues, and ominously colored the growing debate over foreign policy. It was, Corcoran mused long afterward, as though one had a million dollars in the bank and suddenly received notice one was overdrawn. For months, Corcoran remembers, Roosevelt was depressed.[32]

In keeping with his lifelong habits, Roosevelt let no sign of his low spirits appear outside his closest circle. He was correct in thinking that the people were largely with him, and he continued to match his strength with his opponents. He was battered but by no means beaten. The struggle over the court plan had settled constitutional issues for decades to come. The contest with the congressional conservatives continued unabated.[33]

Chapter 19

NEW DEALER WITH BRAKES ON

"I HAVE JUST BEGUN TO FIGHT," Roosevelt had remarked in May, 1937, on his return from a fishing trip. He was alluding both to the struggle over the Supreme Court and his broad agenda of reform. Since he firmly believed that liberals have only brief and infrequent opportunities to achieve change, he wanted to make full use of his electoral mandate while it was still fresh. He had cited Wilson to newspaper editors in April: "You have a liberal administration in Government for eight years and then a conservative lasting sixteen years. Therefore, in eight years you have to accomplish all you possibly can."[1]

Despite his outward militancy, Roosevelt operated with caution, as in his support of striking workers and of blacks seeking their civil rights, even though both groups were components of the New Deal coalition. When the economic recovery plummeted into recession, he continued for months to cling to fiscal conservatism before he consented to renewed government spending. In all these areas his actions lagged behind those of ardent New Dealers. He was careful because of pressures from Congress and the public, but also because he himself was so firmly grounded in the more limited reform tradition of the Progressive Era. Wilson had once seemed a progressive with brakes on; now, in turn, Roosevelt was a New Dealer applying progressive brakes.

Nevertheless, Roosevelt's overall tone was still militant. After the Supreme Court issue was finally put to rest, speaking at Roanoke Island, North Carolina, he paid his respects to his opponents in the Senate. He reminded his audience of the "war between those who, like Andrew Jackson, believed in a democracy conducted by and for a complete cross-section of the population, and those who, like the Directors of the Bank of the United States and their friends in the United States Senate, believed in the conduct of government by a self-perpetuating group at the top of the ladder."[2]

To Senator Josiah Bailey of North Carolina, Roosevelt's address seemed both an affront and a challenge, "an argument for *pure* democracy — which is, of course, dictatorship." Bailey lamented that "the Party is divided hopelessly. . . . The decisive battle will be fought out in the next session."[3]

The big battle within the Democratic party was already under way and, in its focus upon domestic policy, continued unabated through the election of 1938. The alignment involved far more than the court fight. It was largely a split between the traditional agrarian Democrats of the South and West, and the pro–New Deal Democrats of the large cities. Some of Roosevelt's opponents were conservative to the core, like Carter Glass and the surviving Bourbons of the nineteenth century. Many others were Wilsonian progressives with the misgivings about big government and big business that had led Theodore Roosevelt in the campaign of 1912 to label their credo "rural toryism." In the 1930s they became increasingly alarmed over enlarging government, heavy deficits, and especially two manifestations of the election of 1936.

The first and minor fear of the conservative Democrats was over Roosevelt's courtship of the blacks in northern cities. The second and major concern was over the rapid growth of unions in size and power, and the emergence of big labor as a key component of the New Deal coalition. The conservative alliance against Roosevelt in Congress was an informal coalition, continually shifting. At its heart there was the small number of bedrock right-wing Republicans, and, not always cooperating with them, a handful of their counterparts in the Democratic party. The great balance combined with them or opposed them depending upon what issue was being debated. Thus Representative John E. Rankin of Mississippi, the most notorious racist in Congress, was on most questions a New Dealer. He had supported Roosevelt even on the court question, but in 1937 fulminated that the National Labor Relations Board was "conspiring with communistic influences to destroy Southern industries."[4]

Union membership, which had grown by nearly half before the passage of the Wagner Act, increased spectacularly in the years that followed. John L. Lewis, head of the United Mine Workers, and the leaders of the two great garment unions, Sidney Hillman and David Dubinsky, had forced the American Federation of Labor (AFL) craft unionists to consent to the building of industry-wide unions in the huge industries previously unorganized, especially steel, automobiles, and rubber. Not only corporations but also craft unionists began to oppose the massive drives; the Congress of Industrial Organizations (CIO) split off from the AFL by the end of 1935, and by 1937 industrial warfare was at its height. Organizers battled against company guards and sometimes against the police and rival union men, but unlike the era before the New Deal, enjoyed some protection from the National Labor Relations Board. By the beginning of 1937, organizers in the automobile industry were using a spectacular and disconcerting new technique, the occupation of the plants in "sit-down strikes." They had spread to America from France.

The sit-down strikes, with their threat to private property, together with the accompanying labor violence of the massive unionization drives, alarmed a large part of agrarian and middle-class America. Coming at the same time as the court fight, they intensified distrust and bitterness toward Roosevelt. That was ironic, for Roosevelt's own deep-held views were much the same as those of the majority responding to pollsters. Three quarters, the Gallup surveys indicated, favored labor unions. Two thirds also discountenanced sit-down strikes. At the same time, three fourths disapproved of the vigilante citizen committees that were springing up in strike areas.

A minor controversy in Pennsylvania in the spring of 1937 dramatized the rift that sit-down strikes threatened to bring to Roosevelt's political coalition. A CIO-led sit-down strike in the Hershey chocolate factory deprived dairymen in the surrounding countryside of their $14,000-a-day milk market. In response the farmers and nonstriking workers, brandishing knives, clubs, and carrying banners denouncing the CIO, smashed into the factory, beating and throwing out the strikers until belatedly state police halted the melee.[5]

During the labor battles of 1937, Roosevelt, in keeping with his own convictions, quietly and with considerable skill threaded his way through the no-man's-land between the opposing forces. He certainly did not wish to lose the votes of farmers and middle-class supporters, nor did he want the labor leaders to be so strong that they could dominate him. On the other hand, he was keenly aware of the plight of industrial workers in a depression economy.

Roosevelt had firm reasons, therefore, to keep himself as disengaged as possible through the long embroilment of the industrialists and unions. In January, 1937, during the first of the major, dramatic sit-down strikes at Flint, Roosevelt quietly backed Governor Frank Murphy of Michigan as Murphy maneuvered to try to get the workers out of the General Motors plants without bloodshed. Ultimately Murphy in Detroit worked out a tentative settlement between Lewis and General Motors.[6]

Roosevelt's greatest contribution was negative; in tandem with Murphy he resisted pressure to assign government force to oust the workers from the plants. "There have been a number of occasions when, both in Albany and Washington, it took real calm not to call out the troops," he reminisced to Rosenman in 1940.[7] The settlement of the Flint strike temporarily took some of the pressure off Roosevelt. He shared in the general acclaim for Murphy, and while the acclaim soon faded, Roosevelt's rather exaggerated esteem for him did not.

Sit-down strikes continued to plague a number of industries, and the clamor against Roosevelt for not taking action increased throughout the spring. Ironically many of the same leaders, within Congress and outside it, who were assailing Roosevelt for aggrandizement of power in trying to transform the Supreme Court were also attacking him for not taking strong action against the strikers.[8]

Gradually sit-down strikes came to a halt, but labor violence intensified, with Roosevelt receiving much blame from the public and the press. He suffered from the fact that employers and most middle-class Americans considered him pro-labor, while Lewis and other labor leaders were becoming increasingly upset over his neutrality. They needed his support in the continued drive to organize the remainder of the automobile and steel industries. The Ford company continued to repel organizers from the United Auto Workers (UAW), and although United States Steel had come to terms with Lewis, the "little steel" companies under the leadership of the militant Tom Girdler of Republic Steel were aggressively opposing the strikers.

The climax came at the end of May, 1937, when two particularly upsetting confrontations took place. On the overpass where workmen crossed from Ford's huge River Rouge plant, Ford "service men" brutally beat Richard Frankenstein, Walter Reuther, and other UAW organizers while newspaper photographers snapped pictures and Dearborn police stood by uninvolved. The other episode, on Memorial Day, involved a march of strikers and strike sympathizers toward the gates of the Republic Steel Company in South Chicago. When strikers yelled and threw a few rocks at the Chicago police, the police responded by firing their pistols and charging the crowd with clubs. When the melee was over, ten men, none of them policemen, were dead; a hundred were wounded. The La Follette Committee report on the "Memorial Day massacre" asserted that the police had no right to limit the number of pickets at the gate, and that even if they had, they should have used tear gas, not guns and clubs.[9]

The Memorial Day massacre put Roosevelt in an even more uncomfortable spot than before. It was such a blatant violation of the strikers' rights that union leaders seemed entitled to some expression of sympathy. But Mayor Edward J. Kelly of Chicago, who was vehemently defending his police from criticism, was an important ally of Roosevelt, at the moment keeping an Illinois senator in line on votes critical to the president.

It was the end of June before Roosevelt volunteered a comment on the continuing labor violence, and then he did so obliquely. He had just seen Charles Taft of the Mediation Board, and told reporters that he and Taft agreed that "the Nation, as a whole, in regard to the recent strike episodes . . . are saying just one thing, 'A plague on both your houses.' "[10]

Throughout the country, the newspapers proclaimed Roosevelt's comment, "A plague on both your houses." And on Labor Day there came John L. Lewis's retort, also phrased in Shakespearean language: "It ill behooves one who has supped at labor's table and who has been sheltered in labor's house to curse with equal fervor and fine impartiality both labor and its adversaries when they become locked in deadly embrace."[11]

Lewis and Roosevelt continued to drift apart, and by 1940 Lewis was back in the Republican party. Union labor did not follow him. Despite Roosevelt's "fine impartiality," he continued to enjoy the support of organized labor as it became increasingly strong in the basic industries of the North. In the South, textile manufacturers succeeded in thwarting the organizing drives, and Roosevelt's political alliance with the unions continued to be a festering grievance.

Southern white leaders were also becoming increasingly irritated over Roosevelt's silence as blacks, with the vigorous support of advanced New Dealers, struggled for civil rights and economic opportunities. Part of his political friendship and long-lasting alliance with the southern Democrats had been his acceptance of the white supremacy tradition, with all it entailed both socially and economically. White supremacy, along with other notions in a period of acute racism, had been part of Roosevelt's upbringing as a northern patrician. They were the views of his progressive mentors Theodore Roosevelt, Woodrow Wilson, and Josephus Daniels. He never questioned during the Wilson era that the navy should be lily-white except for stewards. During the 1920s, as he tried to recuperate from polio at Warm Springs and built a strong political base in Georgia, he did not at any point challenge local customs.[12]

Yet Roosevelt as a country squire on the Hudson River could feel at ease with blacks in ways contrary to Dixie taboos. On the 1917 junket to Haiti, where he outranked everyone present, he danced with the wives and daughters of black Haitian government officials, while white marine officers, bound by southern traditions, stood on the sidelines.[13]

As president, Roosevelt persisted in these attitudes. He did little specifically for blacks during his first years as president, and while in the White House invariably argued he could not do more because he did not want to offend southern leaders in Congress and jeopardize passage of his legislative program. At Warm Springs, he was, like southern whites of means, a patron of the blacks. He was a kind employer toward three black farmhands, giving them housing and the prevailing wage of $20 per month. He helped obtain a private donation and WPA and PWA funds to build a school for black children, and in 1936 participated with Mrs. Roosevelt in the dedication of "the Eleanor Roosevelt Vocational School for Colored Youth." It was segregated, but also it was infinitely superior to the facilities for other rural black children. When public housing came, the first completed project was in Atlanta, again under Roosevelt's aegis, and entirely for blacks. These improvements represented steps forward at the time, and probably went as far as Roosevelt was willing to go.[14]

The fact that the New Deal included blacks, even in a limited discriminatory way, in the largesse of housing, relief, and farm programs upset defenders of the status quo in the North as well as the South. They blamed Roosevelt as the patron of the blacks, and as with labor, he tried to give the impression that he was not really their partisan.

Roosevelt's indignation over merciless economic exploitation of blacks welled up in 1935 when Governor Eugene Talmadge of Georgia complained to Harry Hopkins that the WPA was paying blacks such high wages that they would not accept farm jobs. Roosevelt dictated an answer, then either out of caution or because he would not give Talmadge the satisfaction of a response from the president, sent it to Hopkins to sign:

"I take it . . . that you approve paying farm labor forty to fifty cents a day . . . for working at least ten and possibly twelve hours." He then worked out what on a yearly basis the total wages would be. Since the work was usually seasonal, "I take it that the man described would actually have to live on from sixty to seventy-five dollars a year.

"Somehow I cannot get it into my head that wages on such a scale make possible a reasonable American standard of living."[15]

Eleanor Roosevelt's awareness of the plight of blacks grew much more rapidly than her husband's, and as her attitudes changed she pressed him toward action. The cause to which she tried to rally him was federal antilynching legislation. The number of lynchings per year in the South was only a fraction of what it had been at the turn of the century, but the eighteen in 1935, some of them especially nauseous in their sadistic barbarity, outraged the nation. While a minority in the rural South still looked upon lynchings as a vital control in the system of white supremacy, an essential safeguard for white women, the overwhelming majority condemned them as the disgrace of their region. The women of the Methodist Episcopal Church, South, passed a unanimous resolution calling for federal legislation.

Within Congress, as Roosevelt well knew, antilynching legislation was the symbol for the attack on the system of segregation, and almost every white southerner was determined to resist to the end. That was the reason Roosevelt gave to Walter White, the secretary of the National Association for the Advancement of Colored People, when Mrs. Roosevelt got White past the southern secretaries to talk to the president. "I did not choose the tools with which I must work," he told White in their first conversation in May, 1934. "But I've got to get legislation passed by Congress to save America."

Roosevelt did extend one bit of encouragement to White, Eleanor Roosevelt has reminisced: "You go ahead; you do everything you can do . . . but I just can't do it."[16]

Mrs. Roosevelt asked the president subsequently if he minded if she said what she thought, and Roosevelt replied: "No, certainly not. You can say anything you want. I can always say, 'Well, that is my wife; I can't do anything about her.' "[17]

Eleanor Roosevelt did more than release trial balloons. She formed a strong alliance with White and the two Senate sponsors of antilynching legislation, Edward Costigan and Robert Wagner, and gradually brought Roosevelt closer to her viewpoint.

Slowly but steadily, sentiment in favor of antilynching legislation grew throughout the country and in Congress. In April, 1937, supporters of a strong bill in the House of Representatives managed to wrest it out of Hatton Summers' Judiciary Committee, and in the aftermath of a blowtorch lynching of two blacks in Mississippi, passed it 227 to 120. Only one southerner, Maury Maverick of Texas, voted for it. The victorious House sponsor commented, "I got very little active support from the White House."

Whatever romantic notion southern senators held that an antilynching bill would be a hot potato for Roosevelt disappeared in January, 1938, when he gave it his firm support. Northern, voting blacks, like workers, had become important to him. Southern senators launched into an impassioned filibuster. Pat Harrison lamented that the Democratic majority was "betraying the trust of the Southern people," predicting that the course of action would lead to legislation abolishing Jim Crow and white primaries. James F. Byrnes developed much the same theme. Others viewed the antilynching bill as proof of the Communist sympathies of New Dealers. And so the speeches went, from January 6 into February, when Roosevelt, in serious need of an emergency relief appropriation to aid victims of the recession, could no longer afford the filibuster. It came to an end on February 21.

The antilynching bill was, as southern senators perceived it to be, basically a symbol of the assault upon second-class citizenship for blacks. Even though the senators could block its enactment, the debates in the Congress and the rise in public indignation against lynching were preparing the way for change. Congress enacted no legislation, but several states, including Mississippi, sought to forestall federal action by passing drastic laws. In 1939 the number of lynchings was down to two.[18]

The virtual elimination of lynchings was only the beginning. Roosevelt with his exceeding caution was aware that in civil rights, as in social security earlier, long years of what he referred to as education of the public were essential to the political process. Just as Eleanor Roosevelt worked year in and year out on her husband's attitudes, so he in turn labored quietly with the public. In March, 1938, several weeks after the end of the filibuster, he passed on to reporters what he said he had told a good many senators. The Senate should at least authorize the attorney general or a standing congressional committee to investigate any instances of mob violence resulting in deaths.

"Would you include all types of violations," a reporter queried, "for instance those labor violations which occurred in Chicago last year?"

"Yes," Roosevelt responded, "in other words, the taking of human life."[19]

Thus Roosevelt combined the cautious protection of two groups of often persecuted supporters, the blacks and the union members. Congress took no action. As for the blacks and workers, many of them deplored the failure of Roosevelt to go further, his refusal to be as militant as Senator Wagner. Yet the fact that he had done more for them than any previous president helped give them hope and insured for him their continued allegiance.

In the spring of 1937, as Roosevelt shifted toward fiscal orthodoxy, he seemed to be stripping another of his constituencies, those on WPA and relief, of almost everything except hope. Steady improvement of the economy turned him toward balancing the budget.

By several indicators the nation had attained substantial recovery compared with the boom year 1929. The real income of farmers was up approximately to the unsatisfactory 1929 level; industrial production was only 7.5 percent lower. Stock dividends were within 90 percent of the 1929 level, and real wages were 10 percent above it. There were flaws. National income and most other aggregate indices were well below those of 1929. The level of construction was only a third of the 1920s peak, and production of durable goods lagged. New issues of stocks and bonds were only a fourth of what they had been in the previous boom. Unlike the twenties, businesses were pessimistic and, although money was cheap, ventured little upon capital investment or expansion of their enterprises. Most serious of all, unemployment continued at a high level, at about 11 percent of the work force (9 percent when seasonally adjusted). That figure included those on work projects — present-day estimates of unemployment do not include such people. However, the crude measurements of the time probably underestimated unemployment. There were still nearly 4,500,000 families on relief.

Roosevelt was delighted with the recovery and dismayed by the continuing heavy relief figures. Pressured by both Congress and Morgenthau, he insisted upon a balanced budget, except for service on the debt, in fiscal 1938 (beginning July 1, 1937). He was determined to balance it in every way the following year. That would necessitate slashing federal relief and recovery programs.

Even before the 1936 election, Roosevelt had been planning to reduce expenditures on the WPA. Hopkins, acting upon his orders, trimmed it by the summer of 1937 to half its previous size. Ickes began phasing out the Public Works Administration. The slashes threw large additional numbers of people onto direct relief, which, as Republican critics had long insisted, was less expensive. The change, especially in southern states, meant being reduced to a miserable level of subsistence.[20]

Yet Roosevelt did not seem to think he was abandoning the poor. Through the spring of 1937, he continued to reassert the imperative to aid the underprivileged third of the populace, but he returned also to the bootstrap formula of 1933 that recovery and reform must come through methods that would not burden the government with further deficits. He was predicating his slashes in relief expenditures on the premise that, as the economy continued to improve, private enterprise must take up the slack in employment. Employers enjoying increasing profits must hire workers. The device to force them to do so should be a federal ceiling on hours, a floor under wages, and the prohibition of child labor, which combined would create more jobs. He suggested to Senate Majority Leader Robinson: "If in some way we can accomplish, by legislation, a shortening of hours for the unskilled, a large part of the unemployed will be taken off the relief rolls."[21]

The idea was not likely to appeal to Robinson and other southern leaders. It was a renewed threat, as both the National Recovery Act and the National Labor Relations Act had been, to the lower pay scales that southerners insisted they must keep in order to compete with the North.

Simultaneously Roosevelt curtailed the Public Works Administration, partly so he could draw upon its funds to finance relief, but above all to curb heavy construction in order to bring down the rapidly rising price of materials, especially copper, which was up to 17 cents a pound, and steel, which had gone up $6 a ton. He was convinced that the increased production of durable goods and accompanying higher prices threatened inflation and recession. "The time has come," he declared, "to discourage Government expenditures on durable goods and to encourage Government expenditures on consumer goods."[22] Economists questioned Roosevelt's decision, taking the view that recovery in durable goods production lagged far behind that in consumer goods.

There was no insincerity in Roosevelt's ardor for financial conservatism in 1937. When Anne O'Hare McCormick talked to him that summer, she correctly noted that "less known but just as real is the Dutch householder who carefully totes up his accounts every month." In a heated interchange with Garner before a cabinet meeting in May, Roosevelt asserted, "I have said fifty times that the budget will be balanced. . . . If you want me to say it again, I will say it either once or fifty times more."[23]

In 1937, that year of disappointments, Roosevelt succeeded in both blocking unwanted spending and obtaining his full $1.5 billion relief appropriation. Fresh disappointment came later, for by the time Congress voted the sum, the nation was already slipping into a recession.

The recession only slowly became apparent, and it caught Roosevelt and the nation by surprise. May marked the apex of the wave of recovery, which, far from carrying a threat of incipient boom and inflation, was so precarious that by August it was quickly residing into a trough. Through the summer, Roosevelt continued to be cautious in spending, slowly deciding which PWA proposals he should authorize to replace schools that were firetraps. By early September he had allocated the final $150 million in grants and loans, and thought he had wound up the PWA.[24]

When, in the fall and winter of 1937–1938 it became all too apparent that the economy had plummeted, Roosevelt let nature take its course. Some of the signs that he had regarded in the spring as indications of a dangerous boom, rises in prices and heavy stockpiling, by the end of the summer were leading to unsold inventories. Into October, as the stock market continued to decline, Roosevelt regarded the drop as a normal correction and saw no reason to fear a serious business reversal. He was intent still on balancing the budget for the 1939 fiscal year, an act that Morgenthau thought would hearten business more than any other step he could take.

By October 19, "Black Tuesday," the market was dropping so dismayingly that the complacency among those around Roosevelt disappeared. By the end of the month the market was steadying, but the recession was well advanced.

It was a grim fall and winter. Abroad there were portents of a new world war, and at home the recession was undoing the advances since 1935. Roosevelt had to confront an increase of nearly two million unemployed between mid-September and mid-December. The WPA estimated another million would lose their jobs after Christmas. Steel production fell to a quarter of what it had been.

It was a Roosevelt recession, proclaimed business and political opponents of the New Deal. They recited a familiar litany of grievances. The basic charges were those they had leveled in the 1936 campaign, that Roosevelt was antibusiness and had been spending the nation into insolvency. Not all businessmen entirely agreed. A few, even before Christmas, were wondering if it would not be well to return to government spending. In their eyes, the Roosevelt administration had erred toward conservatism.

It was indeed a recession Roosevelt brought on through fiscal conservatism, some economists at the time and both Keynesians and monetarists have declared since. In their view, the sharp curtailing of government spending and the deflationary policies of the Federal Reserve and of the Treasury, sterilizing gold (that is, blocking the use of gold flowing in from Europe as a basis for bank credit), precipitated the decline. In 1936, New Deal relief and public works spending, to which Congress added $1.7 billion to pay the veterans' bonus, poured $4 billion in excess of tax receipts into the economy. Then, unexpectedly in 1937, the Roosevelt administration played exactly the reverse role in the economy, reducing funds available to consumers by $4 billion. The soldiers' bonus had pumped money into the economy and then run out, relief and public works spending were cut, and the new Social Security program collected $2 billion in new taxes without returning any of it as yet in benefits. Credit was tightened to stem the rise of prices. The result was a serious decline in consumer buying power. The holders of the inventories, amounting to about $4 billion, had to lower their prices and cut back orders to manufacturers. As in the fall of 1933, the nation went into a major economic decline.

Roosevelt, uncertain, much of the time regarded the recession as he had that earlier one, as due to the selfishness and hostility of a large part of big business. He was well aware of the failure of consumer buying power, but laid it to unjustified speculative increases in prices. Earlier he had asserted that, while the price of copper had risen to 17 cents a pound, many mines in the country could produce it for 5 or 6 cents and still make a profit. The recession seemed to the president proof that he had been right in his worries about monopoly profits and impelled him even more strongly toward a program to control the large corporations. Frankfurter's protégés Thomas Corcoran and Ben Cohen were at the peak of their influence in the White House. Ickes, in progressive fashion, inveighed against America's sixty richest families. Roosevelt was becoming increasingly interested in Robert H. Jackson, an assistant attorney general, whom in 1938 he promoted to solicitor general. During the recession Jackson became the most eloquent administration spokesman for policies that carried echoes of Brandeis' pronouncements and the Wilsonian New Freedom. Antitrust suits could be a prime device to restore competitive pricing.[25]

Yet when wrestling with problems of the economy during his second term, Roosevelt, those around him have recalled, would frequently evoke Theodore Roosevelt. He was no more antibusiness than TR, and indeed like TR was less interested in "busting" trusts than in using the Sherman and Clayton Acts to regulate big business and stimulate competition.

In consequence, Roosevelt was disposed to cajole as well as to threaten the financial and business community if it would help reverse the economic downturn. During the recession winter he not only took preliminary steps to intensify antitrust action but also toyed with the idea of reconstituting the NRA in some form or another. The two approaches were negative and positive aspects of the same policy.

Cooperation with business, the NRA idea, of course was the concept of economic planning that conservative orators had excoriated as fascism, communism, or at best statism. They had so vented their wrath on its exponent, Rexford Tugwell, that he had felt his political usefulness to Roosevelt at an end and had resigned in December, 1936. Tugwell's shift to business, where he became vice president of Charles Taussig's American Molasses Company, did not alter his enthusiasm for planning. In late 1937 he, Taussig, and Thomas W. Lamont, a J. P. Morgan partner, allied themselves in the cause with Adolf A. Berle, who had continued to believe in the NRA "partnership" concept. It seemed, Berle commented, like 1932 all over again. Their mission was to establish new links between business and the New Deal, not an easy undertaking for either industrialists and financiers, on the one hand, or the president on the other.

Morgenthau's speech on November 10, 1937, pledging a balanced budget was a revealing case in point. He was unnerved when, as he reached the key point of the pledge, someone in the audience of business leaders laughed. The story quickly spread that the entire audience had hooted.[26]

There was an even more startling added factor. Two days earlier, Roosevelt had seen Marriner Eccles, head of the Federal Reserve, who came bearing a memorandum by economists blaming cuts in government spending for the recession. Roosevelt seemed impressed. On the afternoon of the tenth, Roosevelt gave Eccles the impression that he agreed that spending was essential to reverse the economic decline. That evening Eccles was surprised to hear Roosevelt's emphatic public pledge, via Morgenthau, to cut spending and balance the budget.

Roosevelt's simultaneous assent both to Morgenthau's call for a balanced budget and to Eccles' for renewed pump priming was a particularly painful illustration of one of his most conspicuous weaknesses as chief executive, his tendency to give almost every pleader the impression that he was in sympathetic agreement. In this instance, Eccles was undoubtedly right when he concluded years later that Roosevelt had assented out of his own deep uncertainty.[27]

Long before 1938 the preponderant leadership of the financial and business community was so wholeheartedly alienated from Roosevelt that even his total return to economic orthodoxy would have done little to mend the breach. A substantial majority of business leaders and members of Congress wanted both a balanced budget and tax cuts, together with painful deletions of New Deal programs. Roosevelt did not want to go that far and fought defensively for the taxes he had worked so hard to obtain.

Through the fall and winter as the recession worsened, Roosevelt appeared to be passive, out of control of events, doing little as four or more sets of advisers battled for his ear. There was some overlap in their ideas, as must have been amply apparent to the eclectic Roosevelt, and he seemed to be disposed to let them engage in give-and-take among themselves while they were undertaking to persuade him. What ensued in policy formulation was the development of rival schemes from below, among the young economists in several federal agencies, and ultimately Roosevelt's selection of a program that would at least be fairly palatable to most of them.

First, Roosevelt, without rejecting other approaches, focused upon the one scheme that would permit him to continue the course of fiscal conservatism Morgenthau announced. He would promote recovery in the NRA fashion through seeking cooperation with the economic community. Beginning in October he consulted with groups of business and labor leaders in a fashion depressingly reminiscent of President Hoover's meetings in the aftermath of the Great Crash. Next, Berle and Tugwell tried to develop their program of cooperation between the economic sector and the New Deal. On December 23, they met with Thomas Lamont, Owen D. Young of General Electric, and, representing the unions, John L. Lewis and Philip Murray.

In mid-January, 1938, Roosevelt talked with that group at the White House and urged them to form an advisory committee. He seemed eager to create the impression that he was seeking better relations with business and labor, but nothing much came of the effort. Disruptive forces then took over. Left-wing leaders in the CIO would not sanction Lewis' cooperation within the group; Lamont and Young feared Roosevelt was using them for his political advantage. Berle, from without, noted, "Corcoran and Cohen think their position is threatened and have started a row."[28] There were unflattering leaks to the press from within the White House.

The advisory committee was stillborn and by mid-February had ceased to function. Yet it made some contributions to solving the problem of recovery. It augmented the respectability of the CIO and helped bolster support for wages and hours legislation. It helped sell Roosevelt on the need to ease credit, and perhaps made him less unhappy over the congressional onslaught against the undistributed surplus and capital gains taxes. In March, Roosevelt discoursed cheerfully on the possibility of stimulating the flow of capital credit, and took seriously proposals to stimulate the expansion of utilities and to end the TVA struggle against Commonwealth and Southern. And, ironically, although Roosevelt's interest in cooperation with business was to avoid fresh deficit financing, the committee's proposals for a large-scale housing program and for appropriations to alleviate suffering among the unemployed, helped divert him from his insistence upon a balanced budget.[29]

On the other hand, Morgenthau was urging Roosevelt to pursue an antimonopoly policy as an alternative to spending. An antimonopoly program would go in the opposite direction from the business advisory committee, but there was a certain consistency to the two approaches. Cooperative business, it was agreed, would rally behind the committee; the profiteers whom Roosevelt held responsible for the recession would suffer from antimonopoly suits. (At the beginning of the century, Theodore Roosevelt in much the same fashion had promoted both the National Civic Federation, representing business and labor leaders, and simultaneously a vigorous trust-busting program.) Not only Morgenthau but also Jackson, Ickes, and Leon Henderson, economic consultant to Harry Hopkins, were blaming the high price structure of monopoly enterprise for the decline in buying power. Roosevelt, after conferring with congressional leaders, decided to embark upon an antimonopoly course, and directed Morgenthau to prepare a statement. The statement and the easing of credit mildly raised the lagging prices of commodities. In dealing with business, threats of discipline seemed to have a better effect than offers of cooperation.[30]

By this time in March, Roosevelt had gone as far as he felt prudent, but the nation continued to suffer from a decline in employment, giving Keynesians ammunition in their campaign for a more drastic remedy. Factory production and farm prices were sinking close to 1933 levels. The president, apprehensive, could not remain unheedful for long. The crisis point came while he was taking a few days' vacation in Warm Springs. He had left Washington in an irascible mood, frustrated anew in his maneuvers against congressional conservatives. On March 23, at Gainesville, Georgia, he gave vent to his feelings. He blamed the failure of the nation in general and the South specifically to attain full prosperity upon the few who, displaying minority selfishness, had blocked his programs. "I, too, wanted to balance the budget but . . . I put human lives ahead of dollars." Wall Street interpreted Roosevelt's sharp words as concern about the recession, and frantic unloading of stocks drove the Dow Jones industrial average down to 98. The new crash shocked Roosevelt into postponing his dream of a balanced budget. The minor palliatives would not suffice. Furthermore, he was coming under pressure to engage in piecemeal bailouts of the worst-affected sectors of the economy.[31]

Pump priming was a lesser evil, and Roosevelt agreed to it while he was vacationing at Warm Springs. It was Harry Hopkins who persuaded him to shift policies. Hopkins, who had been convalescing successfully in Florida from an operation for stomach cancer, had read the accounts of the stock market debacle as a signal that the time had come to stir the president to action. Roosevelt had invited him to visit in Warm Springs, and Hopkins launched a strong campaign to win Roosevelt to spending. Unemployment by March was nearly 2.5 million greater than a year previously; the memorandum Hopkins carried indicated that national income was falling at the rate of $800 million per month. The president, as was characteristic, kept his own counsel. Finally, as he was about to return to Washington, at lunch with Hopkins and Williams, deputy directer of the Works Progress Administration, on April 2, he asserted he would seek a substantial spending program. Once converted, Roosevelt set out energetically on the new course.[32]

Beyond question the dimensions of the crisis had brought the change in Roosevelt's strategy. In the months since congressional leaders had tried to deny Roosevelt a $1.5-billion relief package, the distress of their constituents and the approach of the 1938 election had softened their resistance to spending. Many businessmen, putting survival ahead of traditional economics, were less disposed to protest pump priming. Humanitarianism, as well as the urgent need for a strong recovery measure, swayed Roosevelt. On the way north, as he gazed out the window at some of the dispossessed waiting along the tracks to see his train go by, he commented to one of his entourage, "*They* understand what we're trying to do."[33]

It is more difficult to determine whether Roosevelt had actually, like Paul on the road to Damascus, undergone a conversion at Warm Springs and joined the newly growing ranks of the Keynesians. He liked Keynes, to be sure, but did not pretend to understand his theories. Roosevelt's attitude during the next two years — before massive defense appropriations made the question moot — indicates that countercyclical spending remained for him solely a policy of last resort. What he had learned in the New Deal was that in a major calamity, pump priming would work. When the calamity of 1938 had become sufficiently grave, he was ready to prime the pump once more, and then as the crisis abated revert to his earlier policies. The economist Herbert Stein has concluded that Roosevelt continued to cling "to his belief in a possible structural reform of the economy, compounded of planning, competition, and income redistribution, which would give high employment without deficits except for occasional fluctuations." It was a view, Stein points out, that was standard among the liberals of the era, who regarded "deficit spending only as a second-best and temporary policy."[34]

Since Roosevelt was not binding himself to a single heavy-spending solution to the recession, the question was how much of the other formulas he would accept. Much of what Eccles had proposed, and Roosevelt himself had already accepted, in the realms of easing credit and providing money for loans to aid business and promote housing, was to go into the package.

Planning as a joint venture between government on the one hand and capital and labor on the other had lost out in the debates. In part it occurred because businessmen could not agree among themselves, and as in the period when NRA codes were being formulated, were particularly interested in establishing their own fair trade practices. Small businessmen had squabbled so noisily when they had met with Roosevelt at the beginning of February that when newspapermen asked Roosevelt if there would be more business conferences he laughed heartily. In part the problem was that Roosevelt did not trust the businessmen to preside over a program, and the businessmen did not want a New Dealer sitting at the head of the table.[35]

Roosevelt, having decided upon his course of action, moved firmly with a sure political touch. He requested approximately $2 billion for direct spending and an additional $1 billion for loans and included other devices not requiring fresh congressional action, notably the desterilizing of gold reserves the Treasury held, which would put $2 billion into circulation. Congress had already authorized a fresh $1.5 billion in Reconstruction Finance Corporation loans. The total, therefore, would be an infusion of $6.5 billion into the economy, an enormous sum by 1938 standards. Congressional leaders with relatively little protest accepted the program, vastly larger than the proposals at which they had balked a few months earlier. The fact that many of them would seek reelection in the fall was not lost upon them.[36]

Once enacted, the spending program went into effect quickly. The WPA could expand immediately and the new PWA, unlike 1933, could initiate public works within months, since projects, plans, and personnel were all available. By 1939, before there was any appreciable impact from defense spending, substantial recovery was once more under way.

As for an antitrust program, it, too, immediately went into operation. Already Roosevelt had brought in Thurman Arnold, who with much fanfare increased the antitrust section of the Department of Justice to three hundred lawyers. They had numbered eighteen in the early New Deal. For several years Arnold tried to police both business and labor, undertaking something of the function Roosevelt had sought in vain through the voluntary cooperation of the economic community. Parallel to the antitrust program, Congress established the Temporary National Economic Commission, which ultimately brought out a shelfful of reports; by then the nation was at war and the TNEC had little lasting impact.[37]

Roosevelt never ceased to hope for the cooperation of businessmen. At supper one night in the White House in May, 1939, he was bemoaning this fact, wondering why they lacked confidence in the economy. Mrs. Roosevelt spoke up: "They are afraid of you."[38]

Chapter 20

QUARANTINE OR APPEASEMENT

BETWEEN 1937 AND 1939, Roosevelt's rather nebulous schemes for coping with aggressor nations began gradually to take more tangible form. In keeping with tradition as exemplified by the American eagle, clutching both an olive branch and arrows, Roosevelt sought peaceful settlement of international disputes, and if that failed he was prepared to resort in concert with other threatened nations to a quarantine, a blockade, or some other form of coercion. If warnings of force were to be effective, there must be rearmament, and very slowly Roosevelt started to strengthen the armed forces.

The partners in these policies would be the British and the French. The British Navy, the most powerful (since the United States had not built up to treaty strength), must combine with that of the Americans if Roosevelt were to succeed in restraining Japan. The Royal Navy together with the French Army, reputedly the best in the world, entrenched in the formidable Maginot Line, ought to suffice, with limited American cooperation, to protect the West from Hitler and his allies. There should be efforts to reach comprehensive settlements with the threatening nations — a plausible enterprise, since even if it failed, rearmament in any event would take several years. Then, if need be, the strengthened democracies could resort to collective action. There seemed to be cause for unease but not panic.

Appeasement — the effort to obtain a settlement with the aggressors — a term that has had a bad name since World War II, was a segment of the effort not only of British and French leaders but also of Roosevelt to meet the growing danger. To a large part of the establishment in the western democracies, appeasement seemed a corollary to rearmament and planning for collective action. If indeed, as Hitler emphatically claimed, Germany had been wronged by the Treaty of Versailles, because it ran counter to Wilson's pledges in the earlier Fourteen Points, then, the argument went, an overall rectification would remove the causes of war. It was a logical, Wilsonian approach — just as logical as the assumption Roosevelt had already accepted, that if the United States abandoned its neutral rights on the high seas and took the profits out of both neutrality and war, Americans would be less likely to become involved. The concept of appeasement rested upon the hope that if the aggressors received what might rightfully be theirs, they would thereafter respect the rights of other nations.[1]

Roosevelt was aware how dubious that proposition was, and was privately scornful of those who proposed trading away to the aggressors what belonged to weaker nations. He opposed rewarding treaty breakers with wrongful gains, but had nothing to lose in putting his weight behind the drive to seek an honorable overall settlement with both the European dictators and the Japanese. Failure would by no means prevent him from falling back upon the other scheme he frequently explored: in one way or another the United States from within its bastion of the western hemisphere might cooperate in a blockade of aggressors.

During the late 1930s Roosevelt alternated between seeking a settlement and threatening reprisals short of war. These were his responses as, appalled and almost powerless, he watched the aggressors precipitate crisis after crisis, each with the potential to touch off a world explosion. Both the president and the electorate expected war; both were determined that the United States must remain uninvolved. Roosevelt's "I hate war" speech of August, 1936, represented both his own beliefs and, as public opinion polls indicated, the overwhelming view of those queried.

Much of the time between 1936 and 1939, Roosevelt optimistically thought he could keep the United States out of the impending European conflict yet make some small contributions to peace. At the propitious moment, perhaps, he could call a conference that would bring about a settlement of the economic issues fueling the aggressive tactics of the dictators. He was ready to cooperate with the British and the French, although he remained wary of their hypothesis that Hitler would be willing to abide by a settlement.

The pressures for appeasement were substantial; a large part of the establishment spokesmen in London and Paris, encouraged by Berlin, supported the movement. While Roosevelt's envoy to Germany, William E. Dodd, seldom talked to the Nazi leadership, confining himself to lengthy Jeffersonian warnings to Roosevelt, other ambassadors to Germany, especially the French André François-Poncet and the British Nevile Henderson, were in touch with the more polished of the Nazi leaders and sent dispatches sympathetic to their persuasive arguments. The consensus was that an economic settlement, involving some territorial readjustments in colonies and perhaps in eastern Europe, would succeed. Further, there was the subtle appeal to conservatives, especially in France, that Nazism was preferable to communism and was indeed the vital bulwark against it.[2]

One influential advocate of accommodation was William Bullitt, who had become United States ambassador to France in September, 1936. He had left the Moscow embassy bitterly disillusioned with the Stalin regime and drawn toward the views of the leading French conservatives; he shared the confidence of these men of power. In lively, graphic accounts, he passed on their thoughts to Roosevelt, and urged a strongly isolationist position. In 1937 Roosevelt was never as isolationist as Bullitt wished him to be.

With Britain, the nation Roosevelt most courted, there continued to be irritations and suspicions, but the threats from Germany and Japan gradually warmed relations. Sir Ronald Lindsay, long the British ambassador in Washington, never ceased to report on Roosevelt with mild condescension. That of the British cabinet was even stronger. Prime Minister Stanley Baldwin seemed to his critics to be lumbering along both in domestic and in foreign policy; the strongest figure in his cabinet, Neville Chamberlain, the chancellor of the Exchequer, was no admirer of Roosevelt. In the fall of 1933, Baldwin asked Chamberlain to explain New Deal policies to the cabinet. Chamberlain noted:

"I made a rather humorous story of it representing the Yanks as a barbarous tribe and Roosevelt as a medicine man whose superiority over other medicine men consisted in the astonishing agility with which when one kind of Mumbo Jumbo failed, he produced another. . . . I look upon him as a dangerous and unreliable horse in any team."[3]

Chamberlain's view did not differ greatly from the consensus of the British leadership, that Roosevelt and the State Department were rather friendly but unreliable. They could not or would not back fine words with firm actions. Yet the British felt that in a real crisis they could count upon the Americans for support. As Chamberlain was preparing to become prime minister early in 1937 that was the word that Lord Runciman, president of the Board of Trade, brought back to him from Washington, where he had engaged in conversations preparatory to negotiating a reciprocal trade agreement. Chamberlain informed his sister that Runciman "brought away a general impression that the President (which of course means the Govt for he is more of a dictator than Hitler) is very friendly, very afraid of war, very anxious to avoid it if it came, but likely, if we should be involved, to be in it with us in a few weeks."[4]

Quite possibly Roosevelt, through talk of an embargo, led Runciman to feel that the United States would quickly become involved if Britain went to war. To the British (and indeed to Roosevelt's own admirals when he sounded them out on one or another of his schemes), an American blockade meant inevitably joining in the conflict. Roosevelt doggedly clung to the notion that he could engage in such assistance without embroiling the United States in full-scale war, as indeed he was to demonstrate in 1940–1941. After war with Hitler came in 1939, the misapprehension of the British led them to suffer many months of impatience and disappointment.

The failure of the British and the Americans to mesh their thoughts in planning for a common defense was not the only cause of irritation. Despite the towering threat from Germany and Japan, lesser rivalries, as always, persisted, and at times became entangled with larger defense issues. A prime instance was the scramble between Roosevelt and the British to secure claims to previously inconsequential Pacific islands that might serve as defense bases against the Japanese — and as refueling stops on commercial air routes between the United States and Australia and New Zealand. For a century or more both nations had held tenuous claims to these bits of land. Neither had permanently occupied them, and occupation, Roosevelt insisted, was essential before they could be annexed.[5]

The foremost reason Roosevelt sought to annex the islands was to develop a chain of bases to counter the Japanese. Their extension of power in the Pacific was never far from his mind. He noted with concern the encroachment of Japanese fishermen into Alaskan waters, and ultimately succeeded in closing them. Reports crossed his desk of formidable Japanese settlements in Lower California and perhaps in Central America. All these he had investigated. They proved false. Early in 1938 he sent his friend Vincent Astor and Kermit Roosevelt to visit the Marshall Islands on the yacht *Nourmahal,* ostensibly on a scientific expedition but actually to check on Japanese activities there. Astor reported that while the Japanese were active, they did not seem to be building fortifications; on the other hand there was a sizable naval base at Eniwetok and an air strip being cleared at Wotje.[6]

Already Roosevelt had taken steps to balance the Japanese presence.

In 1935 he ordered the navy secretly to occupy Howland, Baker, and Jarvis islands, and the following year issued a proclamation putting them under the Department of the Interior as part of Hawaii. The British made no formal protest but acted quickly to assert their own claim when in 1937 the United States showed interest in Canton Island in the Phoenix group.[7]

In the end, Roosevelt obtained what he wanted, but his irritation was genuine; and he subsequently repeated more than once his belief that in any negotiations, the British wanted 90 percent and would give only 10 percent. The British, for their part, felt similarly that in an interchange with the United States they would receive far less than their fair share. Minor antagonisms persisted, but events drew the two nations closer and closer. One British official bluntly informed a German diplomat in May, 1939, that if the choice had to be made, he would much rather his country become an American dominion than a German *Gau*.[8]

In 1937 Baldwin retired and Chamberlain became prime minister. In his own right he could assume direct leadership in seeking a settlement with the aggressors, meanwhile increasing armaments in case the settlement failed. Roosevelt learned from Ambassador Robert Bingham that Chamberlain, earlier "not hostile toward us, but uninformed and indifferent, has completely reversed his attitude." So also had "all the members of the Cabinet of sufficient weight to be counted."[9]

Roosevelt, incensed over an ominous development, a fresh Japanese incursion into China, did not wait in 1937 for the British to join in a protest, but unexpectedly delivered his own spectacular warning: aggressors might face a quarantine. He aimed his words more at the Japanese than the European dictators, although he intended his statement to have a global significance. The Japanese Army in July, 1937, used the pretext of a minor clash with Chinese forces at the Marco Polo Bridge near Peking to initiate a new major thrust that by fall had overrun Peking and was threatening Nanking.

The American public reacted with anger and revulsion. Newsreels depicted the ruthless might of the Japanese forces; the American ambassador and his staff fled to American gunboats on the Yangtze, where they witnessed the Japanese bombs dropping on slums along the riverbank.[10]

Roosevelt shared the public indignation, and encouraged by it, became increasingly bold in his reactions. Neither Japan nor China declared war, and Roosevelt did not invoke the Neutrality Act, which would have hurt China worse than Japan. At a cabinet meeting on September 14, Secretary Claude Swanson reported the navy feeling that if

Japan needed to be put in its place, this was the time to do it, since Japan was so fully occupied in China. Ickes noted, "The President said that he was a pacifist. He has no intention of making any warlike moves." After the cabinet meeting, Roosevelt was more candid with the sympathetic Ickes. He said he was thinking of sending a letter to all the nations of the world, except perhaps the "three bandit nations" (Japan, Germany, and Italy), a letter in which, according to Ickes, "he would suggest that, in the future, if any nation should invade the rights or threaten the liberties of any of the other nations, the peace-loving nations would isolate it. What he has in mind is to cut off all trade with any such nation and thus deny it raw materials."[11]

Roosevelt departed a few days later for a trip to the West, and returning over the Great Plains toward Chicago, marshaled his thoughts on the means to contain Japan. Sumner Welles later recalled to Rosenman:

> As you undoubtedly remember, he was talking with the Navy about drawing an actual line in the Pacific to be maintained by the United States, if the British would agree to cooperate, beyond which Japan would be told she would not be permitted to trade or to expand in the event that she persisted in the policy of military conquest of China. . . . The President used the word "quarantine" in connection with that line.[12]

On the train, Roosevelt took a phrase from Norman Davis, "war is a contagion," and to it added the logical but electric word "quarantine." Probably out of shrewdness, since he was as yet in no position to obtain either British or American support for a blockade in the Pacific, neither in the speech nor thereafter did he specify what the word "quarantine" might mean. It was to be pacific — that he made clear — and Roosevelt believed would not involve war. He apparently thought then, as later, that the Japanese government would submit to it rather than launch a retaliatory strike.

In his address before thousands of spectators in Chicago, Roosevelt cited the ruthless bombings in which "innocent peoples, innocent nations, are being cruelly sacrificed to a greed for power and supremacy." That brought him to the point upon which he felt Americans most needed educating:

> If those things come to pass in other parts of the world, let no one imagine that America will escape, . . . that this Western Hemisphere will not be attacked. . . .

> It seems to be unfortunately true that the epidemic of world lawlessness is spreading.
>
> When an epidemic of physical disease starts to spread, the community approves and joins in a quarantine of the patients in order to protect the health of the community against the spread of the disease.

What that quarantine might involve, he did not even hint. Rather, he went on reassuringly,

> It is my determination to pursue a policy of peace, to adopt every practicable measure to avoid involvement in war.[13]

The speech created a sensation both at home and abroad. It almost drove the World Series off the front pages of newspapers. The immediate response was overwhelmingly positive within the United States. Both notables and ordinary people hailed Roosevelt's leadership against war; only a minority felt he was pulling the nation toward conflict. Of almost 500 letters and telegrams that arrived at the White House, 423 favored the speech and 74 opposed it. The normally isolationist Senator William E. Borah lauded "our great President's" speech, interpreting it as a proposal to keep the nation out of foreign wars, although Senator Gerald Nye promised a hot fight against the quarantine concept. Gradually the Hearst papers and isolationist leaders became heated in their denunciations of the quarantine idea, but in total this was not a serious backlash in the weeks that followed. The immediate response within the United States was favorable. Opinion polls both before and after the talk did indicate that Roosevelt had a considerable way to go if he were to persuade the public that he should possess the power against aggressors he most wanted at that time, the right to embargo them and not their victims.[14]

Overseas, there were the expected complaints from the Japanese, toward whom Roosevelt had primarily addressed his remarks, and from the Germans and Italians, to whom the remarks also applied. From the democracies and the Soviet Union came acclaim. A bit later the cautious Prime Minister Chamberlain hailed Roosevelt's "clarion call." In the privacy of a cabinet meeting, the prime minister's reactions to the speech were not flattering. He did not want to be maneuvered into appearing to stand in the way of sanctions if the United States would cooperate, yet "the speech was so involved that it was very difficult to discover its meaning."[15]

The speech, broadcast by shortwave, rallied the League of Nations.

"Its effect in Geneva was instantaneous and put an end to considerable shilly-shally that was going on," wrote Moffat. "We can now regard a nine power conference as almost inevitable." The next day the Assembly voted to condemn Japan's aggression against China and invited the nine powers that had signed the treaty on the Far East in 1922 to confer. The American minister to Switzerland reported that several delegations that might otherwise have abstained had been swayed.[16]

A nine-power conference would give Roosevelt an immediate vehicle to transform the generalities of the quarantine speech into concrete action. Through October, he was optimistic that opinion could be marshaled.

While Roosevelt in his own mind thought of a "quarantine" as a means of avoiding war, fearful isolationists and pacifists, not knowing just what he planned, took the view that it would indeed involve the United States in conflict. Roosevelt in his reassuring remarks to the press and in a Fireside Chat could give no specifics but simply emphasized his peaceful intent.

A reporter asked him the day after the quarantine speech what type of measure he had in mind, and whether it would be collaborative and something more than moral indignation. Roosevelt replied affirmatively.

> Q. "Doesn't that mean economic sanctions anyway?"
> THE PRESIDENT: "No, not necessarily. Look, 'sanctions' is a terrible word to use. They are out of the window."

Roosevelt, while being cryptic, did give some indications of what was on his mind. It was, he granted, an attitude "but it says we are looking toward a program."

Ernest K. Lindley continued to try to pin down Roosevelt.

> "You say there isn't any conflict between what you outline and the Neutrality Act. They seem to be on opposite poles to me and your assertion does not enlighten me."
> THE PRESIDENT: "Put on your thinking-cap, Ernest." . . .

"What is a quarantine?" pressed Lindley.

Mrs. Roosevelt, who was attending the press conference, broke in to say, "I have great sympathy with you, Ernest."

Not surprisingly, the consensus among reporters at the time was that Roosevelt was feeling his way without any clear idea what to do. Many historians have agreed.[17]

Roosevelt, hobbled both at home and abroad, felt firmly that a strong concert of nations could restrain aggression without danger of attack, provided they were sufficiently cohesive. The key to the combination was the British and the French, and his experience with them had not been reassuring.

As soon as Roosevelt returned to Washington, he spent two hours with Secretary Hull, Under Secretary Sumner Welles, and Norman Davis discussing concretely what he hoped to achieve through a nine-power conference. He wanted it to meet in Brussels so that it would not be under British domination, and favored Davis, whose ideas most clearly meshed with his, to head the delegation. (Later Roosevelt decided to send J. Pierrepont Moffat and Stanley Hornbeck, who seemed more cautious, as the two advisers to Davis.) "As to substance, the President is thinking far more in constructive terms than in terms of sanctions," Moffat noted. "He has some definite ideas and will not cross other bridges unless and until necessary."[18]

Already within the State Department, some resistance to Roosevelt's program was coalescing. As Moffat put it, "if effective and Japan were completely downed China would merely fall a prey to Russian anarchy and we would have the whole job to do over again and a worse one." Further, in advising Hull, "those of us who lived abroad were a unit in pointing out that we could not go on to take sanctions, no matter what their form, without risking retaliation." The weight of the department upon Roosevelt was cautionary.[19]

On October 19, 1937, Roosevelt at Hyde Park gave final instructions to Davis before the latter sailed for Brussels (which Davis recorded in his memorandum of the conversation):

> . . . all of the countries which wish to stop this war and to protect themselves from its consequences, or in other words the so-called neutral countries, should band together for their own protection against this contagion. One thing that might be considered would be that . . . the other powers would agree to give China every facility for acquiring arms, and so forth, to defend themselves; although in this case the United States could do nothing because our laws would not permit. Another alternative would be for the neutrals to ostracize Japan, break off relations. This he said would not be practical unless the overwhelming opinion of the world would support it.

Roosevelt was vague about sanctions but left Davis with the belief that as a final resort he might discuss them.[20]

There in essence was what Roosevelt had refused to define for the reporters, the meaning of "quarantine." Moffat, who was accompanying Davis to the conference, read the memorandum and concluded reluctantly that Roosevelt "did not see his way out of the situation any more than did we."

The British had already been sounding out the State Department on whether or not the United States was prepared, if need be, to join with them in an economic boycott of Japan. Chamberlain reported to the British cabinet that he and Foreign Secretary Anthony Eden had concluded that effective economic sanctions could not be put in force without risking war, and that they would be of no use unless they were backed by overwhelming force. Therefore, Chamberlain concluded, "We could not go into sanctions . . . without a guarantee from the United States of America that they would be prepared to face up to all the consequences. . . ." If the conference were ineffectual, it might well serve only to encourage "peace breakers."[21]

When the nine-power conference at Brussels opened in November, it was as foredoomed as the London Economic Conference of 1933 had been. Japan defiantly would not attend; none of the delegates, except perhaps the British, felt that Roosevelt's formula of arousing public opinion and moral indignation, or resorting to measures short of coercion, could have any effect. Davis himself, thinking he was acting in keeping with Roosevelt's instructions, was ready if need be to go further. The State Department was more cautious, creating serious difficulties for him, and Roosevelt, too, seemed to have retreated to a safe but innocuous position. On November 6, Roosevelt discussed with Jules Henry of the French embassy the banning of munitions shipments on the Indochina railroad. "Some of the great powers with territorial interests in the Far East," Roosevelt observed, "were behaving like 'scared rabbits.' " When Henry asked if the United States would come to the assistance of France if Indochina were attacked, Roosevelt responded that he understood Henry's viewpoint perfectly, but had the impression that France might have exaggerated fears. Henry reported that the president had asked rhetorically, ". . . is it not taken into account in France that a Japanese attack upon Hong Kong, or Indochina or the Dutch East Indies would constitute equally an attack against the Philippines? In that eventuality, our common interests would be menaced and we would have jointly to defend them."[22]

These candid remarks were too incautious for Roosevelt to let them stand unaltered. Later he toned them down, initialing a corrected version in which he dismissed the question as hypothetical and refused to comment on what the navy would undertake. When Premier Camille

Chautemps discussed Henry's report with the American ambassador, William Bullitt, he remarked that while France and Great Britain might be behaving like scared rabbits, "the rabbit which was behaving in the most scared manner since there was no gun pointed toward it was the United States."[23]

There was indeed a gun pointed at Roosevelt, but it was from within the United States. In consequence he would have nothing to do with the various bold proposals that Davis took up in private at the Brussels conference after the initial efforts at conciliation failed. Davis was carrying out the president's orders. Nevertheless, with the conference already under way, Roosevelt responded favorably to a suggestion from Admiral Harry E. Yarnell, commander in chief of the Asiatic Fleet, that in case of hostilities with Japan, the navy should pursue an economic war of strangulation. Roosevelt noted that "it goes along with the word 'quarantine' which I used in the Chicago speech last month."[24]

Although Roosevelt's fascination with the idea of restraint continued unabated, Secretary Hull was firmly negative. At the outset of the Brussels conference, Roosevelt made some slight effort to counteract the caution in the State Department. In the days that followed, he succumbed to criticism at home and from overseas. The bombardment from the Senate was particularly strong, and he was always sensitive to it. Davis pleaded with Roosevelt, but received no direct support from him. Rather Davis heard only from the State Department; Hull ordered Davis not even to consider nonrecognition of aggressors. The Brussels conference adjourned fruitlessly on November 24, 1937. Davis returned to the United States bitter, and for some time made scathing remarks within the State Department. In 1938, Roosevelt appointed Davis to head the American Red Cross, and continued to seek his counsel, but never again used him as a key figure in American diplomacy.[25]

Roosevelt, revealed powerless, was himself resentful. It was not his eloquence that had failed him. Rather, events had not yet become grim enough, nor did they for another year, to sway the electorate toward giving him greater authority.

From the summer of 1936 into early 1939, no calamity more clearly illustrated Roosevelt's lack of power than the Spanish Civil War. Like a persistent fire on the edge of a great munitions depot, sometimes smoldering, occasionally flaring, it threatened to touch off a general European conflagration. For the president it created grave dilemmas in both foreign policy and domestic politics, which for the most part he met by doing little or nothing. His response to the war was more canny than dramatic, departing little from the national consensus. He stood on the sidelines, largely as an inactive spectator to the Spanish tragedy.[26]

In retrospect, the issues involved in the war look much simpler than they did at the time. It has seemed to be a first testing of the Nazi and Fascist forces outside the borders of Germany and Italy, and a struggle for survival against them. As "bleeding Kansas" did before the Civil War, the Spanish Civil War seemed a preliminary battle in the impending major conflict.

At first, the revolt of the right-wing Spanish Army officers in July, 1936, must have appeared to Roosevelt a minor peril that he could only hope would disappear in a few days. So indeed it might have, had not the rebel officers been successful in their appeal to Hitler and Mussolini for aid. The rebel forces, calling themselves Nationalists, under the leadership of General Francisco Franco became powerful enough to threaten the capture of Madrid by September, 1936. The government forces, which came to be known as the Loyalists, rallied, received some Soviet aid, and drove the Nationalists back from Madrid. The struggle clearly would be a long and complicated one.

Nor was it a struggle in which it would be easy for Roosevelt to choose sides from a standpoint of policy, conscience, or politics. There was his acute and overweening concern over the threat of the Nazis, which grew rather than diminished during the years of the war. There was, on the other hand, the strong repugnance with which the larger part of his Catholic supporters viewed the Loyalists. He seems for some time to have shared that repugnance. Prior to the outbreak of the war, Spain had been turbulent and there had been outrages committed against Catholic clergy and churches.

When the war broke out, Roosevelt and Hull with good reason assumed a traditional stance of noninvolvement both in word and spirit. Ambassador Claude Bowers heartily supported their views from the outbreak of the war to near the end; it was only afterward that he felt the United States should strongly have aided the Loyalists.

American noninvolvement in the Spanish Civil War did not fit the international law of neutrality, which would have permitted only the legitimate government involved in a civil war — the Loyalists — to purchase arms. Rather, it was in keeping with the efforts of the British and the French to prevent the war from spreading beyond the bounds of Spain, and hence to appease Germany and Italy. When the Germans and Italians began aiding the Nationalists, France was allowing a little aid to go to the Spanish government and the Soviet Union seemed ready to give considerable assistance. Within a few days the British persuaded the French to join with them in establishing a Non-Intervention Committee pledging themselves not to sell arms to either side. The Germans, Italians, and Soviets joined the committee. There followed years of charade in which officially the totalitarian powers were prohibiting aid, while the newly formed Axis powers (Germany and Italy) provided large amounts, and the Soviets rather less. However, the Axis did not send the massive aid to Franco that would have brought the war to an end; they profited from the uncertainties of the drawn-out struggle, and the threat that the war might spread.

For Roosevelt there was the immediate danger in 1936 that the Republicans might develop the Spanish Civil War into a political issue with which to undercut him in the presidential campaign, then in its opening stages. Catholics especially might be susceptible. He turned aside the threatening question first and foremost with his "I hate war" speech, which took care of the electorate in general. As for the Catholic voters, he depended upon eloquent friends in the clergy, especially Father John A. Ryan of the National Catholic Welfare Conference.[27]

During the first year of the Spanish Civil War few Americans took exception to Roosevelt's policy toward Spain. He and the State Department did not resort to traditional neutrality, but rather followed a course in keeping with that of the British and French. The United States would not join the Non-Intervention Committee, but Roosevelt did try to prevent arms sales to either side through a device rhetorical rather than legal, a "moral embargo," which he announced in August, 1936. Since it placed no legal impediment against arms sales, Roosevelt sought from Congress discretionary power, but had to agree to the Spanish Embargo Act of January, 1937, which banned sales to either side. Subsequently a new neutrality law still failed to give him discretionary power. Probably that was all to the good for Roosevelt, since it prevented him from having to choose sides later between Catholic supporters who were pro-Franco and liberal followers, increasingly pro-Loyalist.[28]

At first Roosevelt genuinely wished to block supplies to both sides, but by April, 1937, his sympathies, even if not his policies, seemed to sway toward the Loyalists. He was, however, quite careful about what he said in public. He had firm reasons for being quiet about Italian Fascism. In part, he had hopes that Mussolini could in the end be swayed to move nearer to democracy in Italy and to France and Great Britain in European politics. Further, as a political realist he could not overlook the popularity of Mussolini among the considerable Italian electorate in the United States, even as Italian legions moved into Spain.

An additional complication was the pro-Franco sympathies of the heads of a number of Latin American nations. Aid to the Loyalists, some of the State Department officials feared, might imperil solid support for hemispheric defense.

Within the United States, through 1938, pressures for aid to Loyalist Spain gradually grew as the fortunes of the Loyalists declined. Roosevelt was sympathetic but was reluctant to challenge Congress, the general public, and particularly his strong Catholic following. The isolationist Senator Gerald P. Nye, regarding the embargo as a boon to Franco, introduced a resolution to lift the embargo against the government of Spain (the Loyalists), and maintain it against the Nationalists.

In May, when Ickes aired his outspoken views to Roosevelt, he received a strong retort. Even if the embargo were raised, the president asserted, Spain would not be able to buy munitions. Ickes pressed him further: "Finally the President told me that he had discussed the matter with Congressional leaders that morning. . . . He said frankly that to raise the embargo would mean the loss of every Catholic vote next fall and that the Democratic Members of Congress were jittery about it and didn't want it done."[29]

Yet at that very time Roosevelt was toying with schemes to send covert aid to the Loyalists that would bypass both Congress and the British. France in the spring of 1938 was surreptitiously allowing some military supplies to cross the border into Loyalist Spain. Roosevelt sent word confidentially to the columnist Drew Pearson that he would allow goods destined for Spain to be cleared for France. For a brief while Roosevelt's scheme worked. The American purchasing agent for the Loyalist government, who was involved with Roosevelt's brother-in-law, G. Hall Roosevelt, successfully sent thirty shipments of strategic materials via France during March and April, 1938.

The climax of this operation came in June. Hall Roosevelt located for the Spanish government 150 new and used airplanes. He then discussed the scheme with the president, who (as Hall Roosevelt later explained to Bullitt) "agreed to wink at the evasion of the Neutrality Act" in order to bolster "the resistance of the Spanish Government against Franco." On June 13, the president at a meeting in the White House with Hall and James Roosevelt present, ordered Joseph Green of the State Department not to scrutinize closely whatever falsified papers were presented, and to allow the export of the planes. Nothing was on paper; there was not even a record of an appointment with Green, whom Roosevelt had summoned by telephone. Next went a cable not from Franklin D. Roosevelt, but from Eleanor Roosevelt to Ambassador Bullitt, notifying him that Hall was coming to Paris and asking for his assistance. Before Hall Roosevelt could arrive in Paris, the scheme collapsed. Prime Minister Chamberlain persuaded Premier Edouard Daladier to close the French border to all military shipments. In any event, the time when American supplies might have meant a difference to the Loyalist cause was soon over. In the early months of 1939, Franco forces brought the war to an end.[30]

As Roosevelt's fumbling venture into covert action indicated, from an initially impartial position he had become a partisan of the Loyalists (or more accurately stated, a foe of their opponents). Yet he would have paid too high a price both at home and abroad had he assumed a more open role earlier. His policies throughout the conflict were both unheroic and ineffective, but seldom had his options for action been more limited. The charade of nonintervention in the Spanish Civil War was a facade for appeasement that by 1939 had manifestly failed. The Catholic issue, which had hampered Roosevelt at home, melted away with the end of the war. The American people, like Roosevelt, had to face more starkly the growing Nazi hegemony in Europe and that of the Japanese military leaders in East Asia.

Chapter 21

ADMINISTRATIVE REFORM AND ATTEMPTED PARTY PURGE

ROOSEVELT continued doggedly to seek structural changes to put in place a permanent New Deal. His goals were to modernize the administrative branch and to remake the Democratic party in his own image. He had achieved a transformation in judicial review; the roadblock continuing to face him was in Congress. Even in the best of times a full-fledged reorganization program would have invited protests from many interest groups. In 1938 it led to a fresh full-scale contest between the president and the congressional conservatives, who were less concerned with the merits of the proposals than with grinding down of the president.

Behind Congress there was a discernible conservative trend in the thinking of the electorate. Roosevelt's own popularity remained remarkably high, but opinion polls indicated that enthusiasm for his proposals lagged. The court issue had shaken many voters and strengthened dissent in politics. A note of nastiness, long a minor theme, became more intense and widespread. Roosevelt, sensitive to the attacks, seemed to feel besieged; he was not as disposed as before to respond with hearty laughter to jibes at his expense. In this mood he responded to the jokes of the Washington correspondents at their Gridiron Dinner: "If privately and publicly, you exercise your constitutional right not to hitch your wagon to great ideals, don't cut the traces of your neighbor who is trying to hitch his wagon to a star. At long last those who seek most highly gain most greatly. The people of the United States will see to that."[1]

The basic changes that Roosevelt envisaged in noble terms appeared to his critics as dangerous, self-seeking, and even dictatorial. An irreconcilable gulf was opening, and it grew over an issue that Roosevelt and many sharing his progressive background had for decades insisted should be scientific and technical, not political. That was the reorganization of the administration that he had proposed to Congress in January, 1937.[2]

Most presidents, beginning with Benjamin Harrison in the 1890s, had been seeking modernization, Roosevelt reminded editors of religious journals in the spring of 1938. Administrative machinery was "awfully old-fashioned and sort of grew up like Topsy," he explained. "What we want to do is to put it on the same kind of an efficient basis that we would run an industrial plant or a private charity or even the financial end of a church."[3]

The problem was, as Roosevelt well knew, that as various federal agencies had come into existence they tended to take on a life of their own, independent of the executive department, depending directly upon Congress to nurture them. In return, the powerful committee and subcommittee chairmen in Congress derived many of their prerogatives from their special relationship with agencies under their cognizance. Special interest groups outside the government came to be the clients of these agencies, and these too fought vigorously against any effort to modify them. Presidents and their staffs came and went, but these relationships went on seemingly forever. Congress and the public had not been kind to presidents who tried to alter them through government reorganization. When a reporter asked why certain senators who said there were too many government bureaus were afraid to abolish some, Roosevelt parried, then a few weeks later gave publishers a tart, considered answer:

"When Congress starts to reorganize what happens? We have in this Government six or seven different agencies that are . . . printing maps. . . . Do you think that Congress can ever be got to consolidate that? Oh, no, the pressure from those six or seven bureaus would be too strong."[4]

A good bit of the pressure was coming from Roosevelt's own ordinarily loyal lieutenants. The rivalry among them, which he had so frequently fostered either for his own amusement or to stimulate achievement, was in this instance destructive. Secretary of the Interior Ickes doughtily fought to obtain the Forest Service from Secretary of Agriculture Wallace, who with equal vigor resisted; each thought that Roosevelt was on his side. Meanwhile conservation organizations pleaded with Congress to block any change. Even more fundamental was the conflict between Congress and the president over executive power. Roosevelt sought reorganization in order to promote efficiency, a goal that he had pointed out even during the Hundred Days was more important than any possible savings. He should have remembered that earlier attempts at reorganization had encountered congressional jealousy.

Late in 1936, Roosevelt took a keen interest in the lengthy planning of the reorganization program, enlisting the expertise of three of the foremost American authorities on public administration, Charles E. Merriam, Louis Brownlow, and Luther H. Gulick. He himself, out of his own experience, made contributions to their proposals. Ignoring at first the likely political protests, he wanted the quasi-judicial independent agencies like the Interstate Commerce Commission brought under executive control; by 1938 he was ready to make them an exception. Roosevelt seemed bent upon achieving what from a standpoint of responsible public administration would be an ideal structure, a monument to him, rather than upon placating conflicting political pressure groups. A more practical matter was that Roosevelt needed to prepare his cabinet for forthcoming drastic changes: the establishment of departments of Public Works and Social Welfare, and the changing of the name of the Interior Department to the Department of Conservation.

Roosevelt was acting at the right moment before opposition either to reorganization or to himself could crystallize. Considering the major importance of his message calling for a fundamental renovation of the executive branch of the government, there was surprisingly little response from either Congress or the public. In Congress there was much quiet surprise but little open protest. Numerous congressmen protested in private, because the plan would put under civil service all government employees except those involved in policy-making. Patronage was a vital perquisite that they would not readily abandon.[5]

Perhaps the public did not grasp the purport of Roosevelt's request; it was too technical and too remote from immediate concerns. Only a few people were absorbed in the question of modern public administration. Had not the Supreme Court fight eclipsed the reorganization bill in 1937, it assuredly would have been enacted in some form. As it was, when Roosevelt returned to this major objective in 1938, the attitude of both Congress and the public had changed.

Basically, as those who have analyzed Roosevelt's reorganization fight in 1938 have pointed out, the president's goal and that of the experts assisting him was to make the sprawling administration more responsive to the White House. Roosevelt himself should obtain the services of six administrative assistants, with, to quote the committee, "a passion for anonymity." Bureaus should be moved into departments where they would more logically belong. A hundred-odd agencies could be reorganized.

Congress could within sixty days disapprove of any change Roosevelt recommended. If he vetoed their disapproval, they could override him with a two-thirds vote.[6]

In theory there was nothing in the proposals that strong congressional advocates of reorganization, such as Senator Harry Byrd of Virginia, could find objectionable. Byrd at first seemed neutral, but soon voiced firm objections because the primary result of reorganization would not be economy. As various congressmen expressed dismay over the likelihood of losing patronage or some cherished relationship with a government agency they helped oversee, the overriding issue became apparent. They saw reorganization as weakening their own power and prerogatives in relation to those of the president. They did not want Roosevelt to gain firmer control over his own administration, and in the frightful decade of Hitler, Mussolini, and Franco, the rhetoric quickly escalated to charges that he was attempting to create a dictatorship.[7]

Beyond all principles there was a final reason for the struggle — that opponents of Roosevelt both within Congress and without gradually seized upon the issue as a vehicle for the punishing attacks they had begun over the court plan. At first they made only slight headway. There was some familiar bombast during the House debate in the summer of 1937. Dewey Short of Missouri predicted that the White House assistants would be "theoretical, intellectual, professorial nincompoops who could not be elected dog-catcher." The Republican watchdog of government expenditures, John Taber of New York, assailed the proposed Department of Welfare; it would burden the nation with a "permanent relief set-up," and open new vistas to "experimentalists from Columbia and dear old Harvard." These attacks received little publicity, and the bills embodying the reorganization plans sailed through the House by wide margins. The Senate failed to act, and reorganization was stalled.

By winter, administrative reorganization had lost much of its support. Unlikely voices, including that of the notable conservationist Bernard DeVoto, were warning that the bill would wipe out the barriers to totalitarianism. Opposition was becoming respectable, ready-made for those disposed to launch a new massive assault on Roosevelt.[8]

Frank Gannett, owner of the third largest newspaper chain in the country, founded the ostensibly nonpartisan National Committee to Uphold Constitutional Government, which sent out 900,000 letters urging protests to senators. At a critical point, Father Coughlin joined forces, and turned the flow into a flood. Senator Wagner received 10,000 telegrams and decided to vote against the bill. Nevertheless, after considerable modification, the reorganization plan passed the Senate on March

24. Senator Byrnes, managing the bill, momentarily was distracted and had to agree to send the bill to the House. Foes of reorganization thus staved off defeat, but that became apparent only later.[9]

Roosevelt, vacationing in Warm Springs, received the news of the Senate victory with such jubilation that he forgot his customary wariness. Engaged in banter with reporters, he gave them the rare privilege of quoting him directly: "It proves that the Senate cannot be purchased by organized telegrams based on direct misrepresentation."

Roosevelt had delivered himself into the hands of his enemies. Not only the senators, but also the members of the House who had yet to vote were outraged. One representative remarked, "That really did stir the animals up." Roosevelt had crowed over his Senate victory too soon. When the House several days later again took up the reorganization bill, resentment of many members spilled over against Roosevelt. They defeated the bill by a slim margin, 204 to 196.[10]

Even before the final defeat, Roosevelt was wincing from the accusations that he wanted to be a dictator. Newspapers on March 31 carried the bizarre story that Marvin McIntyre had aroused the reporters at Warm Springs at one o'clock in the morning to hand them a letter in which Roosevelt expressed his denial. It was startling indeed to read Roosevelt's statement to an unknown correspondent: "I have no inclination to be a dictator."

For Roosevelt to have replied openly was a political blunder. The issuing of the statement in the middle of the night was an unfortunate happenstance. The reporters had not gone to bed but had been playing poker, and one of them was particularly eager to obtain the story for his morning paper.

The result was a flurry of uncomplimentary speculation in the news media and ammunition from political detractors. The insinuations persisted. In the winter of 1940, Eleanor's cousin Alice Roosevelt Longworth amused Washington society with her joke that "F.D.R." stood for "Fuehrer, Duce, Roosevelt," thus linking him with both Hitler and Mussolini.[11]

The defeat over reorganization in the spring of 1938 was a temporary, not a lasting crisis for Roosevelt. By trimming back his proposals to what a congressional majority would accept, Roosevelt succeeded in installing the fundamentals of several of his proposals. It was the tactic that Theodore Roosevelt had pursued three decades earlier to obtain railroad legislation, and that the senior senator La Follette had denounced bitingly as a half-a-loaf policy. Yet first for TR and later for FDR, a half-loaf grew in time to something far more substantial.

In 1939 Roosevelt finally obtained some authority to reorganize the administration. Early in July he met once more with his experts to devise a strategy that involved even further concessions. Roosevelt remarked to Farley concerning the 1938 bill that the teeth had been taken out of it, that it was harmless. Now he made it seem even more innocuous by removing every possible point of contention around which special interest groups could rally.[12]

Representative Lindsay Warren of North Carolina counseled extreme caution, and Roosevelt accepted the warnings, letting Warren reduce the measure to a minimum acceptable to most Democratic congressmen. The measure attracted relatively little attention as, under Warren's management, it sailed through the House by a substantial majority. The vote in the Senate was closer, but Byrnes this time was alert in handling the bill, and Roosevelt himself may have intervened. He persuaded Senator Harry S. Truman, a safe administration supporter, to fly back from Missouri, and he won the votes of two key senators from states with large cattle interests, Key Pittman of Nevada and Dennis Chavez of New Mexico, by promising them that he would not transfer the national forests to the Department of the Interior. Western cattlemen who leased enormous areas of grazing land from the Forest Service were adamant that it stay in the Department of Agriculture. The three senators helped defeat a crippling amendment, 46 to 44, and the final measure passed by a wide margin.[13]

The Reorganization Act that Roosevelt finally signed on April 3, 1939, seemed at the time little more than a meaningless sop, comparable to the minimal modernizing of the judicial system that followed the court-packing debacle. The fact that the president had to present his reorganization plans to Congress for approval mollified it. The dropping of the proposed new departments, especially the Welfare Department, alleviated fears that New Deal agencies would be made permanent. It was decidedly weaker than the 1938 legislation, but it gave Roosevelt an opportunity to begin substantial modernization of the federal administration. He was as delighted with it as with a new toy.

Even before the bill was passed, Roosevelt returned with enthusiasm to the public administration committee that had advised him for several years. They had been a political liability until then and he had kept them out of sight. In addition, Roosevelt enlisted Harold D. Smith, the first-rate young director of the Michigan budget, whom Brownlow recommended, to become director of the budget. When the outgoing budget director brought him into the Oval Office, he remarked to the president that Smith was not eager to take the appointment, he had too many bridges to burn in Michigan. Roosevelt handed a folder of matches to Smith and said, "Start burning." It was a felicitous appointment at precisely the right time. Smith undertook administrative reforms and was an influential advocate of Keynesian policies.[14]

On Sunday afternoon, April 23, 1939, Louis Brownlow's committee of public administration experts presented the president with a draft message on reorganization and specific executive orders covering the first step of the program. Roosevelt greeted the committee with gusto. Through his knowledgeability he demonstrated his own qualifications in public administration. He suggested a number of ways to strengthen the message, and proposed collecting all the federal loan agencies, except perhaps Farm Credit, into a single loan administration.[15]

The revolution in the federal administration came with Plan I, which Roosevelt sent to Congress on April 25. It established the Executive Office of the President, gathering under White House control, together with Roosevelt's immediate staff, the Bureau of the Budget. There was nervousness over how Congress would receive the plan. Everyone "seemed to have had the jitters as a result of previous experience with the reorganization proposals," Smith noted. Nevertheless, with surprising speed and little debate, the House upheld the proposals on May 3, and since they required the approval of only one house, they thus gained congressional sanction. Plan II and subsequent proposals also caused little trouble. Most of the transfers of agencies from one department to another proceeded without difficulty.[16]

Roosevelt's greatest gain from reorganization, and his largest contribution to his successors, was the creation of a modern support organization for the White House. The Executive Office of the President was a sound replacement for the improvisations upon which Roosevelt had depended since he took office. He considered it his working force, and hoped Congress would give him latitude in developing it.[17]

Key elements were the Bureau of the Budget and the new assistants. Earlier directors of the budget had been responsive to him, but were located with their staffs in the Treasury Department. Now Smith and his subordinates were in the Executive Office and solely at the president's disposal. The Bureau of the Budget, originally a progressive concept, served when first established in the Harding administration as a conservative device, as William Allen White stated it, "to slash the guts out of reform." Roosevelt reshaped it into one of the most powerful forces in the administrative branch.[18]

Roosevelt particularly needed the full-time assistants so that he would no longer have to depend upon the services of a shifting group of people nominally assigned to other agencies. In July, he appointed Lauchlin Currie, William McReynolds, and James Rowe. It took him a little while to become accustomed to delegating duties to them, but soon they were invaluable. Their long hours of work justified Brownlow's recommendation that they should be persons of "great physical vigor." Roosevelt took seriously the "passion for anonymity" requisite, and warned Rowe when his name appeared in print among those seen at a cocktail party, "If I read this too often, you will need another job." It was Roosevelt's firm instinct not to let anyone come between him and a diversity of sources of information, or to formulate in advance his ultimate decisions. The assistants were an instrument of power for him; he did not become a figurehead behind which they could take control.[19]

In subsequent administrations, the tools Roosevelt had developed could be put to still different uses. What he had conceived of as no more than prudent administration came to be labeled an "imperial presidency." "Roosevelt, for his own part, took the first steps toward the 'institutionalized President,' " the political scientist Richard Neustadt has suggested. "But Roosevelt rarely let himself become its prisoner."[20]

Like administrative reorganization, party reform had been one of Roosevelt's most enduring dreams since he had entered politics, but there was no ultimate victory in his effort to transform the Democratic party. It was ironic that Roosevelt, who only ten years earlier had unified a riven minority party, in 1938 deepened a rift in what he had transformed into the party of a substantial majority.

Roosevelt sought, through running pro–New Deal candidates in the primaries, to defeat conservative Democratic senators who had been thwarting his reform measures, even though in election years they professed their loyalty to the president. For all their forebodings even critics as vehement as Senator Josiah Bailey of North Carolina had no intention of bolting the Democratic party, their vehicle to power. They profited from Roosevelt's popularity, enjoyed much patronage, and then wrought havoc upon New Deal programs.

On the other hand, throughout the country, including to a considerable degree in the South, there were a number of emergent young Democratic leaders who had broken with past traditions and cast their lot unreservedly with Roosevelt. A notable pair of these, Lister Hill of Alabama and Claude Pepper of Florida, fared well at the polls in 1938.

The presence in the Senate of Hill and Pepper, and in the House of comparable New Deal supporters, like Lyndon B. Johnson and Maury Maverick of Texas, was comforting to Roosevelt, since a great deal of his concern was over the blocking of southern programs. Pepper recalled that Roosevelt's conversations with him largely concerned the problems of the South: "Our needs ran almost the gamut of our economy and our society. President Roosevelt couldn't understand why so many Southern Senators and Representatives would oppose his programs to help the South . . . when our needs were so great."[21]

The victories of Hill, and especially of Pepper early in 1938, encouraged Roosevelt to intervene. They brought rejoicing in the White House and dismay among the southern conservatives in Congress. The voters had spoken, and they seemed firmly behind Roosevelt, yet the wages and hours legislation the president sought seemed buried. It continued to be southern gospel, repugnant to Roosevelt, that the prosperity of the South depended upon cheaper wages to bring in industries. As with the reorganization bill, compromise after compromise had been inserted into the Fair Labor Standards (wages and hours) bill to make it more palatable to southern business and agriculture. Farm wages were exempted, yet the Southern Pines Association had published full-page advertisements headed "Farmers! to arms!" warning them that if the bill passed they would have to pay their hands three dollars a day. "That is a lie," Roosevelt asserted to a group of newspaper editors, "and every editor who ran that ad knew it was a lie."

When the news of Pepper's victory reached Capitol Hill, representatives rushed to the well of the House to sign a discharge petition — the honor roll, they called it — and within two and a half hours there were sufficient names on the petition to exhume the bill from John J. O'Connor's Rules Committee, where it had seemed dead. On May 24, the wages and hours bill passed 314 to 97. It survived southern attempts to reinstitute a wage differential in conference committee with the Senate, and was signed by Roosevelt June 25, 1938.[22]

Along with the Reorganization Act of 1939, the Fair Labor Standards Act was one of the two last basic domestic reform measures of the New Deal. It was so watered down and weak that it seemed more symbol than substance. Large categories of the most ill-paid, overworked laborers in both the South and the North were exempted. When it went into effect in October, 1938, it provided for a 44-hour week, to be reduced two hours in each of the following two years, and for a 25-cent-an-hour minimum wage, to go up in steps to 40 cents by 1945. Yet even a 25-cent minimum raised the wages of 44 percent of the workers in southern sawmills, and the 44-hour week ended a 12-hour day in the cottonseed industry. Throughout the entire country, numerous workers benefited, and gained still more through decades that followed as the wage minimum was ratcheted upward and Congress voted to wipe out one exempt group after another. The measure also prohibited the employment of child labor in interstate commerce.[23]

After much wrangling with Senator Pat Harrison of Mississippi over a tax measure, Roosevelt in a Fireside Chat in June, 1938, threw down his gauntlet. There were two viewpoints, Roosevelt suggested. The liberals believed they could solve problems "through democratic processes instead of Fascism or Communism," and were opposed to a "moratorium on reform." The conservative school of thought, on the other hand, did not recognize the validity of government action to meet the new problems. "It believes that individual initiative and private philanthropy will solve them — that we ought to repeal many of the things we have done and go back . . . to the kind of Government we had in the twenties."

The voters, Roosevelt said, should choose between these two groups in the primaries. In his role as president, he would not ask the electorate to vote for Democrats, nor would he take part in Democratic primaries. But, and here he made his challenge:

> As the head of the Democratic Party . . . charged with the responsibility of carrying out the definitely liberal declaration of principles set forth in the 1936 Democratic platform, I feel that I have every right to speak in those few instances where there may be a clear issue between candidates for a Democratic nomination involving these principles, or involving a clear misuse of my own name.[24]

What Roosevelt had in mind was apparent. The operation, which newspapers already were labeling a purge, was to be something more than reprisals against those who had opposed him in the court fight. He and his House leadership were sick of the obstructionism of Representative O'Connor of New York City, who still professed himself a New Dealer, but the Senate was Roosevelt's prime target. There he wanted to insure the reelection of Alben Barkley of Kentucky, the majority leader, and to get rid of several of his most consistent opponents. He had already found candidates to run against Walter George of Georgia and Millard Tydings of Maryland. At the outset, he targeted nine of the twenty-nine Democrats up for reelection. Even if some of these seats were to be lost in November, the victory of New Dealers in the primaries might assure control of the state Democratic organizations in the 1940 election. That was said to be the prime objective.

The South was in the forefront of Roosevelt's attention, even though opposition in Congress was coming as much from the West. Roosevelt shared the zeal of his wife and was determined to better the lives of the southern underprivileged, whether in the mining area of West Virginia or in the hinterland of Warm Springs. Southern leadership in Congress was one of the most formidable obstacles to the eradication of both rural poverty in the area and urban wretchedness in the cities of the North, but it was the South, lagging economically behind the rest of the nation, that Roosevelt especially sought to redeem from the Bourbon Democratic grasp of the past.[25]

In the spring of 1938, a group of idealistic young southern social scientists had provided him with much of the factual ammunition he needed for his political assault upon southern poverty. Clark Foreman, an Atlanta liberal, persuaded Roosevelt to ask for a study of southern conditions; southern social scientists prepared it under the sponsorship of the National Emergency Council. The *Report on Economic Conditions of the South*, appearing in the summer of 1938, summed up the southern scholarly monographs of the decade: "The paradox of the South is that while it is blessed by Nature with immense wealth, its people as a whole are the poorest in the country." In a prefatory letter, Roosevelt asserted, "It is my conviction that the South presents right now the Nation's No. 1 economic problem — the Nation's problem, not merely the South's." He set forth once again, in the language of the planners, an agenda repugnant to those comfortable with things as they were.[26]

Both before and after the appearance of the report, Roosevelt elaborated upon its themes, suggesting the political means to his great social ends. At Gainesville, Georgia, in March, he had labeled the political economy "feudal," and declared there was little difference between a feudal system and a fascist system. "If you believe in the one, you lean to the other."[27]

The southern establishment reacted with outrage against both the report and its political implications. Despite all the years Roosevelt had been visiting Warm Springs, and demonstrating his mastery of southern social and political mores in the guise of a Georgia farmer-politician, he stood revealed now as an outsider, at best a meddler, and at worst a Yankee carpetbagger.

Southern Democratic leaders particularly feared that Roosevelt, egged on by Mrs. Roosevelt, was engaged also in a covert attack upon segregation and the denial of the franchise to blacks. Throughout the South, one of the most powerful tacit weapons of the conservatives was the issue of white supremacy. A Georgia county Democratic official declared, "You ask any nigger on the street who's the greatest man in the world. Nine out of ten will tell you Franklin D. Roosevelt. Roosevelt's greatest strength is with the lower element. That's why I think he is so dangerous."[28]

Roosevelt was well aware that his greatest strength in the South was among the part of the populace with the fewest votes, not only blacks but whites as well. After his Gainesville, Georgia, speech, he commented to Aubrey Williams, the southern liberal, "One difficulty is that three-quarters of the whites in the South cannot vote — poll tax, etc." The Florida victory, in which 70 percent of the votes were pro–New Deal, had come shortly after the repeal of the state poll tax. It remained a bulwark of the conservative organizations in eight southern states. Roosevelt guardedly endorsed repeal in a letter to Brooks Hays of Arkansas, but later insisted he was not intervening in a state matter. The repeal movement failed in Arkansas that November. Beneficiaries of WPA or agricultural aid were, understandably, strongly pro-Roosevelt, but could not be much use to him if they could not vote.[29]

Much was made during the primary battles over the control that Roosevelt and his cohorts exercised over federal spending, and the enormous sums they could pour into critical areas through public works and work relief projects. Within the Democratic South the question long had been which organization would handle funds. In areas where they were under the control of friends of Roosevelt's, like Burnet Maybank of South Carolina, he would have no trouble. Unfortunately, many of the allocations had gone to Democrats whose enthusiasm for Roosevelt was more public than private, more professed than real.[30]

What counted in primaries was not the personal popularity of Roosevelt, which remained high, but the attractiveness and the organizational strength of the candidates he endorsed. Old master of politics that he was, he was ignoring the lessons he had learned from his bouts with Tammany a quarter-century earlier. Nor did he have the support of Farley, who with Roosevelt's consent took the public position that, as chairman of the Democratic National Committee, he must remain neutral. In private Farley was firmly opposed to the purge. By this time Farley all too clearly was eyeing for himself the prize of the 1940 presidential nomination, and was in no way interested in abandoning the party coalition tactics he had so long pursued.[31]

The efforts started with Hopkins, who drew early attacks because of his endorsement of a New Deal opponent of Senator Guy M. Gillette of Iowa. Gillette won the primary. Hopkins got in too deep, Corcoran commented long after. But Thomas Corcoran, Roosevelt's prime political operator in 1938, was not able to invoke the Farley magic among the organizations; Farley himself would have found the task impossible.[32]

Basically, Roosevelt's intervention in the primaries involved sporadic appearances by the president himself, many of them not differing greatly from the veiled endorsements he had previously given before he abandoned the fiction that he would not endorse primary candidates. He had not arranged the solid groundwork that had been such a vital component of campaign successes. Yet, since Roosevelt had made an open challenge, the press made much of each contest as a momentous struggle. Roosevelt was staking his prestige against a series of congressional opponents, most of them far better known, organized, and entrenched than the administration candidates.

In what the *New York Times* columnist Arthur Krock predicted would be the "Gettysburg of the party's internecine strife . . . an unmistakable test of the President's political leadership," Roosevelt was on the winning side. That was the primary contest in Kentucky, involving an affirmation not a replacement, the tense and vital struggle between Senate Majority Leader Alben Barkley and the ambitious governor of Kentucky, A. B. ("Happy") Chandler, an admirer of Senator Byrd, who was mounting a formidable campaign. Barkley won by a decisive 56 percent of a large vote. The contribution of Roosevelt does not seem to have been substantial.[33]

Roosevelt avoided disaster, but unfortunately for him, not embarrassment. It came over the energetic involvement of the WPA and federal employees on behalf of Barkley, arrayed against Chandler's equally militant state forces. The misuse of the WPA ballooned before the end of the primary into a national scandal.[34]

Both conservative Democrats and resurgent Republicans carried into the fall campaign the charge that Harry Hopkins and the "White House Janizaries," as Hugh Johnson, by this time a hostile columnist, labeled them, were trying to buy the election with relief funds. Fortunately for Hopkins, the election was over before the notorious remarks he supposedly made at a racetrack that summer got into print, "We will spend and spend, tax and tax, and elect and elect." The playwright Robert Sherwood years later ran down the source, Max Gordon, who would only say they represented what Hopkins seemed to mean. They have persisted in political memory as the intent of Hopkins and Roosevelt, and in point of fact, relief spending was an even more potent issue than states' rights in the primaries, and spilled over into a basic attack upon the New Deal in the general election. The best that could be said about the Kentucky primary was that Roosevelt had not lost his Senate majority leader. The WPA scandal was a continuing liability.[35]

There was nothing spectacular in the other endorsements Roosevelt made. Thus far, he was on the whole successful, and whatever effort there had been to purge had been on the part of conservatives trying to get rid of New Dealers. Upon Roosevelt's return from a fishing cruise in the Pacific and Caribbean, the purge entered a new and unfortuitous phase as he undertook his long-promised campaign against three southern Senate foes of the New Deal, Walter George of Georgia, Ellison D. ("Cotton Ed") Smith of South Carolina, and Millard Tydings of Maryland.

In previous months, Roosevelt had laid the groundwork in Georgia for his attack upon George, long the friend of the southern power companies, and the opponent of all Roosevelt's major reforms of the previous two years. Roosevelt chose the exorbitant charges Georgia Power was exacting as the issue with which to dramatize his attack, and for the location picked Barnesville, which was now to receive dramatically cheaper power from a new Rural Electrification Administration project. Thirty thousand people had crowded into the town of three thousand. In person he expounded his familiar agenda for southern change, and castigated those individuals and corporations blocking it. Then, turning to Senator George, who was sitting on the platform, he declared, "What I am about to say will be no news to my old friend." He interpolated that he hoped he and George would always be personal friends, but he drew a parallel to Republicans who were friends, but whose views on public questions differed from his as widely as the North Pole and the South. In consequence, Roosevelt was endorsing the New Deal candidate, United States Attorney Lawrence Camp. In conclusion, Roosevelt returned to the dedication of the electrification project, but in his excitement he forgot to pull the switch and inaugurate the electrical service. No lights went on.[36]

Nor did the purge of George, Smith, and Tydings succeed. Roosevelt failed to back candidates with strong enough organizations behind them. George was skillful in developing the states' rights issue, alluding to Roosevelt's campaign as the "second march through Georgia," and subtly played on race and religious prejudices. Cotton Ed Smith, like George, confused the New Deal issue, and resorted emphatically to racial hatred. The primary fight in Maryland was particularly bitter and futile.[37]

The failure to defeat any of the three incumbent senators made the purge appear a fiasco. Roosevelt had been equally unsuccessful in trying to replace the powerful Congressman Howard Smith of Virginia, but did manage to get rid of John J. O'Connor, the chairman of the Rules Committee. Like the victory of Barkley it was of major importance to Roosevelt in smoothing the path of his bills in Congress. "I do not presume that you shed many tears," Speaker Bankhead commented to Majority Leader Sam Rayburn, who responded, "Our trouble . . . is over as far as O'Connor is concerned." Outside factors rather than Roosevelt's strategy seem to have been responsible for the defeat of O'Connor, but Roosevelt, according to Corcoran, took great satisfaction from the coup. "It took the sting out of the purge."[38]

Despite the hullabaloo in the media over the drubbing Roosevelt had taken, Jasper Shannon in his contemporary analysis found that in nine southern states where New Deal forces had been involved in the primaries, they had received 53.4 percent of the total. In addition, even the conservative Cotton Ed Smith and Millard Tydings had been careful not to campaign as opponents of either Roosevelt or the New Deal. Roosevelt's popularity seemed, if opinion polls were to be trusted, to have been little damaged. He simply could not fare well with the rather inexperienced "elimination committee" of Hopkins, Corcoran, and others, nor could lesser-known candidates win against entrenched incumbents with smooth-functioning organizations. That, considering these handicaps, Roosevelt had come out as well as he had in the overall vote, was an indication of the degree to which New Dealers were becoming an ascendant group in the Democratic party.

The November election added sharply to conservative strength in the Congress, bringing in 80 new Republicans in the House and 8 in the Senate; the most significant of the Republican "New Faces" was Robert Taft of Ohio. Still, the election was not the Roosevelt debacle that the opposition press made it appear to be. Democrats won 24 of the 32 Senate contests and still outnumbered the Republicans 69 to 23; they controlled the House 263 to 169.[39]

To a considerable degree the recession was a factor in the Republican upswing of 1938. If the myth that federal spending made the New Dealers invincible had been true, Roosevelt forces would have swept both the primaries and the November election. The effect may well have been the reverse, to cause middle-class voters to swing toward the Republican party not only because of renewed hard times but also in reaction against the unfair spending power of the New Dealers.[40]

There was wide reaction against the WPA politicking in a number of states, and a perception of corruption even though there was no involvement at the national level. Roosevelt's earlier boast held good through all the years of federal relief, WPA, and public works funding: "In spite of all the demand for speed, the complexity of the problem and all the vast sums involved, we have had no Teapot Dome."[41]

Yet the belief that Roosevelt could spend his way endlessly to victory survived the election undiminished by the results. One by-product was the passage in 1939 of the Hatch Act, which, through forbidding federal employees to engage in political activity, further strengthened unfriendly state and local Democratic organizations.[42]

One clear implication that may not have been lost upon Roosevelt was that, with his own popularity still at a high level, he could attain New Deal goals in future elections only if he himself headed the ticket. His glamor did not rub off on others.

Chapter 22

A POWERLESS WITNESS TO MUNICH

As the tide of aggression rose in both Asia and Europe, culminating in the Munich crisis of September, 1938, Roosevelt was a powerless witness, unable to influence events. What he regarded as threats to vital interests, the American people, although well aware of the approach of a new world war, perceived as no clear and present danger. Their prime concern was to stay out.

In and out of Congress, isolationists promoted a device to limit the president even more tightly. Representative Louis M. Ludlow of Indiana proposed a constitutional amendment requiring a national referendum before the United States could go to war — except in the event of an armed attack. Roosevelt, taking seriously the threat of the Ludlow Amendment, set forth emphatically its liabilities, and asked James Roosevelt to pass them on to the Oregon journalist Richard Neuberger: "National defense is a current, day to day problem of administration in the hands of the President under our Constitution, and it has been on the whole wisely administered. The safeguard is that war shall not be entered into except by Congressional sanction."

A president under some circumstances might better shield the nation from war than would an excited public, Roosevelt argued, citing the Spanish-American war, which he thought probably unnecessary. "Under a Ludlow proposition, we would have gone to war anyway. If we [had] happened to have a strong President, he would have averted war."[1]

Arguments for a flexible defense against aggressors did not stem the antiwar movement within the United States, nor was Roosevelt any more successful in influencing minds in the European democracies. He lamented privately in November, 1937, "We cannot stop the spread of Fascism unless world opinion realizes its ultimate dangers."[2]

There was little Roosevelt could undertake beyond his cautious efforts to transform opinion within the United States and present the nation to the world as a moral leader. Without informing the public, he fostered various schemes to bring pressures short of war against aggressors and to arm potential victims. Also, in keeping with his uncertainties at times, he clung to the remote possibility that in both Asia and Europe the aggressors would be willing to accept reasonable settlement of their demands.

Ambassador Bullitt, hoping for a settlement in Europe, urged Roosevelt to lower his voice concerning Japan. "We have large emotional interests in China, small economic interests, and no vital interests," he declared. "The far-off bugaboo of complete Japanese domination of Asia and an eventual attack on us seems to me no basis whatsoever for present-day policy." It was attractive advice at the time Bullitt gave it — December 7, 1937, four years to the day before the attack on Pearl Harbor, and only five days before Japanese airplanes sank the United States gunboat *Panay*.[3]

The sinking of the *Panay,* with two American flags, fourteen by eighteen feet in size, freshly painted on the top decks, was manifestly deliberate. Since the fall of Nanking four days earlier, the vessel had been anchored fifteen miles above the city on the Yangtze River, gathering intelligence with the most modern devices and serving as a refuge for embassy officials and American citizens. According to navy reports to Roosevelt, an attacking force of six Japanese airplanes repeatedly bombed and strafed both it and three Standard Oil tankers. As the survivors headed for shore in sampans, the planes strafed them, wounding two of them, and repeatedly flew over them after they reached shore, forcing them to take cover until dusk. After the *Panay* was abandoned, the crews of two Japanese Army motorboats fired their machine guns at it and briefly boarded it before it sank. Later Japanese divers visited the wreck. Two Americans were killed, and thirty wounded.[4]

The sinking of the *Maine* (now believed to have been due to an internal fire and explosion) had helped precipitate the United States into a war with Spain in 1898. There was no national cry of "Remember the *Panay*" in 1937, despite the revulsion and horror over the sinking and the brutal bombing of civilians in Nanking during the days that preceded it. Rather, there was the chilling fear that the United States might become involved in war. Senator Borah declared he was "not prepared to vote to send our boys into the Orient because a boat was sunk that was traveling in a dangerous zone." Within twenty-four hours of the attack, Ludlow obtained sufficient additional signatures to bring to the floor of the House his proposed constitutional amendment.[5]

The immediate response of the president was to seek a quick settlement rather than to inflame the public, who did not know that the *Panay* had been gathering intelligence. He refused to make any comments at his next press conference, but distributed copies of his memorandum instructing Secretary Hull to inform the Japanese ambassador that he was "deeply shocked and concerned."

The incident had been the work of militant younger Japanese Army officers acting without authority; Hull referred to them as "wild, runaway, half-insane men." Ambassador Joseph Grew acted effectively in Tokyo, and the Japanese foreign minister sent apologies the following day. The question remained whether Japan would make the full amends Roosevelt sought.

Behind his appearance of calm, Roosevelt for the first day or two was excitedly discussing with his cabinet possible measures short of war that he could put into operation if Japan did not comply. Above all, he again pondered possible ways of establishing a quarantine, never far from his mind. Only a month earlier he had commented approvingly to Admiral Leahy, his Chief of Naval Operations, on a memorandum from Admiral Yarnell on how to wage war economically against Japan. It went along, he said, with what he had written in *Asia* magazine in the 1920s and the word "quarantine" he had used in Chicago. Roosevelt cited "an example of successful strangulation — when the United States, without declaring war, strangled Tripoli." He suggested that the navy make plans to convert merchant vessels into a blockading force.[6]

The *Panay* incident gave Roosevelt an occasion to carry these thoughts to his cabinet on December 17. Only one member of the cabinet, Claude Swanson, the feeble, ailing secretary of the navy, wanted war right away while Japan was vulnerable. Roosevelt explained that he wanted the same results as Swanson, "but that he didn't want to have to go to war to get it," setting forth his blockade schemes:

"We don't call them economic sanctions; we call them quarantines. We want to develop a technique which will not lead to war. We want to be as smart as Japan and as Italy. We want to do it in a modern way."[7]

In the aftermath of the *Panay* sinking, Roosevelt, for a few hours, seemed to be ready to put his quarantine device into operation. To the cabinet he described the blockade line in the Pacific that Welles had earlier witnessed him working out on the map. The United States Navy would operate from the Aleutians to Hawaii to Guam, and the British would take over from there to Singapore. It would not be a difficult task requiring a large fleet, he believed, and could bring Japan to her knees within a year. There were two startling departures from reality in Roosevelt's exciting proposal. He believed, on the basis of 1933 legislation, that he could install sanctions without further congressional action, overlooking the uproar sure to break out in the Capitol. More incredible and more significant for the future, despite the way the Japanese Army had just expressed its contempt for American power, he thought somehow that Japan would abide by a light blockade and humbly submit.

Serious afterthoughts came quickly. On the evening of December 17 Morgenthau found that Roosevelt had reverted to his characteristic caution and put away his dream of an embargo. The idea of a blockade is worth noting primarily because it is indicative of the failure of the president, the State Department, and the navy to take seriously the strength of Japan.[8]

The *Panay* incident came to a satisfactory end. On Christmas Eve, Japan formally apologized and acceded to all the American demands. The next day Hull accepted with satisfaction. On the surface, the outcome seemed the opening of a period of rapport. Indeed in Japan the government, press, and army did not seem to feel, at least until 1941, that they were on a collision course with the United States. Japan continued its efforts to dominate East Asia and western Pacific waters, apparently not aware of the consequences. The Japanese leaders and Roosevelt each thought they could pursue their policies energetically without real danger of hostilities.[9]

On the part of the United States, the *Panay* episode led to several significant developments. On December 23, Roosevelt summoned Captain Royal E. Ingersoll, an expert on war planning, and ordered him to London with only the vaguest of guidelines to develop secretly with the Admiralty the scheme for a possible blockade of trade with Japan. The British had responded favorably to Roosevelt's overtures, and engaged in some exchange of information. Both sides were cautious; the British ambassador in Washington, Sir Ronald Lindsay, warned the Foreign Office that Roosevelt, sensitive as he was to public opinion, wanted to avoid "any appearance of collusion or joint action."

It was indeed a delicate time, since the House of Representatives was debating the proposed Ludlow war referendum amendment. Roosevelt warned Speaker Bankhead that it would "cripple any President in his conduct of our foreign relations, and it would encourage other nations to believe that they could violate American rights with impunity." On January 10, 1938, the House rejected it 209 to 188, comfortably short of the required two-thirds majority.

That same day, as the British wished, Roosevelt ordered substantial fleet units to the Pacific, sent three old, light cruisers to Singapore, and advanced the date for maneuvers. But the British were gloomy because Roosevelt could not give them the commitment they most wanted, that the United States would join them in the event of war. For them to have expected Roosevelt to do so was unrealistic. As it was, there were angry protests in Congress when news leaked of the Ingersoll conversations. The long-range consequences were of great importance; they marked the beginning of naval collaboration between the British and Americans. Each was suspicious and guarded vital secrets, but the process was under way.

In two other ways Roosevelt reacted toward Japan after the *Panay* crisis. One was to direct the army and navy to update the plan, code-named Orange, for possible war in the Pacific. The other was some strengthening of the navy to bring it 20 percent above the old treaty limits. Roosevelt's caution was warranted. Even the *New York Times* in supporting the measure admonished, "Millions for defense but not a cent for foreign adventures in collective security." After stiff debate, Congress enacted the navy bill in May, 1938.[10]

While Roosevelt had not openly excited public indignation against the Japanese, neither was he ready to relax his opposition to Japanese expansion. He had gone as far as American opinion would permit, he explained to the cabinet on January 1, 1938, but wanted to be ready if there were a new crisis. He continued to be zealous in his efforts to ban Japanese salmon fishing along the Alaskan coast. Accounts of Japanese atrocities in China so upset him that while he did not want to read them at cabinet meetings, he asked Hull to devise some way to leak them "so that the American people might get the real Chinese background for the sake of the future."

During 1938 and 1939 little came onto Roosevelt's desk concerning Japan — a few matters like the bombing of Chungking and some informal intelligence — but he did form some new impressions of China. In the summer of 1937 he met a marine captain about to go to China, Evans F. Carlson, and asked him to write through Missy LeHand. Carlson sent him seventeen reports. One of them, an account of the 8th Route Army under Mao Tse-tung, was an analysis of the Chinese Communists so intriguing to Roosevelt that at a social occasion he quoted it to Ickes at some length: Mao's army "showed the best training and the highest morale of any army that the writer had ever seen. The Red armies pay for their food, do not rape the women; they carry schoolteachers with their troops." Through this idyllic account, and much military detail, an American president for the first time acquired information on the Chinese Communist forces.[11]

For two years, the thrust of Roosevelt's attention was elsewhere. During long periods, he paid little attention to Japan, and Stanley Hornbeck in the State Department ran day-by-day policy. Hornbeck, to judge by Roosevelt's files, had little access to the president, but he directed affairs in a fashion quite in keeping with Roosevelt's views, and took minor steps that led toward an ultimate clash.

From the beginning of 1938, Roosevelt focused upon Europe, where catastrophe seemed imminent. Even while he firmed his policy toward Japan, he was ready to make one last gesture toward appeasement of Germany and Italy, by trying to promote a small international conference to draft the criteria for a lasting peace. The action, he informed the British in advance, was the only one that the state of public opinion left open to him. He would announce his scheme to all the diplomats in Washington. If their response was favorable, he would invite delegates from European neutral and American states, nine nations in all, to draw up an agreement.[12]

This innocuous Wilsonian proposal seemed to Prime Minister Neville Chamberlain a "bombshell." As he explained to Roosevelt, he was about to embark upon delicate negotiations with the Italians and, he hoped, the Germans. He noted in his diary, "The plan appeared to me fantastic and likely to excite the derision of Germany and Italy. . . . They would see it as another attempt on the part of the democratic bloc to put the dictators in the wrong." Chamberlain's official reply to Roosevelt was more diplomatic. He confided that Britain expected to recognize the Italian conquest of Ethiopia, if it would be of help. Roosevelt responded with emphatic objections to the recognition, contrary to the policy of restraint against Japan. Anthony Eden persuaded Chamberlain to give up the idea of recognition and invite Roosevelt to proceed with his peace plan. Then for three weeks the British waited, but Roosevelt changed his mind and did not act. To Chamberlain, Roosevelt seemed unreliable. Roosevelt for his part did not so much object to the British appeasement efforts as not want to be associated with them. He let Ambassador Lindsay know a few weeks later that he understood that they might be necessary. When the British subsequently recognized Italy's empire in Ethiopia, he raised no objection yet managed to keep the principle of nonrecognition intact in the United States.[13]

Rapidly accelerating events in Europe caught Roosevelt by surprise. Hitler had built his army and air force to a level so strong that he was ready to expand Germany's borders. Taking over control from his more cautious general staff, he proclaimed himself Chief of the High Command, and through February, 1938, brought acute pressure to bear upon Austria. On March 11, Chancellor Schuschnigg of Austria resigned. German troops entered Austria the next morning, and on March 14, Hitler paraded before cheering throngs in Vienna. The union of Germany and Austria was complete, and Czechoslovakia was threatened on three sides.[14]

Chamberlain did nothing, since he did not want to upset the delicate process of appeasement. France, without a government, could not act. The British and French joined in a mild protest. Roosevelt followed Chamberlain's cue and remained quiet, but both the public and press expressed indignation and alarm over Hitler's ruthless move. It could not have been easy for Roosevelt to remain silent at so portentous a time. If ever there had been reason to credit Hitler's benign attentions, the duplicity and brutality accompanying the *Anschluss* had ended it.

The one significant response of Roosevelt was to inaugurate a conspicuous, but unfortunately feeble, rescue program to try to resettle overseas the victims of the Nazis, both Jews and Christians. He had long been under pressure from Jewish leaders and notable publicists like Dorothy Thompson. The tragic invasion of Austria focused attention on the immediate plight of the Jews of Austria, including the famous Sigmund Freud.[15]

The time had come when Roosevelt wanted to aid the Jews, but as in his collective security ventures, he was circumscribed by both Congress and the electorate. While there was little of the virulent anti-Semitism in the United States that wracked parts of Europe, there was widespread prejudice, which excluded Jews from some residential neighborhoods, resorts, and clubs, and made it difficult for them to obtain work in some occupations. In the 1920s many of the elite colleges and universities had instituted quotas. A faculty committee at Harvard University in 1923 had rejected the proposal of a quota and instead recommended that everyone from the top seventh of his graduating class be admitted. When under the new plan 42 percent of those accepted were Jewish, it was modified to limit those from urban areas. Roosevelt, as a member of the Harvard Board of Overseers until 1924, was involved with the question. Despite his warm friendship with the Morgenthaus, Rosenmans, and others, he accepted quotas.[16]

The feelings of Roosevelt were to surface in November, 1941, when he remarked at a cabinet meeting that there were too many Jews among federal employees in Oregon. Morgenthau, disturbed, asked Roosevelt two weeks later if he wasn't giving the cabinet officers the impression that he did not want too many Jews in the government. You have misunderstood, Roosevelt replied in some agitation. He had heard from a number of sources that Oregon Democrats were irritated, so he had to limit the appointments:

> Let me give you an example. Some years ago a third of the entering class at Harvard were Jews and the question came up as to how it should be handled. . . . I talked it over at that time with your father [Ambassador Henry Morgenthau, Sr.]. I asked him whether we should discuss it with the Board of Overseers and it was decided that we should. . . . It was decided that over a period of years the number of Jews should be reduced one or two per cent a year until it was down to 15%. . . .
>
> I treat the Catholic situation just the same. . . . I appointed three men in Nebraska — all Catholics — and they wanted me to appoint another Catholic, and I said that I wouldn't do it. . . . You can't get a disproportionate amount of any one religion.[17]

The opposition to admitting refugees into the United States who would compete for scarce jobs was bitter in the recession year of 1938, and there was danger of serious outbursts of anti-Semitism, even though anger toward the Nazis was vehement. Restrictionists were already agitating because Roosevelt since late 1935 had been expediting the flow of refugees from Germany within the limited quota. As in collective security matters, Roosevelt had to maneuver gingerly with little leeway. He informed the State Department that he wanted to liberalize procedures under existing legislation, to appeal to Latin American republics to take in refugees, and on a long-term basis to expedite travel documents and circumvent legal disabilities.

The immediate effective step was to make full use of the existing quotas. On March 25, 1938, sitting with Ambassador Bullitt in his Ford roadster at the side of the road in Warm Springs, Roosevelt told reporters that since Germany had absorbed Austria, the government had merged their immigration quotas, making it possible for 26,000 refugees per year to come to America. (Actually the number was over 27,000.) When he was asked if that would take care of all who wanted to leave, he said he had no idea, but he did emphasize that Christians as well as Jews would be among those granted sanctuary. The change, which he did not point out, was that he would encourage full use of the German quota. Since the Hoover administration in 1931, as a response to the depression, had placed impediments in the way of immigration, it had flowed far below quota levels. There is little indication that Roosevelt could have done more within the United States, protests in Congress over his mild gesture were so sharp. A July, 1938, *Fortune* poll indicated that less than 20 percent favored Roosevelt's action; more than two thirds agreed that "with conditions as they are we should try to keep them out." Only 4.9 percent were ready to see quotas raised.[18]

Although opinion was against him, Roosevelt persisted in this program, regretting that the United States could accommodate no more than a small proportion of the political refugees. From the *Anschluss* through Pearl Harbor, some 150,000 refugees entered the United States; only Palestine, which admitted 55,000, came close.[19]

Since so few of the refugees could come to the United States, Roosevelt's major effort was to encourage other nations to take them in and to seek private funds to finance the enterprise. Although the League of Nations had a refugee program and there were three international refugee organizations, Roosevelt wished to establish a new entity under his own auspices. The result was the Évian conference; of thirty-two nations he invited, only Italy and South Africa declined. The conferees agreed with Roosevelt's principle that discrimination against minority groups and the disregard of human rights were contrary to accepted standards of civilization, but then delegate after delegate explained why his country could not resettle refugees. Only the Dominican Republic offered considerable areas for agricultural colonization. By June, 1942, nearly 500 refugees were settled there.[20]

The Intergovernmental Committee on Refugees growing out of the conference remained in permanent session, seeking means to resettle those being persecuted by the Nazis. Roosevelt, eager to further its success, after war broke out in 1939 urged the committee to study uninhabited areas, to prepare for the 10 or 20 millions he thought would have to be resettled when the war was over. In 1940, he created the secret "M" Project under an archaeologist and anthropologist, Henry Field, who compiled studies on possible areas for settlement throughout the world. A favorite of Roosevelt's, which often came up in his conversations during the war, was a plan to irrigate the North African deserts with desalinized water and make them habitable for refugees.[21]

The scheme that Roosevelt most energetically pressed was one to settle the grasslands of Venezuela with "a virile, democracy-loving white population over a period of four or five generations." He tried to make his scheme look like something more than a refuge for Jews, but the Venezuelan government nevertheless balked.

Not even Alaska would accept an elaborate proposal Roosevelt baited with the promise of considerable funds for new development. The Alaskan territorial legislature, the Seattle Chamber of Commerce, and Senator Homer Bone of Washington successfully lobbied against bills before Congress. The proposal foundered, historian David Wyman declares, "on the rocks of nativism, anti-Semitism, and economic insecurity."[22]

In the spring of 1938, Roosevelt was worrying about more than the fate of the Jews; he was concerned about the survival of the European democracies themselves. Already Hitler was bringing pressure upon Czechoslovakia on behalf of the more than three million Germans in the Sudeten area.

During the summer, while Hitler was agitating the Sudeten question, Roosevelt was off on a lengthy cruise on the *Houston*. It was of the sort in which Theodore Roosevelt had taken such delight, for he combined fishing with scientific exploration of the Galapagos Islands, taking along a Smithsonian scientist, Waldo L. Schmitt, to collect specimens. Although Roosevelt described the Galapagos and other Pacific islands to his wife as might any tourist, the scientific expedition he sponsored brought back, without fanfare, a marine collection for the Smithsonian Institution, according to Schmitt "fully as important as the animal collection Theodore Roosevelt sent back from Africa." It included some thirty new species, subspecies, and varieties. Schmitt named some species after Roosevelt as sponsor of the expedition, and some as discoverer. Among them were a fish, five species of mollusks, and

Rooseveltia frankliniana — a new kind of royal palm in Cocos Island
Thalamita roosevelti — a crablike creature
Octopus roosevelti — a hitherto undescribed species
Merriamium roosevelti — a species of sponge[23]

Some weeks after his return, Roosevelt in mid-September had to leave the bedside of his son James, recuperating from a serious stomach-ulcer operation at the Mayo Clinic, to return to Washington and face the threat of European war. For months Roosevelt had carried the knowledge that French public opinion was stiffening and armed conflict a genuine possibility. A woman in his social circle who, according to Roosevelt, had "a somewhat intimate access to Mussolini," sent him a message he relayed to Hull: Mussolini on May 29 had received a telegram from Hitler saying that in ten weeks, when he had completed his defense line, he would present an ultimatum to Prague.[24]

Hitler had indeed informed his command on May 30: "It is my unalterable decision to smash Czechoslovakia by military action in the near future." The chief of his army general staff, General Ludwig Beck, was firmly opposed. He warned that the basis for American supply of the British and French was more advanced than in 1914, and the United States would be twenty times more formidable a foe. If it "threw its vast war potential into the scale," which Beck considered probable, "the opposition would receive an increase of power, especially in the case of a long war, which Germany could not oppose." Hitler had long ignored similar warnings from his ambassador, Hans Dieckhoff, and was not disposed to let General Beck stand in his way. Beck resigned on August 18.[25]

With Hitler escalating his demands, the Sudeten Germans in a frenzy, and Chamberlain poised to visit Berchtesgaden to make a desperate try for a settlement, Roosevelt expressed to Ambassador William Phillips in Rome both his pessimism and defiance:

> Chamberlain's visit to Hitler today may bring things to a head or may result in temporary postponement of what looks to me like an inevitable conflict within the next five years.
>
> Perhaps when it comes the United States will be in a position to pick up the pieces of European civilization and help them to save what remains of the wreck — not a cheerful prospect. . . .
>
> You are right in saying that we are an unemotional people over here in the sense that we do not easily lose our heads, but if we get the idea that the future of our form of government is threatened by a coalition of European dictators, we might wade in with everything we have to give.

Roosevelt was more cautious in what he planned if war broke out. He would not ask the American people to be neutral in thought as Wilson had in 1914; he thought 90 percent were anti-Axis. "I would strongly encourage their natural sympathy while at the same time avoiding any thought of sending troops to Europe." And he lamented the "plight of the unfortunate Jews." These were to be important segments of his policy during the next three years.[26]

As it was, for some days in September, 1938, Europe teetered on the edge of war, with Roosevelt unable to take any decisive part in resolving the crisis. He seemed to be wavering between his strong collective security inclinations and the cautious second thoughts that had kept him silent during earlier threats. Speaking in Kingston, Ontario, on August 18, with the Canadian prime minister, Mackenzie King, on the platform, Roosevelt safely took a halfway stance, emphasizing hemispheric security. He was also, as Assistant Secretary of State Berle had urged, setting forth the American position in a fashion sufficiently hazy as to create doubts abroad and thus exercise a moderating effect. At a press conference in Hyde Park on September 9, he parried a correspondent's query whether his speech did not mean that the United States was "allied morally with the democracies in Europe in a sort of 'Stop Hitler' movement." Roosevelt was so fearful of interventionism as an issue in the congressional campaign of 1938 that he labeled the "interpretations [of it] by columnists and editorial writers in the United States" as being "about 100% wrong" — "just a political attempt to misinterpret the fact."[27]

Roosevelt's confidential assurances to the British were quite different. Three days after the press conference, Ambassador Lindsay informed the British foreign minister, Lord Halifax, that Roosevelt, "aroused by Germany's brutal diplomacy," had declared, "you may count on us for everything except troops and loans."[28]

The grim charade proceeded, with Roosevelt able to contribute little from the sidelines. When he learned on September 19 that the British and French were urging Czechoslovakia to cede the Sudeten territories to Germany, he telephoned Ambassador Lindsay to come to the White House for a secret meeting with him — not even the State Department was to know. He spoke appreciatively of Chamberlain's efforts for peace, and said if they were successful he would be the first to cheer. At the same time, his thinking was carrying him forward to how America would act in the event of war.

Once again, in talking to the British ambassador, he seemed to be relying upon the quarantine/blockade scheme. The powers should draw a line through the North Sea and the English Channel to Gibraltar, closing off the Mediterranean at both ends. He could be more helpful if Great Britain and its allies did not declare war on Germany, since if they did so, he would have to impose an arms embargo.

At several times in the conversation, Roosevelt speculated on the possibility that the United States might become involved in a European war. If so, he did not see how he could send troops across the Atlantic "even if his prestige were as high as it had been just after the 1936 election," unless Germany were to invade Great Britain.[29]

A few days later, the crisis took a turn for the worse. On September 22, when Chamberlain met Hitler at Godesberg to arrange details for the transfer of Czech territory, Hitler brusquely dismissed the arrangements as too dilatory and handed Chamberlain an ultimatum demanding extensive areas immediately, and others subsequently after a plebiscite. He was operating not in a way to avoid war, but rather to precipitate if not a major war, at least a little one. If Czechoslovakia would surrender the Sudeten areas, he told his advisers, then he could take over the remainder of the country later, maybe in the spring.

The shocked Chamberlain returned to London on September 24. There was revulsion against the German terms. Both the French and British, despite their weakness in airplanes, pledged themselves to honor their treaty obligations if war broke out. The French called up a half-million reserves, and the British began digging air-raid shelters in London parks.

War seemed imminent. Although Roosevelt had been holding back, he had been under pressure to take a firm stand for peace. The aged Republican internationalist, President Nicholas Murray Butler of Columbia University, wired him: "Only your voice can save the world from the fearful calamity which is impending." Until September 25, Roosevelt accepted the view of the State Department advisers holding a death watch, as Berle puts it, that the United States should "steer clear and keep quiet." Then he decided he could no longer remain silent, but must send a direct appeal to the European nations.[30]

In his appeal, Roosevelt invoked the Kellogg-Briand Pact, by which every civilized nation had pledged to solve controversies only by peaceful means, and asked the leaders not to end negotiations. He sent the message at one in the morning on September 26, and quickly received approving replies from Chamberlain, Daladier of France, and Beneš of Czechoslovakia. That evening, a truculent eighteen-page reply arrived from Hitler, asserting that Germany had been patient and had exhausted the possibilities of a settlement in its memorandum to Chamberlain. Hitler concluded ominously, "It does not rest with the German government, but with the Czechoslovakian Government alone, to decide, whether it wants peace or war."[31]

Hitler, in a frenzy, then delivered a long speech intended to excite the German public, and if possible to separate Czechoslovakia from Great Britain and France. It was Beneš, he concluded, who must choose between war and peace. Actually, Hitler had already decided to order mobilization on September 28 at 2 P.M. and to attack Czechoslovakia two days later. He informed the British on September 27 that the next day at two o'clock he would act, not specifying what action he meant.[32]

Nevertheless Roosevelt kept trying to avert war — he wanted to leave no avenue to peace unexplored, no matter how slight the chance of success. "We began at noon on Tuesday, September twenty-seventh, to put on every pressure we possibly could," he subsequently informed Ambassador Phillips in Rome, "because the Secretary [Hull] and I had a definite feeling that Hitler would not wait until Saturday, October first, but would move his troops before that." He directed the State Department to draft several alternative messages to Hitler, while he himself worked on one to Mussolini. In the message he chose for Hitler, Roosevelt urged a conference of all the nations directly involved, and included a strong emotional appeal. Mussolini did indeed urge Hitler to resume negotiations.[33]

As the messages went off, Berle noted, "We all think there is only one chance in a thousand." Yet the following afternoon came a sudden climax. While Chamberlain was delivering a speech in the House of Commons that was to contain in its conclusion a threat of war, Lord Halifax and Sir Alexander Cadogan slipped behind the speaker's chair and handed a message to the prime minister: Hitler was inviting him, together with Daladier and Mussolini, to meet at Munich the next day. Roosevelt at his desk in the White House penned a cable that Chamberlain received as he departed. It read, "Good man."[34]

War had been averted — for 1938. Suddenly, to the amazement of his own associates, after so stubbornly holding out against many of them, Hitler had changed his mind. He could gain all of his ostensible goals without fighting, and decided to postpone the war that his larger objective, the carving out of *Lebensraum* — living space — in the east, would certainly require. When he saw Mussolini the next day, he set forth emphatically his view that they must fight France and Great Britain in their lifetime.

A number of factors both large and small contributed to Hitler's change of mind: the British naval mobilization, an indication that it would be a major war, not a small, easy one of the sort Bismarck had fought; the less than enthusiastic response of the German people to his exhortations and to army units going through the streets; the opposition of some of his top command and of his chief lieutenants, Goering and Goebbels; and finally Mussolini's plea. Further, Hitler was only postponing war; his exhortation to Mussolini was a veiled warning that next time there would be no peaceful conclusion to a crisis.[35]

Among the pressures upon Hitler, those of Roosevelt, whether direct or indirect, could not have weighed heavily. Perhaps Roosevelt did to some degree encourage Mussolini's shift, but there the British role was certainly more significant. Hitler himself scorned the United States, but maybe the warning of Ambassador Dieckhoff that in the event of war the United States would join the British and French more rapidly than it had the last time contributed to the emphatic fashion with which some of Hitler's advisers opposed what was to be a major European war.

Certainly Roosevelt himself took satisfaction in his role — issuing pleas that were eloquent yet so cautious that they could not bring upon him the wrath of isolationists in Congress. From King George VI, writing in appreciation of Roosevelt's invitation to visit, came warming words: "I must say how greatly I welcomed your interventions. . . . I have little doubt that they contributed largely to the preservation of peace."[36]

As for the agreement reached at Munich, it was a foregone conclusion. Hitler obtained the Sudetenland, leaving Czechoslovakia stripped of its fortifications and defenseless. Several days later, when Poland obtained the Teschen area, Roosevelt sent word to the Polish foreign minister that he was reminded of a fight between a very large boy and a very little boy in which "a third boy stepped forward and kicked the little boy in the stomach."[37]

The Munich crisis became a benchmark in the history of American foreign policy and military policy. Beginning with Roosevelt, generations of American leaders exerted themselves to make sure nothing like Munich would again take place. At the time, the deficiency of French and British airplanes seemed to be the vital factor. Already, as the crisis was escalating, Bullitt had made the crucial point to Roosevelt: "The moral is: If you have enough airplanes you don't have to go to Berchtesgaden." Bullitt had sent the fateful statistics on September 28. The French minister for air had informed him that if war came on October 1, the French would have 600 planes, compared to Germany, which had 6,500 of the very latest types. Later that day, Bullitt received word of the Munich meeting. He wrote Roosevelt he was so relieved, "I wish I were in the White House to give you a large kiss on your bald spot." Even at this euphoric moment, he warned that it was vital for France and England to start building planes immediately to match the German level. Otherwise, Hitler would soon "issue a ukase, and make war." Roosevelt agreed, and not only tried to help the French but moved the United States toward large-scale airplane manufacture. In mid-November he asserted firmly at a meeting in his office, "Had we this summer 5,000 planes and the capacity immediately to produce 10,000 per year, even though I might have to ask Congress for authority to sell or lend them to countries in Europe, Hitler would not have dared to take the stand he did."[38]

For his part, Hitler for the remainder of his life regretted his lost opportunity. He lamented in his Berlin bunker in February, 1945, "We ought to have gone to war in 1938. . . . September 1938 would have been the most favorable date."[39]

Chapter 23

GIRDING FOR HITLER'S ONSLAUGHT

WITHIN WEEKS after the Munich agreements, the sacrifice of Czechoslovakia seemed to have served only to purchase enough time for France and Great Britain to be better prepared for the next major crisis. Idealistically, Roosevelt still searched for the possibility of a general settlement and disarmament. Realistically, he began to strengthen American defenses, aid the French and British, and prepare contingency plans for the outbreak of hostilities.

War in Europe seemed almost inevitable, and when it came the United States must not become a belligerent. This was the view of Roosevelt and almost all the American people. Roosevelt's thinking ranged further to encompass possible projects that would help defeat Hitler without bringing American involvement. In his conviction that the German aggressions presented a real and immediate threat to the western hemisphere and the United States, he was far in advance of public opinion.

Thus far, he had managed to stay on at least fairly good terms with the isolationist leaders in and out of Congress, but it was a fragile relationship. While Roosevelt felt that the United States could best protect itself by bolstering the democracies, leading isolationists like the powerful Senators William E. Borah, Hiram Johnson, and Gerald Nye feared that any support for the democracies might lead to full-scale American involvement. They did not entirely trust Roosevelt, no matter how much he protested both in public and private that the provision of aid was the best way to stay out of war.

Because of isolationist resistance, Roosevelt found it a delicate task to change the attitudes of people without unduly alarming them. In January, 1939, with domestic as well as foreign policy in mind, he lamented that it was "an uphill fight to counteract the overwhelming odds against us created by most of the press and most of the 'leading citizens.' Sometimes I wish the advent of television could be hastened." (At the New York World's Fair in 1939, Roosevelt himself became the first president to appear on television, but it was an experiment and of no help in spreading his views.)[1]

As a first step after the crisis, in October, 1938, Roosevelt explored the possibility that Hitler had made his pledges at Munich in good faith. Perhaps so that Roosevelt would be blameless in the record, he sent futile feelers for disarmament, and then a fruitless query to threatened nations, asking them whether they would accept a collective security quarantine agreement. When he received no favorable response to either idea, he moved toward armaments, as he pointed out in an interview in December, 1939: "We had to [overhaul] our entire preparedness [program] in the light of Munich. . . . First, place more emphasis on the North–South American axis, Second, Revise the neutrality act; Third, Use our diplomatic influence to hamper the aggressors."

The new strategy to meet the threats of Hitler came out of Roosevelt's own close attention to the cables day by day. "The intricate ones on the dollar and the pound I ignored, but I read all the rest. Then I kept in close telephonic and personal touch with Hull, Welles, Moore — sometimes seeing them in the [White] House, sometimes at the office." Occasionally he saw them after breakfast in his bedroom.[2]

There was no more reassuring note that Roosevelt could have sounded in the fall of 1938 than that of hemispheric defense. It calmed not only an apprehensive public and Congress but also the military leaders, zealous to strengthen their own forces rather than to allow arms production to be diverted overseas. Hence, "All signs point 'Home,' " was the theme that Roosevelt stressed in an interview a few days after the Munich crisis.[3]

In November, 1938, after the final disarmament attempt had failed, Roosevelt said to two journalists, Joseph Alsop and Robert Kintner, "we decided on the North–South axis." The following month he dispatched Secretary Hull to Lima, Peru, including in the delegation Alf M. Landon, the Republican candidate for president in 1936, to indicate how important he considered the International Conference of American States. In the aftermath of Munich, the Latin American nations could no longer count upon the protection of either a preoccupied Great Britain or an impotent League of Nations.

Landon voiced emphatically the new interpretation Roosevelt and Hull wished to give to the Monroe Doctrine: The American people would not "tolerate any foreign government's gaining a foothold on this continent." Behind this statement was Roosevelt's fear that in some colonial settlement Hitler might obtain a toehold in the Americas, or that through Nazi subversion, a government under his control might come into power in one of the American nations. In early October, Roosevelt speculated that England might cede Trinidad to Germany, persuade France to give her Martinique, and urge the United States to agree in the interest of world peace. His response, he told Ickes, would be to send the United States Fleet to take both islands.[4]

At the Lima conference, Hull ably overcame Argentinian resistance and returned with the Declaration of Lima, which in careful language provided for consultation in case of threat to the security of any nation in the hemisphere. It was a step forward in securing a hemispheric alliance, but much of Roosevelt's focus in the winter of 1938–1939 was elsewhere.

The chief new emphasis was on arms production, for both the United States and the potential victims of Germany. The course of the United States must be short of war, yet Roosevelt wanted it to be energetic enough that Hitler would accept peace overtures as preferable to the overwhelming weight of arms the United States could rush to the democracies. The German leaders, Roosevelt feared, were making the same mistakes as in 1914–1917 in their expectation that American opinion would not change to favor massive aid. He had the faint hope that it "was not too late to get it through Hitler's head" that American production could shift the weight in the scales against him. Drawing upon *Alice in Wonderland,* he proposed, and Hull and Welles agreed, that they would "speak sharply to the little boy and beat him when he sneezes."[5]

Airplanes, airplanes, and still more airplanes were, Roosevelt believed, the answer to Hitler. Singularly enough, a considerable part of the rather detailed knowledge Roosevelt had acquired on the air strength and deficiencies of European nations had been gathered by Colonel Charles A. Lindbergh, who was to be his most formidable isolationist antagonist. Lindbergh, who had become one of the most acclaimed popular heroes of his generation by flying solo across the Atlantic in 1927, was able as an aviation celebrity to learn much about the air strength of Britain, France, and the Soviet Union, and, of greatest importance, Germany. The American air attaché in Berlin, thinking that Lindbergh could acquire more information than anyone else about airplane manufacture and the Luftwaffe, arranged for Lindbergh to visit in 1936 and 1937. Lindbergh's estimates and evaluations greatly influenced ambassadors Bullitt and Kennedy. During the Munich crisis, Lindbergh wrote

Kennedy, who cabled Hull, that "German air strength is greater than that of all other European countries combined," and that the United States was "the only nation capable of competing."

After Munich, Lindbergh aided in the campaign to build American air strength, but his recommendations differed from Roosevelt's. Lindbergh testified before a House committee that the United States should develop high-quality planes rather than go into early mass production. Roosevelt was eager to do both, not visualizing an America resolutely isolated, as did Lindbergh. There was one meeting between the two just before Lindbergh testified before the House committee. Lindbergh thought Roosevelt pleasant and interesting, but there was something about him that he did not trust. He wanted to work with Roosevelt, but doubted if he could for long.[6]

In the interview with Lindbergh, Roosevelt obtained figures that bolstered his point of view, and used them that very evening talking to the American Society of Newspaper Editors. He had asked Lindbergh if the United States' estimates of German airplanes at the time of the Munich crisis were correct. Lindbergh said they were about 1,000 too small, and that in case of war, the Germans could manufacture 30,000 to 50,000 planes per year and the Italians from 5,000 to 12,000.[7]

While Lindbergh sought a strong air force in an isolated United States, Roosevelt's thrust long since had been to manufacture planes for Europe, where they could serve as an immediate restraint against Hitler. There were ramifications of this difference in the sometimes conflicting aims of the president and of the armed forces.

In January, 1938, Roosevelt had warmly greeted an envoy from the French Air Ministry, Baron Amaury de la Grange, sent to purchase 1,000 of the most modern military airplanes, and thus "harness American industry to the French war machine." American aircraft producers were in no position to fill so large an order. They did not yet possess the machine tools and assembly lines to mass-produce, like the Germans, planes with aluminum frames and skins. Nor could the French government find the money. Against the resistance of the French aviation industry and workers, France decided to order an initial hundred P-36 fighters to be delivered in 1939. The French order and a British one for 400 trainer and transport planes were an initial stimulus to the American aircraft industry. Roosevelt, after Munich, was determined to turn it into the world's largest, and the French by that time were eager for him to do so.[8]

Even before the Munich agreement was signed, Roosevelt was moving toward a massive air program. On September 28, he called a meeting, according to General H. H. ("Hap") Arnold, who was included. To the delight of Arnold, who the next day became chief of the Air Army Corps, the president declared that army plans for expansion, such as the creation of a new regiment of field artillery, would not frighten Hitler in the slightest. What Roosevelt wanted was airplanes to thwart Hitler's aggressive plans; he proposed building air power for the defense of the hemisphere through constructing factories with a capacity of 20,000 planes per year, and an actual production half that size. Arnold pointed out that mass production was not enough, that there had to be continual experimentation and technical improvements to produce the most advanced planes, and there must be training programs for pilots and mechanics, and the building of bases. Although Roosevelt was concentrating upon sending aid to France and Great Britain, he seemed to understand Arnold's suggestions. Arnold left the meeting "feeling that the Air Corps had finally 'achieved its Magna Carta.' "[9]

In Roosevelt's thinking for the immediate future, building the air corps was secondary to turning out sufficient planes for France and Britain to give them at least equality with Germany. Premier Daladier was eager to take advantage of the opportunity and sent the brilliant, resourceful French economist and financier Jean Monnet, whom Bullitt recommended, to talk to Roosevelt. When they met secretly at Hyde Park on October 19, Roosevelt suggested that in case of war the French could circumvent the Neutrality Act through assembly plants in Canada to which American companies could shift parts. There should be plants, one opposite Detroit, and another across from Niagara Falls, which together could turn out 5,000 planes per year.[10]

Several days later, while Roosevelt's friend Arthur Murray of the British Liberal party was visiting Hyde Park, the president had similar conversations with him, sending a verbal message to Lord Tweedsmuir, governor-general of Canada, proposing to appoint an officer to act in liaison with a Canadian counterpart to exchange information on airplane design and manufacture, and keep contract prices down. He asked Murray to convey to Chamberlain assurance that the industrial resources of the United States would be behind him.[11]

Both the British and the French were slow to act. Not until mid-December did Chamberlain express his gratitude for Roosevelt's message. In late May, 1939, the air minister finally replied that they might want to procure at that time nothing more than metal sheets made of light alloys and some navigational instruments. The French interest continued to be intense, but there were serious deterrents within France.

In the United States there was considerable opposition to aid, much of it coming from the armed forces. Roosevelt seemed to be little concerned with balanced development. Rather he wanted to produce the largest number of planes possible, hoping to intimidate Hitler, and gave lesser thought to their use as an integral part of American defense. He further disturbed some of the commanders with plans to use relief apparatus in rearming the nation. He wanted to construct a basic 8,000 airplanes per year in commercial factories, and then assign the WPA to erect seven additional plants. Two would each produce 1,000 planes, and the other five would be held in reserve. (Subsequently he proposed using the National Youth Administration to train large numbers of aircraft mechanics.)

On November 14, 1938, in a momentous meeting, Roosevelt laid out his program for large-scale airplane construction to his top military and naval advisers. Those bold plans for massive shipment of planes overseas could not have been pleasing to many of the generals present, who wanted to build their own forces. Most of them, General George C. Marshall remembered, were "very soothing." Marshall himself was not. When Roosevelt said, "Don't you think so, George?" Marshall responded, "I am sorry, Mr. President, but I don't agree at all." Roosevelt looked startled, and Marshall's colleagues on the way out suggested to him that his tour of Washington was over. Less than a year later, Roosevelt appointed Marshall chief of staff. Marshall continued both to keep his distance and to enjoy Roosevelt's respect; he did not remember Roosevelt calling him "George" ever again.[12]

With considerable difficulty, Marshall and others gradually persuaded Roosevelt to revise his airplane figures downward and to redress the serious deficiencies throughout the armed forces. If indeed they were to be prepared for hemispheric defense, they needed a great strengthening of forces and much modern weaponry. Yet Roosevelt was insistent that the newest airplanes, so vital to the air force, must be shared with France.

Since Secretary of War Harry H. Woodring, ardently isolationist, was opposed to sales abroad of arms that would otherwise strengthen the military at home, Roosevelt delegated the responsibility for negotiating purchase of arms to Morgenthau, who shared the president's views. Ostensibly, Roosevelt turned over the authority to the Treasury Department, because its Procurement Division had experience in large-scale purchases. Of course, it was Roosevelt who suggested or approved Morgenthau's every move.

There were both pluses and minuses in Roosevelt's policy to give priority to aid for the democracies. In the official *U.S. Army in World War II*, historian Mark Watson concludes:

In the ultimate victory over the Axis time would show American factory production to have been an immense factor. Early foreign orders also greatly expedited the enormous development of American industry to the long-range advantage of the Army. Yet this later benefit does not alter the fact that in diverting abroad much of the flow of new equipment those early orders temporarily retarded the equipping and hence the training of the new United Army units whose performance in battle would one day prove a requisite of Allied victory.[13]

In January, 1939, a mishap brought the controversy over airplanes into the headlines, as Congress and the public learned for the first time how Roosevelt was seeking to bolster France. He insisted that the French be helped to procure any types of planes they wished, and General Hap Arnold, not pleased, had to send orders to California to allow the French to fly a new Douglas bomber, after its secret instruments had been removed. On January 23, the bomber crashed and newspapers discovered there had been a Frenchman aboard. At the height of the excitement, Roosevelt was singed by the Senate isolationists. He invited the Senate Military Affairs Committee to the White House to quiet their fears, and instead aroused new ones.

Roosevelt created a furor with his discourse on the threat of Hitler, by this time quite standard in the Oval Office, but firmer and franker than his earlier remarks to congressional bodies. He asked the committee to keep his remarks confidential in order not to create fright, but said he did want Americans "to gradually realize what is a potential danger." War was imminent.

"What is the first line of defense in the United States?" Roosevelt asked rhetorically, and proceeded to answer in terms of various areas of the world. "So soon as one nation dominates Europe, that nation will be able to turn to the world sphere." He named nations surrounding Germany, and went on to say that if the colonies of the British, French, or Dutch fell into German hands the results would be unpredictable. "That is why the safety of the Rhine frontier does necessarily interest us."

A senator queried, "Do you mean that our frontier is on the Rhine?"

"No, not that," Roosevelt responded. "But practically speaking if the Rhine frontiers are threatened the rest of the world is too. Once they have fallen before Hitler, the German sphere of action will be unlimited."[14]

One of the senators talked to a reporter, and throughout the world the word went out that Roosevelt had declared that America's frontier was on the Rhine. Three days later, Roosevelt lamented to the reporters the uproar, over a statement that "some boob got . . . off," which the British and French were applauding and the Germans and Italians were attacking. Two weeks later, off the record, he talked to them again about the way he had been misquoted, and then frankly explained what he had said and why he disliked the version that had been leaked: "Now, suppose I was to say that the continued independence, in a political and economic sense, of Finland is of tremendous importance to the safety of the United States? Now isn't that a very different thing than saying that the frontier of the United States is in Europe?"[15]

Although Roosevelt may have felt bloodied, his policy continued unchanged. Monnet ordered 600 airplanes, and obtained a firm commitment on 1,500 more for early 1940. He ordered double the number of bombers French plants could produce. By the time war broke out in September, France had received a considerable part of the initial orders. As yet Roosevelt had not achieved his goal of providing overwhelming air strength to the French, but he had made a significant beginning.[16]

While Roosevelt was eager to provide arms for the democracies, he was insistent that they gird for war with equal urgency. He was touchy about the isolationist paraphrasing of Admiral Nelson's famous aphorism, that Britain expected every American to do his duty. Roosevelt's patience with Chamberlain's government was becoming strained. One of his Harvard history professors, Roger B. Merriman, hit that sensitive spot in February, 1939, when he sent Roosevelt an extract from a letter by the eminent British historian George Macaulay Trevelyan. Trevelyan asserted:

> The only thing that will stop a war coming pretty soon — since Hitler and Mussolini are both 'rabid' men — would be the U.S. letting them know that you will take part if they make aggression. . . . But whatever you choose to do, *we will put up a jolly good fight*, in which everything I care for will disappear.

Roosevelt responded trenchantly:

> I wish the British would stop this "We who are about to die, salute thee" attitude. Lord Lothian was here the other day, started the conversation by saying he had completely abandoned his former belief that Hitler could be dealt with as a semi-reasonable human being, and went on to say that the British for a thousand years had been the guardians of Anglo-Saxon civilization — that the scepter or sword or something like that had dropped from their palsied

fingers — that the U.S.A. must snatch it up — that F.D.R. alone could save the world — etc., etc.

I got mad clear through and told him that just so long as he or Britishers like him took that attitude of complete despair, the British would not be worth saving anyway.

What the British need today is a good stiff grog, inducing not only the desire to save civilization but the continued belief that they can do it. In such an event they will have a lot more support from their American cousins — don't you think so?[17]

Whether or not Roosevelt intended these stinging words to reach the Foreign Office, they did. In any event they created a flurry, and so strengthened the opponents of Lothian that they almost prevented him from replacing Lindsay as ambassador at the end of the summer. Lothian, who, unlike so many around Chamberlain, was friendly to the United States, became a highly successful envoy.[18]

While many Americans worried about Roosevelt's interest in aiding the democracies, few would have disputed his belief that Hitler was likely to precipitate war. The Munich crisis had left few illusions. At the beginning of October, 60 percent of those Gallup polled thought the outcome would be a great possibility of war.[19]

Kristallnacht, Night of the Broken Glass, on November 9–10, 1938, sent a wave of revulsion across the United States. The Nazis had suddenly rounded up 12,000 Polish Jews in Germany and dumped them without food or shelter at the Polish border. The son of one, in protest, tried to assassinate the German ambassador in France, and instead killed the third secretary of the embassy. In retaliation the Nazi propaganda minister, Goebbels, staged supposed spontaneous anti-Jewish riots across Germany, beating men and women, smashing and looting shops and homes, dynamiting and burning synagogues. In its aftermath, Goering, second in the Nazi hierarchy, imposed a billion-mark indemnity upon Jews. The German government barred them from retail trade and from attending schools and universities, or appearing at theaters, concerts, or in public libraries. They were not even allowed to drive automobiles. In Frankfurt every male Jew between eighteen and sixty was incarcerated. The Nazis were taking a long preliminary step toward the "final solution." The democracies did not yet perceive that ultimate horror, but reacted vehemently. Ninety-four percent of Americans polled said they disapproved of the Nazi treatment of Jews. Ambassador Dieckhoff warned from Washington, "Even the respectable patriotic circles which were thoroughly anti-Semitic . . . begin to turn away from us."[20]

At his press conference, Roosevelt read a statement of protest the State Department had prepared. He had strengthened its cautious words, inserting: "I myself could scarcely believe that such things could occur in a twentieth century civilization." Roosevelt recalled Ambassador Wilson for "report and consultation" — and the United States did not again send an ambassador to the Third Reich.[21]

The American reaction to *Kristallnacht* was of pathetically little help to refugees, but did make easier Roosevelt's moves toward defense. Judged by the polls, Americans were rapidly coming to feel that it was in the national interest to help arm France and Great Britain against the Nazis.[22]

It was a tense winter for the democracies, and Roosevelt tried to guess where Hitler might move next. From private reports, he mistakenly thought west rather than east. Suddenly, with planned precision, Hitler's forces on March 15, 1939, occupied the remainder of Czechoslovakia, negating the solemn pledge at Munich. Throughout the next month, German and Italian militancy escalated. German troops occupied a strip of Lithuania once part of the old Reich, and the Italians on April 7 took over Albania.

Hitler then began to feint toward his real target, Poland, demanding return of a port, the Free City of Danzig (present-day Polish Gdansk), and a route across the Polish Corridor, separating East Prussia from the rest of Germany. Since the British, and doubtless Roosevelt himself, perceived Hitler's new demand as the means of launching a fresh conquest, not an effort to redress a wrong, Chamberlain, finally recognizing the futility of appeasement, signed a mutual assistance agreement with Poland, but failed to obtain a Soviet guarantee of Polish boundaries. War seemed likely at any time.[23]

Roosevelt grew "madder and madder." He publicly warned in both press conferences and a Pan-American Day address that the United States, too, was being threatened and that the dictators must take into account its tremendous force. In a public message to Hitler and Mussolini, he enumerated thirty-one nations and asked for assurance that the Axis would not attack or invade them or their possessions in the next ten years. If Hitler and Mussolini would answer affirmatively, the United States would arrange and take part in a conference to settle questions of disarmament and trade.

The dictators greeted Roosevelt's offer with contempt. Mussolini scoffed at the "Messiah-like messages," and in conversation with Goering agreed that they indicated "an incipient mental disease." Hitler in an address to the Reichstag heaped sarcasm on Roosevelt. It was an address appealing to the American isolationists; Hitler had used some of their arguments, and some of the materials from Nye's munitions investigation in support of the German position.[24]

Some of the isolationists were pleased. "Roosevelt put his chin out and got a resounding whack," wrote Hiram Johnson. "He wants . . . to knock down two dictators in Europe, so that one may be firmly implanted in America." Speaker Bankhead pronounced a view more prevalent in Congress, that Hitler had "no regard whatever for the sanctity or validity of treaties between nations."[25]

War was not to start in the spring, but Roosevelt acted with a greater urgency to prepare the nation for the eventual outbreak of hostilities. A major need was to amend the neutrality legislation so that when war did break out the United States could continue to send aid to Great Britain and France. Ever since German troops had marched into Prague, public opinion polls showed an even larger proportion of the population favoring the change. Since the previous fall, Roosevelt had come to want outright repeal of the legislation, reverting to international law, but had left the matter in charge of Senator Key Pittman, chairman of the Senate Foreign Relations Committee. Pittman was belligerent toward the Axis, but he was also fearful of the isolationists. He was in bad health, and drinking heavily — no person to lead what would be a bitter fight. With little success, in mid-April Roosevelt and Hull took the matter into their own hands. On June 30, when Roosevelt faced certain defeat on neutrality repeal, he telephoned Morgenthau at midnight:

"I will bet you an old hat, and tell your people to spread the word around, that Hitler when he wakes up and finds out what has happened . . . will be rejoicing. . . . I think we ought to introduce a bill for statues of Austin, Vandenberg, Lodge and Taft — the four of them — to be erected in Berlin and put the swastika on them."

These remarks were grossly unfair to four outstanding senators, but they were made in private, and Roosevelt needed to vent his frustration. A dispatch did come from his chargé in Berlin that the Germans looked upon the vote as "a severe defeat for the warmonger Roosevelt."[26]

Toward Japan, on the other hand, Congress and the public were disposed to give Roosevelt far more latitude. That was the answer to the baffling question Ickes had raised in his diary in 1938: "I cannot understand Hull's attitude. He seems to defer unduly to Hitler and Mussolini while he all but rattles the saber when it comes to Japan." There would be no political repercussions. Japan's expansion had kept pace with Hitler's boldness in the months since Munich. Polls indicated that Americans overwhelmingly favored cutting off sales of war matériel to Japan and boycotting its goods. Congress was urging sanctions, but since these would violate the 1911 commercial treaty with Japan, Roosevelt and Hull preferred to give six months' notice and abrogate the treaty. Senator Vandenberg — one of those whom Roosevelt had thought merited a statue in Berlin — introduced such a resolution, and Roosevelt authorized Hull to send notice to Japan. "It is a curious fact," observed Berle, "that the United States, which bolts like a frightened rabbit even from remote contact with Europe, will enthusiastically take a step which might very well be a material day's march on the road to a Far Eastern War." It was indeed a substantial move toward war, and gave pause to Japan. No one had yet decided what to do when the six months' waiting period came to an end.[27]

There were few parts of the world in which Roosevelt failed to perceive danger of Axis penetration. While he focused upon Europe and Asia, he was also keenly interested in South America, where he continued to be worried by reports of spies and settlers from Lower California to Brazil. Friendly Latin American dictators, whom Roosevelt had always encouraged to think of themselves as incipient democrats, received flattering welcomes when they visited the White House. President Anastazio Somoza of Nicaragua left ecstatic that he, "a little fellow," had received the same honor that awaited the king and queen of England. President Getúlio Vargas of Brazil sent word, "Tell your President that we trust him and that he can trust us."[28]

The islands ringing the Pacific continued to figure in Roosevelt's security schemes. In March he sent Welles a lengthy memorandum on Easter Island, which he feared might become an air base, and therefore under no circumstances should be transferred to any nation outside the Americas. He doubted the political wisdom of trying to purchase it from Chile, and wondered therefore if, with its "great recumbent stone figures," it could not be tied together with the Galapagos Islands into a Pan-American trusteeship "to be preserved for all time against colonization and for natural science."

Antarctica absorbed even more of Roosevelt's attention. He had long been fascinated with the expeditions of Admiral Richard E. Byrd and Lincoln Ellsworth, and wished to cap them with American claims. Other nations were active there and he did not wish the United States to lose out, because of not only the scientific importance but also the possible mineral riches of the continent. Welles suggested, and Roosevelt agreed, that executive orders setting forth claims would not be sufficient. In consequence, Roosevelt proposed establishing two bases and manning them through each Antarctic summer.[29]

Royal visitors also fit into Roosevelt's scheme of things, demonstrating to the Axis that the United States supported the regimes of threatened rulers, and helping break down isolationist feelings within the United States. They strengthened him among several national groups. Using the 1939 New York World's Fair as an occasion, Roosevelt not only encouraged Scandinavian royalty to come but was even ready to invite King Boris of Bulgaria. None were to create such a sensation as the unprecedented visit of King George VI and Queen Elizabeth, in response to Roosevelt's invitation of a year before. The American people, having rid themselves of their own monarch over a century and a half earlier, were fascinated with those of Europe. The Roosevelts shared the fascination.

The visit of Norwegian royalty at the end of April served as something of a preview, complete with a picnic on the lawn in front of Roosevelt's new hilltop cottage at Hyde Park, where guests lunched on both smorgasbord and hot dogs. Crown Princess Martha later became a favorite of Roosevelt's.[30]

Both the Roosevelts took seriously the prospect of hosting the British royal couple. Eleanor Roosevelt was rather alarmed by the precise specifications she obtained through the State Department for the comfort of their majesties. Roosevelt, secure in his own role as American head of state, functioned as a coequal. Interested as always in ceremony and protocol, he sent a flurry of chits to the White House social secretary, but at Hyde Park the Roosevelts entertained their majesties as informally as family friends, and they responded accordingly. After a picnic, Roosevelt drove them around in his Ford roadster, with the queen beside him in front, and the king behind.[31]

While the visit was basically ceremonial, a means of arousing American sympathies for the British, it also gave Roosevelt an opportunity to cement further his relations with the British government. At Hyde Park Roosevelt and Prime Minister Mackenzie King talked late into the night with the king. After the conversation, King George knocked on the prime minister's door and remarked, "Why don't my ministers talk to me as the president did tonight? I felt exactly as though a father were giving me his most careful and wise advice."[32]

The summer months were a sunny interlude, although everyone was aware of the thunderheads of war rising ominously on the horizon. By the end of June the cables were disturbing; the consensus was that Hitler was preparing to strike. But Roosevelt felt for the moment that conditions were stable enough for his mother to sail to France, and even at the end of July he told Morgenthau to go ahead and buy steamer tickets for Europe.[33]

With the Nazi threats against Poland becoming more and more serious, he kept watch on preparations for American actions in the event of war. He left few doubts within his administration that the United States would be neutral only within the letter of the law.

With contingency plans in order, Roosevelt feared war was so near that he would have to give up his planned fishing vacation on the USS *Tuscaloosa*, although he was very tired. On the morning of August 12, when he was ready to leave, he received a pessimistic phone call from Bullitt in Paris, and then turned to Welles, who predicted war would come within a week or ten days.

"Oh, in that case I really have a couple of weeks to get a rest," Roosevelt replied, and left, arranging to be on call. While he fished off the coast of Labrador, day by day Welles's cables detailed to him the escalating crisis:

> August 16: "Hitler apparently determined on war with Poland whether Mussolini wanted it or not."
>
> August 17: "Moscow reports . . . Molotov would welcome . . . conversations [with Germany] which might include a non-aggression pact."
>
> August 18: "The German press . . . describes the ruthless terror to which Germans in Poland are being subjected."
>
> August 19: "Daladier . . . thought Hitler was preparing the German army for immediate action but had not yet made up his mind. . . . Daladier added that the French army would immediately attack the Siegfried line in the event of a German attack on Poland."
>
> August 22: "In a conversation with Daladier this afternoon Bullitt was informed that the non-aggression pact [the Soviets had announced they would sign] . . . would place France in a tragic situation since the entire diplomatic structure which France had been preparing was destroyed by this act of the Russians. . . .
>
> "Beck [in Warsaw said] that should Hitler make any move against Danzig Poland would fight immediately. . . .
>
> "Bullitt . . . has instructed consuls in France to advise American citizens that they might well leave Europe."[34]

On August 23 from his boat and the next day from the White House, Roosevelt sent appeals to Hitler, the president of Poland, and the king of Italy. They were ineffective.

Hitler, avoiding what he regarded as his errors of the previous year, now insisted that he would negotiate only with Poland, and alleged that

Poland was refusing his offers. To his associates, Hitler was explaining that he wanted the war with Poland to come by the end of August and to be over in mid-October before the fall rains. It was essential to clear the rear of the Axis for the war against France and Great Britain. If the Soviet Union gained some territory too, that was all right. Hitler and his generals were counting upon fighting a short war, with or without the intervention of Great Britain and France. They possessed the armaments only for a brief campaign of a few months, and had not shifted to a full war economy. Their miscalculation was a repetition of that of the German high command in the fall of 1916, that they could win before the United States, with its enormous potential for arms production, could intervene. When the premier of Hungary relayed American warnings to Hitler in the spring of 1939, Hitler laughed and remarked that "the Americans were mixing up the present situation with that of 1914," and concluded "Roosevelt is fighting for his re-election."[35]

On August 21, with the announcement of a Soviet-German pact, Roosevelt had cut short his trip, heading southward slowly through fog to Sandy Hook. He took a train to Washington. En route, he tried to evaluate "this latest Russian business," which he thought would make things infinitely more difficult for England and France "— though, frankly, I do not believe Russia would have given much substantial aid even if they had not made this non-aggression treaty with Germany." He may well have also pondered the fact that he had sought an exchange of intelligence with the Soviets, and had tried, although unsuccessfully, to arrange the manufacture for them in American shipyards of a battleship and possibly some destroyers. He had hoped to include Russia in his security scheme, and the reverse seemed to have happened.[36]

For several days Roosevelt calmly waited in Washington, occupying himself with preparations for what now seemed inevitable. On August 28, Louis Brownlow entered his office to arrange the last details of an order establishing the Executive Office of the President. Roosevelt greeted him with a facetious "Heil, Hitler," but he was in a serious mood. He added to the order a provision for a liaison office to handle emergency matters in case he proclaimed a national emergency. Executive reorganization was shading off into the creation of a defense administration.[37]

Roosevelt was operating along a thin line between what was legal and what was extralegal. He suggested that in case war broke out, there should be a deliberate flaw in the neutrality proclamation, which the attorney general would detect and which would then take time for the State Department to repair. In that way he hoped to delay issuing the proclamation for about five days, giving the British and French an opportunity to hurry their war materials across the border into Canada or onto ships and beyond the three-mile limit. (Later, despite this bold talk, Roosevelt took more cautious action, and in order not to alarm isolationists delayed the proclamation for only two days.) When Prime Minister Chamberlain broke his usual reserve to send a plea to Roosevelt to provide the Royal Air Force with the superior Norden bombsight, he replied he could not do so under existing legislation without making it available to all other governments. New conditions might change matters. Another concern of Roosevelt's was his fear that a German merchant vessel, the *Bremen,* might leave port to be outfitted as a commerce raider. He ordered the Treasury Department to withhold clearance papers from all ships suspected of carrying armaments until there had been a complete search. With the German government protesting, and both the Treasury and State Departments alarmed over the question of legality, he had the *Bremen* searched so lengthily that even the lifeboats were lowered, and then delayed it even longer. The *Bremen* was two days late sailing. Isolationists were not pleased. Senator Styles Bridges accused Roosevelt of trying to pull the United States into the war before it had even started.[38]

Several days earlier, Berle had delivered to Roosevelt a "full kit of neutrality proclamations and orders." All that remained was to receive news that Hitler had struck.[39]

Chapter 24

THE GERMAN BLITZ AND AMERICAN PERIL

AT TEN MINUTES TO THREE on the morning of September 1, 1939, Roosevelt received a telephone call from Bullitt in Paris relaying word from Ambassador Biddle in Warsaw that German troops were plunging into Poland. At 6:30 he learned that Daladier felt France must fight or lose its last chance to resist. Kennedy in London reported forty-five minutes later that Chamberlain felt Britain too must enter the conflict. These phone calls signaled the beginning of the most frightful war in human history.[1]

Roosevelt, with forebodings that there was a fifty-fifty chance Britain and France might lose, calmly prepared the American response, to aid them and protect the United States. He would call a Pan-American conference to create a security zone against German attacks upon shipping in American waters, and he would summon Congress into special session to repeal the neutrality legislation that would force an arms embargo. He and Hull felt, it was later reported, "that with men's minds suddenly and brutally cleared by war, repeal would be fairly easy."[2]

That afternoon, Roosevelt took up domestic concerns with his cabinet, the prevention of inflation and installation of machinery to marshal the economy for defense. Although he told the cabinet he might have to put the nation on an emergency basis, he asserted, "We aren't going into this war." When the War Department brought him plans that included the equipping of an extraordinary force to Europe, he declared, "You can base your calculations on an army of 750,000 men, for whatever happens, we won't send troops abroad. We need only think of defending this hemisphere."[3]

Thus Roosevelt set what at the time seemed a rather bold course. The

United States turned only slowly from its isolation into a nonbelligerent engaged in quasi-war to defend what the president identified as vital national interests. On the evening of September 3, the day Britain and France entered the war, Roosevelt in a Fireside Chat declared he could not urge Americans, as had Wilson in 1914, to be neutral in thought as well as deed. "Even a neutral," he pointed out, "cannot be asked to close his mind or his conscience." In his peroration he emphasized what almost every citizen wanted most to hear: "I hope the United States will keep out of this war. . . . As long as it remains within my power to prevent, there will be no black-out of peace in the United States."[4]

Two days later, Roosevelt issued the neutrality proclamation required of him and imposed an immediate embargo on the sale of arms and munitions to the belligerents. He needed to proclaim an emergency in order to obtain the powers over the economy inherent in the national defense legislation of the First World War. To reassure the nation, he called it only a "limited emergency."[5]

As yet there was uncertainty over how cataclysmic the war might be. Americans followed with shock, but no feeling of insecurity, the German blitz against Poland, which the French and British could make no effort to deter. In the weeks that followed, with the conquest of Poland soon completed, excitement in the United States gradually sagged, and alarm evaporated. Intelligence reaching Roosevelt gave no assurances that the West might be spared the kind of *Blitzkrieg* that wiped out Poland. It was against the popular view that he had to maneuver in the fall of 1939.

An immediate step in working toward repeal of the arms embargo was Roosevelt's effort to make the issue nonpartisan; he engaged in his first overtures to try to bring into the cabinet the Republican nominees of 1936, Landon and Knox. Landon, after talking to Roosevelt, commended his proposal that Congress adjourn politics in deciding policies toward the European war, but suggested he should remove "the biggest stumbling block of all" by announcing he would not run for a third term. It was impossible to keep politics out, and from then until the 1940 election the "third term" issue colored not only Roosevelt's struggle to obtain repeal of the arms embargo, but much of his handling of foreign relations and aid to Britain and France.

The conversations with the Republican leaders had been half satisfactory. Knox pleased Roosevelt, but Landon, strongly favoring defense and equally vigorously opposing intervention, did not entirely trust Roosevelt. He once remarked, in the terminology of the buffalo and cow country, that he knew there were "bugs under the chips." Colonel

Knox, bluff and hearty, was a type Roosevelt enjoyed and in the course of the winter converted into something of a follower. The conversations were typical of the rapprochement that was developing between Roosevelt and a number of leaders, both Republicans and Democrats, who opposed the New Deal but shared his emphatic feeling that American national interests demanded aid to the foes of Hitler. The Democrat Alfred E. Smith, who had been so bitter in his anti–New Deal polemics, delivered a radio address on behalf of repeal of the embargo.[6]

In Congress, while some who had been staunch supporters of New Deal legislation, like La Follette, moved into the opposition, acerbic old Carter Glass, who for six years had been a thorn in Roosevelt's side, discovered fine qualities in the president.[7]

There was sharp debate both within Congress and outside it. Roosevelt in a meeting with congressional leaders tried to tie the isolationists to the Nazis, claiming that every remark of Borah, Johnson, or Fish was being hailed on the front pages of German newspapers. The hard-core isolationists replied with equal vehemence. "Our boys would follow our guns into the trenches," Borah warned the day war broke out.[8]

One startling attempt Roosevelt made was to win over Lindbergh, a formidable potential opponent, who on September 15 was about to make his first nationwide broadcast opposing involvement in the European war. A few hours before the broadcast, Colonel Truman Smith brought Lindbergh a verbal message that, he noted, "the Administration was very much worried by my intention of speaking over the radio and opposing actively this country's entry into a European war. . . . If I would not do this, a secretaryship of air would be created in the Cabinet and given to me!" It was not an unreasonable feeler, for Lindbergh could have brought strong public support to the air corps and his views differed little from those of its chief, Hap Arnold, whom Roosevelt tolerated. In late spring, 1940, when Lindbergh would assume a commanding role among the most vehement isolationists, Roosevelt was to turn bitter. "If I should die tomorrow, I want you to know this," he exploded to Morgenthau. "I am absolutely convinced that Lindbergh is a Nazi."[9]

At the beginning of November, 1939, Congress repealed the arms embargo by wide margins in each house, freeing Roosevelt to focus upon security. Already he was working to establish naval patrols to bar belligerent ships from American waters, and he thought of seeking bases to help protect the hemisphere. A few days after war began, he had told Morgenthau he was leasing aircraft hangars in Bermuda and was eyeing a base on the French island of St. Pierre in the Gulf of St. Lawrence.[10]

The slowness of the American patrols in beginning operations nettled Roosevelt, but there were insufficient vessels to cover the huge area he visualized. Fortunately, there was as yet no trouble, in part because Hitler wanted to lull the United States, Great Britain, and France into inactivity, or perhaps even into accepting a compromise peace.[11]

Simultaneously with the blitz into Poland, Hitler muted the shrill propaganda against Roosevelt and the United States and restrained the commanding officer of the German navy, Grand Admiral Erich Raeder. Toward the end of the Polish campaign he launched a flurry of peace overtures, mostly through Goering. A *New York Times* headline correctly reported on rumors, "TRUCE PROPOSAL FROM ROOSEVELT WOULD BE ACCEPTED BERLIN HEARS." Roosevelt was interested in peace, but not of this sort. He had long since informed Ambassador Kennedy that the American people would not support any peace move "that would consolidate or make possible a survival of a regime of force and aggression." That, too, was the position of Chamberlain and Daladier.[12]

Hitler was determined, if his peace overtures failed, to launch an attack as soon as possible to the west. He would not try to crack the Maginot Line, the French defense bulwark, but would swing through the Netherlands and Belgium, north of the line. Despite once again facing the opposition of his generals, he set November 15 as his deadline.

As the Germans assembled a formidable number of divisions in the West, invasion of the neutral Low Countries seemed imminent. Roosevelt could only seek unofficial German assurances that they respect the neutrality of the two countries, and offer asylum to the monarchs. Bad weather helped the German generals persuade Hitler to postpone the invasion repeatedly through the winter of 1939–1940.[13]

Instead, on November 30, the Soviet Union launched the "winter war" against Finland. It was the most spectacular step in Stalin's acquisition of a security belt to the west, which had begun with the recent partition of Poland and proceeded to absorb the Baltic states, Lithuania, Latvia, and Estonia. Since the Baltic states remained independent at least in name, there was nothing Roosevelt could do. When Soviet warships and airplanes bombarded Finnish cities and troops began their invasion, Roosevelt in private expressed dismay at "this dreadful rape of Finland" and mused, "No human being can tell what the Russians are going to do next."

The assault evoked indignation and strong pressure for Finnish aid. Some energetic isolationists felt different about a victim of the Communists and complained that Roosevelt's moderate course did not go far enough. Nevertheless, neither the president nor Congress provided any substantial loans or armaments. Primarily Finland obtained popular sympathy so great that its foreign minister declared, "it nearly suffocated us."[14]

The war also created support for Roosevelt's longtime antagonist Herbert Hoover, who chose to become the hero of Finnish war relief rather than to cooperate with Roosevelt and the Red Cross. To present a united, bipartisan response to the foreign threat, Roosevelt, when war broke out in September, extended a feeler to Hoover as he had to Landon and Lindbergh. Roosevelt privately regarded Hoover as the greatest authority on civilian relief and thought of him to head an agency to aid refugees throughout the world. Incongruously, he wanted Hoover to associate himself with Mrs. Roosevelt in the effort. She was enthusiastic about the proposal. Perhaps the Roosevelts' overture was a remaining flicker of the warmth and admiration they had felt toward Hoover during the First World War. Through Norman Davis, head of the Red Cross, Roosevelt invited Hoover to come discuss the possibility, but he declined. "Hoover turned us down," Mrs. Roosevelt informed a friend. "He refused to call on the President." Hoover gave the excellent excuse that he would be busy in 1940 with the presidential campaign, but had he been willing to cooperate, he might ultimately have become head of United Nations relief in World War II. After Pearl Harbor, Hoover, like Lindbergh, offered his services, but never heard from the president.[15]

The Soviet-Nazi pact and the war against Finland also created trouble for Roosevelt within the United States. They gave widespread credence to the charges of disloyalty against factions who continued to follow the Communist line despite the purge and Stalin's pact with Hitler. One such group, the American Youth Congress, was a particularly attractive target for the conservative House Un-American Activities Committee because of Mrs. Roosevelt's interest in it since 1936. Young liberals had established the Youth Congress, but Communists soon won control. Although she had been warned of the Communist influence, she continued to befriend some of its leaders. In February, 1940, at her invitation, the Youth Congress Pilgrimage assembled on the White House lawn to hear the president. Roosevelt, who had written the talk himself, firmly told them: "The Soviet Union, as everybody who has the courage to face the fact knows, is run by a dictatorship as absolute as any other dictatorship in the world. It has allied itself with another dictatorship, and it has invaded a neighbor . . . infinitesimally small." There was brief booing.

Afterward Roosevelt, sensing how embarrassed his wife felt, remarked consolingly, "Our youngsters are unpredictable, aren't they?" When he heard that his wife's secretary, Malvina ("Tommy") Thompson, had reproached the youth leaders for insulting the president, he sent for her and said simply, "Thank you, Tommy."[16]

The Finnish war quickly drew to a close. In March, the Soviets agreed to a peace that gave them strategic areas and brought Finland into the Russian sphere. Roosevelt had been well advised not to channel scarce armaments to that country.

Whatever could be spared, Roosevelt wanted to send to Great Britain and France. The British, it had been agreed in August, were to take "three out of eight units" of total American production, an allotment the armed forces regarded as intolerable. Roosevelt bypassed the military, assigning his secretary of the treasury to work with the unified British and French purchasing missions. Morgenthau developed fine relations with both, but incurred the wrath of the War Department.[17]

Army and air corps resistance to Roosevelt's supplying airplanes to the British and French continued through the winter. In March, 1940, the huge orders began to come in, for 5,000 airframes and 10,000 engines, or double if possible, of the most advanced models of airplanes that would be effective against the Germans in 1941. Secretary Woodring, Assistant Secretary Louis A. Johnson, and General Arnold refused to give permission for the sale of these planes, with their secret designs and equipment. Once more Morgenthau had to go to Roosevelt, who declared forcefully that they would have to conform. "If Arnold won't," he remarked, "maybe I will have to move him out of town." Johnson needed no second prodding. He agreed to announce his enthusiasm for Morgenthau and to pin Arnold's ears back.

In his discussions with Morgenthau, Early, and Edwin M. ("Pa") Watson, military aide and appointments secretary, Roosevelt shrewdly emphasized the benefits to the United States and the Democrats: "Let's be very frank. These foreign orders mean prosperity in this country and we can't elect the Democratic party unless we get prosperity."[18]

This was the first indication that Roosevelt looked upon orders for war materials as a means of pulling the United States out of the depression. As yet they were too small to be of great consequence. The projected British total for the first year of the war was only $720 million. Manufacturers in the United States were reluctant, in the aftermath of the Nye Committee investigation of munition makers, to accept armament orders, and especially to build new plants. They had winced at epithets like "merchants of death" that the Nye Committee had stimulated. More important, they distrusted the New Deal and feared that after they had filled the arms orders they would be saddled with additional idle capacity.[19]

Through the dreary months of the Russo-Finnish War, despite continued alarms over German troop buildups in western Europe, there seemed to be depression politics as usual in Washington, heightened by the approach of a presidential election. Republicans, encouraged by their congressional gains in 1938, saw a strong possibility of winning the presidency in 1940. Two young aspirants, Robert Taft of Ohio and Thomas E. Dewey of New York, were attracting attention, and the older Arthur Vandenberg of Michigan was building support.

The major obstacle to a Republican victory was not Garner, Hull, or Farley, all of them quietly seeking convention delegates, but Roosevelt himself. He appeared to be giving his blessing to one and all to run for the nomination. Farley had his specific sanction. Roosevelt seemed, too, to be seeking a pro–New Deal Democratic candidate; in the early months of 1940, Hopkins, in better health, once again seemed to be the one. But Hopkins had no strength in the public opinion polls, and indeed even Garner, Hull, and Farley did rather poorly when matched against Republicans. The magic name still seemed to be Roosevelt.

Politics in the early months of 1940 revolved around whether or not Roosevelt would challenge the no-third-term tradition. Speculation grew and grew, and Roosevelt shrewdly fed it. At the Gridiron Dinner in December, 1939, the spectacular backdrop for one of the skits was a sphinx eight feet tall, with the visage of Roosevelt, complete with glasses and cigarette holder at a jaunty angle. He was so delighted that he obtained it to display in the new Roosevelt Library.[20]

Roosevelt seemed to be having trouble making up his mind. There is every indication that he was torn between a desire to retire and enjoy the honors and privileges of being an ex-president, and his delight in power and growing concern that no one else could be elected who would fight as effectively as he for the New Deal programs and collective security. No likely Democratic nominee seemed disposed to continue or augment the New Deal. This factor, taken together with his continued popularity in public opinion polls, and the gradual lessening of opposition to a third term as a matter of principle, caused Roosevelt at times to incline toward a third term. His son James feels that at the beginning of 1940 he was definitely planning to run.

Yet James Roosevelt feels equally certain that as of April, before the blitz, his father intended to retire. There is abundant evidence to support that possibility, too. He was a paraplegic, working too hard, and much too confined in the White House to keep in good physical shape as he approached sixty. There was some evidence of moderately high blood pressure, and later at one point Roosevelt suffered from bleeding hemorrhoids. Yet his overall health was robust and there was no physical reason to keep him from running in 1940.[21]

Still, while Roosevelt was maneuvering to guarantee that convention delegates would be committed to him, he was also step-by-step moving toward a retirement to center around the Roosevelt Library. This was another of his administrative innovations, under construction at the estate at Hyde Park, to hold his papers and memorabilia. He would work on the editing of his public papers and addresses. Also, he hoped with the help of the ailing Hopkins to produce a New Deal history — his memoirs. In addition, on January 27, 1940, Roosevelt signed a contract to write for *Colliers* at the same salary he was receiving as president, $75,000 a year.[22]

In private, depending upon his mood or his visitor, he said many different things about a third term. "I definitely know what I want to do," he remarked to Morgenthau in January, 1940. "I do not want to run unless between now and the convention things get very, very much worse in Europe."[23]

Whether he was nursing a cold or feeling fine, Roosevelt continued to encourage speculation over a third term. In this fashion he kept a firm grasp on power, which would have slipped away had he announced he would not run. More important still, he gradually accustomed much of the electorate to the idea of a third term. During the stalemate in Europe, early in February, Gallup polls indicated that 52 percent of those queried thought Roosevelt would run for a third term, and 60 percent thought he could be elected.[24]

If the war of siege had continued in Europe, perhaps Roosevelt would have opted to retire, but pressure was coming from seasoned Democrats, including numbers of those most indignant over his attempted purge of conservatives, who now regarded his renomination as the key to victory at the polls. Their hearts might be with Garner, Farley, or Hull, but they were realistic enough to confide to each other that Roosevelt — whatever their feelings about him — was the answer. Roosevelt could decide later what to do, and within several months the Nazi conquests made the question obsolete.

During the winter months, Hitler's apparently benign attitude toward Great Britain and France was strengthening isolationist feeling within the United States. Even during the campaign against Poland, the lack of air raids or attacks upon the West had given an unreal picture of the war to Americans. One of Senator Borah's last contributions to the debate before his death in January, 1940, had been to give it a name that captured the public imagination, "phony war." That winter two British ladies stopped by American Express in Paris to request a conducted tour of the battlefields.[25]

It was all too easy in the United States to feel no sense of urgency — to believe that at most the war might be a dreary, lengthy siege with the British Navy commanding the seas and the French Army the land, suffering no worse fate than boredom in the Maginot Line. The role of the United States need be no more than to supply whatever additional margin of arms the Allies might need, for cash on the barrel.

There may have been interludes, after Roosevelt received optimistic reports or correspondence, when he leaned toward this comfortable view. Overall, his appraisal was a grim one. Hitler and his generals were in a race to knock out the European democracies before they and the United States could rearm. The question was whether the Allies would be strong enough soon enough. Repeatedly Roosevelt expressed his worry over the prospects in Europe. At the end of January, when he had word that the Germans had massed eighty divisions on the Belgian and Dutch borders, he told the cabinet of the reports that were coming from Poland, and said "that probably nothing in all history exceeds the sadistic cruelty."[26]

Avowing that the prospect for achievement was one in a thousand, Roosevelt decided in late winter, 1940, to send Under Secretary of State Sumner Welles on a peace mission to Europe, comparable to that on which Wilson had sent Colonel E. M. House in 1916. It was an impulsive decision. Roosevelt explained to Assistant Secretary of State Breckenridge Long that he hoped the visit might delay the German spring offensive — even a month or a week would allow the Allies to obtain more supplies. Further, he wanted Welles to find out what he could from Mussolini and Hitler. The visits to Chamberlain and Daladier were simply "window dressing" to give balance to the trip.

Mussolini was sympathetic but not helpful. Hitler talked about the German need for economic supremacy in eastern and southeastern Europe and for the return of its colonies. During his trip, Welles reported directly to Roosevelt in a cipher they had devised before his departure. Not even Hull shared the key, learning only whatever bits of information Roosevelt chose to read him. It was treatment that could only intensify Hull's resentment of the president, and of the under secretary who was bypassing him. The reports were full of foreboding.[27]

In the frightful spring of 1940, the German forces struck one lightning blow after another. The first shock came on April 9, when they invaded Norway and Denmark. For three weeks the British battled along with the Norwegians against the Germans, acquitting themselves well at sea but disastrously on land. Roosevelt, well aware that a German strike against the Low Countries and France was almost certain to follow the German victories in Scandinavia, felt that the United States should be prepared to see the British lose the war.[28]

Roosevelt's forebodings soon were becoming nightmare reality. Hitler on May 10, 1940, launched a full-scale land and air attack upon the Netherlands, Belgium, and Luxembourg. On the eve of the invasion, Roosevelt, thinking of himself as "being of the Netherlands on my Father's side and of Belgium on my Mother's side," informed Ambassador John Cudahy in Brussels that he was "of course, much depressed." He continued to be during the shocking blitz that followed. Hitler sent into the first assault a thousand bombing planes and a million troops. A million more soldiers later joined in the great sweep. Within six days the German forces took over the Netherlands, broke through Belgium, and breached the weak French defenses north of the Maginot Line. The small Dutch Army surrendered on May 15, and Queen Wilhelmina established a government-in-exile in London. She sent Princess Juliana, next in succession, to Canada.[29]

Departing from his prepared text, Roosevelt declared, in a public broadcast on the evening the invasion began: "I am glad we are shocked and angered by the tragic news." The public listened, and their apprehension grew, as it became apparent that France was in deadly peril.[30]

With an appalled public and Congress behind him, Roosevelt moved as rapidly as he had in March, 1933, to respond fully to the emergency. Britain might in a few weeks be fighting alone against Hitler, and if Britain fell, the United States would have to withstand the threats from an Axis possibly allied with the Soviet Union. There was no time to be lost. Roosevelt began immediately preparing the first of what were to be a number of requests to Congress for ever larger armaments appropriations.

Roosevelt's message to Congress two days after the Dutch Army surrendered was forceful and frank: "The Atlantic and Pacific oceans were reasonably adequate defensive barriers when fleets under sail could move at an average speed of five miles an hour. . . . But the new element — air navigation — steps up the speed of possible attack to two hundred, to three hundred miles an hour. . . . So-called impregnable fortifications no longer exist."

The productive capacity for warplanes during the past year had risen, Roosevelt said, from 6,000 to 12,000 per year. He proposed increasing it to at least 50,000 planes per year.[31]

The limited objective Roosevelt set forth was acceptable to most Americans. A Gallup survey during May 18–23 indicated that while only 7 percent favored war, 85 percent believed the armed forces were not strong enough to protect the nation from attack. Congress supported his call for national and hemispheric defense without serious debate — a startling change. As recently as April, General Marshall had argued late into the night with leaders of the House to persuade them to restore an $18 million cutback. By June, Roosevelt was preparing a request for $5 billion more. Congress even broke with long-standing political tradition, and although it was the year of a presidential election, voted new taxes.[32]

Next Roosevelt could move toward his vital objective, to provide as quickly as possible the largest amount of aid to the British and French. In May, only 35 percent of poll samples favored aid at the risk of American involvement; by August, the figure had risen to 60 percent. Congressional isolationists, who in the Senate especially were able to exercise power well beyond their numerical strength, remained a negative force. Roosevelt, well aware of the power of the vociferous dissenters in the Senate, and determined to keep the nation united, proceeded cautiously. Only gradually did he become more open about the massive aid he wished to send the Allies.[33]

Day by day, from the beginning of the attack on the Low Countries, Roosevelt received increasingly urgent pleas for aid. Suddenly both the French and the British realized they were in a struggle for survival in which they needed all possible assistance. Roosevelt had to decide not only what the United States could send, but whether it was in the national interest to do so.

On May 14, Ambassador Bullitt sent fateful news:

> The German tanks had crossed the River Meuse as if it did not exist. They had run through the French anti-tank defenses . . . as if the rails were straw.
>
> Reynaud [the French premier] then said, "at this moment there is nothing between those German tanks and Paris."[34]

The French appeals became increasingly frantic and the French tried to purchase even the most worthless old American equipment. There was not much armament of use to the French that Roosevelt could rush. He proposed sending 2,000 French 75-millimeter guns that had been standard during the First World War.[35]

Day after day, by cable and telephone, Bullitt kept Roosevelt informed of growing calamities and the French pleas for aid. He warned, too, that with the French armies in disarray, Mussolini was preparing to enter the war. Roosevelt futilely marshaled his eloquence to try to persuade Mussolini to stay out.

By late May, the calamitous German breakthrough was driving a considerable part of the French Army, the Belgian forces, and the entire British Expeditionary Force into a trap with their backs against the English Channel. Dark predictions coming from military experts as well as diplomats caused Roosevelt to focus more on Britain, although its cause seemed almost equally hopeless.

While Roosevelt was in urgent communication with the French through Bullitt, he had less direct contact with Joseph P. Kennedy in London. Sympathy between them had not been very high before the outbreak of war when Kennedy had so enthusiastically supported appeasement. With the British forces trapped at Dunkirk, Kennedy suggested to Roosevelt that the Germans might be willing to accept a negotiated peace, "on their own terms, but . . . a great deal better than . . . if the war continues." He was not opposed to Britain, but felt that the United States could provide only too little too late, and that the national interest demanded the husbanding of its armaments.[36]

During the blitz, Roosevelt was in direct, almost daily, communication with the new prime minister, Winston Churchill, and from Churchill he received countering pressure to cast the lot of the United States totally with that of the British. Churchill's arguments were moving and of an audacity that appealed to Roosevelt, but he treated them also with caution.

At the time Churchill became prime minister, Roosevelt shared to some extent the uncertainty in Washington, as well as in London, about how he would turn out. After all, Churchill was sixty-five years old, had been blamed (perhaps unjustly) for the Gallipoli disaster during World War I, and had a capacity for alcohol that was legendary. Roosevelt, when he heard of the appointment, remarked to the cabinet that he supposed Churchill was the best man England had, even if he was drunk half the time.

Churchill's estimate of Roosevelt was no less tentative. In August, 1938, Churchill, although he viewed with pleasure the beginnings of rearmament in the United States, deplored the continuing recession, which he blamed upon the warfare between Roosevelt and big business. There were times in the spring and summer of 1940 when Churchill undoubtedly felt that Roosevelt again was blowing hot and cold, but the relationship was already vital to both of them.

It began after the outbreak of war, when, in September, 1939, Roosevelt sent personal notes both to Prime Minister Chamberlain and to Churchill, who had newly come into the cabinet to head the Admiralty. He invited both of them to keep in touch with him personally. Churchill responded with a series of letters on British naval problems and policies — sent with the approval of the prime minister and the foreign secretary, Lord Halifax, to whom he suggested "that it was a good thing to feed [Roosevelt] at intervals."[37]

Immediately after Churchill became prime minister, the correspondence grew urgent and prolific. "The small countries are simply smashed up, one by one, like matchwood," he informed Roosevelt on May 15. He expected attacks from the air and by airborne troops in the near future. If necessary, Britain would continue the war alone:

"But I trust you realise, Mr. President, that the voice and force of the United States may count for nothing if they are withheld too long. You may have a completely subjugated, Nazified Europe established with astounding swiftness, and the weight may be more than we can bear."[38]

The letter was the opening gambit in negotiations that finally resulted at the end of the summer in the famous destroyers-for-bases deal. In part, the lengthy negotiations indicated the insistence of both Roosevelt and Churchill upon driving a hard bargain, defending their separate national interests and meeting with the approval of their political constituencies. There is an even greater drama involved in the episode, for behind the public facade of optimism and defiance were private fears and even despair shaping the calculations that went into the tough, rather clumsy trading.

In the last days of May, with the likelihood that not only the French but the British troops would have to surrender, Roosevelt had to face the critical problem whether he dared to weaken further the very thin defenses of the United States. The gloomy appraisals that were reaching him plunged him into a state of deep pessimism. To a Canadian envoy he expressed the crux of his concern: "The President has it from what he believes good authority from Germany that Hitler may make an offer of settlement based on turning over of the whole of the [British] colonial Empire . . . and . . . of her fleet as well."[39]

This was the nightmare Roosevelt faced in his planning through May and June, 1940. He explained to his Business Advisory Council on May 23 that a buffer was threatened that had long protected the United States, the British Fleet and the French Army. Without them the nation would face a direct threat, "and so, we have to think in terms of [protecting] the Americas . . . infinitely faster." The only firm line of defense that the United States possessed was its fleet, as Roosevelt kept in the forefront of his thinking. Without control of the Atlantic, the United States would not have time to arm — and General Marshall at the start of the blitz had under him no more than 80,000 men ready for action. The Axis navies augmented by the British and French fleets would far outnumber that of the United States. What was more, American military planners feared that a rapid German thrust across the Atlantic would follow the collapse of France and Britain. The planners estimated that it would take six months for the Germans to prepare and man the captured vessels. Although these projections overestimated the capacities and immediate plans of the Germans, they seemed within the realm of reason at the height of the blitz.[40]

In keeping with what he was learning from his military and diplomatic advisers, Roosevelt faced hard choices on how best to maintain the Atlantic bulwark. The security of the United States seemed to be at stake. He wished to give all possible aid to the Allies in order to keep them in the war, yet should they fail, he wanted to be certain to retain control of the Atlantic. If Britain fell and surrendered its navy to Germany, the United States would lose that control. If Roosevelt lent destroyers to Churchill and then Britain lost, the United States would be still worse off, perhaps catastrophically so. Yet, if the destroyers helped keep the British in the war, they would be of greater value than on American patrol service. That was the dilemma.

The sharp debate over the destroyers continued for several weeks. It was fortunate for the morale of the Americans, reassured by the bold, optimistic public statements of Churchill and Roosevelt during those critical days, that they were not aware of the pessimistic candor that ran through these exchanges. Had they been known, Congress and the American people would have panicked and insisted that the nation retreat into Fortress America, and husband armaments for its own forces. Roosevelt was cautious, knowing that the idea of a hemispheric defense was far more appealing than that of war against the Nazi legions. The British ambassador, Lord Lothian, put his finger on it when he cabled the Foreign Office on May 30, "The expert politician in the President is always trying to find a way of winning the war for the Allies, or, if he fails to do that, of ensuring the security of the United States, without the United States itself having to take the plunge into the war."[41]

The candid discussions began on the evening of May 15, after Roosevelt had received Churchill's request for destroyers. Roosevelt suggested to Lothian and the French ambassador that France would be no worse off if it allowed Germany to occupy all of its territory and then continued to fight from overseas, while the British, French, and United States navies controlled the seas, effectively blockading Germany. Lothian suggested that the position of Britain might soon be analogous, but as with France, the question of the disposal of its fleet could depend upon "whether by the time when the decision was necessary, the United States had thrown its heart and soul into the business of resisting Hitler's aggression . . . and was at war with Germany." Roosevelt replied that the answer would depend upon public opinion, and whether some act of the dictators forced war. He was serious about the possibility of American entry into the war. The next day, in giving Morgenthau permission to send some airplanes vital to the air corps, he remarked, "After all we will not be in it for *60 or 90* days." On May 26, making assumptions to Lothian of the sort Churchill did not want made, Roosevelt suggested that in case of catastrophe No. 10 Downing Street might be transferred to Bermuda. What, Lothian queried, would he do if such a catastrophe impended? "As things were going," Roosevelt responded, "it seemed likely that Germany would challenge some vital American interest in the near future, which was the condition necessary to make the United States enter the war with the necessary popular support."[42]

Understandably Roosevelt was in a state of indecision and confusion. Had he sought a declaration of war, Congress would have vehemently rebuffed him, and the populace would have been outraged. The Republican convention, about to meet, would have certainly nominated the staunchly isolationist Taft or Vandenberg, with every prospect of victory at the polls. He worried, too, that if he gave the destroyers to the British they could not arrive in time to affect the expected German assault in a few weeks, and would needlessly anger Hitler. While Roosevelt might well have thought that the United States would soon be at war, he did not want to incite Hitler while the nation was essentially disarmed.[43]

As the discussion between Roosevelt and Churchill went on, the news from Europe worsened, except for one heartening occurrence. The trapped Belgian armies surrendered, but then the German forces paused to obtain supplies and make repairs to their armored vehicles, giving an opportunity to the encircled British and French. For four days while they held off seven German divisions, the British, using every available boat, successfully evacuated 330,000 troops from Dunkirk to England, although they had to leave behind their arms and equipment. The evacuation made a decided difference in the course of the war. While France staggered still closer to collapse, the British chances for survival rose. But, the American naval attaché in London reported, Britain was "no more fortified or prepared to withstand invasion in force than Long Island." Equipment was even more essential than before. Ambassador Kennedy, despite his isolationist leanings, was eager to help; he even thought Roosevelt could easily obtain congressional approval to transfer the destroyers.[44]

Roosevelt remained unmoved concerning the destroyers, but did order the armed forces "to scrape the bottom of the barrel." Army supply officers, on orders from Marshall, checked through warehouses and found quantities of obsolescent equipment from World War I, most of it British in origin, which would be of help in rearming the British Isles: 500,000 Enfield rifles, 500 75-millimeter guns, 35,000 machine guns, 500 mortars, together with some ammunition.

June was a month of appalling dangers and brave rhetoric. The Royal Air Force, although outnumbered, was successfully attacking the enemy; the British were still masters of the sea. On June 4, Churchill, in the great peroration of his address to the House of Commons, broadcast to the American public as well as the British, asserted that Great Britain could

> ride out the storm of war . . . if necessary for years, if necessary alone; . . . we shall fight on the beaches; . . . we shall never surrender, and, even if . . . this island . . . were subjugated . . . then our Empire beyond the seas, armed and guarded by the British Fleet, would carry on the struggle, until, in God's good time, the New World with all its power and might, steps forth to the rescue and the liberation of the Old.

Lothian was worried that Churchill might be misleading Americans to believe that even if the British were defeated, the United States would obtain the fleet. Churchill at once instructed Lothian to dampen any "complacent assumption" they would "pick up the débris of the British fleet by their present policy. On the contrary they run the terrible risk that their sea-power will be completely over-matched."[45]

Roosevelt engaged in rhetoric of his own several days later when, on June 10, with German tanks crossing the Seine, Mussolini, as expected, declared war on France. That evening, Roosevelt was delivering the commencement address at the University of Virginia, where his son Franklin, Jr., was graduating from law school. Into his speech he penned a startling statement: "On this tenth day of June, 1940, the hand that held the dagger has struck it into the back of its neighbor."

Later that evening, Roosevelt arrived back at the White House, aglow because he had said vigorously what was on his mind. To his listeners the words were electric. Roosevelt was warning the nation of imminent dangers and seeking to counter them by aligning the United States as a nonbelligerent opposed to the Axis. Those fearing American involvement in hostilities were apprehensive, and the disapproval extended into the State Department, but the public response to the White House was favorable.[46]

The French collapse was rapid. Churchill was hopeful that Roosevelt would pledge early United States entry into the war to avert an armistice. Premier Reynaud cabled that if France were to continue the war from overseas he would have to so assure his government. Although there were prominent Americans who would have favored a declaration of war, Churchill was asking the impossible. A day later, he offered Reynaud a union with France, but the French cabinet would not accept it. Reynaud had to give way to the aged Marshal Henri-Philippe Pétain, the hero of the Battle of Verdun in World War I. Pétain declared he would resign unless either the United States declared war or his cabinet agreed to an armistice. On June 17, France sued for peace. Roosevelt immediately signed an order freezing all French assets in the United States. On June 22, the Pétain government signed an armistice with Germany in the same railway car in the Compiègne forest where the Germans had signed in 1918. Before the end of the month, Pétain had established a government in Vichy for the unoccupied southern part of France, and General Charles de Gaulle had formed a French National Committee to carry on resistance from abroad.

To the dismay of both Churchill and Roosevelt, the French Fleet neither escaped to British ports nor was scuttled. The French agreed to return the fleet to ports where it would be disarmed under Axis supervision. There followed a bold British action that Roosevelt approved in advance. On July 3, after French naval officers in Algeria had refused to join the British Fleet or sail to the French West Indies, the British suddenly opened fire, damaging or sinking a considerable part of the French Fleet and killing 1,200 of their erstwhile allies. Roosevelt had assured Lothian that the American public would want the ships forcibly seized rather than allowed to fall into German hands, and indeed the action was acclaimed in the United States. Months later, Hopkins informed Churchill that it was only through the attack on the French Fleet that Roosevelt became convinced that the British possessed the determination to fight on alone against the Axis. The acute danger that the French Fleet might join forces with that of Germany and Italy had been lessened.[47]

That was scant consolation for Roosevelt, since he had to face the fact that Great Britain was standing alone against Germany and Italy with little but its navy and outnumbered air force to protect it from invasion. There were those who expected that Hitler, fresh from parading down the Champs Elysées, would be reviewing troops in Trafalgar Square by August 1. Some of the rhetoric of Churchill's messages of mid-June, urging Roosevelt if not to declare war, at least to send destroyers, must have contributed to the president's misgivings about whether the British could survive alone: "If we go down you may have a United States of Europe under Nazi command far more numerous, far stronger, far better armed than the new [world]."[48]

Some of the military and naval experts were predicting the defeat of Great Britain. If that were to occur, Roosevelt would be open to the charge that he had left the United States relatively defenseless through sending such a large part of the nation's essential armament to Britain. If indeed he sent destroyers and the Royal Navy fell into the possession of Germany, a serious component of America's sea power would pass under Hitler's control.

Roosevelt continued to send all possible armaments and airplanes to the British, despite objections from certain military leaders and from numerous nationalistic isolationists. In spite of some sentiment for building a Fortress America and abandoning Britain, those polled by Gallup and Roper overwhelmingly favored Roosevelt's aid policy.

The destroyers were a different matter. For a number of weeks Roosevelt found various reasons to delay a decision. Perhaps Churchill's inclination to engage in hard bargaining contributed. Roosevelt was not certain for some time if Britain could survive alone. There were also political factors involved. Roosevelt, undoubtedly more through design than inertia, was waiting until both the Republican and Democratic conventions were past, public opinion had solidified, and the strong isolationist minority in the Senate could be contained.[49]

The more compelling problem that faced Roosevelt during the weeks when France was collapsing was to establish a fresh defense policy. The military planners assumed the worst — that the Germans would be able to defeat or blockade Britain — and expected Hitler then to move quickly toward Latin America and European possessions in the Caribbean. Therefore, they recommended to General Marshall that the United States for twelve months should concentrate upon protecting the hemisphere and American territories as far into the Pacific as Midway Island. Marshall shared the fear of a quick Nazi thrust into Latin America, which evidence subsequently available indicates was not among Hitler's plans.[50]

By June 13, Roosevelt was firmly taking the view that the armed forces must do more than prepare for the worst. He presented to the chiefs of Army and Navy Intelligence his own hypotheses, seeking their reaction:

> 1. Time. Fall and winter of 1940.
> 2. Britain and the British Empire are still intact.

Roosevelt went on to guess that while France would be occupied, French resistance would continue from North Africa, and the French Navy would be operating closely with those of the United States and Britain. In less than a week, he was wrong in that optimistic guess. He did better in suggesting that Russia and Japan would still be inactive.

What was most significant was the role that Roosevelt was assigning to the United States — far more energetic than the cautious army plans, and indeed, except for a congressional vote of a declaration of war, the American participation that Churchill was so ardently seeking:

> 7. The U.S. active in the war, but with naval and air forces only. Plane production is progressing to its maximum. America is providing part of Allied pilots. Morocco and Britain are being used as bases of supplies shipped from the Western Hemisphere. American shipping is transporting supplies to the Allies. The U.S. Navy is providing most of the force for the Atlantic blockade. (Morocco to Greenland.)[51]

The scenario set forth the policies Roosevelt hoped to pursue. The army planners and Marshall sought to moderate them. Roosevelt was keeping the fleet at Pearl Harbor rather than returning it to the West Coast, hoping to deter the Japanese from going into the Dutch East Indies. The army feared exactly the opposite result, and also continued to worry about stripping the American forces of equipment and munitions that they desperately needed for training and possible combat.[52]

Above all, Marshall and the army firmly opposed armed intervention until the United States was strong enough to be effective. Until the early fall of 1941, Marshall did not favor war. The chief of naval operations, Admiral Harold L. Stark, on the other hand, was always responsive to Roosevelt's proposals. The army reply to Roosevelt was firm: it declared that entry into the war in the next few months would bring upon the United States attacks from Germany, Italy, and perhaps Japan. "Our unreadiness to meet such aggression on its own scale is so great that, so long as the choice is left to us, we should avoid the contest until we can be adequately prepared."[53]

In the months that followed, into the fall of 1941, Roosevelt, swayed by the logic of the army position and the even stronger political logic of congressional opposition, did indeed avoid premature involvement. At the same time, he moved step-by-step toward the objective he had presented to the army planners in June, 1940, to provide strong aid short of full belligerency to the foes of the Axis.

Chapter 25

THE THIRD TERM CAMPAIGN IN TIME OF CRISIS

DEFENSE AND POLITICS intertwined in Roosevelt's campaign for a third term. In response to the Nazi triumphs of May and June, 1940, he audaciously undertook (in the words of his budget director) "to improvise a new government within a government," essential to put the nation on a defense footing. He felt that if he were to succeed he must be a candidate for a third term. He functioned more as commander in chief than as president, involved during the uncertain summer and fall in the complexities of organizing the nation's defenses and seeking reelection. In his view, both undertakings were vital to protect the nation from foreign perils. Others, sharply challenging his premise, engaged him in passionate debate, which escalated for nearly a year and a half.[1]

While contention grew increasingly heated, Roosevelt, with a national consensus supporting him, devised organizations to stimulate and direct the production of the supplies for hemispheric defense and overseas aid. Fearing bitter arguments in Congress, he bypassed it in creating these initial defense agencies. By utilizing still-valid World War I statutes upon which to base his executive orders, he avoided new legislation. The new agencies were a logical extension of the administrative reorganization in which he had been engaged since the passage of 1939 legislation, and he depended upon the same public administration experts to help design them and put them into operation.

The defense machinery was to be firmly under Roosevelt's own control. That he had determined when, at the outbreak of the war, he had issued the order creating the Executive Office of the President. One section, which he wrote in his own hand, provided for an Office of

Emergency Management. On May 21, 1940, Roosevelt decided to activate the office. Under it would come all other new defense agencies. Thus Congress, in voting what had been thought a meager, almost meaningless authorization to modernize the executive branch, gave Roosevelt power to control defense machinery. He held firm against urgings to entrust it to existing executive departments, convinced they were so bound by bureaucratic rules that they could not act as quickly and audaciously as he wished. Yet Roosevelt at first constituted a weak Council of National Defense and an advisory committee within the Office of Emergency Management that would neither challenge his ultimate authority nor alarm Congress and the electorate.[2]

There was an aroma of politics to Roosevelt's decision in June finally to establish a defense cabinet. He appointed Frank Knox, once one of TR's Rough Riders, and the 1936 Republican candidate for vice president, to be secretary of the navy, and one of the most prestigious Republican elder statesmen, Henry L. Stimson, who had been Taft's secretary of war and Hoover's secretary of state, to be secretary of war. In one stroke Roosevelt brought in two staunch supporters of his defense policy — indeed, a pair who, along with Morgenthau and Ickes, General Marshall and Admiral Stark, would push him to move faster than he deemed prudent.[3]

"Preposterous" was one of the milder expletives Republicans used when Roosevelt's bombshell burst across the front pages only four days before their convention was to meet in mid-June. The Republicans nonetheless came out of the convention strong, proclaiming themselves the party of peace, but rallying behind a candidate hard to distinguish from Roosevelt in his determination to aid Britain. They were hopeful they had found a winner in Wendell Willkie.

Willkie was not the Republican candidate Roosevelt would have chosen to run against. As late as June 4 he thought the most likely nominee was the isolationist Robert Taft. Had the Republican convention not coincided with the fall of France, the guess would probably have been correct. But in the spring of 1940, eastern Republicans had turned toward Willkie, for some months hailed as an eloquent, thoughtful critic of the New Deal yet an advocate of collective security. Willkie, who four years earlier was a delegate to the Democratic convention, had gained fame as the president of the Commonwealth and Southern Utility Company in its struggle against TVA. Like Roosevelt, he was electric and winning in his personality. From the outset of the New Deal they were rivals. When he first confronted Roosevelt at the White House in 1934, he wired his wife, "Charm greatly exaggerated."

At the Republican convention there was stale oratory and a fresh candidate, Willkie. The party was torn between isolationists and interventionists, leading to a platform straddling the defense issue. H. L. Mencken joked, "It will fit both the triumph of democracy and the collapse of democracy, and approve both sending arms to England or sending only flowers."[4]

The question whether or not the United States would become involved in the war in Europe was, of course, the key issue in 1940. Roosevelt was as determined to avoid it as the Republican platform committee. His political instinct was sure but misled him at the outset toward a feeble, ignoble alternative. At the Republican convention, former President Hoover had declaimed, "If man is merely one of the herd . . . Stalin is right, Hitler is right, and God help us for our foibles and our greeds, the New Deal is right." Roosevelt chose to meet this challenge that he was functioning like a dictator rather than face foreign policy questions, and ordered spokesmen "to tie Willkie in with the idea of [Mussolini's] corporate state." It was Roosevelt at his worst — but he had been stung by Republican political jokes.[5]

As the Democratic convention approached, circumstances of politics as well as Nazi assaults dictated the nomination of Roosevelt. No other candidate — certainly not Hull, Farley, Garner, or Paul V. McNutt of Indiana, whose names had been most frequently mentioned — stood any chance of defeating Willkie. There seemed no longer any serious doubt whether Roosevelt would accept the nomination. Yet he refused to reveal his hand, partly out of political showmanship, but also out of lingering misgivings. Finally, the Sunday before the convention he tried to explain to the bitter Farley why he would not abide by his assurance of a year earlier that he would not run. Even then, he opened his shirt to show Farley a lump under his left shoulder, which he said was muscle misplaced because of his illness, and remarked, "You know, Jim, a man with paralysis can have a breakup at any time."[6]

The Democratic politicians so desperately needed Roosevelt that, despite a lack of private enthusiasm among a considerable part of them, he was able to exercise more effective control than before over the convention. He chose Chicago as the site, because he hoped Mayor Edward J. Kelly would pack the galleries with vociferous Roosevelt supporters. While Roosevelt was insisting even to his wife that he was giving the delegates complete freedom to vote as they pleased, he kept the center of power not with Harry Hopkins at the Blackstone Hotel but in his own hands at the White House.[7]

Roosevelt had neutralized several differing Democratic leaders, most notably the fiercely isolationist Senator Burton K. Wheeler, by letting hints reach them that the vice presidential nomination might be theirs. Later, dashed expectations led to sourness. Senator John Bankhead, offering his sympathy to his brother the Speaker, whom Roosevelt correctly considered too ill to become vice president, wrote: "I am wondering if we are going to be as anxious to please FDR *after* Chicago as we are *before*. Personally I think he is the most selfish man of all who have risen to the Presidency. It is all FDR with him or nothing doing."[8]

Through the first day, July 15, 1940, the convention was dull. The delegates, a pro–New Deal newspaper reported, were drafting Roosevelt with all the enthusiasm of a chain gang. The following night, the permanent chairman, Alben Barkley, as Roosevelt had arranged, delivered a statement from the White House that "the President has never had, and has not today, any desire . . . to continue in the office of President" and that "all delegates . . . are free to vote for any candidate."

With these words a great "draft Roosevelt" demonstration was supposed to begin. Kelly's followers went down the aisles carrying signs reading "Roosevelt and Humanity," but Farley's party organization had retained control of the galleries, which remained conspicuously silent. Whatever Roosevelt (listening at his radio in the White House) had hoped to obtain from them, the resourceful Kelly substituted from elsewhere. Out of the loudspeakers came a bellowing voice filling the auditorium: "Illinois wants Roosevelt. . . . New York wants Roosevelt. . . . America wants Roosevelt. . . . The world wants Roosevelt."

The shouting, along with intermittent marching tunes, went on deafeningly for nearly an hour. The *New York Times* correspondent, Warren Moscow, tracked the source to the amplifier controls in the basement of the convention hall, where he found the superintendent of sewers of the city of Chicago, Thomas F. Garry. The "voice from the sewer" became the unedifying symbol of the way in which Roosevelt's convention support had shifted in eight years to the urban bosses who earlier had tried to block him.[9]

Senator Wagner's platform committee, like that of the Republicans, had trouble reconciling interventionist and isolationist pledges. Those fearing war insisted that the planks include, "We will not send our armed forces to fight in lands across the sea." Roosevelt by telephone persuaded the committee to add the words "except in case of attack." It was a hedge that was to run through his mind during the campaign.

Roosevelt won on the first ballot, with 946 votes to 72 for Farley and 61 for Garner. Farley then moved to make Roosevelt's nomination unanimous.

The most difficult hours of the convention lay ahead, for while the organization Democrats had been willing to accept the renomination of Roosevelt in order to stay in power, they were upset and rebellious over word that the president would not allow them to nominate one of their own for vice president, but had decided upon Henry A. Wallace. Roosevelt would have liked to avoid further friction and sought one of the heroes of the regulars, Secretary Hull, who despite his conservative views of domestic matters was popular among liberals as a perpetuator of Wilsonian ideals. Before the convention, on July 3, Roosevelt had urged Hull to join him on the ticket. Hull emphatically refused, and although Roosevelt in the next several days tried to persuade him, continued to refuse. Hull strongly opposed a third term and was resentful over the slights and grievances he believed Roosevelt had inflicted. As late as July 12, Roosevelt was considering another more useful and attractive aspirant, Senator James F. Byrnes, who would have been hailed with enthusiasm by the South and could have continued to help Roosevelt in many ways. Although Byrnes also was to the right of Roosevelt, he was a staunchly loyal and effective political aide. The stumbling block was his religion: he had been born a Catholic and become an Episcopalian. How seriously Roosevelt would have considered him in 1940 had it not been for this question is impossible to say. A Catholic backlash might have followed in some northern states if Roosevelt had chosen Byrnes after eliminating the popular Farley.

As the overtones of Roosevelt's conversations before the convention indicated, he was already focusing, as in the past, upon the progressive Republicans who had been a small but important element in the New Deal coalition. Secretary of Agriculture Wallace, never close to him, was, like Willkie, a tousle-haired, rather rumpled-appearing idealistic progressive; he had not troubled until 1936 to change his registration from Republican to Democratic. Although Wallace had long been in politics, the professionals regarded him as they did Willkie, as an amateur. Roosevelt looked upon him as someone who could strengthen the ticket in the farm belt. The problem was to persuade the convention to nominate him.

Unfortunately, Hopkins and his cohorts had already given the delegates the impression that they themselves could choose the vice presidential nominee, and a number of candidates were energetically rounding up strong followings. They were quite unprepared for the name of Wallace, who did not even have the delegation of his home state, Iowa, behind him. Hopkins phoned that there was a lot of opposition to Wallace, but Roosevelt, eating breakfast in his bedroom, would not budge.

"Well, I suppose all the conservatives in America are going to bring pressure on the convention to beat Henry," Roosevelt told Rosenman, adding firmly, "I won't deliver that acceptance speech until we see whom they nominate."[10]

In Chicago, Roosevelt's workers had difficulty in trying to placate the rebels. Mrs. Roosevelt arrived and delivered a conciliatory speech that helped some, but the delegates expressed their frustrations in the enthusiasm with which they greeted the speeches nominating McNutt, Bankhead, and several other candidates.

At the White House, the president, playing solitaire as he listened to the rebellious clamor, pushed away the cards and wrote on a pad a five-page statement declining the nomination, and handed it to Rosenman to polish. "I may have to deliver it very quickly, so please hurry it up." He turned back to the cards. Roosevelt "had his Dutch up," and was venting his feelings.

When the balloting began, Roosevelt tallied the votes as they came in over the radio. They began to pile up in favor of Wallace. Byrnes had sobered the delegations by warning them that the president would not run unless Wallace was nominated. The vote on the first ballot was Wallace 628, and his nearest rival, Bankhead, 329.

Once more Roosevelt had triumphed, but he looked weary and bedraggled. A few minutes later, freshened, smiling, and jaunty, he went to the broadcast room to deliver his acceptance speech. Everyone around him was jubilant except Missy LeHand, who was in tears; fearing for Roosevelt's health, she wanted him to retire.[11]

In his acceptance address, Roosevelt set forth once more his liberal goals but his emphasis, despite the equivocal plank in the platform, was upon collective security. At the outset he established what was to be the prime issue of the campaign, his own conduct of defense policy. To a certain extent the fact that he was again running for office led him to moderate that policy — as witness his caution in seeking a peacetime draft. For all the Republican fustian against a third term, New Deal spending and radicalism, the campaign centered upon Roosevelt and the Axis peril. There was no subterfuge on that point from either party.[12]

Wily politician that he was, Roosevelt had already settled upon a strategy to counter Willkie's skyrocketing campaign: let the inexperienced Willkie go it alone for weeks and weeks so that his popularity would peak well before the election. Since Roosevelt's justification for seeking a third term was the urgency of the defense crisis, he would stay in Washington or travel only a few hours away to make inspection trips that would emphasize preparedness efforts. In addition, as he explained in his acceptance address, he would, as usual, make periodic reports to the country through press conferences and radio talks. Also, he was canny enough to leave himself a way out if "non-campaigning" was not by itself sufficient. He declared, "I shall never be loath to call the attention of the nation to deliberate or unwitting falsifications."[13]

Roosevelt was indeed working at a hectic pace, not only in meticulous planning for what he expected to be a close, bruising campaign, but also to launch a defense administration, build the armed forces, rush aid to Britain, and obtain crucial legislation from Congress.

Through his new defense organization, Roosevelt was able to delegate responsibilities, especially in the War Department, with Stimson and Marshall there. The navy had gained a vigorous spokesman in Knox and a remarkable administrator in James Forrestal, first under secretary of the navy. Roosevelt had promised the post to Corcoran but Knox rejected him as too political. These new strong defense leaders exerted a continuous conservative influence upon Roosevelt.[14]

An indication of the shift was the subtle way in which Roosevelt mollified several powerful conservative Democrats by phasing out the influential Corcoran and Cohen from both the White House and his 1940 campaign entourage. Their departure was both a gesture to the right, and the reverse, a signal of the ascendancy in Roosevelt's esteem of Harry Hopkins. Although Hopkins had earlier been anathema to the right, he not only survived but became the most trusted adviser. By the spring of 1940, Hopkins had sufficiently recovered from a life-threatening illness to be of service, and he lived in the White House much of the time until late in 1943. He became Roosevelt's intimate in the way no one had been since Louis Howe's heyday two decades earlier, and helped mold international policy, becoming an ardent advocate of Britain's cause. Soon he was in advance of the president in urging all possible aid to opponents of Hitler.[15]

Roosevelt was nervous about Congress and the electorate, but his new prime advisers, and indeed the rapid shift in public opinion, helped pull him along. The enactment of the peacetime draft was an indication of how Roosevelt trailed. When Grenville Clark, leader of the selective service movement, urged a draft upon the president in May, 1940, Roosevelt offered neither encouragement nor objection. Clark and his associates drafted a bill and marshaled support, but for some weeks Roosevelt would not see them, commenting that "the time is not ripe yet." Stimson then nudged Roosevelt to express to Congress his mild support, and in his acceptance speech the president endorsed selective service. Even Willkie aided, committing himself in his own acceptance address. By mid-September, Congress had enacted the Selective Service Act.

Roosevelt would have liked to delay the draft registration it authorized until after the election, but that would have looked awkward. An assistant, James Rowe, cannily warned him not to delay the lottery because trouble would not develop until the local draft boards began operation, which would not be until after election day. So Roosevelt acted, and reaped praise for his political courage.[16]

Though no question of political problems was involved, the mobilizing of science for defense was another instance in which Roosevelt presided over events rather than directing them. In the 1930s Roosevelt had encouraged scientific leaders seeking funds for research, but Congress never voted appropriations. By June, 1940, a sense of urgency existed. Four scientists long involved with Roosevelt, led by Vannevar Bush, president of the Carnegie Institution, persuaded the president to establish a new scientific committee within the Council of National Defense. A year later Roosevelt strengthened it into the Office of Scientific Research and Development. Funds were now forthcoming in abundance, and the scientists, although late in organizing, soon were ahead of the Germans, since Hitler, expecting quick victory, had curtailed scientific research and weapons development. The Americans carried on applied research in innumerable areas, ranging from radar to penicillin. Above all, they were seeking to develop an atomic bomb in advance of the Germans.[17]

As early as the fall of 1939, Roosevelt began to carry in the back of his mind the alarming knowledge that uranium atoms could be split, and that the fission could lead to a chain reaction releasing tremendous amounts of energy. An atomic bomb, with destructive force beyond anything previously known, was within the realm of possibility. Refugees from Hitler, desperately afraid that the Germans would develop such a bomb first, tried to interest the American government. Enrico Fermi from Italy and Leo Szilard, a Hungarian refugee physicist, enlisted the aid of the famous Albert Einstein, who agreed to write a letter for them.

Einstein warned Roosevelt of the need for "watchfulness and, if necessary, quick action," pointing out that Germany had stopped the sale of uranium from Czechoslovakian mines. It was conceivable, though less certain, he wrote, that bombs might be constructed which, "carried by boat or exploded in a port, might well destroy the whole port together with some of the surrounding territory."[18]

The danger and opportunity immediately caught Roosevelt's imagination. New technical possibilities always excited him. He was sufficiently intrigued to establish a uranium committee, yet so cautious that he provided only $6,000 for research. After the fall of France, he worried less about allocating funds, and sanctioned such sizable research contracts that by late 1941 American scientists had completed the groundwork for the building of a bomb. Meanwhile, brilliant refugee physicists in England, excluded from other military research for security reasons, had been free to work on nuclear fission and proved by the summer of 1941 that a bomb could indeed be built in time to be a factor in the war.

In consequence, Roosevelt took very seriously the possibility of constructing an atomic bomb. He authorized Bush and James B. Conant, president of Harvard University, to explore the costs, and finally, on the day before Pearl Harbor, he decided to go ahead. It was a bold decision, diverting considerable numbers of America's most talented scientists and engineers, enormous sums of money, and scarce materials like valves, into an unproven secret project. Had he not taken the decision then, the bomb would not have been ready in time to end the war. What worried him, and the small group who knew of the project, was that Germany might beat the United States and Great Britain in the race for the bomb. At the close of a conversation with the economist Alexander Sachs, who had brought Einstein's letter in October, 1939, Roosevelt remarked, "Alex, what you are after is to see that the Nazis don't blow us up."[19]

In the far more frightening summer of 1940, it was not certain that Roosevelt's new defense establishment would have sufficient lead time to meet the German threat. One could not stop Hitler with money. It had to be turned into contracts, plants had to be built, raw materials obtained, skilled manpower recruited or trained, and finally the output would increase. There were further complications. Manufacturers such as those making automobiles were reluctant to accept defense contracts since they were, thanks to the armament program, being besieged by buyers. On the part of Roosevelt there was no inclination to force the electorate to give up the consumer goods they could now afford to buy, in order to speed defense, nor could he have done so with his relatively toothless defense agencies. Fortunately, Hitler's strategy of planning for one quick war at a time gave him — and Churchill — the time they required. But that became apparent only as the weeks and months went by after the fall of France.[20]

Roosevelt's overall course was to build the American armed forces as rapidly as possible, strengthen hemispheric defenses in both Latin America and Canada, stall Japanese expansion, defer a showdown in the Pacific, give all possible aid to Britain, and resist Hitler. In pursuing these policies, he continued to keep his options as wide as possible, and still, as Lord Lothian had warned, sought to avoid war.

The primary concern had to be defense of the United States. Through the remainder of 1940, that responsibility had to fall heavily upon the navy, since a considerable part of the armaments the army and air force needed for training and possible combat was being diverted to Great Britain. There was, on the other hand, much evidence of the formidable preparations under way in the United States. Frequently Roosevelt escaped from the Washington heat to visit military installations and naval bases undergoing expansion, or to inspect submarine construction. He thus called attention to the work going on, and incidentally dramatized his role as commander in chief.

Perhaps by no coincidence, on August 17, 1940, a scorching day when Willkie was delivering his acceptance address, Roosevelt arrived at Ogdensburg on the St. Lawrence River to inspect the eight divisions, including one of cavalry, that comprised the First Army. "This is the largest gathering of American troops . . . since the close of the Civil War," Roosevelt remarked cheerfully to reporters. There was not much else he could add, for little was on display beyond the 94,000 officers and men. He saw five antiaircraft guns and a few more than a hundred airplanes, at a time when as many as 1,800 German planes a day were attacking Great Britain. There were perhaps a hundred pieces of field artillery from World War I, but no automatic rifles, no antitank guns, and for that matter, no tanks. Trucks covered with canvas and a piece of telephone pole symbolizing the gun represented tanks in the maneuvers. Much of what little equipment there was had gone to bolster the British.[21]

By means of a meeting with Prime Minister Mackenzie King of Canada at Ogdensburg, Roosevelt dramatized the strengthening of the "defense of the American Hemisphere." Under the politically safe umbrella of hemispheric defense, Roosevelt audaciously wrought an agreement to establish with Canada a Permanent Joint Board of Defense. Through this device he openly brought about military staff conversations between the United States and a part of the British Empire. More important, through press conference remarks, he sent visions of new bases for the United States Fleet dancing through the heads of countless Americans who were isolationist, but also nationalist in their convictions. *Time* ran pictures of harbors from Halifax, Nova Scotia, to Trinidad.[22]

Hemispheric defense was more than a clever Roosevelt subterfuge in the summer of 1940. He and his military and naval advisers concentrated for some weeks upon Latin America, taking the view that the odds were three to one Britain would be overrun that summer, and that South America would be the next Nazi target. It was almost defenseless. Once again, Roosevelt tried to rally the Latin American countries into solidarity against the Nazis, and called a Pan-American conference in Havana. Despite a German propaganda barrage at the beginning of the Havana meeting, Hull obtained what he and Roosevelt wanted, authorization to block Axis control of European possessions in the hemisphere.

The Act of Havana, a vaguely worded set of compromise motions, sufficed to empower the United States to seize islands where there was a change of sovereignty, or the threat of indirect control. It was not a form of intervention Roosevelt ever had to undertake. One function of Nelson Rockefeller's interdepartmental committee on inter-American affairs was to counter the German influence. Roosevelt sent some of America's scarce arms and naval vessels to Latin America and authorized bolstering the economies of the area through the purchase of strategic materials. Hitler was not projecting an immediate onslaught against Latin America, but in the fall of 1940 he did ask his staff to draw up plans to seize Atlantic islands as a preliminary step. Roosevelt and the American command were prudent in guarding Latin America, although an attack never came.[23]

During the six weeks following the fall of France, Roosevelt and his military advisers through their focus upon hemispheric defense were treating the British as though indeed they expected an imminent collapse. The much vaunted correspondence between Roosevelt and Churchill lapsed into a single note about the Duke of Windsor. Some months later Churchill recalled, "The Americans treated us in that rather distant and sympathetic manner one adopts towards a friend one knows is suffering from cancer."[24]

As week after week went by and the ominous predictions did not come true, Roosevelt became more optimistic. Hitler had not invaded during the weeks immediately after Dunkirk, when the channel coast of England was almost unprotected on land. What was of major import was the strength of the Royal Air Force (RAF) and the antiaircraft defenses. Although the air assaults on Britain escalated in late July and through much of August, the RAF was not only fending off German bombers but daily attacking barges, harbors, transportation routes, and aircraft plants on the continent.

For the first time, Roosevelt at the beginning of August began to take seriously the possibilities of what evolved into a destroyers-for-bases deal. In his feelers to the British, he was concerned about bases, and still more over obtaining an assurance that the Royal Navy would never be surrendered. He devoted more attention to overcoming resistance within the United States. Roosevelt felt he would need legislation, and was fearful that a small minority in the Senate could filibuster it to death.

Through sophisticated legal arguments and the vigorous support of some Republican leaders, Roosevelt moved circuitously around Congress before the month was out. The arguments were not of the sort that would have necessarily stood up in court, but the aid of the Republicans made that question moot.

There were complications on the British as well as the American side, and there, too, enthusiasts were at work, pushing harder than Churchill, and providing information to the Americans. The destroyers no longer occupied so high a priority in Churchill's thinking, "very serviceable, no doubt, but not vital," and the United States seemed to be asking too high a price. "It doesn't do to give way like this to the Americans. One must strike a balance with them."

Roosevelt was on vacation when the final compromise with the British was reached: two of the bases would be in exchange for the destroyers, and the remaining five would be a gift. The naval and air bases were to be in Newfoundland, Bermuda, the Bahamas, Jamaica, St. Lucia, Antigua, Trinidad, and British Guiana. That, together with the assurances regarding the British Fleet, constituted the final arrangement. Roosevelt did no more than inform Congress of the transaction.

The British received little of immediate tangible value, but much for the future. The old destroyers had to be refitted so extensively that only nine were on antisubmarine patrol by the beginning of 1941. The British gain was, as the Foreign Office argued, something of symbolic value. It was also, as Churchill later stated in his memoirs, "a decidedly unneutral act by the United States."[25]

Roosevelt's efforts to persuade Willkie not to make the destroyer-bases arrangement a campaign issue failed. The president had sought the assistance of the Kansas editor William Allen White, his old friend and election-year antagonist, head of a committee to keep America out of the war by aiding Britain. White obtained an assurance that Willkie would not attack the deal. Subsequently, the isolationist senator Arthur Vandenberg persuaded Willkie to denounce the arrangement, although it had the support of an overwhelming proportion of Congress, the press, and the public. Willkie assailed it as "the most arbitrary and dictatorial action ever taken by any President in the history of the United States." Roosevelt was most vulnerable on the war issue; that had been a significant factor in his slowness to support either the destroyer deal or selective service. Willkie swung national focus toward them.

The early weeks bore promise for Willkie. The first Gallup poll in early August showed Roosevelt with a slight popular lead, but Willkie ahead in twenty-four states with a majority of the electoral votes. Roosevelt, distrustful of public opinion polls, was afraid of manipulation. On October 4 he expressed to Rayburn and McCormack his suspicion that the pollsters were putting Willkie through a bad slump so that Roosevelt would appear ahead:

"Next Sunday, in the Gallup poll, we'll have a great many — too many — votes handed to us. . . . And my judgment is that they are going to start Willkie — pickin' up! pickin' up! pickin' up! . . . and [give] people the idea that this fella can still win."[26]

That was, indeed, what was to happen, without the slightest evidence of any manipulation.

Roosevelt was calculating which states he thought he could carry and which were not worth effort in what he recognized could be a tight finish. He labored hard to try to restore in the Democratic party the unity that he had seriously strained. While Wallace campaigned as an ardent New Deal liberal, Roosevelt sought to pacify the Democratic right. Thus he gave the archconservative Texan Jesse Jones the cabinet post he had coveted, secretary of commerce, and permitted Jones also to continue as head of the Reconstruction Finance Corporation. Neither Roosevelt nor his wife could persuade James A. Farley to stay on, so Roosevelt appointed two Irish Catholics to Farley's positions, Boss Ed Flynn of the Bronx to be national chairman, and the faithful Frank Walker to be postmaster general.[27]

While Roosevelt was trying to create the impression in public that he was above politics, he was in private directing cutting retorts to rough accusations. He was most nettled by the attacks upon his sons because they had already obtained commissions in the armed forces. Political opponents focused their derision particularly on Elliott Roosevelt, who had succeeded in obtaining waivers for bad eyesight and in September was commissioned a captain in the air corps. Some of the Republican youth donned buttons reading, "I want to be a captain too."[28]

A more damaging potential Republican attack worried Roosevelt. That was a number of letters the party leaders had obtained, some genuine and some fabricated, which Wallace, a mystic, had written and headed, "Dear Guru." At the time of the convention, Roosevelt had parried criticisms of Wallace's mysticism by referring to him as a philosopher, but was concerned over the effect the so-called guru letters might have during the campaign. If need be, Roosevelt told his assistant Lowell Mellett, the Democrats could counterattack by spreading stories about a woman friend of Willkie's, "Awful nice gal. . . . But nevertheless, there is the *fact*." Somehow, it did not seem to occur to Roosevelt that he himself was vulnerable because of his past relationship with Lucy Mercer, which had long been Washington gossip.[29]

Roosevelt was indeed in a stiff political fight. Willkie's far from polished campaign style was to some extent an asset — it was in such contrast to that of the "old pro" whom considerable numbers of voters mistrusted. Willkie capitalized on that lack of trust by warning that Roosevelt might involve the United States in war. From the beginning he was hard-hitting. He emphasized that not only had some Republicans been isolationists, Roosevelt had been a prime isolationist and appeaser. At Joliet, Illinois, Willkie went so far as to assert, "Roosevelt telephoned Mussolini and Hitler and urged them to sell Czechoslovakia down the river at Munich." At Boston on October 11, he promised an enormous crowd, including many of Irish and Italian ancestry disposed to bolt the Democratic ticket, "We shall not undertake to fight anybody else's war. Our boys shall stay out of European wars." Subsequently at a congressional hearing, Willkie disavowed such statements as "campaign oratory," but they were sending his ratings so high in the opinion polls that by October 15 he again was threatening Roosevelt in projected electoral votes.[30]

Roosevelt, who had been holding back, felt that the critical moment had come to launch his rebuttal, and on October 18 announced he would deliver five campaign speeches in the next two weeks, ostensibly to correct misstatements.

It was the question of war or peace that made the campaign turn ugly. The nation witnessed the spectacle of the two contending political leaders, both deeply committed to collective security, attacking each other without gloves as each tried to prove the other more likely to embroil the nation in World War II. Willkie seemed to have embraced the entire isolationist wing of the Republican party, together with Colonel Lindbergh. One commentator, Richard H. Rovere, later declared that by late in the campaign, "Willkie was as much in opposition to the man he had been a few months earlier as he was to his opponent." Roosevelt, who had always kept his option of hemispheric defense well in the forefront, was perhaps a bit more consistent, and on domestic policy continued firm in his liberal stance.[31]

Once again Roosevelt, engaging in his favorite sport, was in high spirits as he delivered speech after speech, seeking to counter Willkie's charges that he was the war candidate. At Philadelphia he asserted that he stood on the Democratic platform, which he quoted: "We will not participate in foreign wars and we will not send our army, naval or air forces to fight in foreign lands outside of the Americas except in case of attack."[32]

The pledge was vital in the eastern metropolitan areas, where those of Italian background had resented Roosevelt's "stab in the back" allusion to Mussolini, and where Irish-Americans like Senator David I. Walsh of Massachusetts angrily opposed fighting again upon behalf of the British.

The campaign offensive continued in Madison Square Garden on October 28, when Roosevelt declared that the Republican leaders were playing politics with national security. He enumerated some of those who had voted against repeal of the arms embargo, and then added, "now wait, a perfectly beautiful rhythm — Congressmen Martin, Barton, and Fish." The phrase caught on with the audience, and several minutes later to their roars of delight he repeated it.[33]

The electorate had become so polarized that for some weeks, here and there, Willkie had been the target of eggs, vegetables, ashtrays, and even phone books. Roosevelt, in Boston, was the target of no more than verbal abuse. When he arrived at the apartment of his son John, who was attending Harvard, MIT students next door chanted at Roosevelt in his wheelchair, "Poppa — I wanna be a captain!" When he spoke before a huge sympathetic audience, he paid back his antagonists. Once again he used the phrase "Martin, Barton, and Fish" — his listeners expected it, and by the time the first word was out, joined loudly in the chant. Fear-of-war hysteria, Robert Sherwood remembers, was at its peak, and Roosevelt capitulated to alarmed Democratic politicians who were demanding an absolute guarantee. Abandoning the cautious words, "except in case of attack," he used words that isolationists later threw back at him endlessly:

"I have said this before, but I shall say it again and again and again: 'Your boys are not going to be sent into foreign wars.' "

Willkie, listening on the radio, exclaimed to his brother, "That hypocritical son of a bitch! This is going to beat me."

When, on the campaign train to Boston, Rosenman had pointed out that the usual disclaimer was missing, Roosevelt retorted with words so sharp they betrayed his uneasiness. "Of course, we'll fight if we're attacked. If somebody attacks us, then it isn't a foreign war, is it?"

Willkie continued to press the war issue. On election eve, a Republican radio commercial warned, "When your boy is dying on some battlefield . . . crying out, 'Mother! Mother!' — don't blame Franklin D. Roosevelt because he sent your boy to war — blame YOURSELF, because YOU sent Franklin D. Roosevelt back to the White House!"[34] But the president's firm assurances that he stood for peace were an effective counterattack.

While Roosevelt had jettisoned candor on the war issue, he did not abandon the New Deal. In his final address, at Cleveland on November 2, 1940, he both set forth his defense policy and gave promise of a better postwar nation, in rhetoric that became a model for later declarations:

> It is the destiny of this American generation to point the road to the future for all the world to see. . . .
>
> I see an America where factory workers are not discarded after they reach their prime, where there is no endless chain of poverty from generation to generation. . . .
>
> I see an America whose . . . land and nature's wealth . . . are protected as the rightful heritage of all the people.
>
> I see an America where small business really has a chance to flourish and grow.
>
> I see an America of great cultural and educational opportunity for all its people. . . .
>
> An America where those who have reached the evening of life shall live out their years in peace and security. . . .
>
> I see an America devoted to our freedom — unified by tolerance and by religious faith. . . .

It was a vision that helped rally behind Roosevelt the larger part of those who had long been in his following. It inspired well-educated, liberal supporters and gave hope to the core of his coalition, the poorer people. Despite defections because of the war issue and returning prosperity, Roosevelt succeeded in keeping that core intact.[35]

The prospect of a close election led Roosevelt finally to court seriously one large segment of the coalition, the black voters. For the first time there was a specific plank promising, "We shall continue to strive for complete legislative safeguards against discrimination in government service and benefits, and in national defense forces." It fell short of Republican promises, an indication that Roosevelt was still balancing black votes against those of southern whites. Roosevelt, who unlike his wife had seldom seen black leaders, during 1940 had a half-dozen meetings with them.[36]

By election day, the polls showed Roosevelt well in front, but he was apprehensive, as he had not been in the previous two elections, fearing the effect of both the war and third-term issues upon the vote for him.

He was expecting to win, but had guessed it would be by the narrow margin of 315 electoral votes, not much more than half the total. Willkie did receive far more votes than either of Roosevelt's previous two opponents, but the results were scarcely close: 22 million votes to 25 million, and 82 electoral votes to 449. Samuel Lubell, an authority on the electorate, found that Roosevelt had won basically in the twelve largest cities. His majorities had been greatest among the poorer people. He lost votes heavily among German-Americans and Italian-Americans, but gained proportionately among those, like the Polish-Americans, whose homelands had been overrun by the Germans.[37]

The animus between Roosevelt and Willkie evaporated rapidly. Willkie conceded gracefully and in an Armistice Day broadcast he called upon the nation to cast aside bitterness and give President Roosevelt the respect due his high office. The conflict between Roosevelt and the isolationist leaders intensified in the months ahead, causing Willkie, who returned to his forthright advocacy of aid to Britain, to become more the ally than antagonist of the president.[38]

Chapter 26

ARSENAL OF DEMOCRACY

WITH THE 1940 ELECTION behind him, Roosevelt turned fully to the task of strengthening American defenses and aiding the British. Throughout the ensuing year, he inclined toward intervention, pursuing a cautious course but becoming ever more deeply involved. While isolationists attacked his moves as devious and deceitful, interventionists chafed over his restraint, which they attributed to an inordinate fear of congressional opposition and an unwarranted solicitude over public opinion.

The battering that Congress had inflicted upon Roosevelt in his second term, together with his accumulated fatigue and ailments as he grew older, led him to be slower than before in making up his mind. Furthermore, he faced a fearful responsibility if he took the nation to war. On several occasions he recounted what Wilson had said to him in February, 1917, that if war came with Germany he did not want future historians to place blame upon him. Roosevelt did not wish any more than had Wilson to assume the moral burden of sending American youth to their death. In months ahead, in private he seems to have veered toward the view that there was no other way out, but still he held back until the attack on Pearl Harbor.[1]

The debate in Congress and the nation was particularly sharp over Roosevelt's first crucial proposal after the election, that the United States supply goods to the British and other opponents of the Axis through a device he called "lend-lease." He was well aware that isolationists were sure to make trouble for him if he tried to extend credit through subterfuge. Thus far the British had been able to pay, and Roosevelt demonstrated that the United States was not an easy mark by insisting that they liquidate American assets as assurance of good intentions. There had been complaints after World War I that the British had maintained their assets and trade intact at the expense of the Americans, even while they were borrowing funds they would not repay. The president wanted no repetition. Ultimately the British, as loath to sell off their investments as Roosevelt and Morgenthau were insistent, made one symbolic sacrifice, selling the American Viscose Corporation to a J. P. Morgan syndicate for half its real value.[2]

Roosevelt wanted to develop a scheme to advance credit to them for supplies that would not look like World War I loans, and would be acceptable to Congress. The first hint of a possible formula came from Ickes, who, writing Roosevelt on behalf of the destroyers-bases deal, suggested on August 2, 1940, that Americans were like neighbors who were refusing to sell or lend their fire extinguishers. It was the sort of comparison Roosevelt liked. By the beginning of December, the problem of British credit had become critical, the subject of urgent discussions in both London and Washington. On what seemed a key aspect — the construction of several hundred merchant ships for the British, to replace the frightful losses German submarines were inflicting — Roosevelt, sending up a trial balloon, suggested leasing the ships. He was well aware that the Maritime Commission decidedly would not want the return of these cheap, slow vessels; Roosevelt, on his innumerable trips up and down the Hudson, for years had passed at Tompkin's Cove a tied-up fleet of Hog Island vessels, which had rusted there since the end of World War I until they were useful only as scrap. What was emerging in Roosevelt's thinking was a device to persuade Congress to finance the British, not a practical scheme for the return of ships. As Senator Taft was to observe, "Lending war equipment is a good deal like lending chewing gum. You don't want it back."[3]

Roosevelt mulled over the problem during December while he was on a cruise in the Caribbean. As usual, he spent his days fishing and filled his evenings with movies, poker, and banter. He relaxed, a fresh suntan covered his pallor, and he gave no indication of his inner thoughts.

A lengthy message arrived from Churchill, outlining Britain's long-range strategy and enumerating staggering requirements. For two days, Roosevelt read and reread the letter. "Then," Hopkins later said, "one evening, he suddenly came out with it — the whole program. He didn't seem to have any clear idea how it could be done legally. But there wasn't a doubt in his mind he'd find a way to do it."[4]

At the outset of his White House press conference on December 17, Roosevelt asserted, "The best immediate defense of the United States is the success of Great Britain in defending itself, and . . . it is equally important from a selfish point of view of American defense that we should do everything to help." With this prelude, he proposed to take over British war orders, have manufacturers fill them for the United States, and "either lease the materials or sell the materials subject to mortgage." Then came his famous exposition:

> Now, what I am trying to do is to eliminate the dollar sign . . . the silly foolish old dollar sign. All right!
>
> Well, let me give you an illustration: Suppose my neighbor's home catches fire . . . if he can take my garden hose and connect it up with his hydrant, I may help him to put out his fire. Now, what do I do? I don't say to him before that operation, "Neighbor, my garden hose cost me $15; you have got to pay me $15 for it." . . . I don't want $15 — I want my garden hose back after the fire is over. . . . In other words, if you lend certain munitions and get the munitions back at the end of the war, . . . you are all right.

An old-time newspaperman asked if lend-lease would not increase the likelihood of the United States getting into the war.

"No, of course not," Roosevelt retorted.

In a Fireside Chat at the end of the month, Roosevelt carried that reassuring view directly to his listeners: "The people of Europe who are defending themselves do not ask us to do their fighting." The role of the American people must be to produce the ships, guns, and planes with which the Europeans could defeat the Axis. Borrowing a phrase others had already used, he gave it lasting currency: "We must be the great arsenal of democracy."[5]

A few days later, in his annual message to Congress of January 6, 1941, Roosevelt reiterated these themes, evoking a vision of what immediate sacrifices and successful aid to the Allies could mean in future gains for both the United States and the world. For the nation, he once more enumerated his basic goals: equality of opportunity, jobs, security, and civil liberties, together with a wider, steadily rising standard of living. For other nations, he set forth what came to be heralded as the American war aims, Roosevelt's counterpart to Wilson's Fourteen Points, the Four Freedoms:

> In the future days, which we seek to make secure, we look forward to a world founded upon four essential human freedoms.

> The first is freedom of speech and expression — everywhere in the world.
>
> The second is freedom of every person to worship God in his own way — everywhere in the world.
>
> The third is freedom from want — which, translated into world terms means economic understandings which will secure to every nation a healthy peacetime life for its inhabitants — everywhere in the world.
>
> The fourth is freedom from fear — which, translated into world terms, means a world-wide reduction of armaments to such a point and in such a thorough fashion that no nation will be in a position to commit an act of physical aggression against any neighbor — anywhere in the world.
>
> That is no vision of a distant millennium. It is a definite basis for a kind of world attainable in our own time and generation.

The Four Freedoms raised morale through setting forth positive, idealistic objectives in such simple terms that they could be easily understood. They helped solidify a majority of the nation behind Roosevelt's moderate, careful position that there need be no American blood shed, that it should suffice for the United States to serve as the "arsenal of democracy." It was the ideological justification for lend-lease, as the bill to establish it was debated in Congress.[6] Prime Minister Churchill entered into collaboration with Roosevelt to sway American opinion when Senate isolationists attacked the bill. In a broadcast to the United States, he hailed the unity between the two nations, and like Roosevelt pledged victory without the sacrifice of American lives: "We do not need the gallant armies which are forming throughout the American Union. We do not need them this year, nor next year, nor any year that I can foresee. . . . Give us the tools and we will finish the job."[7]

Only in his most optimistic moments could Roosevelt have believed that the Axis could be overthrown without ordering millions of American soldiers and sailors into combat. Nor would many Americans if they examined the facts, but wishful thinking, their growing sympathy for the British cause, and the spectacle in the press and newsreels of Nazi frightfulness in overrun lands carried them along toward increasingly serious involvement.

The nation took heart from Churchill's rhetoric of optimism and bold defiance and from the pluckiness of the Londoners as the Luftwaffe night after night was blasting and burning the city. At the time Roosevelt proposed lend-lease, newspaper photographs, broadcasts, and films brought evidence of the appalling effects of the bombing. A public opinion poll showed 60 percent of Americans believing that it was more important to help England win, even at the risk of involvement, than to keep out of the war.[8]

Lend-lease, its proponents emphasized, was a patriotic measure to defend America. Sponsors of the bill introduced it as House Resolution 1776. Public sympathy for the British was so strong that the isolationist opponents in Congress, rather than trying to kill the measure outright, sought to substitute a $2 billion loan for the "blank check" that Roosevelt wrote into the bill.

Although Roosevelt had the upper hand, the debate with Congress and throughout the country was ferocious. General Robert E. Wood of Sears, Roebuck, head of the influential America First Committee, opposed to intervention, fulminated that Roosevelt was "not asking for a blank check, he wants a blank check book with the power to write away your man power, our laws and our liberties." Senator Burton K. Wheeler went further in a radio debate when he called lend-lease "the New Deal's triple 'A' foreign policy — it will plough under every fourth American boy." Roosevelt at his next press conference met Wheeler's vilification head-on with an unprecedented outburst: "I regard [it] as the most untruthful, as the most dastardly, unpatriotic thing that has ever been said. Quote me on that."[9]

The lend-lease bill passed the House in February by a vote of 260 to 165, and the Senate in early March, 60 to 31. Senator Vandenberg lamented in his diary the key point, that "we have said to Britain: '*We will see you through to victory.*' " That symbolic significance was not lost on the British. Churchill in Parliament hailed lend-lease as "the most unsordid act in the history of any nation." Behind his rhetoric was his comment to a British Treasury official, "I would like to get them hooked a little firmer, but they are pretty on now."[10]

The immediate material effect of lend-lease was not striking. A newspaperman's remark to Roosevelt when he announced the lend-lease proposal had been to the point: before you loan a hose to your neighbor, you have to have the hose. In 1941, only 1 percent of British arms and munitions came through lend-lease; 7 percent more came from earlier contracts, for which the British paid cash.

In general, financial arrangements with the British were difficult to negotiate. On December 30, 1940, Roosevelt had suggested to the British purchasing agent the literal return of weapons, such as a 3-inch antiaircraft gun. There was no disposition on the part of Roosevelt to let the British off easily. He expected payment for the orders they had made prior to the enactment of lend-lease, and a substantial total settlement in either cash or kind. He even approved trying to negotiate the transfer of rare books, paintings, or prints from British holdings to the Smithsonian or the Library of Congress as part of the lend-lease financial terms.[11]

Of course, no substantial repayment in kind was to come to the United States through lend-lease. Still, Roosevelt had established that he was no dupe of the British — a position vital in his relations with Congress and the public, well in keeping with his own emotions. He and Churchill and their governments were all safeguarding their vital national interests, as reflected in their concern over trade in areas like Latin America, and were jockeying to be in strong postwar economic positions. Of course, the United States, as in World War I, was making substantial gains. Not surprisingly, Roosevelt soon abandoned talk about rare books, though not merchant ships. The question of lend-lease repayment soon became interrelated with that of postwar economic aims, in which Roosevelt was to obtain advantageous concessions from the British.[12]

The move toward lend-lease helped inaugurate a much closer working relationship between the Americans and the British. The sudden death of Lord Lothian and resignation of Joseph Kennedy led to the appointment of two new ambassadors, Lord Halifax, earlier a chief appeaser, who proved himself an exemplary envoy, and John G. Winant, a liberal Republican, a shy, stumbling but sincere speaker, who impressed the British as being Lincolnesque. Neither, despite their popularity, was nearly as important an emissary as Hopkins became.[13]

In December, pondering the many issues in the lengthy letter from Churchill, Roosevelt had remarked, "A lot of this could be settled if Churchill and I could just sit down together." Hopkins volunteered to go to London, and after some days of doubts, Roosevelt dispatched him as the president's personal representative. Upon Hopkins' arrival, he confided to newsman Edward R. Murrow that he had come "to try to find a way to be a catalytic agent between two prima donnas." He quickly won Churchill's full confidence. Hopkins became mediator and interpreter for both leaders, and also a force pushing the hesitant Roosevelt closer toward full hostilities.[14]

Upon Hopkins' return, Roosevelt made him the administrator of lend-lease. In this role Hopkins gradually supplanted Morgenthau and his Treasury team, who had expedited pre–lend-lease supply to the British. To continue liaison in London with Churchill and British leaders, Roosevelt appointed a friend of Hopkins, Averell Harriman, a New York banker and businessman, to go as "defense expediter." When reporters asked what Harriman's relationship to the American embassy would be, Roosevelt retorted, "I don't know, and I don't give a — you know!" Everyone present laughed, but, as with his use of Hopkins, the point was obvious. Roosevelt was bypassing Secretary Hull and Ambassador Winant. Harriman had been associated with the New Deal as early as the NRA days, and from 1941 on was one of Roosevelt's most trusted envoys. The Hopkins and Harriman missions were no substitute for what Roosevelt hoped to undertake, to confer face-to-face with Churchill, but for some months they had to suffice.[15]

The equivocal state of the nation, neither at peace nor at war, was ominous at Roosevelt's third inauguration, on January 20, 1941. There was much of the old and familiar in the pageantry on that chilly, clear day as again he walked slowly to the front of the platform on the arm of his tall son James. But this time James, a captain in the marines, was garbed in a red, gold, and blue dress uniform.

Roosevelt, in elegant generalities, carried the debate over defense policy into his inaugural address. There was a bite to it as he sought to refute Anne Morrow Lindbergh's little book *The Wave of the Future*, setting forth her husband's view that Americans must adjust themselves to an inevitable new order in Europe. Said Roosevelt:

"There are men who believe that . . . tyranny and slavery have become the surging wave of the future — and that freedom is an ebbing tide.

"But we Americans know that this is not true."[16]

There was a new martial note to the inaugural parade. After the lengthy procession of dignitaries, cavalrymen, West Point cadets, Annapolis midshipmen, CCC men, National Youth Administration women, and a unit of black WPA workers, there appeared the beginnings of the new armed forces: tanks, armored cars, and trucks carrying pontoon bridges and antiaircraft guns, shaking the pavement as they sped by.

It was a far from formidable display, not comparable to the endless reviews of Hitler's legions or Japanese combat forces that Americans had so often witnessed in newsreels. Therein lay the problem. The electorate was not yet emotionally ready for land warfare, and if the United States were suddenly to become involved there were not yet the troops, equipment, and shipping to launch overseas missions.[17]

Roosevelt's leadership was carrying the nation slowly toward massive rearmament and aid to the British, but only as new factories and shipyards could come into production. A solid majority accepted his assurances that to serve as the arsenal would suffice; they did not heed the warning of isolationists that Britain was on the brink of defeat, American entry would be futile, and the United States would have to learn to live in an Axis-dominated world.

Yet Roosevelt was by now convinced that the danger was so real and present that he must sooner or later persuade the people to accept entrance into war. The defeat of Hitler would otherwise be impossible. An attack upon the United States could take place at any time, he thought, but he was eager not to provoke one, since the nation as yet was still a year or two away from the strength requisite to fight effectively.

In early 1941 Roosevelt was failing to reveal his strategic projections even to his most bellicose cabinet members like Ickes. These came out only in his conferences with his top commanders and planners. Since the previous June, they had been emphasizing that the United States was so ill armed that "so long as the choice is left to us, we should avoid the contest until we can be adequately prepared." In late 1940, Admiral Harold Stark, chief of naval operations, and his assistants drafted a strategy proposal, which came to be known as Plan D or "Plan Dog," emphasizing that Germany was the most dangerous potential foe, and that if Britain were to be defeated, the United States "might not lose *everywhere*," but possibly "not *win* anywhere." Priority in war must go to operations across the Atlantic; war with Japan should be avoided if possible, and if it came should be limited. Perhaps it could be confined to the sort of blockade Roosevelt had long favored.[18]

In January, 1941, when Roosevelt took up military policy with the secretaries of state, war, and navy and Admiral Stark and General Marshall, he began by speculating that there was about a one-in-five chance that Germany and Japan might attack the United States at any time. If a sudden attack should come, his prime concern was that it should not diminish aid to Great Britain. As for the American role if it were not attacked, he echoed Stark and the planners, directing (according to Marshall's notes) "that the Army should not be committed to any aggressive action until it was fully prepared to undertake it; that our military course must be very conservative until our strength had been developed."

The army was still so ill armed that Marshall was afraid it would have to use dummy weapons again in the maneuvers of the summer of 1941; only the first 128,000 draftees were in training. As late as the early fall, the army had only six divisions ready for combat.

Thus Roosevelt, wisely, was not seeking war, but was undertaking fully to supply the British and at the same time to build the armed forces to meet an uncertain future. He was still in January, 1941, drawing contingency plans on the cautious projection that the British could hold out against the Germans for only six months, and that the United States could then count upon another two months before Hitler could move toward the western hemisphere.[19]

Roosevelt could not share these assumptions with the public, except in the most vague way, without courting greater disaster from the Axis, damaging morale in Britain, and giving isolationists proof of their suspicions. He continued therefore to avoid specific scenarios, simply warning of frightful dangers if Hitler were to triumph.

Warily, in the utmost secrecy, Roosevelt was also directing his military and naval planners in hypothetical discussions with their British counterparts that could lead to joint action if the United States were compelled to enter the war. These American-British conversations went on from January into March, 1941, at the same time as the great national debate over lend-lease, and surprisingly did not leak.

What above all Roosevelt kept privy was his belief, and that of his military leaders, that victory could come only when a huge expeditionary force engaged in massive combat with the German adversaries. The armed forces were already drafting contingency plans to go far beyond the 1941 defensive force of 1.5 million. In the Army Victory Program of October, 1941, they projected forces of over 8 million that could engage the enemy in Europe — but at the earliest in July, 1943.[20]

Politically, Roosevelt would have faced vehement opposition from Congress and throughout the nation if at any time prior to December 7, 1941, he had sought a declaration of war. Only if the United States were to be attacked could he conduct war with unified support. While the opposition of isolationists and a part of the Republicans was that of a minority, it grew increasingly strident and gave no indication that it could be coopted. Lord Halifax, attending a dinner of Republican congressmen in June, noted the bitterness: "One man said that he thought Roosevelt was a more dangerous dictator than Hitler, Mussolini or Stalin, and that he was getting this country to hell just as quickly as he could."[21]

The onslaught from isolationists was equally angry, especially when, in April, Charles Lindbergh began speaking at America First rallies. Lindbergh was relatively mild and careful in what he said, not even mentioning Roosevelt by name, but because of his potential following, he most aroused the president's animus. At a press conference when Roosevelt was asked why he had not asked Colonel Lindbergh to return to active service, he cited Clement L. Vallandigham, leader of the Copperheads (anti-war Democrats) during the Civil War, who had been exiled to the South. "Well, Vallandigham, as you know was an appeaser," he remarked. "He wanted to make peace from 1863 on because the North 'couldn't win.' " Lindbergh indignantly resigned his commission, lamenting in his diary that he was stumping with the pacifists when there was nothing he would rather do than fly with the air corps.[22]

Amid these incessant debates, Roosevelt had to confront a fresh crisis as the British struggled to try to retain control of the Mediterranean shipping lanes and of the Middle East with its oil. What additional supplies could Roosevelt scrape together? Could he order the navy to convoy the merchant vessels carrying them across the Atlantic?

Hitler's immediate threat at the beginning of 1941 was to the supply lines in the Atlantic and the Mediterranean. He hoped to pressure Franco to bring Spain into the war and allow the Germans to attack Gibraltar in February. "Once in possession of Gibraltar, we would be in a position to gain a foothold with strong forces in North Africa," he declared to his generals in January, 1941. Franco refused to cooperate.

Roosevelt had little or nothing directly to do with Franco's gamble that the British, with American aid, would ultimately win the war. On the other hand, Roosevelt did all he could to convince the aged Marshal Pétain, head of the Vichy government, that ultimately the Nazis would lose. In December, 1940, he dispatched Admiral William Leahy, a levelheaded, conservative former chief of naval operations, to serve as ambassador in Vichy and to bring his influence to bear upon both the aged Pétain and his opportunistic new chief minister, Admiral Jean François Darlan. Roosevelt wanted Leahy to be a watchdog, who would warn Pétain of ominous things that could happen if Vichy collaborated with Germany and who would hold out the likelihood of sending medical supplies and milk for French children through the Red Cross.[23]

Meanwhile, Roosevelt also kept a close eye on North Africa, where the talented, also conservative, Robert Murphy, nominally counselor of the American embassy to Vichy, helped influence the French minister of national defense, General Maxime Weygand, to continue his strong opposition to German encroachment. Murphy negotiated an agreement with Weygand to send needed supplies; along with the supplies came American "technical assistants," and the establishment of American influence. It prepared the way for Roosevelt to order complex and significant negotiations a year later.[24]

Both Roosevelt and Churchill had strong reasons to try to thwart Hitler's threatened moves toward French North Africa. Churchill desperately needed to keep open the Mediterranean. Roosevelt was ever aware that Dakar, at the westernmost tip of North Africa, was only a few hours' flight from Brazil.

In the spring of 1941 Roosevelt's interests fared better than those of Churchill. The Germans, quickly defeating Yugoslavia, moved on into Greece and threatened the island of Crete. Both fell despite British aid, leaving the British Army and Navy so weakened that they were no more than a thin bulwark defending Egypt and the approaches to the Middle East against the tanks of General Erwin Rommel's Afrika Korps.

In their fresh plight, the British turned to the United States for additional tanks, antiaircraft guns, and other equipment. It was a period of some fresh tension between Roosevelt and Churchill, but the president in the end accepted the predictions not only of the prime minister but also of Harriman in London that the British would continue to survive, and ordered additional aid.[25]

Nevertheless, Roosevelt gave priority to the Atlantic, in keeping with navy assessments, as he was determined to thwart the German submarines and raiders and deliver supplies to Britain. To the disappointment of Churchill, Roosevelt seemed ready to engage indefinitely in limited naval confrontation without taking the final step of sending a war message to Congress. Hitler, for his part, encouraged the submarine warfare against Britain, but was massing his forces for an attack upon the Soviet Union. A settling of accounts with the United States could wait; he ordered that American merchantmen not be sunk.[26]

The quandary Roosevelt faced seemed less a fear that Hitler might suddenly attack than that isolationists in the Senate would best him. For months he was indecisive about how best to aid the British and continue the buildup of American forces without prematurely taking the nation into the war. The interventionists around him despaired over his caution; in May, Ickes, Stimson, Knox, and Attorney General Jackson met to deplore his failure of leadership. Secretary of State Hull, who for so many of Roosevelt's years in office seemed of minor importance, served through his emphatic and continued caution as a counterforce against the militants. At the beginning of June, when Chief Justice Hughes resigned, Morgenthau proposed to Roosevelt that he elevate Hull to the Supreme Court and make Stimson secretary of state. Roosevelt startled Morgenthau by remarking "that he was not at all sure that Stimson was right in the Manchurian incident and that Hull's tactics might have been better at the time." (Roosevelt was alluding to the "Stimson doctrine" of nonrecognition of Japanese conquests, announced in 1932.) Like Lincoln with his cabinet during the Civil War, Roosevelt was balancing the weight in his saddlebags.[27]

Over the vital question of escorting convoys, Roosevelt pulled first one way and then another. In the winter of 1940–1941 it seemed politically dangerous. He had never considered convoying, he remarked at a press conference on January 21: "Obviously, when a nation convoys ships . . . through a hostile zone . . . there is apt to be some shooting . . . and shooting comes awfully close to war. . . . It might almost *compel* shooting to start."[28]

As a debate went on through the winter, and polls showed opinion edging toward convoying, Roosevelt in April wavered first in favor, then against, a navy plan to provide escorts. He was familiar with the polls; indeed he regularly received advance information through an expert on labor and personnel relations, Anna Rosenberg. The percentages indicated that if he could state the issue appealingly, he could carry a heavy majority with him. Acute damage to shipping inclined him toward escorts; on the night of April 3–4, a wolf pack of German submarines destroyed ten out of twenty-two ships in a convoy. Two events led Roosevelt to decide against escorting convoys. One, kept from the public at the time, was the action of the destroyer *Niblack*, on a reconnaissance mission to Iceland, which while picking up survivors from a torpedoing detected a submarine and dropped depth charges. At worst it could have brought war with Germany, and in any event, if known, would have alarmed isolationists. More serious was a shift in balance in the Pacific as the result of a neutrality treaty that Japan and the Soviet Union signed in April, easing pressure upon Japan and increasing the likelihood of thrusts into Southeast Asia. Roosevelt had just authorized the transfer of substantial fleet units from Pearl Harbor to the Atlantic. In consequence, on April 15, he fell back upon a plan to intensify and extend navy patrols in the Atlantic, which could provide similar protection yet create less uproar at home and be slightly less likely to lead to open war.

The next question was how far the patrols should operate. Roosevelt brought out an atlas, and tried with Stimson to determine a line. He settled upon the twenty-fifth parallel, about halfway between Brazil and Africa; the line later became the twenty-sixth parallel, with a bulge to include all of Iceland. He proposed that the United States should take over the antisubmarine patrol out to that point, leaving the remainder, the far more dangerous half of the Atlantic, for the British to protect.[29]

Roosevelt presented his program to the cabinet as the best way to counter submarines. Wrapping himself in the cloak of his forefathers, he explained that the role of the fleet had been to protect commerce, as witness the undeclared naval wars with the French and the Barbary pirates. By implication, he would not flinch from a new undeclared war on the Atlantic.[30]

Roosevelt's policy of patrolling raised relatively little controversy compared with the explosive issue of convoying, yet in months ahead would lead almost imperceptibly to exactly that, the escorting of vessels. If the Germans fired on American vessels, they would fire back.

Altogether Roosevelt followed a clear enough but rather cautious course, not entirely pleasing to either the navy or army. Admiral Stark commented to the new commander of the Pacific Fleet, Admiral Husband E. Kimmel, that the president had agreed to the escort of convoys, then canceled it "for fear of the Japs." Stark added, "How much a part of our Democratic way of life will be handled by Mr. Gallup is a pure guess." Roosevelt still transferred some ships from Pearl Harbor to the Atlantic and ordered forces into Greenland. His strategy made it necessary for him to await Hitler's moves, and nothing was yet certain.[31]

Reports indicated a vast German buildup to the east; Russia might be the next German target. Not certain in which direction Hitler would strike, Roosevelt on May 22 ordered the army and navy to make preparations to take over the Azores and Cape Verde Islands if, as he thought likely, Germany moved into Spain and Portugal. Both Stark and Marshall pointed out how difficult that operation would be for them. As Stark continued to emphasize the problems, Roosevelt addressed his inquiries to him "with a sort of a mocking or sneering laugh." The armed forces were not prepared for such an amphibious operation, and Roosevelt was irritated.[32]

Yet one point that Roosevelt throughout the spring emphasized to those around him was that he would not be the aggressor. On May 23 he explained to the cabinet that, while the determining factor in the war would be control of the seas, "I am not willing to fire the first shot."[33]

In consequence, Roosevelt, feeling wretched, being hectored by some of those upon whom he most strongly relied, seemed to be passive, avoiding decisions, and not always pleasant. He let it be known that he was suffering from colds and an intestinal complaint. His speech-writer Robert Sherwood, after a long talk with him in his bedroom, told Missy LeHand that the president seemed in fine shape without even a snuffle. Missy suggested that what he was suffering from most was sheer exasperation. In large part it was apprehensiveness over the chess game he was playing in the Atlantic with Hitler.

There were irritations at home as well. John L. Lewis was imperiling the expanding defense production with a coal strike, and was being as gifted as always in his intransigence. It added so greatly to Roosevelt's worries that Fred Shipman, head of the new Roosevelt Library, remembered the president sitting at his desk until quite late one night exhausted, fruitlessly searching for a solution. Finally, Missy began reading him a detective story, and he fell asleep at his desk. Missy herself was under great tension. That summer she suffered a stroke, which left her partly paralyzed and impaired in her speech. She was never able to return to work. Roosevelt was so deeply concerned that he provided a sum in his will to pay for her medical care for the rest of her life, but he gave no outward sign of his feelings. Grace Tully, who also had worked effectively for Roosevelt, took her place. As for the tension over John L. Lewis, the coal strike was settled, but questions concerning other strikes, defense production, the Atlantic, and the Pacific went on and on, increasing in complexity.[34]

Not even a fishing trip had gone well that spring. When Roosevelt arrived at Port Everglades to board the *Potomac,* it was docked next to the German freighter *Arauca,* which had been interned there for fifteen months. For the occasion, the *Arauca* flew from its stern a large swastika flag, flapping in the wind, and German sailors at its railing ogled Roosevelt and his guests drinking cocktails on the afterdeck. With hindsight, the carelessness about security seems appalling. That was not the only carelessness. When the *Potomac* reached the Bahamas, the water was so rough that the shallow-draft vessel rolled ominously, 25 degrees on one side, then 26 degrees on the other. Doughty sailor that he was, Roosevelt looked one morning like a "boiled owl," and confessed he had kept thinking what would happen if a stiff wave should hit the stern. Upon Roosevelt's return, orders went immediately to the navy to stabilize the vessel. Back at Port Everglades they again anchored next to the *Arauca*. Meanwhile word had come to the *Potomac* that the crews of Italian ships were systematically sabotaging them. Roosevelt gave orders to seize all German and Italian vessels to prevent further damage. Shortly after he left the *Potomac,* the Coast Guard boarded the *Arauca* and replaced the swastika flag with the Stars and Stripes.[35]

Slowly, despite Roosevelt's exasperation and the gloomy impatience of his militant advisers, the escalation proceeded — at Roosevelt's pace. During May, he carefully crafted a major speech, apparently to prepare the public for the possible takeover of the Azores. The appearance of the powerful battleship *Bismarck* in the west Atlantic underscored his concern, and led him on May 27 to announce a state of unlimited emergency. That very day the British sank the *Bismarck*. Just what the proclamation might mean no one knew, but Roosevelt's words served their purpose, to alert the public further to the acuteness of the crisis. Only future action would provide the specifics behind the ominous generalities.[36]

Gradually over the summer months the specifics evolved, and the war took some unexpected turns. Again in good health, Roosevelt addressed himself to problems both in the Atlantic and within the United States. Morgenthau was delighted that his mind was clear and that he appeared less harassed. Roosevelt remarked that his red corpuscles were about back to normal. Even when he did not feel too well, he joked about it. On the morning of June 12, when Morgenthau called him, the conversation began:

The President: Hello, Henry. Who do you think I am in bed with?
HM Jr.: I don't know.
The President: Well, I am in bed with a sore throat.

From this lighthearted opening, Roosevelt went on to tell Morgenthau that a German submarine had for the first time sunk an American freighter, the *Robin Moor,* in the South Atlantic bound from New York to Capetown. The vessel was not in a German war zone. Almost miraculously all the passengers and crew survived. The submarine commander, acting contrary to Hitler's orders, had feared that the *Robin Moor* was a British entrapment ship in disguise. Roosevelt issued a strong statement charging Germany with violations of international law, but reaction throughout the country was relatively mild. So were the steps Roosevelt took against Germany. He froze the assets of Germany, Italy, and nations under their domination, and ordered all German consuls and their staffs out of the country. Yet he did not break off diplomatic relations, and unlike Wilson confronted with a sinking in 1916, he did not send an ultimatum. His early impulse was to invoke an "eye for an eye and tooth for a tooth principle" and seize a German vessel somewhere.[37]

Rather, Roosevelt focused on the far more important problem of placing American troops in Iceland, which by this time worried him more than Brazil. Churchill was enthusiastic, envisioning the release of British troops already stationed there. The more militant of Roosevelt's advisers were encouraged. Admiral Stark, in sending orders to Admiral Ernest King, in command of the Atlantic Fleet, wrote, "I realize that this is practically an act of war."[38]

Admiral Stark's German counterpart, Admiral Raeder, was eager for action. For months he had been contending that all-out submarine warfare against both American merchantmen and the United States Navy would bring the British to their knees before American war production could become effective. The likelihood that the Japanese would join in war against the Americans made him especially optimistic. Hitler, still determined to focus upon only one front at a time, firmly restrained

Raeder. The day before Hitler launched Operation Barbarossa against the Soviet Union, he gave orders to avoid further incidents outside the area the United States had proclaimed closed to the German Navy until the success of the invasion became clearer. By that he meant "for a few weeks."[39]

Both the United States and Germany were ready for naval war on the Atlantic, and top advisers on both sides were eager to clash. But because of the restraint of both Roosevelt and Hitler, the war was to develop only slowly.

On the steamy morning of June 22, 1941, Roosevelt awoke to the news that Hitler had launched a massive surprise attack upon the Soviet Union. Both Roosevelt and Churchill had sent warnings to Stalin, but it caught him unaware. For the Roosevelt administration, the greatest likelihood had seemed that Hitler would make demands and that Stalin would agree to them. The rapidity of the German thrust and the disarray of the Russian forces gave credence during the first few days to the pessimism of almost all western experts. The army sent the president its estimate that the conquest of Russia would occupy Hitler for from one to three months.[40]

In consequence, there was no reason that first morning for Roosevelt, in bed again with a throat infection, to look upon the attack as a decisive turning point in the war, comparable to the collapse of France a year earlier. Rather, it seemed to offer a few weeks of extra time to prepare against a German assault upon Britain and into North Africa. The American military attaché in London reported that the earliest date the British had come to expect an invasion was August 31. The more immediate threat for the United States was from Japan. Hitler's attack might embolden the military leaders of Japan to move more rapidly and decisively into Southeast Asia.[41]

There was much for Roosevelt to ponder. He would need to adjust policies toward both Russia and Japan, and he must take into account the widely differing pressures within the United States. Toward Russia, with reason, he was more careful than Churchill, who the evening of the attack broadcast that the British government would give whatever help it could. The British people, relieved to find another power finally joined in the cause, were exhilarated by Churchill's words, and optimistic enough to hope Russia could fight for a year or more.

The American people, neither at war nor immediately beleaguered, were at odds over the proper response to the invasion of Russia. They were, as Walter Lippmann commented, "separated by an ideological gulf and joined by the bridge of national interest." America Firsters, viewing the Soviet system as being at least as repugnant as that of the Nazis, if not more so, hoped that the two great armies would grind each other to bits. Senator Taft asserted that "a victory for Communism would be far more dangerous to the United States than a victory for Fascism." Some of Roosevelt's more militant advisers, including both Stimson and Knox, assuming that the Soviet Union could not long stand up to Hitler, favored not a Russian aid program, but rather, a strong action in the Atlantic. Secretary Knox urged Roosevelt to take advantage of the three months' breather to strike hard on behalf of Britain.

Amid the pressures from both the public and his advisers, Roosevelt was wary. He delivered no ringing Fireside Chat; rather, he issued the requisite proclamations, which had been awaiting signature in the safe of Under Secretary of State Sumner Welles. Then he assigned to Welles the drafting and issuing of a statement. The words, and the voice reading the declaration to the press, were those of Welles, but the thoughts were characteristically Roosevelt's. There was thorough damnation of Hitler's deed, a censorious statement about the Soviet, as well as the Nazi, denial of freedom of worship, and finally a firm alignment with Churchill's position: "Any defense against Hitlerism . . . from whatever source . . . . . will . . . benefit . . . our own defense and security."[42]

Roosevelt could see enormous advantages and few liabilities if somehow the Russians could withstand the Nazi attack. The relations of the United States with the Soviet Union had involved incessant annoyances but no conceivable military threat. To Admiral Leahy in Vichy he wrote on June 26 concerning "this Russian diversion": "If it is more than just that it will mean the liberation of Europe from Nazi domination — and at the same time I do not think we need worry about any possibility of Russian domination."[43]

At his press conference on June 24, when someone asked about the State Department statement, Roosevelt explained in a matter-of-fact way, "Of course we are going to give all the aid that we possibly can to Russia." On actual implementation, he moved cautiously at first. There was the question whether the Soviet forces could survive long enough for either the British or the Americans to supply them with assistance. Still, Roosevelt was risking little in promising aid, since first he must receive Soviet requests, determine what machinery should handle them, and decide what could be sent. In the initial stage, Roosevelt, in keeping with both his customary prudence and strong public opinion (judging by a Gallup poll), expected the Soviets to purchase their supplies. Shipments to the Soviets in July totaled only $6.5 million, and until October 1 were only $29 million.[44]

The impetus toward large-scale lend-lease aid to Russia came in part through Harry Hopkins, visiting in London, who with Roosevelt's hearty approval went on to Moscow at the end of July. He was the first of a number of American dignitaries who enjoyed the warmth and charm that Joseph Stalin could lavish upon those he wished to impress. Stalin talked to Hopkins in detail about Soviet fortunes on the battlefields. What was even more impressive was Stalin's optimistic emphasis, although military realities did not yet justify it, upon a spring offensive he was planning for May, 1942. Indeed, in his first interview with Hopkins, he declared, "Give us anti-aircraft guns and the aluminum and we can fight for three or four years."[45]

Stalin made a remarkable impression upon Hopkins, as he did subsequently in meetings with other Americans, both Democrats and Republicans, including Hull, Willkie, and finally Roosevelt himself. The aura of simplicity, self-confidence in the struggle against the Germans, and sympathetic warmth, encompassing both Stalin and the Russian people, spread in the American news media. Even as the Russian emissaries arrived in large numbers in the United States, not presenting their needs pleasantly and diplomatically like the British, but as stern unwavering demands, the image of "good old Uncle Joe" grew among Americans, who applied it to the entire Russian people. It did not represent the more sophisticated analysis of the Russian specialists in the Foreign Service, nor even the feeling Hopkins brought back. The benign view of Stalin that became current eased the way for Roosevelt to ignore isolationist protests and plan substantial aid, but the compelling reason for the aid was that the Soviets, despite the shocking losses they had sustained in the first few weeks, were already throwing Hitler off his timetable and inflicting heavy damage upon the invading armies.[46]

In September, as the Russians fell back but still maintained their fighting force, Roosevelt and Churchill made plans for long-range coordinated aid to the Soviet Union. With Hopkins ill, Roosevelt sent Harriman to represent the United States at a three-power conference in Moscow. The growing volume of goods still went in return for cash or as part of complicated financial arrangements, since opinion polls showed that while Americans by a substantial margin favored aid to Russia, less than half wished to extend credit. Neither did Roosevelt, until he was sure he had extracted all possible gold from the Soviets. He was as disposed as he had been with the British to drive a hard bargain over assets, nor had he forgotten the long years of irritation that followed recognition of Russia. The Soviet ambassador, Constantin Oumansky, had soon reverted to his customary unpleasantness. After Roosevelt had difficulty in ferreting out of him how large the Russian gold reserves were, he exploded to the cabinet that Oumansky was "a dirty little liar."[47]

Manifestly, Roosevelt would not for long be able to squeeze gold out of the Kremlin. Still fearing an ugly debate, he slowly edged along American opinion toward lend-lease. The optimistic news Hopkins brought back from Moscow helped influence it, and so did a statement Roosevelt obtained from Pope Pius XII, distinguishing between aid to the Soviets and support of communism. In addition, Roosevelt tried to make lend-lease seem overall more palatable by replacing as lend-lease administrator Hopkins, the New Deal spender, with the bland, uncontroversial former chairman of the board of United States Steel, Edward R. Stettinius, Jr. Roosevelt even went so far as to tuck lend-lease into a much larger appropriations bill, including the armed forces, that few congressmen would dare vote not to supply. The tactics worked perfectly. By November 1, he had obtained congressional sanction and wide public backing. He had established policy, but despite the desperate Soviet need through the remainder of 1941, was able to dispatch relatively little aid. Up to the time of Pearl Harbor it totaled only $65 million — small indication of the massive wartime total of $10 billion of goods shipped to the Soviet Union.[48]

Simultaneously with his drive to aid the Russians, Roosevelt in the weeks immediately after the Nazi invasion of the Soviet Union was seeking to contain Japanese expansionist moves, which the engagement of the Soviet forces against the Germans helped trigger.

Franklin D. Roosevelt, aged five, with his mother, Sara Delano Roosevelt, in Washington, D.C., 1887. His long curls had been shorn, and he had graduated from wearing skirts to a kilt in the tartan of his Murray ancestors.

Thirteen-year-old Franklin and his father, James Roosevelt, April, 1895.

Franklin, grown tall and thin, on the second football team at Groton School, October, 1899.

There are no wedding photographs of Franklin and Eleanor Roosevelt together. It would have been too dangerous to have used flash powders to take pictures within the house in New York City. Here they appear, out-of-doors, at the wedding of Franklin's half-niece, Helen Roosevelt Roosevelt, and Theodore Douglas Robinson, on June 18, 1904.

Eleanor and Franklin Roosevelt with their first two children, James and Anna, 1908.

Roosevelt, a notorious tease, playing with the hair of his cousin Jean Delano, at Campobello Island, about 1907.

Roosevelt campaigning with Eleanor Roosevelt in Dutchess County, New York, probably in 1910.

Assistant Secretary of the Navy Roosevelt and Secretary Josephus Daniels, on the balcony outside their offices, looking across at the White House, May, 1918. Roosevelt joked that the photographer had caught "my chief and myself in the act of casting longing glances."

Roosevelt returning from France with President Wilson on the USS *George Washington*, February, 1919.

Roosevelt as vice presidential candidate, parading with the presidential candidate, Governor James M. Cox of Ohio, on the occasion of Cox's acceptance address, in Dayton, Ohio, August 7, 1920.

Roosevelt, displaying his wasted, spindly legs, on a Florida beach with his secretary Marguerite "Missy" LeHand (left) and guests Maunsell Schieffelin Crosby, an ornithologist, and Frances Dana de Rham, wife of a Harvard classmate, February, 1924.

Seated at his desk, Governor Roosevelt warmly greets his predecessor, Al Smith, about 1930, although their relationship had soured since 1928. Roosevelt hung this photograph, which Smith autographed, in his bedroom at Hyde Park.

An enthusiastic crowd surrounds Roosevelt's automobile when, accompanied by his daughter, Anna, and Mrs. Roosevelt, he stops at Warm Springs on his campaign swing through the South, October 24, 1932.

On March 1, 1935, Roosevelt, flanked by Secretary of the Treasury Henry Morgenthau, Jr., and Postmaster General James Farley, buys the first United States savings bond. He is sitting in his second-floor study in the White House, which until the turn of the century had been the cabinet room.

"This morning I came, I saw and I was conquered, as everyone would be who sees for the first time this great feat of mankind," Roosevelt declares as he dedicates Boulder Dam, now known as Hoover Dam, on September 30, 1935. He set forth the case for public improvement projects to bring recovery and contribute lastingly to the national welfare.

Almost no close-up pictures of Roosevelt in a wheelchair exist, although for nearly a quarter century it was his principal means of locomotion. Here he sits at his hilltop cottage in Hyde Park with Ruthie Bie and his Scottish terrier, Fala, in February, 1941.

Aboard the cruiser USS *Houston* off Cocos Island, in August, 1938, Roosevelt poses with his catch. He crowed to his wife, "I caught a 230 lb. shark yesterday — 1 hr. and 35 minutes — so I win the pool for Biggest Fish!"

At the White House on Christmas Day, 1939, Roosevelt embraces two of his grandsons, Franklin D. Roosevelt III and John Boettiger.

In August, 1941, although the United States had not yet entered the war, Roosevelt and Winston Churchill, together with their military staffs, confer aboard warships in Placentia Bay, Newfoundland. They sit for photographs aboard HMS *Prince of Wales*.

On October 27, 1941, Roosevelt, responding to a German submarine attack that killed eleven seamen on the destroyer *Kearney*, warns at a Navy League dinner, "We Americans have cleared our decks and taken our battle stations."

Roosevelt works with Harry Hopkins in the White House study in June, 1942.

Although Roosevelt was enforcing a news blackout as he toured war plants, he could not resist speaking to the workers at a Portland, Oregon, shipyard on September 23, 1942. With him (left to right) are Governor Charles A. Sprague of Oregon and Henry J. Kaiser and Edgar F. Kaiser of the Oregon Shipbuilding Corporation.

Roosevelt takes delight in the surprised reaction of American troops as he reviews them at Rabat, Morocco, January 21, 1943.

Unexpectedly during the press conference at Casablanca, Roosevelt enunciates an unconditional surrender policy. Churchill, surprised by Roosevelt's timing of the announcement, gave it his backing. January 24, 1943.

After considerable difficulties, Roosevelt and Churchill persuade the rival French generals Charles de Gaulle (standing, right) and Henri Giraud to shake hands before photographers at Casablanca, January 24, 1943.

At the Cairo Conference, November 25, 1943, Roosevelt and Churchill met with Chiang Kai-shek and Madame Chiang, who vigorously set forth her husband's policies.

Joseph Stalin, Roosevelt, and Churchill sit for armed services photographers in the portico of the Soviet embassy in Tehran, November 29, 1943.

En route from North Africa to Malta and Sicily, Roosevelt on December 8, 1943, discusses war plans with General Dwight D. Eisenhower, whom he had just chosen to be supreme commander of the invasion of France.

Upon his return to Washington, December 17, 1943, Roosevelt received a warm welcome from Secretary of State Cordell Hull and Director of War Mobilization James F. Byrnes.

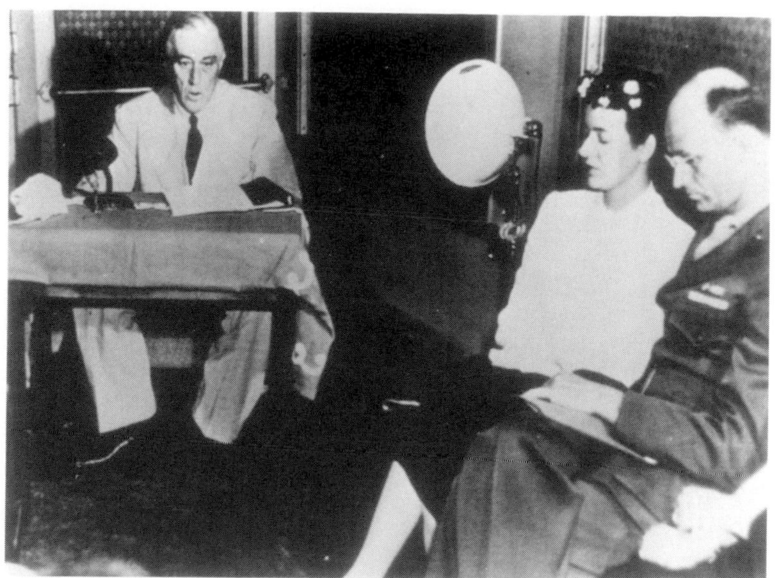

From his private car on a siding at Camp Pendleton near San Diego, Roosevelt on July 20, 1944, broadcasts his acceptance of the nomination to a fourth term. With the president are James Roosevelt and his wife, Romelle Schneider Roosevelt.

In Honolulu on July 28, 1944, Roosevelt confers about Pacific strategy with General Douglas MacArthur (left) and Admirals Chester Nimitz and William D. Leahy.

On the last day of campaigning, November 6, 1944, although the weather is cold and raw, Roosevelt, accompanied by Secretary of the Treasury Henry Morgenthau, Jr., tours in an open car through familiar towns in the Hudson Valley.

Insisting upon a simple wartime ceremony, Roosevelt delivers his fourth inaugural address from the White House balcony, January 20, 1945. With him are the new vice president, Harry S. Truman (left), and James Roosevelt.

Despite his physical condition, Roosevelt presides over the plenary sessions at the Yalta conference. Stalin sits to the left and Churchill is in the right foreground at the session of February 5, 1945.

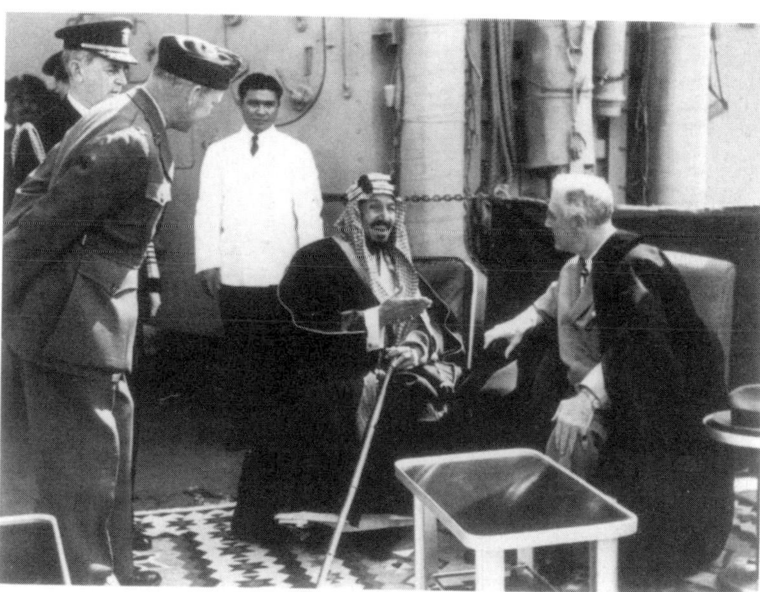

After the Yalta conference, Roosevelt entertains King Ibn Saud of Saudi Arabia aboard the cruiser *Quincy* on February 12, 1945. Colonel W. A. Eddy, minister to Saudia Arabia, standing to the left, serves as interpreter.

Upon his return to the United States, Roosevelt on March 1, 1945, reports to Congress on the Yalta conference. His gaunt appearance and uneven delivery dismay the nation.

Roosevelt, in seriously failing health, had taken pains to bring all his thirteen grandchildren to his inauguration, January 20, 1945; with Mrs. Roosevelt they posed for a final family portrait.

Chapter 27

ESCALATING PRESSURE ON JAPAN AND GERMANY

WHILE ROOSEVELT was focusing his attention upon Hitler's drive into the Soviet Union in the summer of 1941, he was troubled over the fresh opportunities the assault created for the ambitious, restless Japanese military leaders. He feared that the Japanese would attack the Soviets from the rear and also strike British and Dutch possessions in Southeast Asia. His concerns were well founded. There were intelligence reports of Japanese ship movements and of troops being trained on the island of Hainan. On his desk Roosevelt soon had irrefutable evidence in the form of intercepted Japanese diplomatic cables. By August, 1940, an army cryptographer had, through the newly developed "MAGIC" code-breaker, succeeded in cracking the top-priority code. In consequence, Roosevelt's sources were more solid than he could admit when he predicted Japanese moves to the north and south.[1]

As had long been the case, Japan was secondary in Roosevelt's thinking. The great danger was from Hitler, the powerful German armed forces, and the destructive output and potential of German industrialists, engineers, and scientists. Germany, in control of most of western and central Europe, could more quickly replace its losses in weaponry, and it was developing new and more dangerous weapons — among them the atomic bomb.

In contrast, Roosevelt was nervous but not frightened about Japan. During his seven years as assistant secretary of the navy, he had absorbed the view that Japan was a potential, indeed probable, enemy of the United States. Year after year, the opponent in the navy war games was Orange, the Japanese. The navy opinion, which Roosevelt shared, was that in the long run they would be no match for the United States. He was heartened in 1941 by the optimistic predictions of the army that the new American Flying Fortresses (B-17s) would make the Philippines defensible.

On the other hand, some naval officers were well aware of the formidable, indeed superior, quality of the new naval vessels coming off the ways in Japanese shipyards, and the high level of training and competence of Japanese officers and sailors. Admiral James O. Richardson was concerned because the American Fleet he commanded from Pearl Harbor was decidedly weaker than the Japanese Fleet and was diminishing in size as units moved to the Atlantic and into the southeast Pacific. He recommended that the fleet should be returned to the Pacific Coast, which would have left Hawaii with little defense. Roosevelt was not persuaded. On February 1, 1941, he removed Richardson, replacing him with Admiral Husband E. Kimmel, to head the renamed Pacific Fleet. Kimmel had been Roosevelt's aide for a few days in 1915 when Roosevelt visited the Panama-Pacific Exposition in San Francisco, but otherwise Roosevelt had seen little of him. He had a fine reputation, and in Hawaii engaged in rigorous training exercises. But to maintain the morale of his peacetime navy, he brought the vessels back into Pearl Harbor each weekend.[2]

Roosevelt does not seem to have understood how mismatched the Pacific Fleet would be in any early encounter with the Japanese. Rather, his assumption of prior years apparently continued, that in case of war the Pacific Fleet could advance to the Marshall Islands, and from there relieve the besieged Philippines and begin to squeeze Japan. It would be a lengthy war, the hypothesis was, but the United States would be able to build naval vessels in far greater numbers than Japan, and the ultimate victory seemed beyond question.[3]

In any event, Roosevelt's wish was to avoid conflict in the Pacific — or at least to postpone it. His miscalculation was his long-standing view that he could go to considerable lengths toward restraining the Japanese without serious risk of attack. Perhaps MAGIC, with its partial clues to the planning of the Japanese Foreign Office and Navy, gave him the feeling he was privy to all possible Japanese moves, and caused him to become even more overconfident. Gradually, too, the thinking of the public and Congress edged toward the "get tough" approach that the more militant advisers were urging upon Roosevelt.

Ever since he had become president-elect, Roosevelt had favored restraining Japan. He and his advisers viewed the Japanese incursions into the Asian mainland as violations of China's right to self-government.

Now Japan, through aligning itself with the Axis, seemed to imperil not merely Asian but world order. The threat of Hitler led to strong measures against Japan.

In the summer of 1940, the new cabinet of Prince Fumimaro Konoye, as divided over some issues as that of Roosevelt, laid plans in anticipation of an early German victory over Great Britain. The foreign minister, Yosuke Matsuoka, wanted first of all to settle completely the China affair. That meant severing the supply lines of Generalissimo Chiang Kai-shek of China, in part through becoming dominant in French Indochina. It meant also pressuring the Dutch East Indies to supply raw materials — especially oil — to replace those the United States might embargo. The threat of an embargo, Matsuoka argued persuasively, made it imperative for Japan to look southward, which in turn necessitated cooperation with Germany and Italy and a "resolute position" toward the United States.[4]

The Japanese program was irreconcilable with that of Roosevelt, although the president, in response to State Department warnings, was more cautious in limiting the shipment of raw materials to Japan than either some of his more militant advisers or the general public would have liked. Americans were not pleased that freight trains loaded with scrap iron were rumbling into Pacific ports; in the eastern United States, as the new defense needs of Britain and the United States were creating an oil shortage, they were even more unhappy over petroleum shipments to Japan. Most people did not seem to fear that an embargo might result in war. The National Defense Act of 1940 permitted the embargo of all materials for defense. In the fall of 1940, Roosevelt, responding to the Japanese move into Indochina and pressure upon the East Indies for supplies, authorized the total cutting off of scrap. It created problems for the Japanese war industry, and kept before the Japanese cabinet the serious threat of an oil embargo. The State and Navy departments, and the British, Australians, and Dutch all urged Roosevelt not to ban oil shipments for fear that Japan in retaliation might seize the Dutch East Indies. Some irritated citizens looked upon his restraint as weakness. Indeed, it was an indication of the weakness of the armed forces of the United States.[5]

A fresh quandary faced Roosevelt at the end of September, 1940, when Japan signed the Tripartite Pact with Germany and Italy, recognizing their respective spheres of domination in Europe and Asia, and pledging aid to each other in case of attack. It was an implicit threat against the United States. On the morning that news of the pact reached Washington, Roosevelt met in his bedroom with Secretary Hull and

Under Secretary Welles. Hull muttered that Matsuoka was "as crooked as a basket of fishhooks," but favored no rash action. Roosevelt, his jaw jutting, punctuating the air with his cigarette holder, expressed his concern that the Tripartite Pact might be a device of Hitler's to divert the United States. It would not be deflected from the Atlantic, but would stand firm also in the Pacific. Four days later, a recording machine caught Roosevelt in a more excited frame of mind, expressing his indignation over the demand of a Japanese press association official that Wake and Midway islands and Pearl Harbor be demilitarized. "God!" Roosevelt exclaimed. "That's the first time that any damn Jap has told us to get out of Hawaii!"[6]

These offhand remarks, both sober and emotional, summed up Roosevelt's attitude toward Japan in the fall of 1940. He did not want trouble, but was not alarmed over the possibility that it might come. Depending upon Japanese actions, Roosevelt was disposed to offer either an olive branch or a sword, but caution repeatedly tempered his bold thoughts. He fostered Anglo-American naval discussions to plan cooperation in East Asia in the event of war, and sent a few pursuit planes to China, together with some volunteer American pilots, the "Flying Tigers," primarily to defend the Burma Road.[7]

On the other hand, a peaceful settlement seemed not out of the question, although Roosevelt would not retreat from his basic positions. Elements in Japan also sought peace, although they would not countenance any softening of their fundamental stance toward China and East Asia. The result was to be long and confusing negotiations that in the end were futile.[8]

Through parallel official and unofficial negotiations, Japan and the United States sought, from early 1941 to the fateful month of December, to reconcile their differences. Matsuoka sent to Washington a new ambassador, Admiral Kichisaburo Nomura, briefly foreign minister in 1939 but not a professional diplomat, who as naval attaché during World War I had become acquainted with Roosevelt. Nomura feared that the very bad relations were likely to get worse, but gave in to the pressure of naval colleagues eager to avoid war. Nomura, the official envoy, quickly fell under the influence of unofficial negotiators: several concerned Japanese and a pair of American Catholic priests who headed the Maryknoll foreign missions, Father James M. Drought and Bishop James Edward Walsh.[9]

Roosevelt was so interested in what the Maryknoll fathers had to say that he extended an allotted fifteen minutes with them to two hours when they called at the White House in late January, 1941. But he had no serious expectation that either their peace efforts or the negotiations about to begin with Nomura could modify the thrust of events in Japan. Ambassador Joseph Grew, shrewd, judicious, and anxious to maintain peace, warned Roosevelt, "It would be utterly unthinkable for any leader or group of leaders in Japan at present to advocate withdrawal from China and abandonment of their dreams of southward advance."[10]

Roosevelt greeted Admiral Nomura with outward cordiality when Secretary Hull brought him to the White House in February, 1941. Nomura reciprocated. "There is plenty of room in the Pacific area for everybody," Roosevelt declared (Hull noted in an *aide-mémoire*), and "it would not do this country any good nor Japan any good, but both of them harm, to get into a war." Nomura readily assented. Historical evidence indicates that Nomura was indeed sincere at that time and throughout the many months of conversations with Hull that followed.[11]

For some months, while Hull and Nomura engaged in earnest conversations at Hull's apartment, Roosevelt focused upon the Atlantic rather than the Pacific. Nomura had come with no concrete proposals, and neither Roosevelt nor Hull took advantage of the opportunity to set forth a scheme of their own. Roosevelt seemed satisfied to leave Hull occupied with conversations, most useful as a means of delaying war, not of preventing it altogether.

Japan again became of prime concern to Roosevelt when the German invasion of the Soviet Union precipitated a fresh and acute crisis in East Asia. In June, the Japanese Army, aware of the impending German attack upon the Soviet Union, was interested in the opportunity to move southward, and then, when (as was expected) Russia began to collapse, intervene to the north. Matsuoka, put in an embarrassing position by the German attack upon Russia, was eager to respond to Hitler's pressure and attack northward immediately. Not surprisingly, Roosevelt, who had been reading intercepted cables Matsuoka was sending to embassies, was predicting that Japan would strike into Siberia. The Japanese leadership decided otherwise at a conference on July 2 in the presence of the emperor. Within a week Roosevelt had on his desk the Japanese diplomatic circular setting forth in general terms the plans for Southeast Asia. However, this version of the circular did not include the ominous provision, "In case the diplomatic negotiations break down, preparations for a war with England and America will also be carried forward."[12]

Already, plans for a war against the United States (which the imperial government still hoped to avoid) included the audacious scheme of Admiral Isoroku Yamamoto, quite out of keeping with Japanese as well as

American naval policy — a surprise strike at Pearl Harbor. Roosevelt had no notion then or later that the Japanese Navy would resort to so daring an enterprise. Nor did Admiral Stark and his naval command deem it feasible to launch torpedoes from airplanes in such shallow water as that in Pearl Harbor, and had so informed Admiral Kimmel. They could not know that the Japanese were modifying their torpedoes.[13]

In July, 1941, Roosevelt was preparing a firm response to Japanese demands upon Vichy France for key bases in southern Indochina. The Japanese armed forces would thus position themselves to move westward into Thailand and Burma, southward into the oil fields of the Dutch East Indies, perhaps into Malaya, and to threaten the British bastion at Singapore.

Roosevelt sought to restrain Japan with the only effective means at his command, to tighten further the embargo. He had already placed so many restrictions upon Japan that only particularly powerful, and hence dangerous, sanctions remained, chief among them to cut off all petroleum. Ickes, the petroleum coordinator, favored doing so, since already the needs of the British were creating shortages so acute that gasoline rationing was imminent on the Atlantic Coast. Roosevelt blocked Ickes, explaining "It is terribly important for the control of the Atlantic for us to help to keep peace in the Pacific. I simply have not got enough Navy to go round — and every little episode in the Pacific means fewer ships in the Atlantic."[14]

Roosevelt consequently preferred to threaten rather than actually to cut off oil to Japan. As Ickes complained, "He thought that it might be better to slip the noose around Japan's neck and give it a jerk now and then." Roosevelt did not conceal his tactics. He explained them publicly on July 24, speaking extemporaneously to some civilian defense volunteers, and then released his remarks to the press. It was in the self-interest of the United States and Great Britain to allow the export of oil to Japan, in order to prevent an attack on the Dutch East Indies and war in the Pacific.[15]

Oil was the key component in Roosevelt's overall effort to check Japan. In response to the Japanese demands upon Vichy for bases in Indochina, Roosevelt with the support of his cabinet decided to freeze Japanese assets in the United States, and to limit oil exports to the levels of previous years. The announcement of the freezing of assets — apparently the imposition of a full embargo — did not set forth the exception for petroleum. On August 1, the State Department announced that Japan could resubmit applications for petroleum export licenses at levels not to exceed previous years, but two days later Roosevelt left for a meeting with Churchill off Newfoundland, and did not monitor his policy. During his absence, government agencies, in the absence of sufficiently clear guidelines, approved no export licenses. It was early September before Roosevelt realized that a full de facto embargo was in effect, and by this time he felt that he would be displaying weakness if he shifted his policy.[16]

Interestingly, Roosevelt had brushed aside the navy opinion he had solicited. Admiral Kelly Turner, head of the War Plans Division, prepared a recommendation that trade with Japan not be embargoed at that time, and Admiral Stark endorsed it in general. The navy reports, predicated upon a Japanese move into Siberia, warned, "An embargo would probably result in a fairly early attack by Japan on Malaya and the Netherlands East Indies and possibly would involve the United States in an early war in the Pacific."[17]

As the crisis of July, 1941, indicated, both the United States and Japan were on courses virtually irreversible. Roosevelt's rather absent-minded cutoff of oil to Japan evoked more enthusiasm than misgivings in the United States. Opinion polls indicated so favorable a response that Lord Halifax, the British ambassador, assured Churchill he would be able to talk to Roosevelt quite freely about joint action if the Japanese attacked the British or the Dutch. Ambassador Grew in Tokyo lamented in his diary, "The vicious circle of reprisals and counter reprisals is on. . . . The obvious conclusion is eventual war."[18]

Although the crisis with Japan was becoming acute, Roosevelt and his advisers were giving priority to the even more dangerous Atlantic confrontation. U-boats were making the delivery of weapons and supplies ever more perilous. Hence it was imperative to cooperate more closely with the British. Roosevelt also was quietly planning a joint statement of war aims. It would encourage imperiled nations and resistance movements, rally the American public, and commit the British to goals acceptable to the United States. A meeting with Churchill could further these ends.

Slowly, acting with care to carry American opinion with him, Roosevelt had been advancing the navy farther into the Atlantic. At each step, with sophistry, he was justifying his actions as hemispheric defense. Few isolationists objected to protection of the western hemisphere. Iceland was so close to Norway that German patrol planes were flying over it unassailed. In the early summer of 1941, Roosevelt designated it as being within the hemisphere. After negotiations, Iceland finally invited United States protection, and on July 7, 4,400 marines landed to release part of the British garrison. Roosevelt made his case so convincingly that even Senator Wheeler expressed his approval. Encouraged by his success, Roosevelt immediately pressed farther, to protect shipping around Iceland from the numerous German submarines in the area, and authorized the navy to protect convoys bound toward Iceland, "including shipping of any nationality which may join."[19]

When the high command of the German Navy suggested measures to counter the American landing in Iceland, Hitler at his field headquarters declared on July 16 that he was "most anxious to delay the entry into the war by the U.S.A. for another month or two"; hence the navy "should continue to avoid all incidents."[20]

There was no better way to dramatize the struggle on the Atlantic and to cement further the ties between the United States and Britain than for Roosevelt and his staff to meet with Churchill. To judge by the way Roosevelt prepared for this, the first of the summit conferences, his main goal was to gain greater American and world backing for his aims; Churchill's, far more serious, was to seek new commitments that would bring the United States more quickly into the conflict. He thought Roosevelt would not have requested the conference "unless he contemplated some further forward step."[21]

On the contrary, Roosevelt, rather than taking his advisers into his confidence months earlier so that they could prepare detailed plans for coordination with the British, arranged the conference with the secrecy he liked. He wanted the news of the meeting to come with dramatic suddenness not only to the public, but even to his secretaries of state, war, and navy. Roosevelt set up an elaborate charade of pretending to be on a cruise along the New England coast, arranging for someone looking like him to sit on the deck of the *Potomac*, cheerfully waving a long cigarette holder. He must have enjoyed the surprise of Generals Marshall and Arnold and of Admiral Stark suddenly to be heading to a conference, and the irritation and bewilderment of Secretaries Stimson and Knox over their inexplicable absence. Nor could he have been ignorant of the fresh fury he would generate in Secretary Hull, neither informed nor invited, while Under Secretary Welles played a key role.

Actually, Roosevelt with his small entourage was aboard the *Augusta* and a sister cruiser, bound to Argentia Harbor on the south coast of Newfoundland, where the United States was constructing one of the bases obtained in exchange for destroyers. On August 9, amid the pageantry that both leaders so relished, the formidable battleship *Prince of Wales*, still bearing scars of its battle with the *Bismarck*, slowly steamed along a line of American naval vessels displaying the Stars and Stripes, and dropped anchor next to the *Augusta*. On the deck of the British vessel was Churchill. Across on the quarterdeck of the resplendent *Augusta,* Roosevelt waited in his wheelchair. Churchill, accompanied by a staff twice as large as Roosevelt's, stepped aboard the *Augusta* to meet Roosevelt, who stood up grasping the arm of his son Elliott.[22]

Roosevelt, Churchill, and their subordinates achieved a spirit of informal camaraderie at the meeting, which they sustained through the years that followed. It facilitated the hard bargaining over serious differences between the goals of Churchill, bent upon preserving the British Empire, and Roosevelt, seeking to attain the Wilsonian ideals. Churchill garbed his direct, tenacious approach in nineteenth-century eloquence. Roosevelt, equally tenacious, seemed frequently to move off in startling, sometimes frivolous directions, sometimes disguising, but always aiming toward, his ultimate ends. At the initial meetings, Churchill with his staff and meticulous preparation seemed to have outmatched Roosevelt with his casual approach. But Roosevelt kept the conference informal, unlike the wartime ones that were to follow.

Roosevelt reached several significant decisions with Churchill during their four days of meetings. Foremost among the problems worrying them was that of Japan. Roosevelt agreed to join in a stiff warning against further encroachments (which he later modified after his return to Washington), but came to firm agreement with Churchill that war in the Pacific should be delayed as long as possible — at least for thirty days. It seemed vital to contain the Japanese, but also not to fight them if at all possible, since the diversion from the struggle against Hitler would be so serious.[23]

Above all, the meeting focused upon the overall state of the war, and the ways in which the British, with American cooperation, could bring about the defeat of Germany. The first evening, at Roosevelt's request, Churchill delivered one of his overviews of the war, "not his best" in the view of Sir Alexander Cadogan, permanent under secretary of the Foreign Office, but entrancing to the Americans. Churchill was envisaging repeated sorties on the periphery of Axis forces, gradually to encircle and strangle the enemy through blockade, bombing, and aid to resistance groups. He was determined to avoid repeating the slaughter of a generation of British young men that had taken place during the First World War. By implication he was seeking an American declaration of war as soon as possible, and was offering the alluring prospect of a limited conflict — quite in contrast to the plans General Marshall and his staff were developing.[24]

Then and later, Churchill's proposals for peripheral ventures attracted Roosevelt as much as they alarmed his generals. That was particularly true with regard to North Africa. Roosevelt was deeply worried by the infiltration of Nazi agents into the African bulge and their influence in South America, and fearful that Hitler would suddenly strike through the Iberian peninsula into North Africa in the same fashion that he had dashed into Norway. Roosevelt was disposed, therefore, toward the sending of troops not only to the Azores, but even into Africa, especially to the westernmost port, Dakar. The United States Army planners thought African ventures, especially the seizure of Dakar, would require far too much shipping and supplies. To the displeasure of the British, they talked later of sending troops to Brazil and Venezuela.[25]

During the conference, Churchill asserted to Roosevelt on several occasions "that he had rather the United States came into the war now, and that we got no more supplies from the United States for six months, than that supplies from the United States should be doubled but the USA kept out of the war." Roosevelt subsequently dismissed the remarks as exaggerated.[26] Neither Roosevelt nor his army planners were able to accept Churchill's proposition. Marshall, having difficulty in obtaining troops to replace the marine brigade sent to Iceland, felt in no position, if America entered the war, to commit sizable forces to aid the British, as they proposed, in the Middle East and French North Africa. Nor could either Marshall or Stark promise the increased assistance the British sought. The Americans were as reluctant as Pershing had been during World War I to sanction the piecemeal allotment of American troops to units under foreign command. They were noncommittal at the conference, but subsequently the army planners in preparing a reply to the British noted: "Actually we will be more effective for some time as a neutral, furnishing material aid to Britain, rather than as a belligerent. Our potential combat strength has not yet been sufficiently developed." The navy even more strongly held the same view. Hopkins warned Stimson that the navy would never fight Germany if it could avoid it.[27]

Yet Churchill returned from the conference with rather a different impression. Roosevelt had expounded his long-held view on how to thwart aggressors, leading Churchill to report to the war cabinet that Roosevelt was ready to be militant, although he was worried by the narrow margin by which Congress passed further lend-lease appropriations: "The President had said that he would wage war but not declare it, and that he would become more and more provocative. If the Germans did not like it, they could attack the American forces."

Roosevelt had promised that the United States Navy would take over the escort of convoys, and order the patrols to range as far as 300 miles from the convoys to seek out and attack German submarines. "Everything was to be done to force an 'incident' to justify hostilities." Heartened by Roosevelt's strong words, Churchill talked to the cabinet as though Roosevelt would shortly bring the United States into war. In his enthusiasm, Roosevelt may well have been implying more than he intended. Churchill seemed to find in Roosevelt's remarks the assurance of the full belligerency he so eagerly sought, and later told the cabinet, "He was obviously determined that they should come in."[28]

If the United States was not yet a cobelligerent, it was, as Roosevelt did intend, very close to it. There was no clearer indication to the American people and the world than the firm statement of war aims to which Churchill, at war with Germany, and Roosevelt, technically a neutral, jointly subscribed. When, during the first day of the meeting, Roosevelt proposed a statement, Churchill eagerly acceded. Although Welles had come with a draft based on his discussions with Roosevelt, the president agreed that Churchill should produce one. Churchill put Cadogan to work upon a draft and put into it some touches of his own. Subsequently, Welles made some modifications to incorporate Roosevelt's views. Taking pride in his role, Churchill later boasted in *The Grand Alliance* that "the substance and spirit of what came to be called the 'Atlantic Charter' was in its first draft a British production cast in my own words." Rather quickly Roosevelt and Churchill ironed out the differences in their drafts.[29]

The document took the form of a joint press statement to follow the meeting. Although the names of Roosevelt and Churchill appeared at the bottom, no official copy seems ever to have existed to which they affixed their signatures. It bore no resemblance to a treaty; it required no Senate ratification.[30]

In this fashion, on August 14, 1941, Roosevelt and Churchill proclaimed their war aims to the world, making a commitment and attracting attention well beyond what they might have expected during their rather hasty deliberations. The Joint Declaration provided:

> First, their countries seek no aggrandizement, territorial or other;
>
> Second, they desire to see no territorial changes that do not accord with the freely expressed wishes of the people concerned;
>
> Third, they respect the right of all peoples to choose the form of government under which they will live; and they wish to see sovereign rights and self government restored to those who have been forcibly deprived of them . . .;
>
> Fourth, they will endeavor, with due respect for their existing

> obligations, to further . . . access on equal terms, to the trade and to the raw materials of the world . . .;
>
> Fifth, they desire . . . improved labor standards, economic advancement and social security;
>
> Sixth, after the final destruction of the Nazi tyranny, they hope to see established a peace which will afford to all nations the means to dwelling in safety . . . and . . . all the men in all the lands may live out their lives in freedom from fear and want;
>
> Seventh, such a peace should enable all men to traverse the high seas and oceans without hindrance;
>
> Eighth, they believe that all of the nations of the world, for realistic as well as spiritual reasons must come to the abandonment of force. . . . pending the establishment of a wider and permanent system of general security, . . . the disarmament of [aggressor] nations is essential.[31]

Churchill subordinated his misgivings over some of the stipulations to the important gain for Britain in obtaining Roosevelt's subscription to overall war aims. Roosevelt was making a significant commitment, as the head of a neutral nation, in accepting Churchill's words looking forward to "the final destruction of Nazi tyranny."

The informal fashion in which Roosevelt with Churchill quickly formulated the Atlantic Charter was effective. Had the State Department and Foreign Office been alerted in advance, they would have reworked it into a cumbersome, cautious document. In the aftermath, Hull seethed over Roosevelt's ignorance of the trade question; Whitehall experts were dismayed over not only the threat to Britain's imperial holdings, but the protest from Stalin, who feared it implied that the Soviet Union must give up the Baltic republics.

The first three points of the Atlantic Charter gave Roosevelt the reassurances he sought, but opened questions concerning the status of the British Empire that worried Churchill from the outset. The third point, pledging the two nations to "respect the right of all peoples to choose the form of government under which they will live," and "to see sovereign rights and self government restored to those who have been forcibly deprived of them," raised high once more the Wilsonian banner of "self-determination." It would have great appeal to peoples the Nazis and Fascists had overrun, and to others unhappy over the Versailles settlements. But it could also encourage the people of India and elsewhere to break loose from Britain.

Seeking his larger goal, American involvement, Churchill sent the

Atlantic Charter to the war cabinet for approval and informed Clement Atlee, Lord Privy Seal, who had been leader of the opposition, that it was "an interim and partial statement of war aims to reassure all countries of our righteous purpose." Only eight days after announcing the Atlantic Charter, Churchill told the secretary of state for India that it was not intended "that the natives of Nigeria or of East Africa could by a majority vote choose the form of Government under which they live, or the Arabs by such a vote expel the Jews from Palestine." By 1942 Churchill's interpretation of the charter had become an irritating point of contention with Roosevelt.[32]

The meeting at Argentia was a moving occasion that did much to remove previous suspicions and to make future irritations less grave. There was, above all, the Sunday morning religious service on the *Prince of Wales*. Roosevelt used it as an occasion to give what one of the British naval captains recalled as an "impression of great courage and strength of character." Refusing to ride in a wheelchair, he inched his way across the gangplank and along the length of the ship to his seat on the quarterdeck.[33]

Churchill and Roosevelt left the conference admiring each other and pleased with the working relationship they had established.

In subsequent years, the Atlantic Charter and the conference with its combination of fellowship and pageantry have stirred imaginations. The long-range effect was powerful, raising the hopes of conquered people, and countering clever, insidious Nazi propaganda. Its greater impact lay in the future, when the end of the war seemed nearer and consequently its guarantees more tangible.

The immediate response in both Britain and the United States was less positive. The British, longing for an American declaration of war, were little excited. The events had not caught their imagination, Edward R. Murrow broadcast from London. By the time Roosevelt arrived back aboard the *Potomac* on the Maine coast, it was clear that while his supporters were impatient he had not gone further, he had stimulated fresh suspicion and alarm among isolationists.

In response, Roosevelt's approach to the public was remarkably muted. When he first allowed correspondents aboard the *Potomac*, he assured them that the conference involved no more than an exchange of views. At the crux of the interchange was one query, "Are we any closer to entering the war, actually?" Roosevelt responded, "I should say, no."[34]

The prospect was gloomy both in the United States and Britain. While former president Hoover was charging privately that the Roosevelt administration was trying "to get us into war through the Japanese back door," Churchill wired Hopkins, "There has been a wave of depression through Cabinet and other informed circles here about President's many assurances about no commitments and no closer to war &c."[35]

Chapter 28

TO THE BRINK OF WAR

AFTER THE MEETING with Churchill, Roosevelt moved the United States cautiously, step-by-step, into undeclared naval war against the Germans in the North Atlantic. At the same time the embargo against Japan was quietly heightening the likelihood of hostilities in the Pacific. Over several months the nation moved to the brink of global war.

There was strong reason for Roosevelt to proceed slowly. Through much of the summer he had been engaged in a crucial and difficult struggle with the isolationist bloc in Congress to obtain authorization to keep draftees and others on active service longer than twelve months. Otherwise the army would have been limited to troops capable of little more than the defense of the nation's own shores. On the day after the Atlantic conference ended, Roosevelt was victorious, but by only a single vote, 203 to 202, in the House of Representatives.

Draft extension was deeply unpopular, and polls both before and after the Atlantic conference indicated that about 75 percent of the American people wanted to stay out of war with Germany and Japan. Yet Roosevelt seemed to be carrying 60 percent with him in his gradual moves toward undeclared conflict. Publication of the poll results may in itself have created something of a "bandwagon effect," intensifying support for him.[1]

With opinion behind him, Roosevelt could grapple through the next month with problems of increasing defense production. Lord Beaverbrook, the British minister of supply, came to Washington after the conference and emphasized that American production must accelerate enormously. Roosevelt, resisting strong pressure to appoint a production czar — Baruch or someone like him — to speed sluggish armament programs, was receptive to an armed forces proposal urging a threefold increase in production. He asked Stimson, Knox, and Hopkins to provide him with specifications.

The result was the Victory Program, predicated upon large-scale aid and the building of a United States Army of eight million men. That would require an enormous increase in projected defense production. But thanks to the recovery that defense production had brought, corporations, rather than converting their factories, were turning out vast quantities of consumer durable goods. Production of armaments in newly constructed factories would still lag behind that of Britain and Canada until the end of 1943.[2]

While Roosevelt was continually pressing for increased production, he was slow to activate the Victory Program and reluctant to abandon the haphazard techniques he had relied upon during previous years. At one session with planners he said, "I don't want a program made from the top down. . . . I want to start from the bottom, and say I want twice as much of this and twice as much of that, and then get as much as I can."

This technique of Roosevelt's caused General Marshall to complain to Morgenthau: "First the President wants 500 bombers a month and that dislocates the program. Then he says he wants so many tanks and that dislocates the program. The President will never sit down and talk about a complete program and have the whole thing move forward at the same time."[3]

Public opinion seemed to support Roosevelt on the issue of increasing defense production; indeed, much of the pressure from conservatives was for him to act more efficiently and expeditiously. Yet even there, he was cautious and slow in coming to basic decisions. Despite these shortcomings, production did increase rapidly and the Victory Program did serve as the first overall plan.

During these weeks, Roosevelt also, as he had promised Churchill, projected naval strength more strongly into the Atlantic, and soon was engaged in undeclared quasi-war with U-boats. At the conference, Roosevelt had given Churchill the impression he would order the navy to seek and attack German submarines, but had not immediately done so. A British bomber at the beginning of September radioed the location of a German submarine to the USS *Greer*, a destroyer steaming by itself toward Iceland. In keeping with current instructions, for four hours the *Greer* tracked but did not attack the U-boat. When the pilot of the British bomber found that the *Greer* would not attack, it dropped depth charges and left. The German submarine commander, not sure whether the destroyer was British or American or where the depth charges came from, fired a torpedo at the *Greer*. The *Greer* dodged and dropped depth charges.[4]

The time had come to announce a new militant policy in a Fireside Chat. Roosevelt began work on it at once, and announced it for September 8. The day before, while he was visiting at Hyde Park, his mother died, so he postponed it to September 11. By then, Roosevelt had the full facts on the *Greer* incident. The navy reported to him that it had been stalking the U-boat, and that there was "no positive evidence that submarine knew nationality of ship at which it was firing." But he went ahead in his Fireside Chat as though it were a totally unprovoked attack, "piracy, legally and morally," a "determined step towards creating a permanent world system based on force, terror, and murder." In consequence:

"When you see a rattlesnake poised to strike, you do not wait until he has struck before you crush him. These Nazi submarines and raiders are the rattlesnakes of the Atlantic."[5]

The order logically followed, to find and destroy vessels threatening convoys. Thus with relative ease, but leaving troubling questions future critics would debate, Roosevelt brought the navy into the battle of the Atlantic. He was fortunate to do so at a time when Hitler, determined to defeat the Soviet Union before cold weather, refused the requests of his naval commanders to retaliate vigorously. It served the purposes of both Roosevelt and Hitler not to go much further for the time being.

Even before the attack upon the *Greer*, Roosevelt was moving toward more modification of the neutrality legislation, to give the navy and merchant vessels greater freedom in the Atlantic. While debate over the modifying of the Neutrality Act was under way, on October 16–17, during a large-scale submarine wolf-pack attack upon a convoy, the destroyer *Kearny* was torpedoed with the loss of eleven lives. The public was outraged, and the House by a heavy margin (but still with Republicans in opposition, 113 to 39) voted to arm merchantmen. On October 27, Roosevelt, broadcasting a militant Navy Day address before a sympathetic, cheering Navy League audience, whipped both interventionist and isolationist sentiment to new heights:

"America has been attacked. The *U.S.S. Kearny* is not just a Navy ship. She belongs to every man, woman and child in this nation. . . .

"We Americans have cleared our decks and taken our battle stations."[6]

Roosevelt reached a peak of militance in the warlike Navy Day address. Rosenman, who helped draft it, noted that Roosevelt at the time "was convinced that American entry into the war was almost unavoidable." On October 31, shortly before Congress was to give its final approval to modifications in the Neutrality Act, word came that a submarine had sunk the destroyer *Reuben James*, killing over a hundred men, while it was protecting a convoy. Roosevelt's response was remarkably mild, in contrast to his Navy Day speech. When a reporter asked that day if the United States might break off diplomatic relations with Germany, Roosevelt parried that he had heard nothing about it "until you asked the question." He had attained the policy he wanted, and had no interest in going further while he was having to neutralize congressional isolationists, attempting to avert or postpone war with Japan, and strengthening American armaments.[7]

During the fall, Roosevelt was consistent in his thinking and candid among those close to him, in giving reasons for his course of action. On October 10, Halifax reported to Churchill, Roosevelt

> . . . told me what indeed we have always known, that his perpetual problem was to steer a course between the two factors represented by:
>
> (1) The wish of 70 percent of Americans to keep out of war;
>
> (2) The wish of 70 percent of Americans to do everything to break Hitler even if it means war.
>
> He said that if he asked for a declaration of war he wouldn't get it, and opinion would swing against him. He therefore intended to go on doing whatever he best could to help us, and declarations of war were, he said, out of fashion.[8]

Into the first week of December, 1941, Roosevelt was thinking of extending American defenses farther and farther into the Atlantic, and perhaps into southern Ireland, the Azores, or French Africa. He and his chiefs of staff were starting to assemble the enormous forces requisite for an assault on Hitler's European fortress. Although the army was still weak, it already had expanded eightfold. As Hopkins, his family, and others close to him have recalled, Roosevelt was expecting full-scale war in the future, but still had no apparent intention of asking Congress for a war resolution. Many of his advisers, especially Stimson, Knox, Ickes, Morgenthau, and Stark, were chafing under Roosevelt's restraints.

Indeed, Roosevelt continued to be ambivalent. If Hitler were to declare war, that would bring the United States into the conflict, and

Roosevelt was boldly taking steps more and more likely to provoke him. Yet Roosevelt's actions indicated some lingering hope that somehow limited war would suffice.

With the prime focus of the president and nation upon the Atlantic and the uncertainties of the Russian front, the relative calm that had followed the Japanese occupation of Indochina and the ordering of the American embargo in August had been deceptive. Upon his return in mid-August from the Atlantic conference, Roosevelt seemed disposed toward conciliation with Japan, was pleasant in a conversation with Ambassador Nomura, and was receptive to a proposal that he meet with Prime Minister Konoye. Yet, remembering the Munich fiasco, he was wary. He mused, Nomura reported to his foreign minister, over "whether an invasion of Thailand can be expected during those conversations just as an invasion of Indo-China occurred during Secretary Hull's conversations with your Excellency."[9]

Even the intercepted Japanese diplomatic dispatches brought no inkling to Roosevelt and Hull of how seriously Japan was reacting to the oil embargo and moving toward war. The Japanese military chafed increasingly as each day the oil supply, only sufficient for a year and a half of war, dipped another 12,000 tons. It was, one of them lamented, like being a fish in a pond being slowly drained. Another factor pushing the Japanese admirals toward speedy action was the prospect of losing their naval superiority in 1942, when the great buildup of the United States Navy that Congress had authorized after the fall of France would become a reality. Thereafter, the relative strength of the Japanese Navy would decline rapidly. In the fall of 1941, the Japanese Navy was superior to the combined American, British, and Dutch vessels it might encounter in the Pacific. If a surprise blow at Pearl Harbor were successful, Japan would have time to commission new superbattleships, cruisers, and destroyers before the strengthened Allied fleets could assemble against it.[10]

On September 6, 1941, an imperial conference, with the emperor present, once more set forth Japanese conditions for a settlement with the United States — terms that would prove neither new nor acceptable to Roosevelt. The military leaders, without whose support neither Konoye nor any other premier could stay in power, set early October as the deadline for a settlement. If Konoye did not obtain it by then, the armed forces would prepare for hostilities against Great Britain, the Netherlands, and the United States. Weather considerations led the supreme command to favor an attack by December at the latest; conditions would not again be favorable until spring. By then, the oil shortage would be more critical, and American sea and air power stronger.[11]

While Roosevelt had no inkling of this ominous decision, he could read from the dispatches in the *New York Times* and *Herald Tribune* at his bedside each morning almost equally portentous indications. The Japanese government was putting foodstuffs, raw materials, and factory production under its control. Around the imperial palace and throughout Tokyo, air-raid shelters were being excavated, antiaircraft guns put in place, and barrage balloons readied.[12]

Within the United States, there was growing pressure upon Roosevelt to stand firm, coming from the public, the press, and most of his advisers. In September, 67 percent of those polled felt the United States should risk war rather than allow Japan to grow more powerful.[13]

Konoye, as Roosevelt accurately assumed, could make no concessions not acceptable to the military, and negotiations for a meeting with him were petering out during September. Ambassador Grew felt it was the last best chance for peace, and so have some subsequent analysts. However, Roosevelt avoided what could have been a cruel trap through refusing to attend without preconditions. Otherwise, if he had left a meeting without reaching an agreement, the Japanese military leaders could have blamed the failure upon him, and used it as the occasion for war.

In early October, very little was going on in the Hull-Nomura talks, Roosevelt told a British envoy, but he was "gaining useful time." Fundamentally what Roosevelt and Hull wished was for Japan to restrain and withdraw its armed forces from China and Indochina. The Japanese generals thought that since there was no prospect of a settlement, they must prepare for war with the United States; some of the admirals still had misgivings, but in the end would not oppose the army. On October 16, 1941, Konoye resigned, and Hideki Tojo, who had been war minister, became the new prime minister. Tojo continued the discussions between Nomura and Hull, while the army and navy went on with their preparations for war.[14]

On the day the Konoye cabinet fell, Roosevelt jotted longhand notes to Churchill and King George VI. "The Emperor is for peace, I think, but the Jingoes are trying to force his hand," he informed the king. To Churchill he declared, "The Jap situation is definitely worse and I think they are headed North — however in spite of this you and I have two months of respite in the Far East." He was calculating that Japan would not strike southward until Russia was defeated, but was accurate in his estimate of the time remaining to bolster American strength in the Pacific. On the following day, after Roosevelt met with Secretary Hull and his defense advisers, Admiral Stark sent an alert to Admiral Kimmel and General Walter Short in Hawaii:

". . . hostilities between Japan and Russia are a strong possibility. Since the U.S. and Britain are held responsible by Japan for her present desperate situation there is also a possibility that Japan may attack those two powers. In view of these possibilities you will take due precautions."[15]

The next day, Stark assured Kimmel he did "not believe the Japs are going to sail into us," adding, "In fact I tempered the message handed to me considerably."[16]

There was pessimism but not panic in Washington. While Churchill tried to stiffen the United States response to the Japanese, Roosevelt continued to temporize, seeking the time the army and navy needed to so strengthen the Philippine defense that it would be a restraint against Japanese operations toward the south. At a cabinet meeting on November 6, he urged Hull not to let the talks deteriorate. "Let us make no more of ill will," he instructed. "Let us do nothing to precipitate a crisis."[17]

A day earlier in Tokyo, the Privy Council, with the emperor present, decided that if they did not succeed through diplomacy on or about November 25, they should be prepared for war. Since they expected no favorable outcome to negotiations, the statement was little more than a formality. The Japanese chief of naval operations, Admiral Nagano, finally accepted the proposal to attack Pearl Harbor. Operational orders went out the same day: "War with Netherlands, America, England inevitable; general preparations to be completed by early December." The tentative date for attack was December 8, Japanese time (December 7, American time).[18]

The final weeks of negotiation passed amid pessimism on both sides. The Japanese gave the appearance of earnestness by sending a new envoy to join Nomura in the talks. This was Admiral Saburo Kurusu, formerly ambassador to Germany. Foreign Minister Shigenori Togo sent two sets of proposals to Nomura, warning in a cable (that the United States intercepted and Roosevelt soon read), "This time we are making our last possible bargain, and I hope that we can settle all our troubles with the United States peaceably." But a purported concession — to remove troops from China — involved actually no more than moving them to peripheral areas from which they could be quickly recalled, and keeping them thus nearby until 1966. Nor were the trade provisions and the interpretation of the Tripartite Pact likely to be acceptable. The next day, when Nomura presented the proposals at the White House, Roosevelt invoked patience — but time clearly was running out.[19]

The first set of Japanese proposals was dead, although Hull gave no formal reply for several days. Nomura pled with his government not to plunge into war, like Roosevelt urging patience. The foreign minister replied (and Roosevelt read), "The situation renders this out of the question. The deadline for the solution of these negotiations is set . . . and there will be no change."[20]

Yet Roosevelt and Hull did not give up their efforts to obtain at least some sort of temporary truce or *modus vivendi*. The Japanese special ambassador, Kurusu, joined Nomura on November 17. Hull took the two of them to the White House. Roosevelt had no confidence in Kurusu, but the conversation was similar to those before. Roosevelt and Kurusu discussed the three main points of difference, but made no effort to solve them. Tokyo ordered the other scheme, its "Plan B," to be presented, but Hull bridled because that would have required an end to U.S. aid to China.[21]

Roosevelt still did not give up his quest for a stopgap solution. Whether the Japanese generals, the dominant force in Tokyo, would have accepted any concession that would have deprived them of their opportunity to expand the Japanese Empire into Southeast Asia seemed doubtful. Yet there was no certainty of that in Washington, nor was it apparent to Nomura and Kurusu. Hence, Roosevelt's determination to try again. Shortly after November 20 he penciled some notes, probably during a conference with Hull, and handed them to the secretary of state as guidelines for a possible six-month *modus vivendi*, to serve as a response and modification of the Japanese final proposal:

6 MONTHS

1. U.S. to resume economic relations — some oil and rice now — more later.
2. Japan to send no more troops to Indochina or Manchurian border or any place South (Dutch, British, or Siam).
3. Japan to agree not to invoke tripartite pact even if U.S. gets into European war.
4. U.S. to introduce Japs to Chinese to talk things over but U.S. to take no part in their conversations.

Later on Pacific agreements.[22]

Roosevelt's proposals were a remarkable shift from his earlier insistence upon the removal of Japanese troops from China. For several days, from November 21 to 25, Hull and his staff labored energetically to assemble a specific offer of a *modus vivendi* on the basis of the new stipulations.

Neither Roosevelt nor the State Department were sure what the response of the Japanese Army might be. To Ickes, Roosevelt remarked on November 21 "that he wished he knew whether Japan was playing poker or not. . . . whether or not Japan had a gun up its sleeve."[23]

On November 24, Roosevelt, ready to act, sought the support of other involved nations. He sent Churchill details of the State Department draft *modus vivendi*, setting forth the number of Japanese troops to remain in north Indochina and the amount of exports to be allowed Japan, including "petroleum on a monthly basis for civilian needs." Roosevelt by this time was troubled over intercepted Japanese messages instructing Kurusu and Nomura to emphasize that the United States must cut off aid to Chiang Kai-shek, and, although extending the deadline for reaching an agreement to November 29, adding the ominous explanation, "After that things are automatically going to happen." In consequence, at the foot of the proposal he sent Churchill, Roosevelt added a warning:

"This seems to me a fair proposition for the Japanese but its acceptance or rejection is really a matter of internal Japanese politics. I am not very hopeful and we must all be prepared for real trouble, possibly soon."[24]

At first Roosevelt and Hull received encouragement. Army and navy advisers, desperately needing additional time, expressed their satisfaction. Churchill noted his approval to Foreign Minister Anthony Eden. The major interest of the British concerning Japan was, Churchill wrote, "no further encroachments and no war, as we have already enough of this latter."[25]

Then came serious protests that helped tip the scales against the *modus vivendi*. Within the cabinet, Morgenthau and Ickes were outraged, but that could scarcely have affected Roosevelt; it was too commonplace for Ickes to threaten his resignation. Chiang Kai-shek vehemently objected and stirred further objections from several directions. But this was predictable, and Morgenthau heard Roosevelt tell Hull he would see the Chinese representatives and calm them down. Churchill's second thoughts, the first he expressed to Roosevelt, must have had some effect. He inquired:

"What about Chiang Kai-shek? Is he not having a very thin diet? Our anxiety is about China. If they collapse our joint dangers would enormously increase."[26]

The objections of America's client nations, together with the uncertainties concerning Japan, led Roosevelt to abandon the *modus vivendi*. One of the key factors was the certainty that Chiang would create an uproar within the United States and elsewhere, a major factor in leading Hull, even before Churchill's message arrived, to decide in a considerable fury to drop the plan. The other factor, the suggestion that the Japanese were unsure of themselves, must have reinforced Roosevelt's poker-playing reaction that Japan might be bluffing.[27]

Exactly the opposite alternative, that Japan was indeed about to strike southward, had an even stronger, decisive negative effect on Roosevelt. In the forefront of Roosevelt's calculations as early as November 25 was the possibility of a Japanese surprise attack. At noon, when he conferred with Hull, Stimson, Knox, Marshall, and Stark, he broached the idea, according to Stimson, "that we were likely to be attacked perhaps (as soon as) next Monday, for the Japanese are notorious for making an attack without warning, and the question was what we should do. The question was how we should maneuver them into the position of firing the first shot without too much danger to ourselves."[28]

The next morning, November 26, Stimson phoned Roosevelt the news that Army Intelligence (G-2) reported that five Japanese divisions had embarked upon ships and had been sighted south of Formosa. Roosevelt, noted Stimson, "fairly blew up . . . and said that . . . that changed the whole situation because it was evidence of bad faith on the part of the Japanese that while they were negotiating for an entire truce — an entire withdrawal — they should be sending this expedition down there to Indochina."[29]

Roosevelt directed Hull to drop the proposal for a *modus vivendi*. Instead, Hull handed Kurusu and Nomura a lengthy declaration setting forth the long-standing positions of the United States. It was a statement for posterity rather than an effort to reach agreement. Admiral Stark and General Marshall notified the Pacific commands, "Negotiations with Japan appear to be terminated to all practical purposes." Stark warned, "An aggressive move is expected by Japan within the next few days," but he indicated it would probably be "against either the Philippines, Thai or Kra Peninsula or possibly Borneo." Marshall ordered, "If hostilities cannot . . . be avoided the United States desires that Japan commit the first overt act." In none of the messages was there any hint that the attack might be on Hawaii, nor did Roosevelt know that on November 26, the day he scrapped the *modus vivendi*, the Japanese attack force slipped out of its harbor, sailing under strict radio silence, which it never broke.[30]

Subsequent critics of Roosevelt have seized upon Stimson's report of the discussion on how to maneuver the Japanese into firing the first shot. That discussion, and all others in subsequent days, focused upon the assumption that the Japanese attack would be to the south. If war came, Roosevelt was insistent that it be through the Japanese rather than the Americans initiating hostilities. Hence Marshall's warning to army commanders that "the United States desires that Japan commit the first overt act." (MacArthur delayed action in the Philippines for hours after the attack on Pearl Harbor, in keeping with that order.)

There was another possibility in the forefront of the thinking of Roosevelt and his advisers, and that was that the Japanese naval units and troop transports might bypass the Philippines. Would Roosevelt then make good on his past assurances to the British and the Dutch that the United States would join them in war against Japan? That would require him to ask Congress for a declaration of war. Public and congressional sentiment against Japan was so heated that some observers predicted Roosevelt would have no difficulty in obtaining a war resolution. It was a possibility he preferred to avoid. Indeed, up to December 7, it was not entirely certain what he would decide if there were no attacks upon the Philippines. The way his thoughts were turning is clear in Stimson's account of the meeting with his defense counselors to discuss the G-2 report on the Japanese southward movement. "It was agreed that if the Japanese got into the Isthmus of Kra, the British would fight," Stimson noted on November 27. "It was also agreed that if the British fought, we would have to fight."[31]

In the first week of December Roosevelt still did not close off any of his options. On December 3, he learned through MAGIC that the Japanese Foreign Office had ordered key embassies to destroy their codebooks, and that it had sent word to Berlin "that war may suddenly break out between the Anglo-Saxon nations and Japan . . . quicker than anyone dreams." Roosevelt asked for a copy of the dispatch for his files. There was no way for him to know that the Imperial Council had already on December 1 made the final decision for war, but he was certain that a Japanese attack was imminent.[32]

Nonetheless Roosevelt, the press, and the American people seemed to view the crisis almost as if it were unreal, and might at any point evaporate. On the morning of Saturday, December 6, Roosevelt was still projecting a future without full-scale combat. At 11:15, when he met with the director of the budget to review 1943 estimates, he was still restraining the expansion of the marines, paring back the Navy Department request for 40,000 draftees for the Marine Corps.

A telephone call from Secretary of the Navy Knox brought Roosevelt back abruptly to the realities in the Pacific. Knox reported large Japanese convoys and fleet movements. Three Japanese convoys were within striking distance of Bangkok and Malaya. Roosevelt, at the end of the call, remarked to Budget Director Smith "that we might be at war with Japan, although no one knew."[33]

Roosevelt was ready at last, as he had long planned, to send an appeal directly to Emperor Hirohito. If it failed, then he would several days later deliver to Congress the message that was in preparation. In the appeal Roosevelt revived many of the same compromise terms that he had suggested in the discarded *modus vivendi*. The message was transmitted at 9 P.M., Saturday evening, December 6. Later, when Mrs. Roosevelt brought her dinner guests — one of them Judge Justine Wise Polier — upstairs to his study to say goodnight to him, Roosevelt remarked, "Well, Justine, this son of man has just sent his final message to the Son of God."[34]

That same evening, the ultimate Japanese reply to the State Department was arriving at the Japanese embassy. A navy officer brought Roosevelt the first thirteen parts. The critical fourteenth part was to come later, but the sections Roosevelt read were so negative that he exclaimed, "This means war."

Harry Hopkins, who was with him, remarked that it was a shame "we could not strike the first blow and prevent any sort of surprise."

"No, we can't do that," replied Roosevelt. "We are a democracy and a peaceful people. But we have a good record."[35]

Opponents of Roosevelt have insisted that he did not by any means have "a good record," and have attacked it as involving not merely miscalculations but trickery. They began openly from 1945 on to circulate allegations, which in one form or other have persisted, that he was aware of the Japanese attack plans and concealed them from the commanders in Hawaii. They have charged that, unable to sway Congress and the public toward a declaration of war against Germany, he sacrificed the navy at Pearl Harbor to bring the United States into hostilities through the back door.

For Roosevelt thus to have acted would have been wholly out of character. He loved the navy, its ships upon which he had so often cruised; he knew and esteemed most of its top-ranking officers, and had frequently demonstrated an avuncular affection for its seamen. Had he not been president, he would have most wanted to be an admiral. Furthermore, as a father he faced the possibility of painful personal loss in a Pacific war. Of his four sons, two were officers in the navy, and one in the marines. As president and commander in chief, aware of the extreme difficulties and additional burdens war with Japan would create, he had sought, not without errors in judgment but with persistent earnestness, to avoid or at least postpone it.

Hence, on the night of December 6, Roosevelt, feeling secure in his knowledge that all of the commanders in the Pacific had been alerted, awaited developments.

Chapter 29

A DAY OF INFAMY: THE SHIFT TO ACTION

ROOSEVELT was in a troubled mood on the morning of Sunday, December 7, 1941. He had concluded the night before that a Japanese attack was imminent, and was waiting to see where it would be. He did not have to wait long. At 1:50 P.M., while Roosevelt was lunching at his desk with Harry Hopkins, Secretary Knox phoned a message from Husband E. Kimmel, commander in chief of the Pacific fleet: "Air raid on Pearl Harbor. This is not drill." Hopkins thought it must be a mistake, "that surely Japan would not attack . . . Honolulu."

Roosevelt, on the contrary, according to Hopkins, remarked that it was "just the kind of unexpected thing the Japanese would do," that while discussing peace they had plotted war. If the report were true, he felt, it would take the matter out of his hands; the Japanese would have made the decision for him.

At 2:28 came confirmation: there had been a severe attack upon Pearl Harbor. Thus war had come, not in the theater where Roosevelt had wished it, and not in the fashion he would have chosen, but inflicting damage on his beloved navy. The long months of uncertainty were over and his conscience was clear. Instantly he became the commander in chief, the war leader. He directed Admiral Stark to execute the orders prepared in advance in case of an outbreak of hostilities in the Pacific. A half hour later he met with Hull, Stimson, Knox, and Marshall while Stark remained at the Navy Department to relay fresh reports. As Roosevelt conferred, he repeatedly took telephone messages. "With each new message he shook his head," Grace Tully has reminisced, "and tightened the expression of his mouth." Mrs. Roosevelt felt that "in spite of his anxiety," he was "in a way more serene."[1]

Expeditiously the president issued orders placing the nation on a war footing in matters ranging from the disposition of troops to the surveillance of Japanese citizens and the tightening of White House security. He decided to go to Congress the next day to deliver a war message, not a long review of Japanese-American relations, but a concise one. He dictated it incisively and slowly, a statement of less than five hundred words, then went over it with Hopkins, who added a sentence to the peroration.[2]

Churchill telephoned from Chequers, his weekend residence. "We are all in the same boat now," Roosevelt remarked to him, to which he would add in a dispatch the next day, "and it is a ship which will not and cannot be sunk."[3]

When the cabinet and Vice President Wallace assembled in his study at 8:30, forming a ring around him, he remarked it was the most serious session since one Lincoln held at the outbreak of the Civil War. Interestingly, it was in the same room. Afterward they all met with a small group of congressional leaders, including the isolationist Hiram Johnson. What damage had the United States done to the Japanese, Senator Tom Connally inquired.

"It's a little difficult — we think we got some of their submarines but we don't know," Roosevelt replied.

The navy had been asleep, retorted Connally. "Where were our patrols? They knew these negotiations were going on."

Roosevelt could only reply lamely that it was no time for recriminations, that a shooting war was going on in the Pacific.

When the delegation finally left, Roosevelt after midnight, exhausted and angry, vented his feelings to the journalist Edward R. Murrow, with whom he had long had an appointment. Over sandwiches and beer, he recapitulated the losses, and pounding the table lamented that American planes had been destroyed "on the ground, by God, on the ground!"[4]

Even then Roosevelt did not know the full dimensions of the disaster, and it was weeks before he shared most of what he had learned with the public. The Japanese attack had succeeded beyond the greatest expectations of its planners. For obscure reasons, careless rather than sinister — but debated for decades to come — the commanders in Hawaii were caught totally by surprise. The first wave of airplanes hit the naval base at Pearl Harbor at 7:55 Sunday morning; a second wave followed one hour later. The Japanese severely damaged or destroyed 8 battleships, 3 light cruisers, 4 miscellaneous vessels, 188 airplanes, and some shore installations; they inflicted 3,435 casualties. The loss to the Japanese was only 28 airplanes, 5 midget submarines, and fewer than 100 persons. The Japanese vessels withdrew without being detected. Nor would the United States Navy have been powerful enough to pursue them for its strength for the time being was almost obliterated in the Pacific.

Even without the full details, December 7 was a shattering day, yet the next morning Roosevelt said he had slept well. There were fresh dispatches and, as Hopkins noted, "the news is surely not good." Roosevelt jotted it into his message:

> Last night the Japanese forces attacked Hong Kong.
> Last night the Japanese forces attacked Wake Island.
> This morning the Japanese attacked Midway Island.[5]

There was none of Wilson's transcendent idealism in Roosevelt's war message, nor of Churchill's eloquent defiance or Hitler's hysterical bombast, but it was clear and powerful. Again, as in March, 1933, when he had delivered his First Inaugural Address, the Congress and the American public rallied under his leadership. The assembled representatives and senators greeted him with loud acclaim when he entered the House chamber, and punctuated his speech with cheers. Through his simple words he projected a firm confidence, which, like the shocking surprise attack, helped bring together the previously riven nation. For a span of only six and one-half minutes he spoke deliberately and firmly:

> Yesterday, December 7, 1941 — a date which will live in infamy — the United States of America was suddenly and deliberately attacked by the naval and air forces of Japan.

Roosevelt emphasized the treachery of the attack, and reported severe damage and the loss of many American lives in the Hawaiian Islands. He enumerated areas where the Japanese had struck, including the Philippines.

> No matter how long it may take us to overcome this premeditated invasion, the American people in their righteous might will win through to absolute victory.
>
> I asked that the Congress declare that since the unprovoked and dastardly attack by Japan on Sunday, December 7, 1941, a state of war has existed between the United States and the Japanese Empire.[6]

The Congress greeted each of Roosevelt's concluding statements with bursts of applause. For the moment the bitter rift was almost closed. His critic Hoover declared, "We must fight with everything we have." Only the angry Senator Gerald P. Nye had told a Sunday evening audience, "We have been maneuvered into this by the President." He was thus setting instantly what was to become the key accusation of generations of critics. Yet even Nye voted for the war resolution. Within thirty-three minutes both houses had passed it, with only a single dissenting vote, from Jeannette Rankin, a Republican representative from Montana, who had also voted against war in 1917.[7]

The cheers in Congress reflected the national sense of outrage. "I want to beat them Japs with my own bare hands," said the first man in line at the recruiting station in Norfolk, Virginia. Washington streets in the next several days became filled with people in uniform; on Roosevelt's orders those in the services no longer wore their peacetime mufti.

Throughout the nation there was much uncertainty and, as Roosevelt was to note, countless rumors circulated. There was fright on the Pacific Coast where, for all anyone seemed to know, the Japanese might next attack. Unaccustomed blackouts and the piling of sandbags around telephone exchanges fed the hysteria. Resident Japanese, both aliens and citizens, became the targets of suspicion and hatred. Within the first few days a hundred Japanese businesses in the Los Angeles area were sold or closed.

In response to public apprehension and army recommendations, Roosevelt in February, 1942, signed an order directing the army to remove all persons of Japanese ancestry from the Pacific Coast. In consequence, 117,000 Japanese-Americans, two thirds of them United States citizens, were moved to ten relocation centers in remote areas, where they lived uncomfortably behind barbed wire. In June, 1944, Attorney General Francis Biddle informed Roosevelt there was no longer any need to confine the Japanese-Americans, but the president wanted no change until after the election.[8]

Roosevelt shared the anger toward Japan but did not let it distract him from the larger goal toward which he had for so long been working. After returning from delivering the war message, he emphasized to advisers that Germany was still the prime target. Hitler had not declared war, but the president correctly assumed he would.[9]

On December 11, Germany and Italy honored their treaty with Japan. As Foreign Minister Joachim von Ribbentrop testified later at the Nuremberg trials, Pearl Harbor had come as completely as a surprise to the Germans as to the United States. When Hitler returned to Berlin from the Russian front, Ribbentrop presented him with the option of staying out of the war with the United States. The Tripartite Pact bound Germany only in the event of an attack upon Japan. The German Foreign Office was aware of the possible complications for Roosevelt if he sought a declaration of war from Congress. The German chargé in Washington had radioed that Roosevelt would "try at first to avoid sharpening the situation in the Atlantic," and that the military leaders would logically want to avoid a two-front war. Nevertheless Hitler opted for war. Later he explained to followers that the Japanese intervention had come at an opportune time, "at the moment when the surprises of the Russian winter were pressing most heavily on the morale of our people." Grossly overestimating Japanese power and holding the Americans in contempt, he seriously misgauged the future.

Before the Reichstag, Hitler spewed out his pent-up hatred of the president. "I cannot be insulted by Roosevelt, for I consider him mad, just as Wilson was," he declaimed, and argued, like the American isolationists, that Roosevelt was resorting to war to compensate for the domestic failures of the New Deal.[10]

As a consequence, the American declaration of war against Germany (and Italy) came almost as an anticlimax. The president did not again go before Congress but sent a brief message asking it to recognize a state of war with the two Axis powers. Congress unanimously adopted war resolutions. Roosevelt did not deign to call for resolutions against several Nazi satellites that declared war on the United States. It was only months later at Soviet request that he asked Congress to act against Bulgaria, Hungary, and Romania.[11]

Had Roosevelt gone to Congress to request a declaration of war against Germany, he would have faced stiff opposition on the grounds that the enemy that had attacked the United States was Japan. Hitler relieved Roosevelt of that problem; the German war declaration further united the American people. But soon, even as Roosevelt had feared, many of the former America Firsters became "Asia firsters," determined that the war effort should concentrate upon punishing the Japanese for their surprise attack. It was not to be easy for Roosevelt to convince Americans that, despite the grievous setbacks the Japanese were inflicting, by far the most dangerous foe was Nazi Germany, because of its armed might, industrial production, and technological innovations.

Some days later, Roosevelt saw to it that the nation received a fuller and fairly candid report of the destruction at Pearl Harbor. When Secretary of the Navy Knox returned from Hawaii to report to the president, he jotted a succinct outline, which became with small changes

Knox's public statement of the next day. For security reasons Knox had to leave unstated the positive information that all aircraft carriers were elsewhere and that the Japanese planes had not destroyed the indispensable drydocks and other installations.[12]

On the future of war production, Roosevelt in a Fireside Chat on December 9 was with good reason optimistic, but understandably did not mention the serious problem of reallocation. He had been directing production toward aiding nations fighting the Axis, and now had to shift toward filling the needs of the American armed forces. The immediate prospects were bleak but the potential was cheering.[13]

Roosevelt, wrapping himself in his naval cape as commander in chief, zestfully assumed open leadership. Much of what he had undertaken of a military nature had to continue secret, but he no longer had to depend upon makeshifts for economic mobilization, nor to disguise his own role as the supreme war leader. In the immediate aftermath of Pearl Harbor, Congress voted him war powers comparable to those President Wilson had exercised, and unhesitatingly escalated appropriations.

An indication of Roosevelt's inner exhilaration was a memo that on December 11, the day the United States declared war upon Germany, he found time to send Steve Early, his press secretary. Affixed to it was the signature of Grace Tully. It was the first of a number of backward glances toward the First World War, when he was young, energetic, dashing, and in his recollections, performing great feats. The purport was his firm preparation to be wartime commander in chief:

> A good many comments have been made that the President seems to be taking the situation of extreme emergency in his stride, that he is looking well and that he does not seem to have any nerves.
>
> People sometimes forget that this kind of crisis is not wholly new to him; the only difference is that today he is Commander-in-Chief and the final arbiter in all departments and agencies of the Government, whereas during the World War he had to make decisions only for the Navy. . . .
>
> In those early days . . . he personally visited practically all defense activities. . . . But over and above this, he went abroad in the Spring of 1918 on a destroyer and probably saw a greater part of the general war area than any other American.[14]

Within this curious bit of boasting was a significant truth, that Roosevelt had learned much during World War I, even a bit of the rudiments of wartime diplomacy.

Now Churchill and his staff were preparing speedily to come to

Washington. Roosevelt, as a participant rather than as someone being wooed, was about to take a crash course in summit diplomacy and coalition warfare. With the United States fully involved in the war, the relationship had changed. Churchill, the day after Pearl Harbor, parried the cautious approach of a staff member by joking, "Oh, that is the way we talked to her while we were wooing her; now that she is in the harem, we talk to her quite differently."[15]

There was reason for optimism despite spreading disasters in the Pacific. Roosevelt and those about him had been erecting a production and mobilization machine with a potential beyond any the world had seen, but had been forced to limit it to what a peacetime electorate and economy could accept. Now it could operate at full throttle, as it had in 1917–1918.

On the night of Pearl Harbor, Churchill recalled what Sir Edward Grey, foreign secretary during World War I, had said to him years earlier, that America was like a gigantic boiler: "Once the fire is lighted under it there is no limit to the power it can generate." Churchill that night "slept the sleep of the saved and the thankful." He awoke determined to take full advantage of that boiler and to direct its power toward his great ends.

After a rough Atlantic crossing on a new battleship, Churchill and his staff on December 22 flew from Hampton Roads to Washington. Roosevelt greeted them at the airport, standing propped against his automobile. Roosevelt had been apprehensive, Ambassador Halifax had cabled Churchill, that the visit might be "rather too strong medicine" for the previously isolationist American public. Quite the contrary, the nation was wildly enthusiastic; the mission seemed to give promise of positive, dynamic action in contrast to the dreary news of Japanese victories. To the American people, Churchill, his fingers raised to form a V for victory, his voice growling defiance to Hitler, until this point had been their only great hero of the war.

Churchill and the British, seasoned by two years of warfare, came prepared to dominate what was called the Arcadia conference. The British forces and munitions production were at their peak; the great American potential was yet to be realized. On their way to Washington, despite heavy seas, Churchill and his advisers developed position papers, which, after long and vehement debates with Roosevelt and his staff, were to shape Anglo-American strategy.[16]

The American team, as yet unseasoned, was potentially strong. Already Roosevelt possessed in General George C. Marshall a chief of staff of superlative quality, and Marshall, sifting through his long memories of bright young officers and their immediate effectiveness in army maneuvers, was moving upward the most talented. One was a new brigadier general, Dwight D. Eisenhower, whose name had been in Marshall's small black book since 1930. A week after Pearl Harbor he arrived at the War Plans Division to take responsibility for the Philippines, where he had been stationed from 1935 to 1938. Eisenhower put his mind to the impossible task, but soon proved himself more valuable in other ways.[17]

The navy, some of whose top admirals seemed to be demoralized in the aftermath of Pearl Harbor, needed someone of a brilliance and austerity comparable to that of Marshall. The chief of naval operations, Admiral Harold ("Betty") Stark, was intelligent and personally a delight to Roosevelt but not a stern disciplinarian who could run a "tight ship." So it was that Roosevelt turned to Admiral Ernest J. King, who, upon Stark's recommendation, Roosevelt had made commander in chief of the Atlantic Fleet. There King controlled his drinking problem and proved himself a stern, aggressive commander in difficult patrols against Nazi submarines.

A week after Pearl Harbor, Roosevelt appointed Admiral Chester W. Nimitz as head of the Pacific Fleet and promoted King to become commander in chief of the entire United States Fleet. A few months later King became chief of naval operations, and Stark took over command of the Atlantic Fleet. In a naval war that came to center upon aircraft carriers, it was significant that King was the first aviator to attain command of the navy. He quickly proved himself the hard, resourceful leader Roosevelt needed, though one he had trouble keeping within bounds. Like Marshall, King maintained a relationship with Roosevelt that was effective but entirely professional. When Roosevelt died in 1945, he displayed no grief or sense of loss.

Both King and Marshall served the president and the nation well. They had already met and respected the British staff, and were ready to act in unison at the conference. Differences of opinion between the army and navy, as Stimson noted, largely disappeared after the appointment of King. The unity was important, since throughout the war distinct differences did persist between Roosevelt and Churchill and their chiefs of staff.[18]

The relationship was quite different on the British and American sides, Admiral King told Sherwood in 1946:

> Churchill, fancying himself as a great strategist, and being so powerful personally, ruled his Chiefs of Staff with an iron hand,

> forcing them at all times to compliance with the policy as he and the War Cabinet laid it down. . . . Roosevelt, on the other hand, trusted his Chiefs of Staff and thus gave them much more personal authority and immeasurably more freedom of action and of speech than was enjoyed by their British opposite numbers.[19]

At the Arcadia conference Roosevelt and his staff began as the junior partners, weak in strength and lacking in experience, although by the middle of the war they were to be dominant. At Argentia, Newfoundland, the previous August the British had come as supplicants; now they expected to be instructors. Churchill aimed to propose strategies and to make sure that the lend-lease flow of supplies did not slacken. The awaiting American military leaders did not have long-range plans to propose, but immediate measures to try to stem the Japanese. They were wary of the British because of their difficulties during the neutrality period; few of the subordinates were as amenable as Marshall and Hopkins. They were particularly concerned that British demands for lend-lease should not cripple American projects. Marshall commented after the war, "Our people were always ready to find Albion perfidious."[20]

As for Roosevelt, who in time past had been as suspicious and critical of the British as any of his staff, there was the necessity to take a larger view. Throughout the war, as in the neutrality period, he too thought first and foremost of the American national interest, but he did so in more inclusive terms than the generals and the admirals. He was keenly conscious of his dual role as commander in chief and president, and kept balanced in his thinking global and coalition considerations, the demands of each of the services, and of Congress and the public. Almost immediately Congress began to revert to placing sharply critical restraints upon Roosevelt. Roosevelt had to take into account also the public, enjoying a new prosperity but suffering fresh deprivations. He balanced these factors in his thinking and several times in the first two years of the war overruled his military and naval advisers.[21]

Churchill on the evening of his arrival found Roosevelt, unencumbered by any of the reservations that worried his staff, easy to captivate with his prime proposal, that they invade North Africa. Hull, Welles, Stimson, and Hopkins were present, but the American military and naval leaders were not there to raise objections. Churchill's argument was that Hitler, stalled in Russia, might advance through Spain across the Strait of Gibraltar. Roosevelt quickly fell in with the scheme. He agreed to bring pressure upon the Vichy government of France, and then, with or without its approval, to join in an invasion. Churchill was prepared to send 55,000 troops at three weeks' notice.[22]

Beyond question, Roosevelt was being expansive and impulsive, yielding to the euphoria of planning a quick blow against the Nazis within the next several months. Yet there were solid benefits that made the scheme alluring. A landing at Casablanca and a linkage with the British moving west from Libya could clear the south shore of the Mediterranean. Marshall noted that at the conference Roosevelt "considered it very important to morale, to give the people of this country a feeling that they are in the war, to give the Germans the reverse effect, to have American troops somewhere in active fighting across the Atlantic." A public preoccupied with Pearl Harbor would become fully focused on the more dangerous foe only when American troops engaged the Germans in combat. Finally but not least, 1942 would be an election year. Marshall's later conclusion, often quoted, was that he had learned there must always be a military operation in an election year. The remark should be put in context; Roosevelt needed to build strong popular and congressional backing for the war against the Nazis. On the other hand, Marshall, speaking at the Arcadia sessions, noted the perils also, that "a failure in this first venture would have an extremely adverse effect on the morale of the American people." Before the conference closed, news arrived of British reverses in Libya.[23]

If there were to be a North African invasion, it would have to come much later. The American chiefs of staff did not want it at all, since they felt all men and resources that could be rushed across the Atlantic should be concentrated for a thrust into France at the earliest possible time. Roosevelt was not averse to their thinking — if there could be sufficient buildup for a successful landing in 1942, a quixotic notion. Meanwhile he and his advisers agreed to send air squadrons to Britain and divisions to Northern Ireland, where they could complete their training and be poised for action.

At the formal conference sessions the British, compared with the Americans, seemed experienced, highly organized, and far ranging in their proposals. "They knew their stuff," remembered Captain John L. McCrea, soon to be Roosevelt's naval aide, who was the recorder. "They all talked exceedingly well and made much sense. The staff organization was superb, as well." Moreover, they were cordial toward the Americans, who had entered the meetings rather ill at ease, not sure how well they could cope with Churchill's influence over Roosevelt. The tensions soon eased, and although serious differences persisted, the two staffs formed friendships that endured through the war.[24]

That first afternoon, Roosevelt opened the session by presenting the proposals his staff had prepared for him, emphasizing the need to retain key bases and lines of communication while marshaling strength for the future. Churchill was far more positive, outlining the proposals he had aired to Roosevelt the previous evening.

In planning Pacific operations for 1942, Churchill on Christmas Eve, in private, swept Roosevelt along in an optimism greater than the Japanese advance warranted. Churchill reiterated that Singapore would be an impregnable fortress, and Roosevelt impulsively agreed to reroute to Singapore a convoy of seven shiploads of reinforcements and airplanes if it could not break through the Japanese blockade and reach the Philippines. By December 26, MacArthur had to proclaim Manila an open city and withdraw his forces to Corregidor and the Bataan peninsula.[25]

Nothing from the convoy ever reached either the Philippines or Singapore, but Roosevelt's sudden decision, without consulting his chief of staff, was of lasting consequence. Marshall was appalled when on Christmas morning he received from the British a memorandum that Roosevelt recognized that the reinforcements were not likely to reach their destination and wished them used "in whatever manner might best serve the joint cause in the Far East." Marshall, flanked by Arnold and Eisenhower, protested to Stimson, who immediately sent word to Roosevelt that if he continued to make such arbitrary decisions he would need to find a new secretary of war. When Hopkins reported Stimson's anger to Roosevelt and Churchill, they both denied making the agreement. Subsequently, Roosevelt scoffed about incorrect statements, and Stimson silenced the president by reading him the British report. Roosevelt did not again try to bypass his chief of staff.

Marshall, for his part, felt that the only way to avoid similar episodes in the future would be to appoint a supreme commander for the Pacific, in charge of all the forces of several nations, stretched over thousands of miles. The concept of a supreme commander would prepare the way for a unified command in any area to which the United States sent troops. He immediately drafted a proposal, and to make it attractive to the British, suggested their able general Sir Archibald Wavell for the post. Roosevelt gave Marshall his full support. Marshall then won over, after initial opposition, the United States Navy, the British chiefs, and finally, in a dramatic session in Churchill's bedroom, the prime minister. It was a vital achievement into which the president put little time and no effort.[26]

At this point, Roosevelt turned to Admiral King, asking him at lunch who should issue orders to Wavell or any other supreme commander in a theater. It was one of the most difficult problems in undertaking coalition warfare, for each nation would want a voice, and inevitably conflicting views would result in disastrous delays. There was no time to lose, Roosevelt declared; he told King to obtain an agreement from the chiefs of staff that afternoon. However, several days of negotiation between the British and Americans ensued. Roosevelt wanted to create a new organization in which each nation contributing forces, including Australia, New Zealand, and the Netherlands, would have a vote. The British, rather, wanted to set up a committee of the chiefs of staff of the United States and Britain. It would conduct the war; the other nations would have to follow its lead. Both Marshall and King favored the British proposal, and King subsequently obtained Roosevelt's assent. The result was an effective command organization, the Combined Chiefs of Staff, with its headquarters in Washington.[27]

It remained to devise one final piece of machinery to be responsible for allocation of supplies. That machinery was of vital importance to the British, who were more concerned with a continued or even augmented flow of supplies than they were with obtaining American troops. For the chiefs of staff, military control seemed essential, so that civilians would not be able to nullify their decisions by cutting off the flow of matériel. For Roosevelt and the Americans, it was vital for control to remain in the United States. Marshall told Roosevelt that unless the board were under the Combined Chiefs of Staff, he could not continue to meet his responsibilities. Roosevelt supported him against the British, as Robert Sherwood wrote not long afterward, serving "notice on such proud men as Churchill and Beaverbrook that [he] was the boss and Washington the headquarters of the joint war effort." Throughout the war the Munitions Assignment Board performed the difficult and vital function of allocating supplies.[28]

Altogether, Roosevelt and Churchill created organizations for coalition warfare on a global scale. Roosevelt wanted to go beyond this, to establish a grand alliance that would pledge itself not only to fight until victory, but also to attain the idealistic goals he and Churchill had proclaimed in the Atlantic Charter. This would be more than a press release, but a declaration to which representatives of the major powers warring against the Axis would affix their signatures. The idea was Secretary Hull's, and the president was quick to act upon it.

One of the British suggestions delighted Roosevelt, that the small nations as well as large should sign the statement to demonstrate that the war was also being waged upon their behalf. Roosevelt saw it as a "distinct advantage to have as long a list of small countries as possible."

There remained the ticklish question of a suitable name for the group. On the morning of January 1, Roosevelt, excited, had himself wheeled into Churchill's room. According to legend, Churchill emerged from his bath naked, joking that the prime minister had nothing to hide from the president of the United States. (Later Churchill denied the story to Sherwood, saying that he had always at least wrapped a bath towel around himself, and besides the president would have known the statement was not strictly true.) Roosevelt announced that he had found the ideal term, "United Nations." Churchill at dinner that evening declared how much he liked the title and read the manifesto to the guests. A little after ten that evening, Mrs. Roosevelt brought the guests into the Oval Office to witness the signing of the declaration, first Roosevelt, then Churchill, Litvinov, and finally T. V. Soong, Chiang's personal representative, for China. Churchill remarked, "Four fifths of the human race."

In reality, though not in law, Roosevelt had assumed leadership for the United States in a great alliance committed to pursuing the war to final victory. He obtained the adherence of as many nations as possible to the declaration — twenty-six in the next few weeks and twenty more before the war was over.[29]

Yet there was serious tension between Roosevelt and Churchill over the nature of the postwar world, and it was to continue. It did not mar the admiration and affection they held for each other, nor did it interfere with military arrangements. Rather, it was a factor leading to intermittent debate and negotiation. Even before the prime minister departed for London, Mrs. Roosevelt confided to Anna, "I like Mr. Churchill, he's loveable & emotional & very human but I don't want him to write the peace or carry it out."[30]

Even the most fraternal of alliances could raise problems.

Chapter 30

FINAL ARBITER OVER WAR PRODUCTION

As WARTIME COMMANDER IN CHIEF, Roosevelt could exert power over the American economy and society transcending any he had previously wielded, even in the first heady days of the New Deal. He was indeed, as he boasted in the first week of the war, "the final arbiter in all departments and agencies of the Government." The first War Powers Act, which Congress enacted on December 18, 1941, updated World War I legislation and gave Roosevelt vast authority over areas ranging from production controls to censorship. He was able to establish, modify, and reshuffle war agencies, placing them directly under his own purview in the Executive Office of the President.

In peacetime his authority would have seemed to provide an exhilarating opportunity for change; after Pearl Harbor it was of secondary concern. Smooth-running agencies to channel American society, industry, and agriculture toward intensified production were a key to victory, yet understandably Roosevelt focused his time and energies on strategy and diplomacy. On the home front, so far as possible, Roosevelt acted only as final arbiter and came to rely more and more heavily upon his top advisers. Below these were echelons of business and academic experts and New Dealers, some of doubtful worth and others of remarkable ingenuity and enterprise. From their ranks came many of the most effective innovators and administrators.[1]

Roosevelt's administrative techniques were the familiar ones he had so long pursued through the 1930s, compounded of a sense of politics and a tendency to create overlapping lines of authority. More even than before, he expected his administrators to stay out of trouble. Often they failed to do so, and he had to intervene in disruptive quarrels. The clashes of the jousting "war lords of Washington" were spectacular. So too were the related clashes in Congress, the press, and radio.[2]

The struggle was over the drive to meet production goals, and it also reflected the fundamental schism over the nature of the war. Was it to be fought to restore the old order, or to attain the idealistic future Roosevelt from time to time proclaimed? In these terms, the sound and the fury signified much.

Roosevelt, who symbolized the issue as the advocate of a better world, sought nevertheless to bridge the schism by insisting that the immediate overriding concern of the United States was to win the war in the quickest fashion with the fewest casualties. The specifics of the postwar world could be thrashed out later. The urgent, instant need was to raise production as high as possible. Already Roosevelt had proposed figures at what the army and the Office of Production Management regarded as the upper limit, a total of $55 billion. Lord Beaverbrook, in charge of British production, sat with him on Christmas night, 1941, until one in the morning, urging still larger output. He talked, Donald Nelson, in charge of supplies allocations, remembers, "in what seemed at the time to be fantastic figures." Roosevelt accepted them at once, 45,000 tanks and 60,000 planes — 10,000 more than the projection of a year and a half before.[3]

The increased output, Roosevelt told his administrators, must come through curtailing civilian production. Only 35 percent of steel was going into war use, compared with 75 percent in Britain; he wanted to take 60 percent of steel, and 50 percent of all industrial capacity.

To achieve top production, Roosevelt needed to replace the makeshift, inefficient war agencies with new, more effective ones. A consensus was forming that the nation needed a single director to serve as Baruch had during the First World War, but possessing greater power than then. For some days Roosevelt clung to the concept of three directors, thus dispersing power. He was wary and manipulative toward the prestigious, conservative Baruch, who had headed the War Industries Board under President Wilson. Throughout World War II, Baruch exercised influence from the Carleton Hotel and a park bench across Pennsylvania Avenue from the White House. Roosevelt courted Baruch enough to keep him out of the opposition, and followed similar tactics with the Republican Willkie. Both received appointments but little independent power.

Rather, Roosevelt did establish the War Production Board (WPB) with a single director, Donald Nelson, an amiable Democrat and a Sears, Roebuck executive. Nelson, as Roosevelt wished, was sympathetic toward

New Dealers and tried to aid small business, but he could not decide how much steel and other scarce materials the military should receive compared with the civilian economy and make his decision stick. It was with the army that Nelson's troubles gradually intensified, and repeatedly more serious conflicts came before the president. Rosenman witnessed Roosevelt spending hours and days deciding disputes between the WPB and the army. The army almost inevitably won.[4]

Within several months after Pearl Harbor, Roosevelt established or revamped an array of other war agencies and reshuffled personnel who had served previously. Among the most important was the Office of Price Administration (OPA) under Leon Henderson, established in April, 1941, to stem inflation through setting price ceilings and rationing scarce commodities. The mission of all of the agencies, either directly or indirectly, was to foster the production of the materials of war.

The president presented to Congress a first estimate of the cost in the 1943 budget, an almost incomprehensible sum for that time, $59 billion, which on a graph would appear like the peaks of the Rockies looming over the foothills of the New Deal budgets. It was as large as the dollar value of the nation's entire 1939 factory output, yet would account for only half of production, an indication less of inflation than of how far short of potential production the economy had been that year. The budget would involve heavy borrowing and large increases in taxation, a program for the transformation of the nation from the relatively limited defense effort to total war mobilization. There no longer could be both tanks and automobiles, but the OPA was not able to stop the manufacture of automobiles until April 1, 1942.

As always, Roosevelt did not lose sight of the small producers, of the sort with which he was familiar around Hyde Park, and of their need to obtain contracts to keep their workmen on the job. He was concerned about a Poughkeepsie manufacturer of wooden window shades and blinds, for whom he found contracts to build wooden medicine cabinets and other wooden substitutes for steel. In the end, as Roosevelt admitted the following November, it did not work out well: "I tried to get them some orders. Almost impossible because the W.P.B. and the Army and Navy . . . asked for bids on cots and wooden tables and simple chairs and medicine cases. . . . What happens? The bids come in and of course some very, very big company . . . can under-bid this little concern of . . . 30 people in the city of Poughkeepsie."[5]

Roosevelt's efforts on behalf of small business not only reflected his feelings, they were politically popular. Congress that spring voted unanimously to establish a Smaller War Plants Corporation; Senate hearings brought out that up to Pearl Harbor, 71 percent of the defense contracts had gone to a hundred large corporations. Small businessmen continued to suffer, although they obtained some subcontracts from large companies. They were hard pressed for raw materials under the priorities system of allocation. Larger corporations began, in contrast, to thrive as never before. They were most effective in competing for contracts and the priority authorizations with which to seek scarce steel and other components.[6]

With Roosevelt's backing, the WPB undertook to remedy malfunctionings in the priority system. Orders piled up in excess of industrial capacity and available raw materials. In consequence priorities became little more than licenses to hunt for the materials, and there was serious imbalance in the production program.

The WPB stopped construction of some of the superfluous new war plants and shipyards. The need for merchant ships was acute, and until late in the year production did not keep up with submarine sinkings. Nonetheless, projected shipyard capacity was becoming disproportionately large, and in the spring of 1942, Roosevelt, planning a landing across the Atlantic, gave an even higher priority to the construction of landing craft, for the most part being turned out in inland shipyards. On July 4, Roosevelt authorized Nelson to cut back the merchant ship program. The result was the spectacular cancellation of $146 million in contracts and abandonment of the $10-million shipyard that Andrew Jackson Higgins was constructing in New Orleans. Roosevelt was cautious in his comments. Episodes like this were not helpful politically, but contract cancellations and the stopping of construction on a number of war plants helped bring the total production program into better balance.[7]

During the troubled summer of 1942, Ferdinand Eberstadt, chairman of the Army-Navy Munitions Board, helped work out a plan for the rationing of raw materials that Commander John D. Small of the Navy Office of Procurement and Material was suggesting. It allocated precise quantities of raw materials to each manufacturer and made possible a balanced production of exactly the finished products most needed.[8]

With a strong allocation plan and two decisive lieutenants, Nelson by September, 1942, could run the War Production Board more effectively. He brought in Eberstadt and Charles E. Wilson, president of General Electric. It was not an entirely effective system, but despite the inevitable minor problems and strident conflicts, Roosevelt finally had a basic production program in place. By 1943 it was so successful that the focus could turn toward questions of cutbacks and even limited reconversion to civilian needs. Roosevelt did little more than preside over these changes and insist that the quarrels not become too public and disruptive. The effective innovations had come from below.

When the quarreling became too strident between the army and the War Production Board, Roosevelt tried, without openly showing his hand, to quiet difficulties in the WPB between Nelson's two deputies. Wilson had threatened to resign unless he received some of Eberstadt's powers. Nelson capitulated. The problem, the secretaries and under secretaries of the navy and war felt, was with Nelson; and together with Byrnes, Hopkins, and Ickes they pressed Roosevelt to appoint Baruch head of the WPB. Byrnes in February 1943 presented such strong arguments that the appointment would quiet Congress and win the plaudits of the press, that Roosevelt agreed and signed a letter making the offer. But Baruch, undergoing medical tests for cancer, pleaded for time to consider. Days went by with the appointment unresolved.[9]

Roosevelt became swayed by the misgivings of Director of the Budget Smith that Baruch was too elderly and hard of hearing, and perhaps was tied to one of the factions in the dispute. There followed on February 16, 1943, a bizarre episode. At breakfast an assistant informed Nelson that a letter had been drawn up for Roosevelt's signature appointing Baruch chairman of the WPB, and Eberstadt his deputy. The army and navy secretaries and under secretaries were to meet with Roosevelt at two that afternoon, together with Byrnes, to urge Roosevelt to sign the letter. Nelson telephoned Stimson, who confirmed the planned meeting. Next he tried, without success, to reach the president, but failed. He did reach one of the White House staff, who suggested:

"The President expects you to take things in your own hands. . . . This whole row seems to be centering around Eberstadt — yet you've been keeping Eberstadt in your own organization all this time. Do something about *that*, and then see if the Boss doesn't invite you in for a chat."

Nelson immediately requested Eberstadt's resignation and designated Wilson as his chief deputy. Roosevelt's meeting with Stimson and Knox did not take place. Rather, Roosevelt at lunch remarked to Ickes that Eberstadt would be fired that day, explaining that he had failed to get rid of an oil company executive, unpopular in Latin America, who was on the WPB staff. What Roosevelt did not know was that Nelson had advised Eberstadt to do nothing, that he would take up the matter with the president, and then had forgotten to do so. Later that afternoon, Roosevelt told Nelson he was satisfied with the job he was doing, yet for some days still wavered. Baruch's medical tests were negative. He returned to Washington, and expecting to accept the appointment went to the White House. Roosevelt engaged him in conversation on numerous topics, but the WPB was not among them. The president had changed his mind. Nelson remained on as chairman of the WPB and Hopkins saw to it that much of the power was delegated to Wilson. By the summer of 1944, Nelson had become antagonistic toward Wilson, viewing him as agreeing with the army's point of view.[10]

Through all of these episodes involving the WPB and the army, there ran the issue of civilian versus military control over the economy. The question was how much of scarce materials should go to the armed forces. Roosevelt believed in civilian control and repeatedly during the war thwarted efforts of Admiral King to consolidate supply functions within his own expanding domain. Yet what the military wanted, the military seemed to get, regardless of the protests of civilian agencies.[11]

Roosevelt's pride during the First World War in "getting things done" despite the obstacles, persisted during the Second. He wanted quick results without well-publicized dissension. Loath though he was to lose good administrators, he would allow even a gifted Eberstadt to depart if, by doing so, he might bring a modicum of quiet. Undoubtedly the suggestion that Nelson could fire Eberstadt originated with the president himself. On the other hand, Roosevelt also wanted no challenge to his own ultimate authority. This explains why he permitted a not entirely satisfactory Nelson to continue well into 1944. Baruch performed a number of useful, even vital, services for Roosevelt during the war, and in so doing was no threat to the president.

One day early in the war, Roosevelt, nursing a head cold, lunched with Baruch, and gave him a feeling of closeness. Roosevelt remarked, "You think I am too soft." Baruch did not deny it. Yet what Baruch, Stimson, and others saw as softness was Roosevelt's reluctance to use a bludgeon — he could be hard as flint in achieving the same ends in bloodless, almost undetectable ways. The failure of Baruch to head the WPB and the sudden departure of Eberstadt were cases in point.[12]

While Roosevelt was seeking higher and still higher levels of war production, he wanted also to keep a proper balance between it and supplies for civilians. And, of course, he was aware that the base of power in a democracy is its people.

Throughout the war Roosevelt closely watched public opinion polls. Mundane data gave an indication whether programs were working. As the Japanese conquests cut off the supply of natural rubber, he found 77 percent of those polled thought tire rationing necessary. In the fall of 1942, when Gallup sent him a confidential report, Roosevelt was appalled at the percentage of people who had no clear idea what the war was about.[13]

Roosevelt also appraised opinion and conditions through his own observations, especially occasional visits to war plants and conversations with those he trusted. Hopkins, Eleanor Roosevelt, and others served to some extent as ears and eyes for him. He exchanged remarks with his Hyde Park and Warm Springs neighbors, soliciting their views and sometimes arguing with them, but he was so deskbound that it seemed impossible for him to be directly in touch with the thoughts of working people. White House correspondents listened skeptically in April, 1943, as he regaled them with an account of his lecture to a skilled worker, "a very highly skilled mechanic, getting mighty good wages," who passed on to him his wife's complaint because she had had to spend a dollar and a half for a small bunch of asparagus:

> I said, "Look. I am just going to ask you a question — maybe I'm right, maybe I'm wrong. Did your wife ever buy a bunch of asparagus in March before? . . . You know where it came from? It came from Florida. Did you ever eat Florida asparagus in March before?"
>
> He said, "You know, I never thought of that. I will have to talk to my wife about it." . . .
>
> There is a great deal of that in the country, and it comes from the fact that so many people have a great deal more money in their pay envelopes on Saturday night than they ever had before, that they want to go into the luxury business of eating.

All this was to make the point that taxation and savings programs were essential to help tamp down inflation.

More than a year later, at a press conference, Roosevelt returned to the same theme. A friend of his, a foreman, had come to see him that January, he recounted, and said, "I have an awful time when I go home."

> I said, "What's the trouble?"
>
> "The cost of living."
>
> "Well," I said, "what, for instance?"
>
> "Well, last night I went home, and the old lady said, 'What's this? I went out to buy some asparagus . . . five sticks . . . a dollar and a quarter!' "

Merriman Smith of the Associated Press broke in, "Mr. President, is that the same foreman . . . ?"

The correspondents roared with laughter, and Roosevelt joined in.

Smith later wrote, concerning Roosevelt's frequent remarks about mechanics and others dropping in on him, that how they could do so was beyond explanation. "He claimed a lot of friends in comparatively low stations of life," Smith recalled. "I regarded them as his imaginary playmates." And so it seemed.

Surprisingly enough, in this instance Smith was wrong. Years later, Isador Lubin, a labor economist, reminiscing about Roosevelt's broad interests, recalled his own amazement one chilly wartime day when he had accompanied a delegation of workmen into the president's office and witnessed Roosevelt engaging one of them in earnest discussion over the high cost of asparagus.[14]

Roosevelt continued fairly well in touch with his constituency. He hoped to educate them on the fundamental war aims, and from time to time devoted himself to these matters in speeches and in press conference background discussions. But he was also aware of people's day-by-day reactions. For millions of them the war had brought fears and uncertainties on the one hand, and on the other, what they had dreamed of during the depression, well-paying jobs and a far better standard of living. They responded positively to Roosevelt's wartime leadership, but were themselves rather conservative in their aspirations. Public opinion polls from 1936 on had indicated they were more interested in recovery than reform; now they had recovery. They were less concerned with the disappearance of New Deal agencies than with that of consumer goods from the stores.

Roosevelt saw to it that deprivations were not so large as to undermine their morale. He would not force as Spartan an economy upon them as some of the leaders of the armed forces wished. Steel might be short, but he wanted enough allocated to provide bottle caps for soft drinks and beer. He sanctioned the continuation of professional baseball.[15]

He did indeed seek a drastic cutback in those consumer goods competing with war production. More important, he wanted to siphon off much of the new spending power through the heavy taxes he requested from Congress in June, 1942, and through war bond drives. Both taxes and bonds would keep inflation down, and the bonds would serve a further function by providing a cushion to help carry workers through the economic upheaval that Roosevelt expected would follow the war. It was to be a home front of considerable austerity, the pain of shortages and dislocation, and of hard work, mitigated by good incomes and small comforts.

In establishing these policies of sacrifice and reward, Roosevelt sought the cooperation of Congress. On large measures he received it at first; Congress had been quick to grant him the blanket authorization with which he had established the War Production Board and other agencies. Yet on many of the issues that most involved the electorate — wartime taxation, and price and wage stabilization to fight inflation — Roosevelt after 1942 was increasingly at odds with Congress, even though a majority were nominally Democrats.

Like two previous wartime presidents, Lincoln and Wilson, Roosevelt tried to elevate his administration above politics, incorporating in it numbers from the other party. He tried to avoid the trap into which Wilson had fallen in calling for a Democratic Congress in the 1918 election, in contrast telling the press in February, 1942, "When a country is at war we want Congressmen, regardless of party — get that — . . . who have a record of backing up the Government of the United States in an emergency, regardless of party." He added for emphasis, "Put that down again, twice."[16]

Of course, Roosevelt's remarks were themselves viable wartime politics, an effort to create the impression that only support of the administration war effort was legitimate. As for Congress, politics continued little changed from the neutrality years, except that those who had been ardently isolationist now strongly espoused the military efforts, especially against Japan. Those who had been unrelentingly anti-Roosevelt during the 1930s intensified their efforts to wipe out New Deal agencies.

As early as December 26, 1941, Senator Robert A. Taft set forth clearly the credo and agenda of the congressional conservatives. He warned that the Roosevelt administration, under the guise of war, would try to extend its control over the American economy and society. Congress could not assume running the war, he granted, but it should subject postwar proposals to intense public discussion, and it must immediately slash nonwar expenditures. Within six months, Taft believed, Congress could abolish the WPA, CCC, and NYA.[17]

In February, 1942, the Republican leader, Senator Arthur Vandenberg, expressed his irritation to his family:

> Tydings made a grand speech in the Senate today — giving everybody *hell.* It's too early for us to break loose on our side of the aisle. But it won't be long now. Come what may, I'm going to "speak my piece" one of these days. Roosevelt . . . hasn't demobilized a single one of his old "social revolution" units. . . . The country is getting ugly — and I don't blame 'em — *so am I.* Even

we in the Senate can't find out what is going on. This is Roosevelt's private war![18]

With the aid of shrewd advisers like Byrnes, who for so long had been a power in the Senate, Roosevelt could counter adroitly some of the Republican thrusts, but his opponents also enjoyed new advantages. They demonstrated their patriotism through backing the basic war legislation immediately after Pearl Harbor, yet could blame the inefficiencies and conflicts in the war agencies upon the New Dealers. No matter how many Republican businessmen Roosevelt appointed, their outcries continued unabated. Too, they could capitalize upon the mood of the newly affluent electorate, eager to win the war but loath to sacrifice full enjoyment of their gains, and irritated by regulations and dislocations. The same forces were at work beneath the surface of patriotic wartime America in the forties that in the aftermath of the First World War had caused the Harding landslide.[19]

The result was what a historian, John M. Blum, has aptly called "the politics of comfort." Roosevelt and his allies in Congress competed as best they could with the conservatives to maintain a modicum of goods and services flowing to the electorate. The president enjoyed a considerable advantage in that he fought to prevent increases in prices as well as wages, while the conservative alliance was as tolerant of price increases as it was stern in seeking restraints on wages, hours, and unions. Because Roosevelt needed a strong congressional majority and firm backing throughout the country if he were to attain victory, the conservatives undoubtedly exercised a moderating influence.[20]

Roosevelt wasted little time defending targets not of fundamental value to the war effort, such as the Office of Civilian Defense (OCD), in which Mrs. Roosevelt was assistant director. She had worked energetically in 1941 to develop volunteer programs — not unlike her youthful endeavors in the slums of New York City — to improve the nutrition, physical fitness, child care, and recreation that Americans would require during the chaotic rush to defense industries and training camps. Soon after Pearl Harbor both Congress and the press were heaping ridicule and invective upon her for bringing "pinks, downright 'reds' and political hacks" into the OCD, particularly Mayris Chaney, a professional dancer appointed to the physical fitness division. The House voted to deny funds for the teaching of "fan dancing . . . or other public entertainments." On February 7, Roosevelt confided to Biddle that he would like his wife to leave the OCD. Ten days later she resigned. Lamenting the attack on Chaney, she observed, "To know me is a terrible thing."

The bombast diminished but did not end Mrs. Roosevelt's programs. Congress forbade them when it funded the OCD, but some survived in the subsequent Office of Defense Health and Welfare Services.[21]

Of far more consequence was public discontent over wartime shortages and rationing. These inevitably would come, and there was always present in Roosevelt's mind how unpopular they had been in 1918 and how serious their consequences had been for Democratic fortunes. As rationing began in 1942, both he and Mrs. Roosevelt made efforts to brace the public. During 1942, the OPA through local boards issued coupon books entitling users to purchase canned goods, sugar, coffee, meat, fats, and shoes.

The Roosevelts were not always successful in their efforts to discourage hoarding and to make rationing seem the democratic way to guarantee equal supplies for everyone. At a cabinet meeting in March, Nelson cited an occasion when Mrs. Roosevelt told women at a meeting that there would be a scarcity of soap. She urged them not to rush to the stores, but the result had been the opposite, a run on soap. Roosevelt good-naturedly commented, "My wife is too high-minded."

The first acute crisis that developed after Pearl Harbor was a rubber shortage. The Japanese drive into Southeast Asia cut off 90 percent of the supply of raw rubber. The head of the Reconstruction Finance Corporation, Jesse Jones, cautious with money, had built a stockpile of only 500,000 tons, no more than a fraction of projected wartime needs. A ton of rubber went into each tank under construction. Synthetic rubber was so expensive that few factories had been built; capacity was only 40,000 tons per year. To add to the complications, German submarines were concentrating with deadly effectiveness upon tankers bringing oil to the East Coast. At stake was the automobile, at the core of the American way of life, not only for recreation but for the transportation of workers and the trucking of much of the nation's goods. The sale of automobile tires had to be stopped immediately, and soon gasoline was short in the East.[22]

The outward appearance was of an impending disaster, which could ruin the war effort. Roosevelt was fearful that his opponents would seriously damage him with the rubber issue. He remarked facetiously to his cabinet in March, 1942, "that it looked as if his administration might go down in history with a smudge of rubber on it, just as the McKinley administration [during the Spanish-American War] had a smudge of embalmed beef." Nationwide rationing of gasoline would have eased the strain on both oil and rubber, but Roosevelt feared it would be too unpopular. Whence, then, the furor over the "rubber mess"? Bruce Catton, information director for the WPB, concluded bluntly after the war that it was "a refusal to admit that the American public could face the facts without recoiling angrily. . . . The President and Congress simply got scared." Roosevelt tried to function as a champion of voluntarism, set an unpopular 35-mile-per-hour speed limit, fostered an ineffective rubber scrap drive, and finally appointed a blue-ribbon committee to propose solutions to the rubber problem.

The committee proposed a new rubber director under WPB and nationwide gasoline rationing. Roosevelt appointed a strong director, but waited until after the 1942 election before ordering rationing. There was a pinch early in 1943, but soon the crisis was past, because of reduced use of automobiles, soaring synthetic rubber production, and a "Big Inch" pipeline that later in 1943 was delivering 335,000 barrels a day of Texas petroleum to the mid-Atlantic states.[23]

Chapter 31

THE STRUGGLE TO CONTAIN INFLATION

THE ASSAULTS upon wartime inflation controls were, as Roosevelt explained it to the press and public, very much like his wife's view of those on the Office of Civilian Defense — attacks by the privileged few upon the less fortunate. The problem of inflation was, of course, far more complex, involving demands of workers for higher wages and of producers for larger incomes.

It was not an easy contest. While consumers in general were demanding that prices be kept down, some were pressuring their senators and representatives for higher price ceilings on one or another commodity in which they had an interest. Or, on the basis of the rising cost of living, they were demanding that their incomes too be allowed to increase. Inflation could spell economic disaster and, as Roosevelt remembered from his campaign around the country in that inflationary year 1920, political backlash as well. Inflation was a threat he sought throughout the war to try to contain. He negotiated with legislators, worked with his administrators, and through press conference briefings and public speeches, tried to sway the nation. During the first fifteen months of the war he undertook to develop a system that would be both economically and politically viable. It was not easy. "Of course people are sitting up nights trying to invent new methods of accelerating inflation," he lamented to reporters in February, 1942, "and I am sitting up nights trying to block the acceleration."[1]

What Roosevelt was after, he said in June, 1943, was "a very old thing which hasn't yet been solved, and that is keeping the cost of living down." Price and wage instability was the major part of the problem, but there was also what Roosevelt referred to as the unexpended gap at the top of national income. "If people want something they will pay any old price for it, and therefore, the more that gap can be absorbed . . . the less danger of inflation there is." That was the reason for bond drives and heavy taxes. "And what I hope," Roosevelt pointed out, "is that we can get through this war without materially changing the buying power of the dollar that we get in our . . . pay checks."[2]

In the winter of 1942 the Senate had not yet acted on legislation to control prices, and was under pressure from the farm lobby. During the recession years of the later thirties, farm prices had been far below parity, and a majority of farmers in 1942, according to public opinion polls, would have been content with prevailing prices, or parity. Nonetheless, the House added provisions that would send agricultural prices well above 110 percent of parity. Disaster threatened during the week after Pearl Harbor, when, in the absence of controls, speculators forced the price of oils and fats sharply upward. Leon Henderson, an able economist, who since the summer of 1940 had headed the various price control programs, sent Roosevelt a chart delineating the speculative jump. He warned that, worse still, southerners in the Senate were trying to take away from him control over farm prices. Alarmed, Roosevelt turned to James F. Byrnes, who in 1941 had been appointed to the Supreme Court. Byrnes tried with mixed success to rally his old friends in the Senate behind the president.[3]

The various formulas for raising farm prices to 110 percent of parity remained in the completed bill. Roosevelt decided to sign it, since it possessed a number of strong points. As he indicated, it established a single administrator, good enforcement procedures, rent controls, and effective maximum price provisions, except for agricultural commodities. (He did not add what later turned out to be of signal importance, the authorization to pay subsidies.) "Perhaps it is the best we could have got at this time," he concluded. "We will undoubtedly have to step on the toes of a lot of people, which is again another inherent factor in wartime." He served notice that he might return to Congress for improvements in the measure.[4]

Improvements were indeed necessary, as the next few weeks demonstrated. Roosevelt, as expected, appointed the resourceful Henderson to be price administrator, and continued another economist, John Kenneth Galbraith, as Henderson's deputy, but they and other able administrators could not stem the rise in prices through selective controls.

Roosevelt particularly worried about the high ceiling on agricultural commodities. As a makeshift, he had the secretary of agriculture release enough of the large government-owned stocks of grain and cotton to stabilize their prices well under 110 percent of parity. Other anti-inflationary devices were not succeeding entirely. By March, 1942, food cost almost 5 percent, and clothing 7.7 percent, more than on the day of Pearl Harbor; the cost of living had risen 15 percent since September, 1939. Henderson predicted prices might rise 23 percent more by the end of 1942.[5]

The nation, as Roosevelt well realized, was reaching the critical point where, as a result of price increases, demands for wage increases could force spiraling inflation. Since Pearl Harbor, he had been seeking to avoid both major strikes and wage increases. A week and a half after the United States entered the war, he convened a management-labor conference in Washington, and found time to speak to its leaders extemporaneously. He exhorted them to reach unanimous agreement in a day or two on wartime labor policy and the machinery to enforce it. For nearly a week the unions and management were deadlocked over the issue of the closed shop, but Roosevelt told Secretary of Labor Frances Perkins, "Oh, well, I can handle that. We can't expect perfection." The president thereupon announced their agreement that there should be no strikes or lockouts; all disputes should be settled by peaceful means through the War Labor Board.[6]

Roosevelt's solution worked. On January 12, 1942, he created a new National War Labor Board, with authority that its predecessor had lacked, to impose arbitration and adjust general wage levels. It settled the closed-shop dispute by providing that, unless newly employed workers in an industry with a union contract resigned from the union within fifteen days, they had to remain in the union for the duration of the contract. It was a system that helped unions grow phenomenally during the war; their growth gave new fuel to the anger and resentment of those opposed to unions.

Already war workers were receiving what seemed to these critics outrageously large pay envelopes. They were working an average of forty-five or forty-six hours a week and earning time-and-a-half for over forty hours. But the workers were disgruntled because their wages during the defense period had not gone up as prices had increased. Since September, 1941, the steelworkers had been demanding that the four "Little Steel" companies increase their wages a dollar a day. It was the critical question facing the new War Labor Board, since as the Little Steel decision went, so was likely to go the wage level for all war industry.

A big responsibility faced the four public members of the National War Labor Board. Because the representatives of the unions and management would balance their votes against each other, decisions depended upon the public members, who were Roosevelt's appointees. They were a strong group, but before they could establish their new organization, cases piled up.

Workers, despairing because wages remained at low levels while living costs rose, went on wildcat strikes, and moderates as well as conservatives opened fire on Roosevelt. Wendell Willkie, *Time* noted, "blew [a] blistering bazoo at the White House." His were genteel words compared with the blasts by publicists and politicians, who made wild claims that strikes were wrecking vital production. H. V. Kaltenborn, a popular radio commentator, made the startling assertion that 200 bombers could have been built with the time lost in strikes in February, 1942. Roosevelt queried Donald Nelson, who assured him that only two strikes in February had even remotely involved aircraft production; they did not prevent completion of a single bomber.[7]

Simultaneously a widespread campaign was under way to abolish the forty-hour week. The conservative Virginia Democrat Howard W. Smith introduced a repeal amendment in the House. Roosevelt immediately pointed out that the effect would be to eliminate not overtime, but the time-and-a-half pay for it. He declared, "I don't want to have people get less in their pay envelopes than they are getting today, especially with the cost of living going up." Several times Roosevelt did suggest to his administrators that the time-and-a-half for hours over forty per week go to the workers as war bonds, but he never tried to put the scheme into effect. Labor protests would have been vehement and disruptive. What made the anti–forty-hour movement popular among many people, Roosevelt deduced, was a misconception. The antiunion forces had fooled them into thinking that existing legislation forbade a longer work week.[8]

Before opponents could muster majorities in Congress and movements to increase wages and prices became irrevocably strong, Roosevelt had to develop a more comprehensive anti-inflation program. Heavier taxes to drain excess buying power were imperative. As to compliance, there was a basic policy difference between Morgenthau and other administrators. Smith, Henderson of the Office of Price Administration (OPA), and Eccles of the Federal Reserve all felt that there should be a large element of compulsion in the overall program, especially forced savings and a wage freeze. Morgenthau insisted as far as possible upon voluntary programs. Roosevelt was torn between the recommendations. Smith noted, "When the President was confronted with the specific things . . . he showed signs of worrying about some of the details. . . . [They] added up to a pretty stiffly regimented economy for the period of the war."[9]

After lengthy negotiations, Roosevelt announced a seven-point overall anti-inflation program. It was simple, readable, and depended for its effectiveness largely upon powers Roosevelt already possessed. It required only that Congress, as was expected, should enact wartime price increases, and, as was in doubt, lower the ceiling on crop prices. Tax increases, he said, should fall heavily upon profits. There he threw in one of the most controversial of his proposals, that in that time of "grave national danger, when all excess income should go to win the war, no American citizen ought to have a net income, after he had paid his taxes, of more than $25,000 a year."

Americans would have to give up much to which they were accustomed, Roosevelt declared. Living standards would have to come down. He put it more dramatically in his Fireside Chat the next evening, "The price for civilization must be paid in hard work and sorrow and blood."[10]

The immediate effect was administrative measures to make the cost of war fall less hard upon consumers of limited means. The most vital step came on April 28, 1942, the day after the message, when the OPA moved from selective price ceilings to blanket ones. The critical difficulty was the control of farm prices.[11]

Wage stabilization also continued to create problems. While the National War Labor Board was being organized, several other branches of the government tried to set wage scales, often focused more upon stimulating production than restraining inflation. During the debates over policy on the War Labor Board, the labor members became so angered that they threatened to withdraw; Roosevelt personally had to persuade them to stay. Finally, in July, 1942, they reached agreement on the Little Steel formula. The steelworkers would receive a onetime raise to bring their wages up to the 15 percent increase in living costs. There could be exceptions only for those laboring under substandard conditions. Workers favored the formula, a government poll indicated. The OPA administrators opposed wage increases as living costs crept upward, feeling the war required some sacrifice. The *Wall Street Journal* firmly took the same position. The steel workers received not the dollar a day they had sought but 44 cents, raising their wages 17.4 percent. The formula, applied to all industry, would have raised consumer purchasing power $3.5 billion, destroying price ceilings. Chairman William H. Davis of the War Labor Board observed that the trimming of living standards and purchasing power should be the responsibility not of the WLB, but of Congress, which should vote tax increases.[12]

There was no area in which politics more skewed the economic ideal than wartime taxation. Both tax theory and the rhetoric of Congress in the 1930s had set clear guidelines: taxation should be so heavy that it would stifle inflation, drain the profits out of the war, and lighten the tax burden on future generations. Roosevelt persisted in expounding this formula, but it was distasteful to the electorate, which, after years of depression privation, savored the wartime recovery. Roosevelt to a limited degree, and Congress wholeheartedly, acted in response to the voters.

Congress, little affected by the urgencies of war, was as deliberate as in peacetime in considering the 1942 tax bill. Roosevelt, determined to be conciliatory, accepted the minimal Treasury proposal of only $7 billion in new taxes, and stayed with it even after his anti-inflation committee recommended $11.6 billion and $2 billion more in social security levies. As war production soared and the threat of inflation grew, he authorized Morgenthau to up the request by only a billion dollars. Congressional leaders ignored these proposals. Their reluctance might have been attributed to the fact that it was an election year, and even in wartime they worried about reprisals from voters.

Roosevelt was singularly mild and patient. He seemed to have few strongly fixed views on taxes, except for his insistence that somehow personal incomes be limited to $25,000 after taxes. It was an idea to which he gave much effort, but it was not to be. In the fall, he established the $25,000 limit through executive order, and Congress, disposed to act speedily in this instance, legislated it out of existence.[13]

Those at the lower end of the tax bracket also concerned Roosevelt, who insisted they must not carry too much of a burden. He held to his opinion that a sales tax (which if enacted would have had to be 10 percent to raise sufficient revenue) must be a last resort. On the sales tax, there were enough like-thinking Congressmen to bear him out. None of the views of Roosevelt had much impact. Neither was he successful in putting pressure upon Congress to hasten the tax bill. He told reporters he hoped the House Ways and Means Committee would not take it amiss if he said, not as criticism but as a statement of fact, that the Treasury was losing a great deal of money through the delay.[14]

One thing was certain: the New Deal and wartime experiences had not transformed Roosevelt into either a Keynesian or a Hamiltonian. One of his dreams in 1942 was worthy of Jefferson and Jackson. He remarked to Morgenthau in July, 1942, "Supposing we end this war with a debt of $200 billions and I could cut down the expenses of the Government to about $10 billions a year — (I was surprised he used the word 'I') — and our receipts were around $20 billions a year . . . I could wipe out the debt in about 20 years." Several months later he repeated the proposal to his cabinet.[15]

Ultimately in October, Congress passed the Revenue Act of 1942. It provided only an estimated $7 billion in new taxes, not the conservative $8.7 billion the administration had requested. It did raise the top bracket of personal income tax from 77 to 81 percent.[16]

Although the new tax measure was short of what Roosevelt wanted and the nation needed if inflation were to be stopped, it seriously affected almost all Americans. In 1939, only 4 million people had to pay income taxes; by 1942 the number had risen to 17 million, and in 1944 it was up to 42 million. The "Victory Tax," a 5 percent surtax, bore heavily upon those earning little more than the $624 exemption. The escalating higher brackets of the income tax brought Roosevelt's own income down not far above the $25,000 net limit he had sought. "Next year the taxes on $75,000 will leave me only about $30,000 net," he wrote in a memorandum to his wife, "and SOMETHING HAS TO BE DONE!" He felt he had to cut his contribution to the White House food budget from $24,000 a year to $18,000, and suggested that some of the servants who had to be fed be transferred to other government positions.[17]

The failure of Congress to enact sufficiently heavy taxes made more imperative alternate devices to drain off excess purchasing power. Roosevelt in the end favored voluntary purchase of war bonds and savings stamps. Morgenthau told his staff that at a cabinet meeting in July, 1942, "The President said. . . . 'Henry has promised to raise $1,000,000,000 a month and he's got his neck out and', he said, 'let him hang himself if he wants to or else — then he did his (gesture of hand across the throat as if cutting from ear to ear) — 'his head goes caput!' "[18]

Morgenthau not only attained but exceeded his bond sales quota in 1942. Altogether there were, in addition to payroll deduction plans, eight war bond drives, which, although avoiding the sensational, high-pressure tactics of the First World War, left consumers at the end of the war with an estimated $129 billion in liquid savings — a substantial cushion against a new depression. The voluntary system of savings through war bonds was only partially successful in easing inflationary pressure, as such a small proportion of the war borrowing was from small investors.[19]

The major check on inflation had to be price and wage ceilings, and it was manifest in the early summer of 1942 that these bulwarks were in danger of being breached. Congress still refused to reduce ceilings on farm produce to parity, and indeed reaffirmed its support of the 110 percent provision, although a Gallup poll indicated in June that 58 percent of the farmers were satisfied with crop prices. Retailers and consumers were being caught in the squeeze between rising wholesale prices on fruits and vegetables being canned in the summer of 1942 and the frozen retail ceilings. Roosevelt temporarily turned to subsidies. "Pending clarification of the policy of Congress," he wrote Secretary of Agriculture Claude Wickard, "I am asking you to use Commodity Credit Corporation funds."[20]

While making use of this makeshift device, Roosevelt was giving long, cautious thought to a more lasting restraint. At a cabinet meeting on July 10, he noted that the prices of some canned goods had gone up 15 percent, and turning to Miss Perkins, said, "Listen closely, I am going to have an overall ceiling on everything, including labor." Morgenthau responded, "Well, Mr. President, whatever you do you had better do it fairly soon, because this thing is getting away from you."[21]

Although Congress had been reluctant to place firm restrictions upon agricultural prices, Roosevelt still preferred to obtain ceilings through legislation if he could. He showed a draft resolution to the Democratic leaders and, as he informed his cabinet, found they wanted none of it. "There are two ways of doing it . . . ," Roosevelt said to Morgenthau on July 22. "The other way is . . . by getting an opinion from the Attorney General that I have the war powers to do it."[22]

For weeks Roosevelt grappled with the question whether he had adequate power to act without further legislation. Rosenman became nervous and complained to Morgenthau:

"The thing that worries me is the President is so complacent. . . . [and] doesn't devote more than two days a week to the war. . . . I have tried one month to get him to look at this Executive Order, and you heard him this morning. . . . I have been up at Shang-ri-la [Roosevelt's weekend camp] three times and he sits there playing with his stamps."

Morgenthau responded, "Well, maybe he thinks."[23]

Indeed, Roosevelt did have to think — not simply about the anti-inflation program, but simultaneously about several dozen other domestic and military matters. At a single meeting with the assistant director of the budget, Wayne Coy, in August, 1942, Roosevelt set forth his views on training of personnel for postwar military governments, the merger of domestic and international communications systems, the future of overseas air transport, especially in Latin America, rubber conservation and gasoline rationing, construction of the St. Lawrence Seaway, proposed rehabilitation legislation, and the funding of the Office of Strategic Services, Colonel William J. Donovan's intelligence empire. On most of these complex matters, Roosevelt had detailed views. On some others, he was not so sure. He responded to a September memo on one of these questions, "Please get everybody together on this whole matter. I get so many conflicting recommendations that my head goes round."[24]

As for the anti-inflation program, by late August Roosevelt had solved the labor end of his equation. Rosenman brought to the Oval Office the dean of the University of Oregon Law School, Wayne Morse. He was a liberal Republican, and the member of the War Labor Board who had written the Little Steel decision.

Roosevelt told Morse that he was familiar with what he had set forth in the Little Steel decision, and thoroughly agreed with him. Morse had declared, "The war power implies the right to do anything that may seem necessary to carry out the war successfully, even to the extent of performing otherwise unconstitutional acts." Roosevelt then sounded out Morse on whether War Labor Board increases would be inflationary. If so, Roosevelt could then veto them. Morse thought that would take too much time, and would be hard for labor to swallow. He recommended that whatever Roosevelt did should be on as direct a line as possible between his war powers and the War Labor Board. Roosevelt replied, "I think that after I have passed on five or six cases it will be perfectly clear what the policy is. . . . But I don't think it will take so much time. I think that we can get labor to go along with it." Morse was not so sure. "Labor is afraid of an economic dictatorship," he told Roosevelt. "They insist upon their bargaining rights. They want a vote."

If indeed what Roosevelt had in mind was a rollback from the Little Steel decision, Morse was not encouraging. Philip Murray, the head of the United Steel Workers and the CIO, was trying to obtain for the Big Steel unions the same wage increase that had gone to workers in the smaller steel companies. Murray still did not like the Little Steel formula, Morse told the president, but the day before had told the WLB that he had sold it to the union on the basis of a conversation with Roosevelt.[25]

On the question of setting farm price ceilings, Morse was more reassuring. Roosevelt put a question to him: "There is a section in the Price Act (3a) which says that farm parity must be maintained in accordance with the act and cannot be changed by any other power of Government. Do you think that stops me?"

Morse replied, "No. Congress can pass all the laws it wants to, but if you decide that a certain course of action is essential as a war measure, it supersedes congressional action. It is a drastic thing to do." The president agreed, adding, "But I wish you would talk to Sam." Finally Rosenman, who was now legal adviser as well as speech-writer for the president, came to accept the view of the attorney general and Morse, and prepared an executive order.[26]

Accordingly, Roosevelt decided to go ahead with a firm policy toward farmers, flouting an act of Congress, but he abandoned the idea of new, stronger controls over labor. Whether it was his feeling of moral commitment to the Little Steel formula, or his fear of labor outrage and strikes, he stayed with existing arrangements.

When news of the impending action reached Justice Hugo Black, he was so upset that he took the unusual course of pouring out his misgivings to Ickes, who conveyed them to Roosevelt. The president, said Black, had no affirmative powers, and would in effect as commander in chief be brushing aside an act of Congress. He guessed that the courts would be asked to intervene and would hold the action to be unconstitutional. According to Ickes:

"Hugo said that there had been many accusations that the President was attempting to set up a dictatorship, and that if he should claim these powers he would be adding fuel to that flame. He pointed out that while Hitler is exercising the same power, he had at least gone through the formality of obtaining a grant of power from the Reichstag."[27]

Before rumblings could turn into revolt, Roosevelt modified his scheme. On the night of a cabinet meeting, he telephoned Justice Byrnes, who suggested an alternate plan, that the president inform Congress that if it did not act by October 1, he would exercise his power in the belief that he possessed it.[28]

Roosevelt, taken with the idea, presented it to the cabinet immediately as his own: "I have a new thought — to use an old plan which I used three or four years ago when they gave me the power to reorganize, but I had to wait 60 days before putting it into effect. What I am thinking of doing is to use the same plan, but give them only until October 1st."[29]

And so Roosevelt did. First, in a meeting with William Green of the AFL and Philip Murray of the CIO and in a press conference, then in his message to Congress and a Fireside Chat, he undertook to sell his new program as a means of stopping inflation and reconciling the interests of two groups who should not be in conflict, farmers and labor.[30]

In the process of arriving at a freeze of agricultural prices, Roosevelt came under conflicting pressures and, as so frequently, engaged in vacillation and compromise. He accepted the arguments of Henderson of the OPA and Nelson of the WPB in favor of using a small subsidy of $70 to $100 million to keep food prices down. An assistant to the secretary of agriculture lamented, "This episode reveals clearly the

President's weakness, his tendency to let things drift, his preoccupation with politics, and his lack of realization of what good organization means."[31]

In this fashion, Roosevelt negotiated a viable program. He sent a strong message to Congress on September 7, asking specific authorization to stabilize prices of farm commodities, and warning that if it did not act by October 1, he would act under his war powers. He added the reassuring promise that when the war was won, the powers under which he acted would automatically revert to the people.[32]

Roosevelt's summer-long delay in action worked out well. Public pressure had grown to the point that it countered the agricultural interests, and Congress, with elections only two months off, was more responsive than earlier. The powerful Republican Senate leader, Robert Taft, was helpful.[33]

Essentially Roosevelt obtained the authorization he had sought, and signed the Stabilization Act on October 2, 1942. Immediately he acted, as he said, "to stabilize 90 percent of the country's food bill," and to blanket the nation with rent control. The War Labor Board, possessing for the first time affirmative power to limit wages, was able to restrict monthly wage increases to a tenth of a percent, a sixth of what they had previously been.[34]

Under the new, tighter controls disputes among the war agencies and pressures from Congress were certain to continue. Roosevelt, eager to ease the burden of having to decide among the rival claimants with complex arguments that made his head spin, established a new agency, the Office of Economic Stabilization. Its director should serve as a central policymaker, watchdog, and above all mediator. A month before, Morgenthau had proposed Justice Douglas for the position, and Roosevelt countered that he preferred Justice Byrnes, giving the curious reason that "this is a very judicial job." It was also very political, and Byrnes, deeply engaged in the deft handling of Congress, was an ideal choice. Congress, making life miserable for OPA Director Henderson, was seriously threatening stabilization. Roosevelt summoned Byrnes to the presidential bedroom and urged him to take leave from the Supreme Court and become director. Byrnes, feeling that many of the decisions would have political implications, out of propriety resigned from the court.[35]

Byrnes, who had his office in the White House, came to be known as "assistant president" on the home front. Roosevelt, who previously had so jealously guarded his powers, had long since made Hopkins a vital surrogate on some aspects of the conduct of the war. Now he was doing the same with Byrnes, and indeed transferring to Byrnes jurisdiction over some matters that had been on Hopkins' desk.

As Byrnes later remembered it, his working relationship with Roosevelt was smooth. Whenever members of Congress, labor leaders, businessmen, farm spokesmen, and others could, they saw the president to plead their special needs. He would listen, nodding his understanding, and then tell them, "You know, Justice Byrnes is temperamental on this subject. I do not want to talk with him about it but you should go over and see him." Because inequities had to be remedied, and pressures were great, Byrnes had to make upward economic adjustments. In the first six months of the stabilization program the cost-of-living index rose 4.3 percent. "The line was bent in many places," he concluded, "but it held much better than I ever expected."[36]

Roosevelt had his basic machinery for war administration in place.

Chapter 32

STRIKING BACK AMID DISASTERS

THE first months of 1942, a winter of despair for the American people, brought an unalleviated succession of disasters in the Pacific, in the Atlantic, and on the Russian front. Even Roosevelt was not always as buoyant and self-confident as he tried to appear. "FDR is grand," Mrs. Roosevelt informed a British relative, "Stands up even under [the fall of] Singapore without a ripple in his serenity." But at a time of better news in April, Roosevelt confided to his wife that the previous week he had felt disturbed and depressed. During the winter, *Time* reported, he was testy, suffering from war nerves.[1]

It was a serene president who in a February Fireside Chat explained that the nation on all fronts must be active like an eagle, not defensive like a turtle. Yet in fact, activity on all fronts was hardly possible. The price for the bolstering of Britain with weapons and supplies had to be paid in 1942. The United States had entered the war quite unprepared to launch large-scale assaults against either Japan or Germany. It would be a year or two before the armadas and armies were ready.[2]

Despite the lack of adequate forces, Roosevelt resolved to strike unexpected blows against both enemies to throw them off stride and to bolster lagging morale. There was not much the United States could do to save the Philippines, but he and his commanders insisted upon fighting there to the end. When Roosevelt in February rejected firmly President Manuel Quezon's suggestion that the islands be neutralized, Marshall years later recalled, "I decided he was a great man." The president bestowed the Congressional Medal of Honor upon General Douglas MacArthur, by this time a popular hero, for his exploits on the Bataan peninsula, and had him whisked out to Australia. There

MacArthur began developing the forces with which to halt and turn back the Japanese drives southward.[3]

Although Roosevelt was unable to save the Philippines, he tried to muster the support of Asiatic peoples against the Japanese. Early in 1942, he sought particularly to stimulate the resistance of the Chinese and the people of India. For the president, the Chinese government of Chiang Kai-shek, the Kuomintang, appeared to be a source of limitless manpower, which through American financing could be transformed into legions that would tie down Japanese forces. Indeed, that was the role China had been playing in his calculations during much of the 1930s — keeping the Japanese Army endlessly involved as it moved deeper into the countryside but never attained total victory. The involvement of the United States in the war against Japan meant for the rejoicing Kuomintang officials the promise of a flow of money and of supplies with which to build strength for their coming confrontation with the Chinese Communists.[4]

Ignorant of realities, Roosevelt clung to notions that he had cherished since boyhood. "Well, now, we've been friends with China for a great many years," he declared in 1943 to an irritated General Joseph Stilwell, seeking direction. "I ascribe a large part of this feeling to the missionaries. You know I have a China history. My grandfather went out there. . . ."[5]

This was correct as far as it went, but did not take into account the complex politics and problems in Chungking. Chiang lacked the strength to control corruption, yet was too strong for his opponents within the Kuomintang to overthrow. The warning of Ambassador Clarence Gauss that China was not likely to become an effective military ally either did not reach or did not impress the president. Rather, Roosevelt, as his White House assistant Lauchlin Currie had been urging, sought to reform and reinvigorate China, and elevate it to the status of a great nation that could fill the power vacuum that the defeat of Japan would create in East Asia. Roosevelt never fully appreciated what an impossibly weak regime he was trying to strengthen into peacekeeper of postwar Asia.

In the weeks after Pearl Harbor, Roosevelt, intent upon a Germany-first strategy, was vague about the means to transform China. When Chiang sought a billion-dollar loan without any proposals for its expenditure, Roosevelt granted half that amount as a means to cheer Chiang, unhappy over the diversion of lend-lease supplies to the Burma theater. Much of it served not to control but to fuel Chinese inflation, and to fatten the bank accounts of officials and the elite. Little served to strengthen the Chinese Army, or to attain Roosevelt's chief end, turning back the Japanese in Burma and keeping open a road to China. Roosevelt and officials in Washington tolerated the corrupt dissipation of the funds because they hoped for the friendship of China in postwar years.[6]

One immediate gain for the United States was Chiang's agreement that an American officer could come to Chungking to serve as his chief of staff. General Marshall sent him Stilwell, who had spent years in China, spoke Chinese, and was determined to mold its army into a fighting force. Stilwell, whose men with some reason called him "Vinegar Joe," referred to Chiang in his diary as "Peanut" — a code name that qui[illegible] Stilwell failed to respond to the charm of [illegible] his inauspicious beginning, Roo[illegible] policy gradually led to more [illegible]ed to straighten out the [illegible] but more serious crises [illegible] dribbling of aid only

[illegible]ruary, 1942, as the [illegible]a, was the fate of [illegible]urned to Roosevelt [illegible]ntic Charter in Au[illegible]mpathetic. In con[illegible] in September, 1941, [illegible]tish Empire. Roose[illegible]dia committed to war [illegible]British ally. The result [illegible] to Churchill nor to the

[illegible] Asia forced Churchill to budge. He cab[illegible]ernment was considering an offering of dominion status to India after the war. In response, Roosevelt urged that India receive full independence, and suggested that it progress along a path analogous to the fledgling United States, which had begun with the tentative, weak Articles of Confederation government and moved on to the strong new Constitution.[9]

Roosevelt was so proud of this scheme that several times he regaled his cabinet and visitors with an account of it, together with a much expanded lecture on the Confederation period. On one occasion he even asserted that Churchill had repeatedly asked his advice on India.[10]

Churchill saw no parallels. He cited the difficulties among the Hindus and Moslems, and his obligations toward the untouchables and the princely states. None of these concerns seemed to make an impression upon Roosevelt, as he followed closely the negotiations that several missions undertook in India.

The day after Churchill received Roosevelt's proposal, he dispatched a special mission headed by Sir Stafford Cripps, which attracted much attention in American newspapers. Cripps proposed dominion status, and that only after the war.[11]

The offer was far from acceptable to Jawaharlal Nehru, or to Mohandas K. Gandhi, who called it a postdated check. Roosevelt sent a personal representative, Louis Johnson, sympathetic toward the Indians, who tried to negotiate a compromise. When Roosevelt suggested that the deadlock was caused by British unwillingness to concede the right of self-government to the Indians, Churchill reacted explosively. His threat to resign rather than to give in to American public opinion made a marked impression. Firm as Roosevelt's conviction was that India should gradually obtain its independence, his need for Churchill's cooperation in the war was greater.[12]

In the fall of 1942, Wendell Willkie forced Roosevelt to make at least a public gesture toward Indian nationalism. After a globe-circling trip, Willkie alarmed Americans by declaring that the nation was "punching holes in our reservoir of good will . . . by our failure to define clearly our war aims," and gave India as an example. Roosevelt thereupon sent to New Delhi his old friend William Phillips, who to his surprise strongly espoused the Congress party viewpoint. Although Roosevelt did not back Phillips, he did cite his views to prod Churchill, then in Washington. Churchill, annoyed, retorted, "Take India if that is what you want! . . . But I warn you that if I open the door a crack there will be the greatest blood-bath in all history."[13]

By the end of 1942 there was no longer a Japanese threat to India; indeed, there never had been more than a slight likelihood of a serious invasion. Roosevelt's anticolonialism grew in fervor, at least in private, but he seemed reconciled to wait until the end of the war to dismantle the old empires. He was immediately concerned with postwar planning only insofar as it stimulated Asiatics to resist the Japanese.

Early in 1942, when almost all the news was bad, Roosevelt did inspire one joint army-navy action that aroused enthusiasm among the American people. On April 18, sixteen carrier-launched bombers under the command of Lieutenant Colonel James H. Doolittle came in low over Tokyo, dropped their bombs, and flew on toward China. They ran out of fuel before reaching safe airfields, yet all but nine of the eighty men survived. When reporters asked where the planes had come from,

Roosevelt joked that they were from a new secret base in Shangri-la, the locale of James Hilton's utopian novel, *Lost Horizon*. Later Roosevelt gave the name to his new hideaway in the Maryland mountains. President Eisenhower was to rename it Camp David.

"We have had a good crack at Japan by air," Roosevelt crowed to Churchill, but the only achievement at the time seemed to be to create the false impression in the United States that the navy was on the offensive, at the cost of sixteen bombers and the diversion of two carriers needed to counter a coming Japanese offensive in the South Pacific.[14] Yet there were unexpected larger gains. Admiral Yamamoto felt humiliated; the attack ended hesitation over a proposed Japanese attack on Midway Island, to be followed by the invasion of the Hawaiian Islands. That in turn speeded up the Japanese Navy's South Pacific venture, although their move toward Midway left them with only two carriers for an attack on Port Moresby, the only remaining allied base on New Guinea. The United States Navy, successfully cracking some of the Japanese coded messages, was aware of the forthcoming Midway offensive, and dispatched a second carrier to strengthen its meager forces.[15]

In the resulting Battle of the Coral Sea, the navy permanently halted the Japanese drive toward New Guinea. The United States lost the greater tonnage but sufficiently damaged two Japanese carriers to prevent them from participating in the forthcoming crucial engagement at Midway Island.[16]

The stakes in the Japanese assault on Midway Island were enormous. If Admiral Yamamoto had been successful in his main objective, to annihilate the United States Fleet, he would have swept on to occupy Hawaii. The West Coast of the United States would have been vulnerable and the war greatly prolonged. As yet the Japanese forces in the Pacific were more formidable than those of the United States. Consequently, much hinged on how much credence Admiral Nimitz at Pearl Harbor gave to the scraps of Japanese messages that navy cryptographers were cracking. They all pointed to Midway Island, and Nimitz persuaded King to let him act accordingly. The American forces were waiting in strength at Midway, including even the carrier *Yorktown*, damaged in the Coral Sea engagement and hastily repaired.

The Americans achieved victory. Outnumbered, they had engaged in careful planning; the Japanese, confident of victory, were by no means as well trained and effective as they had been at Pearl Harbor. Into the second day of the battle, the Japanese seemed ahead, then in six minutes that changed the course of the war in the Pacific, navy dive-bombers destroyed three Japanese carriers. Later in the day they sank a fourth.

Altogether the Japanese lost four carriers, a heavy cruiser, and 330 planes; the Americans, one carrier — the weakened *Yorktown* — and 150 planes.[17]

Gradually it became apparent that the Japanese Fleet was abandoning its bold strategy. During the summer it moved toward a defensive position, engaging in a war of attrition as the United States pushed back along the edge of the Japanese conquests, preparing to land forces in the Solomon Islands.

Although Roosevelt was intensely concerned with initiating a second front across the Atlantic, he was scarcely involved in the Pacific except to give his approval to Admiral King's proposal in March for a limited offensive in the Solomons. The nightmare campaign began well on August 7, when marines landed on Guadalcanal and two adjacent islands.

Two nights later came a crushing setback. A Japanese cruiser squadron surprised the American Fleet south of Savo Island, sank four cruisers, and damaged another cruiser and two destroyers. To keep the Japanese from knowing the extent of their victory, Admiral King withheld the news, even from the president. That very day, ironically, Roosevelt sent him a teasing note quoting a "sweet young thing" as saying that "the toughest man in the Navy — Admiral King — . . . shaves every morning with a blowtorch."[18]

At first the Japanese Army looked upon the marine landing as a raid, the numbers of the troops were so few and their equipment so inadequate. As the Japanese came to realize the seriousness of the threat they pounded the airfield, renamed Henderson Field, and attacked American pilots, who fought well despite the inferiority of their planes. Congressman Lyndon Johnson, returning from naval service in the Pacific, told Ickes he had found the American airplanes old, heavy, and slow, far poorer than the Japanese Zeros. Ickes asked if he had told this to Roosevelt. "Well," said Johnson, "I spent an hour with him and I told him what I could but you know how it is when you are trying to tell something to the President. He is always trying to tell something to you." Roosevelt had no desire to let Johnson talk about the airplanes in the Pacific, since the newer American planes were being shipped across the Atlantic to engage the Luftwaffe. On the ground the Japanese also had superior strength.[19]

Throughout the fall the attrition the Japanese inflicted in the South Pacific worried Roosevelt and forced the diversion of resources and army units to the area. The Pacific Fleet by November had lost two aircraft carriers and had only the *Enterprise* left. Roosevelt remarked at a cabinet meeting that even if the United States could not hold the Solomon Islands, the delaying action had been of great value.[20]

At this point a naval victory reversed the Japanese tide. At the end of November, Roosevelt informed Stalin that the United States had hit the Japanese very hard in the Solomons and had probably broken the backbone of their fleet, "although they still have too many aircraft carriers to suit me." Bitter fighting continued, the American forces had established their supremacy, and in January, the Japanese high command ordered their troops evacuated.[21]

Despite the heavy fighting in the South Pacific, Americans began to realize that Germany was the most dangerous foe. U-boats throughout the year took a heavy toll among unprotected oil tankers and cargo vessels along the Atlantic Coast. There were little more than five coastal patrol vessels to oppose them, since the destroyers were protecting ships bound for Europe. In March submarines sank twenty-eight vessels; in November overall Allied losses reached an all-time high of more than 600,000 tons. Oil spills, flotsam, and an occasional corpse washed onto beaches from Miami to Cape Cod. The sinkings caused calamitous shortages of oil, and to the irritation of consumers forced the rationing of sugar and coffee. Roosevelt conceded to Churchill, "My Navy had been definitely slack in preparing for this submarine war off our coast." Effective antisubmarine measures were to come only later.[22]

Although the exigencies of 1942 forced Roosevelt to allocate a large part of the nation's armed strength to the Pacific, his imperative objective was to keep Russia in the war through bringing some pressure upon Hitler as soon as possible. Roosevelt and Churchill and their advisers agreed there must be action. But, concealed from the public, they engaged in a vigorous debate through much of the first half of the year about whether it should be a direct thrust across the English Channel or an oblique attack on the periphery of the German and Italian circle of conquests. While Marshall and the head of his war-planning section, Eisenhower, favored striking directly at Germany in order to defeat it most quickly, Churchill sold Roosevelt on a scheme to send troops into French North Africa to forestall a German move across the Strait of Gibraltar.[23]

Marshall, Stimson, and the war planners felt that Churchill was seeking to use American forces not to bring the war to the speediest possible conclusion, but rather to bolster the British Empire. What they overlooked was a critical factor, that the British were so short of troops that they could not undertake an attack across the channel unless it was almost certain to be a success. There was no remaining British margin to permit errors and subsequent assaults. The Americans also failed to take into account that the venture would have to be largely British and that the American forces would be limited in number and unseasoned.

What came about was a strategy for the next two years quite different from what Marshall and his staff wished to pursue. It was the outcome of the most crucial conflict during the entire war between the commander in chief and the generals. Marshall and Eisenhower wished to concentrate upon preparing for a cross-channel invasion, if absolutely necessary in 1942, and firmly in 1943. If the army did not cross the channel in 1942, the men and supplies should remain in Great Britain until the following year, when they would drive toward the heart of Germany. Nonetheless, Roosevelt ultimately ordered North African landings to take place in the fall of 1942 — in the view of Marshall, a diversion that led inevitably to further diversions.

It is easy to view the differences in the spring of 1942 between Roosevelt and his staff, and between the Americans and the British, as being sharper than evidence at the time would indicate. All of them had to maintain a balance among priorities while aiming toward the ultimate cross-channel attack. Roosevelt, as was his custom, behind his facade of quick, dynamic proposals was deliberate, weighing the conflicting demands, again and again turning discussions toward immediate pressures and away from the ultimate objective. Later Stimson remembered his fear of the "trial balloons" Roosevelt was so fond of sending aloft. Marshall concurred. "Roosevelt had a habit of tossing out new operations," he once reminisced. "I called it his cigarette-holder gesture." The president, without making any final commitment, was moving warily toward the major buildup in Britain while he was immediately plugging the global ratholes.[24]

As the thinking of the American planners crystallized, according to Eisenhower, they were of the opinion that a massive invasion of France would not be possible before the spring of 1944. Rather, what they hoped to accomplish was to establish a bridgehead in the fall of 1942, or more likely in the spring of 1943. Already they had identified the area where indeed they ultimately landed, on the Cotentin peninsula leading out to Cherbourg on the coast of Normandy. They hoped to put ashore considerably more force than they were assigning to the Dieppe raid to take place later that summer, seal off the peninsula, and hold it until a major invasion was possible.[25]

At the end of March, Roosevelt sent Marshall and Hopkins to seek the consent of the prime minister. Churchill during the meeting displayed a charming ambiguity comparable to that for which Roosevelt was renowned. He did not want to discourage the buildup, since he feared that otherwise the United States would concentrate upon the Pacific, so he was not open in expressing his preference for a Norwegian or North African diversion. The agreement was in principle, and many of the British expressed one or another reservation. General Sir Hastings Ismay wished in retrospect they had been more candid in expressing their abhorrence of the bloodbath that they thought a 1942 bridgehead attempt almost certainly would become. As it was, Marshall and Hopkins brought back to Roosevelt what seemed to be a firm agreement.[26]

In the spring of 1942, Roosevelt felt briefly that a cross-channel attack that year was both feasible and the best way to ease the German pressure upon Russia. He was worried about the staying power of the Soviet armies and troubled that feelers between the Russians and Germans might lead to a separate peace. He hoped for a summer meeting with Stalin but for fear it might come too late, he persuaded Stalin to send his foreign minister, Vyacheslav Molotov, to visit Washington immediately.

At the time Molotov arrived, Roosevelt felt that he could hold his own in negotiations with the Russians. Stalin had been pressing a treaty upon Churchill guaranteeing the Soviet boundaries as of the time of Hitler's attack. That would mean recognizing the Soviet annexation of the Baltic states and eastern Poland — the fruits of Stalin's pact with Hitler in 1939. Roosevelt objected to it, fearing the wrath of Americans with roots in the annexed areas, and of both Wilsonian idealists and conservatives. The British deleted mention of boundaries from the draft treaty, and surprisingly Molotov while in London obtained Stalin's approval. The obstacle that had concerned Roosevelt and the State Department for months was out of the way.[27]

In his discussions with Roosevelt, Molotov focused upon the second front. He argued that if the Anglo-American forces could divert forty of Hitler's divisions, the Red Army could strike a decisive blow against the German forces. Roosevelt parried by pointing out problems of landing equipment on the beaches, and Marshall emphasized the need to destroy the German air force before operating on the continent. Roosevelt, with Marshall's consent, said Stalin could be informed that the United States was preparing for a second front that year. Marshall wanted to delete the reference to 1942, but Roosevelt overrode his objection. In addition, Roosevelt gave firm assurances covering almost everything Stalin had sought in territorial claims. Assistant Secretary of State Berle lamented Roosevelt's concessions as a "Baltic Munich." The president also proposed to Molotov that the Soviet Union join the United States, Britain, and perhaps China, to act as one of the postwar peacekeepers. Roosevelt, despite his unsatisfactory encounters in earlier years, seemed to feel he could trust the Russians as he did the British.[28]

Concerned over Roosevelt's strong words to Molotov, Churchill and the British acted immediately and energetically to deflect the president from a cross-channel attack in 1942. Lord Louis Mountbatten brought him the sobering news that there were twenty-five German divisions stationed in France; the invasion force could not be large enough to divert additional German divisions from the Russian front. The conversation swung around to North Africa, and Roosevelt remarked how much he had been struck by Churchill's words that they must not lose sight of an operation there. He seemed to accept it as a second choice.[29]

Several setbacks forced a reappraisal of plans in the late spring. Russian forces were floundering, Americans were having trouble sending troops and supplies across the Atlantic, and Field Marshall Erwin Rommel's Afrika Korps was routing the British in Libya. Before Churchill could arrive for fresh discussions, Roosevelt met with his military advisers to express his concern over the Russian plight. He was determined that the United States should not keep sizable forces in reserve in Britain, but engage them before the end of the year against the Germans, either across the channel or in North Africa or the Middle East. If the Russians could hold until December, he felt the United Nations could win the war; otherwise he gave them less than an even chance. Therefore he ordered fresh feasibility studies.[30]

Weeks of debate followed over where the Americans should fight. Marshall and Stimson vigorously opposed North Africa and the Middle East; King, Stimson lamented, "wobbled around." Sir Alan Brooke, the British chief of staff, when he arrived opposed both the North Africa landing and a 1942 bridgehead in France. Churchill and Roosevelt, meeting in June, 1942, at Hyde Park, discussed moving into French North Africa, but their most momentous decision was that the United States should build the large, expensive facilities preliminary to the production of atomic bombs.[31]

The two leaders arrived in Washington to face the shocking news that the British had surrendered at Tobruk. Marshall rushed 300 tanks and 100 105-millimeter guns to the British in Egypt.[32]

The discussions in Washington ran along familiar lines, and Roosevelt and Churchill established a formula not pleasing to their commanders. Preparations for operations on the continent in 1943 must continue with all speed and energy, but there must also be offensive action in 1942. If operations in western Europe seemed destined to fail, the best alternative would be North Africa.[33]

Marshall argued energetically to the contrary, pointing out that another venture could so imperil the buildup for a landing in France that it might not be possible in 1943. Yet Roosevelt did not totally abandon the idea of a cross-channel attack in 1942; preparations for it continued. On the other hand, he was shaken, as his advisers had not been, by Churchill's warnings during his visit. He was readier to accept the reality that a landing in France would be largely a British operation, and that without British approval it could not take place. Gradually the British became more firm and specific in their disapproval. On July 8, Churchill cabled, "No responsible British General, Admiral, or Air Marshal is prepared to recommend [the crossing] as a practicable operation in 1942." Marshall countered, with the support of King, that the United States in this case should shift its forces to the Pacific.[34]

Roosevelt thereupon acted in his tried and true fashion. He dispatched Marshall and King, together with Hopkins, to London and insisted they come home with an amicable agreement. Marshall presented his views there to no avail. He reminisced in 1956: "The British staff and cabinet were unalterable in their refusal. . . . It looked like the Russians were going to be destroyed. . . . Churchill was rabid for Africa. Roosevelt was for Africa. Both men were aware of political necessities. It is something that we [in the military] fail to take into consideration."[35]

In consequence Marshall decided that the expedition into North Africa would be the least harmful diversion. King concurred. The British agreed and the North African plan received the name TORCH.

General Eisenhower lamented at the time that July 22, 1942, when the second front was abandoned, might well go down as the "blackest day in history," particularly if the German drive knocked the Soviets out of the war. In 1947, with hindsight, he came to a different conclusion, admitting to Robert Sherwood that it would have been a mistake to establish a bridgehead in the Cherbourg area. Even if it "had been successful . . . the Germans would have built up such a powerful resistance to further progress . . . that the break-through would have been immeasurably more difficult than it proved to be in July, 1944."[36]

In the late summer of 1942, Eisenhower, who had been strong in his resistance, turned energetically to the planning of the North African campaign, but Marshall and Stimson were as dogged as Churchill had been and for some weeks tried to reverse the decision.[37]

There was little glory for anyone in the protracted, confused struggle over policy. Churchill and the British blocked what undoubtedly would have been a debacle, yet earlier were not firm in their opposition for fear it would lead to a massive American diversion toward the Pacific. Marshall in his unrelenting fight for a 1942 invasion was not serving Roosevelt well.

Roosevelt, as Stimson lamented, was acting in a devious, self-serving, and self-deluding fashion, but so were the others involved. Though he never vetoed a 1942 cross-channel attack, he did overrule the Joint Chiefs of Staff. It was fortunate that he did so.

Chapter 33

INTO NORTH AFRICA

UPON ROOSEVELT fell the responsibility in the fall of 1942 of achieving what had long been his hope — the landing of American troops in North Africa with little bloodshed and the joining of forces with the French to bring them back into the war against Germany. In the process he became involved in some of the complex issues of the war, among them the role of General Charles de Gaulle, the question of unconditional surrender, and the fate of persecuted Jews. There were plaudits for Roosevelt, and not a few brickbats.

When France suddenly collapsed in the spring of 1940, Churchill turned toward the heretofore little-known General de Gaulle, who sought to rally around him Free French fighting forces committed to continuing the war against the Axis. Roosevelt had pursued another tactic, trying to persuade Pétain and his new Vichy government to resist as far as possible German influence and demands. These were not at the time conflicting policies; they were, indeed, complementary. The British and Americans cooperated with each other in developing them.

Roosevelt and the State Department rapidly conceived an antipathy for de Gaulle. They noted that many French leaders who would not serve Pétain's Vichy government also would not join de Gaulle. The problem became worse when the general's and the British assault on Dakar failed, with Frenchmen killing Frenchmen. Finally, at Christmastime 1941, when de Gaulle in violation of Anglo-American commitments seized the tiny islands of St. Pierre and Miquelon in the Gulf of St. Lawrence, he irritated Roosevelt and enraged Hull.

On the other hand, Roosevelt saw useful opportunities in the cultivation both of the aged hero of Verdun, Marshal Pétain, and to a lesser degree of the Falangist victor in the Spanish Civil War, General Franco. Amazingly, Hitler and the Germans seemed to be observing the terms of the armistice with France, not imposing upon it the crushing subjugation that had been the fate of Poland, in the expectation of incorporating France into their new European order. Also, equally surprisingly, although there was only the slightest obstacle on the path to North Africa in the summer of 1940, German divisions stopped at the Spanish border and did not plunge through to Gibraltar and across the strait. Although Franco had accepted German aid during the civil war, he demonstrated a singular unwillingness to allow German forces to cross Spain. He scarcely could have resisted in June, 1940. Later his resistance stiffened, and Roosevelt personally involved himself in making it worth Franco's while to continue to be independent. Fortuitously Hitler had slight interest in taking advantage of his opportunities in French North Africa; his focus even in the summer of 1940 was upon areas to the north and east.

For Roosevelt and both his military and diplomatic advisers, French North Africa was of acute significance, leading them from the beginning to court Vichy, which exercised authority over it, and conversely to be wary of de Gaulle. In private, Roosevelt from time to time declared that there was no legitimate French government, but by virtue of his recognition of the Vichy government he was indeed upholding its legitimacy. Through the American legation in Vichy he was trying to encourage the regime to resist German pressures and to sanction American involvement in North Africa.[1]

From the White House and Hyde Park, Roosevelt personally helped direct the involved intrigues. His most useful informant on the confused, swirling politics of the new government was a gifted young career diplomat, Robert Murphy, chargé d'affaires in Vichy. Roosevelt saw possibilities in reports that there were few Nazis in North Africa but considerable French forces that had sworn allegiance to Vichy. Roosevelt sent for Murphy. With a large map spread out on his desk, Roosevelt engaged him in lengthy conversation, then sent him to North Africa. Next Roosevelt dispatched his chief of naval operations of a few months before, Admiral William D. Leahy, discreet, conservative, and firmly loyal, to serve as ambassador in Vichy and win the confidence of Pétain. Leahy did succeed in establishing pleasant relations with Pétain, who he felt was friendly but helpless because of German restrictions. In North Africa Murphy was able to work out an agreement with General Maxime Weygand, in charge of French troops there, that was acceptable to Pétain in Vichy. A provision permitted the stationing in North Africa of additional consuls, who everyone knew were intelligence agents.[2]

Next Roosevelt began to search for some French leader who had given his allegiance to Vichy, who would assume command of French forces in North Africa, and who would be willing to cooperate with the Americans when they landed. The anti-British Admiral Jean Darlan, who remained commander in chief of the Vichy armed forces, soon hinted that he was ready to negotiate with the Americans, but for months was ignored. Rather, there appeared in Vichy a new prestigious French military leader upon whom Roosevelt and the Americans came to pin their hopes. This was General Henri Giraud, who had escaped from the German castle of Königstein. Giraud was an able, upright military leader, firmly committed to the letter of the law, but, as events were to demonstrate, lacking a sense of politics. Murphy and resistance leaders in Algiers soon succeeded in obtaining Giraud's cooperation. Meanwhile, Murphy was also winning support among sympathetic French in North Africa.

The success of the North African landings might well hinge upon the acquiescence of the French forces. Hence Roosevelt continued personally to involve himself in directing the project. At Hyde Park on August 31, 1942, tieless and in his shirtsleeves, with Hopkins at his side, he briefed Murphy at length. Murphy was to serve as the president's personal representative until the landings took place, and thereafter as head of the civil affairs section and adviser for civil affairs under Eisenhower. (The British later appointed Harold Macmillan as his counterpart.) Roosevelt emphasized, as he had before, that the United States opposed recognizing any person or group as the government of France until the French people could freely make their own choice. That continued to be his firm view. It went directly counter to de Gaulle's vehement conviction that he and his organization were the legitimate government of France.[3]

Through the fall of 1942, as Roosevelt grappled with problems ranging from war production to the heavy Japanese attacks upon Guadalcanal, he waited with concern for the risky landing in North Africa. It was to be an amphibious operation of unprecedented size, involving the carrying of three forces of American and British troops across hundreds of miles of ocean to land them and their equipment on what might prove to be hostile shores. American experience as yet was slight, and the risks substantial.

Roosevelt could by no means be certain that the American courtship of the French would forestall serious fighting against the invasion forces. There had been problems in making arrangements with the underground leaders in North Africa. General Giraud stubbornly insisted, even after the landings began, that he must have command over all forces fighting in North Africa, only belatedly accepting a lesser arrangement, command of all French troops.[4]

On the eve of the invasion, November 7, 1942, Roosevelt, weekending at Shangri-la, seemed preoccupied and tense; he was waiting for an important message, he explained. When finally the call came, his hand shook as he took the receiver. He listened, then replied, "Thank God. Thank God. That sounds grand. . . ." He turned to the guests, "We have landed in North Africa. Casualties are below expectations. We are striking back."[5]

For several days there was a brief interlude of national rejoicing. Not only were the landings successful, but some days earlier, the British under General Sir Bernard L. Montgomery had begun successfully their attack at El Alamein to push Rommel's Afrika Korps out of Egypt. Nevertheless, as Roosevelt predicted to the press that first euphoric November day, there were peaks and valleys in the conduct of the war.[6]

To both the relief and the embarrassment of Roosevelt and the Americans, the key to a relatively bloodless landing in Morocco was Admiral Darlan, earlier premier of the Vichy government. On the day before the invasion, Roosevelt received word that Darlan was in Algiers to visit his son, Alain, ill with polio. Roosevelt's immediate reaction was one of sympathy, and subsequently he sent the young man to Warm Springs for treatment. On the night of the landings, when some French units were firing on Americans, especially at Oran, Murphy confronted Darlan and persuaded him to sign a local cease-fire. When Giraud arrived, he agreed to an arrangement through which he would command the French forces, and Darlan would serve as a sort of high commissioner. Civil government would be under Darlan. Thus came the "Darlan deal," which ended French opposition in North Africa. Darlan persuaded General Pierre Boisson, governor-general of French West Africa, to deliver the port of Dakar, the threat to the Americas that Roosevelt had worried about for so long.

On the debit side, Roosevelt suddenly found himself allied with one of the most notorious of the Vichy collaborators with the Germans, and thus assuming responsibility for continued Vichyite control over the government of French North Africa. To make matters worse, it was a government discriminating against Jews and holding in concentration camps numbers of those who had been opposed to Hitler, Franco, and Vichy. Further, while General de Gaulle was becoming increasingly popular in France and Britain and among the American public, Roosevelt was widening the rift with him.[7]

Roosevelt, far from thinking of himself as bolstering Fascism, continued to expound his formula of democratic self-determination. It was a principle he applied as firmly against Darlan as de Gaulle, refusing to allow Darlan to use official American channels to inform Vichy administrators throughout the world that he was acting only as surrogate for Pétain, who was muted by the German occupation.[8]

"Had you expected Darlan?" Morgenthau asked Roosevelt on November 12. "No, absolutely not," Roosevelt responded, "but he worked out all right and he gave the orders to cease firing." Morgenthau congratulated him on the Roosevelt brains and luck. "The President knocked on wood and said it was a piece of luck."[9]

The luck was not entirely good. There was a flurry of indignation within the United States, where a liberal minority was taken aback that in the war against Nazism and Fascism, Roosevelt for military reasons seemed to be embracing both the former collaborationist Darlan and the Spanish dictator Franco. The Darlan deal cost Roosevelt three fourths of his prestige among the French people, Leon Morandat, a trade union official and underground leader, asserted upon his arrival in London. Churchill reported to Roosevelt, "I ought to let you know that very deep currents of feeling are stirred up by the arrangement with Darlan." It must be temporary, he warned. Roosevelt confessed, "I too have encountered the deep currents."[10]

Before he met correspondents, Roosevelt tried out his justification on Morgenthau. The Darlan deal, he said, meant that instead of taking six to ten weeks to secure French North Africa, "we are going to do it in a couple of weeks with very few lives lost." Later at a press conference he admitted, "I thoroughly understand and approve the feeling that . . . no permanent arrangement should be made with Admiral Darlan."[11]

Roosevelt did not relish the opprobrium. He fumed to the cabinet, noted Ickes, "that, so far as he was concerned, Darlan stank; he was a skunk," but declared he would use Darlan as long as possible, or if Darlan were to try selling out the Americans, clap him into jail. Yet Roosevelt did not feel very kindly toward alternative French leaders. Earlier he had told his cabinet that he had three Kilkenny cats on his hands, Darlan, Giraud, and de Gaulle. Giraud already had proven himself stiffly stubborn and a man with no feel for politics; de Gaulle was difficult.[12]

By undertaking personal supervision of the civilian government of Morocco and Algeria, Roosevelt found himself in the uncomfortable position of being responsible for Jews and political prisoners who had lost their civil liberties. Darlan, on the grounds that Roosevelt's order for a general repudiation of the anti-Semitic Nuremberg Decree might lead to civil war, had been liberating Jews only gradually.[13]

At this point, chance again intervened. On the day before Christmas, a twenty-year-old French monarchist assassinated Darlan. His motives were unclear, perhaps to make the Orléanist pretender, the Comte de Paris, the high commissioner. Within twenty-four hours he was executed. Admiral Leahy, who some months earlier had become Roosevelt's chief of staff, mourned Darlan as "an invaluable asset to the Allied Cause in Africa," but the assassination relieved Roosevelt of a serious political embarrassment. Quickly Roosevelt had Leahy order the elevation of the politically inept Giraud to head French civil as well as military affairs in North Africa.[14]

There would have to be fresh arrangements for the occupation of French North Africa when Roosevelt next met with Churchill there. During the last weeks of 1942 military affairs also had not proceeded as well as Roosevelt had hoped. The Americans were having difficulty in concentrating men and supplies for a drive into Tunisia against the German troops that Hitler had rushed there. What Roosevelt had projected as a few weeks' mopping-up was to develop into a difficult campaign lasting well into the spring.

The basic question, however, was where the United States would next employ the large forces it was sending into North Africa. Once more, Roosevelt and Churchill hoped for a meeting with Stalin, but he excused himself because of the intensity of the Russian siege against a huge German force trapped at Stalingrad. Roosevelt wanted to meet by January 15 in North Africa, commenting to Churchill in allusion to the famous meeting between Napoleon and Alexander I of Russia in 1807, "I prefer a comfortable oasis to the raft at Tilsit." They quickly made their decision. On New Year's Eve, the choice of motion picture shown at the White House suggests Roosevelt savoring his secret. It was Humphrey Bogart and Ingrid Bergman in *Casablanca*.[15]

The flight to Morocco was a daring adventure; it was the first time a president had flown during his term of office. Nor was it an easy mode of transportation for Roosevelt, since he could not brace himself with his legs. "I'm not crazy about flying . . . — rather bumpy both days," he wrote his wife on the way over. Nevertheless, Roosevelt was in a holiday mood. "He acted like a sixteen-year-old" when the requisitioned Pan American clipper rose smoothly from the water at Miami, bound for Brazil, across to Africa, and up to Casablanca. He was airborne for forty-eight hours; for a later generation the trip would take nine.[16]

The poverty and squalor in the British colony of Gambia in West Africa made a serious impression upon him. Along the road to the airport he saw the glum, ill-clothed populace of Bathurst, and learned, according to his log of the trip, "that the prevailing wage rate for unskilled labor . . . was 'one and nine' (one shilling nine pence) per day, together with a half-cup of rice, the main article of diet. . . . Due to the prevalence of disease and general unsanitary conditions, the mortality rate is very high and life expectancy is only about 26 years." The experience fired his anticolonialism and spurred his interest in postwar improvements. On several occasions he recounted the dismaying conditions as a means of assailing Churchill's imperial policies.[17]

Security was tight at Casablanca. He rode from the airfield in a car with mud smeared over the windows so that he could not be seen en route to Anfa, on the outskirts, a resort hotel where he stayed in a luxurious villa. A mile of barbed wire surrounded the estate, and troops, artillery, and planes guarded it.[18]

At Casablanca, military decisions did not so heavily involve Roosevelt as they had earlier. He focused more on the immediate problem of obtaining workable French leadership in North Africa, and on the long-range one of the ultimate peace. The military problems seemed of a rather intermediate sort, involving moves in 1943 rather than the long-term strategy to bring the war to an end, and he was disposed to let his military advisers work out proposals with the British. He had predicted that the British would have a firm plan, and so they did, while the Americans were rather less unified in their thinking.

The American staff felt outmaneuvered at Casablanca. General Albert Wedemeyer, the army planner, flew to Casablanca with three substantial briefing books and the strong feeling that the invasion of North Africa had been a needless diversion. What counted was to cross the channel and drive deep into Germany ahead of the Soviet forces. The British came with a firm case for a Mediterranean policy, backed by a larger staff than the Americans, detailed position papers, and supporting War Office files and file clerks aboard a communications ship anchored in the harbor. The Americans were never underprepared again; it was the last conference the British dominated.[19]

Churchill proposed tactics to the British chiefs of staff before the discussion began. They were to be patient and to allow full discussion — "the dripping of water on a stone." He would follow the same course with the president. But the military program he espoused was not one differing greatly from the objectives of Roosevelt and his advisers except in order of priority: to seize Sicily, move into Burma, undertake a preliminary invasion of France, and above all curb submarine sinkings in the Atlantic. Consequently, while the five days of discussion were at times heated, the conclusions were amicable enough.

The final agreements were short of what General Marshall would have liked, but were acceptable. The cross-channel attack would not take place in 1943, but the buildup would continue, and a staff would begin planning for a major invasion in 1944. Meanwhile, action against Sicily in the summer of 1943 would help prevent recovery of the faltering Luftwaffe. There must be massive efforts to destroy the U-boats in the Atlantic and to bomb German installations and industry. Eisenhower, not involved in the decisions, felt that the "big bosses" had decided well. Roosevelt seemed pleased.[20]

Much of Roosevelt's attention centered upon the problems of the French administration in North Africa. Some arrangements had to be made to lighten Eisenhower's political burdens and lessen the uproar over the political repression. Eisenhower and Murphy came to the conference proposing that Giraud and de Gaulle should share power. The problem was to try to bring the two touchy French leaders together at Casablanca. Giraud was willing, but de Gaulle balked for two days, feeling outraged that he was being invited to come to a conclave of foreign powers on what he considered to be French soil. Roosevelt contemplated the impasse with high spirits, sending an incongruously jocose dispatch to his solemn secretary of state:

"We delivered the bridegroom, General Giraud, who was most cooperative on the impending marriage. . . . However, our friends could not produce the bride, the temperamental lady De Gaulle. She has got quite snooty about the whole idea and does not want to see either of us, and is showing no intention of getting into bed with Giraud."[21]

While waiting for de Gaulle, Roosevelt plunged into the treacherous political currents. One way in which he sought to bring unity among the seriously divided French was to take up a suggestion of Hopkins that the governing structure include, together with Giraud and de Gaulle, a civilian with some administrative skill. On the way to Casablanca, Hopkins had urged upon him Jean Monnet, who possessed these talents, suggesting that Monnet could serve as political adviser to General Giraud. Monnet had long been associated with Hopkins, first in purchasing armaments for France, and since its collapse serving on the British Purchasing Commission. Roosevelt cabled Hull, asking his opinion of Monnet. Hull objected to the suggestion because Monnet had several indirect connections with the de Gaulle organization, so Roosevelt dropped the matter for the time being.[22]

The president was trying to assemble a coalition of varying French views, and found Giraud amenable even though a monarchist. It was upon Roosevelt's recommendation that Giraud subsequently invited Monnet to Algeria, and on the other hand Roosevelt accepted Giraud's wish that Marcel Peyrouton, the former Vichy minister, become governor of Algeria. A howl went up in the American press, for while he was an able administrator he had been a harsh minister of the interior in the Vichy government.

In his efforts to win support from the right, Roosevelt was appalling. He courted General August Noguès, resident-general of Morocco, although he held Noguès in ill-concealed contempt. Noguès had installed the Vichy restrictions upon Jews in Morocco, and now was responsible for erasing them. Roosevelt conversed with him in French about the problem of political prisoners and particularly Jews, declaring (according to his naval attaché, Captain John L. McCrea) that "the number of Jews engaged in the practice of the professions (law, medicine, etc.) should be definitely limited to the percentage that the Jewish population . . . bears to the whole of the North African population." He believed "that his plan would further eliminate the specific and understandable complaints which the Germans bore towards the Jews in Germany, namely, that while they represented a small part of the population, over fifty percent of the lawyers, doctors, school teachers, college professors, etc. in Germany, were Jews."

Roosevelt's remarks that over 50 percent of the professional people in Germany were Jews was an indication of his hazy grasp of the issue, obviously gathered from prejudiced attacks. Jews, between 1 and 2 percent of the German population, had comprised 2.3 percent of the professions; 16.3 percent of the lawyers had been Jewish. The next day Roosevelt expounded the same solution to General Giraud. The ceiling he proposed would have provided few opportunities for Jews in North Africa, where they numbered about 300,000 in a population of more than 13 million.[23]

Several nights later, on January 22, Roosevelt was equally sympathetic toward the sultan of Morocco, to whom he expressed his hope that Morocco could become independent after the war and that the United States could assist in its economic development.[24]

Later that evening, Roosevelt for the first time met with de Gaulle, who in his own time had arrived at the conference, well aware of his strong position as his popularity was spreading in occupied France, Britain, and the United States. Knowing he had the upper hand, he coolly conferred with the cordial Roosevelt. Speaking French, the president, ostensibly alone (but with McCrea listening through a crack in the door and taking notes), set forth his North African policy and his familiar view that for the time being the French people lacked sovereign power.

Both participants considered the meeting a failure. Not surprisingly, de Gaulle responded stiffly to Roosevelt's lecture. "That evening, as on every occasion when I saw him afterwards," de Gaulle wrote, "Roosevelt showed himself eager to reach a meeting of minds, using charm rather than reason to convince me, but attached once and for all to the decisions he had made." Roosevelt complained to Murphy that he had found de Gaulle rigidly concerned with politics, ignoring the urgent need for military victory before there could be a political settlement. Roosevelt was correct in believing that de Gaulle's focus was upon a quick resurgence of France as a major power, and was determined to thwart him. The rehabilitation, he believed then and for many months to come, must proceed slowly. Further, as his remarks to the sultan had demonstrated, he was bent upon dissolving the French Empire as well as that of the British; de Gaulle was determined to preserve it.[25]

In his memoirs, de Gaulle shrewdly appraised Roosevelt:

> Roosevelt meant the peace to be an American peace, convinced he must be the one to dictate its structure, that the states which had been overrun should be subject to his judgment, and that France in particular should recognize him as its savior and its arbiter. . . . It must be added that like any star performer he was touchy as to the roles that fell to other actors. In short, beneath his patrician mask of courtesy, Roosevelt regarded me without benevolence.[26]

As de Gaulle and Giraud maneuvered for power, there continued to be much badinage about forcing a shotgun wedding between the "bride" and "groom." Murphy and his British counterpart, Harold Macmillan, especially labored to bring about an agreement. Giraud was ready to cooperate, on the basis that he would be a political head and de Gaulle his military subordinate. Macmillan reported on the morning of the last day of the conference that de Gaulle had tried to reverse the order of things by proposing to Giraud that he be Foch, the World War I military leader, and de Gaulle be Clemenceau, the civil leader. When Roosevelt heard this report, he remarked, "Yesterday he wanted to be Joan of Arc — and now he wants to be the somewhat more worldly Clemenceau." In one or another version Roosevelt retold the story; it traveled widely, appeared in the American press, and painfully offended de Gaulle. Churchill too could not resist gibes at de Gaulle, replying to a query, "Oh, let's don't speak of him. We call him Jeanne d'Arc and we're looking for some bishops to burn him."[27]

Only a few minutes before a press conference was to begin, de Gaulle and his staff visited Roosevelt. He persuaded de Gaulle and Giraud to go outside to have their pictures taken. They walked into the sunshine, solemn faced, and Roosevelt was carried out in his chair. Then, before the surprised photographers, they posed, for one of the notable photographs of the war.[28]

Afterward de Gaulle prepared a short communiqué announcing the establishment of a permanent liaison with Giraud, who signed it only after de Gaulle changed the phrase "democratic principles" to "human liberties." There had been no real agreement, but the impression of agreement created the effect Roosevelt wished, muting temporarily much, but not all, of the criticism.[29]

Following handshakes for photographers, Giraud and de Gaulle departed, leaving Roosevelt and Churchill to talk to some fifty war correspondents sitting cross-legged on the lawn. Roosevelt spoke carefully from notes, including a topic not in the joint Roosevelt-Churchill communiqué:

> The elimination of German, Japanese and Italian war power means the unconditional surrender by Germany, Italy, and Japan. That does not mean the destruction of the population of Germany, Italy, or Japan, but it does mean the destruction of the philosophies in those countries which are based on conquest and the subjugation of other people.

Churchill was not prepared for the announcement; years later Captain McCrea remembered the startled expression on his face. Yet, he began his remarks by saying, "I agree with everything that the President has said."[30]

"Unconditional surrender" was one of the most momentous and debatable pronouncements of the war. Roosevelt told Hopkins the thought "popped into my mind" as he was talking, but it was in the notes he was following. Churchill was taken by surprise, but there was nothing he could do except to assert unity with Roosevelt. Churchill had known and approved of the unconditional surrender doctrine, although not of the time when Roosevelt would announce it. Thus the president seized the initiative and attention for the United States.[31]

Before the conference, on January 7, Roosevelt had raised the question with the Joint Chiefs of Staff but it brought little reaction and no study. It must have seemed at the time little more than a variant on the theme of "total victory" that Roosevelt and the United States had been emphasizing since Pearl Harbor. "Unconditional surrender" could serve as a new rallying cry, and a reassurance to Stalin that Roosevelt and Churchill would not settle for a negotiated peace. Intertwined in

Roosevelt's mind was the imperative he had been so frequently stating, that there must be no debate over peace terms before the end of the war. After his press conference at Casablanca, he told Harriman that he did not want to repeat Wilson's blunder in issuing the Fourteen Points, which Germany in advance of the armistice had regarded as a basis for the postwar settlement.[32]

At the time there was little criticism of the unconditional surrender doctrine, although the Soviet Union, not consulted beforehand, did not endorse it until late in the year. After the war, attacks became vigorous from many quarters. A military critic, J. F. C. Fuller, asserted that it "transformed the 'soft underbelly' [of Europe] into a crocodile's back, prolonged the war, wrecked Italy and wasted thousands of American and British lives." General Eisenhower in 1964 expressed his conviction that the war would have ended in January, 1945, after the Battle of the Bulge, rather than May had not Hitler "used something from the mouth of our own leader and persuaded the Germans to fight longer."[33] But Churchill, when queried by Robert Sherwood shortly after the war, wrote:

> I would not myself have used these words, but I immediately stood by the President and have frequently defended the decision. It is false to suggest that it prolonged the war. Negotiation with Hitler was impossible. He was a maniac with supreme power to play his hand out to the end, which he did; and so did we.[34]

These debates were for the future. Throughout the Casablanca conference, Roosevelt was in a holiday mood. He took particular pleasure in the surprise of troops he reviewed north of Rabat. As they stood expressionless in keeping with regulations, he noticed a jaw drop here and there, and heard a single word come faintly from one soldier's lips, "J-e-s-u-s."[35]

Chapter 34

VICTORIES — AND THE SHADOW OF STALIN

THROUGH THE SUMMER of 1943, as American forces moved onto the offensive against Japan, and together with the British brought the Italians to the point of surrender, Roosevelt's thoughts were turning more and more toward the peace settlement. One of his continuing concerns was the irritating state of relations with the Soviet Union. The shadow of the absent Stalin loomed over the calculations of Roosevelt and Churchill. They no longer worried, since the debacle at Stalingrad, that Germany might knock Russia out of the war, but the friction with the Soviet Union boded ill for a postwar world in which it would be a dominant power.

Difficulties with Stalin as yet were secondary, and Roosevelt focused upon military ventures. Gradually in 1943 answers came to most of the difficulties, but for the most part without the president playing a prime role. Only in grand strategy and preparations for the peace was he exercising direct control.

Even Roosevelt's beloved navy was an example. The basic strategy in the Pacific was fundamentally the handiwork of Admirals King and Nimitz, General MacArthur, and their subordinates. Roosevelt explained their new policy to the cabinet in February, 1943. Instead of continuing to capture each island on the route to Japan, a process that would take years, the United States would engage in wide flanking movements and thus bypass Japanese garrisons. The name of the chief of naval operations appeared on the White House appointment calendar thirty-two times in 1942, but only eight times in 1943 and nine times the following year. Of course, Roosevelt was in touch through Admiral

Leahy and frequently stopped by the White House map room, where he could monitor movements on the seas of the world.[1]

Roosevelt's overall concern in the Pacific was that the forces be strong enough to win their objectives, and incidentally to placate the public and Congress. Opinion polls indicated that Americans were still more interested in the defeat of Japan than of Germany. Yet Roosevelt insisted the Pacific war must not drain away ships, supplies, and forces essential to success in Europe. Both his head and his heart caused him to concentrate the larger part of his time and attention upon the Atlantic and Germany. For a short while he and Churchill entertained optimistic plans for a cross-channel attack in 1943, but the realities of the shipping shortage caused them to evaporate. For several months more, German submarines continued to inflict serious losses.[2]

At the same time exciting schemes for the postwar world were revolving through Roosevelt's head. During several days of meetings at the White House with Foreign Secretary Eden in March, 1943, new ideas kept popping out on peacekeeping and boundaries. Previously Roosevelt had talked in terms of regional councils; now he and Welles told Eden that the United Nations should be a single worldwide body, with regional councils subordinate to it, and with real decisions being made by the "big four," the United States, Great Britain, the Soviet Union, and China, who for years to come would have to police the world.

Not all of the ideas impressed Eden. One was a suggestion Roosevelt had first floated to a British visitor, Oliver Lyttelton, minister of production, that a new state, to be called "Wallonia," be created out of the Flemish-speaking part of Belgium, together with Luxembourg, Alsace-Lorraine, and part of northern France. It was a farfetched notion, which Eden disparaged, yet in some respects it foreshadowed the economic union, Benelux, which united that area with the Netherlands after the war.

In retrospect, Eden acerbically commented:

> Though I enjoyed these conversations, the exercise of the President's charm and the play of his lively mind, they were also perplexing. Roosevelt was familiar with the history and geography of Europe. Perhaps his hobby of stamp-collecting had helped him to this knowledge, but the academic yet sweeping opinions which he built upon it were alarming in their cheerful fecklessness. He seemed to see himself disposing of the fate of many lands, allied no less than enemy. He did all this with so much grace that it was not easy to dissent. Yet it was too like a conjuror, skillfully juggling with balls of dynamite, whose nature he failed to understand.[3]

Eden's observations were on target. Roosevelt with his high-soaring imagination was happily dreaming of redrawing the map of Europe, indeed of the world. He was disposed to function, to use the term historian Arthur Schlesinger, Jr., later made familiar, as an imperial president. He wanted to restore Hungary and Austria as small independent nations. Roosevelt liked Archduke Otto and his sister, but was firmly against a Hapsburg restoration. Eden seriously questioned whether Roosevelt under the Constitution had the power to establish a new Austria. The president assured Eden he could. In the creation of new states, he had little or no dependence upon Congress; there would be no need for him to negotiate treaties that must run the gauntlet of Senate confirmation.[4]

The reconstruction of Europe was still for the future; strategic matters were of more immediate importance during the talks with Eden. The shipping shortage was forcing a reevaluation of the Casablanca decisions. Roosevelt found himself having to decide whether to supply adequate food and necessities to Britain at the cost of the buildup for a 1943 move into France. The economic well-being and morale of the beleaguered British must come first, he concluded, and he modified plans accordingly, jotting an outline of his tentative proposals for Eden to take back to London:

Germany	No BOLERO [1943 cross-channel attack]. Build long-range bombing to maximum.
Mediterranean	(1) HUSKY [invasion of Sicily]. If HUSKY Italy next and at once. (2) And/or Turkey
Burma	ANAKIM [reopening] out. Keep China going by air.
South West Pacific	Continue as now.[5]

From this point on there was considerable friendly but firm pulling and hauling between Roosevelt and Churchill. Roosevelt, Marshall, and Eisenhower were not disposed to block the invasion of Sicily, but neither did they want to allow Churchill and Brooke to pull them on into a succession of Mediterranean ventures that would prevent crossing the channel not only in 1943, but probably in 1944. Churchill, a bold and imaginative adventurer in proposing peripheral attacks, returned again and again to conservative fears that a direct move into France would cost casualties the British could not afford.

The point of decision about invading Sicily and whatever operations should follow was soon at hand in the spring of 1943, as the British and American forces contained and then began to defeat the Axis troops in

Tunisia. In May, the last German and Italian troops in North Africa surrendered. Altogether the Allies captured 275,000 troops, more than the Russians had at Stalingrad. Of these, 155,000 were German. Hitler, as at Stalingrad, instead of conceding defeat and keeping his losses low, had poured in more and more men and matériel. As a consequence, the Tunisian campaign served not only to provide essential experience for the raw American troops and leaders, but also to weaken further the German forces. The campaign, although under American command, had been preponderantly British, as their casualty figures, double those of the Americans, indicated.[6]

At the time of surrender, Churchill was bound for a fresh conference in Washington, on the high seas aboard the *Queen Mary* together with a staff of a hundred (and, sealed off on the lower decks, five thousand prisoners of war from North Africa). The British hoped at the Trident conference in Washington in May, 1943, to obtain final approval for the invasion of Sicily, and to persuade the Americans to follow it by moving into Italy, and perhaps to the east in the Mediterranean. Roosevelt and his staff were firmly determined not to allow further diversions to prevent a cross-channel invasion in 1944.

Although the Casablanca conference was only a few months before, the relationship between the Americans and British had altered strikingly. Army training camps in the United States were turning out soldiers by the hundreds of thousands; American industry was producing tanks, planes, warships, and munitions in unparalleled quantities — enough to supply both the American forces and the lend-lease demands of Allies. Further, the forces were proving themselves in combat. At Washington in May, America became the leading partner. Roosevelt's advisers, having learned their lessons at Casablanca, were as numerous as the British and equally well prepared.

Roosevelt stood firm at the Washington conference, giving first priority after the campaign in Sicily to whatever would best implement the invasion of France in 1944. Churchill's strategy was to talk in generalities about the peripheral matters at first, moving toward specifics later, but he was realistic enough to accept the power shift. Fairly early at the meeting, he agreed to the proposal that there be an invasion in the spring of 1944. His concern, as he had explained to Harriman during the trip over, was rather that the Americans would not want to utilize their forces further in the Mediterranean after the conquest of Sicily; Churchill was eager to pursue the great opportunities he perceived in the "soft underbelly" of Europe — the mountainous Balkans.[7]

A considerable part of Roosevelt's time at the meetings went into discussion of the critical, though relatively subordinate, question of how to bolster Chiang Kai-shek against the offensive the Japanese were aiming at Yunnan. General Stilwell wanted support for a land operation to reopen the Burma Road into China, but both Roosevelt and the British withheld it, fearing that Allied troops would fight at a serious disadvantage in the jungles.[8]

At the end of two weeks of meetings, Roosevelt and Churchill agreed upon a major invasion of France, given the code name OVERLORD, to begin on May 1, 1944. Reluctantly the British agreed that seven of the divisions would come after November 1 from the Mediterranean area.[9]

The landing at Sicily would be a formidable undertaking, far larger than the North African invasion, but Italy seemed ripe for collapse. The war had gone badly for Mussolini; Germany had become totally dominant in the alliance, and most Italians fought poorly and without heart in what, by the summer of 1943, was clearly a lost cause. Hitler, suspecting that Italy might try to change sides, interspersed among the Italians some German forces with orders in case of defection to block Allied forces from the Po Valley. There were two German mobile divisions among the almost 350,000 soldiers guarding Sicily.

On the evening of July 9, 1943, President Roosevelt during a state dinner for General Giraud announced that American, British, and Canadian forces were landing at Sicily. Their numbers were enormous, some 478,000 men. They met only light resistance from Sicilian reservists, and as they passed through Sicilian towns, the inhabitants handed them fruit and flowers and hailed them as liberators. The initial landings were so successful that Eisenhower's forces should have readjusted their schedules to prevent the escape of any significant number of Axis troops. In this they failed, and 60,000 German troops eluded capture. By August 17, the campaign for Sicily was over, and Mussolini was out of office.[10]

The imminent collapse of the Italian forces foreshadowed a first testing of Roosevelt's unconditional surrender doctrine. By late July, with the new Italian government of Marshal Pietro Badoglio seeking to switch sides, Roosevelt was caught between his formula and his desire to bring Italy quickly to the United Nations side. Unconditional surrender would avoid the trap of an unpopular deal with Badoglio comparable to that with Darlan, but it might protract the fighting. Roosevelt made his way warily. When a reporter asked in May if he had considered the political future of Italy, he tersely responded, "Unconditional surrender." A few days later, he softened his words with explanations to the press, and the Voice of America broadcast his statements to the Italian people.

Roosevelt absolved them from the ruthless acts of Mussolini, and assured them that when the Fascist regime and the Nazis were thrown out they could choose their own kind of nontotalitarian government. Italy would then take her place "as a respected member of the European family of nations."[11]

The fall of Mussolini on July 25 had precipitated rapid political and military realignments. During weeks of uncertainty, Roosevelt and Churchill could only guess at developments. The Germans, mistrusting Badoglio, and having tapped a trans-Atlantic telephone conversation between Roosevelt and Churchill that confirmed their suspicions, were rushing divisions into Italy. Roosevelt and his military staff, unaware of how substantial a military bulwark Hitler was building, accepted Eisenhower's proposal to land forces at Salerno near Naples and dispatch them northward. They expected little resistance until they were beyond Rome, and they did not expect to go farther.

The time had come to prepare for Italian surrender. There was a minor pulling and hauling between Roosevelt and Churchill over the form of the surrender document, growing out of conflicting assumptions. Churchill seemed to feel that Mediterranean matters were primarily a British affair, and that retaining the Italian monarchy would help thwart civil disorders and possibly a Communist takeover. Roosevelt was holding firm to his twin precepts of unconditional surrender and the right of the Italian people ultimately to choose their own government. A sense of practicality brought the two leaders together; both wanted to end the conflict with Italy speedily.

The Italian surrender brought rejoicing in the United States, but was the prelude to a bitterly fought campaign up the Apennine peninsula against German divisions. The surrender negotiations also created suspicions in the mind of Stalin, who suspected Anglo-American treachery in not keeping him better informed. Actually, neither Roosevelt nor Churchill was very clear about what had been transpiring and they were acting toward Stalin in good faith.[12]

Ironically, friction was intensifying at a time when Roosevelt, publicists, and the news media had succeeded in establishing a favorable public image of both Stalin and the Russian people. A glamorous view of the Soviet Union was useful to Roosevelt. It made the war against Germany more attractive to present Russia as a worthy ally and a future collaborator in maintaining the peace.[13]

Roosevelt and Hopkins had been paying little heed to the advice of their own well-seasoned Russian experts in echelons below Welles in the State Department. In the fall of 1942, when Charles E. Bohlen, one of the most notable specialists, came into the department (from internment in Japan) to become assistant chief of the Russian section, he was delighted to find seasoned Moscow hands who favored aid to the Soviet Union and admired its struggle against Germany, but who were apprehensive about its ultimate aims. This was a view not popular then in the White House. When Bohlen first met Hopkins at a dinner party, he asked if Bohlen were part of the anti-Soviet clique and delivered a lengthy discourse on Russian achievements in the war. Hopkins seems to have been testing Bohlen's views, and soon was a strong supporter. One holder of the realistic position who already could penetrate the White House barricades was Averell Harriman, whom Roosevelt in 1943 persuaded to become ambassador in Moscow, a grim, uncomfortable assignment.[14]

A serious and distressing episode went far toward shifting White House policy in favor of the wary attitude of the experts on Russia. That was the shocking claim by the Germans that they had discovered a mass grave in the Katyn Forest near Smolensk, containing the corpses of thousands of Polish officers and enlisted men who had been held in Russian camps. The Russians had professed not to know their whereabouts. Wladyslaw Sikorski's Polish government-in-exile in London reacted to the German broadcasts by requesting the Red Cross to investigate and by asking the Soviet government to comment on the German allegations.[15]

Far from reacting defensively, Stalin turned the incident to his own advantage, using it as the occasion to break off diplomatic relations with the Poles. In March, 1943, Stalin created in Moscow a Union of Polish Patriots, which he ultimately transformed into a pro-Soviet Polish government. By diplomacy as well as force of arms, Stalin was preparing the way for a postwar Poland to his liking.[16]

Roosevelt, concerned with the principles of national self-determination, the Atlantic Charter, and inevitably too with the potential vote of the "several million Poles in the United States," was not pleased, but like Churchill possessed little leverage. As he had made clear in his conversations with Foreign Secretary Eden at that time, he was willing to make territorial concessions to Stalin. But neither then nor later would he countenance efforts to impose a satellite government upon Poland.

The Polish question, so troublesome to Roosevelt, was one of the many problems that caused him in the spring of 1943 again to urge Stalin to meet with him alone. His often stated reason was that he might gain Stalin's confidence more easily without Churchill there. More important was his eagerness to pursue American aims, not on collision course with the British, but decidedly divergent. He sent the pro-Soviet

Joseph Davies to Moscow to plead his case. Davies, friendly but scarcely astute, quickly gained entry to Stalin, who sent back a letter to Roosevelt suggesting they meet perhaps in July or August. He asked Davies to tell the president the location should be Fairbanks, Alaska.[17]

Stalin's smile turned to a frown when in June he received a dispatch from Roosevelt to Churchill postponing the full-scale invasion of France until 1944. He demonstrated his resentment by finding that demands of the military campaign would keep him from meeting with Roosevelt.

There were fears in the West, apparently without substance, that Stalin might try to negotiate a separate peace with Hitler. The German forces were so battered in 1943 that only the slimmest possibility of victory remained, but Hitler, rather than make peace as in 1918, insisted upon fighting to the end. Goebbels noted allegations of peace feelers from the Russians and lamented they were not true.[18] Hitler ordered what was to be the last great offensive against the Soviets, massing three thousand tanks at Kursk, and dispatching them against an equal number of Soviet tanks. The Soviets hurled back the Germans, went on the offensive, and advanced along a broad front until late in the fall.

Contrary to his indignant complaints, Stalin benefited from the campaign in Italy and it became in his interest to improve relations with his allies. The battles had turned so decisively in his direction that the Soviet armies could soon transform his war aims for eastern Europe into accomplished facts. There was no reason for him to toy with the idea of a deal with Hitler when he could gain so much more through negotiation of postwar settlements with Roosevelt and Churchill.[19]

Stalin's truculence had its effect upon atomic diplomacy. In August, 1943, meeting with Churchill in Quebec, Roosevelt took no chances and reaffirmed his pledge to engage in a full exchange of information with Great Britain on atomic energy. His scientific advisers had opposed doing so because they felt the United States would be giving away energy production secrets that would be valuable after the war. Although Roosevelt continued, as in the 1930s, to be a zealous protector of American commercial interests against the British rivals, he took more seriously Churchill's pleas for the atomic bomb as being potentially essential to postwar security. With the weapon, the British could counter the Soviet Union if it threatened to encroach too far west.[20]

The absent Stalin thus was in the back of their thoughts during the great public display at the Château Frontenac, where some six hundred representatives of the United States, Great Britain, and Canada took part in sessions on a large range of topics. Both Brooke and Marshall voiced their suspicions that the Russians might use victory to expand communism and make territorial claims in eastern Europe. Roosevelt seemed to share their view; he asked if studies were under way to move quickly onto the continent if the Germans showed signs of collapsing, since he wanted "United Nations troops to be ready to get to Berlin as soon as did the Russians."[21]

There were reasons for optimism in the enormous American military production, turning out far more tanks than either the Russians or British could absorb, and enough ships to compensate for losses to U-boats. Also, the battle of the Atlantic had turned dramatically against the Germans. Both changes in tactics and the successful cracking of the new German code were inflicting, at least for the time being, devastating losses upon the submarines. For some weeks, Roosevelt and Churchill had jokingly kept each other informed of the sinkings. "The July canaries to date number 35," Churchill had wired July 31; "Let us settle together on the 12th what food our cats are to have." What the press got on August 14 was a joint announcement of over ninety sinkings — nearly one a day — in the previous three months.[22]

The time had come to look ahead to the finale of the Pacific war, when it would be helpful to have, if not the outright aid of the Soviet Union, at least its benevolent neutrality. The American Chiefs of Staff had argued in preparatory discussions that the Soviet Union would be the dominant power in Europe after the defeat of Hitler and that it was imperative to bring it into the war against Japan.

The conference ended with Roosevelt and Churchill both irritated with Stalin, but more than ever disposed to seek his cooperation. On the last day, August 24, two cables came from him, the first complaining that the Soviets were not being kept informed about negotiations with the Italians, and a second one agreeing that the three of them should meet. He had indeed decided to join the party.[23]

Stalin's agreement to confer had a calming effect on Roosevelt. Upon his return to Washington he discoursed philosophically to the cabinet on "the Russian habit of sending him a friendly note on Monday, spitting in his eye on Tuesday, and then being nice again on Wednesday." He said he had come to realize that if he paid no attention to their unpleasant messages, the problems would resolve themselves. He concluded that the Russian diplomatic policy was to be "alternately agreeable and disagreeable."[24]

Roosevelt began to prepare for the meeting with Stalin in a hopeful spirit. His immediate task was to decide whom to send to a preliminary conference of the foreign ministers in Moscow. His first choice was by no means Hull. Roosevelt assured Hull that he wished to send him to the meeting but said that the trip would be too exhausting, since the secretary of state was not in good health and had never flown in an airplane. Rather, with Hull's consent, Roosevelt proposed to send Sumner Welles, as a means of easing him out of the State Department.[25]

For years Hull had resented Welles's favored relationship with the president. Finally, in August, 1943, he forced Roosevelt to choose between Welles and him. Roosevelt, with his keen memory of Wilson's failure to obtain ratification of the Versailles Treaty, did not dare lose the prestigious Hull, who could marshal the support of numerous powerful friends in the Senate. Hull brought pressure upon Roosevelt by means of affidavits alleging that on the train returning from Speaker William B. Bankhead's funeral in September, 1940, Welles, intoxicated, had solicited homosexual services from the porters. Welles's rival, Bullitt, spread the story so widely that by January, 1941, it reached Roosevelt. J. Edgar Hoover, head of the FBI, whom Roosevelt asked to conduct an investigation, reported that the rumors were apparently correct.[26]

Welles was valuable to Roosevelt, his prime means of working with the State Department, but if he was a homosexual could be dangerously susceptible to blackmail. Further, for him to remain in the department could make Roosevelt himself vulnerable to innuendo or even open attack. Roosevelt's solution was to retain Welles, but to have him closely watched to prevent further misadventures.

When the president did not remove Welles, Bullitt in April, 1941, saw Roosevelt and handed him one of the affidavits, arguing at some length how dangerous it was to keep Welles in the State Department. Finally Roosevelt pushed a button summoning his appointments secretary, General Watson. "Pa, I don't feel well," he said. "Please cancel my appointments for the rest of the day."[27]

Just as Roosevelt continued to retain Welles, so also he did not break with Bullitt, sending him late in 1941 as his personal representative to Egypt, and offering him positions less important than he sought. He kept Bullitt dangling just as he had others out of his favor who could be dangerous in opposition. Bullitt continued to be troublesome; twice more he tried to persuade Roosevelt to oust Welles.[28]

Finally, in August, 1943, Hull told the president either Welles must resign or he himself would. Roosevelt summoned Welles to the White House and tried to soften the blow by offering to make him a roving ambassador to Latin America or sending him to the foreign ministers' meeting in Moscow. Welles declined, and sent in his resignation, to take effect in late September.[29]

Although Roosevelt had been capable of carping about Welles, as he did concerning almost everyone from time to time, he took the loss bitterly. Just after Mrs. Roosevelt's return from a trip to the South Pacific in late September, he sent for her one day. White with wrath, he told her that, as he had expected, Bullitt had come to see him to ask for Welles's position as under secretary of state. As she related it with names deleted in *This I Remember*, the president told Bullitt:

> "Bill, if I were St. Peter and you and Sumner came before me, I would say to Sumner, 'No matter what you may have done, you have hurt no one but yourself. I recognize human frailties. Come in.' But to you I would say, 'You have not only hurt another human being, but you have deprived your country of the services of a good citizen; and for that you can go straight to Hell!' "[30]

Rather, Roosevelt chose as his new under secretary of state the loyal, affable Edward R. Stettinius, Jr., former chairman of the board of United States Steel. Stettinius had effectively administered lend-lease and got along well with Congress, Hopkins, and Hull.[31]

As for the Moscow conference, Roosevelt next asked Harriman to serve, but Harriman pointed out that at the rank of ambassador he would not be acceptable. Again, Roosevelt, with Hull's consent, turned to Welles, but at this point Hull became so upset that he changed his mind. Regardless of health or age, said Hull, wherever the conference might meet — anywhere between Washington and Chungking — he would be there. Roosevelt had no choice but to express pleasure.[32]

Above all, Roosevelt wanted Hull to fight in Moscow for an issue Hull also deemed vital: persuading the Soviets to endorse a four-power declaration committing the United States, Great Britain, the Soviet Union, and China to cooperate in maintaining postwar peace and security. Roosevelt, with the presidential campaign of 1944 not far away, was eager to be a strong advocate of collective security, since Republicans in Congress, heedful of the rapid switch of opinion among their constituency, were trying to coopt the issue. Consequently, at Quebec Roosevelt had brought up the draft of such a declaration, suggesting it be an interim arrangement. Churchill agreed that it should head the agenda at the Moscow conference. Subsequently the Russians objected to the inclusion of China as one of the "big four," but Roosevelt directed Hull to insist upon it.[33]

Hull's participation in the Moscow conference of 1943 succeeded far beyond expectations in preparing for the meeting of Roosevelt and Churchill with Stalin. After some days of hard discussion, Soviet Foreign

Minister Molotov agreed that China could sign the Four Powers Declaration, although before the conference he had refused even to allow the matter on the agenda. In private, Roosevelt crowed, "That is my contribution."[34]

At the final banquet, Stalin informed Hull that upon victory in Europe, the Soviets would join in defeating Japan. It was no more than a remark, and Bohlen, head of the Russian desk in the State Department, who was acting as interpreter, was not there to catch it. But it was further than Stalin had ever gone before, and as Hull later emphasized, there were no strings attached.[35]

Through his success in Moscow, Hull became Roosevelt's prime instrument in warming Congress and the public toward his proposal for a postwar peacekeeping organization. There was jubilation over the Moscow Agreement, the communiqué ending the conference, as an assurance of postwar unity. Even before it appeared, Roosevelt acclaimed the conference for its achievements and gave credit to Hull for its spirit. It served Roosevelt's purposes to elevate Hull into the hero of the meeting, and he went to the airport to hail his return. Hull, becoming the first secretary of state to address a joint session of Congress, assured his onetime colleagues, "I found in Marshal Stalin a remarkable personality, one of the great statesmen and leaders of this age." These words, coming from the revered and conservative Hull, raised expectations in Congress and the nation.[36]

Roosevelt needed to capitalize quickly upon that receptivity both at home and on the part of the Russian leaders. No sooner had the secretary of state returned from the Moscow conference than Roosevelt embarked on an Atlantic crossing, not by airplane, but in leisurely fashion aboard the battleship *Iowa*, bound for Tehran.

Chapter 35

THE CONFERENCE AT TEHRAN

WHEN ROOSEVELT in the company of Churchill finally met Stalin in Tehran late in 1943, the president seemed at the time to be strikingly effective. He secured the most important of his military plans for victory and sought to lay the foundations for a peace in which the United States would play a large and mediating role. Yet, even as the conferees disbanded, it seemed as though the one irresistible force in continental Europe was to be Stalin and the Red Army.

Roosevelt's opening gambit was en route to Tehran, at Cairo, where, to the frustration of Churchill and the British, he devoted most of his attention to discussion of China with Chiang Kai-shek and the influential, glamorous Madame Chiang. He thus blocked Churchill from advocacy of his pet schemes, to seize upon what he visualized as easy prizes in the eastern Mediterranean and the Balkans. Further, he forced postponement until the Tehran conference. There he could expect Stalin's backing in the crucial debates over whether to land in France in 1944. Churchill, wretched from a cold and pessimistic in outlook, had growled to his staff before the meeting that he was disposed to tell the Americans, "All right, if you won't play with us in the Mediterranean, we won't play with you in the English Channel." Nevertheless, he again fell under the spell of Roosevelt, and his mood changed. He informed his commanders that he was much pleased by his conversations with the president, and thought the British would not have serious difficulties. Brooke was skeptical, and with reason.[1]

The discussions with the Chinese gave Roosevelt the occasion to develop his East Asian policy in direct negotiations with Chiang. He sought the immediately important goal of trying to persuade Chiang to sanction the further training of forces and to commit them to fight against the Japanese.

The differences between British and American objectives in East Asia and the Pacific were even more pronounced than in Europe and the Mediterranean. Roosevelt tried to give the impression that he was an intermediary between the British and Chiang, although actually Chiang was his client. Churchill especially, and to a certain extent the British command, held as their objective, secondary only to defeating the Japanese, the restoration of the Union Jack over their colonies, from Burma to Hong Kong. They suspected that Roosevelt and the Americans through the device of anticolonialism sought to replace the British Empire, in part through strengthening China, and to build an American economic empire. Some leading American firms, having founded a China-American council in October, 1943, were already jockeying for postwar advantage over the British.[2]

The avowed purpose of Roosevelt in so assiduously courting Chiang was to align China on the Allied side in anticipation of the postwar era. As he had written Mountbatten several weeks earlier, "This will be very useful twenty-five or fifty years hence, even though China cannot contribute much military or naval support for the moment." Further, until it was completely clear that the Soviet Union would throw its weight against Japan after victory in Europe, Roosevelt wanted Chiang to continue as a threat to Japanese troops on the Asiatic mainland. Roosevelt promised Chiang much, and apparently demanded little in return.[3]

Rather, it was Chiang and the Chinese generals who created repeated obstacles, intermittently agreeing, then balking, and escalating their demands for supplies. The irritation became cumulative, having an effect later. On the evening of November 23, Roosevelt was a genial, generous host to the Chiangs. Apparently Hopkins was the only other American present; the only notes on the discussions are those of the Chinese.

The president, according to the Chinese record, declared that China should at once participate on terms of equality in the machinery and decisions of the "big four." He flatteringly proposed that China should undertake prime responsibility for the occupation of Japan, and asked Chiang if he thought the emperor should be removed. Chiang felt China was not equipped to occupy Japan. When Roosevelt raised a favorite topic, Hong Kong, Chiang cautiously suggested that the president should consult the British before further discussion.[4]

Roosevelt's refusal to include Chinese representatives in the deliberations of the chiefs of staff was a note of realism. It indicated how little Chiang could count upon the president's opening assurance that China at once should function fully as a member of the "big four." On the other hand, Roosevelt did clearly hope to use China as a major vehicle for the implementation of a Pax Americana in the Pacific.

The lengthy discussions concerning China were inconclusive, and there was no clear-cut decision on the Burma campaign. Marshall and the chiefs of staff firmly favored the invasion of the Andaman Islands athwart the sea lanes to Burma, holding it vital to Pacific operations and political aims. When Roosevelt left Cairo, Chiang was ready to participate in the Burma operation; the next day, unknown at the time to Roosevelt, he reversed himself, and then before Roosevelt returned from Tehran, re-reversed himself. By then it made no difference, for circumstances had altered Roosevelt's insistence upon the operation.[5]

For Churchill, the first meeting at Cairo seemed largely a waste of time. Roosevelt on November 26, much pleased, prepared to proceed to Tehran.

Well before the meeting, Roosevelt had arrived at rather firm ideas on what to expect from Stalin and the Russians, and what he would be willing to concede to them. After the Quebec conference, on September 3, he had set forth his views to Archbishop Spellman with candor. Churchill was too idealistic, he declared, while he and Stalin were realists. As a realist, Roosevelt expected Stalin would demand, and be able to take, a great deal. "He hoped," Spellman noted, " 'although it might be wishful thinking,' that the Russian intervention in Europe would not be too harsh." He hoped he could persuade Stalin not to annex beyond a certain line, although he counted as gone not only eastern Poland, the Baltic states, and Bessarabia, but also Finland. "So better give them gracefully. . . . What can we do about it?" He also expected Austria, Hungary, and Croatia to fall under some sort of Soviet protectorate, but thought France might escape if it had a liberal government like that of a reform premier in the 1930s, Leon Blum. On the mitigating side, he viewed Russia as having a strong economy, and "he hopes that in ten or twenty years the European influences would bring the Russians to become less barbarian." In any event, according to Spellman, Roosevelt felt that the Americans and British could not fight the Russians. "The Russian production is so big that the American help, except for trucks, is negligible."[6]

On the morning of November 27, Roosevelt departed for Tehran by plane, dipping low to view Jerusalem and Bethlehem, "everything very bare looking," noted Roosevelt, "and *I don't want* Palestine as my homeland." After the plane landed on "a vast plain or saucer with Tehran and its snow peaks to the north," Roosevelt commented, "I am glad we did not go in by train for we saved much time. . . . But I still don't like flying. This is a very dirty place — great poverty."[7]

Unexpectedly, Roosevelt became the guest of the Russians. At midnight Molotov summoned Harriman to warn him that there were German agents in Iran planning to assassinate the three leaders. Harriman was skeptical, but Roosevelt, wishing to demonstrate his goodwill toward Stalin, moved into the heavily guarded Soviet compound. Stalin turned over the main building, a large yellow brick mansion in which he had constructed a new bathroom for the president. The accommodations were especially convenient for Roosevelt, since all the plenary sessions took place in the embassy's conference room.

There was the question of whether the Soviets would eavesdrop on the private conversations of Roosevelt and Hopkins. "We were all agreed that it was probably a Russian trick," General Lord Ismay noted. "I wonder if microphones had already been installed in anticipation!" To Roosevelt it would not have mattered, since his greatest concern was to win over Stalin through gestures of openness and generosity.[8]

Roosevelt arrived at Tehran full of zest and optimism, feeling that he had spent his career reaching accommodations with men and that Stalin could not be so different. Even if he could not persuade him to become a good democrat, Roosevelt thought they could come to a working agreement. It was not a view likely to lift Churchill's gloom, since in order to gain American ends, Roosevelt was quite prepared to court Stalin as he had just been cajoling Chiang. "Sure, we are preparing for a battle at Tehran," Hopkins joked in advance to the British. "You will find us lining up with the Russians."[9]

Roosevelt, staying in the Russian embassy, gained fuller and more informal entry to Stalin than did Churchill at the nearby British embassy. Shortly after Roosevelt arrived, Stalin, accompanied only by an interpreter, called upon him, and Roosevelt for a half hour or more in random fashion brought up one serious matter after another. He said that he wished "it were within his power to relieve the pressure through removing 30 or 40 German divisions from the eastern front — one of the questions he wanted to discuss in Tehran." Stalin replied politely that would be of great value. Roosevelt then switched topics to dangle before Stalin a possible postwar prize, much as he had with Chiang. In this instance it was surplus vessels from the Anglo-American merchant fleet. Stalin responded to the gambit in kind. An adequate fleet would help not only the Soviet Union but also Soviet-American relations, which he hoped would be greatly expanded after the war.

The conversation shifted to Chiang and China; then much of it centered on France. Stalin remarked that France should not get back Indochina. Roosevelt "said he was 100% in agreement . . . that after 100 years of French rule in Indochina, the inhabitants were worse off than they had been." He proposed a trusteeship to prepare Indochina for independence in twenty or thirty years. Stalin agreed.

Continuing on colonialism, Roosevelt tried to be ingratiating concerning India. He "felt that the best solution would be reform from the bottom, somewhat on the Soviet line." Stalin shrugged off the flattery with a bit of realism. He "replied that the India question was a complicated one, with different levels of culture and the absence of relationship in the castes. He added that reform from the bottom would mean revolution."

Bohlen, acting as interpreter for Roosevelt, looked upon the startling remark that India might be reformed "from the bottom, somewhat on the Soviet line" as an indication of Roosevelt's lack of knowledge of the way in which a Bolshevik minority seized power at the top in 1917. Roosevelt was indeed far from sophisticated in his knowledge of the Soviets. His allusion to "the Soviet line" was in such sharp contrast to his reiterated desire to remodel India parallel to the evolution of colonial America into the federal union, that it is a clear indication of the extent to which he would shape his remarks to try to win Stalin's support.[10]

The effort was unnecessary, since — as the plenary session starting a few minutes later indicated — American and Soviet interests coincided. Stalin did not, as Roosevelt and his staff had earlier feared, wish a strong thrust through the Balkans. Rather, like Roosevelt, he wanted his allies to concentrate on the cross-channel invasion.

The first, and in many respects the most crucial, meeting began at four on the afternoon of November 28. Roosevelt, determined to be the dominant figure, had arranged to preside. There was, at this meeting and throughout the conference, no agenda, as Roosevelt requested. He wanted the conferees to be free to bring up whatever they wished, and to keep the sessions relatively informal. Nevertheless, they unfolded much as had those at previous conferences. Each leader sat flanked by his diplomatic and military advisers: Churchill with Foreign Secretary Eden and the British chiefs of staff, Stalin with Foreign Secretary Molotov and Marshal Voroshilov, and Roosevelt with Hopkins and the American chiefs of staff. At the end of the morning, Roosevelt told the chiefs he had nothing planned for the afternoon, but then at lunch changed his mind. It was too late to recall Generals Marshall and Arnold, who had gone sight-seeing to the north of Tehran. Even in Marshall's absence, the meeting went as he would have wished.[11]

Roosevelt launched into a survey of the war, first in the Pacific, then in Europe, from the American point of view. To the British interpreter, Major A. H. Birse, who had not seen him before, he seemed a commanding figure as he sat at the head of the conference table:

> . . . with his broad shoulders and fine head, he had the appearance of a tall strong man, and it was only [his wheelchair] which gave away his infirmity. He beamed on all around the table and looked very much like the kind, rich uncle paying a visit to his poorer relations. While speaking, he would frequently take off his pince-nez and use it to emphasize his point. He spoke firmly, as if sure of his ground, but at the same time he appeared ready to listen to the promptings of his advisers who sat alongside. His manner was pleasing, but I wondered what there was behind that intellectual face.

But as the conference wore on, Birse, like others of the British delegation, felt that Roosevelt was ill informed concerning the Soviet mentality, nor did he like the president "taking sides with Stalin, ostensibly as a joke, but nevertheless tactlessly, in allusion to British colonialism."[12]

When Stalin began to speak, he initially made no comment on Overlord; then to the surprise of the Americans, in casual fashion without raising his voice and while continuing to doodle, he pledged future aid in the Pacific war. It was an assurance Roosevelt and the Joint Chiefs had eagerly sought, but the topic was so sensitive that they had agreed not to discuss it unless the Soviets broached the subject. Once Germany was defeated, Stalin said, the Soviets would sent reinforcements to Siberia and join the common effort to defeat Japan.[13]

Stalin's proposals for the war in Europe were heartening to Roosevelt. The best route to the heart of Germany would be an attack through northern France and even through southern France, although that would be a difficult operation. The president and his advisers had given little thought to a landing along the Mediterranean coast, to be associated with the main invasion in the north, but during the conference as Stalin repeatedly suggested attacking there, they included it in their program.[14]

Each of the three leaders was conciliatory during the meeting, at least making obeisance to the others' points of view. In declaring that he favored the cross-channel attack, Stalin added, according to the Combined Chiefs' notes, that while the Alps would block a successful attack upon Germany from Italy, if Turkey could open the way, a cross-channel attack would be unnecessary. Churchill, concealing his desire to postpone Overlord, reassured Stalin that "both he and the President had never regarded the Mediterranean operations as more than a stepping stone to the main offensive against Germany." And Roosevelt a little later followed in kind with a suggestion that must have been tantalizing to Churchill. Perhaps, he said, an offensive aimed from the northeastern Adriatic toward the Danube would help the Soviets. Already Churchill had made the ingratiating remark that the Communist Tito (Josip Broz) was far more effective in Yugoslavia than his rival Draza Mihailovich. Churchill, who had no thought of dispatching a large army, proposed increasing supplies to Tito. The next day, Roosevelt handed Stalin the favorable report of an American Army officer who had spent six months with Tito. Hopkins, dismayed, jotted a note to Admiral King, "Who's promoting that Adriatic business that the President continually refers to?" King replied, "As far as I know it is his own idea."[15]

Apparently it was an on-the-spot improvisation of Roosevelt's, which grew logically out of the strategy he had discussed that morning with the chiefs of staff to counter demands for troops in eastern Europe with the promise of supplies. At the session, Roosevelt expanded the idea, as he told Marshall, to neutralize Churchill's campaign for an operation against Rhodes. Roosevelt was fearful that once Rhodes fell, the British would insist upon going into Greece.[16]

In the first session, Stalin had come down firmly in favor of the grand strategy that Roosevelt and his chiefs of staff sought. Further, he had gratuitously bestowed upon Roosevelt the promise that after the victory in the west, Russia would enter the war against Japan, an assurance that relieved greatly the pressure to divert American resources to China. Churchill and the British did not fare so well, except to the degree that they had, as Churchill said, always been committed to the cross-channel invasion. Churchill in his quest for prizes in the Aegean was receiving no more than the consolation that he could seek Turkey's entry into the war, which both Stalin and Roosevelt deemed futile. After the session, Churchill, in low spirits, remarked to his physician, "A bloody lot has gone wrong," and General Brooke lamented, "This Conference is over when it has only just begun. Stalin has got the President in his pocket."

As the conference progressed, Churchill was forced into the position of lesser partner to the American and Soviet giants, each representing military might far beyond that of the British. Roosevelt, well aware of the overwhelming size of the Red Army, was not turning anti-British. Hopkins acted quickly to fill in the British accurately on Roosevelt's initial private talk with Stalin, even to the dig that Stalin should not discuss India with Churchill. Rather, Roosevelt, as he and Hopkins kept explaining, was determined, even if he could not transform Stalin into a democratic leader, to win his trust and lay the basis for viable postwar relations. However, as indicated by the quick burial at the first session of any operations that would seriously delay the second front, Roosevelt also profited from Stalin's support for strategies in the American national interest.[17]

During the conference, Roosevelt and Stalin saw a good deal of each other, both at the sessions and dinners and privately. Several times Stalin without warning dropped by Roosevelt's room, smiling, expressing solicitude for his comfort, and engaging in small talk. Each turned his charm on the other.

Stalin, as Roosevelt recalled it, "volunteered his desire to conciliate his neighbors, saying flatly that he had no desire to own Europe. His country, he added, is only half populated and the Russians have plenty to do at home, without undertaking great new territorial responsibilities."[18]

These disarming remarks, which Roosevelt undoubtedly exaggerated in an interview for the *Saturday Evening Post*, were, however, in keeping with the impression Stalin created at Tehran. At the dinner of November 29, when Stalin reminded Churchill how he had tried to destroy the Soviet regime after World War I, Stalin added "that Mr. Churchill need not have worried quite so much as they [the Russians] had discovered that it was not so easy to set up Communist regimes."[19]

During the lively flow of conversation after dinner the first evening, November 28, 1943, before Roosevelt could move into the theme of his plans for peacekeeping, Bohlen recalled that he "suddenly, in the flick of an eye . . . turned green and great drops of sweat began to bead off his face; he put a shaky hand to his forehead. We were all caught by surprise. The President had made no complaint, and none of us had detected any sign of discomfort."

At a signal from Hopkins, Roosevelt was wheeled to his room, where Admiral Ross McIntire, his physician, examined him. His staff was alarmed. The assistant naval aide, William F. Rigdon, remembered, "Our first thought was that his food had been poisoned. Next, that he might have had a heart attack." McIntire diagnosed the attack as nothing more than indigestion, and in his memoir did not mention the episode. The next morning, Roosevelt seemed fine, as vigorous as ever.[20]

When Roosevelt, Churchill, and Stalin assembled with their commanders in plenary session on the afternoon of November 29, the success of the conference seemed to be in doubt because of the British reservations over launching Overlord in May or June. Stalin asked a crucial question about the cross-channel attack, presumably only five or six months in the future. Who would command the operation? he inquired. Roosevelt seemed taken aback; he said it had not yet been decided. "Then nothing will come out of these operations," Stalin retorted. Roosevelt whispered to Admiral Leahy, sitting next to him, "That old Bolshevik is trying to force me to give him the name of our Supreme Commander. I just can't tell him because I have not yet made up my mind." He and Churchill assured Stalin they would decide upon the appointment quickly.

Stalin pressed for a firm date for Overlord, for an operation in southern France (which would be supportive, not diversionary like the campaign against Rome or one in the Balkans), and for the appointment of a commander in chief for Overlord, preferably before the end of the conference. "Until that is done the Overlord operation cannot be considered as really in progress."

In the ensuing debate, Roosevelt followed the same cautious course as on November 28. For his part, Churchill tried to act in a cooperative fashion while clinging to his schemes: "The British Government was anxious to begin Overlord as soon as possible but did not desire to neglect the great possibilities in the Mediterranean merely for the sake of avoiding a delay of a month or two."

Stalin said he wanted to ask Churchill an indiscreet question: "Do the British really believe in Overlord or are they only saying so to reassure the Russians[?]"

Churchill retorted "that if the conditions set forth at Moscow were present it was the duty of the British Government to hurl every scrap of strength across the channel."

Again Roosevelt tried to act as the conciliator.[21]

That evening, November 29, Stalin hosted the dinner, and while giving an appearance of joviality, as Bohlen noted at the time, "lost no opportunity to get in a dig at Mr. Churchill." The president seemed to relish the exchanges — not surprisingly, since Roosevelt had always himself been a conspicuous tease. He later told his cabinet "that Joe teased the P.M. like a boy and it was very amusing." The teasing descended to macabre depths. According to a British account, Stalin declared that fifty thousand Germans must be killed, that their General Staff must go. Churchill retorted, "I will not be party to any butchery in cold blood." Roosevelt interjected with a compromise, that only forty-nine thousand should be shot. Churchill left the room; Stalin followed him, protesting he was only joking. They returned, Stalin grinning broadly, and embraced.

There was one last ominous note, when Churchill tried to draw out

Stalin on his territorial aims. Stalin said, "There is no need to speak at the present time about any Soviet desires, but when the time comes, we will speak."[22]

After the dinner broke up, Hopkins, at the peak of his influence with Roosevelt, went to see Churchill to warn him that both Roosevelt and Stalin were firm in their determination not to delay the invasion of France, that he might best yield with grace.[23]

On Tuesday, November 30, Churchill's birthday, he awoke in a more optimistic mood, and the British did indeed "yield with grace." When the draft conclusions of the Combined Chiefs came before Roosevelt, they read: "Agreed — To inform Stalin that we will launch OVERLORD by June 1st. . . ." Roosevelt wrote in, "during the month of May," thus avoiding argument.[24]

With military commitments firm, Roosevelt could turn his attention almost fully to postwar concerns. Ambassador Harriman in retrospect felt that Roosevelt's prime political aim at the Tehran conference was to win Stalin's support for a new international organization to keep the peace. In his private conversation with Stalin the day before he had broached the plan: a worldwide body of some thirty-five of the United Nations, which would make recommendations to deal with nonmilitary matters to an executive committee consisting of the Soviet Union, the United States, the United Kingdom, and China, together with some six other countries (including one British dominion). In addition there would be the "Four Policemen" to deal immediately with any threat to peace. But, Stalin pointed out, the world organization Roosevelt envisaged, especially the Four Policemen, might also require the stationing of Americans in Europe. Roosevelt then gave one of his most telling answers:

> . . . that he had only envisaged the sending of American planes and ships to Europe, and that England and the Soviet Union would have to handle the land armies in the event of any future threat to peace. He went on to say that if the Japanese had not attacked the United States he doubted very much if it would have been possible to send any American forces to Europe. . . . He saw two methods of dealing with possible threats to peace. In one case if the threat arose from a revolution or developments in a small country, it might be possible to apply the quarantine method, closing the frontiers of the countries in question and imposing embargoes. In the second case, if the threat was more serious, the four powers, acting as policemen, would send an ultimatum to the nation in

> question and if refused, [it] would result in the immediate bombardment and possible invasion of that country.[25]

The high point of amity and optimism came that evening. Churchill hosted a dinner on the occasion of his sixty-ninth birthday, notable for the generous expansiveness of the toasts and the lavish assurances of friendship. Churchill and Roosevelt heaped praise upon each other and upon Stalin, whom Churchill said merited the title "Stalin the Great."

Near the end of the evening Stalin paid the Americans so unique a compliment that Roosevelt embodied it in his presidential log of the conference:

> I want to tell you, from the Russian point of view, what the President and the United States have done to win the war. The most important things in this war are machines. The United States has proven that it can turn out from 8,000 to 10,000 airplanes a month. Russia can turn out, at most, 3,000 airplanes a month. . . . The United States, therefore, is a country of machines. Without the use of those machines, through Lend-Lease, we would lose this war.[26]

There was a full day of negotiations ahead before the gathering dispersed, and there were problems minor as well as major that required agreement. One of the problems, which seemed relatively slight at the time, was to underwrite the independence of Iran, lying between the Soviet Union and the oil fields along the Persian Gulf. Already Roosevelt had met ceremonially to exchange gifts and amenities with the young shah, Mohammed Reza Pahlavi, whose fortunes for decades to come were to be deeply involved with the United States.[27]

Roosevelt also found time for a brief but enthusiastic conversation with the shah's American financial administrator, Arthur C. Millspaugh, who explained that Iranians for the third time since 1910 had sought American administrative aid to strengthen their economic position and maintain their independence from both Russian and British domination. Millspaugh described how the Americans were not only straightening out Iran's finances but also building railroads and highways, promoting irrigation and agriculture, education and public health. Roosevelt, surprised and gratified, declared that Iran was serving as a clinic, demonstrating the practicability of the trusteeships that he hoped would raise living standards and promote democracy after the war. He wanted Americans similarly to serve in other problem areas of Asia.[28]

After lunch on the final day, Roosevelt met privately with Stalin and

Molotov to express views that his interpreter, Bohlen, thought deplorable. According to Bohlen's minutes:

> THE PRESIDENT said he . . . wished to discuss a matter briefly and frankly. He said it referred to internal American politics.
>
> He said that we had an election in 1944 and that while personally he did not wish to run again, if the war was still in progress, he might have to.
>
> He added that there were in the United States from six to seven million Americans of Polish extraction, and as a practical man, he did not wish to lose their vote. He said personally he agreed with the views of Marshal Stalin as to the necessity of the restoration of a Polish state but would like to see the Eastern border moved further to the west and the Western border moved even to the River Oder. He hoped, however, that the Marshal would understand that for political reasons . . . he could not participate in any decision here in Tehran or even next winter on this subject and that he could not publicly take part in any such arrangement at the present time.

Stalin replied he understood. Roosevelt's explanation to Stalin was no doubt frank, but as Eden pointed out, "was hardly calculated to restrain the Russians."[29]

Next, Roosevelt dealt similarly with the question of Soviet absorption of the Baltic states. There were many people of Lithuanian, Latvian, and Estonian origin in the United States, he said, joking that when the Soviet armies reoccupied their homelands he did not intend to go to war with the Soviet Union over that issue. American public opinion, he added, would be concerned that these peoples enjoy the right of self-determination, and he was confident that they would vote to join the Soviet Union. Roosevelt explained that the American public neither knew nor understood. Then, declared Stalin, in terms indicating how different his view of democracy was from Roosevelt's, "they should be informed, and some propaganda work should be done." Roosevelt parried that it would be helpful to him if Stalin would make some public declaration concerning future elections. Stalin replied only that "there would be plenty of opportunities for such an expression of the will of the people."[30]

At the final political meeting, at six o'clock on December 1, Roosevelt opened the session by declaring that the two main questions before them concerned the postwar treatment of Poland and Germany. But first, he and Churchill agreed with the Russian request for part of the captured

Italian war and merchant fleets — a concession that caused much difficulty in ensuing months. Then Roosevelt brought up Poland — not its boundaries, but his hope that the Soviets would reestablish relations with the Polish government-in-exile in London. Stalin hedged, finally declaring that if the government-in-exile would cooperate with the Partisans (i.e., the Communists) in Poland, and sever connections that Stalin alleged existed with German agents in Poland, he would negotiate. On this touchy issue, a portent of the gulf to grow unbridgeable in the future, Roosevelt seems to have made no comment, but Churchill in conciliatory fashion asserted that "the British government wished to see a Poland strong and friendly to Russia."

On the future boundaries of Poland, Roosevelt, as he had forewarned, stayed out of the discussion. But by being present he seemed to be giving his tacit consent. While he sat listening, Churchill suggested again the solution he had broached on that earlier evening after Roosevelt, ill, had left for his bedroom. Churchill had moved three matches across the table, suggesting that while the Russians move their boundary with Poland westward, the Poles in compensation move their own western boundary into what had been German territory, as far as the Oder River.

Roosevelt turned over to Stalin and Churchill a State Department map of the eastern frontier of Poland, with the boundaries before and after 1939 and the proposed British Curzon Line of 1919 marked upon it. Stalin then for the first time asserted a territorial claim against Germany. He wanted to take the ice-free port of Königsberg and the northern part of East Prussia, and then follow the Curzon Line southward, absorbing considerably more Ukrainian territory than that within the 1939 boundary.

During the drawing of the line on the map, Roosevelt abandoned his resolve and entered into the discussion. He inquired if the area Poland would annex from Germany equaled the former Polish territory Russia was acquiring. Stalin said he did not know, but that the Soviet Union did not wish to retain territories that were primarily Polish. Then, pressed Roosevelt, would a voluntary transfer of peoples from mixed areas be possible? Stalin conceded that a transfer would be entirely possible. Thus Roosevelt seemed to be giving sanction to what, with only slight exceptions, became Poland's postwar boundary. The bargain at Tehran, whether or not Roosevelt felt committed to it, was entirely verbal.[31]

With enthusiasm, Roosevelt turned the discussion to postwar Germany and himself entered into the drawing of lines on a European map — but without the lasting effect that Stalin and Churchill had just achieved.

He proposed what for several months had been on his mind, that Germany be divided into five self-governing areas.

A discussion followed as to how Germany could best be dismembered in order not to be a future threat to peace. Churchill inquired whether Stalin envisioned a Europe of small states, "disjoined, separated, and weak." Stalin replied not Europe but Germany, and then, reversing what he had declared earlier in the conference, said that Poland, France, and Italy would be strong. They agreed that the European Advisory Commission should study the dismemberment of Germany. That was the only solid conclusion, and it led to nothing.[32]

It remained at dinner that evening only to put into final form the declaration on Iran and the conference communiqué. The drafting of the Tehran Declaration, a document important for its impact on world opinion, was almost entirely an American undertaking. Roosevelt assigned the task to his son-in-law, Major John Boettiger, a onetime *Chicago Tribune* reporter handling press relations. The declaration was inspiring in its pledge that the three leaders would "seek the cooperation of all nations, large and small, whose peoples in heart and mind are dedicated, as are our own peoples, to the elimination of tyranny and slavery, oppression and intolerance. We will welcome them . . . into a world family of democratic nations."[33]

Roosevelt departed from Tehran well pleased. With the aid of Stalin he had squeezed the reluctant Churchill into an almost irrevocable commitment to strike into France the following spring. Not all of Roosevelt's associates were equally pleased. Admiral Leahy remarked to Hopkins, "Well, Harry, all I can say is, nice friends we have now." Charles E. Bohlen, in a memorandum to Ambassador Harriman on December 15, pointed out that Stalin's remarks gave "a glimpse of the Soviet idea of post-war continental Europe. . . . The Soviet Union would be the only important military and political force. . . . The rest of Europe would be reduced to military and political impotence."[34]

To Stalin, the conference seemed to give a go-ahead signal for political dominance as the Soviet armies moved westward. Churchill alone of the three was quite ambivalent. On the flight out of Tehran he was exhausted and silent, coming down with a serious illness.

In a few hours both Roosevelt and Churchill were back in Cairo. Roosevelt in high spirits sent word to Stalin that the conference had been "an important milestone in the progress of human affairs." That evening, Roosevelt and Churchill continued their strategic debates. On two successive evenings, Churchill tried to persuade Roosevelt to reduce the Andaman Island operations so that the British could seize Rhodes. Roosevelt persisted that he must honor his pledges to Chiang. Neither could sway the other that weekend; Roosevelt by this time had become too familiar with Churchill's eloquence. After his return to Washington, he remarked to Judge Rosenman, "Winston has developed a tendency to make long speeches which he has made before."[35]

Churchill's success would depend in part upon how convincing he could be in his efforts to persuade President Ismet Inönü to bring Turkey into the war. The Rhodes project would, he felt, be the key factor in winning Turkish entry, yet unless Turkey declared war on Germany it would be pointless. Turkey did not enter the war, and by 1947 under the Truman Doctrine would be receiving American aid to stand firm against the Soviets.[36]

Roosevelt as well as Churchill was trying to stave off the inevitable. Yet it was obvious, with the shortage of landing craft a major problem, that if the landings in France were to succeed, the attack on the Andaman Islands (called BUCCANEER) would have to be abandoned. For several days, Roosevelt tried to compromise on scaling it down, then finally, on December 5, while both were in Cairo, Roosevelt sent Churchill a terse message: "Buccaneer is off."

Roosevelt's shift was inevitable. Stalin's assurances that Russia would enter the Pacific war, and his apparent agreement with Roosevelt's plans for an East Asian peace settlement, made the inactive Chiang less important to Roosevelt than he had been before the Tehran meeting. Roosevelt, still not wanting to lose Chiang's goodwill or to seem responsible for China's being knocked out of the war, had reason to argue as long as he did for a limited invasion. He did not want to rely totally upon Stalin. But the Andaman invasion would have been more a sideshow for political effect, and Roosevelt was bent upon dealing Hitler a coup de grace at the earliest possible time. It was vital to marshal every possible landing craft for the invasion of France.[37]

Before he left Cairo, Roosevelt had to come to a decision on the command of the forces that would invade France. In this instance, his postponement had brought resolution of the pros and cons. He had hoped earlier to retain the authority and prestige of General Marshall as chief of staff, able to wield his influence both in American councils and, on the Combined Chiefs of Staff, with the British. This Roosevelt could do if the British would agree that there be a supreme commander over the Anglo-American forces both in the assault against Germany and in the Mediterranean. With Marshall in that position, then General Eisenhower could return to Washington as acting chief of staff. Neither Churchill nor his chiefs of staff would accept such an arrangement. Nor was that surprising, since although American strength was burgeoning, half the troops in the cross-channel attack would be British or Canadian. Churchill had already had to abandon his wish to make General Brooke the invasion commander; he would not also give up control over forces in the Mediterranean, where he still hoped for ventures. Finally, in keeping Marshall in Washington, Roosevelt would put to an end widespread right-wing allegations that he was plotting to remove Marshall from his position of power as chief of staff.[38]

Breaking the news to Marshall was again not the sort of task Roosevelt relished, but he did it skillfully by asking Marshall to decide which position he wanted. It was obvious, as Roosevelt well knew, that Marshall wanted to be the Grant or Pershing of the war, but it was also obvious that Marshall was too loyal and well-disciplined a military leader to act against the wishes of his commander in chief. He offered Marshall his choice, and when Marshall insisted he wanted Roosevelt "to feel free to act in whatever way he felt was to the best interest of the country," Roosevelt assumed the discussion was over, and remarked, "I feel I could not sleep at night with you out of the country." Roosevelt upon his return to Washington took pains to explain his choice in a rather disingenuous way to the thunderstruck Stimson, who had emphatically favored Marshall.[39]

The next morning, Roosevelt flew back to Tunis. Eisenhower met him at the airport, and as they drove off, Roosevelt said, "Well, Ike, you are going to command Overlord." Immediately that afternoon and the next day en route to Malta and Sicily, Roosevelt talked at length with Eisenhower, in part discursively, but also to the point, on the enormous problems Eisenhower would face when he assumed command in London. Eisenhower began immediately planning the choice of his subordinates.[40]

Roosevelt would have liked to visit Naples, but Eisenhower, considering the city too dangerous, managed to divert him to Sicily. At an airfield there, he decorated several officers, and conversed with General George Patton, who was under a cloud. Americans were outraged when the columnist Drew Pearson had published an embellished account late in November of Patton slapping a hospitalized soldier suffering battle fatigue. General Marshall doubted Patton's fitness for a command during the invasion, but Eisenhower considered him too valuable to lose. So did Roosevelt, who told Patton the incident was closed, bringing tears to Patton's eyes.[41]

On December 17, Roosevelt landed refreshed, tanned and jaunty at the Washington Navy Yard, dressed with unprecedented informality in a sweater and blue plaid shirt. His cabinet, the subcabinet, and a number of congressmen of both parties were at the White House to greet him when he was wheeled in from his car. He had been gone five weeks, and had traveled an unprecedented 17,442 miles. Meanwhile, Churchill, exhausted, had become ill in Tunis with pneumonia complicated by a heart condition, so seriously that at one point his physician feared he might not live through the night. Roosevelt in contrast seemed in fine form, bothered only by a nagging cough. To him the Cairo and Tehran conferences seemed a resounding triumph.[42]

In ebullient spirits, Roosevelt recounted his adventures to the cabinet and congressional leaders. Although he was well aware that whatever he said might leak into print, he gave a lively and relatively full account. Attorney General Francis Biddle noted how far Roosevelt went in his hyperbole:

"The President said he thought we would have more trouble in the Post War World with the English than with the Russians. He said that for a year and a half he had been trying to persuade 'Winnie' — as he always calls Churchill to agree to return Hong Kong to the Chinese after the war. Winnie's response had always been a grunt."[43]

The Tehran and Cairo agreements aroused not nearly as much enthusiasm among the American public as had the Moscow agreements. The generalities of communiqués had become too commonplace to be stirring, and while much that transpired at the conference leaked or percolated out from those Roosevelt had briefed, the news that would have caused general rejoicing — Stalin's promise to join the war against Japan — did not become public. Isaiah Berlin of the British embassy informed Whitehall that, in contrast to the excitement over the Moscow agreement and acclaim for Hull, there was no more than "somewhat tepid approval of the President's activities." That was partly because the Moscow statement relieved anxieties, but it also indicated the contrast between the confidence in Hull and "the mixture of admiration for the President's skill in negotiation, with fear of 'cleverness.' " A high State Department official (Hull perhaps?) confided to one reporter "that he feared that the President had given away much of what Hull had secured from the Russians." Berlin did not add that Congress, by rallying behind Hull, was expressing its alienation from Roosevelt. There was plenty involving Congress to occupy Roosevelt in the weeks that followed his return.[44]

Chapter 36

DOCTOR WIN-THE-WAR

BY THE TIME Roosevelt returned from Tehran and Cairo, the next presidential campaign was already in its preliminary stages. Once more he had to focus upon both the electorate and the increasingly alienated Congress if he was to achieve his wartime and postwar goals. Less than a quarter century earlier, President Wilson had failed with the electorate and with the Senate. Roosevelt was determined to avoid both traps.

Inside Congress and out, politicians who did not like Roosevelt — and their number was formidable — were determined in 1944 to rid the nation of both him and the remaining vestiges of his New Deal. Not only the opposition Republicans but also numerous conservative, especially southern, Democrats were no longer worried about winning the war. The electorate was becoming optimistic and turning to the right, public opinion polls indicated. One Gallup survey found 58 percent opposing numerous changes after the war.[1]

The preponderance of hostile feeling in Congress had become news. Roosevelt's shift toward conservative appointees and his delegation of many domestic matters to the cautious James F. Byrnes, one of the most popular southern leaders, did little to mollify the opposition. Privately some of the southerners felt that a Republican victory in 1944 would be no catastrophe, since it would give them four years to evict the New Dealers from the Democratic party.[2]

There was little mystery among the public or within the White House about whether Roosevelt would run in 1944. Unlike 1940, it was a foregone conclusion, which the president disguised only in routine fashion. In early February, 1944, when Ickes remarked he did not think

Secretary of the Navy Frank Knox would back a Democrat for president, Roosevelt replied, "He will support me if I am a candidate."[3]

Roosevelt's leadership in the great wartime coalition would be his biggest asset in the 1944 election. When Raymond Clapper, one of the most influential columnists, acclaimed the unique value of the "big four" conferees at Tehran and Cairo, Henry Luce, publisher of *Time*, complained to Clapper that the column had "stuck with me overnight in a strangely disturbing way. Not like bad oysters. More like some subtle nightmare of premonition.

"Has Ray Clapper now bowed down to the doctrine of the Indispensable Man or Men? Are we hereafter helpless without Fuehrers singular or plural?"[4]

Luce was putting his finger on the paradox of the time, replied Clapper; to preserve the free world the United Nations must work through a "personal quadrumvirate":

"This is the crisis period and it seems to me a very unwise time to change. . . . Can you think of putting my old friend Alf Landon into Roosevelt's shoes to protect our chips in a game with Stalin, Churchill and Chiang?"[5]

Therein lay Roosevelt's greatest strength, and he prudently husbanded it. A Roper poll in the November, 1943, *Fortune* indicated that while no more than 56 percent rated his job on home problems as good, 70 percent favored his conduct of the war and foreign policy. That same month, 58 percent of Republicans queried by Gallup said they favored a bipartisan foreign policy. There was good reason for Roosevelt to be slow in setting forth specifics of his peacekeeping proposals, as he sought to avoid shattering the growing consensus on his international policies.[6]

Rather, from the day of his return from Tehran Roosevelt addressed himself with vigor to the growing crisis in domestic affairs. The war seemed to have been won on the home front in terms of production of munitions, and there was a prevalent expectation, even among Roosevelt's top military advisers, that the fighting might be over as soon as the spring. That would not have been a wild estimate if the heads of the armed forces of Germany and Japan had, like the German staff in 1918, been disposed to sue for peace as soon as all reasonable prospect for victory had evaporated. But even while war production in numerous areas of the United States was being cut back, and reconversion to production for consumers seemed both feasible and imminent, the major American battles against both the Germans and the Japanese had yet to be fought.

The president had returned to a nation in a state both of euphoria and of political deadlock. There was little public pressure upon Congress to enact Roosevelt's tax and price-fixing measures because inflation was relatively mild, and American industry was not only filling war orders but also producing unprecedented amounts of consumer goods (except for prohibited automobiles and household appliances). The volume of Christmas shopping was breaking all records, up 60 percent over the boom years of the 1920s.[7]

The immediate problems confronting Roosevelt were public complacency, labor unrest, and obstruction in Congress. At his first press conference, hours after his return to Washington, the president asked, tongue-in-cheek, "Anything happen here while I was away?" The response was loud laughter. One reporter replied, "That was the trouble." During his weeks away the battle against inflation had gone badly. The latest time bomb was about to explode: economic stabilizer Fred M. Vinson had denied wage increases of more than 4 cents an hour to the railroad brotherhoods, and they voted to strike on December 30. Festering difficulties involving labor, agriculture, and industry had accumulated during Roosevelt's absence. It was up to him to resolve them.[8]

Roosevelt worried that the spreading optimism would lead people to relax in the war effort. "One of the best things that could happen," he remarked to the cabinet, "would be to have a few German bombs fall here to wake us up." Point by point he took up not only economic problems but also political ones. From Oran, he said he had smelled something bad, that southern Democrats were threatening to start a new party. "Cotton Ed" Smith of South Carolina had risen in the Senate to declare, "If the people of the South organize and stand by their self-respect. . . . there will never be another Democratic President — I mean of a certain variety." Roosevelt was concerned, too, by the congressional opposition to the soldiers' vote bill — an opposition that conservatives and southerners based on states' rights, and that transparently rested upon their fears that soldiers' absentee ballots would go heavily to Roosevelt.[9]

In domestic matters, Roosevelt was disposed again to marshal the nation toward more vigorous war efforts, to forgo inflationary wage and price increases and pay higher taxes, although it was a program that would alienate and even anger influential segments of the population. His immediate task was to seek some scheme in negotiations with the railroad workers to pay them side benefits without breaching the ceiling of the Little Steel formula. The brotherhoods were in no mood to give anything, and after several more sessions, Roosevelt announced he had drafted orders to take over the railroads. Two brotherhoods on December 24 accepted Roosevelt's offer to arbitrate, but three others were still balking.[10]

The labor news was still worse after Christmas; Roosevelt, announcing that he could not "wait until the last minute to take action," ordered the army to seize and operate the railroads so that supplies to the fighting men would not be interrupted. The takeover went smoothly; by mid-January all the brotherhoods had accepted Roosevelt's arbitration offers, and the railroads reverted to private operation. The steel workers, hoping arbitration would lift their wages above the Little Steel formula, returned to the mills.[11]

Once more the president personally had helped avert a labor crisis, expending his limited time and energy to do so. More and more, he felt that only a firm solution would forestall disruptions, the enactment of legislation obligating every able-bodied person who might be needed to serve the country in either a military or civilian capacity.

Long before Roosevelt's return from Tehran, many ardent New Dealers were concerned over his insistence upon controls. Congressman Lyndon Johnson saw only disaster ahead for the Democrats, telling Ickes that because he was remaining loyal to the president he doubted if he could carry the primary in his Texas district. Anna Roosevelt Boettiger at lunch with the Ickeses said her father had observed "that politics goes in swings and that it is about time for a swing back to conservatism"[12]

This was the context in which Roosevelt at Christmastime, 1943, announced the retirement of Dr. New Deal and the advent of Dr. Win-the-War. If conservatism were defined as maintenance of wartime controls and restrictions upon the individual, Roosevelt was indeed turning conservative. On the other hand, it was those generally deemed most right-wing among his opponents in Congress who were assuming a libertarian and states' rights stance against him. Not everyone thought that the president was embarked upon a fatal political trajectory. One correspondent, Ernest K. Lindley, observed, "It is at least possible that the politicians who have tied their future to the money-grabbing special interests have guessed wrong."[13]

After the close of his pre-Christmas press conference on the railroad strike, the president dropped the remark to Dilworth Lupton of the *Cleveland Press* that he wished reporters would no longer refer to his program as the New Deal; it was time for some catchy new term like "win the war." It made a striking exclusive story, and at the next press conference, when a correspondent brought up the subject, Roosevelt was ready for him, and indeed afterwards issued an edited version of the comments as a press release.

The analogy was that the New Deal came into existence because the United States, "an awfully sick patient," was suffering from grave internal disorders. Thereupon Roosevelt reminded the nation of "all those ills of 1933," and of the remedies that after a few years brought recovery. Then, on December 7, 1941, there had come "a very bad accident — not an internal trouble, breaking several bones":

> Old Doctor New Deal didn't know "nothing" about legs and arms. . . . So he got his partner, who was an orthopedic surgeon, Dr. Win-the-War, to take care of this fellow. . . . And the result is that the patient is back on his feet. He has given up his crutches. He isn't wholly well yet, and he won't be until he wins the war.
>
> And I think that is almost as simple, that little allegory, as learning again how to spell "cat."

At some length, in no fashion that would give comfort to conservatives, Roosevelt elaborated upon the achievements of "old Doctor New Deal."

The point to all this, Roosevelt concluded, was that at present "the overwhelming first emphasis should be on winning the war":

> And when victory comes . . . it seems pretty clear that we must plan for, and help bring about an expanded economy which will result in more security, in more employment, in more education, in more health, in better housing for all of our citizens, so that the conditions of 1932 and the beginning of 1933 won't come back again.[14]

Whatever Roosevelt intended in retiring the term "New Deal," friends and foes alike interpreted it as a retreat to the right. While Republicans rejoiced that the New Deal white lamb of the 1932 campaign had become the black sheep of 1944, loyal liberals in the Roosevelt administration were dismayed. Budget Director Smith lamented to Ickes that he was so disturbed he wondered whether he should resign, and said his assistant Wayne Coy, an energetic young New Dealer, felt the same. Several weeks later, Coy did indeed leave.[15]

Several diagnosticians, among them Ickes and Eugene Casey, one of the White House assistants, saw Dr. Win-the-War as one more manifestation of the conservative influence of Harry Hopkins, once castigated as the most advanced of New Dealers. For a year, Casey had felt that Hopkins was promoting the army and certain business interests. At the beginning of January, 1944, Casey said that he had urged the president to let Hopkins go, and to invite congressional leaders to the White House on Sunday evenings, not the friends of Hopkins, Stettinius, and

Harriman. Ideology now was under fire, not only from New Deal liberals but also from old-line Democratic politicians like Leo Crowley, head of the Foreign Economic Adminstration.[16]

Hopkins could have been a political liability in 1944, but actually it was his health that caused him to drop out of public view. Until July 4, 1944, he was out of Washington convalescing. Roosevelt, himself not feeling well, missed Hopkins, and in his absence arranged to raise Hopkins' salary upon his return from $10,000 to $12,000 per year. With Hopkins away, Roosevelt on some questions of foreign policy consulted Morgenthau more frequently; on routine matters, he seemed to rely upon his military advisers, particularly the conservative Admiral Leahy.[17]

Larger questions like the dangerous Polish problem deeply involved Roosevelt, and so did some not quite so earthshaking but nonetheless serious, for example, what to print on the currency that the invading American armies would carry into France. Morgenthau and Assistant Secretary of War John McCloy tried to persuade him to agree to "République Française." Roosevelt, propped up in bed, nursing a cold, in a good humor, vigorously balked. The currency was to carry only the French flag and the words *Emis en France* (issued in France). Afterward, McCloy explained to Morgenthau that on various matters the president was quoting Leahy.[18]

On domestic matters, Roosevelt depended upon the smooth administrative talents of Byrnes, director of the Office of War Mobilization. In June, 1944, when Byrnes suggested that the OWM and the War Production Board be merged, Roosevelt flatteringly opposed any transfer of Byrnes's essential tasks: "As you know, you are indispensable on the handling and the actual settling of scores of problems which are constantly arising. You have been called 'The Assistant President' and the appellation comes close to the truth." Yet Roosevelt during Hopkins' absence did not turn to Byrnes for advice on basic domestic policy, and when he worked on his annual message, transparently his election manifesto for 1944, he did not consult Byrnes or show him the draft.[19]

In his 1944 message to Congress, Roosevelt demonstrated two thrusts in his thinking, holding forth as Dr. Win-the-War in a fashion he knew would pain voters, then as Dr. New Deal dangling before them the lure of a better life in a better world. On January 11, 1944, Roosevelt was not well enough to deliver the address in person before Congress; he sent a copy to the Capitol, but that evening, in order to reach the electorate, he read the full address over the radio. It was the most militant of Roosevelt's messages. While he asked for the power to conscript men and women into war work, the strengthening of controls, and raising of taxes, he also lashed out at his conservative opponents.

Finally, Roosevelt cast aside his Dr. Win-the-War cape and spoke once more in the familiar tones of Dr. New Deal. The time had come to plan for a lasting peace and for an American living standard so high that it would not leave "some fraction of our people — whether it be one-third or one-fifth or one-tenth . . . ill-fed, ill-clothed, ill-housed, and insecure." It followed "that true individual freedom cannot exist without economic security and independence." Drawing from the report that in 1942 had led Congress to eradicate the National Resources Planning Board, and from a speech memorandum Chester Bowles, now head of the Office of Price Administration, had sent him, Roosevelt set forth "a second Bill of Rights under which a new basis of security and prosperity can be established for all — regardless of station, race, or creed." It included the right to a job and to "earn enough to provide adequate food and clothing and recreation," the right of farmers to a decent living, of businessmen to be free of unfair competition and monopolies, and:

> The right of every family to a decent home;
>
> The right to adequate medical care and the opportunity to achieve and enjoy good health;
>
> The right to adequate protection from the economic fears of old age, sickness, accident, and unemployment;
>
> The right to a good education.

The president challenged Congress to implement this "economic bill of rights," warning that if it failed to move, the nation would be conscious of the fact.[20]

Thus firmly Roosevelt flung down his gauntlet to the conservative-dominated Congress. There were the conventional paeans of praise from the Democrats. Three hours later the first administration measure of the new year came up, a bill to raise the social security tax; the Senate defeated it 48 to 17, keeping the tax frozen at 1 percent.[21]

Overall, the State of the Union message indicated how clearly Roosevelt was seeking to temper the premature optimism yet address the postwar concerns of the American people. Walter Lippmann, usually critical of the president, assessed it as "good politics in the year 1944 to propose the very things which no other politician has ever regarded as anything but straight political suicide."[22]

The message also seemed at the time to give promise that Roosevelt, aware that for many months he had let domestic matters slide, was now firmly resuming control of the home front. That unfortunately was not the case. He seemed remote and indecisive and chronically unwell, afflicted by continuing grippe and a hacking cough. Some of those who saw him were worried by his appearance, but they often found him in good spirits.

As the fiasco of the 1944 tax bill was to illustrate, Roosevelt was not entirely in control. Even had he been at the peak of his energy and focused upon the bill, he could not have prevailed in an election year when politics took precedence not only in his actions but also in those of adversaries and allies alike on Capitol Hill.

Roosevelt wholeheartedly accepted the view of Treasury Department experts that higher taxes were vital to counter the threat of both wartime and postwar inflation. Already inflation was substantial; prices were up 25 percent over early 1941, and the growing black market and disappearance of low-priced lines of clothing and household supplies were increasing inflation even more. Yet the House Ways and Means Committee in the fall of 1943, listening sympathetically to special interest groups, had drastically trimmed back the Treasury Department's tax proposals. Congress, unmoved by Roosevelt's pleas for increased revenue, in February, 1944, voted a tax bill that contained only $2 billion in increases, not the $10.5 billion he had sought.[23]

A tax increase was no more popular in 1944, however compelling the reasons for it, than in any other year. In the end, Roosevelt decided to veto the bill as inadequate, although the expectation was that Congress would quickly override the veto. The veto message gave him an opportunity to issue a manifesto placing the blame upon Congress for a tax system with which the voters were becoming increasingly unhappy. It enumerated taxpayers' grievances — the withholding tax voted in 1943, forgiving the wealthy their 1942 taxes, the complexity of income tax forms, the failure to drop from tax rolls those at the bottom of the income scale — all these were the fault of Congress. As for the bill, he pointed to the special privileges it provided and denounced it as "a tax relief bill providing relief not for the needy but for the greedy." The language was sure to grate upon raw nerves in Congress.[24]

As the clerk read the president's message, it seemed to Allen Drury in the Senate press gallery that Roosevelt with a succession of blows, "Crack! Crack! Crack! — [was] laying open the backs of his opponents." Roosevelt's longtime adversary Democratic Senator Walter George opened the rebuttal with a resounding denunciation, as in both houses members of both parties expressed eagerness to override the veto.[25]

Majority Leader Alben Barkley had a serious problem; he was one of many southern Democrats aspiring to the vice presidency, and if he crossed Roosevelt he would have to abandon that ambition. Yet if he fought for the president on the tax measure, he would add to his difficulties in winning reelection to the Senate. He opted for the latter, more cautious course, which projected him into the headlines. It made little real difference, since if Barkley had remained loyal to Roosevelt, it would have cost him among the senators. Another contender for the vice presidential nomination, James Byrnes, who earlier had been one of the most popular southerners in the Senate, suffered that backlash as he bore blame for the veto message. One normally mild-mannered senator banged his desk: "You can mark this down in great big black letters: Jimmy Byrnes will never be the vice-presidential candidate."[26]

Dramatically, Barkley resigned as majority leader on February 23. Addressing the Senate for forty-five minutes, he denounced the veto message point by point as a "calculated and deliberate mistake." At Hyde Park when Roosevelt received a report from Wallace on Barkley's attack, he remarked, "Alben must be suffering from shell shock." Later Roosevelt sent word urging Barkley to stay on as majority leader.[27]

Roosevelt's soothing message had its desired effect upon Barkley, but did not defeat the revenue bill. Barkley submitted his resignation; the Democratic senators accepted it, then unanimously reelected him majority leader. Both houses overwhelmingly overrode the veto. Even the previously loyal chairman of the House Ways and Means Committee, eighty-year-old Robert L. Doughton, said self-respect forced him to oppose Roosevelt. For the first time in history, Congress overrode the veto of a revenue bill. More than that, despite the mounting debt and the growing pressure for inflation, it had ended for the duration of the war any further serious effort to obtain increased taxes. Gleefully, Washingtonians sang a parody on the line in a popular nonsense song, "Mairzy Doats":

When Barkley bolts and Doughton bolts
Then F.D.R. eats ivy — poison ivy, too.[28]

Outwardly, relationships returned to normal. Roosevelt and Barkley exchanged the requisite pleasant letters, and throughout the spring Barkley more than once professed publicly his admiration and support. That was no more than window dressing, as Barkley well knew. On the only two further occasions he saw the president that spring, at other legislative conferences, neither mentioned the incident, but Barkley was aware of Roosevelt's "intangible reserve."[29]

In the aftermath of the tax defeat, Roosevelt won only an indirect victory in his long fight to obtain a federal absentee ballot for soldiers. Out of conference between the House and the Senate there came a compromise measure that bore little more than the semblance of a soldiers' vote bill. In April, Roosevelt let "that fool bill" become law without his signature. As its opponents had planned, it was so circumscribed that only 112,000 soldiers cast federal ballots in 1944; but the long, complex efforts of congressional opponents to stall and vitiate the measure so dramatized the voting issue that four million soldiers cast absentee ballots — almost all of them obtained from states — and they heavily favored Roosevelt.[30]

Again through indirection, and with little or no discernible effort on his part, Roosevelt in the spring of 1944 obtained one of the vital segments of his postwar program, a comprehensive array of veterans' benefits, the GI Bill of Rights. It was not the economic bill of rights that Roosevelt had been proposing, but an important segment that was politically viable, a beginning to direct federal aid for education, albeit for a single group, the veterans. Ever since he had begun treatments in Warm Springs, Roosevelt had been concerned with the low quality of education, especially in the South. If the aid were to go to veterans it would be politically irresistible. Working with his planners, who were the targets of congressional conservatives, he projected segments of his overall program that would be of benefit to veterans. Aid to veterans was acceptable to right-wing politicians, but they were wary that the New Deal social planning they were fighting to demolish might result in broader programs.[31]

After the turn of the tide in the war, in the summer of 1943, Roosevelt had taken his postwar plans to the public in a Fireside Chat. The "gallant men and women in the armed services . . . must not be demobilized into an environment of inflation and unemployment. . . . We must, this time, have plans ready."[32] Fortunately for Roosevelt, leaders of veterans' organizations also favored aid to returning veterans. The American Legion brought its clout to the issue, produced its own proposals, and coined the popular appellation "GI Bill of Rights." In January, 1944, the legion sponsored a bill that would provide, as Roosevelt had requested, broad benefits for the veterans, and ever since has taken credit for the GI Bill. As far as enactment of the measure was concerned, the legion might well do so. Roosevelt husbanded his waning influence over Congress and did not spend any of it on this measure, so popular that it was not needed. His near silence was probably beneficial, making the bill less attractive as a conservative target. A considerable segment of Roosevelt's "economic bill of rights" became reality, if not as he had wished for the entire population, for one significant segment of it; and it was a segment that included blacks as well as whites.[33]

Resistance to national service legislation was so great that Congress gave it only slight consideration. In the spring of 1944, as the nation seemed to be doing well without a labor draft, the bill was bottled in committee and seemed dead. Gradually through the spring the armed forces did obtain personnel, and factories and farms adequate numbers of workers. War production had peaked by the beginning of 1944 and was continuing on a high plateau.[34]

With the easing of the manpower shortage, pressure to begin reconversion increased. For Dr. Win-the-War, the answer would have been a simple "no," but Dr. New Deal was well aware that opposition to reconversion could hurt in the presidential election. For months Roosevelt did nothing. Preparations for the climactic invasion were on his mind, and his health seemed to be deteriorating.

As Roosevelt awaited the landings in France, he sought to placate Stalin and steady Churchill until the combined Allied forces could defeat Germany. With victory approaching, the cement of peril that had bound Roosevelt and Churchill so tightly began to soften and they shrewdly maneuvered toward their differing national goals. These were cracks in the grand alliance, not schisms such as that with Stalin over Poland, already foreshadowing the cold war.

Among the old differences there were Churchill's Mediterranean schemes, which as soon as he began to convalesce he again pressed on Roosevelt. He sought to scuttle the landing in southern France, and insisted upon a landing at Anzio to hasten the capture of Rome. The Anzio landing turned out badly. The American commander caught the Germans by surprise, but fearing a trap was so cautious in advancing that the Germans effectively blocked him. That led to further British demands to cancel the landing on the French Riviera.[35]

While the discussion was developing, with Marshall and Eisenhower by no means in agreement, Roosevelt had slipped into chronically ill health. Churchill wanted to meet with him in Bermuda at Easter, but Roosevelt first postponed, and then on doctor's advice apologized that he could not come. Without the conference, and with Roosevelt scarcely involved except to back his generals, the Joint Chiefs of Staff engaged in lengthy and inconclusive debate with the British. The president was leaving military matters largely to them, as they were leaving political questions to him.[36]

Through the spring Roosevelt engaged in much pulling and hauling with Churchill on these political matters. Churchill was justifiably upset because Roosevelt at a press conference remarked that they had promised a third of the Italian fleet to the Soviets, rather than a few vessels, and there was unpleasantness with Stalin before some British and American ships were transferred to Russia. Churchill was also aggrieved because Roosevelt was inserting the United States into questions in the Mediterranean, which the British seemed to regard as *mare nostrum*. Seeking stability, Churchill desired the retention of kings and conservative governments in Italy and the southern Balkans. Roosevelt with reluctance accepted the continued governance in Italy of Marshal Badoglio but only until the fall of Rome. He would not tolerate keeping in power those who had been associated with Fascism. With some caution he did later back Churchill in his efforts to restore the king of Greece to his throne. More amicably, Roosevelt cooperated with Churchill in his rather incongruous policy in Yugoslavia, to bolster the young king in exile, Peter, through supporting the Communist partisan, Tito. The argument was that Tito was fighting the Axis forces; his rival, Mihailovich, was not.[37]

Roosevelt was antagonistic toward Argentina, where a group of army officers who seemed sympathetic toward Hitler were in control and had engineered a coup in Bolivia. Churchill was eager for Roosevelt not to sever diplomatic relations and freeze Argentinian assets, because the British were dependent upon Argentina for a third of their meat. "I would feel the same way if I were a Britisher," Roosevelt granted to Stettinius, and he froze Bolivian assets instead.[38]

Far more serious was the Anglo-American rivalry over Middle Eastern oil. "I am worried about the future supply," he remarked at a press conference in March. "I am thinking of fifty years from now." Churchill was fearful that the Americans would try to seek oil in Iran and Iraq. Roosevelt disclaimed interest, but confessed he was disturbed by a rumor "that the British wish to horn in on Saudi Arabian oil reserves." A preliminary conference seemed to be leading to an amicable settlement, but a final arrangement was scuttled because of both British concerns and those of senators and American oil companies opposed to government intervention in private enterprise.[39]

One of the most unpleasant questions was how much aid to continue to give the British. As a veteran of Anglo-American rivalries and jealousies as far back as the First World War, Roosevelt was not disposed to be generous. In 1944, as opponents in Congress brought pressure, he demonstrated election year sensitivity, tightening lend-lease purse strings and cutting British holdings of gold and dollars. Churchill protested eloquently at being treated worse than Russia and France "at a time when British and American blood will be flowing in broad and equal stream." Once more Roosevelt gave way.[40]

None of these differences between Roosevelt and Churchill were crucial, but they indicated that troublesome questions continued to arise.

During these same months the Soviet Union, whether through Stalin's ambivalence or conflicting pressure within the system, alternated reassuring warmth with coolness and suspicion. Despite fair words, the Soviets stalled on projects for military cooperation that Stalin had promised Roosevelt at Tehran. Harriman at a point of despair in late January commented, "The Russian bear is demanding much and yet biting the hands that are feeding him." A few days later, Stalin was receptive to him and made a complete turnabout. Three bases for "shuttle-bombing" the Germans materialized rapidly. Such was the effect of Stalin's personal intervention.

There was no such ending to the difficulties over Poland, as the Red armies advanced across the border in January. They would give Stalin the final voice in a Polish settlement. Roosevelt used political perils as an excuse for keeping himself on the periphery of the controversy, going no further than to agree to a future visit from Prime Minister Stanislaus Mikolajczyk, head of the London government. He took refuge in the sophistry that his informal assurances to Stalin on Polish boundaries were not binding, and informed Congressman Joseph Mruk of Buffalo, New York, who represented a heavily Polish-American district, that save for military plans he had made no secret commitments at Tehran.[41]

Chapter 37

DECLINING HEALTH AND ESCALATING POLITICS

SLOWLY Roosevelt's physical condition was deteriorating. All his life he had been plagued with pulmonary disorders, but now he did not bounce back into exuberant health as he had always done before. A year earlier, after recovering from the flu, he had informed Churchill he felt like "a fighting cock." He did not feel that way in 1944, although again, as in response to the polio attack, he tried to will himself back into full vigor. He planned to be in Britain at the side of Churchill to witness the mighty assault across the channel.

At first, the illnesses seemed no more threatening than those Roosevelt had weathered since the spring of 1940, and part of the time he seemed to be on the mend. Then, in late March his secretary William D. Hassett noted: "The President not looking so well. . . . Every morning in response to inquiry as to how he felt, a characteristic reply has been 'Rotten' or 'Like hell.' " During a weekend at Hyde Park, Roosevelt had a temperature of 104. Hassett recorded: "looks ill, color bad; but he is cheerful in spirit. . . . Not inclined, however, to take up anything but most pressing business."[1]

During the days when illness drained his energy, Roosevelt delegated power even more than he had earlier in the war. Already he was leaving many domestic problems to his cabinet and subordinates; now he was remote from them and ill disposed to have their differences brought to him for solution. Propped up in bed one morning, perusing memoranda from Morgenthau and Ickes, he remarked "he wished he could get Cabinet members who would do their own work."[2]

Even in reaching military decisions and keeping up with the incessant correspondence with Churchill, Roosevelt depended more and more upon his staff. With Hopkins seriously ailing and absent, Roosevelt relied heavily upon his chief of staff, Admiral Leahy, his naval aide Captain Wilson Brown, and the officers attached to the White House map room. Leahy and Brown would meet Roosevelt each morning when he came down the elevator and brief him as he was wheeled into the Oval Office. There they would go over the maps and dispatches with him. Later, as Roosevelt wished, Leahy would provide "Chip" Bohlen, liaison from the State Department, with copies of cables and replies from Churchill and Stalin that were of foreign policy rather than purely military purport.

Roosevelt entered the map room less often in 1944, but he did continue coming down afternoons to Admiral McIntire's office next door. While Admiral McIntire was treating Roosevelt's sinuses, Captain Brown would brief him upon the day's events. Roosevelt depended upon these briefings and the portfolios of papers and small maps that the staff prepared for him. Increasingly Admiral Leahy and the staff drafted replies.[3]

Especially in 1944 when Hopkins was away ill, the conservative, affable Leahy assumed a vital dominant role, functioniong with discretion. Leahy served both as presidential liaison with, and as chairman of, the Joint Chiefs of Staff. General Marshall's staff prepared the president's message to Congress on the soldier voting bill, yet Marshall went for considerable periods without seeing the president. Leahy was careful not to bypass the State Department. He liked and respected Bohlen, who was bringing into the White House a note of realism and caution in dealing with the Russians. Yet overall, it was the military that profited from the shift.

In another way Roosevelt made life easier for himself when at Christmastime in 1943 he brought his daughter, Anna, to live at the White House. No one had replaced Missy LeHand, who had suffered a stroke two years before. Like Missy LeHand, Anna Roosevelt Boettiger discreetly arranged for him to see personal callers he would enjoy, and turned away those he would be less glad to see. She tried to help her father, but not at the cost of antagonizing her mother, to whom she felt even closer.

Unfortunately, while Franklin and Eleanor Roosevelt continued to be deeply involved with each other, the fatigue and strain of the war heightened the tensions between them. As their daughter put it, "There was no time for relaxation. . . . If Mother felt pushed . . . she might push Father, and then Father would be very abrupt. . . ."

Part of the difficulty was at a humdrum level. Mrs. Roosevelt still brought to her husband numerous concerns of hers, both vital and trivial. Sometimes, as when she urged him to intercede with a southern governor to prevent the execution of a black, she persisted even though he protested he had no power to act. On small matters that assumed importance in her mind, she would hand sheafs of papers to him at cocktail time, when he sought to shed his burdens of the day with lighthearted small talk. He did not take well to these frequent intercessions. Some of those close to him suspected that in order to gain surcease he was encouraging her to undertake long overseas trips. Evidence does not back this surmise; rather he was still, as he had for more than two decades, enlisting her skills as his surrogate. But beyond doubt he was ambivalent about her (as she was about him), and at times that feeling surfaced. In the fall of 1942, on her return from a successful visit to England, she was pleased to find her husband awaiting her at the airport: "I really think Franklin was glad to see me back and I gave him a detailed account of such things as I could tell quickly and answered his questions."[4]

Yet in September, 1943, Roosevelt reacted differently while his wife was on a 26,000-mile trip visiting troops in the South Pacific, which included seeing her protégé and confidant, Joseph Lash, who had been a prominent youth leader. The president was entertaining the ex-empress Zita of Austria-Hungary at Hyde Park. In response to her inquiry, Roosevelt told her his wife would return in a few days. "She will be very tired," commented Zita. "No," said Roosevelt, "but she will tire everybody else." Unpleasantness between the Roosevelts concerning Lash during the months since her return from England may have occasioned the uncharacteristic tart remark.[5]

Difficulties of a serious nature grew out of the long truce in the Roosevelt marriage, the many years in which each sought outlets elsewhere to fulfill intense emotional needs. More than once James Roosevelt witnessed his father hold out his arms to his mother only for her to avoid his embrace. She could forgive others, but not her husband for having fallen in love with Lucy Mercer. She warned Lash, regarding Trude W. Pratt, whom he was courting: she "must be all yours, otherwise you will never be happy." Lash must not "accept ½ a loaf of love." Obviously Mrs. Roosevelt was reflecting her own difficulties.[6]

Only in time of acute crisis could Mrs. Roosevelt relax the physical barrier against her husband. James Roosevelt was to write, "She showed him more affection" in September of 1941, when his mother died, "than at any other time I can recall." A few days later, her brother died, and Roosevelt reciprocated:

> I remember clearly the day she went to father and said simply, "Hall has died." Father struggled to her side and put his arm

> around her. "Sit down," he said, so tenderly I can still hear it. And he sank down beside her and hugged her and kissed her and held her head on his chest. . . . It is too bad they were together like that so seldom.[7]

In a negative way Eleanor Roosevelt betrayed her ambivalence in her ill-repressed jealousy when her husband sought in others the uncritical adulation his wife could not bestow upon him. Trude Pratt came to empathize with Mrs. Roosevelt's irritation. She observed the president at tea in the summer of 1942, and wrote Lash that she was puzzled as to why, as always, Roosevelt had seemed so attracted to Princess Martha of Norway, who "says nothing, just giggles and looks adoringly at him. But he seems to like it tremendously — and there is a growing flirtacious intimacy which is of course not at all serious." Afterward Mrs. Roosevelt explained to Trude Pratt (whom she had enveloped in her warmth and confidence) "that there always was a Martha for relaxation and for the non-ending pleasure of having an admiring audience for every breath."[8]

Roosevelt must have been comparably annoyed by his wife's single-minded devotion to Lash. Mrs. Roosevelt counseled and encouraged Lash and his fiancée, telling them she felt for them much as she did for her own daughter, Anna, and her son-in-law, John Boettiger.

Eleanor Roosevelt, as often is the case with the pure of heart, was indiscreet in her letters to Lash, and even more indiscreet in her visits to him after he was inducted into the army. Although Lash had never been a member of the Communist party, his prominence as a radical youth leader had made him suspect. In the fall of 1941, when he sought to enlist in Naval Intelligence, officers sent word to the president through Admiral McIntire that they did not want him. Roosevelt apparently acquiesced. In the spring of 1942, after Lash was inducted into the Army Air Corps and began training to be a weather observer, Mrs. Roosevelt, although she was aware that Army Intelligence had a file on Lash, visited him several times, and in March, 1943, she spent time with him in her room at the Blackstone Hotel in Chicago. He was so exhausted after dinner that he dozed in the dark while she sat stroking his forehead. Afterward the hotel management informed her that Army Intelligence operatives had bugged the room. She was outraged and upon her return to Washington protested to Harry Hopkins and General Marshall.[9]

Army documents concerning that episode with Lash undoubtedly did reach the president. A few days later Lash and several of his fellow weather forecasters were unexpectedly flown to New Caledonia, to the surprise of the local weather detachment. As for the counterintelligence group that had conducted electronic surveillance of Mrs. Roosevelt without presidential authorization, Roosevelt took the dramatic step of ordering it disbanded. Before Lash was flown out of California, Mrs. Roosevelt saw him to bid him farewell, and she continued her keen interest in him and his welfare. Roosevelt, who had seen much of both Lash and his fiancée, would never for an instant have suspected his wife of having an affair with Lash. His reaction would have been one of fury toward counterintelligence, for stirring further allegations that Mrs. Roosevelt was involved with Communists. Out of both pride and political wariness, he always reacted strongly against attacks on Mrs. Roosevelt.[10]

Later, in 1944, Roosevelt's daughter, Anna, was witness to how Roosevelt could conceal his feelings where Lash was concerned. One day an officer brought her a packet of air letters. He told her they were love letters to Mrs. Roosevelt that censors had intercepted, and asked her to give them to the president. With reluctance Anna entered the Oval Office and handed them to her father. Without saying a word, he took them from her.[11]

Franklin D. Roosevelt's attachments were equally embarrassing to Anna. One day, probably early in 1944, he asked her if she "would mind if he invited a very close friend to dinner." Anna knew instantly that he meant Lucy Mercer Rutherford, recently widowed, whom he had promised Eleanor Roosevelt long before that he would never see again. (He had not kept his pledge, arranging that she attend each of his inaugurations, where she sat unseen, and, beginning during the war years, meeting her from time to time.) Anna had instantly to choose between her conflicting loyalties. As a teenager she had empathized with her mother over the affair, but many years had gone by. Roosevelt must have felt a need to be with the warm, pleasant, uncritical Lucy Rutherford, and occasionally he saw her at the White House, usually with other people around.[12]

Two of these people, with whom Mrs. Rutherford easily blended in so that visitors would not be likely to raise questions, were his cousin Laura ("Polly") Delano and her best friend, a distant cousin of Miss Delano's, Margaret ("Daisy") Suckley. Roosevelt felt comfortable in the presence of these two admiring women, who were so discreet that he did not need to be on guard in their presence. Roosevelt was so devoted to them that he went to Daisy Suckley's for tea on her birthday, and twice visited Polly Delano at her home when she was ill in the fall of 1942. Miss Suckley became an archivist at the Roosevelt Library in the fall of 1941 and throughout the war years aided Roosevelt in sorting through his personal papers and possessions, accessioning those that he was giving to the library. By 1944, Roosevelt was dictating to Daisy Suckley bits of reminiscence that he planned to use in his memoirs.[13]

By March, 1944, only Admiral McIntire seemed oblivious that Roosevelt was not bouncing back from his illnesses, although he was not working as hard as was his habit and had spent several relaxing sojourns at Hyde Park. Both his wife and daughter worried about his poor appearance. McIntire's medical horizons did not seem to extend beyond his specialty. For more than a decade he had been irrigating Roosevelt's sinuses and dosing him with nose drops and sprays. As early as 1937, medical records show, Roosevelt's blood pressure was rising to a level of mild hypertension that called for attention. McIntire gave it none, and the nose drops he dispensed elevated blood pressure.

In 1944, Roosevelt's medical problems clearly extended beyond his nose and throat. His secretary Grace Tully was concerned over the shake in his hand when he lit a cigarette, and his tendency to nod while reading letters or dictating. "He would grin in slight embarrassment as he caught himself and there was no diminution of clarity or sparkle." Miss Tully became so alarmed that she carried her concerns to Anna, who shared them. Anna already had urged McIntire to look into the president's overall health; McIntire sent him for a thorough checkup at the naval hospital in Bethesda, Maryland.[14]

At Bethesda, Roosevelt was wheeled into the office of a young cardiologist in the Naval Reserve, Dr. Howard G. Bruenn, and lifted onto the examining table. Dr. Bruenn later recalled that the president was in good humor, but "appeared . . . very tired, and his face was very gray. Moving caused considerable breathlessness." Dr. Bruenn diagnosed him as suffering from hypertension, hypertensive heart disease, cardiac failure in the left ventricle of his enlarged heart, and acute bronchitis. Admiral McIntire, along with Dr. Bruenn, conferred with leading physicians at the naval hospital. They agreed that Roosevelt must make significant changes in his habits as a means of moderately lowering his blood pressure. He must limit his daily activities, reduce his smoking, go onto a low-fat diet, and as far as possible avoid tensions. Two days later they met with two consultants, Drs. James A. Paullin and Frank Lahey, who went over the X rays, electrocardiograms, and other data. In the afternoon Drs. Paullin and Lahey examined Roosevelt at the White House. Dr. Lahey, particularly concerned with the gastrointestinal tract, did not recommend surgery, but felt Roosevelt's condition was sufficiently grave that he should be fully informed so that he would cooperate wholeheartedly. After some debate, Dr. Bruenn finally won support to administer digitalis to Roosevelt. Overall, the president's ailments were serious but did not seem at the time an immediate threat to his life. His blood pressure in the months ahead fluctuated considerably in response to his physical shape and degree of stress. At its high points it indicated severe hypertension, of a level a patient was not likely to survive for more than a year. Unfortunately, medicine to bring it under control would not be developed until the 1950s. Long afterward Dr. Bruenn would lament that with modern medication Roosevelt might well have served out his remaining years in the White House.[15]

Immediately Admiral McIntire entered into a conspiracy of silence to keep everyone, supposedly even the president, from knowing of his problems with his blood pressure and his heart. McIntire later declared he did not tell Roosevelt of the diagnosis. Neither did Dr. Bruenn, who was under orders from Admiral McIntire to inform no one. It is, however, inconceivable that Roosevelt was not aware of what was wrong with him, expert as he had become at self-diagnosis during his illness with polio. General Eisenhower told Roosevelt in January, 1944, that Lord Moran was complaining that the convalescing Churchill would always forestall him by taking the thermometer out of his mouth and announcing his own temperature. Churchill had explained to Eisenhower, "I believe these doctors are trying to keep me in bed." Roosevelt replied to Eisenhower, "Oh, that's nothing new. I've been doing that for years. I don't trust those fellows either." There is no reason to doubt Mrs. Roosevelt's remark to Morgenthau just after her husband's death that the president had known what was wrong with him and so had she.[16]

Before Roosevelt made his final decision to run for a fourth term, his doctors informed him he "could quite easily go on with the activities of the Presidency." Thirty years later, Anna's husband at that time, Dr. James Halsted, reviewing the evidence, concluded that although there had been no impediments to Roosevelt's running in earlier elections, "on medical grounds alone, he should not have run in 1944."[17]

While Roosevelt from March, 1944, on continued to make only general remarks about his chronic nose and throat problems, Admiral McIntire was a fount of disinformation, again and again announcing that Roosevelt was in a fine state of health. The conspiracy of silence was important if Roosevelt were to run again, as he felt he must, he told his son James in the summer of 1944, "to maintain a continuity of command in a time of continuing crisis."

The imperatives of the war and politics do not mean that Franklin and Eleanor Roosevelt were engaging in fraud. There were times when Roosevelt's colds and bronchitis caused him to feel rotten, as he put it; the muscles he had so persistently built up after the polio attack were deteriorating seriously through lack of exercise, and he consequently felt weak much of the time. But his heart responded to the digitalis treatment and the continuing hypertension caused no pain. When he was well rested, he could intermittently into 1945 feel optimistic and work hard in his customary high spirits, but also there were low points when he could let slip his forebodings. On May 16, 1944, he startled one of his assistants, Jonathan Daniels, by prefacing an account of his conversations with Stalin on Poland with an ominous phrase: "Here is something you should write about if I pop off."

Whether or not Roosevelt kept himself closely informed on his medical problems, he was an exemplary patient, cutting back on his hours of work, increasing his periods of rest, reducing his smoking from a pack or more a day to about six cigarettes (then back up later to a full pack), exercising in the White House swimming pool — which he enjoyed — and adhering to a limited low-salt diet to bring down his blood pressure and his weight. This was the standard treatment for hypertension, which he must have known.[18]

Soon his health improved. On April 5 he told Dr. Bruenn he felt fine. Two days later he was in good humor when he held a press conference; correspondents thought he looked better than a week before. Within two weeks, X rays and an electrocardiogram showed his heart more nearly normal and his lungs clearing.[19]

To speed his recovery, Roosevelt headed south on April 8 for a vacation at Bernard Baruch's plantation, Hobcaw, in South Carolina. For security reasons his whereabouts was secret, but three White House correspondents waited and watched nearby, as they had in Poughkeepsie during his Hyde Park sojourns. He was accompanied by Admiral McIntire, Admiral Leahy, and the military and naval aides, but took with him none of the assistants concerned with domestic or foreign policy.[20]

While Roosevelt was there, his medical problems continued. On April 17, Dr. Bruenn arrived, misidentified even to Admiral Leahy as "an expert dietician." He found Roosevelt in good spirits, eating and sleeping well, although still suffering from elevated blood pressure; but at the end of April and in early May Roosevelt went through a fresh ordeal, suffering two acute gallbladder attacks, which Dr. Bruenn treated with codeine. Admiral McIntire was reassuring at the time, saying the pain was temporary and not serious. (Later in Washington X rays showed gallstones, but Admiral McIntire, again putting the best interpretation on Roosevelt's health, omitted mention of the stones in his medical report.) Dr. Bruenn put Roosevelt on a low-fat diet to lower his weight, at that time 188 pounds. The setback contributed to a decision for Roosevelt to remain at Hobcaw an extra week, until May 6.

Part of Roosevelt's pain seemed to come from his colon. He told Ickes some days after his return to Washington that it had given him some trouble, and he had been fearful there might be a growth. The pain moved several times, from the left side to the right, and back, then disappeared. Roosevelt concluded he did not have a growth, but was looking forward to a complete checkup at the naval hospital.[21]

During Roosevelt's long absence from Washington, rumors were circulating about his physical condition. The most serious, persisting for decades after his death — and difficult to prove or disprove — was that he was a victim of cancer. In January, 1944, a wen had been removed from the back of his head. Rumors of malignancy spread, and Roosevelt was sensitive in such matters. Also, years earlier a New Jersey doctor had written him in some concern because photographs in 1940 showed Roosevelt with a mole over his left eye, growing larger, which the doctor feared might be a melanoma, a dangerous form of cancer. Roosevelt turned the letter over to Dr. McIntire, who replied reassuringly that the mole was being watched. By January, 1941, it had disappeared from his photographs, so obviously had been removed. Since the mole had appeared as early as 1932, and melanoma is fast growing, Dr. Halsted has concluded it is very unlikely the mole was malignant. There were also rumors in the 1940s and later that Roosevelt was suffering from intestinal cancer. Whatever the form of cancer, a biopsy had indicated a malignancy, according to a story circulating among medical men. Perhaps either the wen or the mole had been malignant and the cancer had spread.

It may be, as Dr. Harry S. Goldsmith, who has written on the president's health, points out, that when Roosevelt began in June, as his doctors wished, to lose weight, the rapid and continued loss was due less to the diet than to anorexia and perhaps a malignancy. On the other hand, Dr. Bruenn put him on the low-fat diet to relieve pains from the gallstones at a time when X rays of Roosevelt's stomach, intestine, and colon were normal. Roosevelt took pride in losing about fifteen pounds, boasted that he again had a flat stomach, and stubbornly persisted in staying on the diet. Through the summer, with a few exceptions, he was vigorous and felt well. It may be that his insistence upon bringing his weight even lower than Dr. Bruenn wished was in part self-treatment, comparable to that of the polio years. He boasted to Ickes in mid-June "that he had had high blood pressure . . . but that he was all right again." Roosevelt was seeking to prove both to the American people and to himself that he was in fine health, well qualified to serve another four years.[22]

A renowned medical leader, Dr. Roger Lee of Boston, who apparently had either examined or been consulted about Roosevelt in the spring of 1944, wrote Churchill's physician in January, 1945: "Roosevelt had heart failure eight months ago . . . enlargement of his liver and was puffy. A post-mortem would have shown congestion of his organs." Dr. Lee did not mention the possibility of cancer.[23]

Roosevelt was in fine spirits when he met the correspondents in South Carolina just before he left for Washington. His discourse ranged entertainingly from the bad smell that wafted across the bay from a pulp mill in Georgetown, to a variation on a revolting story he liked to tell about gin being distilled from fish heads. He claimed that near Turin years ago he had seen "a pile as high as a house of decaying figs . . . from all over Italy. . . . That is what Vermouth is made of. Think about that, when you have your next Martini." He was proving his Hasty Pudding Club sense of humor was intact.[24]

On May 8, 1944, Roosevelt appeared back in Washington. He returned, the *New York Times* noted, "with improved color and with some of the tired seams smoothed from his face," but he became instantly the center of attacks and controversy, heightened by the imminence of the 1944 nominating convention. His every word and action, and above all his physical appearance, were the stuff of presidential politics. It was not a time when he could further relax, yet in the months ahead the challenges seemed more often to stimulate than weary him.[25]

By the spring of 1944, rumors were widely circulating about Roosevelt's health. *Time*, in focusing upon his appearance at a press conference on May 9, set one of the most persistent Republican themes of the campaign ahead: "Newsmen were struck by the realization that Franklin Roosevelt at 62 is an old man." In mid-June, Admiral McIntire issued another of his bulletins, declaring that the president was in splendid shape for a man of his age. Voters viewed the announcement in keeping with their political leanings; 84 percent of the Roosevelt supporters believed that the president's health would permit him to serve another four years, but 55 percent of the Republicans disagreed. For voters, what one thought of Roosevelt's health had become a political act of faith. McIntire's assurance removed whatever slight obstacle there might be to Roosevelt's renomination, since Democratic politicians were well aware that unless he headed the ticket, they faced almost certain disaster in November. One public opinion poll indicated that 49 percent of those favoring Roosevelt said that if he did not run they would vote Republican.[26]

Despite the intensifying animus with which conservative Democrats, especially in the South, reacted to Roosevelt during the war years, most of them were reluctantly ready to stand by him through the campaign. Texas politics, which Roosevelt watched closely, indicated once more how precarious his hold was over southern Democratic leaders. The larger part of the Texas Democratic leadership at the state convention participated in the conservative Texas Regulars movement, attempting to deny Roosevelt their electoral vote. Roosevelt was convinced that Jesse Jones, despite his protestations to the contrary, was deeply involved in the maneuver, and was apparently suspicious even of Speaker Rayburn, who had always been loyal to the New Deal.

In the preceding winter months, Roosevelt had demonstrated his own support for Lyndon Johnson, who was endangered by an Internal Revenue Service investigation into the substantial and allegedly illegal campaign contributions of Johnson's sponsor, Herman Brown, through Brown and Root, Inc. Internal Revenue agents wanted to charge the firm over a million dollars in additional taxes. Roosevelt argued to Morgenthau that it was customary in Texas for businessmen to make illegal contributions. "The thing that gets me," Roosevelt complained, "is you go after Congressman Lyndon Johnson." He wanted to know why the IRS did not go after Johnson's opponent, Senator Lee O'Daniel. The Internal Revenue Service had already been ordered to drop the case.[27]

The Texas disaffection disturbed Roosevelt, but the rumblings of dissension there and throughout the South were a gathering storm that did not break until after 1944. There was idle talk in the South of choosing Roosevelt electors who would cast their votes against the president and thus throw the election into the House. There was even some rallying around Senator Harry Byrd of Virginia, but it was so feeble that only fifty-six of an expected two hundred and fifty bothered to attend the luncheon in Atlanta that was to launch his campaign. Throughout the South, although Democratic leaders were antagonistic, and the rank and file disliked many of the administrative policies, Roosevelt continued to be the idol of the electorate.[28]

His own renomination certain, Roosevelt followed the Republican maneuvering in the party primaries out of which would come both a candidate and some of the issues of the campaign. Of key concern to Roosevelt was whether Republicans would favor postwar participation in peacekeeping, or would return to traditional isolationism. Wendell Willkie, long since having antagonized the conservative leaders of the party, plunged into the Wisconsin primary proclaiming his "one world" views. More because of Wisconsin politics than his ideology, he suffered so disastrous a defeat that he dropped out of the campaign. It was a victory not of isolationism but for Wisconsin Republican county chairmen. It seemed an unfortunate portent for Roosevelt.[29]

On the other hand, ultraconservatives and isolationists who stirred a boom for General Douglas MacArthur also precipitated a bust. MacArthur won easily against an unknown in the Illinois preferential primary and placed second in Wisconsin without having given permission for his name to be entered. Then correspondence that a naive freshman congressman from Nebraska made public punctured the small boom. The congressman had urged MacArthur to permit the American people to draft him, declaring that the Roosevelt administration had crucified itself "on the cross of too many unnecessary rules and regulations." MacArthur responded, "I do not anticipate in any way your flattering predictions, but I do unreservedly agree with the complete wisdom and statesmanship of your comments." MacArthur's coy admission of interest in the candidacy was fatal, since attaining it depended upon his total silence.[30]

The Republican primary campaign already had turned into a brief and almost bloodless contest among governors Thomas E. Dewey of New York, John Bricker of Ohio, and Harold Stassen of Minnesota. At first it appeared as though Bricker would gain the isolationist support and Stassen that of the internationalists, leaving Dewey as the candidate of the middle. Rather, with Willkie out of the running, Dewey quietly moved into a position on international affairs scarcely distinguishable from Roosevelt's. Dewey's political rise had been spectacular. Beginning when he was twenty-nine, he became famous as a racket-buster in New York City, obtaining the conviction of several of the most notorious gangsters of the 1930s; in 1940 he had been a leading contender for the Republican presidential nomination; in 1942 he was elected governor of New York, and again demonstrated his efficiency and dynamism. Through the 1944 primaries, he seemed to be functioning as a noncandidate as he won victory after victory. At the same time, he was moving from his earlier isolationist position toward Republican internationalism, in keeping with the party's manifesto, called the Mackinac Declaration, issued the previous September. He told a British envoy that John Foster Dulles, a notable Republican internationalist, was his most intimate friend.[31]

With the campaign more likely to center upon domestic issues, Roosevelt immediately upon his return from Hobcaw had to confront what had so long been a prime Republican theme — the charge that he was a tyrannical oppressor of business. The press and radio were filled in May, 1944, with denunciations of a new episode in the ongoing wartime struggle between business and organized labor, the government seizure of the giant mail-order and retailing firm, Montgomery Ward. The stringent Smith-Connally (War Labor Disputes) Act, which Congress enacted over Roosevelt's veto in June, 1943, had failed to hamstring organized labor or even put an end to troubles with John L. Lewis and the bituminous coal miners. Roosevelt had sought with not much better success to use the measure while he was at Hobcaw to discipline Sewell L. Avery, the vehemently antiunion president of Montgomery Ward, who since 1942 had been defying the War Labor Board. In January, 1944, Avery refused to have further dealings with a CIO union, arguing that a majority of the work force might no longer favor it. In April the union went on strike.

The president under the Smith-Connally Act had the power to take over a strikebound plant if it was "useful" to the war effort. Montgomery Ward, supplying the army and millions of farmers, seemed to Attorney General Francis Biddle to be within this category. Biddle had to fly to Chicago to await Avery in the Montgomery Ward office. Avery arrived and refused to budge, sputtering, "to hell with the government." Two military policemen then ousted Avery. They picked him up, and as they carried him out the main door, a news photographer caught a picture that appeared on front pages throughout the nation. It elicited much sympathy for Avery, and unleashed a torrent of anti–New Deal rhetoric. Some newspapers asserted that the Roosevelt administration was proceeding in the footsteps of Hitler. Later Avery, appearing at a congressional hearing, declared, "Thank heaven I did that! Because the damned photograph resulted." He undermined the favorable impression the picture had created by asserting that the War Labor Board was "that kind of trash" which "must be destroyed." While the attacks on Roosevelt went on, Avery by telephone ran Montgomery Ward as he pleased.[32]

Roosevelt seemed to be in a trap, but by the time he arrived back in Washington he had devised a means to wriggle out. The first press conference opened in cheerful fashion and he kept the reporters laughing all through the session. Roosevelt declared that the union election was taking place that day, and if the union did not have a majority, that would end the case; if it did, since management had declared it would then be willing to continue its contract, that too would end the case. The union won its election that day, so the government withdrew its control, ending the immediate embarrassing political problem for Roosevelt. Avery continued stubbornly to resist War Labor Board rulings, but it was not until December 28, 1944, after the election, that Roosevelt intervened, this time firmly, pushing aside Stimson's fresh objections and preventing Avery from running Montgomery Ward by telephone.[33]

In the same careful fashion, Roosevelt by 1944 was extending support to blacks. One of the unanticipated wartime changes had been a massive movement of blacks from the rural South to the industrial North, the greatest internal migration in American history. The crowding, poor housing, and the irritation of white workers, some of them also fresh from the fields of the South, created tensions, and in the summer of 1943 led to ominous rioting in Detroit and Harlem. Roosevelt made no comments upon the riots, but at his last press conference of 1943, did assert, concerning a case that involved southern railroad employment practices discriminating against blacks, that he would appoint a committee and hope for progress. "I don't think . . . that we can bring about the millennium at this time," he added, but suggested there had been distinct advances in the past decade. He added hesitantly, "I want to continue making advances, although I don't think for a minute that — but hope we can go all the way."[34]

Southern solidarity to preserve white supremacy was the reason for Roosevelt's caution. Even the staunchest New Dealers among the southern senators, like Pepper and Hill, had during each campaign to renew their vows to support it. Opponents of Hill during the Alabama primary had gone so far as to circulate a photograph showing him standing in the Senate men's room side by side with President Tubman of Liberia. Throughout the South, the word spread that Mrs. Roosevelt was responsible for the shortage of low-paid domestic help, that black women were joining "Eleanor Clubs," pledged to put a white woman in every kitchen. (No Eleanor Club ever existed.) In Grenada County, Mississippi, the local editor warned in June, 1944, "The good darkies of the South should remember that, at best, Eleanor will be boss of the U.S. a limited time, while the good white people of the South will be here forever."[35]

The fact that every black moving to the North, and some moving into southern cities like Houston, was gaining access to the ballot, gave Roosevelt a new incentive to make overtures toward blacks. In a close election their votes could be important. In 1943 he had appointed Jonathan Daniels of the *Raleigh News and Observer*, a liberal on the race issue among southerners of that era, to be one of his assistants, assigning him, among other duties, relations with blacks. One of the conspicuous changes was Roosevelt's easing of the proscription against the black press, whom Stephen Early, a southerner, on one pretext or another had banned from press conferences. On February 5, 1944, Roosevelt broke with precedent and invited some fifteen members of the Negro Newspaper Publishers Association to meet with him in a press conference comparable to the one he held each year for the American Society of Newspaper Editors. He pleased them by suggesting they come each year to see him, and by listening to their statement emphasizing their love for the country. In response to their protest against the treatment of black troops, he granted there was definite discrimination and blamed it on white officers. Roosevelt did not promise the publishers he would improve treatment of black troops. "We are up against it, absolutely up against it."

A solution for black problems was in Roosevelt's mind, but rather than state it clearly, which would have been politically hazardous, he told the black publishers an anecdote. Roosevelt said he had been riding southward through the black district of Chattanooga, Tennessee, amid enthusiastic crowds. Suddenly "we came to a place where all the enthusiasm quit. . . . There were a good many colored people on the streets, but . . . they were completely apathetic." He asked the governor of Tennessee what was wrong. The governor told him they had crossed the state line into Georgia. "The great majority of Negroes in Chattanooga are voting," Roosevelt pointed out to the publishers. "They can take part in the life of the community. . . . You get across this invisible line, [and] . . . not one of them can vote." As for the "people of Tennessee" — Roosevelt meant white people — they "are just as well off as before." What he did not add was that black people with the franchise were indeed better off than before.[36]

Far more critical to Roosevelt's success than other components of the electorate were those who favored his program for a new world order. Without them he would not only lose the election but might lose the peace. Yet, as consistently since the fiasco of 1920, he had favored tempering Wilsonian internationalism with a dash of Henry Cabot Lodge nationalism. He sought the support both of idealists who had dreamed of a supranational league powerful enough to enforce the peace, and isolationists who had sought to keep America free from foreign entanglements.[37]

Serious opposition from Senator Vandenberg and other isolationists seemed in the offing. Roosevelt was pessimistic about the Senate isolationists; he had long since feared that Republicans would make proposals for a peacekeeping organization a prime campaign issue, as they did in 1920. Fortunately for him, Secretary Hull was able to play an important role. Congress had hailed Hull as a hero when he returned from Moscow the previous fall and trusted him as it did not Roosevelt. Hull enjoyed the confidence of senators who long since had soured toward the president, and had won a significant concession in April and May when he succeeded in establishing a nonbinding foreign policy liaison with the Senate, meeting repeatedly with a special Senate committee on postwar plans, known as the Committee of Eight. It included two key figures from the isolationist bloc, Vandenberg and La Follette, and the cautious chairman of the Senate Foreign Relations Committee, Tom Connally. Hull showed them in confidence the State Department draft for an international organization. They were gratified that it reserved for the United States and other key nations a veto and did not propose an international police force. "This is anything but a wild-eyed internationalist dream of a world state," noted Vandenberg. "On the contrary it is a framework . . . to which I can and do heartily subscribe."[38]

Yet at the same time that Roosevelt seemed to isolationists to be going too far, there was the danger that to international-minded Republicans like Willkie the president might seem too cautious. For the moment, Willkie was more fearful of the Republican isolationists. "Naturally, as a Republican, I would prefer to work within the Republican party," Willkie wrote the influential radio commentator H. V. Kaltenborn, "but I will be damned if I am going to sit by while the peace of the world is wrecked again as it was in the 20's." Roosevelt would have counted it a coup to have won Willkie and his following.[39]

Now in May 1944 the time had come for Roosevelt to state his views, to court the support of those to whom the international issue was crucial, some of them wavering between him and the newly internationalist Republican candidate-to-be, Dewey. The first publicizing of Roosevelt's aims had been in the planning since mid-March, when he had given an interview to a writer, Forrest Davis; later, he approved Davis's two articles setting forth Roosevelt's account of the Tehran conference and his thoughts on the postwar world order. They appeared in the isolationist *Saturday Evening Post*, which had a huge circulation, on May 13 and 20.

Almost simultaneously Roosevelt began directly to give correspondents his thoughts on international organizations. On May 26, he started with monetary matters, announcing that a conference would meet that summer at Bretton Woods, New Hampshire, to establish an international monetary fund and perhaps a bank for reconstruction and development. Despite the significance of the undertaking, Roosevelt was to be only slightly involved.[40]

On Memorial Day, Roosevelt was ready to talk about peacekeeping. In the morning, Secretary Hull announced that the United States was inviting Great Britain, the Soviet Union, and China to discuss the postwar security problem — what was to become the Dumbarton Oaks conference to draft the United Nations Charter. It was a warm day, and after a short visit to Arlington National Cemetery, Roosevelt met the reporters in his shirtsleeves. The United States, he said, should join with other nations in setting up machinery to maintain the peace. It would not function so that "some other nation would decide whether we were to build a new dam on the Conestoga Creek," but rather to preserve world peace "without taking away the independence . . . or destroying — what's the other word? — the *integrity* of the United States in any shape, manner, or form." If some nation or combination of nations "started to run amok, and seeks to grab territory or invade its neighbors" the purpose of the organization would be to "stop them before they got started."[41]

What seemed at the time most remarkable about Roosevelt's comments on the projected international organization was his conservatism. Nine months earlier in drafting the Mackinac Declaration, the Republican senators Vandenberg and Taft had insisted that the United States must not relinquish its sovereignty to any new world body. Yet internationalists looked upon "sovereignty" as the nationalist concept that led to wars. Roosevelt, as *Time* pointed out, cleverly substituted "integrity" for the proscribed word. Subsequently he explained to an interviewer that he had stressed "integrity" for the benefit of those "tiresome persons who continually brought these words up." Senator Wheeler, renowned for his isolationism, crowed that Roosevelt's plan was not as internationalist as the Mackinac Declaration. On the other hand, as Roosevelt's scheme for the "Four Policemen" became publicized, the small nations of Europe, led by the foreign minister of the Netherlands, voiced their dismay. The new organization would seem to provide them little power except to debate.[42]

There were no surprises when, on June 15, the White House made public the essentials of Hull's draft charter for the United Nations: a council under the domination of the "Four Policemen," an assembly to represent all nations, and the world court. Roosevelt was proposing no "superstate" or international police force. There was disappointment among some internationalists and isolationists, but as *Time* reported, "Most

Americans found the program unexceptionable — what there was of it." Roosevelt, thanks in considerable part to Hull's effective work with the senators, was singularly successful in eliminating the United Nations organization as a campaign issue, just two weeks in advance of the Republican convention.[43]

Chapter 38

A ROOSEVELT-TRUMAN TICKET

FROM THE D-DAY LANDINGS in France to election day in 1944, the demands of the climactic campaigns of the war and national politics absorbed Roosevelt's attention. It was not as dramatic an intermingling as had faced President Lincoln eighty years earlier, in 1864, but to Roosevelt victory both in the field and at the ballot box were requisite to the winning of the peace.

"Over here new political situations crop up every day but so far, by constant attention, I am keeping my head above water," Roosevelt informed Churchill on June 2. But in that nervous week, with only days to go until the invasion of Normandy, Roosevelt's mind must have been far more focused on the tremendous gamble that, against the possibility of foul weather and the certainty of stiff German defenses, the Allies could successfully land and maintain a striking force in France. For months preparation had gone on with little direct involvement on the part of Roosevelt, and not even a great deal by his chief of staff, General Marshall. In London, General Eisenhower and three British commanders were operating the elaborate machinery to launch the attack.[1]

Roosevelt's concern was limited to large general issues, but they were formidable enough. It occupied him to keep Stalin informed, prevent Churchill from engineering any new Mediterranean diversion, and resist doggedly Churchill's pleas that de Gaulle and the French committee be more fully involved in the liberation and governance of French territory. Eisenhower, with the support of Marshall, was also pressing for an amelioration of policy toward de Gaulle. Under the additional pressure from within, Roosevelt modified his policy only to agree that if de Gaulle asked to visit him in Washington he would extend an invitation.

On all these questions as on the unconditional surrender issue, Roosevelt seemed, as he characterized himself, "a stubborn old Dutchman," and budged only with reluctance.[2]

The perils of the attack across the channel were so real that success would be by no means easy or even certain. The landings themselves were risky, and if bad weather were to intervene before sufficient men and matériel had been landed, the German SS Panzer divisions waiting in the interior might well push the Allies into the channel. Only the Luftwaffe was seriously deficient. If the Germans succeeded in repelling the invaders, when if ever would Roosevelt and Churchill be able to launch a new attack? Hitler reasoned that Germany would gain time to turn its full attention to the Soviet Union, and to bring into full production jet airplanes and other dangerous arms that could win the war.

In the back of his mind, Roosevelt mulled the threat from new German weaponry. In September, 1943, when General Omar Bradley, who was to command the American Group in the landings, visited the White House, it was to brief the president on the Sicilian campaign. But Roosevelt then briefed Bradley on the new device the United States was developing that would revolutionize warfare, the atomic bomb. He feared, since the Germans had constructed a large "heavy water" plant near Trondheim, Norway, that they might be nearer to success than the Americans, and wanted to forewarn Bradley of possible nuclear attack during the fighting in France. Roosevelt's private worries may well have been as intense as those Churchill openly voiced, but concerns over the bomb would impel him in the reverse direction, toward early action against Germany.[3]

The days just before the landings were tense ones for the Roosevelts. With four sons in the service they were particularly sensitive to casualties; one of Harry Hopkins' sons had been killed in the Marshall Islands in February. Mrs. Roosevelt articulated her inner thoughts as her husband would not. "I feel as though a sword were hanging over my head, dreading its fall and yet know it must fall to end the war," she wrote Joseph Lash.[4]

On Monday, June 5, there was good news from Italy, where the Fifth Army advancing from Anzio and Cassino finally captured Rome. At ten that evening, Roosevelt announced it over the radio. As he spoke, he knew that Allied forces were on their way across the channel. Already, paratroopers were dropping into the fields of Normandy. Roosevelt told his wife before she went to bed that night that the attack was under way. The next morning, on June 6, the world knew, and Roosevelt, with emotional fervor, read a D-day prayer over the radio.[5]

The landings were enormous beyond anything known before, involving four thousand vessels pouring troops ashore, not where the Germans expected, but along sixty miles of the Normandy coast. American and British airplanes commanded the skies and battleships poured shells into Nazi defenses. The Allies built two artificial harbors out of worn-out ships and special caissons. Unfortunately, Germans had been on anti-invasion maneuvers at Omaha beach, one of the two where Americans went ashore, and inflicted heavy casualties. In the first two weeks the Allies put ashore a million men and the requisite supplies, but the seasoned German divisions that had rushed into the battle fought doggedly behind hedgerows. The Allied forces fell farther and farther behind their projected timetables. Victories came only slowly at first, and at a price.

The president may have been overoptimistic at first; certainly he was displaying renewed energy. Mrs. Roosevelt felt he had become his old self: he "keeps us all a bit undecided by saying he doesn't know what he will do & that when he hears Hitler is ready to surrender he will go to England at once & then in the next breath that he may go to Honolulu & the Aleutians!"[6]

Even before the landings, Roosevelt had been undecided. On May 15, he had asked Admiral Leahy to look into arrangements for an Atlantic crossing in mid-June and for a Pacific voyage leaving Washington July 23. Leahy suggested to him that the visit to Honolulu would have a bearing upon the political campaign — a factor which at the time, as well as since, seemed the prime reason for it. Roosevelt with considerable feeling responded, whether with candor or as camouflage, "Bill, I just hate to run again for election. Perhaps the war will by that time have progressed to a point that will make it unnecessary for me to be a candidate." The next day Roosevelt decided to cancel plans to go to England, and he stuck by his decision.[7]

With American troops in France, and de Gaulle assuming civil authority in liberated areas, Roosevelt slowly began to adjust to new realities. Despite Roosevelt's dogged opposition to recognizing the French provisional government, de Gaulle did come to Washington, and the visit was quite satisfactory. Roosevelt had planned the meetings to be ceremonial rather than substantive, but the visit, except for the lack of a 21-gun salute, was almost indistinguishable from that of a head of state. One day at tea, Roosevelt, in keeping with prior instructions to Anna, engaged only in small talk, regaling his visitor in French about the planning and construction of the Jefferson Memorial; on another, he told reporters, de Gaulle was to brief him on the French underground.

Since there were no agreements to negotiate, for the most part the two discussed their larger views of the role of France and the United States in the postwar world. Roosevelt set forth once more his vision of the "Four Policemen," in which American bases at strategic points would help preserve the peace. Once more he cited Dakar, but this time included Singapore, which he had never mentioned in his discussions with Churchill. Later, de Gaulle passed along this point to the British, arousing Churchill's wrath. To de Gaulle's way of thinking, Roosevelt was moving from the extreme of isolation to that of a permanent system of intervention, based on international law.[8]

A few days later, Roosevelt summed up his impressions in a letter, a copy of which reached the French leader: "De Gaulle and I . . . talked more deeply about the future of France, its colonies, world peace, etc. In relation to future problems he seems quite 'tractable,' from the moment France is dealt with as a world power. He is very touchy in matters concerning the honor of France. But I suspect that he is essentially an egoist." To Churchill, Roosevelt commented only that the visit went very well.[9]

For the public, de Gaulle's visit was that of a popular hero. Admiring people blocked traffic on Pennsylvania Avenue as, towering, he moved in dignified fashion among them, making no acknowledgment of their existence. The only time de Gaulle lost his aplomb was when he visited the aged General Pershing, who persisted in asking after the health of his dear friend Marshal Pétain (who had sentenced de Gaulle to death in absentia). De Gaulle replied, "In 1940, he was really very well considering his age." In his haste to leave, de Gaulle forgot his military cap.[10]

The "stubborn old Dutchman" was changing his course toward de Gaulle and France in keeping with the new realities. He continued some private talk of nonrecognition, of the unworthiness of de Gaulle, of the danger of civil war in France once it was liberated, and even the need as a consequence for American forces to occupy northwestern rather than southwestern Germany. But his subordinates in Washington and Eisenhower in Europe were bringing him around. Through face-saving devices, Roosevelt moved along behind the British. In August when Paris was liberated, it was a French column that first entered the city, and a French general, Philippe Leclerc, who accepted the surrender. By fall, Roosevelt was ready to discard earlier fictions. Finally, on October 23, 1944, the State Department announced full recognition.[11]

There was little drama or surprise when, at a news conference on July 11, Roosevelt finally let it be known that he would accept nomination for a fourth term. The drama came later in the way he engineered the selection of the vice presidential running mate. For weeks Roosevelt had been addressing issues in both domestic and foreign policy areas in ways that seemed preparation for the campaign. Following the Republican convention, a journalist, May Craig, visited Hyde Park and warned Mrs. Roosevelt that with the nomination of Governor Dewey, the campaign theme would be youth versus "a tired old man." Mrs. Roosevelt responded, "Fortunately, he looks pretty vigorous."[12]

The war news was encouraging; the port of Cherbourg had fallen by the end of June. In the Pacific, the great offensive in the Marianas that began in mid-June was quickly but at high cost seizing islands from which the new B-29 bombers would be able to hit Tokyo. In the Battle of the Philippine Sea — the "Great Marianas Turkey Shoot" of June 19 — the largest carrier battle of the war, the Japanese lost two carriers and 346 planes.[13]

The progress of the war and Roosevelt's renewed energy led him in June to take a keen interest again in presidential politics and to engage in numerous behind-the-scenes consultations. Many of them centered upon whether to replace Vice President Wallace, and if so who the new nominee should be. It was not a new question. In December, 1943, Hopkins had already sounded out James Byrnes, telling him that on the way back from Tehran Roosevelt had expressed a strong wish that Byrnes be the vice presidential nominee. Byrnes told Hopkins he was not interested, and Roosevelt did not bring up the subject. In April the announcement that Wallace would visit China and Siberia had led to speculation whether the trip was a buildup or brush-off. Since Wallace would not return until shortly before the convention, Roosevelt gained time to sort out the pros and cons. Before leaving, Wallace reported to him that Hull doubted the value of the trip and Roosevelt replied, "Oh, you must go. I think you ought to see a lot of Siberia."[14]

As a running mate, Wallace embodied serious advantages and disadvantages for Roosevelt. The vice president was loyal and was fighting for the very policies both abroad and at home that the president had stressed in his 1944 State of the Union message. Behind him were rallied some of the strongest, most enthusiastic supporters of the New Deal and the president's foreign policy: northern urban liberals, blacks, and most of organized labor — the hard core of the Roosevelt coalition. Mrs. Roosevelt, pained by Hopkins' movement toward the right, had shifted her allegiance to Wallace.

Unfortunately there was also a negative case, which Edward Flynn, a former chairman of the Democratic National Committee, and Robert

Hannegan, the current chairman, in mid-June pressed directly to the president on behalf of numerous Democratic politicians. Even though the polls gave promise that the Democrats would win in 1944 if Roosevelt were at the head of the ticket, there were also indications, they contended, that the election would be close and Wallace a liability. This charming, brilliant idealist, never a politician's politician, commanded scant power or respect as he presided over the Senate. For conservatives, especially of an isolationist bent, he was an even more conspicuous target than the Republican Willkie. They sneered at his advocacy of aid to the deprived people of the world (quite akin to the programs Roosevelt dreamed of) as constituting "a quart of milk for every Hottentot." Further, Roosevelt had had to remove Wallace as director of the Board of Economic Warfare to end his squabbling with Jesse Jones. Roosevelt felt affection for Wallace, no doubt, but scarcely could have forgotten the 1940 problem over Wallace's mystical "guru letters," likely to surface again. More important, Wallace still seemed lacking in political judgment. While Roosevelt's heart may have been with Wallace, his head was that of a veteran politico bent upon victory.[15]

Months earlier, friend and foe alike among the Democratic leaders had taken the question of dropping Wallace out of Roosevelt's hands. With the president's health so obviously precarious, the vice presidency had acquired powerful allure. Political insiders suspected that Roosevelt would not be able to survive a fourth term. Therefore much quiet winnowing of names and launching of candidates was under way. Some party leaders were seeking to coalesce behind Senate Majority Leader Alben Barkley, their new hero since he had resigned in protest against Roosevelt's veto of the tax bill. Speaker Sam Rayburn was eager for the prize. Byrnes enjoyed even more conservative southern Democratic support. Friends of Senator Harry S. Truman were at work for him, although Truman insisted he was not a candidate. So too did Justice William O. Douglas, who had been head of the Securities and Exchange Commission, for whom Tom Corcoran and his many allies were hard at work.

There were as well some candidates with no hope of winning the nomination who entered the race to try to block Wallace. The moderately conservative spokesman for the cotton interests, Senator John H. Bankhead of Alabama, by the time of the convention was proudly a candidate, in order to sidetrack "that dangerous red by the name of Wallace."[16]

In the complex weighing of political considerations and the maneuvering that went on from late spring into the summer, a simple pattern emerged. The key player of the vice presidential poker game was, of course, Roosevelt himself in his efforts to control the choice. He played his cards with a gusto and effectiveness that surpassed 1940, less out of the indecisiveness that some saw in his strategy than to encourage a number of potential candidates, so many that none would have a clear-cut majority, while he would let his own choice be known so late that those opposed to the person selected would not have time to coalesce and thwart him. In the end this tactic left Roosevelt open to charges that he had been a treacherous, aged tyrant lopping off the heads of those who might dare challenge him.

Through June Roosevelt was purportedly saying that Wallace was indispensable because of his knowledge of international affairs, that even if it cost a million votes, he must stay on the ticket. At the same time through conversations he solicited names of other possible candidates, encouraging his "the more the merrier" strategy.[17]

Roosevelt's duplicity would not have surprised Wallace. In March the president had regaled him with an account of how he had seen Rabbis Stephen S. Wise and Abba Hillel Silver and had refuted their arguments in favor of moving Jewish refugees into Palestine in large numbers: "Do you want to start a Holy Jihad?" Wallace added:

> And yet I knew because Silver had talked to me at length the night before that the bulk of the President's conversation had undoubtedly been to cause Wise and Silver to believe he was in complete accord with them and the only question was the timing. . . . The President certainly is a waterman. He looks one direction and rows the other with the utmost skill.[18]

Roosevelt did not want to fight to retain Wallace. He still was not well enough to relish a battering contest, and justified himself by claiming the price was too high. Roosevelt's chief concern, he made clear to Rosenman at the time, was that he not go through a struggle as he had in 1940: "It will split the party open, and it is already split enough between North and South; it may kill our chances for election this fall, and if it does, it will prolong the war and knock into a cocked hat all the plans we've been making for the future."[19]

Although Roosevelt was willing to abandon Wallace to his conservative Democratic enemies, he had no intention of rewarding them, especially those opening a schism in the South; he would concede just enough to quash their efforts. After the election, win or lose, there would be reprisals, he told Ickes, making a gesture of throat cutting. He was grim over the success of rich Texas conservatives, many of them oil independents, in gaining control of the Texas Democratic convention. Despite the efforts of Speaker Rayburn and Lyndon Johnson, his protégé and Roosevelt's, the conservatives controlled two thirds of the delegates. They refused to endorse Roosevelt, or even Rayburn for vice president, and voted a platform damning the "Communist-controlled New Deal" and advocating restoration of white supremacy. The immediate effect was to destroy the vice presidential candidacy of Rayburn, and to upset Roosevelt as the movement, a forerunner of the Dixiecrat insurgency of 1948, spread in the deep South.[20]

Roosevelt held Jesse Jones accountable, asking him on June 13 what they were going to do about the Texas situation. When Jones said he didn't know, Roosevelt replied, "Well, it seems to me you ought to know." Jones, who had a nephew in the movement, denied any involvement. Late in the day, Roosevelt regaled his assistants with an account of the conversation (no doubt improved by retelling) and concluded that the Texans were trying to wreck the party system. Eugene Casey, one of the assistants, precipitated loud laughter when he commented, "Mr. President, I wish I had 90 per cent of your patience and you had 10 per cent of my ruthlessness."[21]

As the date of the national convention approached, Roosevelt maneuvered to hold together his disparate, rather fragile coalition by settling upon a vice presidential candidate who would be acceptable to their consensus. In his conversations with political leaders, he continued to encourage candidacy after candidacy and to give misleading signals about the direction of his own thinking. This was not all deliberate deception; on Byrnes at least, Roosevelt may have changed his mind. If Roosevelt did not want Byrnes to be the choice of the convention, he did favor him as a stalking horse. The more the better for Roosevelt. Shortly before the convention began, he said "yes" to the candidacy of Senator Scott Lucas of Illinois. Roosevelt was engineering the semblance of an open convention.

For days Roosevelt had been bandying about names in misleading fashion, sounding out insiders, and gradually refining his thoughts. On July 6, eating lunch with Ickes and Rosenman, he indicated the direction in which he was moving. Ickes had already learned that Roosevelt wanted someone who would not be regarded "as a kick in the face by the liberals." Roosevelt now added a new specification. He said he could not see any political sense to Byrnes as a choice; South Carolina was a poll tax state. According to Ickes, "The President did not want anyone below the Mason-Dixon line." This was as near as he came to discussing the growing importance of the black vote in pivotal northern states.[22]

In the final week before the Democratic convention, Roosevelt engaged in complicated maneuvers that brought the result he wished, but not without unpleasantness. First, the bad news had to be conveyed to Wallace, and Roosevelt did not want to do that himself. He dispatched Rosenman and Ickes to see Wallace when he returned to Washington from Asia early on Monday, July 10. Wallace, no fool, refused to talk politics with them, so Roosevelt that afternoon had to take on the task he hated, and he did it badly. He could not be candid to Wallace's face, and assured him he was his choice for a running mate, and was willing to say so in a statement; then Roosevelt warned of the opposition that would make it hard to obtain the nomination, and the cost people said there would be. The figure had now grown, thanks to Flynn's rhetoric, from one to three million votes. Wallace asked Roosevelt if he really wanted him, and Roosevelt said he did, but then tried to make the prospects seem even more grim. Wallace said he was used to difficult situations — and for the time being Roosevelt left the matter unsettled.[23]

On the afternoon of July 10, an hour before that conversation with Wallace, Roosevelt had talked over the vice presidency with Rosenman and Ickes. Ickes noted, "More clearly than ever, the President indicated that he believed Bill Douglas would be the strongest candidate." The next day, Roosevelt hinted differently.[24]

On July 11, while talking with his assistants Daniels and Casey, Roosevelt was candid. Smiling, he asked Casey if he had known Boss Charles Murphy of New York: "Charlie was a wise man. When they asked him who was going to be lieutenant governor, he would always say, 'The convention will decide,' and he got away with it for years."

As Daniels noted in his diary, "Casey said, 'Mr. President, do you mean that the convention will decide *period?*' The President laughed and said, 'Yes. Of course there are some people I wouldn't run with.' "[25]

That evening, Roosevelt met with a group of Democratic leaders to decide upon a vice president. These included Hannegan of St. Louis, Mayor Kelly of Chicago, and Flynn of the Bronx, but no southerner. In advance, Roosevelt had asked Flynn to bring up the name of Truman; Flynn passed the word on to Hannegan, a strong ally of Truman, who found it hard to believe. By the time the meeting took place, the work had been done. They went down a considerable list of names, discussing pros and cons. Roosevelt asked them about Winant and Douglas and elicited little enthusiasm, Flynn remembered. The exception was Mayor Kelly, who championed Douglas.

Flynn later reminisced about the meeting, "Everyone thought he had suggested Truman and that the President had taken his suggestion." During the meeting the president took very little part in the conversation. The question of Senator Truman's association with the Pendergast machine was thoroughly discussed. By the end of the evening there was a consensus, and Roosevelt said firmly, "It's Truman."[26]

As the meeting broke up, Hannegan stayed behind to get a note from Roosevelt, thinking he might need it at the convention. Roosevelt obliged, penning it quickly, and dating it ahead to the time of the convention:

July 19

Dear Bob,

You have written me about Harry Truman and Bill Douglas. I should, of course, be very glad to run with either of them and believe that either one of them would bring real strength to the ticket.

Always sincerely,
Franklin D. Roosevelt

These hasty words required careful reading. Roosevelt was not endorsing Truman, but saying he was acceptable, and was adding the name Douglas to indicate that was true of more than one person, and the convention thus unbossed. Later at the convention the story spread — and has persisted ever since — that originally the letter had read "Douglas and Truman" and that later Hannegan persuaded Roosevelt to reverse the order. The rumor seems to have been no more than part of the "stop Truman" efforts.[27]

Aside from the Pendergast connection, Truman seemed the ideal person for Roosevelt to add to the ticket. He was from a border state, Missouri, had been an army captain in World War I — and it had pained his mother when she first saw him in a Yankee uniform. He enjoyed the confidence and camaraderie of the oligarchy of southern senators. Fortunately for Truman, Roosevelt did not know how pungently Truman shared some of their thoughts about him. Truman was acceptable to the southern Democrats. At the same time, with a few exceptions like the 1944 tax bill, he normally voted for Roosevelt's New Deal and foreign policy measures. He was attractive to union labor, and had taken good care of his black constituency, whose votes had been important for him. He could be useful to Roosevelt as a Senate insider, and would be a scrappy energetic campaigner. That was all Roosevelt sought in the weeks before the convention, when his health and optimism had largely returned. He had not been seeking a likely successor but rather someone who he thought would not cost him votes.[28]

The next two days, the last before Roosevelt entrained for the Pacific coast, were critical ones. He still had to disentangle himself from Byrnes and Wallace, and was not successful with either. There were further interviews with Wallace, and again Roosevelt was "damned careful about language," at least in what he wrote. Orally he was less so. He assured Wallace he would write a letter that afternoon to the permanent chairman of the convention, Senator Samuel D. Jackson. Finally, as Wallace was leaving, Roosevelt took his hand, pulled him down, and said into his ear, "While I cannot put it just that way in public, I hope it will be the same old team."

In the letter to be released at the convention, Roosevelt said concerning Wallace, "I would vote for his renomination if I were a delegate to the convention."[29]

As a result of these tactics, Roosevelt sent both Byrnes and Wallace to a purportedly "open convention," each thinking that the president privately wanted him to win. Each had a strong organization energetically at work. Byrnes, more of a political realist, shrewdly telephoned Truman, whom Roosevelt said the professionals had anointed. Truman, just leaving for the convention, agreed to nominate Byrnes. Truman was already aware, if not of the Tuesday night meeting, of the way Hannegan was moving on his behalf. Amid Truman's reiterated protests that he was not a candidate, during that last two weeks before the convention, he sent word to trusted political friends that Hannegan expected him to be vice president and he would need their help in Chicago. On July 4 he told Forrestal he was being pressed to be the nominee. Truman, who had read much on the Civil War, was assuming the Lincolnesque stance of reticence that Americans so much admired in politics. More important, no "stop Truman" movement could coalesce against him until too late.[30]

The only front-runner who made his reticence stick was Douglas, in the Wallowa Mountains of Oregon. Douglas at convention time sent a letter empowering a friend to withdraw his name and then backpacked into the wilderness, where he was unreachable. He had miscalculated, feeling it was more important to sit on the Supreme Court than to be an impotent vice president, and his backers were aiming him for the presidency in 1948. That fall, Douglas confessed to Ickes that if the president had asked him to run for vice president he would have done so, but he had not heard from Roosevelt either directly or indirectly.[31]

On the evening of July 14, Roosevelt left by train for the West Coast, by way of New Jersey, where he spent much of the next day at the estate of Lucy Mercer Rutherford. In the late afternoon he arrived at Hyde

Park, where Mrs. Roosevelt, concerned about his health and eager to see their sons James and John and families, joined him for the long rail trip ahead.[32]

Traveling under wartime protection of secrecy, Roosevelt and his party arrived in Chicago on Sunday, July 16, two days before the convention opened. Unknown except to a few, he spent several hours in the freight yards in his Pullman car, telephoning and conferring with Hannegan and Mayor Kelly. Later the train rolled on slowly toward California while cruel maneuvering ensued in Chicago. Kelly and Hannegan phoned Byrnes that they had seen Roosevelt, and he had given them "the green light to support you." The next night in Chicago, Hannegan, Kelly, Walker, and others at a dinner seemed firmly behind Byrnes, talking about how to make him the candidate. Then, Byrnes remembered, as the party broke up:

"Hannegan turned to Kelly and said, 'Ed, there is one thing we forgot. The President said, "Clear it with Sidney." ' " The reference was to Sidney Hillman, chairman of the CIO Political Action Committee. (Hillman earlier in the week had been in and out of the White House, and had told Ickes he would accept anyone Roosevelt might suggest.) The next morning, Byrnes got word that Hillman was first for Wallace, then for Truman, and could not be persuaded to support Byrnes. (This led to the derisive chant that the Republicans used against Democrats throughout the campaign and long afterwards, "Clear it with Sidney.")

Next, as the Democratic National Committee was nevertheless about to approve Byrnes unanimously, Flynn intervened, and insisted he must first talk on the telephone to Roosevelt. He and Hillman reached the president at some stop on the way west, and brought back word that Roosevelt would withdraw his approval of Byrnes and accept Truman. An hour later, Truman asked Byrnes to be released from the promise to nominate him, since he was Roosevelt's choice for the vice presidency. Byrnes, embittered, the next day withdrew his candidacy.

Still, Truman did not hear directly from Roosevelt and on Thursday, the day before the convention was to ballot on the vice presidency, was saying he was for Byrnes. The delegates were confused, not sure what to make of conflicting stories. Ickes, outraged at what he saw as boss control, jumped to the support of Wallace, who began to gather strength far beyond what the professionals had warned Roosevelt would be Wallace's limit. Roosevelt on the train was dismayed by Ickes' switch and the way he had been misinformed on Wallace's strength. As the train wound slowly through the west, he telephoned from various stops to see if Hannegan had persuaded Truman, yet did not himself speak to Truman. At the convention there was no longer any illusion that he was uninvolved; his letters to Wallace and Hannegan had both become public. As the train finally arrived in San Diego, the stalemate continued.

With Truman in the room, Hannegan explained to Roosevelt on the phone that Truman still had not consented, and beckoned him to come near the receiver. Truman then heard Roosevelt vigorously assert, "Well, tell the Senator that if he wants to break up the Democratic party by staying out, he can; but he knows as well as I what that might mean at this dangerous time in the world."

"Jesus Christ!" exclaimed Truman. "But why the hell didn't he tell me in the first place?"[33]

By the time Truman won the nomination on the second ballot, Roosevelt's hidden hand was fooling no one. Indeed, it was emphatic evoking of the president's name that brought about the switches in votes. In his machinations, Roosevelt had depended largely upon northern urban bosses, even enlisting the notorious Mayor Frank Hague of Jersey City, to nominate a man with a New Deal voting record, but one also notable for his loyalty to Tom Pendergast of Kansas City. Roosevelt had entered politics as a reform enemy of bosses, and then had learned to use them, like Theodore Roosevelt. Now he gave the public impression that he was one of them.

Byrnes was understandably bitter. At the convention hall, when the voice of Roosevelt came on to deliver his acceptance address, there was a standing ovation. In the presidential box, Byrnes and his wife remained seated. Subsequently Roosevelt tried to make amends to Byrnes by taking him to the Yalta conference.[34]

The trip on the west-bound train was especially slow, since the president did not want to deliver his acceptance address until he got to California, and went along a little-used circuitous route touching the Mexican border. At last, on July 19, Roosevelt, the commander in chief, arrived on his train at Camp Pendleton, the Marine Corps base just north of San Diego. The next night, the convention voted his nomination: Roosevelt, 1,086; Byrd, 89. While floodlights illuminated the empty rostrum in the convention hall, Roosevelt's voice came booming through the speakers. The president was seated in the observation car of his train at Camp Pendleton, covered by a news pool and several photographers. One of the photographers caught him looking down with his mouth open, appearing weak and emaciated, but his voice that night was strong and confident.[35]

Roosevelt, who usually wrote his own stirring conclusion, instead finished with the greatest of American perorations, that of Lincoln's

Second Inaugural: "Let us strive on to finish the work we are in; to bind up the Nation's wounds . . . to do all which may achieve and cherish a just and lasting peace among ourselves, and with all Nations."[36]

The powerful delivery of the speech and some photographs of an animated president were indications of his continued strength; the slack-jawed picture, appearing in newspapers throughout the country, gave warning of his failing health. There was another indication the next day, which fortunately for Roosevelt he was able to keep hidden. Mrs. Roosevelt had flown east; he was in his private car, alone with his son James, about to witness a marine landing exercise in preparation for one in the western Pacific. He was telling James that he was tired but otherwise all right, when suddenly he suffered acute abdominal pains. Previously Roosevelt had had gallstone attacks. He said the pains came sometimes when he ate too fast, or because of his lack of exercise. He did not want a doctor, but had his son ease him onto the floor. There he stretched out for about ten minutes. Gradually he began to feel better, and shortly left, as commander in chief to review the exercises. A photographer caught him with a grin on his face.[37]

Chapter 39

TO THE PACIFIC AND QUEBEC

IN THE SUMMER of 1944, as American forces advanced spectacularly in both Europe and the Pacific, Roosevelt turned his attention away from the election to concentrate upon his role as commander in chief. The best tactic was for him to appear to be too busy for politics, to be wholly concerned first and foremost with cracking Japan's inner defenses in the Pacific. Contemporary observers, particularly the Republicans, viewed his visit to Hawaii to confer with Pacific commanders as being political. It well served that purpose for Roosevelt, but during the trip the presidential election seemed little on his mind and ostensibly he had no plans to campaign later, even in October.

As Roosevelt was about to depart from San Diego, the war in Europe was entering an exciting phase. The First Army, capturing Saint-Lô, brought the battle of the hedgerows in Normandy to a successful conclusion, and several days later began a massive sweep to the south and east into the heart of France. Meanwhile an enormous Soviet offensive was driving westward into Poland. At headquarters in East Prussia, a group of German officers, well aware that the war was lost, narrowly failed in their attempt to assassinate Hitler and thus avoid ruin. When the news reached Roosevelt, he wrote his wife, just before departing, "I might have to hurry back earlier if this German revolt gets worse! I fear though that it won't." Three days before, in reaction to the American victories in the Pacific, the cabinet of Premier Tojo had fallen in Japan.[1]

In part Roosevelt's inspection tour was to reassure those on the West Coast and the "Japan first" enthusiasts everywhere that he had not forgotten the Pacific war. From San Diego he wrote Lord Beaverbrook:

> These good people out here seem to feel a little neglected for to them the Pacific operations seem at least as important as those in Normandy. Their turn will come soon, I hope. . . . Incidentally . . . taking Saipan has been an outstanding success in spite of 15,000 casualties. From there, we will be within thirteen or fourteen hundred miles of the industrial part of Japan — easy bombing range.[2]

Just after midnight on July 22, Roosevelt sailed on the heavy cruiser *Baltimore*. It was a pleasant voyage. With four destroyers guarding against submarines, the cruiser zigzagged in the daytime and sailed straight without lights after dark. Roosevelt napped, read, and in the evening watched motion pictures. By the afternoon of July 26, when the *Baltimore* moored at Pearl Harbor, he was refreshed.

The president gazed out at an armada of warships, the sailors in whites at attention on the decks, and thousands of civilians crowded behind the roped-in area. Since, he remarked, his arrival was obviously no secret, he directed his personal flag to be raised. Admiral Chester W. Nimitz, commander of naval forces in the Pacific, and some forty flag officers of the navy and general officers of the army and navy, all in dress uniform, greeted the president. The only absent figure was General MacArthur. Finally, just as Roosevelt was preparing to disembark, MacArthur, amidst a roar from the crowd, strode up the gangplank and greeted the president.[3]

For three days, Roosevelt divided his time between inspections and sight-seeing, and serious discussions with the Pacific commanders. No member of the Joint Chiefs of Staff was present except for the chairman, Admiral Leahy. Admiral King, who had been in Hawaii meeting with Admiral Nimitz and his subordinates, had not been invited and had hastily departed before the president's arrival. It was, therefore, a most unusual planning session, the only one of its sort in which Roosevelt ever participated. It was particularly remarkable since the president during the past two years had taken little part in naval planning. "He had to show the voters that he was commander in chief," King remarked after the war. MacArthur deemed the conference "purely political," and exclaimed while on the flight from Brisbane, "The humiliation of forcing me to leave my command . . . for a picture-taking junket!"[4]

The meeting in Honolulu would indeed be a major political asset to Roosevelt, sufficient for him to choose it rather than a visit to the Normandy beachhead, which also would have brought acclaim. More than that, Roosevelt as commander in chief was intervening in a debate over the next major target in the Pacific war. In mid-March, the Joint Chiefs had issued a directive providing both that MacArthur should land in November at Mindanao in the southern Philippines and that Nimitz the following February should seize Formosa. Subsequently King strongly favored bypassing the Philippines and attacking Formosa, a proposal that MacArthur energetically argued against as bad strategy and a betrayal of promises to the Filipinos. Nimitz and most of the admirals in the Pacific inclined toward the Philippines. It was a question that must have fascinated Roosevelt, since throughout his career since 1913, his thoughts on a possible Pacific war had centered around expectations of an early loss of the Philippines and its ultimate liberation.[5]

The next day's agenda convinced MacArthur he was right in thinking the meeting political, for from 10:30 to 4:30 he had to ride in an open car sitting on one side of Roosevelt with Nimitz on the other. Leahy rode in the front. MacArthur thought Roosevelt "physically . . . just a shell of the man I had known," but his condition could not be guessed from the schedule.[6]

During the long, rigorous day, Roosevelt chatted and reminisced ingratiatingly with MacArthur, and gave several short extemporaneous talks. At Schofield Barracks, speaking to the seasoned Seventh Division, veterans of Kwajalein and Attu, he contrasted the martial array with what he had witnessed on review ten years previously. His remarks were amusing because of the wild exaggeration: "There were some first World War tanks in it. I think that of the twelve that took part, seven broke down before they could get past. Some difference in ten years! . . . And the aircraft at Schofield — not more than fifteen or twenty — three-fourths of them got past, though whether they got back safely on the earth, I don't know."[7]

When finally Roosevelt returned to the estate on Waikiki Beach where he was staying, he still had sufficient energy to host MacArthur, Leahy, Nimitz, and Admiral W. F. ("Bull") Halsey at dinner. Afterward Halsey departed and Roosevelt settled down to the most serious business of the day. Until midnight they discussed Pacific strategy.

In the debate over whether to land in the Philippines or Formosa, Roosevelt acted as the impartial moderator. The living room of the residence had been transformed into a conference room with huge maps on the walls. Roosevelt opened the discussion by gesturing with a bamboo pointer toward the Philippines and asking, "Well, Doug, where do we go from here?" MacArthur held forth on the moral obligation and military advantages of liberating the Philippines. Nimitz followed with the official plan to go into the southern Philippines, then bypass Luzon to attack Formosa. He argued (as King earlier had with him) that bases to the south of Manila would be as useful and cost fewer lives than a return to Luzon. The next morning the discussion resumed and continued until noon. Even MacArthur felt that the president functioned well as an impartial moderator, doubtful about a Formosa operation but entirely neutral. Leahy admiringly reminisced:

> Roosevelt was at his best as he tactfully steered the discussion from one point to another and narrowed down the area of disagreement between MacArthur and Nimitz. . . . in the end only a relatively minor difference remained — that of an operation to retake . . . Manila. This was solved later when the idea of beginning . . . at Leyte was suggested, studied, and adopted.[8]

The discussions did not settle finally the question whether to make major landings in the Philippines rather than Formosa, but moved toward the choice later of the Philippines. Leahy rejoiced over the cooperative spirit. He noted that both Nimitz and MacArthur agreed that sea and air power could force Japanese surrender without an invasion.[9]

At the conclusion of the discussions, Roosevelt resumed his intensive round of installations and hospitals. Rosenman was moved by the sight of the president in his wheelchair, rolling slowly past the beds of those who had lost arms or legs, giving them a cheery smile and words of encouragement as he displayed his own useless legs.[10]

Surprisingly, Roosevelt managed to breach MacArthur's animus toward him. The first afternoon, he persuaded MacArthur to postpone his return to Australia and accompany him. When Roosevelt parried a query about Dewey by saying he had been too busy to pay attention to politics, MacArthur said, "I threw back my head and laughed. He looked at me and broke into a laugh himself." From the Honolulu meeting on, the relationship between Roosevelt and MacArthur was more pleasant; they exchanged cordial letters.[11]

As Roosevelt sailed northward that night toward the Aleutian Islands and Alaska, he could take satisfaction from the time he had spent combining strategy discussions and morale building among the armed forces, together with the image he gave the electorate of an energetic commander in chief, the friend of the popular MacArthur.

Two days out of Honolulu, sailing through summer seas, Roosevelt received news that Missy LeHand had died. She had never recovered from her stroke of three years earlier. Those with him on the *Baltimore* recorded no impression of his thoughts or feelings; he probably revealed none to them.[12]

On August 3, in fog and drizzle, Roosevelt glimpsed the bright green hills topped with snow of the Aleutian Islands. At Adak, the commanding admiral and general had prepared for him. An army crew under Captain LeRoy Burg had to police the beach twice a day as the tides brought in "flotsam to be deposited as jetsam." Crews were manning the rails of naval vessels as the *Baltimore* moored at a newly constructed dock. Roosevelt, putting on foul-weather gear, went ashore and ate lunch at the mess hall from a regulation aluminum tray. "I like your food. I like your climate," he informed the army, navy, and marine enlisted men, who roared with laughter.

Adak seemed to exhilarate Roosevelt. He was vigorous and feeling well. When the crosswinds were so strong that the navy tugs could not pull the *Baltimore* away from the dock, he donned a rain slicker and boots, was wheeled out into the rainy gusty weather, sat on a stool on the deck, threw a line overboard, and fished for nearly an hour.[13]

While fishing on August 9 with Governor Ernest Gruening at Tee Harbor near Juneau, Roosevelt became intrigued with the possibility of settling returning veterans in Alaska. There was "an abundance of fish and game and timber, together with great possibilities for agriculture," he declared later. Nor were "the climate and the crops . . . essentially different from . . . Norway, Sweden, Finland." He promised that, upon his return to Washington, he would set up a study of Alaska and the Aleutians as areas where veterans could become pioneers. True to his word, he did so.[14]

One small matter annoyed Roosevelt on the return trip. A story began to circulate that when the *Baltimore* finally pulled away from the dock at Adak it left Roosevelt's Scottie, Fala, behind. Supposedly the president sent a destroyer from the escort group to retrieve the dog. Quickly the account spread and became more and more remarkable in its growth. In full size it came to involve both battleships and cruisers, a sortie costing a fortune and removing a naval vessel from the scene of battle, a ship that could otherwise have sunk a Japanese naval vessel that subsequently sank an American transport!

As the story grew it became no joking matter. Representative Harold Knutson, a Michigan Republican, asserted indignantly on the floor of the House that it was rumored that the absence of Fala had not been discovered until the party reached Seattle, and that a destroyer had been dispatched a thousand miles to fetch him. Majority Leader John McCormack called Admiral Leahy and insisted upon the facts. He then quoted to the House Leahy's statement: "The dog was never lost." The irrepressible Knutson thereupon floated a fresh rumor to taunt Mrs.

Roosevelt, "that a certain very high-placed American woman made a trip to Australia in a bomber that it is reported had been remodelled so as to permit the installation of a shower bath." Eventually the Republicans discovered a bona fide Roosevelt dog story. To her subsequent dismay, Anna had approved a directive to ship her brother Elliott's dog home, resulting in two wounded servicemen being bumped from their airplane seats to provide room for the dog in his crate.[15]

From Juneau, Roosevelt sailed down the inland passage aboard the destroyer *Cummings*, which could more easily navigate through several of the straits. Continued bad weather limited sight-seeing, but Roosevelt was relaxing so pleasantly that he devoted little attention to the talk he was to deliver upon his arrival at the Bremerton, Washington, naval yard in Puget Sound. Rosenman had flown back to Washington from Hawaii, so Roosevelt himself dictated the speech to Lieutenant Rigdon, his secretary on the trip. He made only slight changes and no more than glanced at the manuscript an hour or two before he was to deliver it. This was a singular deviation from habit, since the speech was to be broadcast nationally, and although purportedly nonpolitical would obviously have strong bearing on the campaign. Roosevelt intended it to be a folksy report to the American people on his travels, together with some reassurances on the progress of the war and the nature of the peace to come. It was an interesting account told in Roosevelt's way, but lacking the eloquent exhortations and promises that Rosenman or Sherwood would have inserted. Further, Roosevelt departed from the prepared text given to reporters and ad-libbed rather freely.

By no means was the address as weak as Rosenman and others have since suggested. But Roosevelt spoke hesitantly. This, together with his drawn appearance, gave credence to the Republican campaign claims that he was old and in sorry shape. Indeed he was. His halting speech was due in part to his decision to stand. He had not used his braces for a year; they no longer fit well, and cut into his flesh. It was also agonizing for him to put his full weight on his feet. Although his muscles were atrophied, his nerves were sensitive. To add to his difficulties, a stiff wind was ruffling his manuscript as he stood for thirty-five minutes on the sloping bridge of the *Cummings* facing an audience of 10,000 shipyard workers and servicemen. They failed to react to his speech; because of the wind it was hard to hear him over the loudspeakers. The absence of reaction, in contrast to the enthusiasm of the servicemen at Adak, may also have contributed to his lackluster performance.

There was a prime factor that Roosevelt kept secret. During the early part of the speech, as his heart specialist, Dr. Bruenn, revealed years later, Roosevelt began to suffer for the first and only time in his life from an angina attack. An excruciating pain in his chest extended up into both of his shoulders, and only slowly, after fifteen minutes, subsided. Yet he went on talking — a Spartan performance. Afterward he apparently told no one but his doctor what he had undergone while speaking, but he did cancel an inspection of the naval yard. An hour later, Dr. Bruenn gave him an electrocardiogram and checked his white blood count. There were no abnormalities.[16]

On the train trip eastward, Roosevelt bounced back, writing a humorous account of the low-pressure area that followed them from the Aleutians to Chicago. He had turned the attention of the nation to the Pacific war and MacArthur, mollifying an important part of the electorate, and undermining Dewey's argument that the nation would be electing a peacetime president. On the other hand, his performance at Bremerton seemed to substantiate the Republican call for a youthful administration. One facetious cartoon pictured Roosevelt with a beard swirling onto the floor sitting next to Dewey in a cradle. Polls in the next several weeks showed gains for Dewey.[17]

On days when Roosevelt did not feel well he was apathetic. He lamented to a friend, "I shall not weep bitter tears if Dewey wins through a small vote coming out. Neither you nor I have any right to take on more responsibilities." Mrs. Roosevelt believed by this time that his election was essential to preserve liberal policies and encouraged him to be more active. She seated Trude Pratt next to him at a dinner at about that time, to urge him to speak more often and before crowds. Roosevelt said he didn't want to, that his voice was bad; she reassured him that "his ills were imaginary." No doubt Roosevelt relished her concern. He had already announced that he would deliver his first political address before the Teamsters Union, but avowed that he had no intentions of going on a campaign tour. In all of this, he was adhering to his well-established timing in presidential campaigns. One difference in 1944 was his physical condition, which he sought to improve. On a September day, Rosenman entered the president's bedroom to find him wearing his braces, walking back and forth on the arm of Dr. McIntire. He could again stand if he had to, but decided to deliver all of his campaign addresses either seated at a table or in the back seat of his car. Relaxed, he could focus upon what he was saying without risking physical mishaps.[18]

There was still the risk of verbal mishaps. One night when Roosevelt was dining on the south porch of the White House with Dorothy Thompson, the columnist, Anna has reminisced: "I realized at one point he was telling a story toward the end of the meal that he'd already told her toward the beginning. . . . I hadn't noticed this before, but my only feeling was, 'Oh, come off now . . .' but I didn't dare say it." It was more embarrassing on the evening of August 24, when Roosevelt gave a dinner in honor of the first president of the newly independent Iceland. He proposed a toast before President Sveinn Bjørnsson made some remarks, and then afterward absentmindedly toasted him again. The guests were stunned, noted Morgenthau.[19]

Roosevelt fared better in quiet politicking. On the day after his return from Alaska, a bit tired and tense, he was pictured in his shirtsleeves with his running mate, Truman, lunching on the White House grounds under a giant magnolia dating back to Jackson's presidency. Roosevelt looked fine, but his shaking hands shocked Truman. "In pouring his cream . . . he got more . . . in the saucer than he did in the cup." Roosevelt said he was so busy with the war that Truman would have to campaign for both of them. By Labor Day Truman was at work, and in October set out on a 7,500-mile trip. That seems to have been about all Roosevelt saw of Truman during the campaign.[20]

A few days later, Roosevelt again lunched under the Jackson magnolia, this time with the outgoing vice president, Henry Wallace, who loyally was already delivering campaign speeches for Roosevelt. The president assured Wallace that if the election went well he could have any cabinet office he wished except the State Department. Roosevelt did not want to break the heart of that old dear, Hull. At once Wallace asked to take over Jesse Jones's domain, the Commerce Department, the Reconstruction Finance Corporation, and the Foreign Economic Administration. "There would be poetic justice in that," said Wallace. "That's right" commented Roosevelt.[21]

The next noon, Roosevelt in an off-the-record appointment tried to mollify several particularly outraged Wallace supporters from Kentucky who were not as quietly philosophical as their hero. Among them were Mark Ethridge, publisher of the *Louisville Courier-Journal*, and Mary Bingham, wife of Barry Bingham, the owner, on war duty in London. Ethridge had sent a powerful letter to the president. Mrs. Bingham had written Mrs. Roosevelt tactfully that she had heard people at the convention whose devotion to the president was unquestioned using the ugly words "double cross" in "bitterness and disillusion."

The president at the outset of the interview avowed, according to Mrs. Bingham, "that, until he read the Eastern papers he had known nothing about the activities at Chicago attributed to him. We said nothing to this, so there was a rather miserable pause, and I suppose my grief at hearing him utter such a fib was plain to be seen on my unsubtle face." Roosevelt went on to reiterate the same hollow explanation he had given to Wallace the day before — that Wallace did not have the votes — and reminisced about the deal that he, Roosevelt, had had to make with the ill-reputed Hearst forces in order to win the nomination in 1932. His implication was that unsavory deals were the price reformers had to pay if they wished to wield power.

For the rest, Roosevelt repaid them for the trip from Kentucky with speculation about replacing Jones with Wallace, the possibility of more valley authorities like TVA, the need for a development program in Persia, and, interestingly, the apparent apathy of the electorate, even among the armed forces he had visited in the Pacific.

These were the president's reassurances to the troubled liberals. Roosevelt had cast his schedule aside and was again putting in long hours, but in person still gave an impression of dynamism. Mrs. Bingham noted:

> His face in repose looks thin, and about the jaws somewhat sunken. When he is talking, and his face is animated, one does not notice this, but when he is listening there is a . . . sinking of the muscles, and I believe this accounts for some of the very bad pictures. . . . On the other hand, his voicc is powerful, positive, and resonant, and gives one the feeling of . . . strength and equally great control.[22]

Despite their pain over the shell game that Roosevelt had played at Chicago and his subsequent prevarications, Mrs. Bingham and Ethridge remained politically loyal to the president. Roosevelt was not helping his reputation, but he was holding his coalition intact.

While Roosevelt was in the Pacific, Allied armies were making such rapid progress in Europe that victory over Germany seemed only weeks or months away. Yet the advances both in France and on the eastern front were adding to tension and dispute among Roosevelt, Churchill, and Stalin. For Roosevelt and Churchill, still arguing between themselves over strategy, the final phase of "crossing the bridge with the devil" was creating concern and misgivings.

After the first discouraging weeks of the hedgerow war in Normandy, the American and British armies were racing after the Germans across France. Churchill was no longer acquiescing in the agreed-upon plan to land in southern France, wishing instead to send troops through the Ljubljana gap in the mountains of Yugoslavia to beat the Russians into Budapest, Vienna, and Prague. Earlier, his schemes had rested upon military arguments; beginning in the spring of 1944, his motives were also political. Roosevelt backed his generals in their insistence that they seize ports badly needed for landing reinforcements and strike next up the relatively easy Rhone valley.

The landings, when they took place on August 15, were spectacularly easy and hastened the liberation of France. When British criticism continued after the war, Marshall pointed out, "Half of Patton's army was supplied from Marseilles. It was important in the Ardennes period. It helped complete the Eisenhower operations in Normandy."[23]

On August 25, the French Second Armored Division entered Paris early in the morning. Within several days, American troops were passing through the streets of Paris, hailed by cheering crowds, bussed by excited young women. "Can I kiss one too?" one fifteen-year-old asked her father. "No," he replied, pulling her back. In the White House, Roosevelt remarked to Mary Bingham and the Kentuckians that he assumed the troops in Europe "were too busy killing Germans and kissing French girls to care much about voting."[24]

Hundreds of miles farther east, in Warsaw, the Polish underground, loyal to the London government, was fighting helplessly against four armored German divisions. During previous weeks the Red Army had driven 300 miles to the east bank of the Vistula, across from Warsaw. As it approached, the Lublin Committee of National Liberation on July 29 had broadcast from Moscow the signal for the underground to arise against the Germans. They could have done so only with the approval of the Soviets, but when the uprising began on August 1, the Russians gave no aid or encouragement, nor would Stalin allow Churchill or Roosevelt to help.

Churchill and Roosevelt were distressed. On August 20, they sent Stalin a joint message urging him to drop supplies and munitions, or to help Allied planes do so. It was September 9 before Stalin conceded that American and British airplanes dropping aid over Warsaw could then land on Soviet airfields. There were several flights, but few of the supplies reached the underground. Soviet forces still did not move; it was another three months before they entered Warsaw. By October 2, the Germans had wiped out the revolt, killing or wounding nearly a quarter million men, women, and children.

Stalin's callous inaction during the Warsaw uprising, together with the establishment of the Lublin Committee to govern Poland, were symptomatic of the shift that had taken place since his friendly congratulations during the Normandy landings.[25]

Another sign that caused Roosevelt concern came early in the Dumbarton Oaks conference, which met in Washington from August to October, 1944, when Ambassador Andrey Gromyko demanded that each of the sixteen Soviet republics must have a vote in the assembly. Roosevelt exclaimed, "My God," and instructed Stettinius to reply that the demand might keep the public from accepting or the Senate from approving American membership in the new organization. Stettinius persuaded Gromyko not to raise the matter again at Dumbarton Oaks.[26]

The conference was also becoming deadlocked on a question that the Russians, British, and Americans had been debating even before it opened — whether, as the Russians wished, each of the permanent members of the council should be able to exercise a veto. The United States had leaned toward the Russian position but just before the conference opened switched to the British view, that a permanent member should not use the veto in disputes to which it was a party. To back up his position, Roosevelt sent a strong cable to Stalin. He had wanted a husband-and-wife simile in it, but that somehow disappeared in the drafting. Stalin stood firm, citing the earlier American view on voting and the decision at Tehran to insist upon "big four" unity. Roosevelt's private expectation was that he could iron out the problems later in person with Stalin.[27]

Difficulties like these were sufficient to make Roosevelt and his advisers more cautious toward the Russians, but not to bring a change of policy. On September 9, Harriman sent word: "Now that the end of the war is in sight our relations with the Soviets have taken a startling turn evident during the last two months. They have held up our requests with complete indifference to our interests and have shown an unwillingness even to discuss pressing problems. . . ."[28]

Like Roosevelt, Harriman as yet ascribed many of the difficulties to subordinates in the Kremlin. The Americans could not know how monolithic was the power that Stalin exercised, and continued to believe that Stalin, alternately charming and chilling, was open to reason. Only as the Soviet forces advanced did Stalin's basic policy become clear, as he was to tell Tito in 1945: "Whoever occupies a territory also imposes on it his own social system. Everyone imposes his own system as far as his army can reach. It cannot be otherwise."[29]

As yet Roosevelt continued to feel that with firmness and cajoling he could retain Stalin as a reasonably cooperative partner in both the final stages of the war and the future peacekeeping. Indeed, the overall tone of exchanges with the Soviet Union was still favorable. The irritations might nudge Roosevelt to be more concerned that England and the British Empire be strong after the war, but they did not deter him, even as the Warsaw drama was being played out, from supporting a scheme to transform postwar Germany into an agricultural nation. Although he was worried about spreading Russian influence in eastern Europe and the Balkans, he was ready to create a power vacuum in Germany.

In late August, Secretary of the Treasury Morgenthau brought back to Roosevelt from England his concerns, that the British were going broke and were planning to rebuild Germany so it could pay reparations. As for the soft treatment of Germany, Roosevelt replied:

> Give me thirty minutes with Churchill and I can correct this. . . . We have got to be tough with Germany and I mean the German people, not just the Nazis. You either have to castrate the German people or you have got to treat them . . . so they can't just go on reproducing people who want to continue . . . [as] in the past.

Several days later, the president told Morgenthau that he wanted a strong Britain, but worried more about a resurgent Germany than a recalcitrant Soviet Union.[30]

In the belief that he had Roosevelt's support, Morgenthau appointed a Treasury Department committee to draft a program for the postwar treatment of Germany. In persuading Roosevelt, Morgenthau depended heavily upon a proposed "Handbook of Military Government," prepared in London and not yet approved. Roosevelt read the handbook and wrote Stimson in indignation:

> It gives me the impression that Germany is to be restored just as much as the Netherlands or Belgium, and the people of Germany brought back as quickly as possible to their pre-war estate. . . . The fact that they are a defeated nation, collectively and individually, must be so impressed upon them that they will hesitate to start any new war. . . . I see no reason for starting a WPA, PWA or a CCC for Germany when we go in with our Army of Occupation.[31]

Although Roosevelt had difficulty in making up his mind whether or not to pastoralize Germany, he was quite firm that Germans must suffer. The strong objection that Stimson had set forth to Roosevelt, earlier in writing and then at a cabinet meeting, was that the Saar and Ruhr industrial complex was the key to the prosperity of all Europe, including France and Great Britain. He was "utterly opposed to the destruction of such a great gift of nature . . . that . . . should be used for the reconstruction of the world." As the meeting ended, Stimson felt the president had taken his side.[32]

At this point, with the problem not clearly resolved in his own mind, Roosevelt, not at all at his best, weary and suffering from a cold, headed north for a conference with Churchill at Quebec, September 12–16, 1944. It was to be a meeting with the British on the postwar settlement and the Pacific strategy. The military commanders were to be there; both Roosevelt and Churchill brought their wives. The president summoned Morgenthau, who during the summer had become once again one of his mainstays, but left Hopkins behind, ostensibly because of his precarious health.

Since early July, Hopkins had been back at the White House, once more handling foreign policy matters but no longer enjoying his former power or closeness to Roosevelt. While the president still conferred with him, he had not sat with the political leaders when they chose a new vice presidential candidate, nor, as the British soon discovered, could he any longer settle weighty problems for them. Roosevelt was handling the new lend-lease program through Morgenthau, although it had been Hopkins' specialty, and had designated Stettinius rather than Hopkins to serve on the committee.

There was later much speculation that Roosevelt was keeping Hopkins out of the limelight to prevent Republicans from once more making him a campaign issue. That had not deterred Roosevelt in 1940. He may well have felt that Hopkins was exercising too much power in his relations with the British and Russians, authority that Roosevelt wished to wield directly at a time when there were tensions in relations with both Churchill and Stalin. Habitually, Roosevelt seldom kept any one person close to him for very long, and during Hopkins' absence he had become used to working with others. Suddenly Morgenthau, long Hopkins' rival, was again seeing much of the president, and Stettinius was serving day by day as his surrogate at the Dumbarton Oaks conference. Nor was Hopkins a favorite of Roosevelt's influential daughter, who referred to him as "King Harry." Still, during the Quebec conference he handled dispatches from his White House office. Hopkins was a vital assistant, not — as he had earlier seemed — an indispensable partner.[33]

Fortunately for Roosevelt, who for so many months had been avoiding a meeting and intense discussions with Churchill, the sessions at Quebec were brief and amicable. The conference started, as Churchill put it, in "a blaze of friendship." Roosevelt speeded his train so that he would be at the station in time to greet the arriving Churchills. The British were shocked by the appearance of Roosevelt, whose weight had dropped during the summer. Churchill's physician has noted:

> I wonder how far Roosevelt's health impaired his judgment and sapped his resolve to get to the bottom of each problem before it came up for discussion. At Quebec he seemed to have but a couple of stone in weight — you could have put your fist between his neck and his collar — and I said to myself then that men at his time of life do not go thin all of a sudden just for nothing.[34]

Roosevelt's private thoughts may have been much the same, although he was boasting even to the physicians about the weight he had lost during the summer, patting his newly flat stomach. He refused to try to regain weight.[35]

Contrary to the communiqué issued at the end of the Quebec conference, not much military planning took place. The American chiefs of staff had seen no point to the meetings. There was some discussion of the future, but the big decisions seemed already to have been made.

Two acute political problems did make the conference important. Churchill's concern was to obtain strong new lend-lease commitments to cover from V-E day (a term already in use) to the surrender of Japan. Roosevelt's was to obtain agreement upon the Morgenthau plan for Germany.

A Lend-Lease II arrangement, as it was called, was not difficult. Roosevelt wanted it to be generous enough to guarantee a strong postwar Britain, but not so generous that it would enable the British to make inroads on American markets. (He had been indignant when he learned that the British had used American lend-lease pipe to curry favor with Ibn Saud by bringing a water system to his palace.) Churchill won all he could have wished. He enumerated to his assistant John Colville the postwar financial advantage that the Americans were providing. Colville remarked, "Beyond the dreams of avarice," and Churchill responded, "Beyond the dreams of justice."[36]

There may have been some interrelationship between the generous lend-lease arrangements and Churchill's acceptance of the Morgenthau plan. It was the prime project on Roosevelt's mind, and he casually presented it to Churchill at lunch as a means of rehabilitating Britain. He asked the prime minister, who had been glum, "How would you like to have the steel business of Europe for twenty or thirty years?" Roosevelt told Morgenthau "that Churchill seemed much excited over the possibility." That evening at dinner Roosevelt developed his full argument, but went too far for Churchill.

By the next morning, Lord Cherwell, the British scientific adviser, surprisingly had converted Churchill to a rather softened version of the plan — to deprive Germany of its capacity to produce steel on a large scale, some types of chemicals, and electrical machinery, as well as all weapons of war. After attempts by others, Churchill himself drafted the memorandum, and both he and the president initialed it.[37]

With equal suddenness, Roosevelt reversed his long-standing demand for a northern occupation zone in Germany. He still insisted that the American zone be at no point in direct contact with France. The next morning, Morgenthau found Roosevelt alone in his room, marking on a map with red, blue, and green pencils "a very rough suggestion made by me — among others — for a subdivision of Germany after the peace."[38]

Other plans for Europe were also on Roosevelt's mind. One afternoon he had tea with the former empress Zita of Austria and her sons, the two archdukes. He told them that he and Churchill had been looking at maps and concluded that there would be less territorial change than elsewhere in Austria and Hungary. "Our main concern," he asserted, "is now how to keep the Communist[s] out." The equivocation with which Roosevelt discussed the future with a symbol of the imperial past was an indication of his state of mind by the end of the summer of 1944. While he was publicly optimistic about the future with Stalin, he was moving toward a fallback position not so different from Churchill's.[39]

Another aspect of that fallback position was of major concern to Roosevelt when, after the Quebec conference, he entertained Churchill for two days at Hyde Park. That was the future of the atomic bomb and use of atomic energy. The maintenance of peace was in the forefront of Churchill's mind, and if it had to be done through continuation of the Anglo-American military alliance, the atomic bomb could be of crucial importance. A major question was what the approach should be to the Soviet Union. Niels Bohr, the renowned Danish physicist, had gained access to Roosevelt through Felix Frankfurter. Bohr was concerned that there be international control of atomic energy for the benefit of mankind. Roosevelt feared that there might have been a breach of security. He already knew through Stimson that the Soviets had learned by espionage that development of an atomic weapon was under way. During the war, Roosevelt had paid so little attention to Frankfurter that he had sent frequent handwritten notes to Sumner Welles for the drafting of replies. Early in 1944 he saw Frankfurter, trying to find out how much he knew about the atomic bomb, informing him that he was "worried to death," and welcomed help since he and Churchill must find ways to benefit all mankind. Perhaps Roosevelt was using Frankfurter and Bohr to get word back to British scientists, for whom, in fact, Bohr was acting. Further, since Bohr had an important Russian contact, the physicist Peter Kapitsa, who earlier had invited Bohr to come work in the Soviet Union, it is barely possible Roosevelt was also thinking that word of his goodwill might reach the Soviets. It is even more likely that Roosevelt, as was his custom, was simply saying what would please Frankfurter.

On August 26, when Roosevelt met with Bohr, in contrast to Churchill, he was in a warm, receptive mood and talked for an hour and a half. According to Bohr's son, Roosevelt agreed it was necessary to try the approach toward the Soviet Union that Bohr suggested, that Stalin was enough of a realist to understand the revolutionary importance of the bomb. As for Churchill, Roosevelt always managed to come to an agreement with him and would talk to him at their meeting. At Hyde Park Roosevelt had indeed come to an agreement, but one quite different from what Bohr sought.

After arriving at the White House, on September 22 the president met with Leahy, Cherwell, and Vannevar Bush, director of the Office of Scientific Research and Development. According to Bush, Roosevelt declared that he "was very much disturbed in regard to security and wished to know how far Bohr had been taken into the matter, whether he was trusted, and also how Mr. Frankfurter happened to know anything . . . whatever." What seemed to concern Roosevelt was the prospect of immediate disclosure of the secret, possibly as a threat against Germany, together with the questions about postwar control. These views of Roosevelt largely coincided with those of Bush, who throughout the war vigilantly prevented the full sharing of information even with the British, despite Roosevelt's accords with Churchill.

As for the Russians, Roosevelt hoped they had not obtained critical information. Knowledge of their espionage made him more zealous to guard the secrets. Strangely enough, at the Yalta conference Roosevelt, to the dismay of Churchill and Eden, would propose to them that he tell Stalin they were developing an atomic bomb. His reasoning was that if French physicists told de Gaulle what they knew, he might pass the information on to Stalin, and it would be better for word to come directly from Roosevelt. Apparently the British dissuaded the president. It made no difference. In fact, the Soviets had begun a small research program in 1942. In January, 1945, shortly before Yalta, they learned the Americans were close to developing a bomb. It was then they began to give it priority.[40]

The outcome of Roosevelt's discussion with Churchill at Hyde Park the previous September was a memorandum they both initialed, which itself remained top secret for several years. In it they referred to the atomic bomb by its code name, TUBE ALLOYS:

> 1. The suggestion that the world should be informed regarding TUBE ALLOYS, with a view to an international agreement regarding its control and use, is not accepted. The matter should continue to be regarded as of the utmost secrecy; but when a "bomb" is finally available, it might perhaps, after mature consideration, be used against the Japanese, who should be warned that this bombardment will be repeated until they surrender.[41]

Whatever discussion Roosevelt and Churchill engaged in, looking to the dropping of the atomic bomb upon Japan was tentative. They did not contemplate using it against Germany for the obvious reason that they expected that war to end shortly, certainly, Roosevelt believed, by sometime in the spring.

In his discussion on September 22, Roosevelt brought up, according to Bush, the question whether the atomic bomb "should actually be used against the Japanese or whether it should be used only as a threat with full-scale experimentation in this country." Bush recommended postponing the problem until a bomb existed, since it would be inadvisable to make a threat unless it could be followed up. In December, Roosevelt seems to have again expressed his interest in a demonstration and warning, but never made a firm policy statement or wavered in the assumption that the atomic bomb was a legitimate weapon.[42]

Roosevelt was glad to bid farewell to the Churchills when they departed on the evening of Tuesday, September 19. He left word when he went to bed that he wanted to sleep through the morning, but was at work at ten o'clock. He was weary from days of continuous talking, complained that his voice was troubling him, and was nervous about the political speech that he was going to deliver in Washington on Saturday night.[43]

Chapter 40

A FOURTH TERM

FOR ROOSEVELT, the campaign for a fourth term was one of special significance, essential to the winning of the peace. Twenty-four years earlier, fighting for the League of Nations, he had faced an electorate that was indifferent or hostile toward the incapacitated President Wilson, an invalid in the White House. The outcome had been the Harding landslide.

The Republican nominee in 1944, Governor Thomas E. Dewey, was no Harding, but a dynamic young leader in the eastern "internationalist" wing of the party. Nevertheless, the conservative, handsome vice presidential candidate, Governor John W. Bricker of Ohio, was more in the Harding mold on foreign policy, and so were a number of Republican senators running for reelection. The postwar role of the United States in international affairs seemed by no means as certain in the fall of 1944 as it does from the perspective of many decades later, and the specter of Wilson seemed quite real.

The veteran Roosevelt was too shrewd and tight-lipped to voice his feelings about Wilson, but he did give an oblique and involuntary indication. One evening at the Quebec conference he viewed a new motion picture on Wilson that ended with the president stricken and the league fight lost. Dr. Bruenn found the film had pushed Roosevelt's blood pressure notably higher.[1]

The apathy of the electorate was also on Roosevelt's mind, as evidenced by his wisecrack to Mrs. Bingham about the troops in France. It was serious enough throughout the country to draw the attention of political commentators. In *Newsweek* Robert Humphreys called it the "great silence."[2]

Apathy was harmful to Dewey, but far more dangerous for Roosevelt. A considerable part of the voters were in the armed forces, and these younger people were more heavily pro-Roosevelt — hence Roosevelt's fear that, because of the complexities of the soldier voting act, large numbers would not cast ballots. Several millions more had moved to war employment, and while some for the first time could vote without restrictions, all of them had to establish residence and register. That was not always easy. In Maryland one had to certify one's intention to register a year in advance. Among war workers, more likely to vote for Roosevelt, many through inertia might stay away from the polls. Sidney Hillman's CIO Political Action Committee registration drives were vital to Roosevelt's cause.

Linked to the apathy was the effective Republican campaign theme that Roosevelt and the New Dealers were too old and tired, and the rumors that the president was in failing health. The only way Roosevelt could counter was to launch a dynamic, pugnacious campaign. At Quebec, even as he was giving a lackluster appearance of weariness, he was dictating the most effective campaign attack of his career, the satirical riposte about his dog, Fala.[3]

Not only Roosevelt but those around him had been apprehensive since his faltering performance at Bremerton, Washington. He worked for days on what was to be his first frankly political speech of 1944, putting it through draft after draft. The occasion was a dinner for the Teamsters Union and local politicians at the Statler Hotel in Washington, D.C., on the evening of September 23. Seated at the head table, he went over the manuscript once more, marking it with a pencil. Watching him, Anna asked Rosenman, "Do you think Pa will put it over. . . . If the delivery isn't just right, it'll be an awful flop."

The question, as *Time* phrased it, was "has The Old Master still got it?" To those present, he appeared thinner but fit, and ate heartily. The test came when he began to speak, addressing a national radio audience. Before him, to encourage him in his sallies against the Republicans, was an ideal claque, which gave him a six-minute ovation before he even went on the air. Early in his talk he cited those Republicans who attacked organized labor, even labeling it unpatriotic, until an election was at hand when

> they suddenly discover that they really love labor and that they are anxious to protect labor from its old friends. . . .
>
> Can the Old Guard pass itself as the New Deal?
>
> I think not.

> We have seen many marvelous stunts in the circus but no performing elephant could turn a hand-spring without falling flat on its back.

As the audience roared, Roosevelt reacted with one of the most effective performances of his career, ticking off one by one the alleged misrepresentations of the Republican campaigners. After refuting several serious charges, among them that men would be kept in the army after the war because there would be no jobs awaiting them, he turned to the ludicrous rumor that millions had been spent to rescue his dog from the Aleutians. With an air of solemnity he intoned:

> These Republican leaders have not been content with attacks on me, or my wife, or on my sons. No, not content with that, they now include my little dog, Fala. Well, of course, I don't resent attacks, and my family doesn't resent attacks, but Fala *does* resent them. You know, Fala is Scotch . . . — his Scotch soul was furious. He has not been the same dog since.

By this point, Roosevelt's nervous daughter was laughing with everyone else. Then, turning serious, the president enumerated his objectives, to finish the war, establish a lasting peace, and return the armed forces to a prosperous nation in which there would be jobs for everyone.[4]

Roosevelt had erased apathy as a factor in the campaign. Dewey and his advisers decided to strike back in kind, at what they considered one of Roosevelt's most vulnerable areas, his defense record. From his campaign train headed eastward from the Pacific Coast, Dewey sent for item after item, and working until two in the morning, wove them into a stinging attack, which he delivered in Oklahoma City before an ardently partisan and vociferous audience of 15,000.

The Teamsters' speech, Dewey declared, with its "mudslinging, ridicule, and wisecracks . . . plumbed the depths of demagoguery by dragging into this campaign the names of Hitler and Goebbels." Point by point, quoting Generals Marshall, Arnold, and others, he sought to prove that Roosevelt had led a deplorably unready nation into the war.[5]

As in his earlier campaign speeches, Dewey hammered away at facts and figures, reverting to his role of prosecuting attorney. Several days earlier, Roosevelt had remarked to Robert Sherwood, who had returned from his Office of War Information post in London to rejoin the speech-writing team: "You ought to hear him. He plays the part of the heroic racket-buster in one of those gangster movies. He talks to the people as if they were the jury and I were the villain on trial for his life."[6]

Excited Republicans felt that Dewey had revived the campaign, and that Roosevelt had met more than his match. Campaign pledges began to come in. Crowds hailed Dewey at each of his stops on the way east while he poured out his indictment of Roosevelt as an incompetent at home as well as in military policy, and the dupe of "long-haired brain-trusters," city bosses, radical labor leaders, and Communists. Three fourths of the reporters on the campaign train thought Dewey was making headway; half thought he was mastering "the Champ."[7]

Yet on one particularly vulnerable point, Dewey did not attack. That was Pearl Harbor. Already Republicans in Congress had been raising questions seeking to embarrass Roosevelt, and Congress from July through much of October conducted separate investigations into the army and navy roles.

General Marshall became upset in September, 1944, when word reached him that Dewey had learned that the United States had cracked the Japanese diplomatic code. He recognized that Dewey would have much to gain by charging that, although Roosevelt had advance knowledge of Japanese movements, he had failed to counter them. "We were still getting vital information," Marshall later explained, and it involved some German as well as Japanese actions. In consequence, without informing Roosevelt, he sent a colonel to carry a letter to Dewey, warning him of the potential damage. Marshall commented at the time that he hated to put Dewey on the spot, "but see no other way of avoiding what might well be a catastrophe for us." Marshall's courier met Dewey at Tulsa. At first Dewey was incredulous and would not read beyond the first paragraph. After returning to Albany, Dewey was persuaded to read a modified version of the entire letter. As he angrily discussed it with campaign advisers, he looked upon Roosevelt as a traitor, responsible either deliberately or through ineptitude for the heavy loss of ships and lives at Pearl Harbor. Nevertheless, Dewey accepted Marshall's word that this was not a political trick, and kept out of the campaign what could have been an effective Republican issue.[8]

Dewey also chose not to exploit the foreign policy issue, but out of Republican weakness, not forbearance. In August he accepted Cordell Hull's invitation to confer in a nonpartisan spirit on plans for the new international organization. John Foster Dulles represented Dewey in several meetings. Out of them grew a campaign truce on the touchy question whether the United States could commit its armed forces to a United Nations police action without the authorization of Congress. It was a truce that Dewey needed if he were to hold together the divided Republican party.

In early October, Wendell Willkie died suddenly, and without having committed himself to either Dewey or Roosevelt. Senator Joseph Ball of Minnesota, a Willkie Republican who had voted for Dewey at the convention, challenged both Dewey and Roosevelt on the police action question. Roosevelt seized the opportunity two weeks before the election in an address before the Foreign Policy Association. Although the occasion was bipartisan, he delivered a vigorous campaign speech, taking aim at the isolationists in the Republican party, from Senator Hiram Johnson through House Minority Leader Joseph Martin, and explicitly gave the answer that Ball and Republican internationalists wanted to hear:

> A policeman would not be a very effective policeman if, when he saw a felon break into a house, he had to go to the Town Hall and call a town meeting to issue a warrant before the felon could be arrested. . . . if the world organization is to have any reality at all, our American representative must be endowed in advance by the people themselves, by constitutional means through their representatives in the Congress, with authority to act.

Ball endorsed the president, and campaigners for Dewey fumed. A score of years later, Dewey commented that Roosevelt "broke his commitment" not to bring foreign policy into the campaign. "I have been proved right, and he won the election."[9]

On another foreign policy issue, Roosevelt emerged from widespread public discussion almost unscathed. He was scarcely back from the Quebec conference before news of the Morgenthau plan to impose a Carthaginian peace upon Germany leaked. One unnamed opponent within the administration declared that even the airing of the plan would cost lives through stiffening German resistance. Indeed, German radio began proclaiming, "Morgenthau wants to see 43,000,000 Germans exterminated."

While Roosevelt made no comment on the politically negative side of the Morgenthau plan, he in effect pleaded nolo contendere when Stimson finally confronted him about it in person on October 3: "He grinned and looked naughty and said 'Henry Morgenthau pulled a boner' or an equivalent expression." Roosevelt went on, Stimson recorded, to say he had no intention of returning Germany to agriculture, but meant to obtain for Britain some of the proceeds of Ruhr industry. Stimson stopped this line of rationalization by reading several lines from the memorandum Roosevelt and Churchill had initialed at Quebec, concluding that "this programme for eliminating the war-making industries in the Ruhr and in the Saar is looking forward to converting Germany into a country primarily agricultural and pastoral." Roosevelt "was frankly staggered . . . and said he had no idea how he could have initialed this; that he had evidently done it without much thought."[10]

The peace to be imposed upon Germany was to be stern at the outset, but the Morgenthau plan was moribund. Several days before seeing Stimson, Roosevelt had obliquely abandoned it when asked at a press conference about accounts of a cabinet split on policy. "Every story that has come out is essentially untrue in the basic facts," he asserted, then stopped further queries by suggesting correspondents emphasize the adjective "essentially."[11]

The campaign may also have led Roosevelt to temper his China policy in favor of Chiang Kai-shek, who enjoyed strong support within the United States. He had been disgusted with Chiang's continued inaction, refusal to cooperate with Communist forces at Yenan, and insistence upon hoarding rather than utilizing lend-lease supplies. Nor did he like the corruption among Chinese officials. At Cairo in December, 1943, he had told General Stilwell, "If you can't get along with Chiang, and can't replace him, get rid of him once and for all. You know what I mean, put in someone you can manage." Stilwell took this as a signal that Roosevelt wanted Chiang assassinated, and his subordinate Colonel Frank Dorn devised a scheme to sabotage Chiang's airplane. Roosevelt never gave final approval, so the scheme was abandoned, but into the fall of 1944 his displeasure with Chiang escalated.

On July 6, 1944, Roosevelt cabled Chiang that Stilwell must receive "command of all Chinese and American forces . . . including the Communist forces." Roosevelt's concern about the Communists came in part from his fear that if civil war broke out, the Soviet Union would seize Manchuria. Chiang conceded that Stilwell should receive the command but insisted upon delay and asked for a special emissary to explore the future. General Marshall, wishing to protect Stilwell, persuaded Roosevelt to send a flamboyant Republican, General Patrick J. Hurley, to serve as a buffer between Chiang and Stilwell.

The result was the opposite of what Roosevelt and Marshall had sought. At first Chiang so vigorously resisted Hurley's demands that Roosevelt sent an ultimatum the army staff had drafted: Stilwell must receive full power or American aid would end. Hurley, surprisingly, engineered the opposite result, endorsing Chiang's message that he would accept an American commander, but not Stilwell. The central problem, Hurley asserted, was Stilwell. For some days Roosevelt pondered the dilemma. Hurley brought an effective argument to bear upon him: "If we permit China to collapse . . . all the angels in heaven swearing that we were right in sustaining Stilwell will not change the verdict of history." Roosevelt capitulated and on October 18 recalled Stilwell, who already had recorded in his diary his anger that "old Rubberlegs" was slitting his throat again. When Stilwell got back to Washington, Marshall counseled silence and true to his army training he complied. In 1944, Roosevelt averted China as a campaign issue; in subsequent years it returned to harry his successor.[12]

With the election only about a month away, Roosevelt's vitality ebbed, then returned, in his day-by-day activities. At the end of September and in early October, he was suffering from a cold. Although he felt wretched and was apparently taking penicillin, he tried to continue business as usual with long, exhausting days. During his press conference on Friday, September 29, Roosevelt was not smoking, his head was stuffed up, and his voice hoarse. On October 5, he delivered a radio talk aimed primarily at exhorting Democratic precinct workers to get out the vote. It was a cogent but rather sober talk, carefully constructed and demonstrating Roosevelt's concern with the electorate in the cities of the north. Yet compared with the speech before the raucously appreciative Teamsters, it seemed lackluster.[13]

The campaign continued to focus on the precarious health of Roosevelt versus the vitality of his youthful challenger — "Buster," as the White House speech-writers referred to him derisively. Since only relatively small differences separated Roosevelt's avowed policies from those of Dewey, both sides were becoming nasty and vituperative.

All indications pointed toward a close race, and Roosevelt jotted down his own prognosis of a narrow win, keeping it secret until after the election. Gallup polls showed the candidates within two or three percentage points of each other. It was against the law for pollsters to query members of the armed forces, 4,300,000 of whom had applied for ballots; they could add to Roosevelt's majority.[14]

Dewey, although lacking the charm and mass appeal that Willkie had demonstrated four years earlier, was far better organized, cool, and tough minded, a more formidable opponent. He had moved beyond his earlier statesmanlike approach to arouse the emotions of conservative listeners with his rough attacks on Roosevelt. He poured onto Roosevelt serious charges and specious ones, bolstered with quotations sometimes apt, often out of context, and always painful to the New Dealers. He claimed again and again that Roosevelt was accepting Communist support, and after the president disavowed it, Dewey pointed out that the Communists liked him — "their aims can best be served by unemployment and discontent." Repeatedly throughout the campaign he linked Roosevelt with the Communist leader Earl Browder, and vilified Sidney Hillman and the CIO Political Action Committee as being Communist tainted. He struck home when he charged Roosevelt with bungling in establishing and dismantling a succession of defense agencies, and stung when he quoted Winston Churchill of 1937: "The Washington administration has waged so ruthless a war on private enterprise that the United States . . . is actually . . . leading the world back into the trough of depression."[15]

During the give-and-take, Roosevelt came to detest Dewey, but rose to the challenge. The burden of proof was upon him to demonstrate that he was still capable of being a dynamic leader.

In mid-October, the issue of the president's health came out into the open. Two Republican newspapers in New York, the *Sun* and the *Daily News*, speculated on their front pages about Roosevelt's condition. "Let's not be squeamish," declared the *Sun* editorial, ". . . six presidents have died in office." Roosevelt's counterattack was quick and thorough. Admiral McIntire in an interview once again described the president as being in glowing health. He had suffered from the sniffles for several days, said McIntire, but that was over, and he had not been in the swimming pool since before going to Quebec, but would now start again. And in New York, the Democratic National Committee chairman, Hannegan, announced that Roosevelt would take an extended tour of the city that Saturday before addressing the Foreign Policy Association. "After the people have seen him," he declared, "they can make up their own minds about his vigor and health."[16]

In the last two weeks before the election, through a combination of skill and luck, Roosevelt gave the most spectacular campaign performances of his career. Normally he would have wanted excellent weather. Now he faced bad weather, which would test him, and turn what could have been an ordinary demonstration of energy into a spectacle. In addition, events in the Pacific war focused attention upon the commander in chief and added to the aura of excitement around him.

On the morning of October 20, the nation awoke to headlines proclaiming that General MacArthur had landed in the Philippines. "There were extremely light losses — these operations in Leyte," Roosevelt told correspondents that morning. "The enemy was caught strategically unaware." When asked if the plan had been drawn up while he was at Pearl Harbor, Roosevelt modestly said only that he had gone over the plan with MacArthur and after his return it was officially agreed upon and ordered. Next he was asked about his campaigning the next day. "Rain, and a fifty-mile gale in New York, which is not cheerful," he replied.

> Q. Are you going to wear your navy cape?
>
> THE PRESIDENT: I suppose so. (Laughter) About the best garment I have got. . . . this is about the third I have had since 1913.

In dodging a question at the end of the press conference, Roosevelt amid even more laughter declared, "I'm tough this morning," and added a final word, "I hope you don't get wet, those who are going."[17]

Indeed Roosevelt was tough. At 9:50 the next morning, October 21, he left his train at the Brooklyn Army Base and was helped into his black Packard touring car with bulletproof windows. He kept the windows up but ordered the canvas top to be taken down, and with only his navy cape and old campaign hat to protect him, started out in an incessant, driving rain. Even Admiral McIntire had urged him to cancel the trip and save himself for the evening dinner, but Roosevelt had no intention of disappointing the crowds waiting along the fifty-one-mile route, becoming more and more cold and soaked. Their teeth chattered as they waved at the president. He too was getting soaked, the water rolling down his cheeks and trickling up his sleeve as he waved and grinned at the sodden spectators. So also was Mrs. Roosevelt smiling through the rain. It was agreeable only for their "little dog, Fala." Roosevelt, stopping just once for a quick change of clothes, rode for four hours through Brooklyn, Queens, the Bronx, and finally Manhattan. The largest crowds greeted him along Broadway and in the garment district, where ticker tape and confetti came floating down in the rain. Police estimated that between 1,500,000 and 3,000,000 people had seen him, although it had rained two and a half inches that day.[18]

Roosevelt ended his campaigning at Washington Square. There for the first time he went with Mrs. Roosevelt to her apartment to rest. After a hot bath, a third dry suit of clothes, and several hours' relaxation, he was ready for the evening.

Appearing at the Foreign Policy Association banquet, before two thousand members and guests, Roosevelt delivered one of his major campaign speeches, smiling and waving at his applauding audience. He was sufficiently relaxed to ad-lib two paragraphs into the speech being nationally broadcast. It was a success in content as well as delivery. Isaiah Berlin, the British analyst, reported to the Foreign Office that it "was fairly widely acknowledged as being an authoritative, courageous and masterly performance for which the public had been waiting."

The test of strength in New York seemed to have exhilarated Roosevelt, and at his next press conference he boasted, "I haven't even got the sniffles!" *PM* polled the accompanying reporters and found that a majority of them had not fared so well.[19]

The trip to New York City was so effective and enjoyable to Roosevelt that he repeated it elsewhere several times in the remaining days of the campaign. In the wake of more spectacular news, the smashing defeat of the Japanese Navy in the Battle of Leyte Gulf, he began a swing through Pennsylvania into the Middle West by train and automobile. On October 27, he rode for four more hours in an open car, greeting the people of Philadelphia, despite intermittent rain and a near-freezing wind. Although blue from the cold, the crowds greeted him in a carnival spirit. That evening he spoke from his automobile, driven up on a special ramp, at a baseball park. His theme was his role as commander in chief. To the accompaniment of cries from the bleachers of "pour it on," he enumerated the American victories down through the landings in the Philippines.[20]

Through the night the thirteen-car campaign train headed westward, and the next day passed through Ohio and Indiana on its way to Chicago. Roosevelt arrived in Chicago too late to parade through the flag-decked streets, but as Mayor Kelly had promised, spoke at the biggest political rally in the city's history. People, some of whom had lined up six hours in advance, filled the 110,000-seat stadium; 150,000 more jammed the area outside. They cheered him for ten minutes before he began excoriating the Republican campaigners:

> Well, they say in effect, just this:
>
> "Those incompetent blunderers and bunglers in Washington have passed a lot of excellent laws about social security and labor and farm relief and soil conservation — and many others — and *we* promise that if elected we will not change any of them."
>
> And they go on to say, "Those same quarrelsome, tired old men — they have built the greatest military machine the world has ever known, which is fighting its way to victory; and," they say, "if you elect us, we promise not to change any of that, either."
>
> "Therefore," say these Republican orators, "it is time for a change."[21]

On the way back to Washington, Roosevelt succumbed to pleas and stopped at Clarksburg, West Virginia, where he spoke extemporaneously and ably about reforestation and conservation. At the beginning of his trip he had spoken from the rear platform at Wilmington, Delaware. Altogether in his whirlwind tour he had been seen in seven different critical states; later, when Ohio reelected Senator Robert Taft by a close margin, he regretted that he had not also spoken there. On Monday morning, Hassett found "the Big Boss brisk as a bee. . . . not a trace of a cold . . . since he undertook these tours."[22]

The following weekend, the last of the campaign, Roosevelt was off again, to the New England states. Again the train slowed down going through towns where crowds were awaiting; at Hartford and Springfield he talked from the rear platform. At Worcester he took aboard the isolationist Senator David I. Walsh, no friend, who rode into Boston but would not accompany Roosevelt to Fenway Park. No matter. Roosevelt's concern was to answer some of the charges of Dewey and other Republican campaigners that most rankled him. He was particularly irritated by the incessant attacks upon Sidney Hillman, which he felt carried implications not only of union and Communist influence but of religious and racial overtones. Some radio stations every hour were broadcasting the line, "Clear everything with Sidney." Roosevelt reminded his Boston audience that he had campaigned there in 1928 on behalf of Al Smith. Bostonians had never lost their affection for Smith, who had died earlier that fall. All the bigots in 1928, he reminded them, "were gunning for Al Smith":

> Religious intolerance, social intolerance, and political intolerance have no place in our American life. . . .
>
> Since this campaign developed, I tell you frankly that I have become most anxious to win — and I say that for the reason that never before in my lifetime has a campaign been filled with such misrepresentation, distortion, and falsehood. Never since 1928 have there been so many attempts to stimulate in America racial or religious intolerance.[23]

All that remained was familiar, pleasant ritual. On the afternoon before the election Roosevelt took a final tour along the Hudson River valley in the open car, although it had been snowing that morning. He bundled himself in a heavy overcoat with a beaver collar, taking with him Admiral Leahy and Morgenthau, shivering in a light topcoat. He visited Beacon, where he had first spoken when he ran for the state senate in 1910, crossed the Hudson to Newburgh, where the Delanos had lived, and went up to Kingston, where, he informed his audience, a militiaman ancestor in 1660 had taken up a musket to repel the Indians. In Poughkeepsie, as in earlier years, he ended what he referred to as "another sentimental journey." In the evening he made a final radio appeal and, Leahy noted, went to bed "in a very happy frame of mind, confident of re-election."[24]

The next morning Roosevelt went to the polling place in the Hyde Park firehouse, announcing his occupation to be "tree farmer." From within the voting booth came the sound of clanking levers and a familiar voice, "The goddamned thing won't work." An official adjusted the cable on the voting machine, and Roosevelt pulled the lever. He subsequently protested he had said no more than "damned," but six reporters and photographers insisted they had heard otherwise.[25]

That evening after the traditional supper of scrambled eggs, his "lucky dish," Roosevelt went through his ritual of tabulating the returns. At no point did he show any sign of apprehension, and the early returns from the northeast were favorable. At 11:15, to the music of fifes and a drum, a torchlight procession of Hyde Park neighbors and two busloads of Vassar students arrived at the front door. Roosevelt, in high spirits, spotted some children up in one of the giant evergreen trees, and reminisced how he too had climbed in them as a little boy. He had seen his first torchlight parade right there in 1892 when Cleveland was re-elected, and came down in his nightgown, wrapped in an old buffalo robe. "The reports that are coming in are not so bad," he told them, and it looked as though he would be having "to come back . . . from Washington for four more years."[26]

At 3:15 the next morning, Dewey conceded publicly, but sent no message as yet, which riled Roosevelt. At 4 A.M. as Roosevelt was going to bed he still was full of the fire of battle and remarked to Hassett, "I still think he is a son of a bitch." Three days later, Dewey sent Roosevelt his hearty congratulations, and received a terse but correct reply.[27]

Roosevelt won by the narrowest margin in popular votes since Wilson's reelection in 1916, but in decades since, it would not have been considered a close election. He received 53.5 percent of the popular vote to 46 percent for Dewey and 432 electoral votes to 99. At his next press conference he hunted in his desk drawer until he found his pre-election estimate: 335 to 196. "So I wasn't very accurate, was I?" The total number of votes, especially in large cities, while down from 1940 was larger than earlier predicted. The registration drive of Hillman's Political Action Committee had indeed hurt the Republicans, and Roosevelt's campaign appearances in the open car had had a salutary effect. The southern revolt had fizzled, having no effect on the electoral college, but the percentage of Republican votes in some states like Louisiana was the highest since Reconstruction. The Roosevelt coalition had remained firm, and the rumblings from the South were as yet no more than an omen.

Of great significance to Roosevelt was the voters' rejection of several of the most conspicuous isolationists in both houses of Congress, including his own congressman, Hamilton Fish. Isaiah Berlin reported to London, "The press, even anti-Roosevelt sections of it, report the defeat of isolationists and the 'clear mandate on foreign policy' now given to the President without bitter or uneasy undertones." Roosevelt had avoided the trap into which Wilson had fallen; the election of 1944 was not an analogue of the debacle in 1920.[28]

Upon his triumphal return to Washington on the Friday after the election, Roosevelt received a rousing reception at the Union Station and along Pennsylvania Avenue on the way to the White House, as once more he rode slowly through the rain in an open car. This time, Vice President–elect Harry Truman was at his side. Eight bands were playing along the route. Roosevelt joked that he hoped "the papers won't intimate that I expect to make Washington my permanent residence for the rest of my life."

It was a day of jubilation, and it was also a return to work.[29] Immediately he held a press conference. "Happy Fourth Term!" one of the correspondents shouted. In the afternoon he told the cabinet that his wish to meet with Stalin and Churchill was frustrated thus far because Stalin refused to take a long trip, and he himself did not want to go through the Black Sea to disease-ridden Odessa.[30]

The imperative need to hold a "big three" meeting was in the forefront of Roosevelt's thinking. During the presidential campaign the Soviets had advanced so rapidly in eastern and southeastern Europe that Churchill had urged an immediate conference to determine control over those territories. The prime minister, feeling he could not wait until the American election was over, planned to go to Moscow early in October. Roosevelt, preoccupied with the election, was disposed to remain uninvolved in the talks. Bohlen cautioned Hopkins that Stalin might believe Churchill was speaking for Roosevelt, and Hopkins, alarmed, persuaded the president to send Stalin a disclaimer. Roosevelt warned:

"I am sure you understand that in this global war there is literally no question, military or political, in which the United States is not interested. I am firmly convinced that the three of us, and only the three of us, can find the solution of the questions still unresolved."[31]

In Moscow, on October 9, 1944, Churchill amicably worked out a deal with Stalin to allocate British and Russian interests in the Balkans and Hungary. He proposed, "How would it do for you to have ninety percent predominance in Rumania, for us to have ninety percent of the same in Greece, and go fifty–fifty about Yugoslavia?" He jotted the figures on a piece of paper, adding fifty–fifty for Hungary and twenty-five–seventy-five for Bulgaria. Stalin made a check mark upon the sheet.[32]

Roosevelt would never countenance such an agreement, Harriman warned Churchill several days later. The arrangement was dead.

Roosevelt's gratitude to Hopkins for suggesting a warning to Stalin that Churchill could not commit the United States was, Robert Sherwood writes, one of the factors in restoring Hopkins to his earlier position as the indispensable foreign policy adviser. If Roosevelt in the summer had feared Hopkins was too pro-British, that apprehension was gone.

Rather, after the election, with Secretary of State Hull so seriously ill that he had to resign, Roosevelt presided over an overhaul of the State Department to coordinate it more effectively with Hopkins, Leahy, and the president himself. In keeping with ritual, Roosevelt lavished praise upon Hull when he resigned, but ignored his wish that James Byrnes become the new secretary. Roosevelt decidedly did not want a strong-minded secretary of state with his own power base. He immediately forestalled pressures from the Senate by nominating Edward Stettinius, already under secretary, an able and amiable manager whose credentials as former president of United States Steel made him impervious to attacks from the right. Stettinius, who earlier in the war as a protégé of Hopkins had been administrator of lend-lease, considered himself apolitical and was unquestioning in his loyalty to Roosevelt and Hopkins. At the same time he created a good public image. Bohlen deemed him "a decent man of considerable innocence." Irritated Senate leaders could do little but accept Stettinius; Senator George, outsmarted, granted he was "a nice enough lad if not too bright."[33]

During Stettinius' tenure as under secretary, he had already made the State Department more effective in serving Roosevelt, especially in Soviet affairs. Now Bohlen became assistant secretary of state for White House liaison, an appointment that would have been impossible under the jealous Hull. Ambassador Harriman continued influential. The White House by this time was expertly informed, and while Roosevelt no longer possessed sufficient vigorous curiosity to become involved in detailed briefings, he listened sympathetically.[34]

The price Roosevelt had to pay for this improved system was a State Department reorganization, which brought in several conservatives. After the election and before Hull's resignation, Roosevelt authorized Stettinius to rid the department of deadwood and appoint new assistant secretaries. There was only one appointment Roosevelt himself wanted to designate, that of Archibald MacLeish, poet, Librarian of Congress, and a valued presidential speech-writer. Of the incumbents, Stettinius wished only the conservative Dean Acheson to remain. He proposed two other conservatives: Lewis Douglas, highly successful in running wartime shipbuilding; and Will Clayton, biggest cotton broker in the world, an assistant secretary of commerce closely allied with Secretary of Commerce Jesse Jones. Clayton in 1936 had been a member of the Liberty League. Roosevelt was ready to accept Douglas, who did not want to take an appointment, but for the moment balked at Clayton. He still had his score to settle with Jones.

Since the appointments had to run the gauntlet of a hostile Senate, Roosevelt gave in and nominated Clayton, together with two additional nominees: the former protocol expert of the department, General Julius Holmes, who had been an aide to Eisenhower; and a wealthy career diplomat, James Dunn, who had long played croquet with Hull.[35]

There was something in the package of nominees for every politician and publicist to denounce. Senator "Happy" Chandler of Kentucky, usually anti–New Deal, turned populist and declaimed, "Instead of poor folks obtaining jobs, the Wall Street boys are . . . and we are clearing everything with Harry Hopkins." Champ Clark of Missouri amused himself by citing incongruous lines of MacLeish's poetry to his colleagues, and tried to bait MacLeish at the confirmation hearings. Conservatives concentrated upon trying to defeat MacLeish. Roosevelt dug in his heels, vowing that if the Senate failed to confirm MacLeish he would resubmit his name in January.[36]

Liberals were even more unhappy with the package, tying General Holmes to the Darlan deal, and Dunn to the wartime courtship of the Spanish dictator, Franco. Mrs. Roosevelt was so distressed that she sent a lengthy protest to her husband at Warm Springs. She was nervous because Roosevelt had argued with her that he did not care what Dunn thought because he would do what Roosevelt ordered, and she wrote, "for three years you have carried the State Department and you expect to go on doing it. . . . With Dunn, Clayton and Acheson under Secretary Stettinius, I can hardly see that the set-up will be very much different from what it might have been under Dewey. . . . I hate to irritate you and I won't speak of any of this again but I wouldn't feel honest if I didn't tell you now."[37]

All the nominees won approval in the Foreign Relations Committee,

MacLeish only after some maneuvering. As Senator Claude Pepper and others prepared to filibuster, Roosevelt by intervening directly saved the nominations. The Senate voted confirmation and adjourned for Christmas.

The day that Roosevelt cajoled Pepper into line, a correspondent, May Craig, asked him whether he was moving to the left or the right. He responded that, as throughout his presidency, he was "going down the whole line a little left of center." How could he match that with his six appointments? someone else inquired. "Very well." Could he call them a little left of center? "I call me — myself — a little left of center."[38]

Roosevelt did indeed move back to that position in two even more controversial appointments he subsequently sent to the Senate: of Wallace to succeed Jesse Jones as secretary of commerce, and of Aubrey Williams, an ardent New Dealer, to head the Rural Electrification Administration. Some observers thought Pepper and his cohorts had played a useful role in helping nudge Roosevelt back toward left of center; others more cynical wondered if, in his support of Wallace and the flamboyant Williams, by trailing his cape so provocatively in front of the bull he indicated that he was not seriously concerned that they be confirmed. Maintenance of balance among his working coalition doubtless played a part in his motivation, as it had consistently. He told reporters, "I have got a lot of people in the Administration — oh, I know some of them are extreme right and extreme left, and everything else . . . and I cannot vouch for them all. They work out pretty well."[39]

Fear of upsetting that balance, and a deep reluctance to fire anybody, led Roosevelt for weeks after the election to postpone the settling of accounts with Jesse Jones. There was no ruthless bloodletting of the sort he had vowed months in advance. Jones, whose supporters came close to commanding a majority in the Senate, created a difficult problem. Roosevelt, who would continue to face serious difficulties in getting a positive program through Congress, would have preferred, despite his animus toward Jones, to leave him in office. On the other hand, if he reneged on his promises to Wallace, he would alienate the basic coalition that had brought his reelection. An indication of his ambivalence came on November 10, when he sounded out Stettinius on sending Wallace to be ambassador to China. The easiest course was the one Roosevelt took, to postpone action until after his inauguration.[40]

The amount of attention that Roosevelt could give to his presidential duties varied dramatically during the months after the election. Upon his return to Washington he worked long hours, even well into the evenings, involving himself in a wide variety of questions. He had strained his back while participating in Armistice Day ceremonies at the Tomb of the Unknown Soldier, but did not let that slow him down. In one November session Stettinius went to him with a work sheet covering fourteen items, ranging from postwar rehabilitation and foreign economic policy to a possible visit of Princess Juliana to Venezuela. The president checked off every item.[41]

By November 18, Roosevelt's physical condition was again deteriorating. He looked tired; his blood pressure, which during the campaign had been lower than before, was up. He had lost his appetite, and although he was fed eggnogs, his weight had slipped to 165 pounds from the earlier 188. On November 27 he left for almost three weeks in the relaxing environment of Warm Springs, where he did little work except for going through the daily pouch of dispatches. After about a week he tried swimming and enjoyed it, but his blood pressure shot up alarmingly — which brought almost to an end the rehabilitation and recreation that had meant so much to him. He went into the pool only three times. His appetite remained poor — "can't eat — cannot taste food" — and except for a slight lowering of blood pressure, his physical condition did not improve.[42]

Nevertheless, Roosevelt inspired optimism, perhaps in himself and certainly in those around him, when he returned to the White House on December 19 and plunged into a heavy schedule for several days. He demonstrated patience when conferring with Ickes and others on a number of problems. At a cabinet meeting he had to face some very worrisome ones, above all the great counteroffensive that Field Marshal Karl R. G. von Rundstedt had launched against thinly held lines in Belgium and Luxembourg, driving twenty or thirty miles through, and threatening to recapture Antwerp. This was the frightening Battle of the Bulge, which brought gloom at Christmastime and caused Roosevelt and Stimson to worry anew about deficient American manpower.

After five intense days in Washington, Roosevelt returned to Hyde Park in time to broadcast a Christmas Eve message, again more full of hope than of cheer. There were all the traditional festivities. Two of his children, Anna and Elliott, newly a brigadier-general, were present, and a daughter-in-law, Mrs. Franklin, Jr., and a number of grandchildren. At dinner, Roosevelt sat at one end of the table, a gaunt old patriarch, and Mrs. Roosevelt at the other. Roosevelt's secretary Hassett, who was among the guests, lamented, "To me the President seemed . . . weary — not his old self as he led the conversation."[43]

Roosevelt's conversations around this time were as far ranging and anecdotal as ever, but often he seemed to miss the point toward which he had embarked. Wallace, recording in some detail a lengthy session with him on December 20, concluded that "he is losing considerable of his old power of focus. His mind isn't very clear anymore." On some topics, his information was wildly erroneous — he cited a single entrepreneur in Brazil who had been clearing ten million acres a year to plant cotton. Wallace interposed that could not be true since the United States planted only twenty million acres a year. Wallace concluded that Roosevelt's extraordinary discursiveness might earlier have served him well, "but as he gets older it makes him less and less capable . . . and more and more irritating to administrators."[44]

On days when Roosevelt was feeling better, his inability to make a point or to grapple with a difficult problem disappeared. Nor was there anything new about his tendency to hold forth with a wide variety of stories and reminiscences, more remarkable for their color than their accuracy.

Back in Washington at the beginning of the new year, Roosevelt again worked effectively for long hours. On January 2, 1945, when he met with the House and Senate Democratic leaders, Wallace thought he "looked unusually well and was in excellent spirits." His State of the Union message contained little that was controversial. It did reiterate near the conclusion Roosevelt's interest in a postwar economic bill of rights, in reconversion, and in full employment. He sent the message to Congress, where a clerk read the full 54 minutes' worth in lifeless fashion to lawmakers, inattentive in the absence of Roosevelt. That night the star performer delivered a crisp 25-minute version to the radio audience.[45]

The inauguration was in keeping with wartime simplicity. The deletion of most of the pomp and parading minimized the strain on Roosevelt. Inauguration Day, January 20, 1945, was solemn and Spartan. It had snowed in the night, turning to sleet by daybreak. The one happy sight early that morning was Roosevelt grandchildren, bundled in snowsuits, coasting down the slight slope on the White House lawn. Roosevelt and the cabinet, as always, attended religious services, this time in the East Room. His mentor, Peabody of Groton, had died, and the Episcopal bishop of Washington, Angus Dun, led the prayers, including one for the enemy.

The brief inaugural ceremonies took place on the balcony of the south portico of the White House. By an effort of will, Roosevelt rose to his feet, and on the arm of his son James walked to the podium. He was wearing his braces. Although the wind was bitter, he refused the cape James offered him and stood, bareheaded, in a blue business suit. Around him were dignitaries and families; Henry Wallace had just sworn in Harry Truman as vice president. On a staircase were the baker's dozen of his grandchildren; he had insisted they all be there. Below in the mud and slush on the lawn were nearly eight thousand shivering guests, including some wounded servicemen. In the distance, beyond the fence, on the ellipse, were three thousand more spectators. Once more Roosevelt took the Oath of Office on the Dutch family Bible. This time Chief Justice Harlan F. Stone administered the oath.

The inaugural address was the shortest of any president's, only 573 words. It was not destined to become a classic like Lincoln's Second Inaugural and was immediately forgotten. Yet it made two simple points. First he quoted from his old schoolmaster, Peabody, that things in life will not always run smoothly, but that the trend of civilization was upward, a reaffirmation of his progressive ideals. Next he set forth the firm lesson that was emerging from the two world wars, a newly accepted truth at the time, commonplace in the decades since:

> Today, in this year of war, 1945, we have learned lessons — at a fearful cost — and we shall profit by them.
>
> We have learned that we cannot live alone, at peace; that our own well-being is dependent on the well-being of other Nations.[46]

After the ceremonies, Roosevelt spent some time alone with his son. He wanted to talk about his will (James was to be one of the three executors) and to tell him there was a letter in the safe giving funeral instructions. He also told James he wanted him to have the family ring and hoped he would wear it. In previous months he had assigned heirlooms to various members of the family and given keepsakes to those working for him. At the time, his father's conversation seemed to James to be simple prudence, and so perhaps it was.

Although several senators returning from the inaugural commented on how unsmiling everyone had seemed, it was a day of optimism for Roosevelt. When James exclaimed to him that he looked like hell, he retorted that he was only a little tired, that a few days' rest would restore him. "At the reception that evening," writes Dr. Bruenn, "he appeared to be in excellent spirits."[47]

On the afternoon of Inauguration Day, Roosevelt as a prelude to sailing off for his conference with Churchill and Stalin tossed a lighted firecracker to the Senate he was leaving behind — the nomination of

Wallace to be both secretary of commerce and head of the financial agencies Jesse Jones had run.

After postponing for so long his confrontation with Jones, Roosevelt relished it. The next day, a few hours before leaving, he told Ickes he would like to relate a few facts about the Jones matter "in case . . . he was torpedoed." Jones, declared Roosevelt, had insisted upon seeing him on Sunday at the White House, and begged to be kept as head of the RFC. Roosevelt refused, but offered to make him either a member of the Federal Reserve Board or ambassador to France. Jones declined. Ickes recorded: "[Jones] told the President that he 'represented business and finance in the Government.' The President remarked that this was a total giveaway by Jones. . . . [and asked,] 'Don't you have any feeling that you represent the people?' "[48]

In Jones's account, the basic facts were the same but the flavor was different. Jones had come to the White House at the request of Roosevelt, who suggested that he "go to France and reconstruct that country, or Italy." Jones declined, saying he was not in sympathy with the "plan to give those people everything we have, probably to the point of bankrupting ourselves." Then Roosevelt asked Jones "to take over the Federal Reserve Board, and build it up to do the big job it would have to do postwar." Again Jones said he was not interested, because he would clash with Morgenthau, and Roosevelt would side with his secretary of the treasury.[49]

Wallace had wanted Jones's head on a platter; ultimately he received it but almost lost his own in the process. It was satisfying recompense for his defeat in the Board of Economic Warfare squabble of the summer of 1943 and some slight compensation for the humiliation he had undergone in losing the vice presidency. Roosevelt, having tilted strongly toward the right in the State Department appointments, by favoring the left now reassured his liberal supporters, including his wife. The result was what might have been expected, even if Roosevelt had been in Washington. Senate leaders made it clear immediately that Roosevelt would have to sign a bill Walter George had introduced, removing the loan agencies, before Wallace could be confirmed solely as secretary of commerce. Pleas went to the president at sea, even one from Mrs. Roosevelt, but on security grounds he would not break radio silence (although he did to approve another bill). Finally he sent his assurance on February 1 when he was off Algeria. Wallace with much difficulty won confirmation solely as secretary of commerce.[50]

In his relations with Congress, Roosevelt's fourth term thus began as the third term had ended. At times he was a bit left of center, but he was above all cautious. The Senate blocked the liberal Aubrey Williams, nominee to head the Rural Electrification Administration. Roosevelt would not even nominate David Lilienthal for another term at TVA, Senator McKellar of Tennessee was so vehemently opposed; Truman, his successor, would do so, amused at the thought of McKellar's indignant reaction.[51]

Chapter 41

YALTA

TWO DAYS after his fourth inauguration, Roosevelt quietly left the White House on an arduous journey to meet Churchill and Stalin at Yalta. The time of departure, the route, and the destination were secret, but the American people, indeed the world, had been aware for weeks that a great conference was impending. At press conferences, Roosevelt had even joked about whether it was to be, perhaps, at the North Pole or the South Pole. With the war moving toward an end, there was a sense of excitement almost comparable to that preceding the Versailles conference twenty-six years earlier.[1]

At his last cabinet meeting before departing, Roosevelt's thoughts went back to the failing Wilson of 1919. He told the cabinet he would be gone for four or five weeks, taking Stettinius with him, and would have no objections if the next-ranking cabinet member, Morgenthau, wished to call a meeting. Wilson, he reminded them, had suffered a stroke while campaigning for the League of Nations in 1919. Secretary of State Robert Lansing then called a cabinet meeting, and Wilson was so enraged he forced Lansing to resign. Roosevelt reassured his secretaries that he was not going to make commitments; he told them he wanted time to study the British and Russian requests and confer with Congress.[2]

As to his foreign policy aims, Roosevelt enjoyed the support of the nation, and even of the Senate, to a degree Wilson had not in 1919. Some felt he was no more than following a consensus that publicists like Lippmann had advocated. Actually, during his many years in the presidency, he was continually projecting himself in front of opinion, but seldom too far in front, as he adroitly advocated his blend of Theodore

Roosevelt nationalism and Wilsonian collective security. To be sure, he was not a World Federalist, and avoided schemes that would impinge upon American sovereignty, but the projected world organization he had been influential in shaping at Dumbarton Oaks was winning wide acceptance. A March Gallup poll found 81 percent favorable.[3]

Roosevelt took with him a strong staff of State Department experts and a substantial briefing book, one of several prepared for the conference. The Joint Chiefs of Staff were similarly ready. Hopkins, Harriman, and Leahy were among Roosevelt's chief diplomatic advisers; he directed Leahy to attend all of the political meetings. Secretary of State Stettinius also came along — Hull had not been invited to either Casablanca or Tehran. Bohlen was now both interpreter and an influential adviser. Alger Hiss, later so controversial, came as a specialist on the United Nations organization; his chief contribution was to circulate a memorandum arguing against including any of the Soviet republics among the initial members, since they were not sovereign states under international law.[4]

Because Hiss was later accused of working for the Communists at Yalta, Bohlen's reminiscences are significant:

> I do not believe that Roosevelt had any prior acquaintance with Hiss. . . . But I can testify with certainty that Roosevelt never saw Hiss alone during the entire proceedings of the conference . . . because, as Roosevelt's interpreter, I had to stay close to him in anticipation of a possible suggestion from Stalin for a meeting. Hiss sat in on the big conferences but never at any of the private meetings that the President had with Stalin or Churchill.[5]

The occasion also served Roosevelt in his efforts to conciliate James Byrnes, angry, deeply hurt, and in a position to wreak political damage, because Roosevelt had passed him over for both vice president and secretary of state. The president invited Byrnes to the meetings, where, utilizing his old skill as a court reporter, he took full notes. Both Eleanor and Anna Roosevelt wanted to attend the conference. Roosevelt told Eleanor he could not bring her because wives would not be attending, but when he found Churchill and Harriman were each bringing daughters, he included Anna in the party. Anna, as she had in the White House, saw to it that he was comfortable.[6]

Aboard the cruiser *Quincy*, Roosevelt settled into what for him was one of the happiest of routines. He took the captain's quarters for himself, because, he explained to Anna, he always preferred the starboard side, and allotted the admiral's quarters to Anna. They should have gone to Leahy, a five-star admiral, but, Roosevelt explained, it would be embarrassing for her to be below decks where the men liked to run around in their underpants. Unfortunately, Roosevelt boarded the *Quincy* with a runny nose and tickle in his throat, which developed into a light cold that kept him in his quarters for several stormy days. Seasoned sailor that he was, he slept well and enjoyed himself. Each day he talked over with Admiral Leahy some of the issues he would face at the conference. Bohlen later lamented that Roosevelt had not mastered the detailed briefing books, but that had never been his custom while at sea.[7]

On several occasions Roosevelt displayed his old liveliness. On January 25, Anna told her father that, although the seas were running high, she was going to watch the crew drop a mail pouch on a long rope, sealed in an empty torpedo casing, for a destroyer to pick up. He insisted upon going with her in his wheelchair. She wrote in her diary:

> We had slowed up to a point where we were only keeping steerage way and were rolling very heavily. FDR's chair has no arms so he had to clutch the wire railing for dear life. The destroyer assigned to pick up [the mail pouch] . . . plowed and wallowed. . . . Sometimes the waves hid all but her mainmast from our view.[8]

The weather turned calm and warmer. Roosevelt sunned himself and enjoyed the merriment of deck games, and on January 30 celebrated his sixty-third birthday with a convivial dinner. Churchill sent several dire messages warning of health conditions and a treacherous mountain road that would have to be traversed in the Crimea, but Roosevelt would not alter his plans.[9]

By the end of the voyage, "The President seemed rested and calm," Stettinius noted. "He said he had been resting ten hours every night since leaving Washington but still couldn't understand why he was not slept out."[10]

On the morning of February 2, as the *Quincy* slowly slipped through the narrow harbor entrance at Malta, Churchill, Eden, and the British chiefs of staff, together with their American counterparts with whom they had been conferring, stood in welcome along the railings of HMS *Orion*. Eden recalls, "While the bands played and amid so much that reeked of war, on the bridge, just discernible to the naked eye, sat one civilian figure. . . . All heads turned his way and a sudden quietness fell." Roosevelt, wearing a tweed cap, was wheeled to a sunny spot on the deck to receive his own military and diplomatic leaders, then Churchill and Eden. Neither at a pleasant lunch nor at dinner would Roosevelt discuss issues involving the Russians.[11]

As he arrived in Malta, Roosevelt was well aware of the explosive irritation with which Churchill had viewed the president's less than full cooperation and unpleasant cables during recent British intervention in Athens on behalf of the king. Nevertheless, the Greek episode was of minor importance to Roosevelt.

What was vital was to parry the British efforts to modify American strategy. Roosevelt could best do so through avoiding lengthy debate with Churchill. The British had a poor opinion of Eisenhower and his commanders. While Eisenhower wanted to bring German resistance to an end by massive pressure in both the northern and central sectors of the western front, the British proposed launching only a single attack under Field Marshal Montgomery in the north. Nor were the Americans pleased by Churchill's continued pressure to reassign forces to areas in which the British would have a postwar interest. At the end of 1944, Roosevelt, after examining Stimson's data showing that the British had sent some of their troops as far away as Athens, asserted, "Churchill is always a disperser."[12]

Before Roosevelt's arrival, the American and British staffs, already in Malta, engaged in their last great strategy debate of the war, and the Americans won. Marshall, in a closed session with no notes taken, argued against Montgomery's requirements of elaborate preparations and overcaution in advancing. He also protested against Churchill's pressure upon Eisenhower. Marshall carried the meeting. While Montgomery fought in the north, the Americans advanced toward bridgeheads along the Rhine and the Ruhr industrial area beyond. By this time, the Americans and British were confronting as many German divisions as the Russians on the eastern front.[13]

During a session aboard the *Quincy,* Roosevelt avoided arguments with Churchill as the American and British chiefs of staff reviewed the military decisions they had reached. At lunch Churchill found Roosevelt very friendly, and was touched that the president had placed a small candle on the table so he could light his cigar. "Pleasant but no business," Eden noted. "So a dinner was arranged specifically for this purpose. . . . Impossible even to get near business." Eden was dismayed, since they would be negotiating "with a Bear who would certainly know his mind."[14]

The flight to the Crimea took a toll on Roosevelt. After dinner there was scant time for him to sleep before he took off at 3:30 A.M. on a new four-motored transport, a C-54, especially fitted for him with an elevator and bedroom, the first of the specifically presidential airplanes. Newspapermen dubbed it the "Sacred Cow." The seven-hour flight left him visibly in a state of exhaustion; he did not sleep well because of the noise and vibration. His condition dismayed those who saw him when, after landing on the icy runway at Saki airport, sitting in a Jeep, he reviewed a goose-stepping Russian guard of honor. He was, observed Churchill's physician, Lord Moran, "looking straight ahead with his mouth open, as if he were not taking things in." (Members of the family explained Roosevelt's open mouth, which had become rather frequent, as a result of his sinus problem.) Even Bohlen, who had gone for only two weeks without seeing the president, was shocked by the way his physical condition was deteriorating. After several days' observation, Lord Moran noted, "To a doctor's eye, the President appears a very sick man. He has all the symptoms of hardening of the arteries on the brain in an advanced stage, so that I give him only a few months to live."[15]

Yet Roosevelt, as in previous months, marshaled his faculties to meet challenges as they arose at the conference. The British were shocked by what they regarded as his deficiencies in presiding over the sessions, and were critical at the time and later. Churchill lamented that it was difficult to engage Roosevelt in serious discussion, but Roosevelt for his part felt that Churchill's powers were declining. At one session as Churchill began speaking, Roosevelt jotted a note to Stettinius, "Now we are in for ½ hour of it." Each thought the other rambled; each had become familiar with the other's favorite anecdotes. So too their own subordinates would complain, Eden about Churchill and Hopkins about Roosevelt. Hopkins remarked to Lord Halifax after Roosevelt's death that the president had not followed half of what was going on at Yalta. Roosevelt was indeed in decline, but his difficulty with Churchill was that the early fascination was gone, and their aims were conflicting.[16]

The American estimate of Roosevelt's performance at Yalta was favorable. Leahy felt that the president presided over the sessions with great skill and dominated the discussions. "The President looked fatigued as we left, but so did we all." Bohlen, who was close to Roosevelt throughout the conference, concluded "that while his physical state was certainly not up to normal, his mental and psychological state was certainly not affected. He was lethargic, but when important moments arose, he was mentally sharp. Our leader was ill at Yalta . . . but he was effective. I so believed at the time and still so believe."[17]

Hopkins had suffered such a serious relapse in his stomach condition that he was in worse shape than Roosevelt. While at Yalta he lost eighteen pounds. Throughout the conference he had to stay in bed, leaving only to go to sessions, where — as at Tehran — he served as adviser and prompter to the president. Once again his status was high.

The Soviets assigned Roosevelt to the Livadia Palace, where Czar

Nicholas II and his family had spent much time, two miles south of the town of Yalta. The Germans had stripped the palace of even its plumbing fixtures, but in three weeks the Soviets had fully refurbished it and brought in staff from three Moscow hotels. Roosevelt occupied a suite on the first floor, the only one with a private bath. Nearby were the banquet hall and ballroom where the sessions were to take place. Since Stalin had not arrived, Roosevelt was able to dine and sleep before beginning five arduous days of negotiations.[18]

Each of the three leaders came with his own agenda, with some overlapping of viewpoint among them. Roosevelt was placing his hopes primarily upon a United Nations, in which American membership, if it served no other purpose, would commit the United States to a collective security policy during the postwar period when there might be isolationist reaction. He and his Joint Chiefs of Staff still were eager to obtain specific commitments and arrangements for Soviet participation in the war against Japan, even though during the conference a powerful United States naval task force was able to sail along the shores of the main island, Honshu, bombarding it. Nor was there any certainty that the atomic bomb, to be ready that summer, would actually work. As for the British, Roosevelt was suspicious of imperial schemes, less than enthusiastic about spheres of influence, and not entirely friendly toward Churchill's desire to balance Russian force on the European continent with a strong France and a rehabilitated industrial Germany. About the Soviets, Roosevelt, thanks to his briefings from Harriman and Bohlen, was better informed than earlier, well aware that they were establishing firm control in areas their troops were occupying, but hopeful that participation in the United Nations would temper their suspicions.

In talking to Democratic and Republican Senate leaders on January 11, 1945, Roosevelt had been unusually candid, stating "that the Russians had the power in Eastern Europe, that it was obviously impossible to have a break with them and that, therefore, the only practicable course was to use what influence we had to ameliorate the situation." In reply to an inquiry from Senator Vandenberg, he said there was no economic bargaining weapon because to cut down on lend-lease would hurt the United States as much as the Russians.[19]

As at earlier conferences, the agenda at Yalta was flexible, with topics of concern popping up for discussion, sometimes being settled, but more often being referred back for consultation, perhaps to the foreign ministers, and later being returned for discussion. Once more Roosevelt put in arduous hours, at first skipping his periods of rest, to consult with his own staff, or participate in the formal sessions beginning at four in the afternoon and dinners that could run long into the night.

The negotiations began with deceptive camaraderie like that of a poker game for high stakes, when at four o'clock on February 4, Roosevelt again met Stalin. They shook hands and smiled like two old friends. Roosevelt opened by remarking that he had made several wagers on shipboard whether the Soviets would reach Berlin before the Americans took Manila (the next day they did indeed enter North Manila). The Soviet Army on the Oder was only fifty miles from Berlin. Stalin did not inform Roosevelt that that very day he had ordered it to halt; rather, the forward movement of the Russian troops was around Budapest and toward Vienna, securing central Europe for the Soviets. Instead, Stalin answered that certainly the Americans would reach Manila first, since there was very hard fighting along the Oder. Only an hour before, Stalin had assured Churchill that the Oder was no obstacle; the Red Army was across it at several points and encountering only raw troops.[20]

As at Tehran, Roosevelt in his conversation sought to be ingratiating toward Stalin and to suggest views differing from the British on treatment of the Germans and France. The extent of the German destruction in the Crimea caused him, he told Stalin, to be more bloodthirsty than earlier; "he hoped that Marshal Stalin would again propose a toast to the execution of 50,000 officers of the German army." Concerning France, Roosevelt aired his preference for a northwest zone of American occupation in Germany, not requiring transit, "but the British seem to think that the Americans should restore order in France and then return political control to the British." Stalin inquired if he thought France should have a zone of occupation; Roosevelt said it would not be a bad idea, but should go to France only out of kindness.[21]

In opening the first plenary session at five o'clock, Roosevelt remarked that there would be much to discuss, indeed the whole map of Europe. Marshall said that the Allies had regained all the terrain lost in the German Ardennes offensive, and in March should be crossing the Rhine. Stalin declared that the Russians had launched their winter offensive early in order to help the British and Americans even though they had not pressured him to do so. It was "our duty as allies." Roosevelt proposed that with the armies approaching each other in Germany, they should more closely coordinate their operational plans. Stalin suggested the staffs should discuss plans for a summer offensive, since he was not sure the war would be over by then.[22]

At the outset, Roosevelt made a poor impression; at other times during the conference, he was fine. Major Birse, the British interpreter, felt that Roosevelt functioned ineffectively throughout. "Sitting at the round-table he looked worn-out and almost disinterested. It was Stettinius and Byrnes who appeared to be putting the words into his mouth."

On the other hand, while General Laurence S. Kuter, representing the air force, felt Roosevelt was not mentally alert at the first session, he noted that at subsequent meetings "his improvement and comeback were almost spectacular." An evening or two later, Kuter attended a small dinner with Roosevelt and his daughter. Only Americans were present, and both General Marshall and Admiral King were elsewhere. Roosevelt mixed four-to-one martinis, and held forth on what poor condition Churchill had been in that afternoon, his nap having been interrupted:

> According to the President, the Prime Minister had sat at the table and drifted off into a sound sleep from which he would awake very suddenly making speeches about the Monroe Doctrine. The President said he had to tell him repeatedly that it was a very fine speech, but that it was not the subject under discussion.[23]

Roosevelt's jovial liveliness then was in contrast to his fatigue and irritation the first evening. He was the host and too weary to mix cocktails. The conversation was cordial and light until near the end, when Stalin began to discuss the rights and responsibilities of the three great powers in relation to the smaller nations. He felt that since the big three had borne the brunt of the war they had the right to preserve the peace, "but that he would never agree to having any action of the Great Powers submitted to the judgment of the small powers." Roosevelt "said he agreed . . . and that the peace should be written by the Three Powers."[24]

Hard bargaining began with the second plenary session, which focused on the future of Germany. Roosevelt was far from incisive in opening the discussion, giving a rambling discourse on his memories as a small boy of a bucolic, premilitarist Germany before Berlin diminished the power of small semiautonomous states. Stalin paid little attention; Churchill toyed with his cigar. Roosevelt may have been vague because while he was still saying he thought the dismemberment of Germany was a good idea, he no longer seemed really to favor it. Nor did Churchill, now seeking counterweights to Soviet power. Stalin seemed cautiously to be trying to commit Roosevelt and Churchill to partition; after the war Soviet propagandists told Germans that Stalin had never favored it. Although Roosevelt introduced a map at the session, and a committee was assigned to consider the question, the idea of dividing Germany was abandoned. The committee never met.[25]

The question whether France should administer a zone of occupation was relatively easy to settle. Churchill argued strongly for it, suggesting that it was questionable how long the United States would maintain an occupation force, and that the British could not bear the full cost or provide the manpower. Stalin objected to changing the tripartite control of Germany into four-nation control. Roosevelt agreed with Stalin that France must not hold a seat on the control commission, but warned that he probably could not persuade Congress to authorize American troops to stay in Europe much beyond two years.

In giving this warning, Roosevelt was not playing into the hands of Stalin, Bohlen points out. The context was not "a divided Germany with rival occupation armies facing each other" but united allies seeking to prevent a resurgence of German military strength.

The arguments of Bohlen and H. Freeman Matthews, head of the State Department European Affairs Division, swung Roosevelt toward a council seat for France. At a subsequent session he proposed it. Stalin, not wanting to offend the French, threw up his arms and exclaimed, "I surrender."[26]

Reparations were a far more difficult question, because of the growing concern of Churchill and to a lesser degree of Roosevelt that Germany should participate in bringing economic rehabilitation in Europe, and become a possible barrier against Soviet power. The Soviets sought $10 billion in reparations in kind — to remove 100 percent of Germany's plants used for military production, and 80 percent of its heavy industry — which would have led to a result much like the Morgenthau plan. Churchill vigorously protested, pointing out how little German reparations had benefited the Allies in the 1920s, and that smaller countries also had claims against Germany. If a horse was to pull a wagon, concluded Churchill, one had to give it fodder.

Roosevelt, seeking to act as mediator, added that the United States had lost heavily through the loans, providing over $10 billion to the Germans, which kept the reparations functioning. The United States did not want capital or industrial plants from the Germans, and also did not want to help keep the Germans from starving. He sympathized with the Russian claims for reparations; the German living standard should not be higher than that of the Russians. The problem was that although he wished to see restoration of all the areas German armies had devastated, reparations could not possibly be sufficient to cover the undertaking.[27]

The reparations problem went back to the foreign ministers, and again on February 10 came before Roosevelt, Churchill, and Stalin for debate. Stettinius had proposed that an Allied Reparations Commission should, as the Soviet Union wished, consider the Russian request for $10 billion in reparations. The British opposed any mention of figures until the commission determined them; Bohlen agreed. Hopkins, on the contrary, scribbled a note to Roosevelt at the final session, "The Russians have given in so much at this conference that I don't think we should let them down." The final protocol provided that the commission in its initial studies should take the Soviets' proposed sum — 50 percent of the $20 billion total — as a basis for discussion. Harriman has noted, "That fifty percent was to plague us at Potsdam."[28]

Without great difficulty, Roosevelt obtained a settlement of the voting problems threatening the United Nations. On February 6, it was the first order of business at the plenary session. Stettinius made a well-crafted persuasive presentation of the American proposal, that each member of the Security Council should have one vote, but all decisions on preservation of the peace require the unanimous approval of the permanent members. Stalin wanted the working of the proposal explained to him.

It was Churchill, not Roosevelt, who obliged. If China wished the return of Hong Kong, he pointed out, Great Britain could preserve its interests through exercising the veto power. Stalin inquired what would happen if Egypt sought the return of the Suez Canal. Egypt, Churchill explained, would have the right to speak. He concluded "that because of our great power, which is still protected by the veto if we do not agree, we should allow others to be heard."

Stalin declared that his concern was less over voting procedure than with lasting unity. The three of them "knew that as long as . . . [they] lived none of them would involve their countries in aggressive actions, but after all, ten years from now none of them might be present. . . . If unity could be preserved there was little danger of the renewal of German aggression." He seemed worried that nations raising complaints against the great powers "would not be without friends or protectors in the assembly."

Unity was one of the prime aims, Roosevelt responded, and the American proposal "promoted rather than impaired this aim." If differences arose among the great powers they would become fully known to the world, regardless of the voting procedure. "In any event, there was no method of preventing discussions of differences in the assembly."[29]

Later in the conference, Molotov announced acceptance of the American formula for a veto in the Security Council. He then requested that three Soviet republics, the Ukrainian, White Russian, and Lithuanian, receive votes in the Assembly, not the full sixteen Soviet republics as the Russians had demanded at Dumbarton Oaks. Roosevelt carefully countered that the proposal would require study since it "might prejudice the thesis of one vote for each nation." Churchill, who, as the

Americans knew, wished to include India in the United Nations, declared his "heart went out to mighty Russia which though bleeding was beating down the tyrants in her path." Before the end of the conference, Roosevelt reluctantly agreed to the admission of the Ukraine and White Russia. On the advice of Byrnes, who feared an adverse congressional reaction, Roosevelt later wrote both Stalin and Churchill requesting three American votes. Both agreed, but when word leaked in Washington, the reaction was so derisive that the United States never claimed extra votes. At Yalta, Roosevelt also arranged that a conference to organize the United Nations should shortly take place in San Francisco. Subsequently, Bohlen looked upon the settlement of the Security Council voting procedure as "the one solid and lasting decision of the Yalta Conference," without which "there would hardly have been a United Nations."[30]

The most difficult problem that Roosevelt faced at Yalta was Poland, as he battled for some formula which would enable him to return to the United States asserting that he had defended principles of democratic self-determination. The reality that the Soviet Army occupied all of Poland made Stalin and Molotov ill disposed to accept any infringement upon their power and control. All that would be possible would be to obtain some face-saving device.

By February 8, Roosevelt was so worried and upset over the trend of discussions on Poland, Dr. Bruenn noted, that he was obviously fatigued and his blood pressure for the first time was showing irregularity. Bruenn cut him off from visitors each day until noon and insisted upon at least an hour's rest before the afternoon conferences. Within two days his blood pressure and appetite had improved, he was in fine spirits, and had obtained an agreement concerning Poland that on the surface was satisfactory.[31]

The question of Polish frontiers was secondary, and to the east had been basically settled at Tehran as being along the Curzon Line of 1919. Roosevelt tried to persuade Stalin to concede to the Poles the city of Lvov and adjacent oil fields just beyond the line. "Most Poles," said Roosevelt, "like the Chinese, want to save face." Stalin interrupted to inquire, "Who will save face, the Poles in Poland or the *emigré* Poles?" Roosevelt went on, "It would make it easier for me at home if the Soviet Government could give something to Poland." Stalin gave nothing. Churchill worried about extending Polish boundaries so far to the west as to incorporate some six million Germans, "stuffing the Polish goose to the point of indigestion." Stalin retorted that most of the Germans had already run away from Soviet forces.[32]

The stumbling block was Roosevelt's insistence, with the backing of

Churchill, upon free elections in Poland — the right of the people to a government of their own choosing, even if it should be Communist. Roosevelt still had some reason for hope, on the basis of Stalin's relatively lenient treatment of Finland, abutting Russia's northern border. (Stalin had heeded Churchill's pleas at a lunch with Roosevelt during the Tehran conference.) It was a misplaced hope, since Stalin had no intention of budging from support of the Lublin provisional government he had established for Poland. There was no other issue during the conference about which he argued so lengthily or skillfully, pacing behind his chair as he made his points.

Bohlen, functioning as both interpreter and adviser to Roosevelt, has summed up Stalin's tactics: "The task of the Soviet diplomacy . . . was to retain a tight grip on Poland without causing an open break [with Roosevelt and Churchill]. . . . Stalin displayed considerable astuteness . . . and a tenacity in beating back one Western attempt after another to create conditions for a genuinely democratic government."[33]

Roosevelt and Churchill continued to fight for the creation of a new interim government combining moderate Poles from abroad with the Lublin, Moscow-dominated Poles. After a futile discussion on February 6, Roosevelt had Bohlen draft a letter to Stalin, elaborating on Roosevelt's proposal for a council of leaders to form a temporary government that all three countries could recognize. It was a scheme that Mikolajczyk, head of the London government, had proposed to Roosevelt.

The next day, February 7, Stalin rejected Roosevelt's plan, suggesting instead the addition to the Lublin government of leaders from outside of Poland. Roosevelt and his advisers saw in the scheme the basis for a compromise, if they could write in adequate safeguards. Roosevelt succeeded in referring the problem to the foreign ministers, who at a meeting that evening drafted an agreement. It provided for the enlarging of the existing provisional government. The reorganized government, the agreement stated, "shall be pledged to the holding of free and unfettered elections as soon as possible on the basis of universal suffrage and secret ballot. In these elections all democratic and anti-Nazi Parties shall have the right to take part and put forward candidates."

The meaning seemed straightforward enough at the time, but Bohlen lamented later that they did not take longer to add precision to the language. Stalin had assured Roosevelt that a free election could be held perhaps within a month, but no election was to take place in Poland until 1947 and then under circumstances quite different than Roosevelt and Churchill had visualized.[34]

Roosevelt's intentions were certainly clear enough to Stalin. On

February 10, Roosevelt proposed a Declaration on Liberated Europe, drafted in the State Department, which provided that the three governments would help "form interim governmental authorities broadly representative of all democratic elements in the population and pledged to the earliest possible establishment through free elections of governments responsive to the will of the people; and . . . to facilitate where necessary the holding of such elections."[35]

Stalin proposed only one amendment, on behalf of pro-Soviet elements, to provide for the support of those people who had actively struggled against the German occupation. Roosevelt and Churchill would not accept the change, and nonetheless Stalin agreed to the declaration. The declaration would include Poland, and since the State Department had crafted it carefully without the time pressure of the Yalta conference, it had no apparent loopholes. The Soviet government simply ignored it in dealings with Poland, Romania, Bulgaria, and other nations, never consulting the United States or Great Britain. It seems most improbable that harder bargaining and more specific wording of the Polish agreement would have altered future Soviet actions.

On the other hand, if Stalin had carried out the agreements, the result might well have been independent nations rather than satellites. At the time, Stalin may not have objected to free elections, thinking they would lead to Communist governments, but when signs of opposition appeared he interpreted the agreement in ways of his own choosing. In November, 1945, when he allowed a free election in Hungary, Communists polled only 17 percent of the vote. There were no more free elections in Hungary.[36]

The warm cooperativeness of Stalin in military planning at Yalta, especially for the entrance of the Soviet Union into the war against Japan, buoyed the western participants and helped create an overall atmosphere of optimism and camaraderie. Stalin agreed to point after point to improve cooperation in the final battles against Hitler's forces, except to insist that liaison among the Americans and British and the Russians must not be direct but in slower, less satisfactory fashion, through Moscow.

The Americans were particularly happy over Russian plans for energetic participation in the war against Japan. Although the struggle was going well, the dogged, suicidal resistance of Japanese troops gave promise that an invasion of the main islands of Japan might cost 500,000 casualties. Although the Joint Chiefs of Staff were well advanced with their plans for it, the prospect was not pleasant. They thought that the main Japanese forces were in North China and Manchuria, and that it would be important for the Soviets to engage them so they could not return to defend Japanese shores. Admirals Leahy and King opposed the invasion of Japan, hoping that naval blockade and incessant bombing could bring surrender. There was no expectation that the atomic bomb would be the key factor. Leahy still believed it unworkable. Others of the chiefs expected it to be of no greater force than the total tonnage dropped in one of the almost daily bombing raids, and thought there might be no more than one atomic bomb by the end of the summer.

Hence the ardent courtship of the Soviet armed forces at Yalta. Stalin was receptive, since he had ambitions in East Asia as well as in eastern and central Europe. At Tehran he had remarked that at the proper time he would make known Soviet aims; at Yalta he gave Roosevelt his list. In an ironic counterpart of Churchill's allocation of percentages of influence when he met Stalin in Moscow, Roosevelt, without Churchill present, assented to Stalin's requests. They came to him as no surprise, since Harriman had reported from Moscow in mid-December, 1944, that Stalin wished return of the Kurile Islands and the lower half of Sakhalin Island, and again to lease warm-water ports and the Chinese Eastern Railway in Manchuria. Two State Department memoranda opposed the return of southern Sakhalin and the southern Kuriles; there is no evidence that either Roosevelt or Stettinius ever saw them.[37]

On February 4, 1945, when Roosevelt met with the Joint Chiefs, Harriman reported on Stalin's expected demands. The military advisers thought the price too high to "sweeten Stalin," that southern Sakhalin would have been enough, but since their sphere was military policy, they did not sway Roosevelt. When the two of them met he did not make concessions to Stalin on the spur of the moment; he had considered them for months.[38]

At the outset of the session on February 8, Roosevelt obtained from Stalin assent to various requests from his chiefs of staff: two American bases in the maritime provinces of Siberia, and perhaps others later in Kamchatka after the Japanese consul had left; planning sessions between the Soviet and American staffs; the use of air bases near Budapest to carry out bombing operations in Germany, and a survey by United States experts of bombing effects in eastern and southeastern Europe. Stalin in return asked about purchase of surplus ships, and Roosevelt, saying he hoped the Soviet Union would become interested in shipping in a big way, offered ships on credit in such a way that twenty years' depreciation would wipe out the debt. This was the prelude to Stalin's discussion of the political conditions upon which the Soviet Union would enter the war against Japan, which he had already communicated through Harriman.

Roosevelt gave quick, clear replies to Stalin. He saw no difficulty in the postwar return of the southern half of Sakhalin Island and the Kuriles. Concerning a warm-water port and the Russian use of rail lines across Manchuria, he could not speak for the Chinese since he had not yet discussed the matters with Chiang. One option would be for the Soviets to lease both the ports and the rail lines. Another would be to operate the railroad under a commission of one Chinese and one Soviet representative. Roosevelt would prefer for Dairen to be made a free port under an international commission.

Stalin replied, according to Bohlen's minutes, "that it is clear if these conditions are not met it would be difficult for him and Molotov to explain to the Soviet people why Russia was entering the war against Japan." Roosevelt's answer was "that he had not had an opportunity to talk to [Chiang] and he felt that one of the difficulties in speaking to the Chinese was that anything said to them was known to the whole world in twenty-four hours." Stalin agreed, saying it was not yet necessary to speak to the Chinese, but he wished to leave Yalta "with these conditions set forth in writing agreed to by the three powers."[39]

Subsequently, Molotov handed to Harriman an English translation of Stalin's requirements. Roosevelt sought to amend them with two stipulations, that Dairen and Port Arthur, both of which Stalin sought, should be free ports, and that the arrangements would not be finally settled until Chiang had concurred. Stalin agreed concerning Dairen, but wanted a lease on Port Arthur so it could serve as a Soviet naval base. With this and other small changes, the document was revised. Harriman tried to persuade Roosevelt to delete several Soviet phrases that the Soviets could use as authorization for further aggrandizement, but Roosevelt argued the words meant only that the Russians had a greater interest in the area than the British and Americans. The Joint Chiefs of Staff raised no objections; indeed Admiral Leahy commented on the Soviet war plans, "This makes the trip worthwhile."

For months the agreement was locked in the president's personal safe. The Chinese, when they learned of the agreement in May, after Roosevelt's death, accepted Truman's excuse that it had been withheld to maintain military secrecy. They agreed to the terms as a means of resisting stiffer demands from Stalin.[40]

The sanction Roosevelt thus gave to the Soviet Union in East Asia became in later years the target of criticism exceeding even that over the Polish arrangements. It was no casual, ad hoc agreement on Roosevelt's part, but the result of deliberate consideration, in part going back as far as Tehran.

The conference ended, as Roosevelt wished, with a rush. He had feared it might drag on for days with endless arguments over the wording of agreements. As he had forewarned Churchill, he had arranged in advance to meet "three kings" in Egypt. On February 10, Roosevelt announced he must leave the next day. "Franklin, you cannot go," Churchill protested. "We have within reach a very great prize." When Stalin also asked for more time, Roosevelt agreed to stay longer if necessary, but on Sunday, February 11, the three approved the communiqué, leaving it to foreign ministers to deal with problems of wording. Additional time would have allowed Roosevelt and Churchill to work out agreements with more precision, but it is unlikely they would have altered future developments.[41]

As it was, Roosevelt, who never had any great faith in precise wording, was extending to Stalin two great incentives to be cooperative. A merchant shipping fleet at no cost, proffered at Yalta, was the lesser one. He could also expect a $6 billion reconstruction loan at low interest rates. The size can be measured by that of the subsequent loan to the British of $3 billion. For some time the Soviet Union, which had originally proposed the loan, had been negotiating about it with the United States. Roosevelt deliberately did not bring it up at Yalta, reserving it to head off problems in the future.[42]

When the conference came to an end, Churchill left already pessimistic and Roosevelt realistic enough not to be euphoric. "We have wound up the conference — successfully I think," he wrote his wife. "I am a bit exhausted but really all right."[43]

Chapter 42

ROOSEVELT'S TRIUMPH AND TRAGEDY

THE WORDS "triumph and tragedy," which Churchill used as the title of his final volume on World War II, apply also to the last weeks of Roosevelt. He returned from the apparent triumph of Yalta as victory in Europe was coming within grasp. The tragedy lay in the rapid disintegration of the agreements with Stalin and the irreversible decline of Roosevelt's health.

In his first venture on the way back from the conference, Roosevelt flew to Egypt. Aboard the USS *Quincy*, anchored in Great Bitter Lake in the Suez Canal, he entertained King Farouk of Egypt, Emperor Haile Selassie of Ethiopia, and King Ibn Saud of Saudi Arabia. Churchill was so disturbed at these meetings as a potential threat to British dominance in the area that he arranged also to meet the three rulers on subsequent days.

The visits with Haile Selassie and Farouk were little more than social, involving the exchange of pleasantries and gifts, allowing Roosevelt to expound his schemes to raise the living standards of the Ethiopian and Egyptian peoples. The luncheon with Farouk on the *Quincy* did raise a minor problem for Anna, when the king invited her to be his guest at his palace that evening. Anna remembered "being petrified," wondering how she could handle Farouk with his unsavory reputation. "Well, I didn't have . . . a second to worry because father had . . . been listening." He graciously expressed appreciation to the king for his thoughtfulness, but since Anna was doing some important work for him, it would be impossible for her to accept.[1]

Great Bitter Lake, called Mara in biblical times, was an ironic location for Roosevelt's debate with Ibn Saud over the fate of Jewish refugees, for (as he knew) Moses had stopped there with the Israelites on the flight from Egypt toward the promised land. The meeting, Roosevelt commented afterward, "was perfectly amazing." It began when the destroyer *Murphy* appeared carrying Ibn Saud, in the words of one witness, "a spectacle out of the past on the deck of a modern man-of-war." Royal bodyguards armed with long rifles and unsheathed scimitars were arrayed along the forecastle while, as Roosevelt described it, "the King, a great big whale of a man . . . [was] sitting in a Louis Quinze chair, up on the forward gun deck, on a great pile of Turkish carpets." In the bow was a large tent where the king stayed with a retinue of over forty people, including an astrologer and a food tester. At the stern was a flock of some eighty sheep to provide food. The crew received an unwanted thrill when they discovered one of the servants cooking on a brazier at the open entrance to an ammunition magazine.[2]

The meeting began amicably when Ibn Saud, who Roosevelt later said had been wounded nine times in battle, limped aboard, and expressed an interest in the wheelchair in which the president was sitting. Roosevelt presented him with one, and also gave him a C-47 airplane; the king gave the president rich robes, perfumes, and a sword in a diamond-studded scabbard.

The shock came when Roosevelt turned the conversation toward Jews. It was a topic that had not gone well at dinner on February 10, when Stalin had asked Roosevelt what he planned to give Ibn Saud. Roosevelt joked then that he might offer the king the six million Jews in the United States. That had led Stalin to make some unpleasant remarks about Jews, and also led some ardent Zionists in later years to charge that Roosevelt had been serious, and an anti-Semite. In actuality, Roosevelt was stubbornly pro-Zionist, and had a difficult time with Ibn Saud when he tried to persuade the king to accept 10,000 more Jews in Palestine. The king responded emphatically in words that Roosevelt would not repeat when he talked to reporters on the *Quincy:* "It was perfectly terrible."[3]

Ibn Saud retorted that the Jews should return to live in the countries from which they had been driven. "The President seemed not to fully comprehend," Hopkins noted later, "for he brought the question up two or three times more and each time Ibn Saud was more determined than before." Roosevelt then turned to his favorite topic, the greening of Arabia through irrigation projects, which decades later did lead to the growing of wheat in the desert. Ibn Saud thanked him for his interest "but said that he himself could not be much interested in agricultural and public works projects if this prosperity would be inherited by the

Jews." Roosevelt tried to be conciliatory, warning he could not prevent discussion in Congress or the press, but pledging "he would do nothing to assist the Jews against the Arabs and would make no move hostile to the Arab people."[4]

Arabs and Jews were on a collision course, Roosevelt warned Stettinius in Alexandria the next day. He planned to meet with congressional leaders and to reevaluate Palestine policy in search of some new formula to prevent warfare. He never succeeded.[5]

It was a time for leave-takings, significant in retrospect. Aboard the *Quincy*, moored off Alexandria, on February 15, Roosevelt enjoyed a pleasant lunch with Churchill, who had flown in from Athens where he had addressed a huge cheering throng in Constitution Square. In the afternoon he took up with Roosevelt and Hopkins a proposal for postwar British research on atomic bombs. Roosevelt, according to Churchill, made no objection. He remarked that commercial use of atomic power seemed less likely than it had seemed earlier, and that the first important testing of an atomic weapon would come in September, 1945. Churchill, remembering Roosevelt's "placid, frail aspect," wrote later, "This was the last time I saw Roosevelt. We parted affectionately. I felt he had a slender contact with life."

Roosevelt was in stable physical condition after the one episode at Yalta that had concerned Dr. Bruenn. He continued to fare well through the long voyage back to Washington, except that his blood pressure was variable and he was depressed.[6]

The ill health of several of those around him upset Roosevelt. As he arrived in Alexandria, "Pa" Watson, whose banter had long cheered him, was below decks, barely clinging to life, a victim during the voyage of congestive heart failure and a cerebral hemorrhage. After they sailed, Hopkins was too ill to leave his cabin, and had to act through Bohlen to persuade Roosevelt to tone down a scathing retort to General de Gaulle. Although de Gaulle had earlier sent word to Roosevelt that he would be happy to meet him anywhere on French soil, he curtly declined to come to Algeria, although it was then a French *département*.

Roosevelt was further upset when Hopkins decided he was so ill that he must leave the ship at Algiers and fly back to the United States. Roosevelt had been relying upon Hopkins to help him prepare his message to Congress on the Yalta conference. To compound his irritation, Bohlen agreed also to leave the *Quincy* and accompany Hopkins. Roosevelt's daughter remembered acting as an emissary from her father to Bohlen and failing to persuade him to stay. As was so typical of Roosevelt, he did not simply ask Bohlen to remain and assist him. Bohlen has reminisced that he had no knowledge the president wanted him, or of course he would have complied. Before departing, Bohlen dictated hasty notes on the conference and its significance to help Rosenman, summoned from London, draft the address. Roosevelt, petulant, seemed to feel that Hopkins was abandoning him to escape the boredom of the voyage, and was not pleasant in his farewell. He never saw Hopkins again. To compound Roosevelt's distress, two days later, on February 20, Watson died.[7]

Roosevelt was so upset over Watson's death that he talked about it as he had not about the loss of his mother or Missy LeHand. Those on shipboard with him feared he was thinking also of his own declining health. Day after day he would sit on the deck for an hour or more, not reading or conversing with Anna, but staring wooden-faced out to sea. Then he would nap. Only over cocktails and dinner would he become animated and amusing.[8]

Toward the end of the voyage, Roosevelt finally went to work with Rosenman and put in long hours on a second and third draft of the Yalta report. In the process he expressed his feelings about the conference and Churchill to both Rosenman and the three press correspondents aboard. One of them queried him on de Gaulle's statement that French Indochina was soon to be liberated. Off the record, Roosevelt talked about his efforts to place Indochina under a trusteeship to prepare it for self-government. The British, he said, didn't like the idea: "It might bust up their empire, because if the Indo-Chinese were to work together and eventually get their independence, the Burmese might do the same thing to the King of England."

As for Churchill, Roosevelt remarked that he was "mid-Victorian on all things like that," and again, "Dear old Winston will never learn."[9]

Churchill and the British were indeed, as Roosevelt claimed, ready to back de Gaulle in resisting what Cadogan called the president's "sinister intentions" to oust the French from Indochina. The Foreign Office also echoed the argument that France must be strengthened "as a counterweight to Russian influence in Europe."

De Gaulle was adamant in opposing American interference, announcing that he would build "a large land, air and naval base" at Dakar at the tip of West Africa, which Roosevelt had earmarked as an international peacekeeping base. De Gaulle told the Indochinese, celebrating their New Year, that France wanted to make the development of Indochina a principal aim of "reborn power and greatness." In March he expressed his indignation that American forces were under orders not to send aid to French units fighting the Japanese in Indochina. "We do not want to fall into the Russian orbit," he protested to the American ambassador, "but I hope that you will not push us into it." Soon Churchill and de Gaulle persuaded the United States. Roosevelt's dream of a trusteeship and ultimate independence for Indochina did not survive him.[10]

The greatest prize Roosevelt believed he was bringing home from Yalta, he explained in his leisurely talk with the three correspondents, was a United Nations organization that would work. Could it be the foundation of world peace for more than the generation creating it? he was asked. His answer was an affirmation tinctured slightly with realism: "We can look as far ahead as humanity believes in this sort of thing. The United Nations will evolve into the best method ever devised for stopping war." Moreover, it could be the agency to bring agricultural development and a higher living standard to impoverished areas of the world.

As for Germany and Japan, Roosevelt felt they should remain permanently disarmed. He hoped they would turn away from militarism and become members of the United Nations. Again, he evoked an idyllic premilitary Germany and the subsequent centralization and appearance of uniforms. "Now if a nation can do that in fifty years," he reasoned, "why couldn't you move in the opposite direction?" He applied the same optimistic proposition to Japan.[11]

Roosevelt's first order of business, upon his return to Washington, was to mollify the Senate. In years previously he had broadcast messages to Congress to the American people, using the Congress as the backdrop. With the Yalta report he reversed the order. He tried to disarm correspondents by saying he would go in person rather than having the address read to Congress, in order to avoid having to broadcast it that evening. It was twenty-six months, before the Casablanca conference, since he had appeared in person. Now he was willing to reveal his deteriorated physical condition by displaying himself before the members of both houses.

On March 1, 1945, only thirty-six hours after the trip ended, Roosevelt entered the packed House chamber. As he was rolled toward the dais in his small armless wheelchair, there was an immediate hush, then loud cheering. Just before he appeared, he remarked, referring to Churchill's report to the House of Commons, "I hope to do in one hour what Winston did in two." There was little new left to tell them, and he avoided extravagant claims, as he went over with them, and a world audience linked through the dozen microphones in front of him, the familiar points in the previously released communiqué. It was not an oration of Churchill's eloquence, but simple, direct, and casual. He ad-libbed incessantly, to the despair of Rosenman, as he brought to his speech the direct flavor of his earlier Fireside Chats, or his meetings with congressional leaders. "I come from the Crimea Conference with a firm belief that we have made a good start on the road to a world of peace," Roosevelt declared. He hailed it as marking the beginning of "a permanent structure of peace upon which we can build."[12]

The prime target of the speech, the members of the Senate, seemed disappointed, it contained so little new and seemed rather lifeless. When Vice President Truman was queried, Allen Drury, covering the Senate, noted, he remarked, "One of the greatest ever given," then laughed heartily. The reporters joined in. But the concept of a United Nations organization was receiving almost unanimous support in the Senate, and the listening public was favorable.

Only half the interest of the nation was in what Roosevelt said; there was equal concern over his physical condition. Newsreels taken at Yalta, showing him slack-mouthed and emaciated, were causing talk. Roosevelt sought to counter them with his report, yet through his appearance and delivery confirmed them. At the outset of his speech he apologized for sitting: "It makes it a lot easier for me not to have to carry about ten pounds of steel around the bottom of my legs." He added that he was "refreshed and inspired," that "I was not ill for a second, until I arrived back in Washington, and there I heard all of the rumors which had occurred in my absence." Yet at this very period, *Time* was to report in late April, superiors informed the Secret Service the president could go at any time, and a bodyguard began twenty-four-hour duty with Vice President Truman.[13]

Well into March, Roosevelt worked long hours and violated Dr. Bruenn's rules despite the efforts of his daughter to protect him. He saw numerous people, and concerned himself with a variety of issues both large and small.[14]

Roosevelt relaxed with notables and royalty, since he could engage in reminiscence and air his dreams for the future instead of addressing difficult issues. That was true even with Mackenzie King of Canada, who arrived on March 9. The prime minister, sitting on a sofa between the Roosevelts, was upset over the president's appearance. Mrs. Roosevelt, appearing worried, lamented the pressures upon him; she wished he would move his cabinet meetings to Hyde Park for the summer. Roosevelt expressed the view that he would be fine if only he were out of office and unencumbered by duties. Nevertheless, after lunch the next day he sketched for Mackenzie King elaborate plans for a trip to Europe in June. He wanted to stay at Buckingham Palace, visit Churchill at

Chequers, address Parliament, visit Queen Wilhelmina at The Hague, inspect troops on the battlefields, and perhaps visit Paris.

Roosevelt also spun out a new scheme for retirement. At the end of the fourth term he would like to establish a four-page newspaper containing only news — no editorials or advertisements. Through radio photography he would distribute it through the United States. The price would be one cent.[15]

On March 13, Mackenzie King again returned to the White House. Roosevelt seemed very weary, but rather than working on his correspondence, he wanted to talk, and urged the prime minister to stay. Mrs. Roosevelt was away. "He said for dinner he was having just his daughter and her husband and another relative Mrs. Rutherford." Mackenzie King found her "a very lovely woman and of great charm." He added, "I should think she has an exceptionally fine character." Roosevelt's reminiscences that evening ranged from the 1939 visit of the king and queen through his recent trip to Russia and Egypt. The Boettigers opened some suitcases and displayed some of the garments, harem gowns, and jewels that King Ibn Saud had presented to the Roosevelts.[16]

Saturday, St. Patrick's Day, marked the Roosevelts' fortieth wedding anniversary. They celebrated with a family luncheon, including only Anna and her small son, John. That evening they were hosts at a small state dinner for the governor general of Canada, the Earl of Athlone, with Princess Juliana of the Netherlands also present. On the table were St. Patrick's Day decorations that women on the White House staff had made for them. As the party broke up, Roosevelt said he would sleep until noon the next day.[17]

Some of Roosevelt's apparently casual comments to visitors during these days could be of serious import. That was the case when he welcomed to his March 9 press conference a group of French correspondents who had been touring America, and afterward talked to them. He was trying to smooth over a presumed thrust against de Gaulle that he had slipped into his address on the Yalta conference; referring to troubles with Yugoslavia, where Tito was assuming power, he had added, "we have to remember that there are a great many prima donnas in the world." It was useful diplomacy, therefore, to say a few words to the journalists in his "Roosevelt French." He assured them of his affection for France, reminiscing about his bicycling adventures as a teenager, transferring the locale from the German to the French countryside. As for the supposed friction with de Gaulle, it was the invention of journalists; their relations had been particularly cordial when de Gaulle had come to Washington. "We are great friends."

"Roosevelt does not look at all like his photos," reported the correspondent for *Le Figaro*, Jean-Paul Sartre, later renowned as an existentialist. "What is most striking is the profoundly human charm of his long face, at once sensitive and strong. . . . He smiled at us and talked to us in his deep, slow voice." Sartre asserted that the meeting with Roosevelt made the American trip worthwhile.[18]

Whatever Roosevelt's inner thoughts about de Gaulle might be, he was seeking a more cordial relationship, because already, within a month of the Yalta conference, relations with the Soviet Union were turning sour. He was having to retreat tentatively toward the very balance-of-power, sphere-of-influence politics that he had decried in his address to Congress. It had long been his fallback position. At the same time he was optimistic enough to think that the unity among the "big three" that he had proclaimed would indeed prevail.

Message after message was arriving at the White House map room from American commanders, diplomats, and an increasingly dismayed Churchill. Their theme was the same, in matters large and small: the Soviets seemed to be ignoring their Yalta commitments, or construing the agreements in a fashion that appeared to the Americans quite out of keeping with intentions. Stalin, ignoring his pledges to broaden the Lublin government and hold early elections, was consolidating his power in Poland, and would not even, as promised, allow western observers into the country. Some of the arrangements with the military fared not much better. At the beginning of March, Roosevelt protested to Stalin against the difficulties being encountered in locating and evacuating American prisoners of war and aircraft crews stranded within the Russian lines, many of them in Poland. "There is now no accumulation of U.S. prisoners of war on Polish territory or in other areas liberated by the Red Army," Stalin replied. Stalin, paying no attention to the Declaration on Liberated Europe, was similarly closing off other eastern European nations. At about the same time, he seemed to indicate how slight his interest was in the United Nations organization by sending word that Foreign Minister Molotov would be too busy to attend the San Francisco conference. The young ambassador Andrey Gromyko was to represent the Soviet Union.[19]

With Hopkins gravely ill at the Mayo Clinic, the task of advising Roosevelt on foreign policy fell heavily on Leahy and Bohlen. Although Roosevelt "could call on reserves of strength whenever he had to meet with . . . public figures," Bohlen recalls, he was succumbing to "weariness and general lassitude." His hands shook so badly he could hardly hold a telegram. Roosevelt was becoming more dependent than before upon the good judgment of his advisers. They would discuss dispatches with him and draft replies in keeping with his decisions. It bothered Churchill that in response to his urgent messages came cables worded in the officialese of Leahy, without even the flourishes that Roosevelt so often had added. A most affectionate personal message went for several weeks unanswered. Churchill, pained, could not fathom how seriously Roosevelt's strength was declining.[20]

There was some gratification for Churchill in the fact that Roosevelt was becoming so disillusioned with the Russians that he was closing ranks with the British. On March 23, Roosevelt declared to Anna Rosenberg, a public relations expert, that Harriman was right, "We can't do business with Stalin. He has broken every one of the promises he made at Yalta." He remarked to Anne O'Hare McCormick of the *New York Times* on March 29 that he had entirely believed what he told Congress about the Yalta conference, but Stalin was either not a man of his word or not in control in the Kremlin. That same day he sent Churchill a copy of his message to Stalin warning that a thinly disguised continuation of the existing Polish government "would be unacceptable, and would cause our people to regard the Yalta agreement as having failed." Churchill immediately informed Roosevelt, "I am delighted with our being in such perfect step. I have bunged off my [protest] to the Bear."[21]

Intertwined with the messages protesting Soviet intransigence on Poland were more explosive ones leading to an ominous altercation with Stalin. It developed over feelers a German SS general, Karl Wolff, had initiated at Bern, Switzerland, in a very secret, noncommittal way with Allen Dulles, an Office of Strategic Services agent, to discuss the possibility that Marshal Albert Kesselring might negotiate the separate surrender of the German forces in Italy. Roosevelt, with the consent of Churchill, authorized discussions but did not tell Stalin, fearing that Soviet involvement would destroy the delicate maneuvering toward a meeting between Kesselring and the Allied commander, Marshal Alexander. Churchill informed Stalin, arousing his suspicions. Roosevelt assured Stalin that, if the feelers led to any surrender negotiations between Allied and German officers, Soviet representatives would be welcome. Stalin replied that "the Germans have already taken advantage of the talks . . . to move three divisions from Northern Italy to the Soviet front." Roosevelt retorted that any movement of German troops from Italy to the eastern front had begun more than two weeks before any hint of surrender.[22]

In response, Stalin revealed his dark side, alleging that the feelers had led to an arrangement in which Kesselring would allow Anglo-American troops to move east into Germany in exchange for easier armistice terms: "And so what we have at the moment is that the Germans on the Western Front have in fact ceased the war against Britain and America. At the same time they continue the war against Russia." He tempered his allegation only with the preface that he assumed Roosevelt was not fully informed.[23]

Roosevelt, outraged, authorized Admiral Leahy, who together with General Marshall and Bohlen had been drafting the correspondence, to prepare a stern reply. He expressed his astonishment to Stalin over the allegation that there had been a deal with the Germans:

> and I feel that your information . . . must have come from German sources which have made persistent efforts to create dissension between us. . . .
>
> Frankly I cannot avoid a feeling of bitter resentment toward your informers, whoever they are, for such vile misrepresentations of my actions or those of my trusted subordinates.[24]

Although Roosevelt, as a diplomatic historian, Warren Kimball, points out, still was not answering the key question why the Soviets had been excluded from the talks in Bern, his firm reply was reassuring to Stalin. In a final defense of the sources of his data, Stalin backed down sufficiently to declare that he had never doubted the integrity or trustworthiness of Roosevelt or Churchill. That was sufficient for Roosevelt.[25]

On April 11 Roosevelt sent Churchill the only letter he personally wrote in their interchanges of the period:

> I would minimize the general Soviet problem as much as possible because these problems, in one form or another, seem to arise every day and most of them straighten out as in the case of the Bern meeting.
>
> We must be firm, however, and our course thus far is correct.[26]

It was his final estimate of Stalin.

During March, Roosevelt was also having Russian troubles with the press and Congress. His agreement at Yalta that the Soviets should have three votes in the United Nations Assembly — an agreement that he had firmly refused to mention in his report to Congress — was becoming known to a number of people. Secretary of State Stettinius felt that before it became too late, he should take the delegation to the San Francisco conference into his confidence and explain the agreement.

On March 24, Roosevelt did so, giving them a colorful but misleading account. He did not admit his firm commitment, but rather claimed he had told Stalin, in words reminiscent of his equivocal backing of Wallace in 1944, "if he were a delegate at San Francisco that he personally would favor the Soviet proposal." Roosevelt's distortion represented a change in his thinking since Yalta. He had asked Stettinius on March 12 to see if there were not some way to avoid the concession; if not, the United States must have the same number of seats.

Word of the extra seats appeared in the *New York Herald Tribune* on March 29, stimulating questions whether there had been further secret agreements at Yalta. Roosevelt, in the White House for a few hours, en route from Hyde Park to Warm Springs, hastily assigned Daniels and MacLeish to prepare a press statement. Daniels remembered going with MacLeish to the upstairs Oval Office, where Roosevelt was working with his secretary Grace Tully, tediously signing papers, indicating what he wanted to take with him:

> [Roosevelt] looked bone-tired, haggard, almost torpid. . . . With seeming precision he made a slight change in the first paragraph and pushed the paper back to me. We departed in haste. Then — when we reached the elevator . . . we discovered the change he had made in the first paragraph turned into confusion the rest of the statement. We had to go back. . . . Without any rebuke to either of us, the President corrected the paper.[27]

By mid-March Roosevelt's pace had already become too much for him and his physical condition was again taking a dip. While his blood pressure and the condition of his heart changed little, he had lost his appetite, complaining he could not taste his food, and seemed to be losing weight. By the end of the month, he was so tired that he felt he needed to go to Warm Springs once more to recuperate. Then on April 25, he would appear in San Francisco to open the United Nations conference.

Nevertheless, he arrived at Warm Springs on the afternoon of March 30 with enough bounce to get behind the wheel of his automobile and drive to the "Little White House." There in warm sunshine, in surroundings he loved, he began to pull back, relishing almost daily rides in the countryside. The level of his blood pressure varied widely, but his appetite improved so decidedly that he began asking for second helpings, and seemed to be putting on a little weight. He was in a better mood and more active. His color and vigor were at their best in the morning; after lunch he seemed worn and fatigued.[28]

Hassett, dropping his false front of optimism, began recording his apprehension that Roosevelt was slipping away. He had a long conversation with Dr. Bruenn, who guardedly, "reluctantly admitted the Boss in a precarious condition, but his condition not hopeless. He could be saved if measures were adopted to rescue him from certain mental strains and emotional influences, which he mentioned." Years later, talking to Dr. James Halsted, Anna Roosevelt's husband by this time, Dr. Bruenn was more candid. Dr. Halsted jotted down his account of Mrs. Roosevelt's calling her husband at Warm Springs "during the final trip a week or two before his death and talking 45 minutes urging help for Yugoslavia. This resulted in rise of B[lood] P[ressure] of 50 points. His veins stood out on his forehead. Obviously the necessity to deny her request and the long telephone conversation was a major strain."[29]

Domestic affairs, as well as overseas ones like aid for Tito and problems with Stalin, accompanied Roosevelt to Warm Springs. He dispatched much correspondence, little of his own drafting, but for the most part representing his decisions. As always, they gave the impression that he was in fine form. "I am getting a ten-day vacation, more for catching up with mail than for a rest," he assured Senator Claude Pepper on April 9. To James F. Byrnes went a soothing acceptance of his resignation as chief administrator of the war economy. Roosevelt disliked losing Byrnes's talents, but had not been pleased by a tantrum at Yalta, and remarked as he affixed his signature, "It's too bad some people are so primadonnish." He sent a joking note to the economist Isador Lubin bound for Moscow to discuss reparations, "Be sure to keep your rubbers on!" That had also been his parting injunction to Rosenman, returning to London. By telephone he approved Stettinius' announcement that the United States would not seek three votes in the United Nations Assembly. Excitement over the issue soon evaporated. While the Russians obtained their two extra seats at the San Francisco conference, the United States dropped its claim.[30]

April 11 was a fruitful, happy day for Roosevelt. He busied himself with a Jefferson Day address that he was planning to deliver over the radio on April 13. Robert Sherwood had sent him a draft, which he used as the basis for a new draft he dictated. After it was typed, as for so many decades had been his habit, he worked on the peroration. The last typed sentence read, "The only limit to our realization of tomorrow will be our doubts of today." He penned in, "Let us move forward with strong and active faith." In the afternoon, accompanied by Polly Delano and Daisy Suckley, he took a two-hour drive with Lucy Rutherford to one of his favorite mountaintop spots, Dowdell's Knob, and sat on a fallen log, pouring out to her his dreams for a better postwar world.[31]

Ironically, Secretary Stimson had a bad afternoon because of the Roosevelts. He returned with great enthusiasm from the Oak Ridge atomic facility to find a memorandum from the president awaiting him, asking him to talk to John Boettiger about the army's refusal to commission Sergeant Joseph Lash. General Marshall, who had been blocking Lash, had dumped the problem upon Stimson. After a long, inconclusive talk with Boettiger, Stimson was so upset that he could not sleep and got out of bed at midnight to drive down to Mount Vernon and back.[32]

At about 7:30 that evening, Morgenthau joined Roosevelt for cocktails and dinner. Roosevelt's hand shook so badly he knocked over the glasses, and Morgenthau had to hold the glasses as he poured. After two cocktails and some Russian caviar, Roosevelt seemed to feel better. Morgenthau noted: "I have never seen him have so much difficulty transferring himself from his wheelchair to a regular chair, and I was in agony watching him." After dinner, although Morgenthau found that Roosevelt's memory was bad and he was confusing names, they discussed Morgenthau's wish to keep Germany economically weak. Roosevelt declared, "Henry, I am with you 100 percent." When Morgenthau left, Roosevelt was sitting laughing and chatting with his four women guests, Polly Delano, Daisy Suckley, Lucy Rutherford, and Madame Elizabeth Shoumatoff, whom Mrs. Rutherford had brought to Warm Springs to paint a portrait of Roosevelt. "I must say the President seemed to be happy and enjoying himself." Later that evening, Roosevelt telephoned Anna to inquire about his grandson John, who had been seriously ill. As usual he made no mention of his own health, but, Anna remembered, he "couldn't have been more vigorous or full of details . . . [of] what he was doing" and of a barbecue he would attend the next afternoon.[33]

Roosevelt began April 12 with laughter over a remark of his black maid, who weighed two hundred pounds and said that in her next life she would like to be a canary bird. He told Dr. Bruenn he had a slight headache, but "he had a very good morning, and his guests commented on how well he looked." He sat in his favorite leather chair by the fireplace, joking as he worked on a card table signing letters and papers. "Here's where I make a law," he remarked as he signed a bill to continue the Commodity Credit Corporation. While he did his paperwork, Mme. Shoumatoff worked on her watercolor portrait.

At about 1:15 P.M., Roosevelt said, "I have a terrific headache," and slumped over. Dr. Bruenn arrived a few minutes later to find the president unconscious, breathing heavily. He had suffered a massive cerebral hemorrhage. Dr. Bruenn got him into bed, but nothing could have any beneficial effect. Miss Delano and Miss Suckley remained in the living room; Mrs. Rutherford and Madame Shoumatoff hastily packed and left. At 3:35, Dr. Bruenn pronounced the president dead.[34]

The news sent waves of shock across the country and around the world. Miss Delano had alerted Mrs. Roosevelt in Washington, phoning her that the president had fainted and been carried to bed. Dr. McIntire, not alarmed, urged her to go on with her afternoon engagements; they would fly to Warm Springs that evening. While at a benefit party, she received another call from Stephen Early, upset, and asking her to come home immediately. There she learned the news. She wired their sons, "Father slept away. He would expect you to carry on and finish your jobs." Stunned, and also determined to do her duty, she changed into black. When Harry Truman arrived at the White House and asked what he could do for her, she responded by asking what she could do for him. With the assembled cabinet and staff she watched Truman take his oath of office as president. Mrs. Roosevelt later said to Morgenthau that her husband had "died a soldier's death and perhaps his death will be an example for the rest of us to do even more."[35]

The nation was stunned by the suddenness of Roosevelt's death. When Washington reporters, who had been working frantically for hours, left the teletypes and telephones, Drury noted, they bought papers headlined ROOSEVELT DEAD, read them, and still could not believe it. Yet the abrupt death had been in some ways a blessing, for Roosevelt's health had been deteriorating to the point where he might have lost his competence, or could have suffered Wilson's fate and lived on helplessly. He had expressed to Miss Suckley the hope that that would never happen.[36]

Coming near the climax of the Second World War, Roosevelt's death seemed to the American people to symbolize their losses and suffering. Newspapers published his name in casualty lists; Yale University, from which he had received an honorary degree, included him on its roster of war dead. The news sent a shock throughout the nation and the world. Millions of Americans for decades could remember where they had been when they heard the news, whether at home or on some distant battlefield.

Eisenhower and his commanders in Europe pondered the effect upon the peace to come. It was after midnight; they went to bed, Eisenhower has reminisced, depressed and sad: "In his capacity as leader of a nation at war," he writes, "he seemed to me to fulfill all that could possibly be expected of him."[37]

Churchill, working late, heard the news at about the same time and was distressed. "I am much weakened in every way by his loss," he lamented in private. Edward R. Murrow broadcast from London that Churchill had told him, tears in his eyes, "One day the world, and history, will know what it owes to your President." Churchill made arrangements to fly to the services, but his cabinet insisted he remain in London.[38]

Without speaking, Stalin held Ambassador Harriman's hand for about thirty seconds when Harriman called the next evening. He was much concerned about the circumstances of Roosevelt's death and sent a message to the State Department asking that an autopsy be performed to determine if the president had been poisoned. Following routine procedure, Michael F. Reilly of the Secret Service had already sent the remains of Roosevelt's breakfast to a chemical laboratory, which found nothing. Nor was there an autopsy, since Mrs. Roosevelt felt her husband would not have wanted one. Harriman did use the occasion to persuade Stalin to reverse himself and send Molotov to San Francisco as a public gesture of continuing Soviet collaboration.[39]

There was both pomp and simplicity in the days of mourning that followed. A procession accompanied his coffin through Warm Springs, with muffled drums and two thousand servicemen from Fort Benning. On the long train ride to Washington, Mrs. Roosevelt sat sleepless through the night, looking out at the mourners standing along the tracks and gathered at stations where the train slowed down. On a bright Saturday morning, six white horses pulled the caisson bearing the flag-draped coffin down Pennsylvania Avenue past thousands of silent people, some of them crying.

At four o'clock, Bishop Angus Dun conducted the funeral service in the East Room of the White House, and as Mrs. Roosevelt requested, quoted from the First Inaugural, "The only thing we have to fear is fear itself." Mrs. Roosevelt also wished the quotation inscribed on the stone over her husband's grave, but found he had left instructions that he wanted it to bear only his name and that of his wife, whom he wished to have buried beside him.

The final services took place the following day at Hyde Park. There was a twenty-one-gun salute, the final playing of "Hail to the Chief," the committal service, and the coffin was lowered into a grave in the rose garden within a hemlock hedge, where he had played as a boy.[40]

ABBREVIATIONS AND SHORT TITLES USED IN CHAPTER NOTES

Blum, *Morgenthau Diaries*	John M. Blum, *From the Morgenthau Diaries* (3 vols., 1959–1967)
C&R	*Churchill and Roosevelt: The Complete Correspondence*, Warren F. Kimball, ed. (3 vols., 1984)
Dallek, *Roosevelt and Foreign Policy*	Robert Dallek, *Franklin D. Roosevelt and American Foreign Policy 1932–1945* (1979)
DNC	Democratic National Committee mss., FDRL. Most are in boxes designated by state.
ER	Eleanor Roosevelt
FDR	Franklin Delano Roosevelt
FDR & FA	*Franklin D. Roosevelt and Foreign Affairs: January, 1933–January, 1937*, Edgar B. Nixon, ed. (3 vols., 1969), cited by volume and page number; *Franklin D. Roosevelt and Foreign Affairs*, Donald B. Schewe, ed. (in 2 editions, one of 10 vols., one of 16 vols., with index, 1979; also available in microfilm); cited by document number
FDRL	Franklin D. Roosevelt Library. All manuscript materials, unless otherwise cited, are in the library.
FL	Family Letters
FO	British Foreign Office
FRUS	United States, Department of State, *Foreign Relations of the United States*
Gallup Poll	*The Gallup Public Opinion Poll*, George H. Gallup, ed. (3 vols., 1972)
GO	Governor's Official File, FDRL
HU	Harvard University
Ickes, *Secret Diary*	Harold L. Ickes, *The Secret Diary of Harold L. Ickes* (3 vols., 1953–1954)
Lash, *Eleanor and Franklin*	Joseph P. Lash, *Eleanor and Franklin* (1971)

LC	Library of Congress
NARA	National Archives and Records Administration
OF	President's Official File, FDRL
PC	Press conference transcripts, 25 vols., FDRL. Available in both microfilm and printed form.
PL	*F.D.R., His Personal Letters*, Elliott Roosevelt, ed. (3 vols., 1947–1950)
PPA	*Public Papers and Addresses of Franklin D. Roosevelt*, Samuel I. Rosenman, ed. (13 vols., 1938–1950); cited by year covered by volume, i.e., *PPA*, 1933, etc.
PPF	President's Personal File, FDRL
PRO	Public Record Office, London, England
PSF	President's Secretary's File, FDRL
Perkins, *Roosevelt I Knew*	Frances Perkins, *The Roosevelt I Knew* (1946)
Rosenman, *Roosevelt*	Samuel I. Rosenman, *Working with Roosevelt* (1952)
Sherwood, *Roosevelt and Hopkins*	Robert E. Sherwood, *Roosevelt and Hopkins* (1950)
Tully, *FDR My Boss*	Grace Tully, *FDR: My Boss* (1949)
YU	Yale University

CHAPTER NOTES

Chapter 1: THE UPBRINGING OF A GENTEEL REFORMER

1. Interview with ER. The critical view is in John T. Flynn, *Country Squire in the White House* (1940).
2. On the Roosevelt genealogy, see Timothy F. Beard and Henry B. Hoff, "The Roosevelt Family," *New York Genealogical and Biographical Record* (October, 1987), 118:193–202; (January, 1988) 119:19–34; FDR, "The Roosevelt Family in New Amsterdam before the Revolution" (December, 1901), ms.
3. FDR to Philip Slomovitz, March 7, 1935.
4. FDR to Stephen Early, October 19, 1939, *PL*, 1928–1945, 2:942.
5. David Mearns to Jonathan Daniels, April 9, 1945, Daniels mss., cited in Geoffrey C. Ward, *Before the Trumpet* (1985), 18.
6. Frank Freidel, "The Dutchness of the Roosevelts," in J. W. Schulte Nordholt and Robert P. Swierenga, eds., *A Bilateral Bicentennial: A History of Dutch-American Relations, 1782–1982* (1982), 156–158; *PPA*, 1944–1945:406–407.
7. Frank Freidel, "Roosevelt's Father," *FDR Collector* (November, 1952).
8. Frank Freidel, *Roosevelt: The Apprenticeship* (1952), 20–34; Sara Delano Roosevelt, *My Boy Franklin* (1933). Roosevelt's boyhood letters are in *PL*. The fullest account of FDR's boyhood is in Ward, *Before the Trumpet*, 109–177. Interview with ER.
9. Freidel, *Apprenticeship*, 35–51; Frank D. Ashburn, *Peabody of Groton* (1944), 112–113, 317–325; Sherrard Billings to Richard Cobb, after May 21, 1900, *Harvard University Gazette*, September 21, 1984. Conversation with Frances Perkins.
10. Freidel, *Apprenticeship*, 52–73; FDR, undated response on a questionnaire, *Harvard Crimson*, Harvard Crimson office.
11. On the young ER, see especially Joseph P. Lash, *Love, Eleanor* (1982), 1–36; J. William T. Youngs, *Eleanor Roosevelt* (1985), 23–66; ER, *This Is My Story* (1937). On her education of FDR, conversation with Mary Dublin, March, 1983.
12. Ward, *Before the Trumpet*, 252–255; Lash, *Love, Eleanor*, 35–36.
13. Lash, *Love, Eleanor*, 40–41; Ward, *Before the Trumpet*, 313. On the cipher

diary entries, see Nona S. Ferdon, "Franklin D. Roosevelt: A Psychological Interpretation of His Childhood and Youth," University of Hawaii Ph.D. dissertation, 1971.

14. Freidel, *Apprenticeship,* 69–71, 77–81; ER, *This Is My Story,* 162.
15. Walter Tittle, *Roosevelt as an Artist Saw Him* (1948), 95–96.
16. Lash, *Love, Eleanor,* 56; ER, *This Is My Story,* 139–165. ER continued to hold these views. Interview with ER, May 1, 1948. For a psychological interpretation, see Bernard Asbell, *The F.D.R. Memoirs* (1973), 221–227.
17. Freidel, *Apprenticeship,* 74–77, 82–84; Esca C. Rodger, "Want to be a Lawyer? . . . ," *American Boy* (June, 1927), 28:3; Grenville Clark in *Harvard Alumni Bulletin* (April 28, 1945), 47:452.

Chapter 2: A PROGRESSIVE APPRENTICESHIP

1. *San Diego Union,* April 14, 1914.
2. *PPA,* 1941:457–460.
3. Frank Freidel, *Roosevelt: The Apprenticeship* (1952), 87–89; *PPA,* 1933:338; John E. Mack interviewed by George A. Palmer, February 1, 1949.
4. Theodore Roosevelt to A. R. Cowles, August 10, 1910, in Elting E. Morison, ed., *Letters of Theodore Roosevelt* (8 vols., 1951–1954), 7:110.
5. George Mowry, *Theodore Roosevelt and the Progressive Movement* (1946), 134–155.
6. Enclosure in FDR to Edward Hayden, September 12, 1910.
7. *Poughkeepsie News-Press,* October 27, 1910; FDR, address at Hyde Park, November 5, 1910, longhand ms.
8. Freidel, *Apprenticeship,* 97–105.
9. *New York Tribune,* May 31, 1911; *New York Times,* May 31, 1911.
10. *New York Post,* April 1, 1911; *The Nation* (April 6, 1911), 92:334–335; FDR to Ferdinand Hoyt, April 12, 1911; FDR to James Barkley, April 4, 1911.
11. Freidel, *Apprenticeship,* 117–133; Watertown, New York, newspaper, about May 30, 1913, in FDR scrapbook; FDR to Thomas J. Comerford, August 26, 1914.
12. FDR, *The Happy Warrior: Alfred E. Smith* (1928), 6.
13. Freidel, *Apprenticeship,* 120–122.
14. Freidel, *Apprenticeship,* 136–137.
15. Freidel, *Apprenticeship,* 153–154; Liberty Hyde Bailey to FDR, January 31, 1913; FDR to Bailey, February 4, 1913.
16. Abram I. Elkus to FDR, February 6, 1913; FDR to Elkus, February 13, 1913.
17. *Poughkeepsie News-Press,* March 5, 1912.
18. FDR to Thomas Pendell, January 24, 1912; see also FDR senatorial mss., Box 9.
19. Ernest K. Lindley, *Franklin D. Roosevelt* (1931), 120; Freidel, *Apprenticeship,* 134, 138–146.
20. On the FDR–Howe relationship, Alfred B. Rollins, Jr., *Roosevelt and Howe* (1962), is definitive.
21. John Keller and Joe Boldt, "Franklin's On His Own Now . . . ," *Saturday Evening Post* (October 12, 1940), 213:42.
22. Interview with ER, May 1, 1948; Lindley, *Roosevelt,* 110; Josephus Daniels,

The Wilson Era, Years of Peace (1944), 124–127; Daniels diary, March 6, 9, 1913; Daniels to Woodrow Wilson, March 11, 1913, Daniels mss., LC.

23. *PL,* 3:467.
24. Freidel, *Apprenticeship,* 168–171; FDR to Hamilton Fish, July 20, 1914.
25. FDR to George S. Bixby, March 24, 1913; *New York Times,* December 15, 1914; interview with Daniels, May 29, 1947.
26. Freidel, *Apprenticeship,* 185–187.
27. Freidel, *Apprenticeship,* 338–340; *Washington Post,* July 5, 1917; *New York Tribune,* February 11, 1918.
28. Daniels, *Wilson Era, Years of Peace,* 126.
29. Freidel, *Apprenticeship,* 192–206.
30. Freidel, *Apprenticeship,* 211–214.
31. Daniels autobiography, draft, Daniels mss.; McGowan to FDR, August 7, 1916; Frank Freidel, *Roosevelt: The Ordeal* (1954), 160–161.
32. ER, *This Is My Story* (1937), 199–203.
33. Yates Stirling, *Fundamentals of Naval Service* (1917), 80–83; the flag is in the museum of FDRL.
34. Villard to FDR, March 14, 1913.
35. U.S. Secretary of the Navy, *Annual Report, 1913* (1913), 5.
36. FDR to Alfred Thayer Mahan, June 16, 1914; FDR memorandum [spring, 1913]; Senate Naval Affairs Subcommittee, *Naval Investigations, 1920,* 1:758, 808–809; *Minneapolis Tribune,* April 16, 1914.
37. FDR, "Trip to Haiti and Santo Domingo 1917"; George Marvin, "Notes on Franklin D. Roosevelt as Assistant Secretary of the Navy," [1946]; Freidel, *Ordeal,* 81–82, 135–136.
38. *PL,* 2:243; Augustus P. Gardner to FDR, November 17, 1914; FDR to Gardner, November 25, 1914, not sent; *Hearings . . .* (1915), 1059.
39. Wilson to FDR, January 3, 1917, Wilson mss., LC.
40. *PPA,* 1939:117.
41. Freidel, *Apprenticeship,* 292–295.
42. Interview with ER, May 1, 1948; FDR to Daniels, February 14, 1941, Daniels mss.; Theodore Roosevelt to FDR, September 13, 1918.
43. Freidel, *Apprenticeship,* 312–314.
44. *PL,* 2:407–418. At one point the quotation follows a slightly different wording from that in the ms.
45. Freidel, *Apprenticeship,* 349–351, 357–358, 362–364; Daniels diary, September 3, 5, 10, 1918, Daniels mss.
46. Freidel, *Ordeal,* 3–15.
47. *Time,* May 28, 1923.

Chapter 3: YEARS OF TESTING

1. Conversation with Raymond Corry. There are varying accounts of the crisis in Bernard Asbell, *The F.D.R. Memoirs* (1973), 228–233, based in part on Anna Roosevelt Halsted's recollections; Lash, *Eleanor and Franklin,* 220–227, in part based on ER's discussion with him; James Roosevelt, *My Parents* (1976), 99–104; Elliott Roosevelt and James Brough, *An Untold Story* (1973), 83–86, 95–

96; Joseph Alsop, *FDR, A Centenary Remembrance* (1982), 70. The search in Sara Delano Roosevelt's diary took place in 1952.

2. On Alice Sohier, see Geoffrey C. Ward, *Before the Trumpet* (1985), 252–255. Interviews with Anna Roosevelt Halsted and James Roosevelt.
3. ER, *This Is My Story* (1937), 162, 173; interviews with ER.
4. William Phillips, *Ventures in Diplomacy* (1952), 70.
5. Alsop, *FDR*, 67; Geoffrey C. Ward, *A First Class Temperament: The Emergence of Franklin Roosevelt* (1989), 449, places the episode in 1919.
6. Michael Teague, *Mrs. L: Conversations with Alice Roosevelt Longworth* (1981), 157–158; Photographic Files, FDRL. I am grateful to the Roosevelt Library staff for their research on the circumstances of the photograph.
7. Jim Bishop, *FDR's Last Year* (1974), 245.
8. Interview with ER.
9. ER, *This Is My Story*, 254–267, 322–327.
10. Freidel, *Roosevelt: The Ordeal* (1954), 31–35.
11. Freidel, *Ordeal*, 39–50.
12. Freidel, *Ordeal*, 51–69.
13. Claude Bowers to Cox, in James Cox, *Journey Through My Years* (1946), 241–242; *New York Times*, July 15, 1920.
14. *New York Times*, August 19, 29, 1920.
15. Freidel, *Ordeal*, 79–91.
16. Freidel, *Ordeal*, 81–82.
17. Freidel, *Ordeal*, 92–93, 138–159.
18. Freidel, *Ordeal*, 152–158.
19. *PL*, 2:517–522; FDR to Charles H. McCarthy, July 26, 1923.
20. Clipping, July 28, 1921, FDR scrapbook.
21. Earle Looker, *This Man Roosevelt* (1932), 111–112; Marguerite LeHand to ER, August 23, 1921. On FDR and polio, see especially Ward, *First Class Temperament*, 579–756; Hugh G. Gallagher, *FDR's Splendid Deception* (1985); and Richard T. Goldberg, *The Making of Franklin D. Roosevelt* (1981).
22. Interview with Frances Perkins, May, 1953; ER, *This Is My Story*, 331–332; *PL*, 2:524–525.
23. Robert W. Lovett to George Draper, September 12, 1921, Lovett mss., Harvard Medical School.
24. Interview with Admiral William D. Leahy, May 24, 1948; interviews with ER, May 1, 1948, September 3, 1952.
25. FDR to Bessie G. Norwalk, August 17, 1921; Kathleen Lake to Lovett, March 17, 1922, Lovett mss.
26. Lake to Lovett, December 17, 1921; FDR to G. S. Barrow, December 8, 1921, Lovett mss.
27. Ross T. McIntire, *White House Physician* (1946), 32. Clinical details are in Lovett mss.
28. ER, *This Is My Story*, 339–340.
29. Lake to Lovett, March 17, 1922, May 6, [1922]; Draper to Lovett, March 25, June 9, 1922, Lovett mss.
30. Lake to Lovett, May 6, [1922]; Lovett to FDR, August 14, 1922; FDR to Lovett, September 22, 1922, Lovett mss.

31. Edna T. Rockey to Lovett, November 12, 1922; FDR to Lovett, November 13, 1922, Lovett mss.
32. *PL,* 2:535–536; FDR to Carter Glass, March 27, 1923.
33. FDR to Lovett, April 27, 1923, encl. memorandum, Lovett mss.
34. Lake to Lovett, May 24, 1923, Lovett mss.
35. Tully, *FDR My Boss,* 338–340.
36. *Weona II* log; FDR to Henry Noble MacCracken, March 27, 1923.
37. Looker, *Roosevelt,* 118–119; Donald S. Carmichael, *FDR Columnist* (1947), 9; FDR to Byron Stookey, September 4, 1924. On Warm Springs, see Turnley Walker, *Roosevelt and the Warm Springs Story* (1953), and Theo Lippman, Jr., *The Squire of Warm Springs* (1977).
38. *PPA,* 1934:487–488; FDR to Livingston Davis, April 25, 1925.
39. *PL,* 2:261.
40. *New York Post,* November 7, 1928.
41. Winston S. Churchill, *The Hinge of Fate* (1950), 377. I am indebted to Charles McLaughlin for sharing his insights on FDR's freedom behind the wheel of an automobile. See McLaughlin's remarks in Wilbur J. Cohen, ed., *The New Deal Fifty Years After* (1984), 78–81.

Chapter 4: THE POLITICAL COMEBACK: GOVERNOR OF NEW YORK

1. Herbert Pell to FDR, October 2, 1921.
2. FDR to Caroline O'Day, January 18, 1922.
3. Mrs. Charles Hamlin, "Some Memories of Franklin D. Roosevelt," ms.
4. Frank Freidel, *Roosevelt: The Ordeal* (1954), 235–237.
5. Freidel, *Ordeal,* 160–183: on the Democratic party, see David Burner, *Politics of Provincialism* (1968).
6. FDR to Willard Saulsbury, December 9, 1934.
7. Warren Moscow, *Politics in the Empire State* (1948), 15.
8. *New York Times,* June 28, 1928. On Smith see Oscar Handlin, *Al Smith and His America* (1958).
9. Howe to FDR, telegram, September 25, 1928; *New York Herald Tribune,* October 21, 29, 1928; Ernest K. Lindley, *Franklin D. Roosevelt* (1931), 11; *PL,* 2:646; ER, *This I Remember* (1949), 44–45, 367–368.
10. Howe to FDR, telegram, October 2, 1928; ER to FDR, telegram, October 2, 1928.
11. *New York Post,* October 2, 1928; Lindley, *Roosevelt,* 21.
12. Freidel, *Ordeal,* 261–267.
13. *Los Angeles Times,* November 21, 1928; Rosenman, *Roosevelt,* 26; Edward J. Flynn, *You're the Boss* (1947), 71–72; James A. Farley, *Behind the Ballots* (1938), 53.
14. Rosenman, *Roosevelt,* 16.
15. *PL,* 3:772; interview with Frances Perkins, May, 1953; Perkins, *Roosevelt I Knew,* 51–53.
16. *New York Times,* December 17, 25, 1928; Perkins, *Roosevelt I Knew,* 54–55.
17. FDR to Adolphus Ragan, April 6, 1938, unsent, *PL,* 2:772–773.
18. *New York Times, New York Herald Tribune, New York World,* all of January 2,

1929; State of New York, *Public Papers of . . . Governor* (4 vols., 1930–1939), 1:11–15; *PL,* 3:773.

19. Frank Freidel, *Roosevelt: The Triumph* (1956), 29–34; cf. Bernard Bellush, *Franklin D. Roosevelt as Governor of New York* (1955).
20. Freidel, *Triumph,* 35, 37–41.
21. Freidel, *Triumph,* 43–46, 100–119.
22. Freidel, *Triumph,* 74–75, 123–127, 186–192, 196.
23. Freidel, *Triumph,* 30–31, 60–63, 121–122.
24. Raymond Moley, *After Seven Years* (1939), 2.
25. *PL,* 3:43; *Public Papers of . . . Governor,* 1:745.
26. *New York Times,* April 14, 1929.
27. *New York Times,* June 11, 13, 17, 18, 19, 21, 1929; FDR to William G. Howard, June 21, 1929, FL.
28. Freidel, *Triumph,* 85–87.
29. *New York Times,* January 22, 23, 1930; Perkins, *Roosevelt,* 93–96.
30. *New York Times,* July 1, 6, 1930; a complete transcript appeared in a supplement to the *United States Daily,* July 14, 1930.
31. FDR, message to legislature, March 25, 1931, *Public Papers of . . . Governor,* 3:130.
32. *Public Papers of . . . Governor,* 3:173, 174–180; Jesse Isador Strauss to Herbert Lehman, October 7, 1931, and attached memorandum, GO; Robert Sherwood, *Roosevelt and Hopkins* (1948), 17, 32.
33. TERA, Report, October 15, 1932; TERA, *Five Million People, One Billion Dollars; Final Report . . .* (1937).

Chapter 5: WINNING THE PRESIDENCY

1. Frank Freidel, *Roosevelt: The Triumph* (1956), 141–146. On the 1932 campaign see Freidel, *Triumph;* Elliot A. Rosen, *Hoover, Roosevelt, and the Brains Trust* (1977); and Rexford G. Tugwell, *The Brains Trust* (1968).
2. Stimson diary, October 23, 24, 1930, Stimson mss., YU; *New York Times,* October 26, 28, 29, November 2, 1930; Rosenman, *Roosevelt,* 43–44.
3. Stimson diary, October 28, 1930, Stimson mss.
4. Dr. Edgar W. Beckwith to FDR, October 21, [1930], Howe mss.; *New York Times,* October 18, 19, 1930.
5. Rosenman, *Roosevelt,* 42–43; James A. Farley, *Behind the Ballots* (1938), 54–55; Mary Dewson scrapbook, "Politics, 1932–1933," Dewson mss.
6. State of New York, *Public Papers of . . . Governor* (4 vols., 1930–1939), 3:762; Rosenman, *Roosevelt,* 42.
7. James Malcolm, ed., *New York Red Book 1931* (1931), 393, 404, 406.
8. Farley, *Behind the Ballots,* 62; *New York Times,* November 7, 1930.
9. Freidel, *Triumph,* 170–176.
10. Rosenman, *Roosevelt,* 56–59; Raymond Moley, *After Seven Years* (1939), 6–15; interview with Moley, June 2, 1955.
11. Moley, *After Seven Years,* 20–21.
12. Interview with Rexford G. Tugwell.
13. Freidel, *Triumph,* 255–260.
14. FDR to Arthur Krock, July 3, 1931, *PL,* 3:204–205, 207.

15. Walter Lippmann, *Interpretations, 1931–1932* (Allan Nevins, ed., 1932), 257–259.
16. Lippmann, *Interpretations,* 300, 303–305; "Friends of Al Smith" pamphlets in FDR mss.
17. *Chicago Herald and American,* January 3, 1932; FDR, address before the New York State Grange, February 2, 1932, *Public Papers of . . . Governor,* 4:550–552. Excerpts in *PPA,* 1928–1931:155–157, omit sections on the league and war debts.
18. House to Farley, February 10, 1932, House mss., YU; Mrs. Charles Hamlin to Daniels, March 1, 1932, Daniels mss., LC.
19. FDR to Clark Howell, March 31, 1931, *PL,* 2:186–187.
20. Bernard Bellush, *Franklin D. Roosevelt as Governor of New York* (1955), 270–276; *Public Papers of . . . Governor,* 4:287–293; FDR to House, June 4, 1932, Governor's Personal File, partly in *PL,* 2:281; Lippmann, *Interpretations,* 251.
21. *New York Times,* June 22, 1932.
22. *PPA,* 1928–1932:624–627, 639–647; *New York Times,* April 15, 1932.
23. Freidel, *Triumph,* 276–290.
24. Freidel, *Triumph,* 291–293; Robert Jackson to FDR, April 7, 1932, DNC, New Hampshire.
25. Farley, *Behind the Ballots,* 116–119; *New York Times,* June 25, 27, 28, 1932.
26. Henry L. Mencken, *Making a President* (1932), 105; on the "Stop Roosevelt" movement, see Rosen, *Hoover, Roosevelt, and the Brains Trust,* 26–38, 212–242, 245–251.
27. Freidel, *Triumph,* 304–307.
28. Freidel, *Triumph,* 307–311; Bascom Timmons, *Garner of Texas* (1948), 165–166; interview with Farley, August 7, 1954; interview with Burton K. Wheeler, July 8, 1954.
29. Timmons, *Garner,* 166–167.
30. FDR memorandum, March 25, 1933, speech files, FDR mss.; Rosenman, *Roosevelt,* 77; Moley, *After Seven Years,* 33–34.
31. *PPA,* 1928–1932:647–649.
32. Rosenman, *Roosevelt,* 78.
33. *Proceedings of the Democratic National Convention* (1932), 596–597; Moley, *After Seven Years,* 35; Lela Stiles, *Man Behind Roosevelt* (1954), 166.
34. *PPA,* 1928–1932:674–675.
35. Stimson diary, July 5, 1932, Stimson mss.
36. Theodore Joslin, *Hoover Off the Record* (1934), 330; Claude Bowers to FDR, July 29, 1932; FDR to Bowers, August 1, 1932, DNC, NYC.
37. *New York Times,* July 28, 29, 30, 1932; Roger Daniels, *The Bonus March* (1971).
38. Ickes to FDR, July 8, 1932, GO.
39. Freidel, *Triumph,* 333–336; FDR to Frankfurter, August 24, 1932; interview with Moley, September, 1954; Moley to author, April 4, 1956.
40. Robert W. Bingham to FDR, September 5, 1932, DNC, Kentucky; Farley, *Behind the Ballots,* 172–178; Edward J. Flynn, *You're the Boss* (1947), 106–109.
41. Freidel, *Triumph,* 338–359.
42. Moley, *After Seven Years,* 53; *Brooklyn Eagle,* September 25, 1932.

43. *PPA*, 1928–1932:704–709.
44. *PPA*, 1928–1932:742–756.
45. William Starr Myers, ed., *The State Papers . . . of Herbert Hoover* (2 vols., 1934), 2:451–452.
46. Moley, *After Seven Years*, 65.

Chapter 6: THE INTERREGNUM CRISIS

1. Edmund Wilson in *New Republic* (February 1, 1933), 320; (March 22, 1933), 154; Jane Addams to Mrs. Raymond Robbins, February 20, 1933, Robbins mss., University of Florida.
2. FDR, "The New Deal — an Interpretation," *Liberty* (December 10, 1932), 7–8.
3. 72 Cong., 2 Sess., Senate Finance Committee, *Investigation of Economic Problems* (1933); Frank Freidel, *Roosevelt: Launching the New Deal* (1973), 51–59.
4. Herbert Hoover, "My Personal Relations with Mr. Roosevelt," September 26, 1958, FDR file, Hoover mss., Hoover Library; interview with Hoover, December 28, 1951; interviews with ER.
5. Freidel, *Launching*, 31–45.
6. Stimson diary, January 9, 1933, Stimson mss., YU; *New York Times*, January 18, 1933.
7. Freidel, *Launching*, 46–59.
8. Josiah Bailey to Clarence Poe, January 10, 1933, Bailey mss., Duke University.
9. *PPA*, 1928–1932:627–639.
10. Freidel, *Launching*, 83–101.
11. This version of his remarks is in the original stenographic report, Edgar Nixon, ed., *Roosevelt and Conservation* (2 vols., 1957), 1:133. Cf. *PPA*, 1928–1932:888–889.
12. *Literary Digest*, February 4, 1933; *New York Times*, February 3, 1933.
13. Freidel, *Launching*, 169–174; *New York Times*, February 17, 1933; interview with Moley, October 22, 1958; *Time*, February 27, 1933.
14. Hoover to FDR, February 18, 1933, PSF; William S. Myers and Walter H. Newton, *The Hoover Administration* (1936), 338–341; Moley diary, February 18, 1933, Moley mss., Hoover Institution; Raymond Moley, *After Seven Years* (1939), 140–141. Susan Estabrook Kennedy, *The Banking Crisis of 1933* (1973), is definitive.
15. Thomas W. Lamont to FDR, letter and enclosed memorandum, February 27, 1933, PPF 70; Freidel, *Launching*, 177–188.
16. Hoover to FDR, February 28, 1933; FDR to Hoover, February 20, 28, 1933, with stenographic notes, PSF.
17. *Wall Street Journal*, March 4, 1933; Freidel, *Launching*, 189–195.

Chapter 7: THE HUNDRED DAYS

1. Frank Freidel, *Roosevelt: Launching the New Deal* (1973), 196–202; FDR to Charles Cropley, February 25, 1933; FDR to Hughes, February 25, 1933, PSF (Inauguration 1933). See James E. Sargent, *Roosevelt and the Hundred Days* (1981).
2. *PPA*, 1933:11–16.
3. Interview with ER, July 13, 1954.

4. Anne O'Hare McCormick, *The World at Home* (1956), 132.
5. Interview with ER, July 13, 1954.
6. Freidel, *Launching*, 213–236.
7. Freidel, *Launching*, 237–241.
8. *PPA*, 1933:49–51.
9. Ernest K. Lindley, *Roosevelt Revolution* (1933), 91; Howard McBain to Moley, November 14, 1932, Moley mss., Hoover Institution; *PPA*, 1933:66–67.
10. James F. Byrnes to F. H. Griffin, June 27, 1933, Byrnes mss., Clemson University; Morgenthau diary, June 12, 1933; PC, June 14, 1933, 1:391–392.
11. Freidel, *Launching*, 248–252.
12. Feis to Stimson, March 15, 1933, Feis mss., LC; *New York Times*, March 17, 1933; Raymond Moley, *After Seven Years* (1939), 165.
13. FDR, *On Our Way* (1934), 62.
14. Freidel, *Launching*, 320–326.
15. PC, April 19, 1933, 1:155.
16. *Christian Science Monitor*, May 8, 1933; Moley diary, April 18–19, 1933, Moley mss.; Lindley, *Roosevelt Revolution*, 123.
17. *PPA*, 1933:74.
18. Van L. Perkins, *Crisis in Agriculture* (1969), 36–78; Gilbert C. Fite, *Peek and the Fight for Farm Parity* (1954), 248–249.
19. Ellis W. Hawley, *New Deal and the Problem of Monopoly* (1966), 3–34; Charles F. Roos, *NRA Economic Planning* (1937), 1–54; Irving Bernstein, *New Deal Collective Bargaining Policy* (1950), 29–33; Robert F. Himmelberg, *Origins of the National Recovery Administration* (1976).
20. Hiram Johnson to sons, June 4, 1933, in Robert E. Burke, ed., *Diary Letters of Hiram Johnson* (7 vols., 1983), vol. 5; Freidel, *Launching*, 439–453.
21. Freidel, *Launching*, 454–469.

Chapter 8: A TIGHTROPE FOREIGN POLICY

1. Josephine Young Case and Everett Needham Case, *Owen D. Young and American Enterprise* (1982), 637. Dallek, *Roosevelt and Foreign Policy*, is detailed and authoritative.
2. Frank Freidel, *Roosevelt: Launching the New Deal* (1973), 359–365; James Warburg diary, May 29, 1933, Kennedy Library.
3. J. P. Moffat to Hugh R. Wilson, April 22, 1933, Moffat mss., HU.
4. James A. Farley, *Jim Farley's Story* (1948), 34, 39; Rexford G. Tugwell, diary, January 17 [should be 19], 1933; interview with Herbert Hoover, December 28, 1951. On Japan in 1933, see Dorothy Borg, *The United States and the Far Eastern Crisis of 1933–1938* (1964).
5. Paul Claudel to Paul-Boncour, January 11, 1933, *Documents Diplomatiques Français, 1932–1939* (Paris, 1966), Series I, 2:414–417; Freidel, *Launching*, 21–23, 135–136. On the background of the war debts/reparations problem, Stephen A. Schuker, *American "Reparations" to Germany, 1919–1933* (Princeton Studies in International Finance, No. 61, 1988), is indispensable.
6. Sir Ronald Lindsay to Sir John Simon, January 30, 1933, C 853/1/62, PRO.
7. Theodore Marriner to J. P. Moffat, October 3, 1932, Moffat mss.
8. Andreas Hillgruber, *Germany and Two World Wars* (1981), 57.

9. Freidel, *Launching,* 390–395.
10. Claudel to Paul-Boncour, April 5, 1933, *Documents Diplomatiques Français,* Series I, 3:148–149.
11. *Time,* May 29, 1933; *Documents on German Foreign Policy, 1918–1945* (1957); Series C (4 vols.), 1:447, 451–455.
12. Henry Morgenthau, Jr., diary, May 22, 1933; *FRUS,* 1933, 1:146–151, 156; PC, 1:266; *New York Times,* May 17, 1933.
13. Morgenthau diary, May 9, 1933; *New York Times,* May 18, 1933.
14. Roosevelt to Phillips, June 19, 1933; *FRUS,* 1933, 1:647–649; Raymond Moley, *After Seven Years* (1939), 236; *FDR & FA,* Nixon, ed., 1:248–250.
15. *FRUS,* 1933, 1:658, 660–661, 663.
16. Morgenthau diary, June 30, 1933; Moley diary, June 29, 1933, Moley mss., Hoover Institution; Charles Hurd, *When the New Deal was Young and Gay* (1965), 166–171.
17. *FDR & FA,* Nixon, ed., 1:268–270; British in Berne to Simon, July 7, 1933, W 8354, PRO; Herbert Feis, *1933* (1966), 224–225, 238–240; Moley diary, July 24, 29, 1933; Freidel, *Launching,* 470–489.
18. Feis, *1933,* 255; Moley diary, July 14, 1934, Moley mss.; George Harrison, telephone call to Montagu Norman, July 14, 1933, Harrison mss., Columbia University; Morgenthau diary, December 13, 1944.
19. D'Arcy Osborne to Sir Robert Vansittart, August 27, 1933, with comments, A 6330/252-45, PRO.

Chapter 9: INSTALLING THE NEW DEAL PROGRAMS

1. *PPA,* 1933:164.
2. PC, August 9, 1933, 2:159; January 15, 1934, 3:68.
3. *PPA,* 1933:165.
4. On appointments, see Frank Freidel, *Roosevelt: Launching the New Deal* (1973), 137–160; Peter H. Irons, *New Deal Lawyers* (1982); James A. Farley, *Behind the Ballots* (1938).
5. Susan Ware, *Beyond Suffrage: Women in the New Deal* (1981); Ware, *Partner and I: Molly Dewson* (1987).
6. Frank Freidel, "Hoover and Roosevelt and Historical Continuity," in Arthur S. Link, ed., *Herbert Hoover Reassessed* (1980), 279–290.
7. Martin Fausold, *Presidency of Herbert Hoover* (1985), 240.
8. Freidel, *Launching,* 267–298; J. P. Moffat diary, March 28, 1933, Moffat mss., HU.
9. Lester G. Seligman and Elmer E. Cornwell, Jr., eds., *New Deal Mosaic . . . National Security Council* (1965), 2.
10. PC, July 21, 1933, 2:75.
11. *PPA,* 1933:358–359.
12. *PL,* 2:358.
13. *PPA,* 1933:341. On the NRA and related programs, see Ellis Hawley, *New Deal and the Problem of Monopoly* (1966); Bernard Bellush, *Failure of the NRA* (1975); Louis Galambos, *Competition and Cooperation* (1966); and Theda Skocpol and Kenneth Finegold, "State Capacity and Economic Intervention in the Early New Deal," *Political Science Quarterly* (1982), 97:255–278.
14. *PPA,* 1933:302.

15. Ickes, *Secret Diary,* 1:110 et passim.
16. *PPA,* 1933:341.
17. *PL,* 2:395.

Chapter 10: THE FAILURE OF BOOTSTRAP RECOVERY

1. PC, 1:80–85, 251–253.
2. See Van L. Perkins, *Crisis in Agriculture* (1969).
3. PC, 2:282.
4. PC, 2:279–280.
5. Blum, *Morgenthau Diaries,* 1:59 et seq.
6. Blum, *Morgenthau Diaries,* 1:61–77.
7. *PL,* 2:371–373.
8. See Bonnie Fox Schwartz, *Civil Works Administration* (1984).
9. Lester G. Seligman and Elmer E. Cornwell, Jr., eds., *New Deal Mosaic . . . National Security Council* (1965), 165, 169; PC, 3:178.
10. Seligman and Cornwell, eds., *New Deal Mosaic,* 168.
11. PC, 3:295–297; cf. PC, 3:371–373.
12. PC, 3:372, 4:45–46.
13. PC, 2:538.
14. Allan S. Everest, *Morgenthau, the New Deal and Silver* (1950).
15. *PPA,* 1934:141–142; Ralph F. de Bedts, *The New Deal's S.E.C.* (1964); Michael E. Parrish, *Securities Regulation and the New Deal* (1970).
16. *PL,* 2:401; *PPA,* 1934:290–291, 312 et seq.
17. *PL,* 2:417; George Wolfskill, *Revolt of the Conservatives* (1962).
18. Alan Brinkley, *Voices of Protest* (1982).
19. *PPA,* 1934:21–22.
20. Sherwood, *Roosevelt and Hopkins,* 65.

Chapter 11: A NEW DEAL FOR THE DISPOSSESSED

1. A caustic account, based on a Harvard case study, is Dwight Macdonald, *Henry Wallace* (1948).
2. Arthur M. Schlesinger, Jr., *The Coming of the New Deal* (*Age of Roosevelt,* vol. 2, 1959), 378; PC, 4:46–47.
3. Abraham Holtzman, *Townsend Movement* (1963).
4. Alan Brinkley, *Voices of Protest* (1982), 82–142.
5. James A. Farley, *Behind the Ballots* (1938), 240–242; interviews with Frances Perkins. On Long see also T. Harry Williams, *Huey Long* (1969).
6. On the poll, see James A. Farley, *Jim Farley's Story* (1948), 51; on the threat from the left, David H. Bennett, *Demagogues in the Depression* (1969).
7. Lester G. Seligman and Elmer E. Cornwell, Jr., eds., *New Deal Mosaic . . . National Security Council* (1965), 359, 387.
8. Michael E. Parrish, *Securities Regulation and the New Deal* (1970), 145–155.
9. Tugwell diary, November 22, 1934; Ickes, *Secret Diary,* 1:194; Bell memorandum, October 10, 1934, in Morgenthau diary.
10. Bell memorandum, October 1, 1934, in Morgenthau diary.

11. Bell memoranda, October 1, 10, 1934, in Morgenthau diary; Blum, *Morgenthau Diaries,* 1:235–240.
12. Bell memorandum, October 1, 1934, in Morgenthau diary, December 10, 11, 1934; Ickes, *Secret Diary,* 1:256; Federal Emergency Administration of Public Works, "Proposed National Construction Program . . . ," November 30, 1934, in Morgenthau diary.
13. Ickes, *Secret Diary,* 1:256; Morgenthau diary, December 3, 1934.
14. Edwin Witte, *Development of the Social Security Act* (1962), 18, 45, 66; PC, 5:84. See also J. Douglas Brown, *Genesis of Social Security in America* (1969).
15. Luther Gulick, Memorandum on Conference with FDR concerning Social Security Taxation, Summer, 1941, FDR Memorial Foundation mss.
16. *PPA,* 1935:19–20.
17. *PPA,* 1935:98–99.
18. FDR to Arthur Pierce Butler, March 14, 1935, PPF, 2312.

Chapter 12: A LOW-KEY INTERLUDE

1. See, for example, James T. Patterson, *New Deal and the States* (1969), and Lyle W. Dorsett, *Roosevelt and the City Bosses* (1977).
2. *PL,* 2:466–467.
3. Dallek, *Roosevelt and Foreign Policy,* 95–97.
4. Ickes, *Secret Diary,* 1:255–260, 274–276 et passim.
5. Lester G. Seligman and Elmer E. Cornwell, Jr., eds., *New Deal Mosaic . . . National Security Council* (1965), 450, 459–460.
6. FDR to Josephus Daniels, March 1, 1935, Daniels mss., LC.
7. See J. Joseph Huthmacher, *Senator Robert F. Wagner and Urban Liberalism* (1968).
8. See Martha H. Swain, *Pat Harrison* (1978).
9. *PPA,* 1935:138.
10. PC, 5:189. For a new interpretation see Stanley Vittoz, *New Deal Labor Policy* (1987).
11. PC, 5:266; *Time,* May 13, 1935; George Norris to Ben V. Stephens, May 20, 1935, Norris mss., LC.
12. PC, 5:944. On Norris, Richard Lowitt, *George W. Norris* (2 vols., 1963–1971), is definitive.
13. PC, 5:299.
14. Irving Bernstein, *New Deal Collective Bargaining Policy* (1950), and Bernstein, *Turbulent Years* (1969).

Chapter 13: THE FIGHT FOR THE REFORM PROGRAM

1. Frank Freidel, "The Sick Chicken Case," in John A. Garraty, ed., *Quarrels That Have Shaped the Constitution* (1964), 191–209.
2. Box 22, Frankfurter mss., LC.
3. PC, 5:305–306.
4. PC, 5:309–337.
5. *PPA,* 1935:274; Freidel, "Sick Chicken Case," 191–209.
6. *Literary Digest* (June 29, 1935), 3–4.
7. T. Harry Williams, *Huey Long* (1969), 812, 836, 837.

8. *Today* (July 6, 1935), 19.
9. Raymond Moley, *After Seven Years* (1939), 310; *Today* (July 6, 1935), 19.
10. *Literary Digest*, August 10, 1935; *Time*, June 24, 1935.
11. Blum, *Morgenthau Diaries*, 1:343–354.
12. *Literary Digest*, June 29, 1935.
13. PC, 5:379–380, 390–391.
14. *Time*, August 12, 1935.
15. *Literary Digest*, July 13, 1935.
16. James T. Patterson, *Congressional Conservatism and the New Deal* (1967), 52; Frankfurter to FDR, undated, PSF 6.
17. PC, 6:32–33.
18. *PPA*, 1935:328–329.
19. Edward F. Taylor to William B. Bankhead, August 31, 1935, Bankhead mss., Alabama Archives; *Literary Digest*, August 31, 1935.
20. *PPA*, 1935:325.

Chapter 14: SEEKING SECURITY SHORT OF WAR

1. Raymond Moley, *First New Deal* (1966), 393–402, 411–419; Herbert Feis, *1933* (1966), 132–152; Frederick W. Leith-Ross, *Money Talks* (1968), 160–177.
2. On the recognition of Russia and its aftermath, see Robert P. Browder, *The Origins of Soviet-American Diplomacy* (1953); Edward M. Bennett, *Recognition of Russia* (1970); Beatrice Farnsworth, *Bullitt and the Soviet Union* (1967); and Donald G. Bishop, *Roosevelt-Litvinov Agreements* (1965).
3. Stimson diary, November 9, 1932, Stimson mss., YU.
4. Browder, *Soviet-American Diplomacy*, 99–108; Farnsworth, *Bullitt*, 89–94; Bennett, *Recognition of Russia*, 87–104.
5. Adam Ulam, *Stalin* (1973), 363–364.
6. Farnsworth, *Bullitt*, 32–70.
7. Phillips diary, November 6, 9, 10, 1933, Phillips mss., HU.
8. James A. Farley, *Jim Farley's Story* (1948), 43–44; Phillips diary, November 11, 1933, Philips mss.
9. Robert I. Gannon, *Cardinal Spellman Story* (1962), 156–157, 425; see also Farley, *Story*, 43–44, and Perkins, *Roosevelt I Knew*, 143.
10. Bennett, *Recognition of Russia*, 127.
11. Orville H. Bullitt, ed., *For the President . . . Correspondence Between Roosevelt and Bullitt* (1972), 63–64.
12. Bullitt, *Correspondence*, 67, 69.
13. Bishop, *Roosevelt-Litvinov Agreements*, 231.
14. *FDR & FA*, Nixon, ed., 2:493; Bullitt, *Correspondence*, 113; *PL*, 2:476.
15. Bullitt, *Correspondence*, 157, 160, 163, 167; Dallek, *Roosevelt and Foreign Policy*, 144–145.
16. George F. Kennan, *Memoirs* (1967), 49–60; Charles Bohlen, *Witness to History* (1973), 23–24, 32–36.
17. W. P. Crozier, *Off the Record* (London, 1973), 4–5.
18. John Campbell White to Moffatt, November 27, 1933, Moffatt mss., HU;

Documents Diplomatiques Français, 1932–1939 (Paris, 1966), Series I, 3:496–497.

19. PC, 4:59–61.
20. On comparisons between the New Deal and Hitler's domestic program, see John A. Garraty, "The New Deal, National Socialism, and the Great Depression," *American Historical Review* (October, 1973), 78:907–944, and Garraty, *The Great Depression* (1986), 182–211.
21. Gerhard L. Weinberg, *Foreign Policy of Hitler's Germany: Diplomatic Revolution in Europe 1933–1936* (1970), 143–144; Weinberg, "Hitler's Image of the United States," *American Historical Review* (July, 1964), 69:1006–1012; Andreas Hillgruber, *Germany and the Two World Wars* (1981), 49–50; *FDR & FA*, Nixon, ed., 2:27–28.
22. Interview with Herbert Hoover, December 28, 1951; Frank Freidel, *Roosevelt: Launching the New Deal* (1973), 457.
23. Douglas MacArthur, *Reminiscences* (1964), 101.
24. *FDR & FA*, Nixon, ed., 1:595, 610, 641, 654–658.
25. Akira Iriye, *Across the Pacific: An Inner History of American–East Asian Relations* (1967), 176–177, 181–182; Charles E. Neu, *Troubled Encounter: United States and Japan* (1975), 142–145.
26. FDR to Daniels, October 3, 1934, Daniels mss., LC; Robert Divine, *Illusion of Neutrality* (1962), 69–73.
27. Divine, *Illusion of Neutrality*, 83.
28. *FDR & FA*, Nixon, ed., 2:381.
29. Divine, *Illusion of Neutrality*, 86–87; *FRUS*, 1935, 1:363–364, 370–371; *FDR & FA*, Nixon, ed., 2:608.
30. *PPA*, 1935:410–411, 412–418.
31. *PL*, 2:472–473.
32. *FDR & FA*, Nixon, ed., 2:488–489; Phillips diary, March 22, 1935, Phillips mss.

Chapter 15: THREATS FROM LEFT AND RIGHT

1. Alan Brinkley, *Voices of Protest* (1982), 80–81.
2. *Gallup Poll* contains findings of all Gallup polls, 1935–1971; see 1:2.
3. Morgenthau diary, December 2, 1935.
4. Morgenthau diary, September 6, 1935.
5. Morgenthau diary, September 13, 1935; *PPA*, 1935:358; Brinkley, *Voices of Protest*, 628.
6. Ickes, *Secret Diary*, 1:433; *Time*, September 23, 1935.
7. Ickes, *Secret Diary*, 1:422.
8. *PL*, 2:537–538.
9. Rosenman, *Roosevelt*, 132.
10. Bruce M. Stave, "Pittsburgh and the New Deal," in John Braeman et al., eds., *The New Deal* (2 vols., 1975), 2:391–393; *Gallup Poll*, 1:18–19.
11. *Time*, October 7, 1935; Ickes, *Secret Diary*, 1:444; *PPA*, 1935:379–381.
12. *PPA*, 1935:400–401.
13. *Time*, October 7, 1935. On the CCC, see Frank Freidel, *Roosevelt: Launching*

the New Deal (1973), 259–266; John A. Salmond, *The Civilian Conservation Corps* (1967).

14. J. F. T. O'Connor diary, O'Connor mss., University of California.
15. *PPA*, 1935:412–415.
16. *Time*, October 14, 1935.
17. Bell memorandum, September 12, 1935, Morgenthau diary.
18. PC, 7:6–12.
19. *Time*, January 13, 1936.
20. *PPA*, 1935:437; PC, 7:84.
21. *PPA*, 1936:67; *Time*, February 3, 1936.
22. PC, 7:165–175. On tax policy, see Mark Leff, *Limits of Symbolic Reform: New Deal and Taxation 1933–1939* (1984).
23. PC, 7:280; *Time*, February 23, 1936.
24. Early to Block, December 13, 1935; Block to Early, December 18, 1935, PPF 3069.

Chapter 16: THE PEOPLE APPROVE

1. *PPA*, 1936:12–14; *Time*, January 13, 1936.
2. *PPA*, 1936:63; *Time*, January 27, 1936.
3. *Time*, February 2, 1936.
4. Morgenthau diary, February 6, 1936; *Time*, January 6, 27, 1936.
5. John Keller and Joe Bolt, "Franklin's On His Own Now," *Saturday Evening Post* (October 12, 1940), 134; James A. Farley, *Jim Farley's Story* (1948), 61; *Time*, April 27, 1936; *Today*, May 9, 1936.
6. Tully, *FDR My Boss*, 201.
7. Farley, *Story*, 61–62.
8. *PPA*, 1936:194–222; *Time*, June 22, 1936.
9. *Time*, June 22, 1936.
10. Donald R. McCoy, *Landon of Kansas* (1966).
11. Arthur Krock, column of April 10, 1936, *In the Nation* (1966), 36.
12. Rosenman, *Roosevelt*, 103–105.
13. Conversation with Moley.
14. Tully, *FDR My Boss*, 202; Michael F. Reilly and William J. Slocum, *Reilly of the White House* (1947), 99–100; James Roosevelt and Sidney Shalett, *Affectionately, F.D.R.* (1959), 157, 158; Raymond Clapper notes, July 29, 1936, Clapper mss., LC.
15. *PPA*, 1936:230–236; Raymond Moley, *After Seven Years* (1939), 344–345.
16. Interview with Alf M. Landon, June 21, 1954.
17. William E. Leuchtenburg, "Election of 1936," in Arthur M. Schlesinger, Jr., and Fred L. Israel, eds., *History of American Presidential Elections* (4 vols., 1971), 3:2832–2833.
18. *PPA*, 1936:288–289; Clapper notes, August 3, 1936, Clapper mss.
19. Rosenman, *Roosevelt*, 110–111; *Time*, October 12, 1936.
20. Clapper notes, October 27, 1936, Clapper mss.
21. Interview with Landon, June 21, 1954.
22. *PPA*, 1936:362–363.

23. *PPA,* 1936:568–569.
24. Rosenman, *Roosevelt,* 137–138.
25. *PL,* 2:626.

Chapter 17: THE GOOD NEIGHBOR PROMOTES HEMISPHERIC DEFENSE

1. See Irwin F. Gellman, *Good Neighbor Diplomacy* (1979); Bryce Wood, *Making of the Good Neighbor Policy* (1961); E. O. Guerrant, *Roosevelt's Good Neighbor Policy* (1950).
2. *FDR & FA,* Nixon, ed., 3:230–232.
3. *FDR & FA,* Nixon, ed., 3:198–199.
4. *FDR & FA,* Nixon, ed., 3:233, 238.
5. *PPA,* 1933:14.
6. *PPA,* 1933:129–132; Wood, *Good Neighbor,* 124.
7. Irwin F. Gellman, *Roosevelt and Batista* (1973); Gellman, *Good Neighbor,* 17, 35.
8. Gellman, *Good Neighbor,* 22–26; *FDR & FA,* Schewe, ed., documents #218, #689.
9. Gellman, *Good Neighbor,* 47–48; Francis B. Sayre, *Way Forward* (1939); George N. Peek, *Why Quit Our Own?* (1936).
10. *PL,* 2:625; Ickes, *Secret Diary,* 2:7.
11. *PL,* 2:632.
12. *PL,* 2:634–635.
13. Beatrice B. Berle and Travis B. Jacobs, eds., *Navigating the Rapids, From the Papers of . . . Berle* (1973), 119–120.
14. *PPA,* 1936:607.
15. *Time,* December 14, 1936.
16. *Time,* December 14, 1936; *PL,* 2:635–637.
17. J. Manuel Espinosa, *Inter-American Beginnings of U. S. Cultural Diplomacy, 1936–1938* (1976), 170, 303.
18. *PPA,* 1943:405–406.

Chapter 18: THE STRUGGLE TO TRANSFORM THE SUPREME COURT

1. Morgenthau diary, April 20, 1936; Charles W. Eliot II, Notes re Conference with the President, February 20, 1936, Ickes file, NRPB, Record Group 48, NARA.
2. Ickes, *Secret Diary,* 2:15, 63.
3. Ickes, *Secret Diary,* 2:8.
4. Clapper notes, November 16, 1936, Clapper mss., LC.
5. Ickes, *Secret Diary,* 2:14.
6. PC, 9:217.
7. PC, 8:208–209.
8. *PPA,* 1937:4–5.
9. *Time,* February 1, 1937; PC, 9:99.
10. Rosenman, *Roosevelt,* 144.

11. Memorandum of conversation with Roosevelt, December 2, 1935, George Fort Milton mss., LC.
12. Barry Karl, *Executive Reorganization and Reform in the New Deal* (1963), 192.
13. Joseph Alsop and Turner Catledge, *The 168 Days* (1938), 20, 27–32; PC, 9:164. This account follows the reporting in Alsop and Catledge, *168 Days*, and *Time*. On the issues, see William E. Leuchtenburg, "Franklin D. Roosevelt's Supreme Court 'Packing' Plan," in Harold Hollingsworth and William Holmes, eds., *Essays on the New Deal* (1969); Paul L. Murphy, *The Constitution in Crisis Times* (1972), 128–169; and Robert H. Jackson, *The Struggle for Judicial Supremacy* (1949).
14. Alsop and Catledge, *168 Days*, 35–36.
15. Rosenman, *Roosevelt*, 147; interview with ER.
16. *PPA*, 1937:55; Alsop and Catledge, *168 Days*, 66–67.
17. *Time*, February 15, 22, 1937; Alsop and Catledge, *168 Days*, 68–78.
18. *PPA*, 1937:120, 123; Alsop and Catledge, *168 Days*, 88–111.
19. Burton K. Wheeler, *Yankee from the West* (1962), 325.
20. Alsop and Catledge, *168 Days*, 106–134.
21. Alsop and Catledge, *168 Days*, 135–174.
22. PC, 1937:260–263.
23. Alsop and Catledge, *168 Days*, 153.
24. Alsop and Catledge, *168 Days*, 155–156, 159–160.
25. Alsop and Catledge, *168 Days*, 204.
26. Alsop and Catledge, *168 Days*, 205–214.
27. *PL*, 2:685–686.
28. Alsop and Catledge, *168 Days*, 216–267.
29. *PPA*, 1937:305–308; Martha H. Swain, *Pat Harrison* (1978), 158–163.
30. Alsop and Catledge, *168 Days*, 279, 283, 294.
31. Alsop and Catledge, *168 Days*, 308–312.
32. Interview with Thomas Corcoran.
33. Anne O'Hare McCormick, *World at Home* (1956), 303.

Chapter 19: NEW DEALER WITH BRAKES ON

1. PC, 9:270, 363.
2. *PPA*, 1937:329.
3. Josiah Bailey to Joseph O'Mahoney, August 22, 1937, O'Mahoney mss., University of Wyoming.
4. Martha H. Swain, *Pat Harrison* (1978), 163.
5. *Time*, April 19, 1937.
6. Irving Bernstein, *Turbulent Years* (1969), 536–551.
7. *PL*, 2:1078.
8. *Time*, April 12, 1937.
9. *Time*, August 2, 1937.
10. PC, 9:467.
11. *New York Times*, September 4, 1937.
12. Frank Freidel, *Roosevelt: The Ordeal* (1954), 30.

13. George Marvin, "Notes on Franklin D. Roosevelt as Assistant Secretary of the Navy," [1946].
14. Frank Freidel, *F.D.R. and the South* (1965), 68–69, 81–82; PC, 9:284–285. On blacks in the FDR years, see Nancy Weiss, *Farewell to the Party of Lincoln* (1983); Harvard Sitkoff, *A New Deal for Blacks* (1978); and Bernard Sternsher, ed., *The Negro in Depression and War* (1969).
15. Freidel, *F.D.R. and the South*, 68–69.
16. Walter White, *A Man Called White* (1948), 169.
17. Freidel, *F.D.R. and the South*, 87.
18. Sitkoff, *New Deal for Blacks*, 290–295.
19. PC, 11:245–246.
20. Blum, *Morgenthau Diaries*, 1:276–282.
21. *PL*, 2:653.
22. PC, 9:239–242.
23. Anne O'Hare McCormick, *World at Home* (1956), 306–307; Ickes, *Secret Diary*, 2:144.
24. Ickes, *Secret Diary*, 2:185, 189; PC, 10:64–65.
25. PC, 9:241–244, 253; 10:382, 385, 438–441; Blum, *Morgenthau Diaries*, 1:360.
26. Jordan A. Schwarz, *Liberal: Adolf A. Berle* (1987), 110–113; Blum, *Morgenthau Diaries*, 1:380–432; Bernard Sternsher, *Tugwell and the New Deal* (1964), 322.
27. Sidney Hyman, *Marriner S. Eccles* (1976), 240–241. See especially Dean May, *From New Deal to New Economics* (1982).
28. Beatrice B. Berle and Travis B. Jacobs, eds., *Navigating the Rapids, From the Papers of . . . Berle* (1973), 154–161.
29. Berle and Jacobs, eds., *Navigating the Rapids*, 163–168.
30. Blum, *Morgenthau Diaries*, 1:411.
31. *PPA*, 1938:166–167; *Time*, March 28, April 4, 18, 1938; PC, 11:284.
32. Joseph Alsop and Robert Kintner, *Men Around the President* (1939), 148–150; *Time*, May 2, 1938.
33. James MacGregor Burns, *Roosevelt: The Lion and the Fox* (1956), 328.
34. Perkins, *Roosevelt I Knew*, 225–226; Herbert Stein, *The Fiscal Revolution in America* (1969), 117.
35. PC, 11:136.
36. *PPA*, 1938:221, 243–244.
37. E. W. Hawley, *New Deal and Problem of Monopoly* (1966), 404–494.
38. Jerre Mangione, *An Ethnic at Large* (1978), 247.

Chapter 20: QUARANTINE OR APPEASEMENT

1. See David Reynolds, *Creation of the Anglo-American Alliance 1937–1941* (1982), 1–9 and notes.
2. See essays by Franklin Ford and Felix Gilbert in Gordon Craig and Felix Gilbert, eds., *The Diplomats, 1919–1939* (1953), 437–476, 537–554, 555–578.
3. Neville Chamberlain to Ida Chamberlain, October 28, 1933, Chamberlain mss., Birmingham University. I am indebted to Stephen Schuker for this and the following quotation.
4. Neville Chamberlain to Ida Chamberlain, February 6, 1937, Chamberlain mss.

5. M. Ruth Megaw, "The Scramble for the Pacific: Anglo–United States Rivalry in the 1930's," *Historical Studies* (October, 1977), 17:458–473.
6. Jeffery M. Dorwart, "The Roosevelt-Astor Espionage Ring," *New York History* (July, 1981), 312–314.
7. *FDR & FA*, Nixon, ed., 3:203, 294–295.
8. Reynolds, *Anglo-American Alliance*, 13–16.
9. *FDR & FA*, Schewe, ed., 1937, #349.
10. *Time*, September 20, 27, October 4, 11, 1937.
11. Ickes, *Secret Diary*, 2:211, 213.
12. Rosenman, *Roosevelt*, 164.
13. *PPA*, 1937:406–411.
14. Kenneth Hechler in *Washington Post*, September 29, 1957; *Newsweek*, October 25, 1937; *Life*, October 18, 1937; John M. Haight, "Roosevelt and the Aftermath of the Quarantine Speech," *Review of Politics* (April, 1962), 24:233–259; Dorothy Borg, "Roosevelt's 'Quarantine Speech,' " *Political Science Quarterly* (1957), 72:405. The classic overall study is Borg, *The United States and the Far Eastern Crisis of 1933–1938* (1964).
15. PRO, CAB 23/89 9110, pp. 255–256; *FDR & FA*, Schewe, ed., 1937, #535; *Newsweek*, October 18, 1937; *Life*, October 18, 1937; *FRUS*, 1937, 4:87–88, 120.
16. Moffat diary, October 5, 1937, HU; Haight, "Quarantine Speech," 24:239–240.
17. PC, 10:248–249.
18. Moffat diary, October 8, 1937.
19. Moffat diary, October 8–10, 1937.
20. Norman Davis mss., cited in Borg, *Far Eastern Crisis*, 406.
21. PRO, CAB 23/89 9110, p. 297.
22. *FRUS*, 1937, 4:170; *Documents Diplomatiques Français, 1932–1939* (Paris, 1966), Series II (1936–1939), 3:355–356; Borg, *Far Eastern Crisis*, 635.
23. *FRUS*, 1937, 4:173; Borg, *Far Eastern Crisis*, 421.
24. *FDR & FA*, Schewe, ed., 1937, #599, #599a, #607; Waldo Heinrichs, "The Role of the U.S. Navy," in Dorothy Borg and Shumpei Okamoto, eds., *Pearl Harbor as History* (1973), 212–213.
25. Moffat diary, November 18, 1937; Borg, *Far Eastern Crisis*, 439.
26. Richard P. Traina, *American Diplomacy and the Spanish Civil War* (1968), is the prime source for this section. See also F. Jay Taylor, *The United States and the Spanish Civil War* (1956), and Stanley Weintraub, *The Last Great Cause: The Intellectuals and the Spanish Civil War* (1968).
27. George Q. Flynn, *American Catholics and the Roosevelt Presidency* (1968), 227–228, 231–234.
28. Traina, *Spanish Civil War*, 86–92.
29. Ickes, *Secret Diary*, 2:388; Wayne S. Cole, *Roosevelt and the Isolationists* (1983), 235–237.
30. *FDR & FA*, Schewe, ed., 1938, #1166; Orville H. Bullitt, ed., *For the President: Correspondence between Roosevelt and Bullitt* (1972), 274–276; Traina, *Spanish Civil War*, 279.

Chapter 21: ADMINISTRATIVE REFORM AND ATTEMPTED PARTY PURGE

1. Harold Brayman, *From Grover Cleveland to Gerald Ford . . . The President Speaks Off the Record* (1976), 326.
2. See Barry Karl, *Executive Reorganization and Reform in the New Deal* (1963), and Richard Polenberg, *Reorganizing Roosevelt's Government* (1966). For the proposals, see The President's Committee on Administrative Management, *Report* (1937).
3. PC, 11:323–324.
4. PC, 11:303.
5. *PPA*, 1936:668–681; Herbert Emmerich memorandum, January 10, 1937, Merriam mss., University of Chicago.
6. *Time*, March 28, 1938.
7. PC, 11:302–303.
8. Polenberg, *Reorganizing*, 49–51.
9. Polenberg, *Reorganizing*, 144–145; *Time*, April 4, 1938.
10. PC, 11:259–260; Polenberg, *Reorganizing*, 138–159; *Time*, April 18, 1938.
11. *PPA*, 1938:181, 191–192. For a full postmortem, see Polenberg, *Reorganizing*, 162–180.
12. James A. Farley, *Jim Farley's Story* (1948), 129.
13. Hiram Johnson to Hiram Johnson, Jr., March 19, 1938, Robert E. Burke, ed., *Diary Letters of Hiram Johnson* (7 vols., 1983), vol. 6; David L. Porter, *Congress and the Waning of the New Deal* (1980), 89–108; Polenberg, *Reorganizing*, 184–187.
14. Blair Moody, "Mr. Smith Doubles for Roosevelt," *Saturday Evening Post* (March 27, 1943), 24, 56.
15. Harold Smith diary, April 23, 1939.
16. Louis Brownlow, *A Passion for Anonymity* (2 vols., 1958), 2:415–416; Polenberg, *Reorganizing*, 187–188.
17. Smith diary, January 24, 1940.
18. William Allen White to Judson King, March 24, 1942, White mss., LC.
19. Smith diary, May 12, June 16, 1939; *Washington Post*, January 27, 1982.
20. Richard Neustadt, *Presidential Power* (1960), 160.
21. Claude Pepper to author, March 2, 1982.
22. George B. Tindall, *Emergence of the New South, 1913–1945* (1967), 534; see pp. 545–649 on the New Deal. PC, 11:340.
23. Tindall, *New South*, 535–537; William E. Leuchtenburg, *Roosevelt and the New Deal* (1963), 262–263.
24. *PPA*, 1938:398–399; Martha H. Swain, *Harrison* (1978), 175–183.
25. Porter, *Congress and the Waning of the New Deal*, 138–140; Ronald L. Feinman, *Twilight of Progressivism: Western Republican Senators and the New Deal* (1981), 136–156; Ronald A. Mulder, *Insurgent Progressives in the United States Senate and the New Deal* (1979), 273–279, 311–313.
26. United States National Emergency Council, *Report on Economic Conditions of the South* (1938), 1–2, 8; Tindall, *New South*, 575–599.
27. *PPA*, 1938:167–168.

28. Ralph J. Bunche, *The Political Status of the Negro in the Age of FDR* (Dewey W. Grantham, ed., 1973), 206.
29. Tindall, *New South*, 626, 639–640.
30. Harry F. Byrd to Hiram Johnson, August 18, 1938, Johnson mss., University of California, Berkeley; Marvin Cann, "Burnet Maybank and Charleston Politics in the New Deal Era," South Carolina Historical Association, *Proceedings* (1970), 39–48.
31. Farley, *Story*, 120–121; Virginia V. Hamilton, "The True-blue Democratic," *American Heritage* (August, 1971), 42.
32. Interview with Thomas Corcoran, October 20, 1957.
33. Farley, *Story*, 143–144.
34. Polly Davis, *Alben W. Barkley* (1979), 53–71.
35. Thomas L. Stokes, *Chip Off My Shoulder* (1940), 517–518; Sherwood, *Roosevelt and Hopkins*, 102–103; Arthur Krock, *Memoirs* (1968), 216–217.
36. *PPA*, 1938:463–471; *Time*, August 22, 1938.
37. Luther H. Zeigler, Jr., "Senator Walter George's 1938 Campaign," *Georgia Historical Quarterly* (1959), 333–352; Jasper B. Shannon, "Presidential Politics, II," *Journal of Politics* (1939), 1:286–352.
38. Interview with Thomas Corcoran, October 20, 1957; William Bankhead to Sam Rayburn, September 29, 1938; Rayburn to Bankhead, October 3, 1938, Bankhead mss., Alabama Archives; Richard Polenberg, "Franklin Roosevelt and the Purge of John J. O'Connor . . . ," *New York History* (July, 1968), 306–326.
39. Shannon, "Presidential Politics, II," 1:295–297.
40. James T. Patterson, "The Failure of Party Realignment in the South, 1937–1939," *Journal of Politics* (August, 1965), 27:612.
41. *PPA*, 1936:484.
42. Leuchtenburg, *Roosevelt and the New Deal*, 270.

Chapter 22: A POWERLESS WITNESS TO MUNICH

1. *FDR & FA*, Schewe, ed., 1937, #774; see *Gallup Poll*, 1:71.
2. *FDR & FA*, Schewe, ed., 1937, #604.
3. *FDR & FA*, Schewe, ed., 1937, #654.
4. *FDR & FA*, Schewe, ed., 1937, #682, #703a.
5. Wayne S. Cole in Dorothy Borg and Shumpei Okamoto, eds., *Pearl Harbor as History* (1973), 314–315.
6. *FDR & FA*, Schewe, ed., 1937, #607; Dallek, *Roosevelt and Foreign Policy*, 153–155; PC, 10:409; *PPA*, 1942:541–542; Waldo Heinrichs in Borg and Okamoto, eds., *Pearl Harbor as History*, 119–120.
7. Blum, *Morgenthau Diaries*, 1:489.
8. Dallek, *Roosevelt and Foreign Policy*, 154–155; Ickes, *Secret Diary*, 2:273–275; Stephen Pelz, *Race to Pearl Harbor* (1974), 200.
9. Akira Iriye in Borg and Okamoto, eds., *Pearl Harbor as History*, 213–214; Iriye, *Across the Pacific* (1967), 195.
10. Waldo Heinrichs in Borg and Okamoto, eds., *Pearl Harbor as History*, 213–214; James R. Leutze, *Bargaining for Supremacy: Anglo-American Naval Collaboration, 1937–1941* (1977), 21–28; David Reynolds, *Creation of the Anglo-American Alliance* (1982), 60; *PPA*, 1938:70–71; *New York Times*, March 8, 1938, in Keith D. Eagles, *Ambassador Joseph E. Davies* (1985), 282.

11. Presumably FDR was quoting from Evans F. Carlson to LeHand, December 24, 1937; see *FDR & FA*, Schewe, ed., 1937, #885; Ickes, *Secret Diary*, 2: 279, 296, 302, 327.
12. Lindsay to Eden, January 11, 1938, FO 371-21526 8342, PRO.
13. Reynolds, *Anglo-American Alliance*, 19–20; Eden to Lindsay, January 13, 1938, FO 371-21526 8342, PRO; *FDR & FA*, Schewe, ed., 1938, #899a.
14. On developments leading to the Munich agreement, see Arnold A. Offner, *American Appeasement, 1933–1938* (1969); Gerhard L. Weinberg, *Foreign Policy of Hitler's Germany, 1937–1939* (1980); and James V. Compton, *The Swastika and the Eagle* (1967).
15. David Wyman, *Paper Walls* (1968), is the basis for this section. See also Henry L. Feingold, *Politics of Rescue* (1970), and Barbara McDonald Stewart, *United States Government Policy on Refugees from Nazism, 1933–1940* (1982).
16. David O. Levine, *The American College and the Culture of Aspiration* (1986), ch. 7; Marcia G. Synott, *The Half-Opened Door* (1979), 92, 107, 110, 202.
17. Morgenthau diary, November 26, 1941.
18. PC, 11:249–250; Wyman, *Paper Walls*, 46–47.
19. Wyman, *Paper Walls*, 209.
20. Wyman, *Paper Walls*, 6, 49–50, 61–62; *PPA*, 1938:169; *FDR & FA*, Schewe, ed., 1938, #1005, #1005a.
21. Wyman, *Paper Walls*, 59; PPA, 1939:548–550.
22. *FDR & FA*, Schewe, ed., 1938, #1134, #1153, #1223, #1243, #1278; Ickes, *Secret Diary*, 3:56–57; Wyman, *Paper Walls*, 99–111.
23. *PL*, 2:799; Sidney Hyman interview with Waldo L. Schmitt, July 25, 1949, FDR Memorial Foundation mss.
24. *FDR & FA*, Schewe, ed., 1938, #1190.
25. Offner, *American Appeasement*, 252–255; Weinberg, *Foreign Policy, 1937–1939*, 369–371, 384, 408–409.
26. *FDR & FA*, Schewe, ed., 1938, #1277.
27. *FDR & FA*, Schewe, ed., 1938, #1225; *PPA*, 1938:492–493; PC, 12:83–84.
28. Offner, *American Appeasement*, 258.
29. E. L. Woodward and Rohan Butler, eds., *Documents on British Foreign Policy, 1919–1939* (1954), 3d series, 7:627–629.
30. *FDR & FA*, Schewe, ed., 1938, #1286; Beatrice B. Berle and Travis B. Jacobs, eds., *Navigating the Rapids: From the Papers of . . . Berle* (1973), 186–187; Nancy H. Hooker, ed., *The Moffat Papers* (1956), 211–213.
31. *PPA*, 1938:531–535.
32. Weinberg, *Foreign Policy, 1937–1939*, 450–451.
33. *FDR & FA*, Schewe, ed., 1938, #1360.
34. Berle and Jacobs, eds., *Navigating the Rapids*, 187; David Dilks, ed., *Diaries of Sir Alexander Cadogan* (1972), 109; *FDR & FA*, Schewe, ed., 1938, #1309.
35. Weinberg, *Foreign Policy, 1937–1939*, 456–458.
36. *FDR & FA*, Schewe, ed., 1938, #1333.
37. *FDR & FA*, Schewe, ed., 1938, #1313; Whitney H. Shepardson, *United States in World Affairs, 1938* (1939), 84–85.
38. *FDR & FA*, Schewe, ed., 1938, #1288, #1306, #1306a; Reynolds, *Anglo-American Alliance*, 42.

39. Weinberg, *Foreign Policy, 1937–1939*, 463.

Chapter 23: GIRDING FOR HITLER'S ONSLAUGHT

1. FDR to Frank P. Graham, January 21, 1939, PPF, 530; *New York Times*, May 1, 1939.
2. Joseph Alsop and Robert Kintner, interview with FDR, December 23, 1939, Alsop mss., LC.
3. Anne O'Hare McCormick, *World at Home* (1956), 390.
4. Beatrice B. Berle and Travis B. Jacobs, eds., *Navigating the Rapids, From the Papers of . . . Berle* (1973), 193; PC, 13:307–314; PC, 15:275–281; Whitney B. Shepardson, *United States in World Affairs, 1938* (1939), 280–288; Ickes, *Secret Diary*, 2:484.
5. Joseph Alsop and Robert Kintner, *American White Paper* (1940), 18.
6. Wayne S. Cole, *Lindbergh and the Battle Against American Intervention* (1974), 27–48, 68.
7. PC, 13:314–316.
8. John M. Haight, *American Aid to France, 1938–1940* (1970), 3–12 et seq. is indispensable.
9. H. H. Arnold, *Global Mission* (1947), 173, 177–179; Thomas M. Coffey, *Hap, Military Aviator* (1982); Blum, *Morgenthau Diaries*, 2:48–49. The September date has been questioned; a more crucial meeting took place on November 14. It seems likely that Arnold's notes cover both meetings.
10. Jean Monnet, *Memoirs* (1978), 118; Haight, *Aid to France*, 25, 27–37.
11. Lord Ellibank [Arthur Murray], "Franklin Roosevelt: Friend of Britain," *Contemporary Review* (June, 1955), 188:362–368; *FDR & FA*, Schewe, ed., 1939, #1826.
12. Blum, *Morgenthau Diaries*, 2:48–49; Forrest Pogue, *George C. Marshall* (4 vols., 1963–1987), 1:322–323.
13. Mark S. Watson, *The War Department: Chief of Staff; Prewar Plans and Preparations (U.S. Army in World War II*, Series 4, vol. 1, 1950), 300; Keith D. McFarland, *Harry H. Woodring* (1975), 140–141, 300.
14. Wayne S. Cole, *Roosevelt and the Isolationists* (1983), 304–306; Alsop and Kintner, *American White Paper*, 30–31.
15. PC, 13:117, 139–140.
16. Blum, *Morgenthau Diaries*, 2:76–78; Monnet, *Memoirs*, 122.
17. Frank Freidel, "FDR on the British," *M.H.S. Miscellany* (May, 1972), 1–2; Ickes, *Secret Diary*, 2:571.
18. David Reynolds, *Creation of the Anglo-American Alliance* (1982), 46–47; Reynolds, "FDR on the British: A Postscript," *Proceedings of the Massachusetts Historical Society* (1978), 90:106–110.
19. *Gallup Poll*, 1:121–147.
20. David Wyman, *Paper Walls* (1968), 71–72; Henry L. Feingold, *Politics of Rescue*, (1970), 41; *Time*, November 21, 1938; Saul Friedländer, *Prelude to Downfall: Hitler and the United States* (1967), 7–9.
21. *FDR & FA*, Schewe, ed., 1938, #1408; PC, 12:227–228; Wyman, *Paper Walls*, 731.

22. *Gallup Poll*, 1:141, 145, 149.
23. *FDR & FA*, Schewe, ed., 1939, #1708, #1798; Shepardson, *U.S. in World Affairs, 1939*, 23–30; Dallek, *Roosevelt and Foreign Policy*, 182–184.
24. *PPA*, 1939:195–205; Günther Moltmann, "Franklin D. Roosevelts Friedensappell," *Jahrbuch für Amerikastudien*, 9:91–109; Friedländer, *Hitler and the U.S.*, 13.
25. Hiram Johnson to Hiram Johnson, Jr., April 29, 1939, in Robert E. Burke, ed., *Diary Letters of Hiram Johnson* (7 vols., 1983), vol. 7; Dallek, *Roosevelt and Foreign Policy*, 186–187.
26. Morgenthau diary, June 30, 1939; Friedländer, *Hitler and the U.S.*, 21–22.
27. Ickes, *Secret Diary*, 2:348; Berle and Jacobs, eds., *Navigating the Rapids*, 231–232; Dallek, *Roosevelt and Foreign Policy*, 194–196.
28. *FDR & FA*, Schewe, ed., 1939, #1815, #1843, #1789a.
29. *FDR & FA*, Schewe, ed., 1939, #1513, #1887, #1888, #1969, #1916, #1920; Byrd to Grace Tully, PPF, 201; Moffat diary, May 11, 1939 et seq., Moffat mss., HU.
30. *New York Times*, April 30, 1939.
31. *PL*, 2:889–890; Lash, *Eleanor and Franklin*, 579–580.
32. John W. Wheeler-Bennett, *King George VI* (1958), 389. See notes on FDR's assurances, 390–392.
33. Berle and Jacobs, eds., *Navigating the Rapids*, 229; Morgenthau diary, July 26, 1939.
34. *FDR & FA*, Schewe, ed., 1939, #1879–#2001; Alsop and Kintner, *American White Paper*, 54.
35. Gerhard L. Weinberg, *Foreign Policy of Hitler's Germany, 1937–1939* (1980), 598–599; Friedländer, *Hitler and the U.S.*, 17–19.
36. Alsop and Kintner, *American White Paper*, 54–55; Keith D. Eagles, *Ambassador Joseph E. Davies* (1985), 194, 280; *FDR & FA*, Schewe, ed., 1939, #2023, #2028.
37. Harold Smith diary, August 28, 1939.
38. Berle and Jacobs, eds., *Navigating the Rapids*, 244–247; Ickes, *Secret Diary*, 2:700–702; *FDR & FA*, Schewe, ed., 1939, #2018, #2019, #2060; Moffat diary, August 29, 1939, Moffat mss.; Morgenthau diary, August 31, 1939.
39. Berle and Jacobs, eds., *Navigating the Rapids*, 247.

Chapter 24: THE GERMAN BLITZ AND AMERICAN PERIL

1. Joseph Alsop and Robert Kintner, *American White Paper* (1940), 58–60; PC, 14:130–131.
2. Alsop and Kintner, *American White Paper*, 60–63; Morgenthau diary, September 25, 1939.
3. Harold Smith diary, September 4, 1939; Alsop and Kintner, *American White Paper*, 64–65; Ickes, *Secret Diary*, 2:716–717.
4. *PPA*, 1939:460–464.
5. *PPA*, 1939:488–489.
6. Donald R. McCoy, *Landon of Kansas* (1966), 414–415; interview with Landon, June 21, 1954; Eliot Janeway, *Struggle for Survival* (1968 ed.), 101; Ickes, *Secret Diary*, 3:23, 93.

7. Glass to Harry Byrd, September 12, 1939, and in contrast, Glass to FDR, September 30, 1942, Glass mss., University of Virginia.
8. Wayne S. Cole, *Roosevelt and the Isolationists* (1983), 322, 326 et seq.
9. Charles A. Lindbergh, *Wartime Journals* (1970), 257–258; Cole, *Roosevelt and the Isolationists,* 329; Wayne S. Cole, *Lindbergh and the Battle Against American Intervention* (1974), 73–74; Morgenthau diary, May 20, 1940.
10. Morgenthau diary, September 18, 1939; *PL,* 2:995, 1002–1003.
11. *PL,* 3:936–937; Saul Friedländer, *Prelude to Downfall: Hitler and the United States* (1967), 57–61; Patrick Abbazia, *Mr. Roosevelt's Navy, 1939–1942* (1975), 61–75.
12. Friedländer, *Hitler and the U.S.*, 37–39; Cordell Hull, *Memoirs* (2 vols., 1948), 1:711–713; William L. Langer and S. Everett Gleason, *Challenge to Isolation* (1952), 250.
13. Hull, *Memoirs,* 1:712–713; Langer and Gleason, *Challenge to Isolation,* 259–267; *PL,* 2:952, 971.
14. Langer and Gleason, *Challenge to Isolation,* 321–329; *PL,* 2:961, 965; PC, 14:332–333; Dallek, *Roosevelt and Foreign Policy,* 208–212. See Travis B. Jacobs, *America and the Winter War, 1939–1940* (1981), for a full study.
15. Langer and Gleason, *Challenge to Isolation,* 329–342; Ickes, *Secret Diary,* 3:9, 95–96; Lash, *Eleanor and Franklin,* 635; Bernard Asbell, ed., *Mother and Daughter: Letters of Eleanor and Anna Roosevelt* (1982), 112.
16. Lash, *Eleanor and Franklin,* 598–607; Lash, *Love, Eleanor* (1982), 280–294; *PPA,* 1940:85–93; Irving Howe and Lewis Coser, *American Communist Party* (1957), 348–353, 358, 361.
17. Blum, *Morgenthau Diaries,* 2:110–113; H. Duncan Hall, *North American Supply* (1955), 69–72.
18. Blum, *Morgenthau Diaries,* 2:115–119; Morgenthau diary, March 12, 1940, 3:50 P.M., 5:30 P.M.; March 31, 1940.
19. Hall, *North American Supply,* 97, 114.
20. Morgenthau diary, January 24, 1940; Harold Brayman, *From Grover Cleveland to Gerald Ford . . . The President Speaks Off the Record* (1976), 324–355.
21. Howard G. Bruenn, "Clinical Notes on the Illness and Death of President Franklin D. Roosevelt," *Annals of Internal Medicine* (April, 1970), 72:580; interview with James A. Halsted, July, 1983; *Time,* April 15, 1940; James Roosevelt, *My Parents* (1976), 162–163.
22. Rosenman, *Roosevelt,* 193; Archibald MacLeish to FDR, April 8, 1940, MacLeish mss., LC; John Gunther, *Roosevelt in Retrospect* (1950), 308–309.
23. Morgenthau diary, January 24, 1940.
24. *Gallup Poll,* 1:208–211.
25. Sumner Welles, *Time for Decision* (1944), 75: *Time,* March 18, 1940.
26. PC, 15:284; Ickes, *Secret Diary,* 3:129.
27. Fred L. Israel, ed., *War Diary of Breckinridge Long* (1966), 64; Welles, *Time for Decision,* 77–145; Morgenthau diary, March 3, 31, 1940; Beatrice B. Berle and Travis B. Jacobs, eds., *Navigating the Rapids, From the Papers of . . . Berle* (1973), 295.
28. Morgenthau diary, April 29, 1940.
29. *PL,* 2:1024; Wilhelmina, *Lonely But Not Alone* (1960), 149–180; *Time,* May 20, 1940.

30. *PPA*, 1940:184.
31. *PPA*, 1940:198–202.
32. *Gallup Poll*, 1:226; Forrest Pogue, *George Marshall* (4 vols., 1963–1987), 2:22–32.
33. On public opinion polls during this period, see Jerome S. Bruner, *Mandate from the People* (1944), 22; *Gallup Poll*, 241; Hadley Cantril, ed., *Public Opinion* (1951), 968–973.
34. Orville H. Bullitt, ed., *For the President: Correspondence between Roosevelt and Bullitt* (1972), 414–420.
35. Bullitt, ed., *For the President*, 427.
36. Arthur M. Schlesinger, Jr., *Robert Kennedy and His Times* (1978), 31–36; Michael R. Beschloss, *Kennedy and Roosevelt* (1980), 206–207; James E. Leutze, *Bargaining for Supremacy: Anglo-American Naval Collaboration, 1937–1941* (1977), 89–91.
37. See especially, for its notes as well as the correspondence, *C&R*. Francis L. Loewenheim, Harold D. Langley, and Manfred Jonas, eds., *Roosevelt and Churchill: Their Secret Wartime Correspondence* (1975), is a useful selection. Joseph P. Lash, *Roosevelt and Churchill, 1939–1941* (1976), is a lively narrative.
38. *C&R*, 1:37.
39. J. W. Pickersgill, *The Mackenzie King Record* (4 vols., 1960), 1:116–117.
40. Stetson Conn and Byron Fairchild, *The Western Hemisphere: Framework of Defense* (*United States Army in World War II*, Series 12, vol. 1, 1960), 34–36; Morgenthau diary, May 10, 1940.
41. David Reynolds, *Creation of the Anglo-American Alliance* (1982), 116.
42. Llewellyn Woodward, *British Foreign Policy in the Second World War* (2 vols., London, 1970–1975), 1:270–271, 343–344; Morgenthau diary, May 16, 1940.
43. Reynolds, *Anglo-American Alliance*, 109–116; Leutze, *Bargaining for Supremacy*, 72–78; Ickes, *Secret Diary*, 3:199–200; Woodward, *British Foreign Policy*, 1:342–345.
44. Leutze, *Bargaining for Supremacy*, 83; Woodward, *British Foreign Policy*, 1:344–345.
45. Woodward, *British Foreign Policy*, 1:214, 345; Lash, *Roosevelt and Churchill*, 149.
46. *PPA*, 1940:263; Berle and Jacobs, *Navigating the Rapids*, 322; Israel, ed., *Diary of Long*, 104–106.
47. Reynolds, *Anglo-American Alliance*, 119; Lash, *Roosevelt and Churchill*, 165.
48. *C&R*, 1:50.
49. Reynolds, *Anglo-American Alliance*, 117–120.
50. Pogue, *Marshall*, 2:124.
51. Maurice Matloff and Edwin M. Snell, *Strategic Planning for Coalition Warfare, 1941–1942* (*United States Army in World War II*, Series 4, vol. 3, 1953), 13–14.
52. Matloff and Snell, *Strategic Planning, 1941–1942*, 14–15.
53. Pogue, *Marshall*, 2:120–122, 125–126.

Chapter 25: THE THIRD TERM CAMPAIGN IN TIME OF CRISIS

1. Robert Sherwood, interview with Harold Smith, November 1, 1946, Sherwood mss., HU.

2. Harold Smith diary, May 22, 1940; PC, 15:384–390. Singularly, the transcript of the first meeting of the advisory committee appears in PC, 15:395–424.

3. Elting E. Morison, *Turmoil and Tradition: . . . Henry L. Stimson* (1960), 477–482; Morgenthau diary, June 19, 1940. For a critical view, see R. N. Current, *Secretary Stimson* (1954).

4. On Willkie, see Steve Neal, *Dark Horse: . . . Wendell Willkie* (1984). On the campaign, see Donald B. Johnson, *The Republican Party and Wendell Wilkie* (1960); Herbert S. Parmet and Marie B. Hecht, *Never Again: A President Runs for a Third Term* (1968); Bernard F. Donohoe, *Private Plans and Public Dangers: FDR's Third Term Nomination* (1965); and Robert E. Burke, "Election of 1940," in A. M. Schlesinger, Jr., and F. I. Israel, *History of American Presidential Elections* (4 vols., 1971), 4:2917–3006.

5. Ickes, *Secret Diary*, 3:220–221; James A. Farley, *Jim Farley's Story* (1948), 243–244; Moffat diary, January 16, 1940, Moffat mss., HU.

6. Morgenthau diary, June 28, 1940; Farley, *Story*, 246–258.

7. *Time*, July 29, 1940; Farley, *Story*, 224–225; Burton K. Wheeler, *Yankee from the West* (1962), 361–364.

8. John Bankhead to William Bankhead, July 8, 1940, W. B. Bankhead mss., Alabama Archives.

9. Donohoe, *Private Plans*, 168–170; Parmet and Hecht, *Never Again*, 188–189; Warren Moscow, *Roosevelt and Willkie* (1968), 117–121.

10. Rosenman, *Roosevelt*, 212–213; Donohoe, *Private Plans*, 174–175.

11. Rosenman, *Roosevelt*, 214–219.

12. *PPA*, 1940:293–303.

13. Ickes, *Secret Diary*, 3:238; *PPA*, 1940:298.

14. Robert G. Albion and Robert H. Connery, *Forrestal and the Navy* (1962), 1–9; PC, 15:600.

15. Rosenman, *Roosevelt*, 226–227; Sherwood, *Roosevelt and Hopkins*, 121–122, 173.

16. John O'Sullivan, *From Voluntarism to Conscription: Congress and Selective Service* (1982), 1–105; *PPA*, 1940:295, 431; PC, 16:193.

17. Irvin Stewart, *Organizing Scientific Research for War* (1949), 3–40; James Phinney Baxter, *Scientists Against Time* (1946), 8–9, 14–15, 124, et passim.

18. Donald Fleming, "Albert Einstein, Letter to Franklin D. Roosevelt, 1939," in Daniel Boorstin, ed., *An American Primer* (1966), 857–861. On the topic, see Richard Rhodes, *The Making of the Atomic Bomb* (1986).

19. Richard G. Hewlett and Oscar E. Anderson, *History of the United States Atomic Energy Commission* (1962), 1:9–52; James B. Conant, *My Several Lives* (1970), 274–281; Vannevar Bush, *Pieces of the Action* (1970), 58–61.

20. Barton J. Bernstein, "The Automobile Industry and the Coming of the Second World War," *Southwestern Social Science Quarterly* (June, 1966), 22–23.

21. PC, 16:130–131; *Time*, August 26, 1940.

22. *PPA*, 1940:331; *Time*, August 26, 1940; J. W. Pickersgill, *The Mackenzie King Record* (4 vols., 1960), 1:131–139.

23. Beatrice B. Berle and Travis B. Jacobs, eds., *Navigating the Rapids: From the Papers of . . . Berle* (1973), 330; PC, 16:96–97; *Time*, August 26, 1940; Ickes, *Secret Diary*, 3:289.

24. David Reynolds, *Creation of the Anglo-American Alliance* (1982), 120.

25. Reynolds, *Anglo-American Alliance*, 121–127; James R. Leutze, *Bargaining for Supremacy: Anglo-American Naval Collaboration, 1937–1941* (1971), 97–127; *Time*, July 29, August 26, September 2, 1940.
26. Burke, "Election of 1940," 4:2940–2941; Robert J. C. Butow, "The FDR Tapes," *American Heritage* (February–March, 1982), 18–19.
27. *Time*, September 2, 19, 1940.
28. *Time*, October 14, 1940; Morgenthau diary, October 31, 1940.
29. Butow, "FDR Tapes," 21; Neal, *Willkie*, 37–44, 144; Edward L. and Frederick H. Schapsmeier, *Henry A. Wallace* (2 vols., 1968), 1:273–276.
30. Burke, "Election of 1940," 4:2941–2943; Johnson, *Republican Party and Willkie*, 135–149; Moscow, *Roosevelt and Willkie*, 144–146.
31. Neal, *Willkie*, 159–160.
32. *PPA*, 1940:485–489.
33. *PPA*, 1940:499–506; Rosenman, *Roosevelt*, 240.
34. *PPA*, 1940:517; Sherwood, *Roosevelt and Hopkins*, 191, 198; Ellsworth Barnard, *Wendell Willkie* (1966), 258.
35. *PPA*, 1940:551–552.
36. Nancy Weiss, *Farewell to the Party of Lincoln* (1983), 272–281.
37. Morgenthau diary, October 29, 1940; Samuel Lubell, *Future of American Politics* (1951), 51–57.
38. Neal, *Willkie*, 175, 181–182.

Chapter 26: ARSENAL OF DEMOCRACY

1. *PPA*, 1939:117–118; PC, 16:356–357.
2. David Reynolds, *Creation of the Anglo-American Alliance* (1982), 159, 166; Ickes, *Secret Diary*, 3:597–598; Blum, *Morgenthau Diaries*, 2:235–241.
3. On lend-lease, see especially Warren F. Kimball, *The Most Unsordid Act: Lend-Lease, 1939–1941* (1969), 77–104; *PL*, 2:1072; Blum, *Morgenthau Diaries*, 200–201; John E. Wiltz, *From Isolation to War* (1968), 85–86.
4. *C&R*, 3:102–109; Sherwood, *Roosevelt and Hopkins*, 224; Kimball, *Lend-Lease*, 119.
5. PC, 16:340–344, 350–360; *PPA*, 1940:640–643.
6. *PPA*, 1940:671–672.
7. Joseph P. Lash, *Roosevelt and Churchill, 1939–1941* (1976), 284; Dallek, *Roosevelt and Foreign Policy*, 259–260.
8. *Gallup Poll*, 1:260.
9. PC, 17:76–77; Manfred Jonas, *Isolation in America, 1935–1941* (1966), 241–242; Wayne S. Cole, *Roosevelt and the Isolationists* (1983), 412–414.
10. Arthur H. Vandenberg, Jr., ed., *The Private Papers of Senator Vandenberg* (1952), 9–10; Reynolds, *Anglo-American Alliance*, 168; Kimball, *Lend-Lease*, 236.
11. Purvis to Morgenthau, December 30, 1940; FDR to Morgenthau, March 17, 1941, Morgenthau diary.
12. Reynolds, *Anglo-American Alliance*, 272–280; H. G. Nicholas, ed., *Washington Despatches 1941–1945* (1980), 246–247; PC, 22:86–88.
13. Bernard Bellush, *He Walked Alone: Winant* (1968), vii–viii, 156–159.
14. Sherwood, *Roosevelt and Hopkins*, 230–231, 236 et seq.

15. PC, 17:128–131; W. Averell Harriman and Elie Abel, *Special Envoy to Churchill and Stalin, 1941–1946* (1975), 3.
16. *PPA*, 1941:3; Anne Morrow Lindbergh, *The Wave of the Future* (1940).
17. *Time*, January 27, February 10, April 28, May 5, 1941.
18. Maurice Matloff and Edwin M. Snell, *Strategic Planning for Coalition Warfare, 1941–1942* (*United States Army in World War II*, Series 4, vol. 3, 1953), 15–18.
19. Matloff and Snell, *Strategic Planning, 1941–1942*, 28–29; Forrest Pogue, *George Marshall* (4 vols., 1963–1987), 2:159.
20. Reynolds, *Anglo-American Alliance*, 184–185; James R. Leutze, *Bargaining for Supremacy: Anglo-American Naval Collaboration, 1937–1941* (1977), 216–252; Pogue, *Marshall*, 158–160; Matloff and Snell, *Strategic Planning, 1941–1942*, 58–62.
21. Halifax diary, June 23, 1941, Churchill College, Cambridge University.
22. Cole, *Roosevelt and the Isolationists*, 459–462; Wayne S. Cole, *Lindbergh and the Battle Against American Intervention* (1974); PC, 17:293.
23. William D. Leahy, *I Was There* (1950), 6–10; Leahy diary, LC.
24. William L. Langer and S. Everett Gleason, *The Undeclared War, 1940–1941* (1953), 360–381.
25. Langer and Gleason, *Undeclared War*, 413–418; Reynolds, *Anglo-American Alliance*, 195–199.
26. On the battle of the Atlantic, see Thomas A. Bailey and Paul B. Ryan, *Hitler vs. Roosevelt: The Undeclared Naval War* (1979), and Patrick Abbazia, *Mr. Roosevelt's Navy: The Private War of the U.S. Atlantic Fleet, 1939–1942* (1975), both of which utilize German as well as American sources.
27. Ickes, *Secret Diary*, 3:512–513; Morgenthau diary, June 4, 1941.
28. PC, 17:86-87; Langer and Gleason, *Undeclared War*, 243, 266–267.
29. Hadley Cantril, ed., *Public Opinion* (1951), 1127–1128; *Gallup Poll*, 1:275; *PL*, 2:1158; Langer and Gleason, *Undeclared War*, 445–446, 520–521; Abbazia, *Roosevelt's Navy*, 153–155; Morgenthau diary, April 2, 1941.
30. Ickes, *Secret Diary*, 3:466, 481–482, 491–492.
31. Abbazia, *Roosevelt's Navy*, 154.
32. Morgenthau diary, May 17, 22, 1941.
33. Abbazia, *Roosevelt's Navy*, 155–156.
34. Conversations with Fred Shipman; Sherwood, *Roosevelt and Hopkins*, 293.
35. *Time*, March 31, April 7, 1941; Ickes, *Secret Diary*, 467–469.
36. Morgenthau diary, May 22, 1941; Sherwood, *Roosevelt and Hopkins*, 296–297; *PPA*, 1941:181–193; PC, 17:362, 368–369; *Time*, June 9, 1941.
37. Morgenthau diary, June 4, 1941; Ickes, *Secret Diary*, 3:533; Bailey and Ryan, *Hitler vs. Roosevelt*, 138–144, 147.
38. Sherwood, *Roosevelt and Hopkins*, 290; Halifax diary, June 15, 30, 1941.
39. Langer and Gleason, *Undeclared War*, 245, 322, 494–495; Bailey and Ryan, *Hitler vs. Roosevelt*, 146–147.
40. Langer and Gleason, *Undeclared War*, 533–537; Forrest Davis and Ernest K. Lindley, *How War Came* (1942), 238; Sherwood, *Roosevelt and Hopkins*, 335; *Time*, June 30, 1941.
41. James Leutze, ed., *The London Journal of General Raymond E. Lee, 1940–1941* (1971), 331.

42. Davis and Lindley, *How War Came,* 243, 245; Langer and Gleason, *Undeclared War,* 538–539.
43. *PL,* 2:1175.
44. PC, 17:408–411. On aid, see George C. Herring, Jr., *Aid to Russia, 1941–1946* (1973), and Robert H. Jones, *The Roads to Russia: United States Lend-Lease to the Soviet Union* (1969).
45. Sherwood, *Roosevelt and Hopkins,* 319–328.
46. Sherwood, *Roosevelt and Hopkins,* 328–345; Davis and Lindley, *How War Came,* 244–245; *Life,* September 8, 1941.
47. Ickes, *Secret Diary,* 3:360; Herring, *Aid to Russia,* 13.
48. Herring, *Aid to Russia,* 15–29.

Chapter 27: ESCALATING PRESSURE ON JAPAN AND GERMANY

1. Roberta Wohlstetter, *Pearl Harbor: Warning and Decision* (1962), 172–173.
2. Leonard Baker, *Roosevelt and Pearl Harbor* (1970), 277–278.
3. On the relative strength of the two navies, see Stephen E. Pelz, *Race to Pearl Harbor* (1974). On the interrelationship of FDR's policies toward Japan and Germany, see Waldo Heinrichs, *Threshold of War* (1988).
4. William L. Langer and S. Everett Gleason, *The Undeclared War, 1940–1941* (1953), 4–5.
5. Langer and Gleason, *Undeclared War,* 9–21; Wayne Cole in Dorothy Borg and Shumpei Okamoto, eds., *Pearl Harbor as History* (1973), 313; *PL,* 2:1077.
6. Forrest Davis and Ernest K. Lindley, *How War Came* (1942), 154–157; Henry L. Stimson and McGeorge Bundy, *On Active Service in War and Peace* (1948), 385; Robert J. C. Butow, "The FDR Tapes," *American Heritage* (February–March, 1982), 22:10, 12, 16–17.
7. Langer and Gleason, *Undeclared War,* 42–47, 296–305.
8. Akira Iriye, *Power and Culture: The Japanese-American War, 1941–1945* (1981), 12–13; Langer and Gleason, *Undeclared War,* 311–312.
9. For a detailed account, see Robert J. C. Butow, *The John Doe Associates: Backdoor Diplomacy for Peace* (1974).
10. Butow, *John Doe Associates,* 8–10; Waldo Heinrichs, *American Ambassador: Joseph C. Grew* (1966), 340.
11. *FRUS,* 1941: *Japan,* 2:387–389.
12. Butow, *John Doe Associates,* 214–216; *Pearl Harbor Attack,* Part 20, 4018–4019, in Herbert Feis, *The Road to Pearl Harbor* (1950), 215–216, 219.
13. Gordon W. Prange et al., *At Dawn We Slept: . . . Pearl Harbor* (1981), 9–17, 157–159; Wohlstetter, *Pearl Harbor,* 369–370.
14. Ickes, *Secret Diary,* 3:543–546, 558, 567.
15. Ickes, *Secret Diary,* 3:588; *PPA,* 1941:277–281.
16. Dallek, *Roosevelt and Foreign Policy,* 275; Feis, *Road to Pearl Harbor,* 242–250. On the oil embargo, see especially Jonathan G. Utley, *Going to War with Japan, 1937–1941* (1985), 95–101, 126–133, 151–156.
17. *Pearl Harbor Attack,* Part 5, 2382–2384, in Feis, *Road to Pearl Harbor,* 231–232.
18. Dallek, *Roosevelt and Foreign Policy,* 275; Heinrichs, *Grew,* 337–338.
19. Maurice Matloff and Edwin M. Snell, *Strategic Planning for Coalition Warfare, 1941–1942* (*United States Army in World War II,* Series 4, vol. 3, 1953), 49–

51; Mark S. Watson, *The War Department: Chief of Staff: Prewar Plans and Preparations* (*United States Army in World War II*, Series 4, vol. 1, 1950), 487–490.

20. Counselor Etzdorf notes, July 16, 1941, *Documents on German Foreign Policy, 1918–1945* (1957), Series D (13 vols.), 13:102.
21. Joseph P. Lash, *Roosevelt and Churchill, 1939–1941* (1976), 391.
22. See Theodore A. Wilson, *The First Summit: Roosevelt and Churchill at Placentia Bay, 1941* (1969); also H. V. Morton, *Atlantic Meeting* (1943), and Elliott Roosevelt, *As He Saw It* (1946).
23. Wilson, *First Summit*, 160–169, 208–209.
24. Wilson, *First Summit*, 103–107.
25. Richard W. Steele, *The First Offensive, 1942* (1973), 21–24.
26. Martin Gilbert, *Winston S. Churchill: Finest Hour, 1939–1941* (1983), 1173; Wilson, *First Summit*, 288.
27. Stimson diary, August 19, 1941, Stimson mss., YU; Forrest Pogue, *George Marshall* (4 vols., 1963–1987), 2:144–145; Matloff and Snell, *Coalition Warfare*, 53–55.
28. Gilbert, *Churchill: Finest Hour*, 1167–1168; Lash, *Roosevelt and Churchill*, 401–402.
29. *FRUS*, 1941, 1:342; see notes in Francis L. Loewenheim, Harold D. Langley, and Manfred Jonas, eds., *Roosevelt and Churchill: Their Secret Wartime Correspondence* (1975), 149–151; Langer and Gleason, *Undeclared War*, 679–680; Davis and Lindley, *How War Came*, 265–266; Gilbert, *Churchill: Finest Hour*, 1161–1162; Winston S. Churchill, *The Grand Alliance* (1950), 434.
30. See note, *FRUS*, 1941, 1:367
31. *FRUS*, 1941, 1:367–369.
32. Gilbert, *Churchill: Finest Hour*, 1162–1163; Llewellyn Woodward, *British Foreign Policy in the Second World War* (4 vols., 1970–1975), 2:207–208.
33. David Dilks, ed., *The Diaries of Sir Alexander Cadogan, 1938–1945* (1972), 399; Wilson, *First Summit*, 100–101, 109.
34. Wilson, *First Summit*, 230–232; PC, 18:76–84.
35. Gilbert, *Churchill: Finest Hour*, 1176.

Chapter 28: TO THE BRINK OF WAR

1. Theodore A. Wilson, *The First Summit: Roosevelt and Churchill at Placentia Bay, 1941* (1969), 265–267.
2. William L. Langer and S. Everett Gleason, *The Undeclared War, 1940–1941* (1953), 735–741.
3. Morgenthau diary, October 23, 25, 1941; Blum, *Morgenthau Diaries*, 2:274–276.
4. Samuel Eliot Morison, *The Battle of the Atlantic* (1947), 79–80; Thomas A. Bailey and Paul B. Ryan, *Hitler vs. Roosevelt, The Undeclared Naval War* (1979), 168–173.
5. *PPA*, 1941:389–391; Rosenman, *Roosevelt*, 290–293; David Reynolds, *Creation of the Anglo-American Alliance* (1986), 216–217.
6. *PPA*, 1941:438, 444.
7. *PPA*, 1941:444; PC, 18:268; Bailey and Ryan, *Hitler vs. Roosevelt*, 205–209.

8. Halifax to Churchill, October 11, 1941, in Joseph P. Lash, *Roosevelt and Churchill, 1939–1941* (1976), 422.
9. Nomura to Foreign Office, August 28, 1941, *Pearl Harbor,* part 17, 2794; cf. *PL,* 2:1197; *FRUS,* 1941: *Japan,* 2:572. On the negotiations, see especially Robert J. C. Butow, *The John Doe Associates: Backdoor Diplomacy for Peace* (1974), and Jonathan G. Utley, *Going to War with Japan* (1985).
10. Robert J. C. Butow, *Tojo and the Coming of the War* (1961), 234–237, 243–245; Stephen Pelz, *Race to Pearl Harbor* (1974), 217–218, 221–224.
11. Butow, *Tojo,* 246–259.
12. Butow, *John Doe Associates,* 270–271; Herbert Feis, *The Road to Pearl Harbor* (1950), 282.
13. Dallek, *Roosevelt and Foreign Policy,* 302–303.
14. Butow, *John Doe Associates,* 276–277; Butow, *Tojo,* 262–309; Feis, *Road to Pearl Harbor,* 286–287.
15. *PL,* 2:1223–1224; Roberta Wohlstetter, *Pearl Harbor* (1962), 132–133.
16. Wohlstetter, *Pearl Harbor,* 146.
17. Ickes, *Secret Diary,* 3:635; Stimson diary, November 6, 7, 1941, Stimson mss., YU.
18. Langer and Gleason, *Undeclared War,* 853–854.
19. Langer and Gleason, *Undeclared War,* 855–858; Butow, *Tojo,* 322; Feis, *Road to Pearl Harbor,* 304; *FRUS,* 1941: *Japan,* 2:718.
20. Feis, *Road to Pearl Harbor,* 305–306.
21. *FRUS,* 1941: *Japan,* 2:740–753; Cordell Hull, *Memoirs* (2 vols., 1948), 2:1070.
22. *FRUS,* 1941, 4:626.
23. Ickes, *Secret Diary,* 3:649–650; *FRUS,* 1941: *Japan,* 2:758–759, 761–762.
24. *C&R,* 1:275–276; *FRUS,* 1941, 4:661–664.
25. Lash, *Roosevelt and Churchill,* 468.
26. *C&R,* 1:277–278.
27. James C. Thomson, Jr., in Dorothy Borg and Shumpei Okamoto, eds., *Pearl Harbor as History* (1973), 103–104.
28. Stimson diary, November 25, 1941.
29. Stimson diary, November 26, 1941.
30. For a careful, detailed refutation that the Japanese did break radio silence and FDR was cognizant of it, see Robert J. C. Butow's review of John Toland, *Infamy: Pearl Harbor and Its Aftermath* (1982), in *Journal of Japanese Studies* (Summer, 1983), 9:411–420.
31. Stimson diary, November 27, 1941; R. N. Current, "How Stimson Meant to 'Maneuver' the Japanese," *Mississippi Valley Historical Review* (June, 1935), 40:67–74.
32. Feis, *Road to Pearl Harbor,* 329.
33. Harold Smith diary, December 6, 1941; Wohlstetter, *Pearl Harbor,* 271–272.
34. *FRUS,* 1941: *Japan,* 2:784–786; Lash, *Roosevelt and Churchill,* 48.
35. *Pearl Harbor,* part 10, 4661ff; Wohlstetter, *Pearl Harbor,* 273.

Chapter 29: A DAY OF INFAMY: THE SHIFT TO ACTION

1. U.S. Congress, Joint Committee on the Investigation of the Pearl Harbor Attack, *Report* (1946), 439; Sherwood, *Roosevelt and Hopkins,* 430–431; Tully, *FDR My Boss,* 254; ER, *This I Remember* (1949), 233.

2. Sherwood, *Roosevelt and Hopkins*, 432; Tully, *FDR My Boss*, 254–255; Morgenthau diary, December 7, 1941.
3. Joseph P. Lash, *Roosevelt and Churchill, 1939–1941* (1976), 490; *C&R*, 1:283; Tully, *FDR My Boss*, 256.
4. Sherwood, *Roosevelt and Hopkins*, 432–434; Dean Albertson, *Roosevelt's Farmer: Claude Wickard* (1961), 246–248; James MacGregor Burns, *Roosevelt: The Soldier of Freedom* (1970), 164–165.
5. Sherwood, *Roosevelt and Hopkins*, 436.
6. *PPA*, 1941:514–515.
7. *Time*, December 15, 1941; Rosenman, *Roosevelt*, 308.
8. *Time*, December 15, 1941.
9. Rosenman, *Roosevelt*, 308. See especially Roger Daniels, *Concentration Camps USA: Japanese Americans and World War II* (1971).
10. William L. Shirer, *The Rise and Fall of the Third Reich* (1960), 893–899.
11. *PPA*, 1941:532; FDR to Hull and Welles, December 12, 1941, PSF, Box 22.
12. *PL*, 2:1253–1254.
13. *PPA*, 1941:522–530.
14. *PL*, 2:1255–1256.
15. Burns, *Roosevelt: Soldier of Freedom*, 172.
16. Winston S. Churchill, *The Grand Alliance* (1950), 2:607–608, 625–662; Charles Wilson (Lord Moran), *Churchill: From the Diaries of Lord Moran* (1966), 10–11; Dallek, *Roosevelt and Foreign Policy*, 318.
17. Forrest Pogue, *George Marshall* (4 vols., 1963–1987), 2:89, 235–239.
18. Thomas B. Buell, *Master of Sea Power: . . . Ernest J. King* (1980), 127, 149, 152–161, 488; Henry L. Stimson and McGeorge Bundy, *On Active Service in War and Peace* (1948), 396.
19. Notes on interview with Ernest J. King, May 24, 1946, Sherwood mss., HU.
20. Pogue, *Marshall*, 2:264.
21. Kent R. Greenfield, *American Strategy in World War II* (1963), 80–84. On FDR as commander in chief see also Eric Larrabee, *Commander in Chief* (1987); William R. Emerson in Ernest May, ed., *The Ultimate Decision* (1960); and Samuel Eliot Morison, *Strategy and Compromise* (1958).
22. Churchill, *Grand Alliance*, 664–665.
23. Pogue, *Marshall*, 2:288; Greenfield, *American Strategy*, 59.
24. Buell, *King*, 162–163; Pogue, *Marshall*, 2:270.
25. Stephen E. Ambrose, *The Supreme Commander: The War Years of General Dwight D. Eisenhower* (1970), 9–11; Maurice Matloff and Edwin M. Snell, *Strategic Planning for Coalition Warfare, 1941–1942* (*United States Army in World War II*, Series 4, vol. 3, 1953), 72–73, 82–84.
26. Matloff and Snell, *Strategic Planning, 1941–1942*, 95; Pogue, *Marshall*, 2:265–266, 275.
27. Buell, *King*, 167–169; Pogue, *Marshall*, 2:282–284.
28. Sherwood, *Roosevelt and Hopkins*, 470–473; Pogue, *Marshall*, 2:285–287.
29. Churchill, *Grand Alliance*, 374–375, 683; Sherwood, *Roosevelt and Hopkins*, 442–443; Lash, *Roosevelt and Churchill*, 20.
30. Bernard Asbell, ed., *Mother and Daughter: Letters of Eleanor and Anna Roosevelt* (1982), 141.

Chapter 30: FINAL ARBITER OVER WAR PRODUCTION

1. *PL,* 2:1255. On the home front see John M. Blum, *V Was for Victory* (1976), and Richard Polenberg, *War and Society* (1972).
2. On defense agencies and their conflicts, see Eliot Janeway, *The Struggle for Survival* (1968 ed.); Bruce Catton, *War Lords of Washington* (1948); Torbjörn Sirevåg, *Eclipse of the New Deal* (1985); U.S. Bureau of the Budget, *The United States at War* (1946).
3. Donald Nelson, *Arsenal of Democracy* (1946), 185.
4. Byrnes, Memorandum on War Production Board, January 13, 1942, Byrnes mss., Clemson University; James F. Byrnes, *Speaking Frankly* (1947), 15–17; Janeway, *Struggle for Survival,* 218–223; Blum, *V Was for Victory,* 121.
5. PC, 19:24–26, 20:218.
6. Blum, *V Was for Victory,* 124–128; Bureau of the Budget, *U.S. at War,* 112–115.
7. PC, 20:170–171, 189–190; Bureau of the Budget, *U.S. at War,* 117–120.
8. Ickes diary, November 15, 1942, LC; Robert H. Connery, *The Navy and Industrial Mobilization in World War II* (1951), 157–173.
9. Byrnes to FDR, February 5, 1943, enclosing draft of FDR to Baruch, February 5, 1943, Byrnes mss.; *PL,* 2:1396–1397; Janeway, *Struggle for Survival,* 244.
10. Harold Smith diary, February 15, 1943; Ickes diary, February 20, 1943; Stimson diary, February 18, 1943, YU; Catton, *War Lords,* 206; Janeway, *Struggle for Survival,* 244–247; see also Nelson, *Arsenal of Democracy,* 388–389.
11. David Novick, Melvin Anshen, and W. C. Truppner, *Wartime Production Controls* (1949), 298–299.
12. Ickes diary, February 22, 1942.
13. Hadley Cantril, ed., *Public Opinion* (1951), 588, 864; *PL,* 2:1349.
14. PC, 21:265–267, 23:200–201; Merriman Smith, *Thank You, Mr. President* (1946), 72; conversation with Isador Lubin.
15. PC, 20:98; *PPA,* 1942:62.
16. PC, 19:114.
17. 77 Cong., 1 Sess., *Congressional Record,* A5709–A5711, cited in Richard N. Chapman, *Contours of Public Policy* (1981), 143–144.
18. Arthur H. Vandenberg, Jr., ed., *The Private Papers of Senator Vandenberg* (1952), 76.
19. Roland Young, *Congressional Politics in the Second World War* (1956), 12–13; Chapman, *Contours of Public Policy,* 144.
20. Blum, *V Was for Victory,* 221 et seq.
21. Lash, *Eleanor and Franklin,* 639–640, 644–653; Chapman, *Contours of Public Policy,* 168–174; Young, *Congressional Politics,* 47–48; Memorandum, February 7, 1942, Biddle mss., LC.
22. Polenberg, *War and Society,* 14–15.
23. Catton, *War Lords of Washington,* 151–157, 173–175; Ickes diary, March 7, 1942; *PPA,* 1942:162–163; PC, 19:331, 20:93–94; Conference with the President, June 5, 1942, Harold Smith mss.; Polenberg, *War and Society,* 17–19.

Chapter 31: THE STRUGGLE TO CONTAIN INFLATION

1. PC, 19:176.
2. PC, 21:388–394.

3. FDR to Byrnes, December 29, 1941, enclosing Henderson chart and letter; Byrnes to FDR, December 31, 1941, Byrnes mss., Clemson University; U.S. Bureau of the Budget, *The United States at War* (1946), 241–246; *PPA*, 1941:288–289. On the overall problem, see Lester V. Chandler, *Inflation in the United States 1940–1948* (1951).
4. PC, 19:103–105; *PPA*, 1942:67–73; John Kenneth Galbraith, *A Life in Our Times* (1981), 151.
5. Bureau of the Budget, *U.S. at War*, 248–253; *Time*, April 20, 1942.
6. *PPA*, 1941:558–563, 592–593.
7. *Time*, February 23, 1942; *PL*, 2:1301.
8. PC, 19:171–173, 234, 267; Hadley Cantril, ed., *Public Opinion* (1951), 292.
9. *Time*, April 13, 1942; Morgenthau diary, April 15, 1942; Blum, *Morgenthau Diaries*, 3:36–37; Rosenman, *Roosevelt*, 333; Harold Smith diary, March 4, 25, April 1, 4, 16, 1942.
10. *PPA*, 1942:216–224, 227.
11. Bureau of the Budget, *U.S. at War*, 254–257.
12. Bureau of the Budget, *U.S. at War*, 262–264; *Time*, July 27, 1942.
13. *PPA*, 1942:219–221; Blum, *Morgenthau Diaries*, 3:39–40. On wartime taxation, see Blum, *Morgenthau Diaries*, 3:33–76, and Randolph E. Paul, *Taxation for Prosperity* (1947).
14. Morgenthau diary, June 16, 1942; PC, 19:396–397.
15. Morgenthau diary, July 7, 1942; Ickes diary, October 25, 1942, LC.
16. Paul, *Taxation for Prosperity*, 318–321.
17. *PL*, 2:1352.
18. Morgenthau diary, April 5, 1942.
19. Blum, *Morgenthau Diaries*, 3:22, 23–42; Chandler, *Inflation in the United States*, 142–143, 154–180.
20. Bureau of the Budget, *U.S. at War*, 254–257, 259–262.
21. Morgenthau diary, July 10, 1942.
22. Morgenthau diary, July 22, 1942; Ickes diary, July 26, 1942.
23. Morgenthau diary, August 25, 1942.
24. Wayne Coy, memorandum for the file, August 6, 1942; Coy to Grace Tully, September 15, 1942, Harold Smith mss.
25. Morse memorandum, August 21, 1942; telephone conversation between Morse and Davis, August 21, 1942; telephone conversation among Morse, Davis, Graham, and Taylor, August 21, 1942, Morse mss., University of Oregon.
26. Morse memorandum, August 21, 1942; Morse to Rosenman, August 22, 1942, Morse mss.; Ickes diary, September 12, 1942.
27. Ickes diary, September 6, 1942.
28. Ickes diary, September 12, 1942.
29. Morgenthau diary, September 4, 1942.
30. PC, 20:68–69, 82.
31. Dean Albertson, *Roosevelt's Farmer: Claude Wickard* (1961), 304–308.
32. *PPA*, 1942:364–365.
33. Bureau of the Budget, *U.S. at War*, 266, 269–270; James T. Patterson, *Mr. Republican . . . Robert A. Taft* (1972), 258.
34. *PPA*, 1942:404–406.

35. James F. Byrnes, *Speaking Frankly* (1947), 17–18.
36. Byrnes, *Speaking Frankly,* 19; Sherwood, *Roosevelt and Hopkins,* 634.

Chapter 32: STRIKING BACK AMID DISASTERS

1. Joseph P. Lash, *Love, Eleanor* (1982), 376, 379; *Time,* February 23, 1942.
2. *PPA,* 1942:105–116; Rosenman, *Roosevelt,* 4; *Time,* March 2, 1942; PC, 19:157.
3. Forrest Pogue, *George Marshall* (4 vols., 1963–1987), 2:247–248. On the Pacific war, see two overviews, Ronald H. Spector, *Eagle Against the Sun* (1985) and, on the naval role, Samuel Eliot Morison, *The Two-Ocean War* (1963). On MacArthur, see D. Clayton James, *Years of MacArthur* (2 vols., 1970–1975).
4. Michael Schaller, *The U.S. Crusade in China, 1938–1945* (1979). See also Tang Tsou, *America's Failure in China* (1963); Herbert Feis, *The China Tangle* (1953); and, on Anglo-American relations in East Asia, Christopher Thorne, *Allies of a Kind* (1978).
5. Theodore H. White, ed., *The Stilwell Papers* (1948), 251.
6. Schaller, *Crusade in China,* 97–99.
7. Schaller, *Crusade in China,* 93–95. See also Barbara Tuchman, *Stilwell and the American Experience in China* (1971), and, on the financing of China, see Blum, *Morgenthau Diaries,* 3:102–122.
8. Gary R. Hess, *America Encounters India, 1941–1947* (1971), 26–32, 60–62. See also Thorne, *Allies of a Kind,* 233–251, and, on larger issues, William Roger Louis, *Imperialism at Bay: The United States and the Decolonization of the British Empire, 1941–1945* (1978).
9. *C&R,* 1:374–375, 400–404.
10. Ickes diary, March 22, 1942, LC; the most detailed account is in the Davies mss., LC.
11. Winston S. Churchill, *Hinge of Fate* (1950), 214; Hess, *America Encounters India,* 44–45.
12. Hess, *America Encounters India,* 45–52; *C&R,* 1:446–449.
13. Phillips, *Ventures in Diplomacy,* 343–396; Thorne, *Allies of a Kind,* 245.
14. Spector, *Eagle Against the Sun,* 154–155; H. H. Arnold, *Global Mission* (1947), 298–300; Stimson diary, December 14, 1941, Stimson mss., YU; William Hassett, *Off the Record with FDR* (1958), 40–41; PC, 19:292, 380; *C&R,* 1:466.
15. Gordon W. Prange et al., *Miracle at Midway* (1982), 24–27; for a contrary view, see Thomas B. Buell, *Master of Sea Power . . . Ernest J. King* (1980), 196.
16. Morison, *Two-Ocean War,* 140–146.
17. Prange, *Miracle at Midway;* Morison, *Two-Ocean War,* 146–163; E. B. Potter, *Nimitz* (1976), 91–107.
18. Buell, *King,* 221–223; *PL,* 2:1339.
19. Ickes diary, July 26, 1942; Spector, *Eagle Against the Sun,* 184–218; Samuel B. Griffith II, *The Battle for Guadalcanal* (1963).
20. Ickes diary, November 1, 1942.
21. FDR to Stalin, November 26, 1942, *Correspondence Between the Chairman of the Council of Ministers of the USSR and the Presidents of the USA . . .* (Moscow, 1957), 2:40.
22. Maurice Matloff and Edwin M. Snell, *Strategic Planning for Coalition Warfare,*

1941–1942 (*United States Army in World War II*, Series 4, vol. 3, 1953), 311–312.

23. On the decision to land in North Africa, see especially Matloff and Snell, *Strategic Planning, 1941–1942;* Richard W. Steele, *The First Offensive, 1942* (1973); and Pogue, *Marshall*, vol. 2.
24. Henry L. Stimson and McGeorge Bundy, *On Active Service in War and Peace* (1948), 414; Pogue, *Marshall*, 2:306.
25. Robert Sherwood, interview with Eisenhower, January 14, 1947, Sherwood mss., HU; Robert Ferrell, ed., *The Eisenhower Diaries* (1981), 72.
26. Churchill, *Hinge of Fate*, 323–324; Pogue, *Marshall*, 2:319–320; Matloff and Snell, *Strategic Planning, 1941–1942*, 188–189.
27. Dallek, *Roosevelt and Foreign Policy*, 240–245.
28. *FRUS*, 1942, 3:569–570, 575–577; Sherwood, *Roosevelt and Hopkins*, 564, 568–569, 577; Cordell Hull, *Memoirs* (2 vols., 1948), 2:1165–1169; PC, 19:382–390.
29. Pogue, *Marshall*, 2:327; Sherwood, *Roosevelt and Hopkins*, 582–583.
30. Sherwood, *Roosevelt and Hopkins*, 580–581; Pogue, *Marshall*, 327–328.
31. Stimson to FDR, June 19, 1942, in Stimson diary, Stimson mss.; Churchill, *Hinge of Fate*, 377–382.
32. Pogue, *Marshall*, 333; Churchill, *Hinge of Fate*, 382–383.
33. *FRUS, Conferences at Washington, 1941–1942, and Casablanca*, 434–438.
34. *C&R*, 1:520; Pogue, *Marshall*, 2:340–341.
35. Pogue, *Marshall*, 2:346; Steele, *First Offensive*, 167–179.
36. Harry C. Butcher, *My Three Years with Eisenhower* (1946), 29; Sherwood, interview with Eisenhower, January 14, 1947, Sherwood mss.
37. See unsent letter to FDR, August 10, 1942, Stimson diary, Stimson mss.

Chapter 33: INTO NORTH AFRICA

1. On Vichy policy, William L. Langer, *Our Vichy Gamble* (1947), an unofficial defense, utilizes interviews, Leahy's files, and OSS materials; Robert Murphy, *Diplomat Among Warriors* (1964) contains additional source materials; William D. Leahy, *I Was There* (1950), closely follows his files. See also Arthur Layton Funk, *The Politics of Torch* (1974); R. T. Thomas, *Britain and Vichy* (1979); and Milton Viorst, *Hostile Allies: FDR and de Gaulle* (1965).
2. Murphy, *Diplomat Among Warriors*, 66–70; Leahy, *I Was There*, 8–9, 443–446.
3. Langer, *Vichy Gamble*, 277–283; Murphy, *Diplomat Among Warriors*, 101–102, 105–106.
4. Murphy, *Diplomat Among Warriors*, 110–123; Stephen E. Ambrose, *The Supreme Commander: The War Years of General Dwight D. Eisenhower* (1970), 111–116.
5. Tully, *FDR My Boss*, 264.
6. PC, 1942:221; *Time*, November 26, 1942; *C&R*, 1:636.
7. Murphy, *Diplomat Among Warriors*, 124–142.
8. Leahy diary, November 20, 1942, LC.
9. Morgenthau diary, November 12, 1942.
10. See, for example, *Christian Century* (December 2, 1942), 1475–1476; *New Re-*

public (February 8, 1943), 170; *New York Times,* November 20, 1942; *C&R,* 2:7–8.

11. Morgenthau diary, November 17, 1942; PC, 20:244–247.
12. Ickes diary, November 15, 22, 1942, LC.
13. Stimson diary, December 27, 1942, Stimson mss., YU.
14. Peter Tompkins, *The Murder of Admiral Darlan* (1965), 185–190; Leahy diary, December 24, 25, 26, 1942.
15. Stalin to FDR, December 6, 1942, *Correspondence Between the Chairman of the Council of Ministers of the USSR and the Presidents of the USA . . .* (Moscow, 1957), 2:43; *C&R,* 2:54–55; Sherwood, *Roosevelt and Hopkins,* 665.
16. *PL,* 2:1393, 1395; Michael F. Reilly and William J. Slocum, *Reilly of the White House* (1947), 161; Log of the Trip of the President to the Casablanca Conference.
17. Log of the Trip of the President, January 14, 1943; Elliott Roosevelt, *As He Saw It* (1946), 75.
18. Sherwood, *Roosevelt and Hopkins,* 673; Reilly and Slocum, *Reilly of the White House,* 148–152.
19. Albert C. Wedemeyer, *Wedemeyer Reports* (1958), 170–171, 185, 192; Arthur Bryant, *Turn of the Tide* (1957), 443; Murphy, *Diplomat Among Warriors,* 167–168.
20. Minutes of the meetings of the Combined Chiefs of Staff, and of the (American) Joint Chiefs of Staff are in *FRUS, Washington and Casablanca,* 536–722; Final Report of the Combined Chiefs of Staff . . . , January 23, 1945, in *FRUS, Washington and Casablanca,* 791–798; Forrest Pogue, *George Marshall* (4 vols., 1963–1987), 3:30–31.
21. *FRUS, Washington and Casablanca,* 816; Jean Monnet, *Memoirs* (1978), 207; Murphy, *Diplomat Among Warriors,* 171–172.
22. See André Kaspi, *La Mission de Jean Monnet à Alger, Mars-Octobre 1943* (1971). *FRUS, Washington and Casablanca,* 809.
23. *FRUS, Washington and Casablanca,* 606–608. On Jews in German professions, see David S. Wyman, *Abandonment of the Jews* (1984), 313.
24. Murphy, *Diplomat Among Warriors,* 173; *FRUS, Washington and Casablanca,* 693.
25. Charles de Gaulle, *War Memoirs* (2 vols., 1964), 2:84–87; Sherwood, *Roosevelt and Hopkins,* 685. On de Gaulle's role in the conference, see Arthur Layton Funk, *Charles de Gaulle, The Critical Years, 1943–1944* (1959), 54–100.
26. De Gaulle, *War Memoirs,* 2:88–89.
27. Sherwood, *Roosevelt and Hopkins,* 686, 691; Murphy, *Diplomat Among Warriors,* 175; Funk, *De Gaulle,* 73; Kenneth Pendar, *Adventure in Diplomacy* (1945), 151.
28. Sherwood, *Roosevelt and Hopkins,* 693.
29. De Gaulle, *Memoirs,* 2:94–95.
30. PC, 21:89–90; interview with Admiral John McCrea, February 8, 1964.
31. Sherwood, *Roosevelt and Hopkins,* 696; Halifax diary, November 20, 1942, Churchill College, Cambridge University.
32. Combined Chiefs of Staff minutes, January 18, 1943, *FRUS, Washington and Casablanca,* 506, 635; W. Averell Harriman and Elie Abel, *Special Envoy to Churchill and Stalin, 1941–1946* (1975), 190; Raymond G. O'Connor, *Diplo-*

macy for Victory; FDR and Unconditional Surrender (1971), 1–53. See also the negative Anne Armstrong, *Unconditional Surrender* (1961), based upon extensive German writings and interviews.

33. *New York Times*, December 21, 1964, quoting Eisenhower.
34. Sherwood, *Roosevelt and Hopkins*, 696.
35. William Hassett, *Off the Record with FDR* (1958), 152.

Chapter 34: VICTORIES — AND THE SHADOW OF STALIN

1. Ickes diary, February 7, March 6, 1943, LC; Ronald L. Spector, *Eagle Against the Sun* (1985), 226–228; Samuel Eliot Morison, *The Two-Ocean War* (1963), 272–273; Thomas B. Buell, *Master of Sea Power: . . . Ernest J. King* (1980), 244.
2. Buell, *King*, 315–318; *C&W*, 2:133, 134.
3. Sherwood, *Roosevelt and Hopkins*, 708–717; Anthony Eden, *Memoirs: The Reckoning* (1965), 373–374.
4. Sherwood, *Roosevelt and Hopkins*, 711, 719–720; *FRUS*, 1943, 3:35; Ickes diary, March 20, 1943.
5. *C&W*, 2:156.
6. Stephen E. Ambrose, *The Supreme Commander: The War Years of General Dwight D. Eisenhower* (1970), 166–190; Forrest Pogue, *George Marshall* (4 vols., 1963–1987), 2:179–192. See also the army history, George F. Howe, *Northwest Africa: Seizing the Initiative in the West* (1967).
7. W. Averell Harriman and Elie Abel, *Special Envoy to Churchill and Stalin, 1941–1946* (1975), 205–206.
8. Theodore H. White, ed., *The Stilwell Papers* (1948), 204–206.
9. For a summary of the conference, see Pogue, *Marshall*, 3:193–213; official minutes, position papers, and correspondence are in *FRUS, Conferences at Washington and Quebec*, 1:387.
10. Ambrose, *Supreme Commander*, 218–233; C. L. Sulzberger, *World War II* (1970), 205–211.
11. *FRUS, Washington and Quebec*, 326–331; PC, 21:335, 373–374.
12. Dallek, *Roosevelt and Foreign Policy*, 409–418; Stalin to FDR and Churchill, August 22, 1943, *Correspondence Between the Chairman of the Council of Ministers of the USSR and the Presidents of the USA . . .* (Moscow, 1957), 2:84.
13. Allan M. Winkler, *Politics of Propaganda, Office of War Information* (1978), 68–71; *Gallup Poll*, 1:366, 367.
14. H. G. Nicholas, ed., *Washington Despatches 1941–1945* (1980), 163; Charles E. Bohlen, *Witness to History* (1973), 121–122; Sherwood, *Roosevelt and Hopkins*, 706; Harriman and Abel, *Special Envoy*, 198.
15. Herbert Feis, *Churchill, Roosevelt, Stalin* (1957), 192–194. A subsequent British investigation verified the German charges, but lowered the body count to 4,510. *C&R*, 2:192–193.
16. Stalin to FDR, April 21, 1943; FDR to Stalin, April 26, 1943, *Correspondence*, 2:60–61; Adam B. Ulam, *Stalin* (1973), 583–584; *C&R*, 2:193, 198.
17. Harriman and Abel, *Special Envoy*, 216–217; FDR to Stalin, May 5, 1943, *Correspondence*, 63–64. Details of Davies' 1943 mission are in Keith Eubank, *Summit at Teheran* (1985), 68–69. See also diary and correspondence in Davies mss., LC.

18. Sherwood, *Roosevelt and Hopkins,* 734; Feis, *Churchill, Roosevelt, Stalin,* 143.
19. Ulam, *Stalin,* 170.
20. Martin J. Sherwin, *A World Destroyed: The Atomic Bomb and the Grand Alliance* (1975), 78–87; Barton J. Bernstein, "The Quest for Security: American Foreign Policy and International Control of Atomic Energy, 1942–1946," *Journal of American History* (March, 1974), 60:1003–1010.
21. *FRUS, Washington and Quebec,* 910–911, 942.
22. *C&R,* 2:368, *FRUS, Washington and Quebec,* 833.
23. Stalin to Roosevelt and Churchill, August 22, 24, 1943, *Correspondence,* 1:148–150.
24. John M. Blum, ed., *The Price of Vision: Diary of Henry A. Wallace, 1942–1946* (1973), 245.
25. Cordell Hull, *Memoirs* (2 vols., 1948), 2:1253–1255.
26. Ted Morgan, *FDR* (1985), 677–686.
27. Orville H. Bullitt, ed., *For the President: Correspondence between Roosevelt and Bullitt* (1972), 512–514.
28. Bullitt, ed., *For the President,* 514–516; Morgenthau diary, August 28, 1943.
29. Hull, *Memoirs,* 2:1227–1231, recounts Welles's many derelictions in Hull's eyes.
30. ER, *This I Remember* (1949), 63.
31. Thomas C. Campbell and George C. Herring, *Diaries of Edward R. Stettinius, Jr., 1943–1946* (1975), xiii–xxiii.
32. Harriman and Abel, *Special Envoy,* 227, 230; Hull, *Memoirs,* 2:1254–1256.
33. Dallek, *Roosevelt and Foreign Policy,* 419–420; Hull, *Memoirs,* 2:1256–1257; William Hassett, *Off the Record with FDR* (1958), 219; *PL,* 2:1468.
34. Hassett, *Off the Record,* 219.
35. *FRUS, Conferences at Cairo and Tehran, 1943* (1961), 58.
36. Hull, *Memoirs,* 2:1314–1315.

Chapter 35: THE CONFERENCE AT TEHRAN

1. Arthur Bryant, *Triumph in the West* (1959), 47.
2. Christopher Thorne, *Allies of a Kind* (1978), 313–314, 718–724.
3. *PL,* 2:1468; Maurice Matloff and Edwin M. Snell, *Strategic Planning for Coalition Warfare, 1943–1944* (*United States Army in World War II,* Series 4, vol. 4, 1959), 325–326, 348.
4. *FRUS, Cairo and Tehran,* 296, 322–325, 748.
5. Matloff and Snell, *Strategic Planning, 1943–1944,* 351–352.
6. Robert I. Gannon, *The Cardinal Spellman Story* (1962), 222–224.
7. Keith Eubank, *Summit at Teheran* (1985), 170–176.
8. W. Averell Harriman and Elie Abel, *Special Envoy to Churchill and Stalin, 1941–1946* (1975), 264–265; Charles E. Bohlen, *Witness to History* (1973), 135–136; Eubank, *Summit at Teheran,* 190; Hastings L. Ismay, *Memoirs of General Lord Ismay* (1960), 337; *Time,* December 13, 1943.
9. Charles Wilson (Lord Moran), *Churchill: Taken from the Diaries of Lord Moran* (1966), 142.
10. Bohlen, *Witness to History,* 136–141; *FRUS, Cairo and Tehran,* 483–486.
11. *FRUS, Cairo and Tehran,* 487; Forrest Pogue, *George Marshall* (4 vols., 1963–1987), 3:310.

12. A. H. Birse, *Memoirs of an Interpreter* (1967), 155.
13. Wilson, *Churchill,* 146: Thomas B. Buell, *Master of Sea Power . . . Ernest J. King* (1980), 430.
14. *FRUS, Cairo and Tehran,* 506–507.
15. *FRUS, Cairo and Tehran,* 501–504, 529, 606–615; Sherwood, *Roosevelt and Hopkins,* 780.
16. *FRUS, Cairo and Tehran,* 478–480; Pogue, *Marshall,* 3:309–310.
17. Wilson, *Churchill,* 143, 145.
18. Forrest Davis, "What Really Happened at Teheran," *Saturday Evening Post* (May 13, 1944), 216:12.
19. *FRUS, Cairo and Tehran,* 837.
20. Bohlen, *Witness to History,* 143–144; William H. Rigdon, *White House Sailor* (1962), 84; Ross T. McIntire, *White House Physician* (1946), 173.
21. William D. Leahy, *I Was There* (1950), 208; Harriman and Abel, *Special Envoy,* 271; *FRUS, Cairo and Tehran,* 533–552.
22. Bohlen, *Witness to History,* 146; Wilson, *Churchill,* 146, 152–153; Stimson diary, December 17, 1943, Stimson mss., YU; *FRUS, Cairo and Tehran,* 554–555.
23. Bohlen, *Witness to History,* 148.
24. Wilson, *Churchill,* 153; *FRUS, Cairo and Tehran,* 564, 565.
25. *FRUS, Cairo and Tehran,* 531–532.
26. *FRUS, Cairo and Tehran,* 469, cf. 584–585.
27. Eubank, *Summit at Teheran,* 375–388.
28. Arthur C. Millspaugh, *Americans in Iran* (1946), 8, 206; *FRUS, Cairo and Tehran,* 470, 629–630.
29. Anthony Eden, *Memoirs: The Reckoning* (1965), 428; *FRUS, Cairo and Tehran,* 594.
30. *FRUS, Cairo and Tehran,* 594–595.
31. *FRUS, Cairo and Tehran,* 599–600, 604 (a color reproduction of the map appears opposite p. 601). Bohlen, *Witness to History,* 151–152.
32. *FRUS, Cairo and Tehran,* 600–603.
33. John R. Boettiger, *Love in a Shadow* (1978), 250; David Dilks, ed., *Diaries of Sir Alexander Cadogan* (1972), 581, 586–587; *FRUS, Cairo and Tehran,* 634–641.
34. Bohlen, *Witness to History,* 152–154; *FRUS, Cairo and Tehran,* 846.
35. *FRUS, Cairo and Tehran,* 785; Leahy diary, December 2, 3, 1943, LC.; Rosenman, *Roosevelt,* 406–407.
36. *FRUS, Cairo and Tehran,* 713.
37. *FRUS, Cairo and Tehran,* 706, 803–804; Pogue, *Marshall,* 3:316–317; Ismay, *Memoirs,* 342; Winston S. Churchill, *Closing the Ring* (1951), 409–412.
38. Pogue, *Marshall,* 3:319–322.
39. Sherwood, *Roosevelt and Hopkins,* 803; Stimson diary, December 18, 1943, Stimson mss., YU.
40. Pogue, *Marshall,* 3:222; Dwight D. Eisenhower, *Crusade in Europe* (1948), 207–208.
41. Eubank, *Summit at Teheran,* 399; Ambrose, *Supreme Commander,* 311–312; Leahy, *I Was There,* 215.
42. Stimson diary, December 17, 1943.

43. Biddle notes, December 17, 1943, Biddle mss., LC; Ickes diary, December 19, 1943, LC; John M. Blum, ed., *The Price of Vision: Diary of Henry A. Wallace 1942–1946* (1973), 279–284.
44. H. G. Nicholas, ed., *Washington Despatches 1941–1945* (1980), 283, 287–288.

Chapter 36: DOCTOR WIN-THE-WAR

1. *Gallup Poll,* 1:402–403. On the national move to the right, see John M. Blum, *V Was for Victory* (1976).
2. Allen Drury, *A Senate Journal* (1963), 4; *Time,* December 20, 1943.
3. Ickes diary, February 6, 1944, LC.
4. Henry R. Luce to Raymond Clapper, December 4, 1943, Clapper mss., LC.
5. Clapper to Luce, December 6, 1943, Clapper mss.
6. Hadley Cantril, ed., *Public Opinion* (1951), 762; *Gallup Poll,* 1:425.
7. H. G. Nicholas, ed., *Washington Despatches, 1941–1945* (1980), 292–293.
8. PC, 22:216; *Time,* December 27, 1943; *Newsweek,* December 27, 1943.
9. John M. Blum, ed., *The Price of Vision: Diary of Henry A. Wallace, 1942–1946* (1973), 281–282; Ickes diary, December 19, 1943, LC; *Time,* December 20, 1943.
10. PC, 22:230–234; William Hassett, *Off the Record with FDR* (1958), 222.
11. *PPA,* 1943:563–569; Hassett, *Off the Record,* 226–227.
12. Ickes diary, November 21, December 19, 1943.
13. *Newsweek,* December 29, 1943.
14. *Time,* January 3, 1943; PC, 22:245–247, and edited version in *PPA,* 143: 569–575.
15. Ickes diary, January 1, 1944; Nicholas, ed., *Washington Despatches,* 315.
16. Blum, ed., *Wallace Diary,* 140, 289; Ickes diary, January 1, 1944.
17. George McJimsey, *Harry Hopkins* (1987), 313–314, 332; Morgenthau diary, March 7, 1944.
18. Morgenthau diary, January 8, 1944.
19. *PL,* 2:1515; Ickes diary, February 6, 1944.
20. *PPA,* 1944:32–44; Rosenman, *Roosevelt,* 423–426.
21. Drury, *Senate Journal,* 46.
22. *Time,* January 24, 1944; Nicholas, ed., *Washington Despatches,* 307.
23. Randolph Paul, *Taxation for Prosperity* (1947), 143–160.
24. *PPA,* 1944:80–83.
25. Drury, *Senate Journal,* 86–91.
26. Wallace to Barkley, June 26, 1954, Barkley mss., University of Kentucky; Polly Davis, *Alben W. Barkley* (1979), 137–155; Blum, ed., *Wallace Diary,* 299, 301; Drury, *Senate Journal,* 97.
27. Hassett, *Off the Record,* 235–236.
28. Paul, *Taxation for Prosperity,* 161–162.
29. Davis, *Barkley,* 153–158.
30. Richard Polenberg, *War and Society* (1972), 195–197.
31. Rosenman, *Roosevelt,* 394–395. See Davis R. B. Ross, *Preparing for Ulysses: Politics and Veterans during World War II* (1969).
32. *PPA,* 1943:333.

33. Ross, *Preparing for Ulysses*, 53–61 et seq.; Polenberg, *War and Society*, 96–97; *PPA*, 1944–1945:180–185.
34. Polenberg, *War and Society*, 178–180; Byron Fairchild and Jonathan Grossman, *The Army and Industrial Manpower* (*United States Army in World War II*, 1959), 226–237.
35. *C&R*, 2:632–633, 636, 638; Forrest Pogue, *George Marshall* (4 vols., 1963–1987), 3:330–331.
36. *C&R*, 3:53, 59–60.
37. On the Italian ships, see *C&R*, dispatches in 2:654–702 and 3:15–28; interchanges with Stalin in *Correspondence Between the Chairman of the Council of Ministers of the USSR and the Presidents of the USA* . . . (Moscow, 1957), 2:117–129; and PC, 23:70–71. On the Italian government, see *C&R*, 2:723, 3:28–29, 31–32, 42, 176, and Ickes diary, March 21, 1944. On Yugoslavia, see *C&R*, 3:80–82, 115–116, 131–133. On Greece, see Dallek, *Roosevelt and Foreign Policy*, 504–505.
38. Randall B. Woods, *Roosevelt Foreign Policy Establishment and the 'Good Neighbor'; United States and Argentina, 1941–1945* (1979), 111–127; *C&R*, 2:678–679; Thomas C. Campbell and George C. Herring, eds., *Diaries of Edward R. Stettinius, Jr.* (1975), 24–25.
39. PC, 23:72; Ickes diary, March 20, 1944; *C&R*, 2:744–745, 3:14, 17, 26–27, 169, 187, 511–512.
40. *C&R*, 2:527, 743–744, 3:34–35; Campbell and Herring, eds., *Diaries of Stettinius*, 45.
41. W. Averell Harriman and Elie Abel, *Special Envoy to Churchill and Stalin, 1941–1946* (1975), 296; *PL*, 2:1498.

Chapter 37: DECLINING HEALTH AND ESCALATING POLITICS

1. William Hassett, *Off the Record with FDR* (1958), 239–241.
2. Hassett, *Off the Record*, 247.
3. George M. Elsey, interview, February 4, 1987; Elsey to author, February 22, 1987. For indications of who drafted replies, see dispatches in *C&W;* Elsey, "Memoir: Some White House Recollections, 1942–53," *Diplomatic History* (Summer, 1988), 12:357–364.
4. Interviews with Anna Roosevelt Halsted; interview with Anna Roosevelt Halsted, 1975, COHC; Lash, *Eleanor and Franklin*, 668.
5. Hassett, *Off the Record*, 200.
6. Joseph P. Lash, *Love, Eleanor* (1982), 384.
7. James Roosevelt, *My Parents* (1976), 113.
8. Lash, *Love, Eleanor*, 399.
9. Lash, *Love, Eleanor*, 368–369, 447–448, 450–451.
10. Lash, *Love, Eleanor*, 489–491, 500, 505.
11. Conversation with Anna Roosevelt Halsted, July 31, 1975.
12. Anna Roosevelt Halsted interview, 1975, COHC; conversation with Anna Roosevelt Halsted, July 31, 1975; Geoffrey C. Ward, *A First Class Temperament: The Emergence of Franklin Roosevelt* (1989), passim.
13. Hassett, *Off the Record*, 137, 139–140, 147; *PL*, 2:1488, 1540–1541; Lash, *Eleanor and Franklin*, 694; William R. Emerson to author, January 28, 1988.
14. Howard G. Bruenn, "Clinical Notes on the Illness and Death of President Franklin

D. Roosevelt," *Annals of Internal Medicine* (April, 1970), 75:579–580. In 1937, FDR's blood pressure was 162/98. Hugh C. Gallagher, *FDR's Splendid Deception* (1985), 179–180; interview with Anna Roosevelt Halsted, July 31, 1975; Anna Roosevelt Halsted interview, COHC; Hassett, *Off the Record*, 240–241.

15. Bruenn, "Clinical Notes," 580–581; Dr. James Halsted to author, November 14, 1983; Dr. Bruenn's comment to author; Robin M. Henig, "Defining Hypertension," *New York Times Magazine*, January 24, 1988, 32–33.
16. Gallagher, *FDR's Splendid Deception*, 182; Ross T. McIntire, *White House Physician* (1946), 57; Bruenn, "Clinical Notes," 583; *New York Times*, January 19, 1944; Morgenthau diary, April 12, 1945.
17. McIntire, *White House Physician*, 143; Halsted to Jim Bishop, December 5, 1974, copy in author's possession.
18. James Roosevelt, *My Parents* (1976), 278; Jonathan Daniels, *White House Witness* (1975), 220; Bruenn, "Clinical Notes," 584–586.
19. Bruenn, "Clinical Notes," 582–583; *New York Times*, April 8, 1944.
20. *New York Times*, April 11, 1944.
21. Ickes diary, May 20, 1944; McIntire, *White House Physician*, 185.
22. PC, 23:20–21; James A. Halsted to author, June 18, 1982; *New York Times*, February 5, 1944, April 13, 1945; Harry S. Goldsmith, "Unanswered Mysteries in the Death of Franklin D. Roosevelt," *Surgery, Gynecology & Obstetrics* (December, 1979), 149:899–908.
23. Charles Wilson (Lord Moran), *Churchill: Taken from the Diaries of Lord Moran* (1966), 242–243.
24. PC, 23:146–147.
25. *New York Times*, May 8, 1944.
26. *Time*, May 22, 1944; *Gallup Poll*, 1:460.
27. Morgenthau diary, March 7, 1944; FDR to Morgenthau, February 24, 1944; Herbert Gaston, memorandum to Morgenthau, March 1, 1944, in Morgenthau diary; Robert A. Caro, *The Path to Power* (*Years of Lyndon Johnson*, vol. 1, 1983), 745–753.
28. *Time*, April 24, 1944.
29. H. G. Nicholas, ed., *Washington Despatches 1941–1945* (1980), 343–344, 347.
30. PC, 23:148; *Time*, April 24, 1944; Arthur Vandenberg, Jr., ed., *The Private Papers of Senator Vandenberg* (1952), 85.
31. *Time*, April 16, July 3, 1944; Nicholas, ed., *Washington Despatches*, 348–349.
32. Francis Biddle, *In Brief Authority* (1962), 308–318; Jesse Jones, *Fifty Billion Dollars* (1951), 478–481; Richard Polenberg, *War and Society* (1972), 167–175; *Time*, May 8, 22, June 29, 1944; PC, 23:147, 153–160.
33. Polenberg, *War and Society*, 174–175.
34. PC, 22:252.
35. *Time*, June 29, 1944.
36. *PPA*, 1944–1945:66–70; PC, 23:23–35.
37. See Robert A. Divine, *Second Chance: The Triumph of Internationalism in America During World War II* (1967).
38. Vandenberg, ed., *Vandenberg Papers*, 96; Divine, *Second Chance*, 194–198; Cordell Hull, *Memoirs* (2 vols., 1948), 2:1658–1660.
39. Willkie to H. V. Kaltenborn, May 9, 1944, enclosing Turner Catledge, "La

Follette Goes Isolationist," *New York Times,* May 9, 1944, Kaltenborn mss., Wisconsin State Historical Society.

40. PC, 23:176–177; Blum, *Morgenthau Diaries,* 3:252–278.
41. Hull, *Memoirs,* 2:1671–1674; PC, 23:191–197.
42. Nicholas, ed., *Washington Despatches,* 365; *Time,* June 12, 1944.
43. Divine, *Second Chance,* 206–208; *Time,* June 12, 26, 1944.

Chapter 38: A ROOSEVELT-TRUMAN TICKET

1. *C&R,* 3:161; Forrest Pogue, *George Marshall* (4 vols., 1963–1987), 3: 379–387.
2. Alfred D. Chandler, Jr., et al., *The Papers of Dwight D. Eisenhower* (*The War Years,* 5 vols., 1970), 3:1794–1795. On all these issues, see *Eisenhower Papers,* 3:1794–1907, and *C&R,* vol. 3.
3. Max Hastings, *Overlord: D-Day and the Battle for Normandy* (London, 1984), 28, 30, 58–59; Omar N. Bradley, *A Soldier's Story* (1951), 178–179.
4. Lash, *Eleanor and Franklin,* 700.
5. Rosenman, *Roosevelt,* 433–434; *PPA,* 1944–1945:152–153.
6. Lash, *Eleanor and Franklin,* 701.
7. Leahy diary, May 15, 1944, LC.
8. Charles de Gaulle, *War Memoirs* (2 vols., 1964), 2:269; interview with Anna Roosevelt Halsted, July 31, 1975.
9. De Gaulle, *Memoirs,* 2:272; *C&R,* 3:238. On the visit, see also Julian G. Hurstfield, *America and the French Nation, 1939–1945* (1986).
10. H. G. Nicholas, ed., *Washington Despatches 1941–1945* (1980), 384.
11. Hurstfield, *America and French Nation,* 207–224.
12. Lash, *Eleanor and Franklin,* 708.
13. Samuel Eliot Morison, *The Two-Ocean War* (1963), 322–343.
14. James F. Byrnes, *All In One Lifetime* (1958), 219; Nicholas, ed., *Washington Despatches,* 349; John M. Blum, ed., *The Price of Vision: Diary of Henry A. Wallace, 1942–1946* (1973), 310–315.
15. Rosenman, *Roosevelt,* 438–439; Edward J. Flynn, *You're the Boss* (1947), 180; Ickes diary, June 18, 1944, LC.
16. D. B. Hardeman and Donald C. Bacon, *Rayburn* (1987), 291–292; Byrnes, *All In One Lifetime,* 214; John H. Bankhead to Marie B. Owen, December 17, 1943; Bankhead to Oscar Johnston, July 5, 26, 1944, Bankhead mss., Alabama Archives. See also Corcoran mss., Douglas mss., and Ickes diary, LC.
17. *Newsweek,* May 8, July 3, 1944.
18. Blum, ed., *Wallace Diary,* 313.
19. Rosenman, *Roosevelt,* 439.
20. Ickes diary, April 29, June 18, 1944; Hardeman and Bacon, *Rayburn,* 295–296.
21. Jonathan Daniels, *White House Witness* (1975), 227–228; Ickes diary, June 18, 1944.
22. Ickes diary, June 25, July 9, 1944; "Periscope," *Newsweek,* May 29, July 10, 1944.
23. Blum, ed., *Wallace Diary,* 360–362.
24. Ickes diary, July 16, 1944.

25. Daniels, *White House Witness,* 235.
26. Rosenman, *Roosevelt,* 445; Flynn, *You're the Boss,* 181; Roger Biles, *Big City Boss: Edward J. Kelly* (1984), 129.
27. Rosenman, *Roosevelt,* 447; Richard Lawrence Miller, *Truman: The Rise to Power* (1986), 384–385.
28. Blum, ed., *Wallace Diary,* 365–367, 371.
29. Rosenman, *Roosevelt,* 449.
30. Miller, *Truman,* 385; Walter Millis, ed., *The Forrestal Diaries* (1951), 5.
31. Abe Fortas to William O. Douglas, July 25, 1944; Francis Maloney to Douglas, July 10, 1944; Eliot Janeway to Douglas, August 4, 1944, Douglas mss., LC; Douglas, *The Court Years, 1939–1975* (1980), 281–284; Ickes diary, October 7, 1944, LC.
32. Jim Bishop, *FDR's Last Year* (1974), 94–95.
33. Byrnes, *All In One Lifetime,* 226–230; Flynn, *You're the Boss,* 182–183; Rosenman, *Roosevelt,* 450–451; Miller, *Truman,* 386; Robert Donovan, *Conflict and Crisis* (1973), xii–xiii; Bert Cochran, *Truman and the Crisis Presidency* (1973), 6–21.
34. Daniels, *White House Witness,* 238–239.
35. Rosenman, *Roosevelt,* 450–453; William M. Rigdon, *White House Sailor* (1962), 111–113; *Time,* July 31, 1944.
36. *PPA,* 1944–1945:201–206.
37. James Roosevelt, *My Parents,* 278–279; James Roosevelt and Sidney Shalett, *Affectionately, F.D.R.* (1959), 351–352.

Chapter 39: TO THE PACIFIC AND QUEBEC

1. *PL,* 2:1525.
2. *PL,* 2:1524.
3. Leahy diary, July 21–26, 1944, LC; William M. Rigdon, *White House Sailor* (1962), 116–117; Rosenman, *Roosevelt,* 456–457.
4. Thomas B. Buell, *Master of Sea Power . . . Ernest J. King* (1980), 467; D. Clayton James, *Years of MacArthur* (2 vols., 1970–1975), 2:527.
5. Buell, *King,* 444–447, 463–468.
6. James, *MacArthur,* 2:533.
7. *PPA,* 1944–1945:206–207.
8. William D. Leahy, *I Was There* (1950), 251; Rigdon, *White House Sailor,* 117; Leahy diary, July 27, 1944.
9. Leahy diary, July 29, 1944.
10. Rosenman, *Roosevelt,* 458.
11. James, *MacArthur,* 2:534–535; PC, 24:33; *PL,* 2:1541.
12. Rosenman, *Roosevelt,* 459; James Roosevelt, *My Parents* (1976), 283. See *PPA,* 1944–1945:212.
13. Rigdon, *White House Sailor,* 124–125; *PPA,* 1944–1945:213–216; Leahy diary, August 3, 1944; Maclyn Burg to author, May 29, 1984.
14. *PPA,* 1944–1945:223; Ickes diary, August 20, 1944, LC; FDR to Ickes, August 17, 1944, copy in Wickard mss., LC.
15. Rigdon, *White House Sailor,* 126; Rosenman, *Roosevelt,* 455–456; Richard Nor-

ton Smith, *Thomas E. Dewey and His Times* (1982), 416; Leahy diary, September 1, 1944.

16. Rigdon, *White House Sailor,* 128–131; Howard G. Bruenn, "Clinical Notes on the Illness and Death of President Franklin D. Roosevelt," *Annals of Internal Medicine* (April, 1970), 72:586; *Seattle Post-Intelligencer,* August 13, 1944; *Time,* August 21, 1944; *PPA,* 1944–1945:216–228. On the problems from not being used to being on one's feet, see Jane E. Brody, *New York Times,* March 24, 1988.

17. *Time,* August 21, 1944.

18. FDR to Frederick B. Adams, September 4, 1944, *PPF,* 914; Rosenman, *Roosevelt,* 474; Lash, *Eleanor and Franklin,* 710.

19. Interview with Anna Roosevelt Halsted, July 31, 1975; Morgenthau diary, August 25, 1944; *PPA,* 1944–1945:236–240.

20. *Time,* August 28, 1944; Harry S. Truman, *Memoirs* (2 vols., 1955), 1:193; William Hassett, *Off the Record with FDR* (1958), 265, 267.

21. John M. Blum, ed., *The Price of Vision: Diary of Henry A. Wallace, 1942–1946* (1973), 381–384.

22. Mark Ethridge to FDR, July 25, 1944; Mary Bingham to ER, July 25, 1944; ER to Mary Bingham, August 3, 1944; Mary Bingham memorandum [after August 30, 1944]; Mary Bingham to Barry Bingham, September 4, 1944, Bingham mss., Schlesinger Library, Radcliffe College.

23. Forrest Pogue, *George Marshall* (4 vols., 1963–1987), 3:411–420.

24. Mary Bingham, memorandum [after August 30, 1944], Bingham mss.

25. W. Averell Harriman and Elie Abel, *Special Envoy to Churchill and Stalin, 1941–1946* (1975), 335–349; FDR and WSC to Stalin, August 20, 1944; Stalin to WSC and FDR, August 22, 1944, *Correspondence Between the Chairman of the Council of Ministers and the Presidents of the USA . . .* (Moscow, 1957), 1:254–255.

26. Thomas C. Campbell and George C. Herring, eds., *Diaries of Edward R. Stettinius, Jr., 1943–1946* (1975), 110–114, 117–118.

27. Campbell and Herring, eds., *Stettinius Diaries,* 128–131; FDR to Stalin, September 8, 1944, *Correspondence,* 2:159.

28. *FRUS, Second Quebec Conference,* 198–200.

29. Harriman and Abel, *Special Envoy,* 334–349; Milovan Djilas, *Conversations with Stalin* (1962), 114.

30. Morgenthau diary, August 19, 25, 1944.

31. FDR to Stimson, August 26, 1944, Stimson diary, Stimson mss., YU.

32. *PL,* 2:1535; Stimson diary, September 6, 1944.

33. George McJimsey, *Harry Hopkins* (1987), 343; Morgenthau diary, September 9, 1944; Ickes diary, September 17, 1944; Daniels, *White House Witness,* 17, 244.

34. Hastings L. Ismay, *Memoirs of General Lord Ismay* (1960), 373; *FRUS, Second Quebec Conference,* 285; Charles Wilson (Lord Moran), *Churchill: Taken from the Diaries of Lord Moran* (1966), 192.

35. Bruenn, "Clinical Notes," 587.

36. *FRUS, Second Quebec Conference,* 344–345, 348, 361; Martin Gilbert, *Winston S. Churchill: Road to Victory* (1986), 964.

37. *FRUS, Second Quebec Conference,* 323–328, 360–362; 466; Wilson, *Churchill,* 190–191.
38. *FRUS, Second Quebec Conference,* 392 and map in color.
39. *FRUS, Second Quebec Conference,* 367–369.
40. See Richard Rhodes, *Making of the Atomic Bomb* (1986), 525–538; Barton Bernstein, "Roosevelt, Truman, and the Atomic Bomb: A Reinterpretation," *Political Science Quarterly* (Spring, 1975), 90:27–34; Martin J. Sherwin, *A World Destroyed; The Atomic Bomb and the Grand Alliance* (1975); and Daniel Yergin, *Shattered Peace* (1977); Stimson diary, September 9, 1943; *New York Times,* August 19, 1960.
41. *FRUS, Second Quebec Conference,* 493.
42. Bernstein, "Roosevelt, Truman, and the Atomic Bomb," 90:32–34.
43. Hassett, *Off the Record,* 272.

Chapter 40: A FOURTH TERM

1. Howard G. Bruenn, "Clinical Notes on the Illness and Death of President Franklin D. Roosevelt," *Annals of Internal Medicine,* (April, 1970), 72:587.
2. *Newsweek,* September 25, 1944.
3. Ickes diary, October 6, 1944, LC.
4. *PPA,* 1944–1945:284–292; Rosenman, *Roosevelt,* 474–477; *Time,* October 2, 1944.
5. Richard Norton Smith, *Thomas E. Dewey and His Times* (1982), 421–422; *Time,* October 2, 1944.
6. Sherwood, *Roosevelt and Hopkins,* 821; Barry K. Beyer, *Dewey: A Study in Political Leadership* (1979), 209.
7. Smith, *Dewey,* 424–425.
8. Forrest Pogue, *George Marshall* (4 vols., 1963–1987), 3:470–473; Smith, *Dewey,* 425–430.
9. *PPA,* 1944–1945:350; Smith, *Dewey,* 412–415.
10. *Time,* October 2, 1944; Stimson diary, October 3, 1944, Stimson mss., YU.
11. PC, 24:134.
12. Michael Schaller, *The U.S. Crusade in China, 1938–1945* (1979), 147–175; PC, 24:204–210.
13. *Time,* October 9, 16, 1944; Stimson diary, October 3, 1944; PC, 24:139; *PPA,* 1944–1945:317–325; Jonathan Daniels, *White House Witness* (1975), 280; William Hassett, *Off the Record with FDR* (1958), 276–277.
14. *Gallup Poll,* 1:458–467; *Time,* October 23, 1944.
15. *Time,* October 23, 1944; Beyer, *Dewey,* 230–231.
16. *Time,* October 23, 30, 1944; PC, 24:181.
17. PC, 24:186–188, 191.
18. *New York Times,* October 22, 1944; *Time,* October 30, 1944.
19. *PPA,* 1944–1945:342–354; PC, 24:192; Rosenman, *Roosevelt,* 482–484; H. G. Nicholas, ed., *Washington Despatches 1941–1945* (1980), 441.
20. Rosenman, *Roosevelt,* 486–487; *New York Times,* October 28, 1944.
21. *PPA,* 1944–1945:369–370; *Time,* November 6, 1944.
22. *New York Times,* October 29, 1944; PPA, 1944–1945:378–382; Rosenman, *Roosevelt,* 498; Hassett, *Off the Record,* 287.

23. *PPA*, 1944–1945:397–398; Rosenman, *Roosevelt*, 499–503; Hassett, *Off the Record*, 289–290; Leahy diary, November 4, 1944, LC.
24. *PPA*, 1944–1945:406–413; Leahy diary, November 6, 1944.
25. Letter section, *Time*, December 11, 1944; PC 24:252.
26. *PPA*, 1944–1945:413–414; Hassett, *Off the Record*, 292–294; Leahy diary, November 7, 1944.
27. Hassett, *Off the Record*, 294; Smith, *Dewey*, 436–437; *Time*, November 13, 1944.
28. Leon Friedman, "Election of 1944," in Arthur M. Schlesinger, Jr., and Fred L. Israel, eds., *History of American Presidential Elections* (4 vols., 1971), 4:3037–3038; Nicholas, ed., *Washington Despatches*, 456–458; *Time*, November 20, 1944; PC, 24:219.
29. *PPA*, 1944–1945:418; Hassett, *Off the Record*, 295–296.
30. PC, 24:217; Thomas C. Campbell and George C. Herring, eds., *Diaries of Edward R. Stettinius, Jr., 1943–1946* (1975), 167–168.
31. FDR to Stalin, October 4, 1944, *Correspondence Between the Chairman of the Council of Ministers of the USSR and the Presidents of the USA . . .* (Moscow, 1957), 1:162; *C&R*, 3:343–344; Sherwood, *Roosevelt and Hopkins*, 833–834.
32. Winston S. Churchill, *Triumph and Tragedy* (1953), 227–228.
33. Nicholas, ed., *Washington Despatches*, 465, 469–470; Charles E. Bohlen, *Witness to History* (1973), 166.
34. Campbell and Herring, eds., *Stettinius Diaries*, 185–186; Bohlen, *Witness to History*, 165–167.
35. Campbell and Herring, eds., *Stettinius Diaries*, 169–170; Nicholas, ed., *Washington Despatches*, 474–475; *Time*, December 18, 1944.
36. *Time*, December 18, 1944; R. H. Winnick, ed., *Letters of Archibald MacLeish* (1983), 325.
37. Lash, *Eleanor and Franklin*, 713–714.
38. Allen Drury, *A Senate Journal* (1963), 305, 315; *Time*, January 1, 1945; PC, 24:262–263.
39. PC, 24:264; *Time*, February 5, 1945; Nicholas, ed., *Washington Despatches*, 507.
40. Campbell and Herring, eds., *Stettinius Diaries*, 170.
41. Hassett, *Off the Record*, 303; PL, 2:1556.
42. Bruenn, "Clinical Notes," 587–588; Hassett, *Off the Record*, 305–306.
43. *PPA*, 1944–1945:444–445; Hassett, *Off the Record*, 307.
44. Blum, ed., *Wallace Diary*, 406–413.
45. *PPA*, 1944–1945:457–517; PC, 25:11; Blum, ed., *Wallace Diary*, 420; Drury, *Senate Journal*, 331.
46. *PPA*, 1944–1945:523–525; Hassett, *Off the Record*, 312–313; *Time*, January 29, 1945.
47. Hassett, *Off the Record*, 312–313; James Roosevelt, *My Parents* (1976), 281–284; Ickes diary, January 21, 1945, LC; Bruenn, "Clinical Notes," 588.
48. Ickes diary, January 27, 1945.
49. Jesse Jones memorandum, March 20, 1945, Jones mss., LC.
50. Anna Roosevelt Boettiger diary, February 1, 1945; Leahy diary, January 29, 1945; Daniels, *White House Witness*, 257; Drury, *Senate Journal*, 345–355, 360; Bascom N. Timmons, *Jesse H. Jones* (1956), 351–356.
51. Daniels, *White House Witness*, 286–287.

Chapter 41: YALTA

1. PC, 25:3.
2. Jesse Jones memorandum, February 11, 1945, Jones mss., LC; Ickes diary, January 21, 1945, LC; Walter Millis, ed., *The Forrestal Diaries* (1951), 27.
3. *Time,* January 29, 1945; *Gallup Poll,* 1:485, 488, 497.
4. Thomas C. Campbell and George C. Herring, eds., *Diaries of Edward R. Stettinius, Jr., 1943–1946* (1975), 215–216; Charles E. Bohlen, *Witness to History* (1973), 194.
5. Bohlen, *Witness to History,* 194–195.
6. James F. Byrnes, *Speaking Frankly* (1947), 21–22; Edward J. Flynn, *You're the Boss* (1947), 185–186; Reminiscences of Anna Roosevelt Halsted, COHO.
7. Howard G. Bruenn, "Clinical Notes on the Illness and Death of President Franklin D. Roosevelt," *Annals of Internal Medicine* (April, 1970), 72:588; Anna Roosevelt Boettiger diary, January 23, 1945; William D. Leahy, *I Was There* (1950), 292; Bohlen, *Witness to History,* 178.
8. Anna Roosevelt Boettiger diary, January 25, 1945.
9. Anna Roosevelt Boettiger diary, February 1, 1945; Bruenn, "Clinical Notes," 588; *C&R,* 3:518, 521.
10. Campbell and Herring, eds., *Stettinius Diaries,* 235.
11. Anthony Eden, *Memoirs: The Reckoning* (1965), 511.
12. Stimson diary, December 31, 1944, Stimson mss., YU.
13. Forrest Pogue, *George Marshall* (4 vols., 1963–1987), 3:516–517.
14. Charles Wilson (Lord Moran), *Churchill: Taken from the Diaries of Lord Moran* (1966), 234; Eden, *The Reckoning,* 512.
15. Wilson, *Churchill,* 242; Bohlen, *Witness to History,* 171.
16. Campbell and Herring, eds., *Stettinius Diaries,* 184.
17. Leahy, *I Was There,* 321; interview with Admiral Leahy, May 24, 1948; Bohlen, *Witness to History,* 172.
18. Leahy, *I Was There,* 296–297; Pogue, *Marshall,* 3:520–521; *FRUS, Conferences at Malta and Yalta, 1945* (1955), 549–552.
19. Campbell and Herring, eds., *Stettinius Diaries,* 213–214.
20. W. Averell Harriman and Elie Abel, *Special Envoy to Churchill and Stalin, 1941–1946* (1975), 394.
21. *FRUS, Malta and Yalta,* 570–573.
22. *FRUS, Malta and Yalta,* 578–581.
23. A. H. Birse, *Memoirs of an Interpreter* (1967); Laurence S. Kuter, *Airman at Yalta* (1955), 128–129, 171–172.
24. *FRUS, Malta and Yalta,* 589; Bohlen, *Witness to History,* 181.
25. *FRUS, Malta and Yalta,* 611–616; Bohlen, *Witness to History,* 183.
26. Bohlen, *Witness to History,* 184–185; *FRUS, Malta and Yalta,* 899–900.
27. *FRUS, Malta and Yalta,* 616–622.
28. Harriman and Abel, *Special Envoy,* 403–405; Bohlen, *Witness to History,* 185–186; Sherwood, *Roosevelt and Hopkins,* 860.
29. *FRUS, Malta and Yalta,* 660–667.
30. *FRUS, Malta and Yalta,* 711–715; Bohlen, *Witness to History,* 193–195.
31. Bruenn, "Clinical Notes," 589.

32. *FRUS, Malta and Yalta*, 667, 677, 717.
33. Bohlen, *Witness to History*, 150–151, 187; *FRUS, Malta and Yalta*, 667–670.
34. Bohlen, *Witness to History*, 190–192; *FRUS, Malta and Yalta*, 781.
35. *FRUS, Malta and Yalta*, 972.
36. Harriman and Abel, *Special Envoy*, 414–415.
37. *FRUS, Malta and Yalta*, 378–383, 385–388.
38. *FRUS, Malta and Yalta*, 567.
39. *FRUS, Malta and Yalta*, 768–769; Bohlen, *Witness to History*, 196–197.
40. Harriman and Abel, *Special Envoy*, 398–400; Bohlen, *Witness to History*, 198–199.
41. Campbell and Herring, eds., *Stettinius Diaries*, 278.
42. Bohlen, *Witness to History*, 192–193; Harriman and Abel, *Special Envoy*, 412–414.
43. *PL*, 2:1570.

Chapter 42: ROOSEVELT'S TRIUMPH AND TRAGEDY

1. Interview with Anna Roosevelt Halsted, July 31, 1975.
2. PC, 25:49–50; William H. Rigdon, *White House Sailor* (1962), 165, 167.
3. Charles E. Bohlen, *Witness to History* (1973), 203. FDR's joke was omitted from the published Yalta transcripts. PC, 25:50.
4. Sherwood, *Roosevelt and Hopkins*, 872; Colonel William A. Eddy *aide mémoire* in Rigdon, *White House Sailor*, 170–172; Bohlen, *Witness to History*, 203–204.
5. Thomas C. Campbell and George C. Herring, eds., *Diaries of Edward R. Stettinius, Jr., 1943–1946* (1975), 289–290.
6. Martin Gilbert, *Winston S. Churchill: The Road to Victory* (1986), 1222–1223; Howard G. Bruenn, "Clinical Notes on the Illness and Death of President Franklin D. Roosevelt," *Annals of Internal Medicine* (April, 1970), 72:589. Dr. Bruenn did not note FDR's depression.
7. Sherwood, *Roosevelt and Hopkins*, 873–874; interview with Anna Roosevelt Halsted, July 31, 1975; Bohlen, *Witness to History*, 205–206; Rosenman, *Roosevelt*, 521–522.
8. Rosenman, *Roosevelt*, 522–524; interviews with Anna Roosevelt Halsted.
9. Rosenman, *Roosevelt*, 526–527; PC, 25:70–73.
10. *Time*, February 26, 1945; Christopher Thorne, *Allies of a Kind* (1978), 621–626.
11. PC, 25:58–63.
12. *PPA*, 1944–1945:570–586; Jonathan Daniels, *White House Witness* (1975), 266–267; Rosenman, *Roosevelt*, 527–529; *Time*, March 12, 1945.
13. *Time*, April 23, 1945; *PPA*, 1944–1945:570; Allen Drury, *A Senate Journal* (1963), 373.
14. Daniels, *White House Witness*, 264; William Hassett, *Off the Record with FDR* (1958), 318.
15. J. W. Pickersgill, *The Mackenzie King Record* (4 vols., 1960), 2:325–326; Mackenzie King diary, March 10, 1945, Archives of Canada, Ottawa.
16. Mackenzie King diary, March 13, 1945; Daniels, *White House Witness*, 271.
17. Hassett, *Off the Record*, 324–325.

18. Annie Cohen Solal, *Sartre* (Paris, 1985), 316–317, citing *Le Figaro,* March 11, 12, 1945; *Time,* March 19, 1945.
19. FDR to Stalin, March 3, 1945; Stalin to FDR, March 5, 1945, *Correspondence Between the Chairman of the Council of Ministers of the USSR and the Presidents of the USA . . .* (Moscow, 1957), 2:194–195; *C&R,* 3:541–542.
20. Bohlen, *Witness to History,* 206–208; *C&R,* 3:542–598; W. Averell Harriman and Elie Abel, *Special Envoy to Churchill and Stalin, 1941–1946* (1975), 420–431.
21. Harriman and Abel, *Special Envoy,* 444; *C&R,* 3:599–602; FDR to Stalin, received April 1, 1945, *Correspondence,* 2:201–204.
22. FDR to Stalin, received March 25, April 1, 1945; Stalin to FDR, March 29, 1945, *Correspondence,* 2:198–205.
23. Stalin to FDR, April 3, 1945, *Correspondence,* 2:205–206; *C&R,* 3:610.
24. FDR to Stalin, April 4, 1945, *Correspondence,* 2:207–208; *C&R,* 3:609, 611–612.
25. Stalin to FDR, April 7, 1945, *Correspondence,* 2:208–210.
26. *C&R,* 3:630.
27. Campbell and Herring, eds., *Stettinius Diaries,* 297, 306–307; Daniels, *White House Witness,* 277–278.
28. Hassett, *Off the Record,* 327–329, 333–334.
29. Hassett, *Off the Record,* 328; James Halsted notes, March 8, 1967, Anna Roosevelt Halsted mss. I am grateful to Geoffrey C. Ward for providing me with a copy of these notes.
30. Claude D. Pepper, *Pepper* (1987), 139; *PL,* 2:1578–1579, 1581; Hassett, *Off the Record,* 329; Rosenman, *Roosevelt,* 539–540; PC, 25:120–121.
31. Rosenman, *Roosevelt,* 551; Hassett, *Off the Record,* 333; confidential source.
32. Stimson diary, April 11, 1945, Stimson mss., YU.
33. Morgenthau diary, April 11, 1945; interview with Anna Roosevelt Halsted, July 31, 1975.
34. Hassett, *Off the Record,* 333–336; Bruenn, "Clinical Notes," 590; conversations with Margaret Suckley.
35. Morgenthau diary, April 12, 1945; ER, *This I Remember* (1949), 343–344; *Time,* April 23, 1945.
36. Drury, *Senate Journal,* 412; conversations with Margaret Suckley.
37. Dwight D. Eisenhower, *Crusade in Europe* (1948), 409–410.
38. Gilbert, *Road to Victory,* 1291–1294; Donald P. Geddes, ed., *Franklin Delano Roosevelt: A Memorial* (1945), 55.
39. Harriman and Abel, *Special Envoy,* 440–442; Michael F. Reilly and William J. Slocum, *Reilly of the White House* (1947), 234; *C&R,* 3:631, citing *FRUS,* 1945, 5:836–839.
40. ER, *This I Remember,* 345–347; Hassett, *Off the Record,* 339–345; Drury, *Senate Journal,* 412–413; *Los Angeles Times* editorial in Geddes, ed., *Roosevelt,* 84.

BIBLIOGRAPHICAL NOTE

The literature on Franklin D. Roosevelt and related topics is rich and enormous. Among the biographies are the two volumes by James MacGregor Burns, *Roosevelt: The Lion and the Fox* (1956), and *Roosevelt: The Soldier of Freedom* (1970), and a multivolume work by Kenneth S. Davis, *FDR* (3 vols. thus far, 1972–). Frank Freidel, *Franklin D. Roosevelt* (4 vols., 1952–1973), covers into July, 1933, and is much fuller in text and notes than the present one-volume biography. Geoffrey Ward's two volumes, *Before the Trumpet* (1985) and *A First Class Temperament* (1989), cover their subject into 1928 and are particularly detailed on Roosevelt's personal life and family. Joseph P. Lash, *Eleanor and Franklin* (1971), portrays Roosevelt's relationship with his wife, primarily from her papers. William E. Leuchtenburg, *In the Shadow of FDR* (1983), traces his impact since his death, focusing upon his effect upon subsequent presidents.

On Roosevelt within the panorama of the New Deal, Arthur M. Schlesinger, Jr., *The Age of Roosevelt* (3 vols. thus far, 1957–), is classic. The standard brief assessment is William E. Leuchtenburg, *Franklin D. Roosevelt and the New Deal, 1932–1940* (1963). A readable reference work is Otis L. Graham and Meghan Robinson Wander, eds., *Franklin D. Roosevelt: His Life and Times, an Encyclopedic View* (1985).

Key surveys of Roosevelt's first two terms are Anthony J. Badger, *The New Deal: The Depression Years, 1933–40* (1989), an appraisal based upon scholarly monographs and papers, with a full annotated bibliography; and Robert S. McElvaine, *The Great Depression: America 1929–1941* (1984), an account of the American people. On the home front in World War II, John M. Blum, *V Was for Victory* (1976), is a stimulating interpretation. On foreign affairs, Robert Dallek, *Franklin D. Roosevelt and American Foreign Policy, 1932–1945* (1979) is authoritative; Frederick W. Marks III, *Wind Over Sand; The Diplomacy of Franklin Roosevelt* (1988), based upon broad research, differs from Dallek's book and this study in some of its conclusions. Eric Larrabee, *Commander in Chief, Franklin Delano Roosevelt, His Lieutenants and Their War* (1987), is a luminous survey.

The Roosevelt record both in print and in manuscript is massive. There are large manuscript holdings in the Roosevelt Library, the National Archives, and in foreign archives. Scores of other libraries contain materials. Many of these collections are cited in the notes. Contemporary accounts, diaries, memoirs, and oral history interviews are other prime sources. Some of the most important material, for example, the Roosevelt-Churchill correspondence, is in print; even more, like the Morgenthau diaries, is available in microfilm or microfiche form. Notes in this volume refer wherever possible to the location in print of letters and documents rather than to an archive or manuscript collection. The notes also contain citations to specialized studies on many aspects of Roosevelt's life and career.

ACKNOWLEDGMENTS

Many people and institutions have been of essential help to me in writing this volume. I am particularly grateful to Richard N. Current and Alan Brinkley for their many comments upon the finished manuscript, to Stephen A. Schuker for his guidance on foreign policy questions, and to Dr. Lawrence Z. Freedman for his insight into the personalities of the Roosevelts. A number of historians have provided me with materials and suggestions. Among them are Saul Benison, Barton Bernstein, John M. Blum, Robert Burke, Robert Butow, Roger Daniels, Irwin Gellman, Richard Harrison, Gary Hess, Barry Karl, Bradford Lee, Mark Leff, William Leuchtenburg, Richard Lowitt, Nancy Weiss Malkiel, Ernest May, Thomas Paterson, James T. Patterson, David Reynolds, Mario Rossi, Arthur M. Schlesinger, Jr., David Shannon, James Thomson, Geoffrey Ward, David Wyman, and William Youngs.

Numerous archivists and librarians have guided me to materials and offered their hospitality. I owe much to the directors of the Roosevelt Library, from the late Fred Shipman through the current director, William E. Emerson, and to many members of the Roosevelt Library staff, including Susan Y. Elter, Audiovisual Archivist; and to Benedict Zobrist, director of the Truman Library, Thomas Thalken, former director of the Hoover Library, David Wigdor of the Manuscripts Division of the Library of Congress, Y. T. Feng, Roy E. Larsen Librarian of Harvard College, F. Nathaniel Bunker, Charles Warren Bibliographer at the Harvard library, Elizabeth Mason of the Columbia Oral History Collection, and Karyl Winn, curator of the manuscripts division, University of Washington Library.

I am grateful for the expert assistance of Betsy Goolian and Janet

Schwartz and the research assistance of Richard Seitz at the University of Washington, and for the typing of Susan Hunt and Victoria Cox Buresch at Harvard University.

Time and funds for research and writing have come from the Bullitt Chair in American History at the University of Washington, the Charles Warren Center for Studies in American History at Harvard University, and through a fellowship from the National Endowment for the Humanities.

At Little, Brown and Company, Roger Donald, Trade Publisher, contributed much to the shaping of the manuscript; Jennifer Josephy, Senior Editor, Betsy Pitha, Manager of Trade Copyediting, and Ann Staffeld, Copy Editor, demonstrated rare skill in preparing it for publication.

From my wife, Madeleine Freidel, have come incisive criticism and unflagging encouragement.

INDEX

Absentee ballots. *See* Soldiers' vote bill
Acheson, Dean, 8, 133, 570
Act of Havana, 351
Adak, 543, 544
Adams, Henry, 24
Addams, Jane, 79
Administrative reform, 96, 97, 221, 223, 224, 228, 273–280, 281; advisers on, 275, 278, 279, 341; criticism/opposition, 276, 277, 280; defense and, 319, 341–342; goal of, 275; passage of, 276–277, 279; personnel and, 278–280. *See also* Executive Office of the President
Admiralty, British, 292, 333
Adriatic, 483
Africa, 369, 389; FDR's anticolonialism and, 461, 462; TR and, 298. *See also* Africa, French North; Africa, French West; Ethiopia; South Africa
Africa, French North, 367, 386, 456; Allied invasion, 412–413, 447–448, 449, 450–452, 469; Churchill and, 386, 412–418; FDR's strategy for, 373, 386, 394; French government/forces in, 454, 455–458, 459, 460–461; French nationalists in, 339, 367; Hitler's plans for, 367, 373, 386, 454; as refugee settlement site, 297. *See also* Casablanca conference; Egypt; Libya; Tunisia
Africa, French West, 456, 458, 596
Afrika Korps, 368, 450, 456
Agricultural Adjustment Administration (AAA), 103, 141; constitutionality rulings on, 191–192, 193; farm organizations and, 154; income redistribution and, 127; modifications in, 148, 192; as New Deal mainstay, with NRA, 126–127, 147; planning and passage of, 83, 84, 85–86, 100, 101, 103–104, 105, 228; problems with, 126, 128, 130–134, 136, 145; processing tax to fund, 130, 133; prototypes for, 123, 136; Thomas amendment to, 133. *See also* Agriculture: crop control; Farm Relief Act
Agriculture, 7, 93, 139; blacks and, 245–246; business and, 104, 126–127, 128; commercial/large-scale, 154, 206; crop control, 57, 73, 77, 85, 86, 103–104, 111, 116, 130, 131, 147, 191–192, 193; depression and, 60, 75; discontent, 133–134, 144; FDR's Georgia farm, 47, 51; FDR's relationship with, 20, 21, 54, 57, 58–59, 67, 70, 83, 154, 227, 242, 345, 440, 500; income of, 205, 248; international, 111, 115, 116, 597; labor and, 242, 438; mortgages and loans/foreclosure, 21, 70, 73, 85–86, 100, 103, 105, 134; prices, 57, 75, 79, 85–86, 101, 102, 103, 104, 116, 128, 131–134, 192, 206, 430–431, 433, 435–436, 437–439; purchasing power of, 70, 85, 127, 128; relief for, 123, 138, 565; Republicans and, 18; southern, 245–246, 281, 281; strikes, 133–134; surpluses, 131–132, 215; wartime, 417, 496. *See also* Agricultural Adjustment Administration (AAA); Farm Board
Agriculture, Department of, 123, 136, 278
Aid, U.S, 309–311, 312, 313, 341, 347; air program, 308, 309, 310, 311, 312, 326, 335, 338; to Asia, postwar, 219; to Britain, 299, 303–304, 305, 309, 314, 315, 319, 322, 326, 329, 331, 333–336, 338, 339, 342, 347, 349, 350, 352, 355, 357, 358–360, 361–364, 365, 367, 368, 375, 379, 382, 386, 391, 392, 412, 415, 441, 450, 473, 505–506; to Britain, postwar, 552; to

Aid, U.S. (*cont.*)
China, 380, 398, 399, 442–443, 469, 478, 483, 561; cold war and, 219; covert, French plan, 309–311; covert, in Spanish Civil War, 271–272; as defense, 321, 322, 323, 358, 359, 361, 386; defense/rearmament vs., 306, 308, 309–311, 326, 333–334, 338, 339, 409, 412, 441; to Europe, 307, 314, 321, 329, 330, 334, 335, 339–340 (*see also* Aid, U.S.: to Britain; to France); to Europe, postwar, 219; to France, 299, 303–304, 305, 308, 309, 310, 311, 312, 314, 315, 319, 322, 326, 329, 331–332, 367, 460, 596; to Iran, 487; to Latin America, 218–219, 220, 351 (*see also* Good Neighbor policy); neutrality legislation and, 309, 315, 319–320; oil shortage and, 379, 382; to Soviet Union, 374–375, 375–376, 471, 473, 479; to Tito, 604; to Turkey, postwar, 491; for underprivileged of world, 530. *See also* Destroyers-for-bases deal; Lend-lease; Munitions Assignment Board; Red Cross
Aircraft, 436; in Allied invasion of France, 527; British, 301, 303, 307, 308, 309, 548; B-17s, 378; B-29s, 529; C-47s, 594; C-54s, 580; disarmament and, 111; FDR on, 330; FDR's personal use of, 73, 458, 580; French, 301, 303, 307; French purchase of U.S., 308, 309, 310, 311, 312; German, 303, 307–308, 526; Italian, 308; Soviet, 307; Spanish Civil War and, 271; U.S., 303–304, 405, 446, 548; as U.S. aid, 308, 309, 310, 311, 312, 326, 335, 338; U.S. bases, 261, 323; U.S. rearmament program, 307–311, 312; U.S. war production and, 330, 339, 432
Air force/air corps, U.S., 323, 326, 335, 339, 350, 352, 353, 355, 367, 413. *See also* Aircraft; Armed forces, U.S.; Destroyers-for-bases deal; "Flying Tigers"
Air force, British, 320, 336, 338, 351
Air force, German, 449. *See also* Luftwaffe
Airmail regulation, 139
Alabama, 87, 520; congressmen/senators from, 74, 132, 152, 168, 238, 280, 530
Alaska, 472; FDR in, 542, 543, 546; Japanese offshore fishing, 261, 293; as settlement area, for refugees and veterans, 298, 543
Albania, 314
Albany, New York, 18, 19, 24, 55, 56, 57, 66, 72, 76, 150, 242, 559
Aleutian Islands, 292, 527; FDR's trip to, 542, 543, 545, 558
Alexander, Marshal, 601
Alexander I, 458
Alexandria, Virginia, 595
Algeria, 337, 457, 460, 461, 575, 595
Algiers, 455, 456
Allenwood School, 12
Allied Reparations Commission, 585
Allies, 329, 331, 334, 339, 360, 547, 583. *See also* Great Britain; Soviet Union; United States
Alps, 482
Alsace-Lorraine, 466
Alsop, Joseph, 306
Amberjack II, 115, 116
"America First," as slogan for isolationists, 68
America First Committee, 362, 366, 373–374, 408
American Agriculturist, 57
American Construction Council, 40
American Federation of Labor (AFL), 156, 159, 161, 241–242, 438
American Fleet, 350, 378, 411, 445, 446. *See also* Pacific Fleet
American Flying Fortresses (B-17s), 378
American Group, 526
American Labor party, 204
American Legion, 96, 503
American Molasses Company, 252
American Museum of Natural History, 196
American Society of Newspaper Editors, 308, 521
American Tobacco, 15
American Viscose Corporation, 359
American Youth Congress, 325
Amtorg, 172
Anacostia River, 75
ANAKIM (Burma opening), 467
Andaman Islands, 479, 491
Andrew, Abram Piatt, 10
Anfa (Casablanca), 459
Angell, James R., 210
Annapolis, 10, 179, 364
Anschluss, 295, 296, 297
Antarctica, 316
Anti-Comintern pact, 217
Antigua, 352
Antilynching bill, 148, 246–247
Anti-Semitism; in Europe, 112, 295; FDR and, 112, 594; in French North Africa, 456, 457, 461; of Hitler/Germany, 107, 112, 113, 179; Jewish emigration and, 295, 296–297; refugee resettlement plan and, 296, 298; in Romania, 112; Roosevelts' name change and, 4; in U.S., 112, 146, 295–296, 298, 313. *See also* Jews
Antiwar movement, 289. *See also* Disarmament; Isolationists
Antwerp, 572
Anzio, 504, 526
Appeasement, 112, 258–260, 269, 272, 294, 295, 314, 332, 363; FDR and, 259, 354; Spanish Civil War and, 269, 272
Appenine peninsula, 470

Arabia. *See* Saudi Arabia
Arabs, 389, 594–595. *See also* Saudi Arabia
Arauca, 371
Arcadia conference, 410–416; British domination of, 410, 412, 413; coalition warfare issues, 414–416; strategic issues, 410–414
Ardennes, 548, 583
Argentia, Newfoundland, 384, 389, 412. *See also* Atlantic (Argentia) conference
Argentina, 213, 215, 216, 219, 307, 505
Arizona, 84, 96
Arkansas, 198, 237, 284
Arlington National Cemetery, 523
Armaments. *See* Atomic bomb; Disarmament; Munitions Assignment Board; United States: rearmament/war preparedness; War production
Armed forces, German, 377
Armed forces, U.S., 179–180, 331, 407, 411, 412, 504, 521, 559; in Africa, 455, 467–468; in Britain, 413, 450; preparedness/strength, 180, 310, 347, 349, 366, 364, 368, 370, 379, 386, 394, 396, 445, 446; voting in, 496, 503, 547, 557, 562. *See also* Air force, U.S.; Army, U.S.; Marines, U.S.; Navy, U.S.; Selective service
Armistice, 31, 33, 37, 93
Arms embargo. *See* Embargo
Army, Belgian, 332, 335
Army, British, 368, 447–448, 492, 547
Army, Chinese, 293, 443
Army, Dutch, 330
Army, 8th Route (China), 293
Army, First, 539
Army, French, 258, 318, 329, 332, 333, 548
Army, German, 324, 329, 335, 450
Army, Japanese, 262, 290, 291, 292, 381, 382, 442, 446
Army, Red, 583
Army, Soviet, 583; in Poland, 587
Army, Spanish, 269
Army, U.S., 321, 326, 350, 370, 386, 399, 411, 498; budget and, 97, 180; FDR's defense policy and, 326, 339–340, 355; French invasion, 448, 547, 548; Japan and, 293, 444–445, 559; strength/preparedness of, 364, 365, 366, 392, 394, 397, 446, 468; war production and, 419, 421. *See also* Armed forces, U.S.; Army Air Corps; Selective service
Army Air Corps, 309, 510. *See also* Air force/air corps, U.S.
Army Intelligence (G-2), 339, 400, 401; surveillance of ER, 510, 511. *See also* Intelligence, U.S.
Army-Navy Munitions Board, 420
Army Victory Program, 366
Arnold, H. H. ("Hap"), 309, 311, 323, 330, 384, 414, 481, 558
Arnold, Thomas, 8
Arnold, Thurman, 256–257
"Arsenal of democracy," 360–361. *See also* Aid, U.S.
Articles of Confederation, 443
Arts, WPA support for, 187–188
Ashurst, Henry F., 229, 234
Asia, 188; European possessions in, 377; Japan and, 79, 109, 110, 272, 289, 290, 292, 316, 369, 373, 377, 378, 379, 380, 381, 398, 395, 398, 427, 442, 443, 444; Soviet Union and, 590, 591; U.S. and, 215, 219, 408, 478, 487; war threat in, 172, 180, 181. *See also names of individual countries*
Asia magazine, 291
Asiatic Fleet, 268
Asquith, Lord, 194
Associated Gas and Electric Company, 151, 166, 167
Associated Press, 39, 423
Astor, Vincent, 261
Athens, 580, 595
Athlone, Earl of, 599
Atlanta, 245, 283, 517
Atlantic: *Bismarck* sinking, 371; British in, 359, 368, 369, 371; convoys and patrols in, 368–370; FDR's prewar strategy in, 330, 334, 339, 368–370, 371, 372, 374, 378, 380, 381, 382, 383–384, 386–387, 391, 392–394, 394–395; FDR's wartime strategy in, 408, 441, 446, 447, 450, 459, 460; Germans in, 351, 367, 372–373, 447, 473; *Greer* incident, 392–395; *Robin Moor* sinking, 372; in World War I, 37
Atlantic Charter, 383, 387–390, 415, 443, 471
Atlantic (Argentia) conference, 384–389, 391, 392, 395, 412
Atlantic Fleet, 411
Atlee, Clement, 389
Atomic bomb, 348–349, 377, 450, 472, 526, 553–555, 582, 590; use vs. demonstration, 555
Attu, Aleutian Islands, 541
Augusta, 384, 385
Austin, Warren, 315
Australia, 216, 261, 379, 415, 542, 544; MacArthur in, 441–442
Austria, 467, 479, 553; *Anschluss*/German invasion, 111, 295, 296, 297; Soviet Union and, 479
Austria-Hungary, 509
Automobile industry: strike, 242–243; during World War II, 419, 427
Avery, Sewell L., 519, 520
Axis, 184, 270, 299, 311, 314, 315, 316, 317, 319, 330, 334, 337, 340, 346, 351, 358, 360, 361, 365, 366, 379, 385, 408,

Axis (*cont.*)
409, 415, 453, 468, 496, 505. *See also* Germany; Hitler; Italy; Japan; Mussolini
Azores, 370, 371, 386, 391

Bad Nauheim, 7
Badoglio, Pietro, 469, 470, 505
Bahamas, 158, 352, 371
Bailey, Josiah, 84, 241, 280
Bailey, Liberty Hyde, 21
Baker, Newton D., 33, 66, 68, 71, 72
Baker, Ray Stannard, 153
Baker Island, 262
Baldwin, Stanley, 260, 262
Balkans: Churchill and, 468, 477, 505, 568–569; FDR and, 505; Soviet Union/Stalin and, 481, 485, 550, 568–569
Ball, Joseph, 560
Baltic Sea, 111
Baltic states, 324, 388, 449–450, 479, 480
Baltimore, 540, 542, 543
Bangkok, 402
Bankhead, John H., 132, 133, 153, 344, 530
Bankhead, William B., 153, 315, 286, 292, 344, 346, 474
Banking, 101, 127, 139, 146, 203; crisis/runs on, 79, 88–90, 94–95; FDR's frustration with, 90, 94–95; FDR's legislation/reform, 58, 94–95, 98, 100, 123, 128–129, 141, 143, 158, 167, 170; federal insurance of deposits, 95, 105, 128; international, 181, 523. *See also* Federal Reserve
Bank of America, 95
Bank of New York, 4
Bank of the United States, 240–241
Barkley, Alben, 169, 237, 238, 282, 285, 286, 344, 501–502, 530
Barnard College, 59
Barnesville, Georgia, 286
Barton, Bruce, 355
Baruch, Bernard, 60, 103, 192, 391, 418, 514; WPB appointment, 421–422
Bataan peninsula, 414, 441. *See also* Philippines
Bathurst, 458
Batista, Fulgencio, 213, 214
Beacon, New York, 566
Beard, Charles A., 66, 141
Beaverbrook, Lord, 391, 415, 418, 539
Beck, Ludwig, 299, 318
Beer bill, 96, 97
Belgium: German invasion/blitz, 324, 329, 330, 335, 572; postwar, 550; Wallonia and, 466
Bell, Daniel, 148
Bellau Wood, FDR on, 30–31
Benelux, 466
Beneš, Edvard, 301
Berchtesgaden, 299, 303
Berle, Adolf A., Jr., 66, 216, 300, 301, 302, 316, 320, 449–450; economic planning and, 252, 253
Berlin, 178, 184, 259, 304, 307, 315, 316, 401, 408, 473, 583, 584; -U.S. relations, 107; in World War I, 28
Berlin, Isaiah, 493, 564, 568
Bermuda, 323, 335, 352, 504
Bern, Switzerland, 601, 602
Bessarabia, 479
Bethesda, Maryland, 512
Bethlehem, 479
Biddle, Francis, 8, 321, 407, 426, 493, 519
Biddle, George, 9
"Big four," 466, 475, 478–479, 495, 549
"Big Inch" pipeline, 428
Billings, Reverend Sherrard, 9, 10
Bingham, Barry, 546
Bingham, Mary, 546–547, 548, 556
Bingham, Robert W., 76, 107, 262
Birse, A. H., 482, 583
Bismarck, 371, 384
Bismarck, Otto Eduard Leopold von, 302
Bjørnsson, Sveinn, 546
Black, Hugo L., 104, 167, 168, 238–239, 438
Blacks, 160, 173, 244–245, 520, 521, 534; armed forces and, 504, 521; ER and, 123, 245, 246, 283, 356, 508–509, 520; FDR and, 9, 123–124, 148, 214, 240, 241, 244, 247, 284, 356, 364, 520–521, 532; FDR's personal relationships with, 245, 605; New Deal and, 122, 245, 529; in the South, 123–124, 173, 245–246, 283–284; voting rights, 247, 284, 520, 521. *See also* Antilynching bill; South: black issues/civil rights
Black Sea, 568
Blackstone Hotel, Chicago, 343, 510
Black Thursday, 60, 250
Blitzkrieg, 322
Block, Paul, 194, 206
Blockade, 171, 258, 259, 261, 263, 291, 292; Churchill's strategy for, 385; of Germany, 183, 184, 335, 339; of Japan, 365, 590; U.S.-British secret plan for, 292. *See also* Quarantine
Blum, John M., 426
Blum, Leon, 479
Board of Economic Warfare, 530, 575
Board of Trade, 260
Boettiger, Anna Roosevelt. *See* Roosevelt, Anna
Boettiger, John, 490, 510, 599, 605
Boettiger, John, Jr., 599, 605
Bohlen, Charles ("Chip") E., 177, 470–471, 476, 481, 484, 485, 488, 490, 508, 568, 569, 602; foreign policy and, 600; at Yalta

conference, 578, 579, 581, 582, 585, 586, 587, 588, 591, 595–596
Bohr, Niels, 553, 554
Boise, Idaho, *Statesman*, 165
Boisson, Pierre, 456
BOLERO (1943 French invasion), 467
Bolivia, 505
Bolshevik Revolution, 171, 174, 176
Bolshevism, 39, 173, 174, 176; FDR's knowledge of, 481; fear of, 39
"Bombshell message," 117
Bone, Homer, 298
Bonus Army, 75
"Boondoggling," 135
Borah, William E., 96, 161, 232, 236, 264, 290–291, 305, 323, 328
Boris, King of Bulgaria, 317
Borneo, 400
Boston, 9, 13, 70, 354, 355, 566
Boston Transcript, 165
Boulder Dam, 189–190
Bourbons, 241, 283
Bowers, Claude, 38–39, 75, 269
Bowles, Chester, 500
Boycotts, 171, 184; of Japan, 267, 315. *See also* Embargo; Quarantine; Sanctions, economic
Bradley, Omar, 526
Brain trust, 66, 84, 86, 223, 559
Brandeis, Louis D., 121, 144, 161, 251; judicial reform and, 231, 234
Brazil, 7, 367, 369, 372, 386, 458; Axis threat and, 316; FDR's visit to, 216, 217; Good Neighbor policy and, 213, 219
Bremen, 320
Bremerton, Washington, speech, 544, 557
Bretton Woods, New Hampshire, economic conference, 522
Brewster, Ralph Owen, 168
Bricker, John W., 518, 556
Bridges, Styles, 320
Brisbane, Australia, 540
British Empire, 333, 339, 350, 385, 443, 447, 478, 549; Atlantic Charter and, 388, 443; FDR's anticolonialism and/opposition to, 462, 478; Pacific Island claims, 261, 262. *See also* Antigua; Bermuda; British Guiana; Burma; Hong Kong; India; Singapore; Trinidad
British Expeditionary Force, 332
British Fleet, 333, 334, 336, 337, 352
British Foreign Office, 292
British Guiana, 352
British Purchasing Committee, 460
Bronx, 57, 353, 533, 564
Brooke, Alan, 450, 467, 472, 477, 483, 492
Brooklyn, New York, 160, 564
Brooklyn Navy Yard, 25
Browder, Earl, 563
Brown, Herman, 517
Brown, Wilson, 508
Brown and Root, Inc., 517
Browning, Elizabeth Barrett, 13
Brownlow, Louis, 275, 278, 279, 280, 319
Broz, Josip (Tito), 483
Bruenn, Howard G., 512, 513, 514, 515, 544, 545, 556, 574, 587, 595, 598, 604; FDR's death and, 605–606
Brussels, 330
Brussels conference, 266–267, 268; plan for nine-power conference, 265, 266
Bryan, William Jennings, 7, 24, 181
B-17s, 378
B-29s, 529
BUCCANEER (Andaman Islands attack), 491
Buckingham Palace, 598
Budapest, 547, 583, 590
Budget, Bureau of the, 279–280
Budget, federal, 94, 199–200, 256, 257, 419; armed forces and, 179–180, 210; balancing, 77, 78, 79–80, 81, 83, 84, 88, 96, 99, 104, 128, 30–131, 138–139, 140, 147, 150, 191, 192, 199–200, 222, 248–249, 252, 254; Congress and, 252–253; cuts in, 78, 96, 97, 138–139, 191, 248–249, 222; deficits, 61, 104, 128, 179, 191, 192, 193, 221, 241, 249, 254, 256; emergency, 130–131
Buenos Aires conference (1936), 209, 215–217, 218
Buffalo, New York, 54, 58, 506
Bulgaria, 317, 408, 569, 589
Bulge, Battle of the, 464, 572
Bullitt, William C., 290, 296, 303; as French ambassador, 260, 268, 271, 307, 309, 318, 321, 331–332; Soviet Union and, 172, 173–177, 260; Welles controversy and, 474, 475
Bull Moose party, 76, 199
Bureau of Supplies and Accounts, 26
Burg, LeRoy, 543
Burma, 382, 442–443, 459, 467, 478, 479, 596
Burma Road, 380, 469
Bush, Vannevar, 348, 349, 554, 555
Business, 93, 94, 248, 431, 478, 498; big, 241, 251; FDR and, 75, 97, 104, 141, 142, 196, 201, 250–252, 426, 500, 519; FDR's career in, 15, 40; FDR/New Deal opposition in, 138, 139, 143, 144, 147, 151, 158–159, 160, 163–164, 250, 332, 440; recession advisory committee, 253–254; Republicans and, 97, 426; small, 136, 137, 143, 145, 157, 159, 162, 164, 202, 206, 356, 419–420; wartime issues, 420, 431–432, 433. *See also* Holding companies; Industry; Labor; National Recovery Administration; Unions

Business Advisory Council, 333
Butler, Nicholas Murray, 301
Butler, Smedley, 28
Byrd, Harry, 232, 276, 285, 517, 537
Byrd, Richard E., 316
Byrnes, James F., 222, 247, 426, 430, 502, 569; administrative reorganization and, 277, 278; as "assistant president," 439–440, 494, 499; as FDR's supporter in Senate, 99–100; judicial reform/Supreme Court, 235, 237, 438; Office of Economic Stabilization head, 439–440; United Nations proposal and, 584; as vice presidential nominee, 345, 346, 529, 530, 532, 535, 536, 537; WPA and, 421; at Yalta conference, 578, 583, 604
Byrns, Joseph, 153

Cadogan, Alexander, 302, 385, 387, 596
Cairo conferences (1943), 494, 495, 561; before Tehran conference, 477–479; following Tehran conference, 490–492
California, 141, 145, 231, 311, 511; Bank of America and, 95; Democratic support in, 70, 72, 190; FDR in, 537; Japanese spy rumors in, 261, 316
Camp, Lawrence, 286
Camp David, 445. *See also* Shangri-la
Campobello Island, New Brunswick, 6, 27, 35, 41, 42, 116
Camp Pendleton, 537
Canada, 300, 309, 320, 330, 333, 598, 599; defense and, 349, 350, 392 (*see also* Hemispheric defense); electric power in, 58, 64, 147; French invasion and, 492; at Quebec conference, 472; wheat agreement with U.S., 86
Canton Island, 262
Cape Verde Islands, 370
Caracas, 218
Cardozo, Benjamin, 161
Caribbean, 11; FDR's trips to, 11, 359. *See also specific places*
Carleton Hotel, Washington, 418
Carlson, Evans F., 293
Carnegie Institution, 348
Carter, Ledyard and Milburn, 15
Casablanca, 413
Casablanca conference, 458–464, 467, 468, 578, 597
Casey, Eugene, 498, 532, 533
Cassino, Italy, 526
Castro, Fidel, 214
Catholicism/Catholics, 51, 146, 345; FDR, as anti-, 20, 51; FDR and, 36, 269, 270, 271, 272, 296, 353, 380–381, 454; Soviet Union and, 173, 175, 376; Spanish Civil War and, 269, 270, 271, 272
Catton, Bruce, 428
Censorship, 417
Central America, 51, 261. *See also* Good Neighbor policy; Latin America; Mexico; Nicaragua
Central Statistical Board, 125–126
Centrists, 161, 230, 571, 575
Cermak, Anton, 72, 73; death of, 87–88
C-47, 594
C-54, 580
Challenge to Liberty (Hoover), 140
Chamber of Commerce, Seattle, 298
Chamber of Commerce, U.S., 158, 159
Chamberlain, Neville, 262, 272, 294, 295; Czechoslovakian crisis and, 300, 301, 302–303; FDR and, 260–261, 294, 300, 301, 312, 313, 320, 333; Hitler and, 295, 299, 301, 314, 324; Japan and, 264, 267; Munich conference, 302; Poland and, 314, 321; U.S. and, 309, 329
Champs Elysées, 338
Chandler, A. B. ("Happy"), 285, 570
Chaney, Mayris, 426
Chattanooga, Tennessee, 521
Chautauqua, FDR speech at, 205
Chautemps, Camille, 267–268
Chavez, Dennis, 278
Chequers, 405, 599
Cherbourg, 448, 451, 529
Cherwell, Lord, 553, 554
Chiang Kai-shek, 379, 416, 442–443, 469, 480, 490, 491, 495, 561–562; at Cairo conference, 477–479; Soviet Union and, 591; U.S. assassination plans, 561; U.S.-Japanese negotiations and, 399–400
Chicago, 72, 76, 79, 510, 519, 533, 545; Democratic conventions in, 70, 343, 344, 346, 535, 536–537, 546, 547; FDR's 1944 campaign trip through, 565; FDR's quarantine speech in, 263–264, 268, 291; Memorial Day massacre, 243–244, 247
Chicago, University of, 61
Chicago Tribune, 140, 490
Child labor, 20, 21, 157, 249, 282; NRA regulation of, 127, 137, 161
Chile, 213, 316
China, 139, 571; "big four" and, 478–479; at Cairo conference, 477–479; communism in, 266, 293–294, 442, 561; FDR and, 109, 442, 477–479; Hong Kong and, 493, 586; Japan vs., 83, 106–107, 109, 110, 181, 262–263, 265, 266, 293, 378–379, 380, 381, 396, 397, 398, 399–400, 442–443, 467, 469, 477–479, 589; postwar world/ United Nations and, 450, 466, 475, 478–479, 486–487, 523; Roosevelts' and Delanos' business with, 5, 8, 10, 109, 442; Soviet Union and, 266, 480, 591; U.S. relations with, 266, 290, 483, 491, 529,

561–562. *See also* Chiang Kai-shek; Manchuria; Nanking
China-American Council, 478
Chinese Eastern Railway, 590
Christian Science Monitor, 161
Christian Socialist movement, 8
Chungking, 293, 442, 443, 475, 516, 593
Churchill, Winston, 332–333, 334, 372, 478, 491, 495, 505; at Arcadia conference, 410–416; at Atlantic conference, 384–390, 392; atomic bomb and, 553, 554, 555; Balkans and, 477, 505; at Cairo conference, 477, 478, 479; at Casablanca conference, 463; chiefs of staff and, 411–412; de Gaulle and, 453, 462, 525, 596, 597; destroyers-for-bases deal and, 352; Egypt and, 59; ER on, 416; FDR and, 31, 117, 332–333, 351, 364, 372, 385, 389, 392, 396, 397, 410, 413, 445, 450–451, 459, 465, 472, 473, 507, 508, 525, 528, 551–553, 563, 568, 569, 574, 592, 595, 598–599, 602; FDR and, differences between, 368, 386–387, 389, 411, 416, 443–444, 447, 459, 467, 478, 490–491, 504–506, 547–548, 580, 582, 593, 596; FDR and, personal relationship, 48, 415–416, 504–506, 580, 581, 601, 606–607; FDR on, 3, 581, 584; French invasion, 447, 448–449, 450, 466, 467, 468, 477, 482–483, 484–485, 486, 490, 492, 504, 526; Germany and, 550, 552–553, 584–585, 585–586; Greece and, 505, 595; health, 493, 513; Hong Kong and, 493; Hopkins and, 363, 364; as imperialist, 385, 388, 389, 447, 459, 478, 493, 582, 593, 596; India and, 443–444, 586–587; Italy and, 468, 470, 504, 505, 601; Japanese threat, 396, 397; on lend-lease, 361, 362; Mediterranean and, 367, 468, 470, 477, 483, 485, 492, 504, 505, 525; North African invasion, 367, 386, 447–448, 448–449, 450, 451, 452, 457–458, 459; Poland and, 489, 548, 587, 588; postwar goals, 363, 416, 468, 470, 475, 504–506, 528, 560–561, 568–569, 580, 584–585, 585–586, 590; at Quebec conference, 551–553, 560–561; speeches/speaking style, 336, 361, 385, 491, 597; Stalin/Soviet Union and, 373, 374, 375, 449, 471, 472, 473, 480, 482, 483–484, 485–486, 568–569, 583, 590, 601, 602; at Tehran conference, 477, 479–490; at Trident conference, 468; unconditional surrender, 463, 464; United Nations and, 415–416, 586–587; U.S. and, 333, 334–335, 336, 338, 351, 352, 359, 505–506; U.S. public opinion and, 361, 410; U.S. war involvement, pressure for, 332, 337, 338, 339, 362, 368, 383, 384, 385, 386, 387, 389, 390, 394, 405; war strategy, 349, 447, 504, 580; Yalta conference and, 554, 574, 577, 579, 578, 581, 582, 583, 584–585, 586–587, 588, 589, 592
Cities, 20, 57, 67, 137, 146, 149, 222, 283; blacks in, 241, 520; Democrats in, 189, 241; FDR's support in, 206, 344, 357, 537, 562, 567; New Dealers in, 241, 529; reform and, 20, 21; rural planning and, 85
Civilian Conservation Corps (CCC), 100, 102, 180, 190, 364, 425, 550
Civilian defense, 382
Civil liberties. *See* Civil rights; Four Freedoms
Civil rights, 240, 244, 247
Civil service, 122, 275
Civil War, 5, 92, 109, 269, 350, 366, 368, 405, 535
Civil Works Administration (CWA), 134–135, 149–150
Clapper, Raymond, 495
Clark, Champ, 570
Clark, George Rogers, 198
Clark, Grenville, 15, 347
Clarksburg, West Virginia, 565–566
Clayton, Will, 570
Clayton Anti-Trust Act, 251
Clemenceau, Georges, 31, 462
Cleveland, Grover, 3, 16, 17, 18, 144, 121, 206, 567
Cleveland, Ohio, 193, 356
Cleveland Press, 497
Coal industry, 104, 193; Delanos' business in, 5, 8; NRA and, 157, 167; strike, 370, 371; unions and, 519
Coast Guard, 371
Cohen, Benjamin V., 120, 161, 251, 253, 347
"Cold turkey cabinet," 58
Cold war, 219, 504
Collective bargaining, 20, 104, 137, 138, 140, 143, 148, 156, 57, 158; NRA and, 158, 161. *See also* Labor; Unions; Wagner Act
Collective security, 80, 84, 106, 117, 118, 171, 172, 177, 178, 82, 258, 259, 293, 295, 296, 300, 306, 327, 342, 346, 354; European view of, 178; isolationism and, FDR's theory, 172, 177, 182, 184; postwar, 475, 582; Wilson and, 578. *See also* Good neighbor policy; Hemispheric defense
Colliers, 328
Colonies/possessions: European, Hitler's threat to, 307, 311, 334, 338, 351; German, 329
Colorado, 153
Colorado River, 189
Columbia University, 66, 84, 124, 276, 301; Law School, 66; FDR in, 14
Columbus, Ohio, 74
Colville, John, 552

Comintern, 173, 174, 175
Commerce, interstate, 160, 161, 163
Commerce Department, 546
Committee on Economic Security, 150
Commodity Credit Corporation, 133, 436, 605
Commodity dollar, 133–134, 139
Common Counsel Club, 24
Commonwealth and Southern Utility Company, 254, 342
Communism/Communists, 247, 252, 282, 376, 470, 489, 505, 510; in China, 266, 293–294, 442, 561; Dewey's accusations of, 562–563, 566; ER accused of, 426, 511; European colonialism/imperialism and, 596, 597; FDR accused of, 206–207, 559; free elections/self-determination and, 588, 589; Hiss and, 478; isolationists and, 324; Nazism/fascism vs., 260, 374; U.S. views on, 172, 374; in U.S., 325. *See also* Bolshevik Revolution
Communist Internationale, 173. *See also* Comintern
Compiègne forest, 337
Conant, James B., 349
Conboy, Martin, 76
Congress, 51, 104, 197, 392, 395, 466, 475, 476, 577; administrative reform and, 224, 273, 274, 275, 276, 278, 279, 342; agricultural legislation, 86, 100, 101, 103–104, 105, 435–436, 437, 438; antilynching legislation, 246–247; banking legislation, 89, 90, 95, 128–129; beer bill and, 96–97; budget cuts and, 249, 251, 252–253, 255; conservatives in, 86, 153, 222, 227, 229, 231, 233, 239, 240, 241, 254, 273, 281, 287, 412, 425, 426, 500, 503; defense spending, 330–331; Democrats in, 79, 81, 88, 89, 122, 128, 144, 146, 152, 153, 166, 222, 223, 239, 247, 271, 278, 280, 425, 494, 496, 497; Democratic party purge, 221–222, 223; disarmament and, 114; draft and, 347–348, 391; economic issues and, 96–97, 101, 102, 134, 257, 419, 430, 432, 433, 438, 439, 500; electric power legislation, 100, 105; ER criticized by, 426, 427; executive power vs., 93, 98, 274, 467; FDR and, fourth term, 575–576; FDR and, second New Deal, 152, 154–155; FDR's blanket authorizations, 97, 131, 425; FDR's defense strategies, 311, 341–342, 347; FDR's messages to, 151, 360, 405, 406–407, 595, 597, 600, 601, 602; FDR's opponents in, 169, 241, 243, 273, 282, 286, 295, 297, 298, 358, 412, 432, 493 (*see also*: Congress: conservatives in; Congress: right wing in); FDR's strategies/working relationship with, 80, 83, 85, 92, 96–99, 102, 103, 124, 158, 160, 166, 169, 182, 200, 222–224, 230, 237, 341, 347, 352, 376, 412, 440, 498, 571; foreign aid/lend-lease, 183, 270, 271, 303–304, 341, 352, 358–359, 361, 362, 363, 376, 386, 505; holding-company "death penalty," 166, 167–169; industrial legislation and, 104–105; isolationists in, 114, 115, 117, 171, 289, 303, 305, 331, 362, 391, 394, 425, 568; Japan and, 315–316, 397, 399, 401, 402, 466; judicial reform bill and, 224, 227, 229, 230–233, 234, 236, 238, 241, 276; labor issues and, 158, 164, 274, 281–282, 425, 432, 519; Nazi refugee program, 295, 297, 298; neutrality legislation and, 183, 321, 323, 394; New Deal, influence on, 98, 99, 152, 153; New Deal and, 122, 139, 149, 154, 155, 187, 233, 249, 251, 252–253, 255; New Deal passage, 92, 95, 97–100, 101, 102–103, 104, 105, 115, 120, 139; New Deal passage, "second," 152–153, 154–157, 158, 159, 164, 165–170, 183, 185, 230, 232; New Deal supporters in, 152–153, 155, 229, 230, 323; nonpartisan approach to war, 322, 323; NRA and, 136, 164; patronage and, 187, 275, 276; progressives in, 94, 105, 229; public pressure on, 222, 227; railroad legislation, 103, 104; Republicans in, 141, 153, 196, 241, 327, 475; right wing in, 170, 497; securities regulation, 100, 102–103, 105, 139; social security and, 150, 154, 155–157, 164, 207; soldiers' voting bill, 508; southerners in, 154, 166, 245, 281, 282, 286; Soviet relations and, 171–172, 324–325, 602–603; special interest groups and government agencies, 274, 276; State of the Union messages to, 195, 499–501, 573; Supreme Court and, 162, 164; taxes and, 164–166, 169, 191, 192, 253, 425, 433–435, 496, 501, 502; trade agreements and, 214–215; veterans' legislation and, 75, 96, 97, 105, 192, 193, 251, 503; war debts and, 110, 171; war involvement and, 293, 306, 323, 335, 340, 366, 368, 378, 394, 402; war powers, 437–438; war resolutions, 407, 408; work relief and, 149, 151, 154, 155; World War I investigations, 37, 38; World War II, and FDR's war message, 405, 406–407; World War II issues, 220, 289, 292, 322, 323, 330–331, 412, 418, 419, 421, 424–427, 428, 430, 432, 559, 585. *See also* Elections; House of Representatives; Senate
Congressional Medal of Honor, 441
Congress of Industrial Organizations (CIO), 242, 437, 438, 519; Political Action Committee, 536, 557, 563, 567
Connally, Tom, 405, 522

Conservation, 73, 85, 192, 193, 274, 565, 566; FDR's support for, 6, 20, 21, 67; TR and, 17, 196. *See also* Soil Conservation Act
Conservation, Department of, 275
Conservatives, 23, 59, 86, 87, 94, 145, 146, 198, 200, 222, 240, 260, 273, 279, 367, 426, 454, 518, 530, 570; black issues and, 283, 284; defense program and, 347, 392; economic issues and, 77, 88, 94, 96, 97, 100, 101, 102, 103, 128, 133, 139, 165, 186, 191, 193, 240; FDR, influence on, 3, 4–5, 16, 61, 83, 494, 497, 498, 499, 508; FDR/New Deal opposition, 19, 70, 85, 102, 103, 120, 140, 144, 188, 224, 230, 241, 273, 285–286, 425–426, 498, 562; FDR on, 52, 138, 282, 345–346, 497; FDR strategy with, 79, 80; FDR support from, 53, 77, 80; Hull as, 345, 476; judicial reform and, 232, 233, 235, 238, 239; labor issues and, 20; Robinson as, 235, 236; in the Senate, 153, 156; soldiers' legislation and, 496, 503; southern, 281, 517, 530; Soviet relations and, 173, 449; State Department reorganization and, 569–571, 575; on Supreme Court, 225, 235, 236; Willkie and, 518, 562; World Court and, 182. *See also* House Un-American Activities Committee
Constitution, 4, 16, 443; democracy and, 225, 226; FDR and, 225, 226, 227, 467; judicial reform, 232, 234, 238; judiciary and, 230–231; minimum wage and, 234; New Deal and, 144, 157, 160, 161, 162, 163, 167, 191–192; Supreme Court's views on, 226. *See also* Judicial reform; Ludlow Amendment; Supreme Court
Construction, 40, 60, 127, 149, 248, 249, 349, 420. *See also* Public works
Consumer issues, 58, 104, 130, 144, 147, 429; NRA codes, 126, 127; war production, 424, 495, 496. *See also* Economy: purchasing power
Consumers' League, 12
Convoying, 367, 368–369, 370, 393, 394, 414; escorting, 384, 386–387
Coolidge, Calvin, 51, 52, 68, 85, 110, 182
Copper industry, 115, 139, 251, 249
Coral Sea, Battle of, 445
Corcoran, Thomas G., 120, 123, 161, 168, 222, 239, 347, 530; as FDR's speechwriter, 201, 202; influence, 251, 253; purge and, 284, 287
Cornell University, 21, 100
Corporate income tax, 164, 167, 192
Corregidor, 414
Corry, Raymond, 33
Costigan, Edward P., 148, 246
Cotenin peninsula, 448
Coughlin, Reverend Charles E., 141, 145, 146, 154, 165, 182, 204, 276
Council of Economic Advisers, 126
Council of National Defense, 29, 342, 348
Court Disapproves, The (FDR), 144
Courts. *See* Judicial reform; Supreme Court
Cox, James, 38, 39
Coxey's Army, 7
Coy, Wayne, 436, 498
Craig, May, 529, 571
Crete, 368
Crime, 58, 59
Crimea, 579, 580, 583, 598. *See also* Yalta conference
Cripps, Stafford, 444
Croatia, 479
Crowley, Leo, 499
Cuba, 212, 213–214
Cudahy, John, 330
Cummings, 544
Cummings, Homer, 186, 227, 228
Curley, James Michael, 70
Currie, Lauchlin, 289, 442
Curzon Line, 489, 587
Cutting, Bronson, 8
Czechoslovakia: Germany vs., 314, 315, 348, 354; Sudetenland crisis, 295, 298, 299, 300, 301–304, 305

Dairen, 591
Dakar (French West Africa), 367, 386, 453, 456, 528, 596
Daladier, Edouard, 272, 309, 318, 329; German threat and, 301, 302, 321, 324
Daniels, Jonathan, 514, 520–521, 533, 603
Daniels, Josephus, 181, 155, 208, 244; as secretary of navy, 23, 24, 26, 28, 29, 30, 31, 37, 38
Danube, 483
Danzig, Free City of, 314, 318
Darlan, Alain, 456
Darlan, Jean François, 367, 455; FDR's deal with, 456–458, 469, 570
Darrow, Clarence, 136
Darrow Report, 136, 137
Davies, Joseph E., 177, 472
Davis, Forrest, 522
Davis, Jefferson, 87
Davis, John W., 52, 140
Davis, Norman H., 51, 84, 114, 263, 325; Brussels conference/nine-power conference and, 266, 267, 268; Hitler and, 177–178
Davis, William H., 433
D-day, 525, 526
Dearborn, Michigan, 243
Debts. *See* Economy: national debt; War debts
Declaration on Liberated Europe, 589, 600
Deflation, 80, 81, 89, 102. *See also* Depression, Great

de Gaulle, Charles, 337, 453, 554; Allied invasion of France and, 525, 527; at Casablanca conference, 461–463; colonialism/imperialism of, 596–597; FDR and, 453, 454, 455, 456–457, 462, 525, 527–528, 595, 596–597, 599, 600; North African invasion and, 453, 454, 460, 461–463; support for, 456, 461; U.S. recognition of government, 527, 528

Delano, Frederick, 221

Delano, Laura ("Polly"), 511, 604, 605, 606

Delano, Sara. *See* Roosevelt, Sara Delano

Delano, Warren, 3, 5, 8, 10, 109, 566

Delaware and Hudson Railroad, 5, 6

Democracy, 375, 470; "arsenal of," 360, 361; FDR and, 203, 217, 221, 232, 240–241, 402, 422, 456–457, 487, 488; in Latin America, 209, 212, 216, 218; postwar, 487, 587–588, 589; Supreme Court vs., 221, 224–226, 232. *See also* Self-determination

Democratic Committee (New York), 57, 58

Democratic Executive Committee, 49

Democratic National Committee, 67, 71, 74, 121, 122, 284, 529, 536, 563

Democratic party, 16, 54, 37, 41, 65, 68, 74, 88, 127, 135, 141, 144, 153, 166, 189, 197, 204, 288; campaign funds of, 203–204, 205; conservatives in, 19, 52, 67, 71, 79, 83, 121, 122, 140, 146, 153, 169, 185, 200, 227, 230, 240, 241, 280, 285, 328, 347, 432, 494, 531 (*see also* Democratic party: right wing); depression and, 52, 63, 64; ER and, 49–50; FDR and, 17, 42, 49, 50–51, 52, 54–55, 58, 65, 79, 81, 139, 166, 187, 190, 198, 200, 204, 223, 239, 278, 328, 436, 499, 516–517; FDR's first speech, at 1920 Dutchess County Democratic picnic, 17; FDR's influence in, 19, 22, 23, 24, 25, 32, 190, 223, 224, 239, 343–344, 346; FDR's opposition in, 169, 185, 221–222, 425, 494, 501, 517; FDR's support in, 57, 73, 143, 196, 224, 343, 356, 500; judicial reform bill and, 229, 231, 232 233, 237, 239; New Deal/New Dealers and, 121, 140, 152, 153, 200, 240, 241, 280, 287, 323, 327, 494; in New York, 18–19, 20, 22, 25, 50, 53, 54–55, 57, 64, 204; 1910 election, 17–18; 1912 election, 22; 1920 election, 38; 1924 election, 51–52, 71; 1928 election, 53; 1932 election, 65, 69, 70–74, 200; 1934 election, 141; 1936 election, 190, 194, 196, 197, 198, 200–203, 207–208, 342; 1938 election, 287; 1940 election, 201, 327, 328, 338, 343–346, 353–354, 355, 531; 1944 election, 495, 497, 546, 547, 562, 529–531, 532, 533, 534, 536–537; progressivism and, 17, 22, 25, 32, 37, 83, 168, 231; purge of, 273, 280–287, 328; right wing, 144, 241, 353; Roosevelt family in, 17, 22; southern, 52, 67, 144, 146, 201, 230, 241, 244, 494, 496, 502, 517, 530, 531, 534; unity issues, 51, 52, 63, 67, 75, 81, 190, 240, 280, 284, 353, 356, 531; urban, 51, 67, 189; war issues, 323, 326418, 427; women in, 49–50, 64, 122. *See also* Congress: Democrats in; Senate: Democrats in

Denmark, 329–330

Depression, Great, 60–62, 93, 106, 119, 122, 164, 196, 242, 297, 424; artists and, 188; as campaign issue, 63, 64–65, 70, 73, 74; causes of, 60, 61, 78; FDR's approach to, as governor, 60–62; FDR's expectation/prediction of, 52, 53, 60; FDR vs. Hoover on, 65, 75, 78, 80, 81–83, 86, 88–89; future prevention of, 80, 142; national morale and, 88, 92; public demand for change, 92, 94; recovery and setback, 119; war/defense production and recovery, 326, 392, 408, 424, 426, 434; worldwide, 79, 102, 213, 563. *See also* Banking: crisis in; Economy; New Deal; Recession; Stock market

"Depression clinic," 81

Depression(s): Democrats' popularity during, 52; of late 1800s, 5, 7

Destroyers-for-bases deal, 333–336, 338, 351–352, 359, 384

Detroit, 62, 243, 309; 1943 riots in, 520

DeVoto, Bernard, 276

Dewey, George, 23

Dewey, John, 17, 93

Dewey, Thomas E., 327, 518, 522, 529, 542, 545, 562, 570; attacks on FDR, 558–559, 562, 566; FDR on, 558–559; FDR's postelection attitude toward, 567; as presidential candidate, 556, 557, 558–560

Dewson, Mary (Molly), 64, 122

Dieckhoff, Hans, 299, 303, 313

Dieppe, 448

Disarmament, 110, 111, 113, 114–115, 117, 177–178, 183, 210, 305, 306, 314; Atlantic Charter on, 388; FDR's hope for, Buenos Aires conference and, 215–216; Geneva conference on, 82, 111, 113–114, 210; postwar, for Germany and Japan, 597

Division of Eastern European Affairs, 173

Dixiecrat insurgency, 532

Dodd, William E., 107, 218, 259–260

"Domestic allotment" plan, 86

Dominican Republic, 297, 313

Donovan, William J., 436

Doolittle, James H., 444

Dorn, Frank, 561

Doughton, Robert Lee, 155–156, 157, 502

Douglas, Lewis, 96, 97, 101, 138, 140, 570
Douglas, Paul, 61
Douglas, William O., 123, 439; Supreme Court appointment, 239; as vice presidential nominee, 530, 533, 534, 535
Douglas bomber, 311
Dowdell's Knob, 604
Draft. *See* Selective service
Draper, George, 41, 43, 44
Dred Scott case, 162
Drought, Father James M., 380
Drury, Allen, 501, 598, 606
Dubinsky, David, 241
Dulles, Allen, 601
Dulles, John Foster, 518, 559
Dumbarton Oaks conference, 523, 548–549, 551, 578, 586
Dun, Bishop Angus, 573, 607
Dunkirk, 332; evacuation of, 335, 351
Dunn, James, 570
Du Pont, 53, 140
Dutch East Indies. *See* East Indies, Dutch
Dutchess County, New York, 17, 48, 56, 57

Early, Stephen, 39, 123, 182, 194, 223, 228, 326, 409, 521, 606
East Indies, Dutch, 267, 339, 379, 382, 383
Easter Island, 316
Eastern front, 547, 580, 601
Eberstadt, Ferdinand, 420, 421, 422
Eccles, Marriner, 167, 252, 256, 43
Economy, 66, 80, 96, 127, 128, 221, 248, 249, 252, 417, 526; agriculture as base of, 85; "commodity dollar" theory and, 133–134, 139; conservatism in, 77, 88, 94, 96, 97, 100, 101, 102, 103, 128, 133, 139, 165, 186, 191, 193, 240; conservatism of FDR, 61, 94, 96, 97, 100, 128, 130, 133, 139, 186, 240, 248–249, 250, 252, 253; currency stabilization, 84, 102, 105, 111, 113, 115, 116, 117, 118 (*see also* Economy: dollar, value of/stabilization); deficits, *see* Budget, federal: deficits; dollar, value of/ stabilization, 89, 90, 101, 102, 116, 117–118, 130, 133, 134, 138, 248, 430 (*see also* Economy: currency stabilization); FDR and, 10, 17, 66, 78, 126, 127, 134, 248–249, 255–256, 322, 417, 434; FDR's bill of rights, 500, 503, 573; fundamentalism, 81, 102; gold and silver purchases, 133–134, 139; government regulation of, 10, 16–17, 24, 77, 80, 93–94, 139, 143, 147, 193, 219, 231, 239 (*see also* New Deal); indices on, 75, 79, 95, 100, 102, 119, 131, 134, 135, 136, 143, 248; Keynesian approach, 117, 128, 133, 192, 250, 255, 279, 434; laissez-faire approach, 16, 61, 81, 100, 121; national debt, 100, 130, 134, 165, 206, 248; national income, 248, 255, 430; nationalism vs. internationalism, 78, 84, 102, 104–105, 106, 107, 115, 117; New Deal and, 96–97, 130–131, 136–136; politics and, 433–434; postwar, 363, 424, 498, 500; public works funding and, 127–128; pump priming, 130, 252; purchasing power, 70, 85, 127, 128, 192, 251, 349, 424, 430, 432, 433, 435; reconversion, 495, 504; recovery, 84, 110, 119, 147, 192–193, 206, 240, 248, 249–250, 253; redistribution of wealth, 127, 164, 167, 129, 256; war production and, 326, 392, 408, 418, 419, 421, 424, 425, 426, 434; worldwide, 79, 82, 83, 102, 110, 113, 522–523, 552. *See also* Banking; Budget, federal; Depression, Great; Gold; Gold standard; Inflation; London Economic Conference; Monetarism; New Deal; Recession; Tariffs; Tax(es); Trade; War debts
Eden, Anthony, 267, 294, 399, 471, 481, 488; FDR's postwar ideas and, 466–467; at Malta, 579, 580; at Yalta conference, 554
Education, 498, 500, 503
Egypt, 368, 450, 456, 474, 586, 592; FDR's visit to, 593–595, 599
8th Route Army, 293
Einstein, Albert, 348, 349
Eisenhower, Dwight D., 411, 414, 445, 467, 491, 513, 528, 570, 580, 606; French invasion and, 447, 448, 492, 504, 525, 548; in Italy, 469, 470; North African invasion and, 447, 448, 451, 455, 460; Philippines and, 411; on unconditional surrender, 464
El Alamein, 456
"Eleanor Clubs," 520
Eleanor Roosevelt Vocational School for Colored Youth, 245
Elections: barnstorming, 76–77; disability and health, as issues, 54, 55, 64, 76, 82, 516, 544, 545, 557, 562; FDR's campaign tactics, 76–77, 195, 196–197, 197–198, 200–203, 204, 205, 346–347; FDR's "lucky dish," 567; *1910*, 17, 18; *1912*, 22, 25, 197, 241; *1914*, 25; *1918*, 26, 425; *1920*, 38–40, 82, 429; *1928*, 51, 52–53, 54–55, 82, 196, 566;1930 presidential/ gubernatorial, 63–65; *1932*, 52, 63, 65–78, 81, 199, 200, 241, 547, 498;1932 campaign issues, 67–70, 73–74, 75–76, 82; 1934 congressional, 141, 142, 144, 153, 154, 199, 223; *1936*, 40, 52, 146, 153–154, 163, 166, 169, 185–186, 195–197, 197–208, 221, 222, 224, 238, 248, 306; 1936 campaign issues, 188, 191, 193–194, 198, 200, 203, 204–205, 205–206; 1938 congressional, 223, 273, 280–287, 300, 327; *1940*, 201, 282, 284, 325, 327–328, 335, 338, 341, 342–347, 350, 352–357, 494, 531, 567; 1940 campaign

Elections (*cont.*)
issues, 327–328, 352–353, 354–356, 496; *1942*, 413, 428, 434, 439; *1944*, 486, 494–495, 499, 513–514, 516–517, 524, 525, 527, 528–538, 539, 544, 556–560, 561, 562–567, 567–568; 1944 campaign issues, 475, 498, 517–518, 519, 524, 529, 544, 545, 551, 557, 562, 563; torchlight parade, 567; two-thirds rule and, 65, 70, 71, 72, 201. *See also* Inaugurations
Electric power, 57–58, 59, 67, 71, 77, 87, 147–148, 190, 286; rates, 57–58, 64. *See also* Holding companies; Tennessee Valley Authority
Elizabeth I, Queen of England, 61, 317
Ellsworth, Lincoln, 316
Embargo, 181, 182–183, 261, 264, 292, 486; arms and war supplies, 105, 109–110, 115, 181, 209, 300, 355; FDR and, 109–110, 115, 183; on gold, 101; against Japan, 109–110, 379, 382–383, 391, 395, 396, 398, 399; legislation on, 177, 321, 322, 323; Spanish Civil War and, 270, 271
Emergency Banking bill, 95
Emergency Council. *See* National Emergency Council
Emergency Railroad Transportation Act, 103
Emmet, Grenville T., 40
Empire State Democracy, 22
England, 3, 4, 8
English Channel, 300, 332, 447, 477. *See also* France: Allied invasion of
Eniwetok, 261
Enterprise, 446
Erie Canal, 59
Estate taxes, 164, 165, 167
Estonia, 324, 488
Ethiopia, 593; British vs. U.S. policy on, 294–295; Italian invasion of, 154, 181, 182, 184, 191, 294
Ethridge, Mark, 546, 547
Europe, 260, 307, 308, 528; anti-Semitism in, 112, 295; dictators of, 181, 184, 230, 259, 260, 262; FDR's travel to, 7, 598–599; German threat/war imminent, 111, 113, 154, 172, 177, 179, 191, 204, 210, 215, 219, 250, 259, 268, 289, 290, 294, 295, 298, 299–300, 301, 304, 318, 327; Nazism, rise of, 112, 113, 272, 333, 338; occupation forces, 584–585; postwar, 219, 466–467, 482, 484, 486, 488, 489–490, 523, 568–569, 583, 584–585; Soviets/Stalin and, 472–473, 477, 479, 550, 582, 583, 585, 590, 596, 600; U.S./FDR and, 89, 215, 117, 215, 216, 218, 301, 316–317, 318, 321, 398, 606; war in, 343, 354, 360, 366, 398, 466, 482, 483, 539, 547, 548, 568, 590, 593, 606. *See also names of individual countries*
European Advisory Commission, 490
Évian conference, 297
Exchequer, British, 260
Executive branch. *See* Administrative reform
Executive Council, 125
Executive Office of the President, 279, 319, 341–342, 417
Ezekiel, Mordecai, 123

Factory Investigating Commission, 21
Fair practics codes. *See* National Recovery Act: codes
Fair Labor Standards Act, 281–282. *See also* Wage(s); Work hours/work week
Fairbanks, Alaska, 472
Fairhaven, Massachusetts, 10
Farley, James A., 57, 65, 127, 146, 154, 174, 185, 187, 189, 235, 237, 278, 353; FDR's campaigns and, 64, 65, 71, 72, 197, 198, 200; New Deal appointees and, 121–122; as presidential nominee, 284, 327, 328, 343, 344, 345
Farley, Thomas M., 69
Farm Board, 133
Farm Bureau Federation, 86
Farm Credit Administraton, 133, 172, 279
Farmer's Holiday Association, 131
Farm Relief Act, 103
Farouk, King of Egypt, 593
Fascism, 146, 252, 282, 374, 388; FDR and, 290, 457; French North Africa and, 456–457; Italian, 269, 270, 470, 505; Latin America and, 218, 219; southern feudal system as, 283; in Spain, 269, 457
FBI, 219, 474
Federal Communications Commission, 139
Federal Deposit Insurance Corporation, 95, 167
Federal Emergency Relief Administration (FERA), 100, 135, 187
Federal Housing Act, 139
Federal Reserve, 25, 139, 167, 250, 252, 432, 575; banking crisis and, 90, 95; modifications to, 147, 148
Federal Trade Commission, 160
Feis, Herbert, 99, 117
Fermi, Enrico, 348
Fidelity and Deposit, 40
Field, Henry, 297
Fifth Army, 526
"Final solution," 313
Finland, 312, 543; Soviet Union and, 324–325, 326, 327, 429, 588; war debts of, 171
Fireside Chats, 99, 162, 374, 598; answering critics in, 141; on anti-inflation program, 438; on FDR's 1938 candidates, 282; on *Greer* incident, 393; on lend-lease/"arsenal of democracy," 360; on NRA, 126; origin

of, 58; on postwar world, 503; on quarantine, 265; during World War II, 322, 409, 433, 441; on WPA and social security, 158
First Army, 350
First Hundred Days, 92–105, 108, 117, 119, 124, 143, 222, 224, 275; legislation rush, 92, 95, 97–100, 101, 102–103, 104, 105; public support during, 92, 98
Fish, Hamilton, Jr., 25, 173, 323, 355, 568
Fitzgerald, John J., 25
Flandin, Pierre, 178
Flint, Michigan, strike, 242
Florida, 280, 284
"Flying Tigers," 380
Flynn, Edward, 353, 529–530, 533–534, 536
Foch, Ferdinand, 462
Food stamps, 132
Ford, Henry, 127
Ford Company, 243
Foreign Affairs, 51
Foreign Economic Administration, 499, 546
Foreign Office, 111, 313, 118, 334, 352, 385, 564, 596; Atlantic Charter and, 388
Foreign policy, 50–51, 79; FDR's goal of international cooperation, 50, 215, 220, 415; FDR as personal diplomat, 106, 108–109, 172, 173, 174; in First Hundred Days, 106–118; U.S. as "good neighbor" to world, 178, 183. *See also* Good Neighbor policy; *names of individual countries*; Nationalism: internationalism vs.; State Department; United Nations
Foreign Policy Association, 560, 563; FDR 1944 campaign speech at, 564–565
Foreign Service, 107, 375
Foreman, Clark, 283
Forest Service, 274, 278
Formosa, 400, 541, 542
Forrestal, James, 347, 535
Fort Benning, 607
Fortress America, 334, 338
Fortune, 297; poll on FDR, 495
Four Freedoms, 360–361
"Four Policemen," 486–487, 523, 528
Four Powers Declaration, 476
Fourteen Points, 259, 360, 464
France, 178, 242, 267, 313, 317, 466, 505, 527, 550, 554, 583, 584; aircraft of, 301, 303, 307, 308, 309, 310, 311, 312; Allied invasion of, 413, 447–449, 450–452, 459, 466, 467, 468, 469, 472, 477, 481, 482–483, 484–486, 490, 491–492, 499, 504, 507, 525, 526–527, 539, 547, 548, 553; *Anschluss,* reaction to, 295; appeasement and, 258, 259–260, 269; British relations, 299, 301, 303; colonies/colonialism, 307, 311, 462, 481, 528, 596–597 (*see also* Africa, French North; Africa, French West; Algeria; Indochina, French; Martinique; West Indies, French); Czechoslovakian crisis and, 300, 301, 302; de Gaulle's provisional government, 527, 528; economy, 116, 134; FDR's forebears in, 4, 5; German prewar relations/war threat, 113, 114, 176, 177, 183, 184, 268, 298–299, 302, 305, 307, 318, 319, 324, 328–329; German war/fall of, 330, 331–332, 333, 334–335, 336, 337, 338, 339, 342, 349, 351, 373, 367, 395, 450, 453, 454, 482–483, 525, 526, 527; Italy and, 183, 270; at London Economic Conference, 116, 117; Nazism vs. communism, 260; invasion, 318, 321, 322; postwar, 490, 582, 583, 584–585; Soviet Union/Stalin and, 479, 481, 490, 596, 597; Spanish Civil War and, 269, 270, 271, 272; U.S./FDR's relations with, 31, 110, 111, 114–115, 124, 178, 180, 258, 259, 266, 267, 299, 301, 303, 312, 337, 367, 457, 599; war debts and, 110, 111, 113, 115; in World War I, 29, 31. *See also* Africa, French North; de Gaulle, Charles; Vichy government
Franco, Francisco, 269, 270, 271, 272, 276, 456, 570; FDR and, during World War II, 454, 457; Hitler and, 367, 454; popularity in Latin American, 270, 271
François-Poncet, André, 260
Frank, Jerome, 145
Frankenstein, Richard, 243
Frankfurt, Germany, 313
Frankfurter, Felix, 76, 121, 168, 169, 226, 239, 251, 553–554; Schechter case and, 161, 162, 164
Free French Fighting Forces, 453
French Air Ministry, 308
French Fleet, 334; fall of France and, 337. *See also* Navy, French
French National Committee, f337
French Second Armored Division, 548
French West Africa. See Africa, French West
French West Indies. *See* West Indies, French
Freud, Sigmund, 295
"Friends of Smith," 68
Fuller, J. F. C., 464
Fundy, Bay of, 41, 42, 168

Gainesville, Georgia, 254, 283, 284
Galapagos Islands, 298, 316
Galbraith, John Kenneth, 430
Gallipoli, 332
Gallup, George, 185; on WPA patronage, 189; 1936 Republican campaign issue, government spending, 191; on unions, 242
Gallup polls, 185, 313, 328, 331, 338, 353, 370, 374, 422–423, 435, 494, 495, 562, 578. *See also* Public opinion/polls
Gambia, 458

Gandhi, Mohandas K., 444
Gannett, Frank, 276
Gardner, Augustus P., 28, 29
Garner, John Nance, 152, 249; judicial reform bill and, 229, 233, 237, 238; as presidential/vice presidential nominee, 68, 69, 70, 71, 72, 73, 74, 201, 327, 328, 343, 344
Garry, Thomas F., 344
Gauss, Clarence, 442
Gdansk, 314. *See also* Danzig
Gellman, Irwin, 213
General Electric, 253, 420
General Motors, 53, 242–243, 243
Geneva, 265; disarmament conference, 82, 111, 113–114, 210
Gennerich, Gus, 218
George, Walter, 282, 286, 501, 569, 575
George VI, King of England, 31, 303, 317, 396
Georgetown University, 173
George Washington, 31
Georgia, 64, 70, 245; blacks in, 521; congressmen/senators from, 282, 286; FDR's contact with residents of, 124; FDR's farm in, 47, 51
Georgia Power, 166, 286
Gerard, James W., 25
German-Americans, 39, 357
German Foreign Office, 408
German SS Panzer divisions, 526
Germany, 313, 447–452, 480; air strength, 303, 307–308, 309, 350; anti-Comintern pact, 217; Anzio and, 504; Atlantic, 351, 367, 372–373, 447, 473; atomic bomb and, 348, 349, 377, 526, 555; Austria and, 111, 295, 296; Belgium and, 324, 329, 330, 335, 572; blitz (1939–1940), 321, 322, 324, 327, 329, 330, 331, 332, 333, 334, 335–336, 338; bombing of, 460, 506; Britain and, 112, 113, 183, 184, 262, 268, 299, 300, 301, 302–303, 305, 307, 311, 319, 410, 464; Britain and, war with, 324, 328, 329–330, 331, 332, 333, 334, 335, 337–338, 350, 351–352, 359, 361–362, 365–366, 367, 368, 371, 373, 379, 387, 450, 602; Britain's postwar plans for, 550, 582, 583, 584–586; collective security and, 178; colonies of, 329; Crete, Greece, defeat of, 368; Czechoslovakia and, 295, 298, 299, 300, 301–304, 305, 314, 315, 348, 354; Denmark and, 329–330; economy of, 79, 96, 100, 178, 319, 329; Egypt, 368; emigration/refugees from, 295, 296; European colonies/possessions and, 307, 311, 351; expansionism/*lebensraum*, 111, 179, 295, 302; FDR's strategy on, 215, 218, 263, 264, 300, 312, 314, 324, 328–329, 407, 413, 463, 467, 583; FDR's strategy, "Germany first," 110, 294, 315–316, 365, 377, 381, 382, 383, 384, 407, 408, 442, 446, 447, 466, 539; FDR's travel to, in childhood, 7; France and, 113, 114, 176, 177, 183, 184, 268, 298–299, 302, 305, 307, 311, 318, 319, 324, 328–329, 330, 331–332, 333, 334–335, 336, 337, 338, 339, 342, 349, 351, 373, 367, 395, 450, 453, 454, 482–483, 525, 526, 527; Gibraltar and, 367; Iceland and, 384; industry, 308, 377, 408, 526, 550, 553, 560–561, 582, 585; Italy and, 469, 470, 601–602; Japan and, 373, 376, 379–380, 397, 408; Jews and anti-Semitism in, 313–314, 461 (*see also* Anti-Semitism: *Kristallnacht*); Latin America and, 338, 307, 350–351; Lithuanian occupation, 314; Luxembourg, 330; Mediterranean strategy, 367; militarism/military strength, 7, 111, 112, 299, 314, 377, 408, 472, 597; Netherlands, 311, 324, 329, 330; *Niblack* incident and, 369; North Africa and, 367, 386, 412–413, 454, 458, 468; Norway and, 329–330, 386; occupation zones, 553; Pearl Harbor and, 407–408; Poland and, 111, 314, 318–319, 320, 321, 322, 324, 357, 548, 550; populace, and reaction to war, 302; in Portugal, 370; postwar plans for, 488, 489–490, 550–551, 582, 583, 584–586, 597; postwar, Morgenthau plan, 550, 552, 552–553, 560–561, 605; press/newspapers in, 318, 323; rearmament, 113, 114, 178, 179, 181, 295; ships of, U.S. seizure of vessels, 371; Soviet Union and, 173, 174, 176, 177, 217, 368, 370, 373–374, 376, 377, 381, 393, 412, 449–450, 451, 465, 471, 472, 485, 489, 526, 582, 585, 589; Soviet non-aggression pact with, 318, 319, 325, 449; Spain and, 367, 370, 412, 454; Spanish Civil War and, 269, 270, 454; surrender in Italy, 601–602; threat from, 106, 171, 172, 177, 178, 179, 217, 260, 261, 305, 307, 311, 1335, 339, 349, 365, 447; Turkey and, 491; U.S.-Britain-France as potential enemy, 299, 303; U.S. relations with, 107, 111–114, 177–178, 218, 314–315, 320, 348, 372, 391, 394 (*see also* Germany: threat from); U.S. war with, 386, 402, 407–408, 409, 441, 447–452, 470, 495, 504, 547, 580, 528, 590; U.S. and, in Atlantic, 368, 369, 370, 372, 391, 392–394; unconditional surrender and, 463; United Nations organization and, 597; Versailles Treaty and, 39, 173, 183, 259; view of FDR/U.S., 307, 315; war reparations, 585–586; in World War I, 29, 195, 307, 358, 464; Yugoslavia and, 368. *See also* Hitler, Adolf; World War II

GI Bill of Rights, 503–504
Gibraltar, 300, 367, 454; Strait of, 412, 447
Gibson, Hugh, 107
Gillette, Guy M., 284
Giraud, Henri, 455–456, 457, 458, 460–461, 462–463, 469
Girdler, Tom, 243
Glass, Carter, 45, 167, 229, 230, 233, 241, 323
Godesberg, 301
Goebbels, Joseph, 302, 313, 472, 558
Goering, Hermann, 302, 313, 314, 324
Gold, 102, 116; banking crisis and, 95; bonds, 130; British holdings, 505; "commodity dollar" theory and, 133–134, 139; presidential power for regulating, 90; sterilizing of, 250, 256; U.S. reserves, 101, 117. *See also* Gold standard
Gold Reserve Act, 134
Goldsmith, Harry S., 515
Gold standard, 82, 88–89, 90, 100–101, 102
Gompers, Samuel, 158
Good Neighbor policy, 209–220; Buenos Aires conference, 209, 215–217, 218; collective security and, 212, 216, 219, 220; cultural exchanges, 215, 216, 218, 219, 220; dictatorships and, 214, 216; evolution of, 51, 211–212; FDR on, 215, 216–217, 218, 219, 220; as model of international cooperation, 215, 220; nonintervention policy of, 211, 212, 213–215; postwar criticism, 219; success of, 219–220; trade and, 212, 214–215, 220; U.S. aid and, 218–219, 220; war threat in Europe and, 215, 218. *See also* Central America; Hemispheric defense; Latin America; ***names of individual Latin American countries***; South America
Gordon, Max, 285
Governors Conferences, 61
Grand Alliance, The (Churchill), 387
Grange, Amaury de la, 308
Grange, New York State, 21, 57, 68
Grassy Point, New York, 57
Great Bitter Lake, 593–594
Great Britain, 564; air strength, 301, 303, 307; *Anschluss,* reaction to, 295; appeasement and, 258, 259–260, 263, 269, 294; in Atlantic, 359, 368, 369, 371; atomic bomb/atomic issues and, 349, 472, 554, 595; bombing of, 350, 351, 361–362; China and, 477, 478; colonies and imperialism, 261, 262, 307, 311, 333, 377, 382, 383, 398, 458, 482, 493, 580, 582, 596 (*see also* British Empire); Czechoslovakian crisis and, 300, 301, 302–303; de Gaulle and, 456, 461; disarmament plan, 114; economy of, 82, 89, 118, 134; in Egypt, 456, 593; FDR and, 4, 5, 31, 110, 111, 115, 118, 205, 260–261, 262, 294, 312–313, 412, 482, 581, 583, 601 (*see also* Churchill, Winston: FDR and); FDR's strategy vs. surrender of, 333–334, 335, 336, 338, 351–352; France and, 299, 301, 303, 330, 337, 338, 453, 528, 582, 583; French invasion and, 447–448, 448–449, 450–451, 452, 459, 466, 467, 468, 469, 477, 484–485, 486, 490, 492, 504, 507, 525, 527, 548; German prewar relations, 112, 113, 183, 184, 262, 268, 299, 300, 301, 302–303, 305, 307, 311, 319; German war with, 324, 328, 329–330, 331, 332, 333, 334, 335, 337–338, 350, 351–352, 359, 361–362, 365–366, 367, 368, 371, 373, 379, 387, 450, 602; German war with, predictions of defeat, 330, 332, 333, 334, 335, 338, 351, 352, 365, 366, 379; Germany, postwar plans for, 550, 582, 583, 584–586; Greece and, 368, 569, 580; Hitler, views on, 177, 314 (*see also* Great Britain: appeasement and); Hong Kong and, 586; in Iceland, 372, 384; India and, 443–444, 587; industry and war production of, 392, 410, 418, 550, 560; Iran and, 487; Italy and, 183, 270, 294–295; Japan and, 263, 264, 267, 292–293, 377, 379, 381, 382, 383, 395, 396–397, 399, 401; Latin America and, 306; in Libya, 413, 450; Mediterranean strategy, 367, 459, 505; Middle East and, 386, 593; morale in, 366, 373, 467; North African invasion and, 453, 455, 459; in Norway, 329–330; Poland and, 314, 321, 322, 489; postwar plans, 450, 466, 475, 478, 505, 506, 523, 549, 550, 552, 553, 582, 583, 584–586, 560; rearmament, 335–336; royalty of, U.S. visit, 317, 599; Soviet Union/Stalin and, 373, 374, 375, 449, 483, 505; Spanish Civil War and, 269–270, 271; in Tunisia, 467–486; United Nations and, 466, 486–487; U.S. aid repayment/debt record, 82, 110–111, 113, 115, 171, 358–359, 362–363, 375, 592; U.S. prewar relations, 107, 110–111, 114–115, 118, 178, 261, 262, 292, 293, 294, 299, 300, 301, 303, 312–313, 317, 347, 362, 363–364, 366, 383, 384, 385, 392–393; U.S. prewar relations, war involvement issue, 259, 260, 261, 267, 293, 312, 332, 335; U.S. wartime relations, 410, 412, 413, 450, 459, 468, 471, 472–473, 528, 551, 569, 580; World War I and, 29, 31, 385. *See also* Aid, U.S.: to Britain; British Empire; Chamberlain, Neville; Churchill, Winston; Destroyers-for-bases deal; Lend-lease
"Great Marianas Turkey Shoot," 529
Great Wall of China, 109
Greece, 368, 483, 505, 569, 580

Green, Joseph, 271
Green, William, 156, 159, 438
Greenland, 339, 370
Greer, USS, 392–393
Grenada County, Mississippi, 520
Grew, Joseph, 8, 107, 180, 291, 381, 383, 396
Grey, Edward, 410
Gridiron Dinners, 59, 327
Griffin, Charles, 218
Gromyko, Andrey, 549, 600
Groton School, 8–10, 11, 12, 16, 19, 20, 23, 216, 537
Gruening, Ernest, 543
G-2 (Army Intelligence), 400, 401
Guadalcanal, 446, 455
Guadelupe Hidalgo, Treaty of, 211
Guam, 292
Guffey, Joseph, 188
Guffey Act, 167, 193
Gulick, Luther H., 150, 275

Hague, Frank, 537
Hague, The, 599
Haile Selassie, 183, 593
Hainan Island, 377
Haiti, 28, 39, 214, 245
Half Moon, 7
Halifax, Lord, 300, 302, 333, 363, 366, 383, 394, 410, 581
Halifax, Nova Scotia, 350
Halsey, W. F. ("Bull"), 541
Halsted, James, 513, 515, 604
Hamilton, Alexander, 434
Hamilton, John D. M., 206
Hamlin, Bertie, 50, 69
Hannegan, Robert, 529–530, 533, 534, 535, 536, 537, 563
Hapsburgs, 467
Harding, Warren G., 38, 39, 40, 107, 279, 426, 556
Harlem, 520
Harriman, Averell, 8, 363–364, 368, 464, 468, 490, 499, 506, 549, 569, 590, 601; FDR's death and, 607; Soviet relations and, 375, 471, 475; State Department reorganization and, 569; Tehran conference and, 480, 486; Yalta conference and, 578, 582, 586, 590, 591
Harrison, Benjamin, 199, 274
Harrison, Pat, 153, 156, 157; black issues and, 247; judicial reform and, 233, 237–238; tax proposal and, 166, 167, 282; vs. FDR, 222, 224
Hartford, Connecticut, 566
Harvard Crimson, 11, 107
Harvard University, 180, 276, 312, 349, 355; anti-Semitism at, 295–296; Board of Overseers, 295–296; FDR at, 8, 10–11, 12, 15, 107, 180; FDR honors from, 59; FDR speeches at, 37, 206; Law School, 76, 121
Hassett, William D., 507, 566, 567, 572, 603–604
Hasty Pudding Club, 516
Hatch Act, 287–288
Havana, 351
Hawaiian Islands, 292, 378, 380, 397, 400, 402, 405, 406, 445, 540, 544; expansion of, 262; FDR's visit to, 539; Japanese hypothecated attacks on (1933), 109
Hays, Brooks, 284
Hearst, William Randolph, 68, 72, 182, 199, 264, 547
Hemispheric defense, 209–210, 300, 306–307, 309, 310, 321, 323, 331, 334, 338, 341, 349, 350–351, 354, 383; in Atlantic, 383; European war and, 321; Iceland and, 383–384, 386; Spanish Civil War and, 271. *See also* Canada; Good Neighbor policy; Latin America
Henderson, Leon, 254, 419, 430, 431, 432, 438, 439
Henderson, Nevile, 260
Henderson Field, 446
Henry, Jules, 267, 268
Hermitage, The, 226
Herriot, Eduard, 113, 115
Hershey strike, 242
Hickok, Lorena A., 132
Higgins, Andrew Jackson, 420
High, Stanley, 201, 202
Hill, Lister, 280, 281, 520
Hillman, Sidney, 241, 536, 557, 567; Dewey's attacks on, 563, 566
Hilton, James, 445
Hirohito, 402
Hiss, Alger, 578
Hitler, Adolf, 111–114, 276, 300, 303, 347, 354, 364, 473, 558; anti-Semitism and, 112, 113; appeasement of, 259–260, 294; Argentina, support in, 505; assassination attempt, 539; Atlantic strategy, 334, 351, 367, 370, 372, 373, 393; Austria, strategy in, 295; Belgium and, 324, 329, 330; Britain and, 299, 301, 302, 319, 328–329, 330, 333, 338, 351, 361, 368, 410, 464; British view of, 177–178, 259, 312; Caribbean and, 338; Chamberlain and, 299, 301; Churchill and, 410, 464; Czechoslovakia and, 298, 299, 301–304, 314, 315; disarmament conference at Geneva and, 113–114, 117; eastern Europe, strategy in, 111, 302; FDR and, 258, 305, 306, 307, 311, 365, 366, 370, 394–395, 491; FDR compared to, 178–179, 261, 277, 343, 366, 438, 519; FDR's conference plan, 205, 215, 216, 218; FDR's messages/warnings

to, 302–303, 314–315, 318, 319; FDR's view of, 113, 178, 179, 209, 259, 313, 324, 329, 335; final battles, in Soviet Union, 589; France and, 302, 319, 324, 328–329, 330, 338, 454, 527; French views on, 177–178, 259; Gibraltar, 367; goals of, 111, 177–178, 179; isolationist strategy and, 314–315; Italy and, 469, 470; Japan and, 373, 376, 379–380, 408; Jews opposed to, in French North Africa, 456; Latin America and, 307, 338, 350–351; Lithuanian occupation, 314; Luxembourg, 330; Mediterranean strategy, 367; Mussolini and, 184, 299, 302, 318; Netherlands and, 324, 329, 330; North Africa and, 367, 386, 412–413, 454, 458; Norway, conquest of, 386; Poland and, 314, 318–319, 320, 321, 322; in Portugal, 370; racism/nationalism, 178; rise to power, 79, 93, 106, 111–114, 179; in Scandinavia, 329–330; scientific research/weapons development and, 348; Soviet Union/Stalin and, 368, 370, 373–374, 376, 377, 381, 393, 412, 449, 472, 526, 589; Spain and, 367, 370, 412, 454; Spanish Civil War and, 269; speeches, 301, 314, 406; tactics of, 181, 295, 314, 317, 322, 324, 328, 329–330; tactics of, benign image/peace, 114, 177–178, 324, 328–329; tactics of, one war at a time/fighting until end, 301, 349, 372, 384, 468, 472; threat from, 154, 215, 218, 258, 306, 307, 311, 349–350, 365, 366, 377, 385; unconditional surrender and, 464; U.S. and, 307, 309, 310, 313, 323, 329, 333, 334–335, 338, 349–350, 365, 366, 368, 372–373, 394; U.S. and, war declaration, 407–408; Versailles Treaty and, 183, 259; view of FDR and U.S., 299, 303, 314, 319, 324, 408. *See also* Germany; Munich agreement

Hobart College, 59

Hobcaw, 514, 515, 519

Holding companies, 147–148; FDR's "death penalty" for, 166, 167–169, 170; James Roosevelt as president of first, 5

Holland Society, 5

Holmes, Julius, 570

Holmes, Oliver Wendell, 24, 226

Holmes, Reverend John Haynes, 69

Hong Kong, 109, 267, 406, 478, 493, 586

Honolulu, 404, 527; naval planning session in, 540–542. *See also* Pearl Harbor

Honshu, 582

Hoosac Mills Corporation, 191

Hoover, Herbert, 40, 53, 55, 58, 59, 60, 63, 108, 226, 327, 342; agriculture and, 86, 133; Asian policy, 109; banking crisis plan, 95; Bonus Army incident, 75; depression/economic policies, 65, 70, 74, 75, 78, 79, 80, 81–83, 86, 88–89, 127; disarmament and, 111; FDR and, 40, 82, 61, 107, 109, 325; as FDR/New Deal critic, 77, 88–89, 90, 123, 140, 141, 199, 205, 343, 389–390; Good Neighbor policy and, 212; immigration and, 296; New Deal prototypes under, 122, 123; 1932 campaign and election, 67, 74, 75, 77–78; 1936 campaign and, 198; war debts and, 110; World War II and, 325, 407

Hoover, J. Edgar, 80, 474

Hoover Dam, 189

Hoover Farm Board, 123

Hopkins, Harry L., 141, 155, 337, 390, 392, 394, 455, 423, 460, 463, 475, 508, 510, 526, 529, 600; at Arcadia conference, 412, 414; at Cairo conference, 478; Churchill-Stalin meeting and, 568, 569; in Egypt, 594, 595; FDR and, 187, 189, 347, 363, 498–499, 551, 569, 581; Ickes vs., 150, 154, 186, 187; influence of, 124, 439–440; Japan and, 402; lend-lease, 359, 376; to London as emissary, 363, 364; New Deal history, 328; 1940 election, 343, 345; Pearl Harbor and, 404, 405, 406; purge and, 284, 287; relief programs, 132, 133, 134–135, 148, 149, 186, 187, 188, 245, 248, 285, 421; Soviet relations and, 375, 376, 470, 471; State Department and, 569, 570; at Tehran conference, 480, 481, 483–484, 486, 490, 581; as TERA administrator, 61–62; war strategy, 386, 448–449, 451; Yalta conference and, 578, 581, 586, 595, 596

Hornbeck, Stanley, 110, 181, 266, 294

House, Colonel Edward M., 68–69, 84, 123, 134, 139, 140, 172, 183, 184, 329

House Judiciary Committee, 229, 246

House Naval Affairs Committee, 28–29

House of Commons, 114, 302, 336, 443, 597

House of Lords, 194

House of Representatives, 235, 308, 517; administrative reform and, 276, 277, 278, 279; agricultural reform and, 86, 103; antilynching bill, 246, 247; Atlantic strategy and, 393; defense spending and, 331; Democrats in, 65, 141, 282, 287, 573; draft extension, 391; economy bill and, 96; embargo, 109, 183; ER and, 426; Fala story, 543; FDR and, 96, 98, 155, 280, 597; FDR's opposition in, 168, 169, 240–241; FDR's war message and, 406; holding-company bill, 168, 169; judicial reform and, 229, 240–241; labor issues, 281, 432; lend-lease passage, 362; Ludlow Amendment, 291, 292–293; New Deal, "second," and, passage of, 153, 155–156, 156–157; price control legislation, 430; Republicans

House of Representatives (*cont.*)
in, 287, 393; social security and, 156–157, 170; soldiers' vote bill, 503
House Resolution 1776, 362. *See also* Lend-lease
House Rules Committee, 281, 286
House Un-American Activities Committee, 325
House Ways and Means Committee, 156, 434, 501, 502
Housing, 50, 245, 439, 498, 500, 520. *See also* Mortgages
Houston, Sam, 198
Houston, Texas, 53, 520
Houston, USS, 138, 191, 298
Howe, Louis McHenry, 21, 22, 52, 114, 116, 123, 347; FDR's gubernatorial campaign, 53, 54; FDR's relationship with, 42, 43, 47, 49, 197; in Navy Department with FDR, 25, 26; 1932 presidential campaign and, 65, 72; speechwriting, 73
Howells, William Dean, 15
Howland Island, 262
Huddleston, George, 168
Hughes, Charles Evans, 93, 160, 161, 162, 234, 368,
Hull, Cordell, 107–108, 112, 113, 269, 293, 299, 302, 321, 368, 412, 453, 460, 529, 559, 578; Atlantic Charter and, 388, 415; Brussels conference/nine-power conference and, 266, 268; defense, prewar, 307, 308, 315, 316; FDR and, relationship with, 107–108, 212, 214, 345, 364, 384; illness and resignation, 569, 570; Japan and, 180, 291, 292, 315, 316, 379–380, 381, 395, 396, 397, 398, 399, 400, 404; Latin American policy and, 212, 213–214, 215, 306, 307, 351; at London Economic Conference, 115–116, 214; Moley vs., 107, 108, 116; presidency and, 327, 328, 343; as senator, 83, 84; Soviet Union/Stalin and, 172, 173, 174, 375, 473–474, 475–476, 493, 522; trade program of, 115, 116; UN charter, 523–524; Welles vs., 108, 212, 329, 474, 475 and,
Hull House, 79
Humphreys, Robert, 556
Hundred Days. *See* First Hundred Days
Hungary, 319, 348, 408, 467, 479, 553, 569, 589
Hurja, Emil, 185
Hurley, Patrick J., 63, 561–562
HUSKY (Sicilian invasion), 467
Hyde Park, New York, 11, 37, 42, 43, 48, 78, 90, 180, 186, 207, 212, 266, 300, 309, 393, 419, 423, 450, 454, 455, 502, 507, 509, 512, 514, 529, 535–536, 572, 598, 603; bird collection, 7, 14; Churchill's visit to, 553, 554, 555; Dutch Colonial architecture in, 5; entranceway, as shrine to FDR, 13–14; FDR's funeral services, 607; FDR's neighbors, 99, 124, 211, 419, 423, 567; FDR voting in, 567; Roosevelt estate/residence at, 4, 50; Roosevelt Library at, 328; royal family visit to, 317

Ibn Saud, King of Saudi Arabia, 552, 593–595, 599
Iceland, 369, 392, 546; U.S. protection/hemispheric defense, 372, 383–384, 386
Ickes, Harold L., 127, 215, 218, 221, 222, 223, 251, 263, 294, 307, 315, 438, 446, 457, 494, 497, 498, 507, 515, 572, 575; defense policies, 342, 359, 365, 368; Farley vs., 154; FDR and, 186, 189, 399; Hopkins vs., 150, 154, 186, 187; Japan and, 382, 399; 1944 election/campaign, 531, 532, 533, 535, 536; public works and, 135, 148, 149–150, 186, 187, 189, 248, 421; as Republican, 76, 186; as secretary of interior, 121, 274; Spanish Civil War and, 271; war involvement, 394
Idaho, 165
"I hate war" speech, 205, 259, 270
Illinois, 69, 244, 354, 518, 532
Immigration quotas, 296, 297. *See also* Refugees from Nazism
Imperialism/colonialism, 528, 582, 596, 597; FDR's opposition to, 458–459, 461, 478, 481, 491, 596, 597; U.S. and, 31, 211, 213, 217. *See also* British Empire; Colonies/possessions; Self-determination
"Imperial presidency," 280, 467
Inaugurations, 4, 9–10, 56–57, 90, 92–93, 224–226, 364, 573–574; addresses, 90, 93–94, 98, 211, 224, 225, 364, 406, 574, 607; Lucy Mercer's presence at, 36, 511
Income tax, 19, 128, 164–165, 167, 192, 435, 501
India, 388, 389, 442, 443–444, 481, 484, 587
Indian Congress Party, 443, 444
Indiana, 189, 289, 343; delegates, 69; FDR's 1944 campaign trip through, 565
Indianapolis, 117, 216
Indochina, French, 267, 379, 382, 395, 396, 400, 481, 596–597
Industrial Board (NY), 56
Industry, 20–21, 85, 149, 242, 496; FDR's legislation on, 104–105; New Deal opposition, 326–327; production, 61, 74, 93, 104, 119–120, 131, 143, 248, 249; recovery, 100, 119, 248; unions vs., 241–244. *See also* Business; Child labor; Labor; National Recovery Administration; Strikes; Unions; Wage(s); Work hours/work week
Inflation, 77, 88–89, 90, 249, 250, 321; controlled, to counter deflation, 100–102, 103,

104, 134; FDR's program, 432–438; in Germany, 96, 100; gold and silver purchases, 133–134, 139; postwar, 501, 503; post–World War I, 38, 39, 40; wartime, 419, 423, 424, 425, 429–439, 496, 501, 502
Ingersoll, Royal E., 292, 293
Inheritance taxes, 164, 165, 167
Inönü, Ismet, 491
Insull, Samuel, 87, 147
Intellectuals, and FDR, 67, 77, 145
Intelligence, U.S., 319, 339, 436, 559; army, 510; code-breaking, 377, 378, 381, 473, 445, 559; on Germany, 322, 473, 559; on Japan, 377, 378, 381, 395, 397, 399, 400, 401, 445, 559; navy, 109, 510; North African invasion and, 454; *Panay* and, 290, 291. *See also* MAGIC
Inter-American Conference (Montevideo), 173, 209, 215–217, 218
Intergovernmental Committee on Refugees, 297
Interior, Department of, 262, 275, 278
Internal Revenue Service, 517
International Conference of American States, 306
Internationalism, 105, 518, 521, 522, 523, 556, 560; League of Nation and, 68; UN draft charter and, 523. *See also* Collective security; Economy: nationalism vs. internationalism; Nationalism: internationalism vs.; Isolationists
Interstate commerce, 282
Interstate Commerce Commission, 275
Iowa, 476
Iowa, 72, 284, 345
Iran, 480, 487, 490, 505. *See also* Tehran conference
Iraq, 505
Ireland, 394
Ireland, Northern, 413
Irish-Americans, 20, 39, 57, 354, 355
Ismay, Hastings, 449, 480
Isolationists, 38, 106, 107, 171–172, 184, 260, 271, 310, 317, 320, 335, 342, 405, 410, 518, 528, 530, 560, 566, 582; Atlantic Charter and, 389; Britain and, 312; as campaign issue, 68, 69, 343, 344, 568; in Congress, 114, 115, 117, 171, 289, 303, 305, 331, 358, 362, 391, 394, 425, 568; European war and, 322, 328–329; FDR and, 39, 68, 69, 105, 260, 305–306, 320, 354, 355, 357, 366–367, 368, 375, 391, 394; FDR's security guarantee and, 114–115; hemispheric defense and, 209, 383; Hitler/Nazis and, 314–315, 323, 408; Japanese embargo and, 110; *Kearny* incident and, 393; Lindbergh as spokesman for, 307, 323; neutrality legislation and, 315; *Niblack* incident and, 369; in postwar world, 521–522, 523; quarantine and, 264, 265; Republican, 343, 354; Soviet Union and, 172, 324; UN draft charter and, 523; U.S. aid and destroyers-for-bases, 311, 331, 336, 338, 350, 352, 358, 361, 364–365, 366, 368, 375; World War II and, 425. *See also* America First Committee; Ludlow Amendment
Israel. *See* Palestine
Italian-Americans, 270, 354, 355, 357
Italy, 93, 112, 147, 291, 297, 348, 447, 482, 505, 526, 575; air strength, 308; in Albania, 314; appeasement, 294; British relations with, 294–295, 338; embargo against, 183; Ethiopian invasion, 154, 181, 182, 183, 184, 190, 191, 294–295; Fascism in, 269, 270; FDR and, 215, 218, 263, 318, 463; FDR's World War I visit, 31; French relations with, 332, 336, 337; Germany and, 184, 469, 470, 601–602; Japan and, 379–380; militancy, 314; in North Africa, surrender of, 468; postwar, 470, 490, 505; quarantine plan and, 263, 264; Soviet Union and, 488; Spanish Civil War and, 269, 270; unconditional surrender and, 464, 469, 470; U.S.-British invasion of, 465, 467, 468, 469, 472; U.S. relations with, 177, 294–295, 312, 339, 371, 372; U.S. war with, 407, 408. *See also* Anzio; Mussolini, Benito; Rome; Sicily

Jackson, Andrew, 65, 85, 98, 201, 206, 226, 240, 434, 546
Jackson, Garner, 145
Jackson, Robert H., 251, 254, 368
Jackson, Samuel D., 535
Jamaica, 352
James, Henry, 8
Japan, 290–294, 377–379, 379–383, 395–403, 441–447, 471; Allied/Anglo-American strategy, 412, 589–590; anti-Comintern pact, 217; appeasement and, 259; in Asia, 109, 292, 379, 395, 398, 427; atomic bomb and, 555, 590; bombing of, 540, 582, 590; Britain and, 263, 264, 267, 292–293, 377, 379, 381, 382, 383, 395, 396–397, 399, 401; in China/Manchuria, 83, 106–107, 109, 262–263, 265, 266, 397, 398, 442–443, 469, 477–479; economic depression in, 79; emperor, 395, 396, 397, 402, 478; fall of premier/cabinet, 396, 539; Hitler and, 373, 376, 379–380, 408; imperialism/expansionism and, 79, 173, 181, 315, 349, 376; India, threat to, 442, 443–444; in Indochina, 379, 382, 395, 396, 400, 596; Netherlands and, 377, 379, 383, 395, 397, 389, 400; oil shipments and embargo, 109–110, 379, 382–

Japan (*cont.*)
383, 391, 395, 396, 398, 399; in Pacific, 261, 292, 339, 414, 445–447, 482, 486, 529; postwar plans for, 597; quarantine/blockade of, 184, 263, 267, 268, 291–292, 292–293, 590; Soviet Union and, 172, 173, 176, 369, 377, 381, 383, 396, 397, 473, 476, 478, 482, 483, 491, 493, 582, 589–590, 591; threat of/strength of, 109, 171, 172, 217, 261, 364, 377–382, 445, 446, 597; unconditional surrender, 463; United Nations organization and, 597; U.S. and "Germany first" vs. "Japan first" policy, 110, 315–316, 425, 466; U.S./FDR prewar policies, 28, 51, 106–107, 109–110, 171, 172, 177, 180–181, 215–216, 258, 260, 261–262, 263, 271, 290–292, 293, 315–316, 339, 365, 368, 372, 373, 377–382, 391, 394, 395, 396–403, 404, 405, 407, 441; U.S. war with, 406, 407, 408, 422, 427, 455, 465–466, 473, 476, 478, 482, 483, 486, 493, 495, 539–540, 542, 552, 565, 582; U.S./FDR prewar negotiations with, 380–381, 395, 396, 397–400, 402, 404; war preparations of, 395–398, 400–403
Japanese-Americans, 405, 407
Japanese Fleet, 378, 446. *See also* Navy, Japanese
Japanese Foreign Office, 378, 401
Jarvis Island, 262
Jefferson, Thomas, 5, 124, 227, 434; influence on FDR, 85, 98, 121
Jefferson Day addresses, 5, 70, 139, 604
Jefferson Memorial, 527
Jersey City, 537
Jerusalem, 479
Jews: Arabs vs., 594–595; in Austria, 295; FDR and, 4, 50, 112, 295–297, 299, 461, 593–595; in French North Africa, 456, 457, 461; German/Nazi violence against, 112, 113, 179, 313–314, 453; in Palestine, 389, 531; Polish, 313; refugees from Nazism, 295, 296–297, 314, 531, 593–595; in U.S., 112, 295–296, 594. *See also* Anti-Semitism
Johnson, Hiram, 98–99, 105, 110, 171, 172, 305, 315, 405, 560; judicial reform and, 231, 238
Johnson, Hugh, 285, 126, 136, 137
Johnson, Louis A., 323, 326, 444
Johnson, Lyndon B., 235, 280, 446, 497, 517, 532
Johnson, Tom, 66
Johnson Act, 171
Joint Chiefs of Staff, 451, 508, 540, 541; French invasion, 504; Japan, strategy against, 582, 589–590, 591; Malta strategy debate, 580; unconditional surrender and, 463; Yalta conference, 578, 582, 590
Joliet, Illinois, 354
Jones, Jesse H., 517, 530, 532, 546, 547, 570; as secretary of commerce/RFC head, 95, 121, 123, 353, 427; Wallace to replace, 571, 575
Journal de Genève, 117
Judicial reform, 221, 223, 224–239, 240, 241, 242, 243, 273, 275, 278; compromise and, 235, 238; democracy/underprivileged issue, 221, 223, 224–225, 232–233; FDR and, in New York State, 58; opposition to, 229–232; retirement age issue, 233, 236; strategy for passage of, 227–228, 230, 231, 232, 234; support for, 229, 232. *See also* Supreme Court
Juliana, Princess of the Netherlands, 330, 572, 599
Juneau, 543, 544
Justice, Department of, 186, 226, 227, 257

Kaltenborn, H. V., 432, 522
Kamchatka, 590
Kansas, 77, 198, 199, 262, 352
Kansas City, 537
Kapitsa, Peter, 554
Karl, Barry, 226
Katyn Forest, 471
Kearny, USS (destroyer), 393
Keenan, Joseph, 235
Kelley, Robert F., 173
Kellogg-Briand Pact, 210, 301
Kelly, Edward J., 244, 343, 344, 533, 536, 565
Kennan, George, 177
Kennedy, Joseph P., 72, 139, 200, 307–308, 321, 324, 332, 336, 363
Kentucky, 132, 237; congressmen/senators from, 282, 285, 570; Wallace support in, 546–547, 548
Kesselring, Albert, 601, 602
Keynes, John Maynard, 117, 133. *See also* Economy: Keynesian approach
Kimball, Warren, 602
Kimmel, Husband E., 370, 378, 397; Pearl Harbor and, 382, 404
King, Ernest J., 372, 411, 422, 445, 446, 450, 451, 465, 540, 541, 542, 584; at Arcadia conference, 414–415; Japanese invasion, opposition to, 590; at Tehran conference, 483
King, Mackenzie, 300, 317, 350, 598, 599
Kingsley, Charles, 8
Kingston, New York, 5, 566
Kingston, Ontario, 300
Kintner, Robert, 306
Kirby, Rollin, 74
Kirov, Sergei, 176
Knox, Frank, 206, 384, 392, 421, 495; defense policy, 342, 347, 368, 374; FDR and, 40, 322–323; Japan and, 400, 402;

Pearl Harbor and, 404, 408–409; war involvement, 394
Knutson, Harold, 543–544
Königsberg, East Prussia, 489
Konoye, Fumimaro, 379, 395, 396
Kra Peninsula, 400
Kremlin, 175, 176, 376, 549, 601
Kristallnacht (Night of the Broken Glass), 313–314
Krock, Arthur, 200, 205, 285
Ku Klux Klan, 51, 238–239
Kuomintang, 442
Kurile Islands, 590, 591
Kursk, 472
Kurusu, Shigenori, 397, 398, 399, 400
Kuter, Laurence S., 584
Kwajalein, 541

Labor, 50, 206, 241–244, 534, 559, 565; agriculture and, 438; business/industry vs., 104, 138, 143, 242–243, 519; FDR and, 20–21, 26, 54, 58, 138, 141, 159, 203–204, 206, 227, 240, 242–244, 247–248, 432, 440; FDR's anti-inflation program and, 435, 437, 438; -management conference, on wartime policy, 431; New Deal and, 158, 241, 529; NRA and, 137–138, 143; problems/unrest, 100, 496–497; Republicans and, 557. *See also* Child labor; Collective bargaining; Fair Labor Standards Act; National Labor Relations Act; National War Labor Board; Strikes; Unions; Wage(s); Wagner Act; Work hours/work week
Labor, Department of, 121
Labor's Non-Partisan League, 203
Labrador, 318
La Follette, Robert M., 52, 153, 155, 165, 167, 231, 277, 323, 522
La Follette Committee, 243–244
La Guardia airport, 187
Lahey, Frank, 512
Laissez-faire approach, 16, 61, 81, 100, 121
Lake, Kathleen, 43, 44, 45
Lamont, Thomas W., 90, 252, 253
Landon, Alf M., 495; European war and, 322, 325; in Latin America for FDR, 306–307; as presidential candidate, 198, 199–200, 203, 204–205, 206, 207
Lansing, Robert, 577
Larooco (Lawrence, Roosevelt, and Company), 45
Lash, Joseph, 509, 510–511, 526, 605
Latin America, 349, 421, 436, 474; democracy in, 209, 212, 216; dictators in, 209, 216, 219, 316; FDR as hero of, 216, 217, 218, 220; Hitler/Nazi threat to, 215, 306, 316, 338, 350–351; as refugee settlement area, 296; Spanish Civil War and, 271; U.S./British national interests and, 363; U.S. postwar relations with, 219; U.S. relations with, 51. *See also* Central America; Good Neighbor policy; Hemispheric defense; *names of individual countries*; South America
Latvia, 324, 488
Lawrence, John S., 45
League of Nations, 31, 50, 71, 178, 210, 265, 297, 306, 521; as campaign issue, 38, 39–40, 67, 68, 78; FDR as advocate of, 31, 556; FDR's disavowal of, 68–69; Japan and, 83, 109, 264–265; Mussolini and, 183, 184; U.S. and, 38, 107; Wilson and, 577
Leahy, William D., 291, 454, 458, 465, 490, 514, 527, 543, 554, 569, 590, 602; conservative influence on FDR, 499, 508; as FDR's foreign policy adviser, 600, 601; 1944 campaign, 566, 567; at Pacific planning session with FDR, 540, 541, 542; at Tehran conference, 485; as Vichy ambassador, 367, 374; Yalta conference and, 578, 579, 581, 591
Lebensraum (living space), 111, 179, 302
Leclerc, Philippe, 528
Lee, Robert E., 198
Lee, Roger, 516
Left wing, 141; FDR and, 129, 144–145, 147, 152, 153, 154, 161, 164, 165, 223, 230, 575; New Deal and, 140–141; pressure on FDR, 142, 143, 146, 147
LeHand, Marguerite (Missy), 46, 123, 205, 293, 346, 370–371, 508, 542, 596
Lehman, Herbert, 56, 204
Lemke, William, 204, 207
Lend-lease, 361–363, 366, 375, 376, 386, 442, 468, 475, 487, 551, 505, 552, 561, 569, 582; defense vs., 412; financial arrangements of, 362–363; origins of, 358–360
Lenin, 174
Leo XIII, 146
Lewis, John L., 167, 203, 241, 243, 244, 253, 370, 371, 519
Leyte, 542, 563; Battle of, 565
Liberal party, British, 309
Liberals, 96, 112, 146, 153, 270, 325, 345, 353, 363; Coughlin and, 146; ER and, 545; FDR and, 154, 240, 282, 346, 354, 356, 457, 532, 547, 575, 576; judicial reform and, 230–231; New Deal and, 145, 498, 499, 529; in South, 283, 284; State Department reorganization and, 570
Liberia, 520
Libertarianism, 497
Liberty League, 140, 196, 203, 570
Liberty Loan drives, 136
Liberty magazine, 80
Library of Congress, 363, 570
Libya, 413, 450

Lilienthal, David, 576
Lima, Peru, 306; conference, 306–307
Lincoln, Abraham, 405, 525, 535, 574; FDR compared to, 92, 198, 368, 425; FDR paraphrasing, 85; Second Inaugural, quoted by FDR, 537–538
Lindbergh, Anne Morrow, 364
Lindbergh, Charles A., 307–308, 323, 325; FDR on, as Nazi, 323; as isolationist, 354, 366–367
Lindley, Ernest K., 265, 497
Lindsay, Ronald, 111, 260, 292, 294, 300, 313
Lippman, Walter, 11, 169–170, 577; as FDR critic, 64, 67–68; on FDR's agricultural program, 86; on FDR's fiscal plan, 96; on Jimmy Walker investigation, 69; on 1944 State of the Union, 500; on Soviet Union, 373
Literary Digest, 196, 205
Lithuania, 314, 324, 488, 586
"Little Entente," 184
Little Rock, Arkansas, 198, 236
"Little White House," 603
Litvinov, Maxim, 174, 175, 176, 416
Livadia Palace, 581
Livingston, Robert, 198
Ljubljana gap, Yugoslavia, 547
Lloyd George, David, 31
Loans. *See* War debts
Lodge, Henry Cabot, 24, 28, 315, 521
London, 102, 107, 214, 259, 292, 301, 321, 332, 335, 359, 363, 368, 373, 375, 389, 449, 451, 457, 467, 492, 525, 546, 596, 604, 607; bombing of, 361; Dutch government-in-exile, 330; FDR in, during WWI, 31; Polish government-in-exile in, 471, 489, 506, 588
London Economic Conference, 106, 110, 113, 115–117, 214, 267; effect of FDR's absence, 115–116
London Naval Conference of 1935, 181
Long, Breckenridge, 329
Long, Huey, 71, 141, 146, 154, 155, 165, 166, 185, 186, 204, 320; death of, 186
Long Beach, California, 145
Long Island, New York, 56
Longworth, Alice Roosevelt, 35, 277
Los Angeles: earthquake, 130, 135; FDR's visit to, 190; Japanese in, 407
Los Angeles Times, 55
Lost Horizon (Hilton), 445
Lothian, Lord, 312, 313, 334, 335, 336, 337, 350, 363
Louisiana, 567–568; Long and, 71, 146, 186
Louisville Courier-Journal, 76, 107, 546
Lovett, Robert W., 41, 42, 43, 44, 45
Low Countries, 324, 330, 331. *See also* Belgium; Luxembourg; Netherlands
Loyalists, Spanish, 269, 270, 271, 272
Lubec, Maine, 41
Lubell, Samuel, 357
Lubin, Isador, 424, 604
Lublin Committee of National Liberation, 548
Lublin government, 588, 600
Lucas, Scott, 532
Luce, Henry, 495
Ludlow, Louis M., 289, 291. *See also* Ludlow Amendment
Ludlow Amendment, 289, 291, 292–293
Luftwaffe, 361, 446, 460. *See also* Air force, German
Lupton, Dilworth, 497
Luxembourg, 330, 572; Wallonia and, 466
Luzon, 541
Lvov, 587
Lynching. *See* Antilynching bill
Lyttelton, Oliver, 466

McAdoo, William Gibbs, 25, 71, 72, 190
MacArthur, Douglas, 111, 172, 441–442, 518, 545; in Australia, 441–442; FDR and, 180, 540, 541, 542, 564; Pacific strategy, 541, 542, 465; in the Philippines, 401, 414, 441, 563–564
McCarran, Pat, 187
McCloy, John, 499
McCormack, John, 353, 543
McCormick, Anne O'Hare, 121, 249, 601
McCormick, R. R., 140
McCrea, John L., 413, 461, 463
MacDonald, Ramsay, 112, 113, 115
McDuffie, John, 74
McGowan, Samuel, 26
McIntire, Ross, 484, 508, 510, 512, 513, 514–515, 516, 545, 563, 564, 606
McIntyre, Marvin, 123, 190, 277
Mackinac Declaration, 518, 523
McKellar, Senator, 576
McKinley, William, 11, 213, 427
MacLeish, Archibald, 570, 571, 603
Macmillan, Harold, 455, 462
McNary, Charles L., 48, 86, 232
McNutt, Paul V., 343, 346
McReynolds, James C., 162, 227
McReynolds, William, 280
Madison Square Garden, 207, 355
Madrid, 269
"MAGIC" code-breaker, 377, 378, 401. *See also* Intelligence, U.S.: code-breaking
Maginot Line, 258, 324, 329, 330
Mahan, Alfred T., 10
Maine, 41, 72, 168, 207, 389
Maine, 290
Malaya, 382, 383, 402
Malta, 492; FDR and Churchill at, 579–580
Manchuria, 368; Japanese in, 83, 109, 181,

398, 589; Soviet Union and, 561, 590, 591
Manhattan, 58, 564
Manila, 23, 204, 414, 542, 583
Manufacturing. *See* Business; Industry
Mao Tse-tung, 293–294
Mara, 593. *See also* Great Bitter Lake
Marco Polo Bridge, 262
Marianas, 529
Marines, U.S., 401, 537, 538; Cuba and, 213; FDR's son in, 402–403; in Guadalcanal, Solomon Islands, 446; in Haiti, 28, 39, 214, 245; in Iceland, 383–384, 386; in Nicaragua, 51; in 1913, 27–28
Marion, Massachusetts, 50
Maritime Commission, 359
Marrakesh, 48
Marseilles, 548
Marshall, George C., 310, 331, 334, 336, 367, 386, 410–411, 443, 508, 510, 548, 558, 559, 584, 602, 605; Allied invasion of France and, 447, 448–449, 450, 451, 452, 459–460, 491–492, 504, 525; Arcadia conference, 410–411, 412, 413, 414, 415; Atlantic conference, 384, 385; as chief of staff, return to Washington, 491–492; China and, 561, 562; defense policy, 338, 339, 342, 347, 365; FDR and, 310, 392; FDR's bypassing, on Singapore, 414; on FDR's greatness, 441; Japan and, 400, 401; at Malta, U.S. strategy vs. British, 580; Mediterranean strategy, 467; North African invasion, 447, 448; Pacific strategy, 479; Pearl Harbor and, 404; Soviet Union and, 449, 472–473; at Tehran conference, 481, 483; at Yalta conference, 583
Marshall, John, 227
Marshall Islands, 261, 378, 526
Martha, Princess of Norway, 317, 510
Martin, Joseph, 103, 355, 560
Martinique, 307
Marvin, Langdon, 40
Maryknoll missions, 380
Maryland, 232, 282, 286, 445, 512, 557
Massachusetts, 10, 50, 70, 103, 355
Massachusetts Institute of Technology (MIT), 355
Matsukata, Otohiko, 180
Matsuoka, Yosuke, 379, 380, 381
Matthews, H. Freeman, 585
Maverick, Maury, 198, 229, 247, 280
Maybank, Burnet, 284
Mayo Clinic, 298, 600
Means, Gardiner C., 66
"Means test," 135
Mediation Board, 244
Mediterranean: Churchill's and British strategy in, 367, 468, 469, 477, 478, 483, 485, 504, 525; FDR strategy in, 300, 467, 478, 485; French invasion landing area and, 482; North African invasion plan and, 413; supreme commander for, 491–492. *See also* Greece; Sicily
Mein Kampf (Hitler), 178–179
Mellett, Lowell, 353
Memorial Day massacre, 243–244, 247
Mencken, Henry L., 72, 343
Mercer, Lucy. *See* Rutherford, Lucy Mercer
Merriam, Charles E., 221, 275
Merriman, Roger B., 312
Methodist Episcopal Church, South, 256
Meuse River, 331
Mexico, 28, 155, 213
Miami, 87, 458
Michigan, 278, 279; banking crisis and, 89; congressmen and senators from, 198, 327, 543; Democratic party in, 204; FDR support, at 1932 Democratic convention, 72; strikes in, 242
Middle East, 367, 368, 386, 450, 505. *See also* Palestine; Saudi Arabia
Midway Island, 338, 380, 406, 445–446
Mihailovich, Draza, 483, 505
Mikolajczyk, Stanislaus, 506, 588
Mills, Ogden, 63, 89
Millspaugh, Arthur C., 487
Milton, George Fort, 226
Mindanao, 541
Minimum wage. *See* Wage(s): minimum
Mining, 139, 167, 251; unions and, 519. *See also* Copper industry; Gold; Silver
Minnesota, 518, 560; 1932 Democratic delegation, 71
Miquelon, 453
Missionary Society, 9
Mississippi: congressmen and senators from, 156, 233, 237, 241, 282; FDR support, 72; racism/lynchings in, 246, 247, 520; underprivileged in, 222
Missouri, 276, 278, 534, 570
Moderates. *See* Centrists
Modern Corporation and Private Property, The (Berle/Means), 66
Moffat, J. Pierrepont, 107, 265, 266, 267; on FDR's style in foreign affairs, 108–109
Mohawk Valley, New York, 54
Moley, Raymond, 59, 76, 77, 78, 99, 104, 109, 114; as assistant secretary of state, 107; banking crisis, 90; brain trust and, 66, 223; campaigns, 73, 74; economic policies, 84; FDR and, 66, 87–88, 124; as FDR's speech-writer, 120, 124, 201, 202; Hull vs., 107, 108; industrial reform and, 104; at London Economic Conference, 116, 117; New Deal planning, 84, 86; as Republican and New Deal critic, 201; *Today* editor, 201

Molotov, Vyacheslav, 318, 476, 488; San Francisco conference, 600, 607; Tehran conference and, 480, 481; U.S. negotiations with, 449–450; at Yalta conference, 586, 587, 591
Monetarism, 102, 147, 250
Monnet, Jean, 309, 312, 460
Monopolies, 16–17, 251, 500
Monroe, James, 29
Monroe Doctrine, 114, 215, 217, 306, 584. *See also* Hemispheric defense
Montana, 103, 146, 168, 407; senators from, 71, 76, 139; Wheeler and, 231
Montana State University, 103
Montevideo, 173, 214
Montgomery, Alabama, 87
Montgomery, Bernard L., 456, 580
Montgomery Ward, 519
Moore, Robert Walton, 306
Moran, Lord, 513, 581
Morandat, Leon, 457
Morgan, J. P., 19, 90, 102, 252, 359
Morgenthau, Henry, Jr., 57, 114, 115, 116, 118, 172, 185, 186, 221, 292, 296, 310, 315, 317, 323, 328, 368, 372, 392, 434, 439, 507, 513, 517, 546, 550, 551, 553, 575, 577, 605, 606; agricultural legislation, 57, 86; anti-inflationary program and, 432, 433, 435, 436; campaigns, 566; Darlan deal and, 457; defense policy, 342; economy and, 248, 250, 252, 253, 254; Federal Reserve Board and, 167; foreign policy and, 499; Germany, postwar plan for, 550, 552, 560–561, 585, 605; on Ickes's methods with PWA, 149; Japanese negotiations and, 399; as secretary of treasury, 133; U.S. aid and, 326, 335, 359, 363; war involvement, 394; work relief bill and, 148
Morgenthau, Henry, Sr., 296
Morocco, 339, 456, 457, 458, 461
Morse, Wayne, 437–438
Mortgages, 70, 73, 100, 103, 105, 134
Moscow, Warren, 344
Moscow, 175, 176, 177, 196, 260, 318, 375, 376, 471, 472, 473, 474, 548, 604; Churchill-Stalin 1944 meeting in, 568–569, 590; U.S.-British-Soviet liaison point, 589
Moscow conference, 473–474, 475–476, 485, 493, 522
Moscowitz, Belle, 55, 56
Moses, Robert, 55–56
Mountbatten, Lord Louis, 450, 470
Mount Charleston, Nevada, 190
Mount Holyoke College, 210
Mount Vernon, 605
"M" Project, 297
Mruk, Joseph, 506
Mugwumps, 3, 16
Munich agreement, 289, 302, 303, 305, 306, 307, 308, 313, 314, 315, 354, 395. *See also* Czechoslovakia: Sudetenland crisis
Munitions. *See* War production
Munitions Assignment Board, 415
Murphy, 594
Murphy, Charles F., 18–19, 20, 25, 26, 38, 533
Murphy, Frank, 204, 239, 242–243
Murphy, Robert, 367; North African invasion and, 454, 455, 456, 460, 462
Murray, Arthur, 309
Murray, Philip, 253, 437, 438
Murrow, Edward R., 363, 389, 405, 607
Muscle Shoals, Alabama, 87
Mussolini, Benito, 93, 112, 146, 269, 276, 312, 318, 332, 354, 470; Ethiopian invasion, 154, 181, 182, 183, 184, 190, 191, 294–295; fall of, 469, 470; FDR and, 205, 215, 216, 218, 270, 302, 314–315, 332; FDR compared to, 277, 366; France and, 332, 336, 337; Hitler and, 184, 299, 302, 318; Italian-Americans and, 270, 355; Munich conference, 302; U.S. and, 315, 329; Willkie compared to, by FDR, 343. *See also* Italy
My Day (ER), 218

New Hampshire, 146
NAACP. *See* National Association for the Advancement of Colored People
Naboth's Vineyard (Welles), 213
Nagano, Admiral, 397
Nanking, 262, 290
Nantucket, 116
Naples, 470, 492
Napoleon, 458
National Association for the Advancement of Colored People (NAACP), 124, 214, 246
National Association of Manufacturers, 137, 158, 159, 165
National Bureau of Standards, 97
National Catholic Welfare Conference, 270
National Civic Federation, 254
National Committee to Uphold Constitutional Government, 276
National Defense Act (1940), 379
National Emergency Council, 125, 135, 137, 155, 283
National forests, 278
National Industrial Recovery Act, 77. *See also* National Recovery Administration
Nationalism, 523; economic, 78, 102, 104–105, 117; internationalism vs., 78, 84, 102, 104–105, 106, 107, 115, 117. *See also* Economy: internationalism vs. nationalism; Internationalism
Nationalists, Spanish, 269, 271

National Labor Relations Act, 148, 159, 170, 194, 234, 249. *See also* Wagner Act
National Labor Relations Board, 140, 159; critics of, 241, 242
National Power Policy Committee, 147
National Recovery Administration (NRA), 104–105, 136–138, 143–144, 167, 364; AAA linked to, 126–127; codes/fair practice standards, 104, 120, 126, 127, 136, 137, 144, 159, 160, 161, 167, 170, 193; cost/financing of, 130; criticism of, 141, 143–144, 158–159, 252; as emergency legislation, 143; extension of, 151, 154, 157–158, 159; FDR and, 127, 136–137, 147, 157–158, 252; postage stamp, 127; problems with/monopolistic tendencies, 126, 130, 136–138, 147, 157; recession and, 252, 253; redistribution of wealth and, 127; small business and, 145; as social justice campaign, 126; strikes as by-product of, 137–138; supporters of, 161–162; Supreme Court and, 160–164, 170, 193, 194, 226, 228; wages and, 194, 249; workers and working conditions, 145, 157–158. *See also* Business; Industry; Supreme Court: NRA rulings
National Recovery Review Board, 136
National Resources Committee, 221
National Resources Planning Board, 140, 500
National War Labor Board, 431–432, 433
National Youth Administration, 310, 364, 425
Natural resources. *See* Coal; Conservation; Oil
Naval Intelligence, 109, 339, 510. *See also* Intelligence, U.S.
Navy, British, 28, 258, 329, 333, 334, 335, 338, 368; during Czechoslovakian crisis, 302; FDR's strategy vs. British surrender, 333–334, 335, 336, 338, 351–352; quarantine plan and, 292; strength of, 28, 395; U.S. collaboration with, 293, 359. *See also* British Fleet
Navy, Dutch, 395
Navy, French, 334, 335, 339
Navy, German, 28, 29, 30, 324, 371, 372, 373, 384, 393. *See also* Submarines: German
Navy, Italian, 31
Navy, Japanese, 378, 565; at Midway Island, 445–446; in South Pacific, 445, 446–447; superiority of, 395. *See also* Pearl Harbor
Navy, U.S., 27–28, 97, 191, 213, 244, 293, 334, 335, 339, 347, 384, 386, 411, 414, 419, 446; bases, 350, 352 (*see also* Destroyers-for-bases deal); buildup/strengthening of, 179–180, 180–181, 293, 350, 395, 397, 401; convoy escorts and patrols, 323, 324, 334, 367, 368–369, 369–370, 384, 386–387, 393, 394, 405–411; FDR and, 10, 24, 51, 179, 180, 355, 404, 447; FDR's sons in, 402–403; Germany and, 372; *Greer* incident, 392–393; Honolulu planning session with FDR, 540–542, 563–564; Japan and, 180, 292, 378, 399, 582, 590; Midway Island and, 445; quarantine/blockade plans and, 263, 268, 291, 292–293; Tokyo, 444–445. *See also* American Fleet; Atlantic; Navy Department; Pacific; Pacific Fleet; Pearl Harbor; Submarines
Navy Day address, 393–394
Navy Department, 28, 37, 123, 404; FDR as assistant secretary of, 16, 23–24, 25, 26–32, 28–31, 37–38, 73, 82, 109, 377, 409, 421; post–World War I investigations of, 37–38, 41; TR as assistant secretary, 23. *See also* Navy, U.S.
Navy League, 393
Navy Office of Procurement and Material, 420
Nazism, 107, 111–112, 325, 328, 349, 367, 411, 413, 457, 470, 550, 588; Atlantic Charter and, 388, 389; communism vs., 260; economic demands, and British-French sympathy toward, 259–260; Europe and, 112, 113, 333, 338; expansionism, 183; FDR's views on, 111–114, 118, 367, 374, 393; isolationists and, 323; in Latin America, 218, 219, 307, 338, 351, 386; in North Africa, 386, 454; Poland and, 318; rise of/threat of, 79, 111, 112, 113, 114, 269, 272, 341, 343; satellites of, 408; Soviets and, 173, 374; U.S. public opinion/views on, 107, 296, 361, 374; victims of, 112, 183, 313–314. *See also* Anti-Semitism; Germany; Hitler, Adolf
Neblett, William E., 190
Nebraska, 296, 518
Negro Newspaper Publishers Association, 521
Nehru, Jawaharlal, 444
Nelson, Donald, 312, 432, 438; as head of WPB, 418–419, 420, 421–422, 427
Netherlands, 311, 415, 466; FDR's roots in, 4, 5, 249, 330, 525, 528; German invasion/blitz, 324, 329, 330; Japan and, 377, 379, 383, 395, 397, 398, 400; postwar world, 523, 550. *See also* East Indies, Dutch
Netherlands-America Foundation, 5
Neuberger, Richard, 289
Neurath, Konstantin von, 114
Neustadt, Richard, 280
Neutrality, 181, 259, 322, 386, 387, 388, 412; destroyers-for-bases deal and, 352; FDR on, 195, 322; FDR opposed to, in World War I, 28, 29, 30; international law of, 269; Japanese-Soviet treaty on, 369; legislation on, 154, 181, 182–183, 315, 319–

Neutrality (*cont.*)
320, 321, 393, 394; Spanish Civil War and, 269, 270. *See also* Isolationists
Neutrality Act, 262, 265, 271, 306, 309, 393, 394
Nevada, 139, 187, 278; FDR visit to, 190
Newark airport, 187
New Bedford, Massachusetts, 224
New Brunswick, 6
Newburgh, New York, 5, 566
New Caledonia, 511
New Deal, 78, 93, 94, 139–140, 216, 434; administrative methods of FDR, 120–121, 125–126; blacks and, 122, 240, 241, 244, 245; business and industry and, 143, 326–327; coalition approach, 143, 144, 159, 240, 241, 244, 345, 356, 529; criticism/opposition, 77, 81, 103, 123, 132, 133–134, 140–141, 143–144, 144–145, 147, 151, 161, 178, 188, 189, 198, 199, 201, 229, 233, 247, 248, 250, 280, 282, 284, 285–286, 287, 323, 326–327, 342, 343, 346, 362, 408, 425, 494, 503, 519, 532, 570; conservatives/right wing and, 96, 102, 144, 233, 280, 285–286; deflationary effect of, 100–102, 103, 104; FDR on, 356; FDR's plans to write history of, 328; FDR's shift to right, 142; funding, 96–97, 130–131, 133, 165, 183, 199–200, 233, 240, 249, 252, 287, 356, 419; goals of, 288, 500; influences on, 16, 98, 99, 142; installing, 119, 120–123, 125–129; left wing and, 144–145, 147, 153; origin of term, 73–74; personnel/appointments, 93, 120–123, 123–124, 137, 223; planning/shaping, 84–85, 99, 100; politics of, 100, 121–122, 139, 142, 150, 187; problems with, 126–128, 130–134, 145; progress of/effect of, 126–129; prototypes for, 62, 93, 95, 107, 123, 178, 212; Republicans and, 198, 199, 248, 346, 557; South and, 286, 287, 520, 532; supporters/New Dealers, 76, 110, 139–140, 141, 199–200, 201, 229, 230–231, 240, 241, 244, 280, 282, 284, 287, 323, 344, 362, 364, 376, 417, 419, 426, 497, 498, 499, 517, 520, 529, 562, 571; Supreme Court vs., 144, 157, 159, 160–164, 170, 191–192, 193, 194, 226, 227, 228, 229, 230, 232, 234–235, 236, 239; as temporary measure, 122, 273, 278, 424; Truman and, 534, 537; wealth redistribution and, 127, 129, 164, 167; as "win the war," 497–498, 499, 500; women and, 122; youth and, 121, 280. *See also* Administrative reform; Agricultural Adjustment Administration; Civil Works Administration; Congress: New Deal passage; Congress: New Deal passage, "second"; Judicial reform; National Recovery Administration; Public Works Administration; Social security program; Tennessee Valley Authority; Works Progress Administration
"New deal" speech, 73–74
New Delhi, 444
Newfoundland, 352, 383, 384, 412. *See also* Atlantic conference
New Freedom, 16, 24–25, 104, 251
New Guinea, 445
New Hampshire, 522
New Haven, 207
New Jersey, 69, 535
New Left, 129
New Mexico, 278
New Nationalism, 16, 24–25, 104, 578
New Orleans, 27, 420
Newport, Rhode Island, navy base, 38, 40
Newspapers: on FDR's death, 606; FDR's retirement plan to start, 599; FDR's use of, 18, 29, 39, 50, 99, 147, 162, 567; reporters/correspondents, and FDR, 99, 247, 256, 363–364, 423–424, 571, 523, 594, 597, 606. *See also names of individual newspapers*
Newsreels, 195, 262, 361–362, 364, 598
Newsweek: on electorate's apathy, 556
New York City, 13, 54, 88, 282; corruption in, 63–64, 67, 69–70; Dewey in, 518; ER's work in, 12, 426; FDR's forebears in, 4; FDR's residence in, 50; FDR support in, 51, 63, 64, 204, 563, 564–565
New York Daily News, 563
New York Herald-Tribune, 161, 396, 603; criticism of FDR, 67–68
New York Post, 54
New York State, 17, 50, 55, 57, 64, 69, 124, 138, 160, 506; Dewey and, 327, 518; FDR and Wilson campaign in, 22; FDR as governor of, 17–23, 33, 38, 54–62, 63–65, 90, 99, 123, 150; FDR as state senator, 17–23, 25; Isaac Roosevelt as senator of, 4; Smith as governor of, 38, 51–52, 55, 58; TR as governor of, 11; women in politics in, 49, 50. *See also* Democratic party: in New York
New York State Police, 218
New York Stock Exchange, 90
New York Sun, 563
New York Times: on Democratic politics, 53, 285, 344; on economy, 75, 133, 135; on FDR, 121, 163, 200, 516; FDR to, on Stalin, 601; on war issues/defense, 205, 293, 324, 396
New York Tuberculosis and Health Associations, 61
New York World, 64
New York World's Fair (1939), 306, 317
New Zealand, 216, 261, 415
Niagara River, 58

Niblack, 369
Nicaragua, 5, 51, 214, 316
Nicholas II, Czar of Russia, 581–582
Nigeria, 389
Night of the Broken Glass (*Kristallnacht*), 313–314
Nimitz, Chester W., 411, 445, 465, 540; Pacific planning session with FDR, 541, 542
Nobel Peace Prize, Hull and, 214
Noguès, August, 461
Nomura, Kichisaburo, 380, 381, 395, 396, 397, 398, 399, 400
Non-Intervention Committee, 270
Non-Partisan League, 204
Norden bombsight, 320
Norfolk, Virginia, 407
Normandy, 448, 525, 526, 539, 540, 547, 548. *See also* France: Allied invasion of
Norris, Frank, 8
Norris, George, 77, 87, 98–99, 158, 159
North Carolina, 84, 156, 240, 241, 278, 280
North Dakota, 204
North Sea, 30, 300
Norway, 317, 329–330, 383, 386, 449, 510, 526, 543
Nourmahal, 261
Nova Scotia, 350
Nuclear weapons. *See* Atomic bomb
Nuremberg Decree, 457
Nuremberg trials, 407
Nye, Gerald P., 182, 264, 271, 305, 407; Nye Committee, 181, 182–183, 315, 326

Oak Ridge atomic facility, 605
O'Connor, D. Basil, 40
O'Connor, J. F. T., 190
O'Connor, John J., 281, 282; defeat of, 286–287
O'Daniel, Lee, 517
O'Day, Caroline, 50
Oder River, 488, 489, 583
Odessa, 568
Office of Civilian Defense (OCD), 426–427, 429
Office of Defense Health and Welfare Services, 427
Office of Economic Stabilization, 439
Office of Emergency Management, 341–342
Office of Inter-American Affairs, 219
Office of Price Administration (OPA), 419, 427, 432, 433, 438, 439, 500
Office of Production Management, 418
Office of Scientific Research and Development, 348, 554. *See also* Council of National Defense
Office of Strategic Services, 436, 601
Office of War Information, 558
Office of War Mobilization (OWM), 499
Ogdensburg, New York, 350
Oglethorpe University, 70
O'Gorman, James A., 19, 25
Ohio, 189, 287, 518, 556, 566; FDR in, 74, 565; progressives in, 66; Taft from, 327,
Oil, 104, 162; Japanese shipments and embargo, 379, 382–383, 391, 395, 396, 398, 399; in Middle East, 367, 487, 505; in Texas, 531–532; U.S. companies, in Latin America, 214; wartime shortage, 379, 382, 427, 447
Oklahoma, 101
Oklahoma City, 558
Old-age insurance/benefits, 61, 145, 156–157, 159
Old Guard Republicans, 18, 557
Omaha beach, 527
"One world" movement, 518
"Only thing . . . to fear is fear itself" speech, 93, 607
Ontario, 58
Operation Barbarossa, 373
Oran, 456, 496
Orange plan, 293, 377
Oregon, 289, 296, 535
Oregon Law School, University of, 437
Orion, 579
Osborne, Thomas Mott, 37
Otto, Archduke, 467
Oumansky, Constantin, 375–376
OVERLORD, 469, 482–483, 484–485, 486. *See also* France: Allied invasion of
Oyster Bay, 10

Pacific, 330; Allied strength vs. Japanese, 395; Churchill's attempts to keep FDR's focus from, 449, 452; disarmament in, 215–216; FDR's strategy in, 261–262, 378, 379, 380, 381, 382, 414, 467, 539–543, 547; Japan and, 215, 261, 292, 293, 349, 391, 400, 404, 414, 445, 446–447; Japanese-Soviet neutrality treaty and, 369; navy in, 180, 262, 293, 377–378, 382, 383, 414, 465, 446–447; South, ER's trip to, 475, 509; Soviet Union/Stalin and, 369, 473, 478, 482, 483, 491, 493; supreme commander for, 414–415; U.S. focus on, vs. North Africa invasion, 449, 451, 452; U.S. in, prewar, 180, 396–397, 400–401, 542; U.S.-Japanese war in, 383, 402–403, 410, 441, 478, 482, 483, 529, 538, 539, 541, 545, 563, 565. *See also* Japan; Pacific Islands; *Panay*, sinking of; Pearl Harbor; Quarantine
Pacific Fleet, 370, 378, 404, 411, 446. *See also* American Fleet; Navy, U.S.
Pacific Islands, 261–262, 316; FDR's strategy and, 261–262, 316; FDR's travels to, 298; Japan and, 406; U.S.-British claims to, 261–262; U.S. protection of, 338; U.S. se-

Pacific Islands (*cont.*)
cret occupation of, 261. *See also* East Indies, Dutch; Hawaiian Islands; Midway Island; Wake Island
Pacifists, 179, 209, 210, 263, 265, 367
Pahlavi, Reza Mohammed, 487
Palestine, 297, 389, 479, 531, 594, 595
Palisades Interstate Park, 41
Pan-American conference: FDR's plan for, 321; in Havana (1940), 351
Pan-American Day address, 211, 314
Panama Canal, 214
Panama-Pacific Exposition, 378
Panay, sinking of, 290–292, 293
Paris, Comte de, 458
Paris, 259, 271, 272, 318, 321, 329, 331, 599; FDR in, during WWI, 31; liberation of, 528, 548
"Parley on Pan-American Peace," 210
Parliament, 362, 599
Passamaquoddy, 168
Patronage, 280; Democrats/FERA and, 187; FDR and Wilson, 23; FDR's administrative reform and, 275, 276; FDR's use of, 25, 99, 153, 166, 186, 187, 197, 222, 224, 232; work relief/WPA and, 187, 188, 189
Patterson, James T., 153, 169
Patton, George, 492, 548
Paullin, James A., 512
Peabody, Rector Endicott, 8–9, 9–10, 16, 23, 573, 574
"Peanut" (code name for Chiang Kai-shek), 443
Pearl Harbor, 378, 380, 404–407, 408–409, 430, 431, 442; attack on, 290, 297, 325, 349, 358, 376, 382, 395, 397, 401, 402–403, 404–407, 408–409, 410, 411, 413, 417, 419, 420, 426, 427, 445, 463; attack story in 1934 Japanese comic book, 109; congressional investigations of, 559; FDR at, for naval planning session, 540–542, 563–564; fleet transfer to Atlantic, 369, 370; future debate on, 400–403, 405, 407; German reaction to, 407–408; hysteria/rumors following, in U.S., 407; U.S. fleet at, 339; U.S. losses/casualties, 405–406
Pearson, Drew, 271, 492
Pedagogical Institute, Caracas, 218
Peek, George, 103, 215
Peking, 110, 262
Pendergast, Tom, 534, 537
Pennsylvania, 188, 242, 565
Pensacola navy yards, 27
People Approve, The (Roosevelt), 195
People's Mandate to End War Committee, 210
Peoples, Christian J., 26
Pepper, Claude, 280–281, 520, 571, 604
Perkins, Frances, 20, 41, 56, 60, 122, 150, 157, 431, 436
Permanent Joint Board of Defense, 350
Pershing, John J., 97, 386, 528
Persian Gulf, 487
Peru, 139, 306
Pétain, Henri-Philippe, 337, 367; de Gaulle and, 528; FDR and North African invasion strategy, 453, 454, 457
Peter, King of Yugoslavia, 505
Petroleum. *See* Oil
Peyrouton, Marcel, 461
Phi Beta Kappa, 59
Philadelphia, 202; Democratic convention, 200, 201; FDR's 1940 speech, 354–355; FDR's 1944 campaign in, 565
Philippines, 204; convoy rerouted by FDR, 414; Eisenhower and, 411; fall of, 441–442; Japan and, 109, 267, 400, 406; MacArthur in, 414, 563–564, 565; strategy on, 541–542; U.S. defense of, 378, 397, 401
Philippine Scouts, 180
Philippine Sea, Battle of, 529
Phillips, William, 35, 107, 174, 184, 299, 302, 444
Phoenix islands, 262
"Phony war," 329
Pinchot, Gifford, 21, 188
Pittman, Key, 139, 182, 190, 278, 315
Pittsburgh, 189, 206
Pius XII, 376
Plan D ("Plan Dog"), 365
Platt Amendment treaty, 214
Poland, 471, 499, 600; Britain's mutual assistance agreement with, 314; FDR's appeals to president of, 318; free election agreement, 588, 589; Germany and, 321, 322, 324, 328, 329, 454; government-in-exile in London, 489, 506, 548, 588; Hitler's plan for, 314, 318–319; Partisans/Communists in, 489; partition of, 324; postwar, 471, 488–489, 490, 506, 587–588, 589; Soviet Union/Stalin and, 314, 324, 449, 471, 479, 488–489, 506, 514, 539, 548, 587; Teschen and, 303; underground/Warsaw uprising, 548, 550; Yalta agreement on, 591, 600
Polier, Justine Wise, 402
Polish-Americans, 357, 471, 488, 506, 587
Polish Corridor, 111, 314
Poll tax, 284, 532
Populism, 7, 71, 101, 129, 146, 570
Porcellian Club, 11
Port Arthur, 591
Port Everglades, 371
Port Moresby, New Guinea, 445
Portsmouth naval prison, 37–38
Portugal, 370

Potomac, 371, 384, 389
Potsdam, 586
Poughkeepsie, New York, 5, 419, 514, 567
Po Valley, 469
Prague, 299, 315, 547
Pratt, Trude W., 509, 510, 545
Price fixing, 126, 136, 157, 167, 496
Prince of Wales, 384, 389
Prison reform, 37–38, 58, 59
Processing tax, 86, 130, 133, 191–192
Progressive Era, 3, 16, 63, 94, 164, 202, 240
Progressives, 10, 16–17, 20, 22, 23, 24, 25, 26, 28, 33, 52, 58, 66, 136, 146, 199, 279; administrative reform and, 274; business and NRA, 159; economy and, 128; FDR and, 3, 8, 19, 21–22, 31, 32, 37, 57, 60, 61, 70, 73, 77, 83, 94, 97, 128, 154, 186, 193, 196, 199, 274, 574; FDR supporters, 51, 87, 165–166, 227, 229; issues of, 58; judicial reform bill, 230–231, 239; labor and, 20, 157; New Deal/NRA opponents, 161; public works and, 104; racism and, 244; recession and, 251; in Republican party, 18, 144, 345; Schechter case and, 161; on Supreme Court, 161; Wilson as, 24, 71, 240, 241; work relief bill and, 155 Prohibition, 20, 51, 54, 63, 65, 73, 136, 140, 144
"Protection of Lands, Forests, and Public Parks" bill, 21
Prussia, East, 314, 489, 539
P-36 fighters, 308
Public Service Commission, 58
Public opinion/polls: FDR's ability to sway, 58–59, 108, 162, 224, 247, 268, 290, 293, 305–306, 369, 383, 384, 391, 429; FDR's popularity, 65, 88, 92, 93, 98, 99, 120, 143, 165, 166, 216, 217, 218, 220, 222, 231, 273, 280, 284, 287, 288, 341, 407, 419, 517, 558, 564, 565, 568, 574, 607; influence on FDR, 242, 243, 244, 358, 370, 376, 412, 422–424, 428. *See also* Gallup polls; Roper polls
Public Utility Holding Act, 169
Public utility holding companies, 147–148
Public works, 123, 127, 128, 141, 142, 149–150, 153, 179; budget cuts and, 191, 222, 251; business opposition to, 138; FDR and, 60, 73; funding, 127–128, 138, 251, 287; Hoover and, 60, 61; in South, 284. *See also* Public Works Administration
Public Works, Department of, 275
Public Works Administration (PWA), 100, 104, 186, 187, 198, 245, 248, 249, 250, 550; budget cuts, 248, 249; criticism of, 149; Civil Works Administration vs., 135; FDR's legislation on, 104, 105; funding, 250; projects, 187, 189–190, 250; work relief vs., 186. *See also* Civil Works Administration
Puget Sound, 544
Pullman strike, 7
Punch, 9

Quarantine, 258, 262, 263–267, 268, 291, 300, 306, 486; FDR's Chicago speech on, 263–264, 264–265, 268; origin/meaning of term, 263, 265, 267; *Panay* and, 291–292. *See also* Blockade; Embargo; Sanctions, economic
Quebec conference, 472–473, 475, 479, 551–553, 556, 557, 560–561
Queen Mary, 468
Queens, New York, 564
Quezon, Manuel, 441
Quincy, USS, 579, 580, 593, 594, 595

Rabat, 464
Radio broadcasts, 323, 418; criticism of FDR and, 154; FDR's use of, 53, 58, 70, 76, 99, 195, 198, 347, 499–500, 519, 526, 557–558, 562, 566, 567, 573, 597, 604; on European war, bombing, 361–362; regulation of, 139. *See also* Fireside Chats
Raeder, Erich, 324, 372–373
Railroad Retirement Act, 157, 162
Railroads, 71, 149, 520; brotherhoods/strike, 496–497; depression and, 93; FDR travel by, 6, 39, 76–77, 189–190, 479–480, 551, 565, 566; reform and, 84, 103, 104; Roosevelt family investment in, 5, 8; TR's legislation, 146, 277
Rainey, Henry, 128–129
Raleigh News and Observer, 520
Rankin, Jeanette, 407
Rankin, John E., 241
Raskob, John J., 53, 71, 74
Rationing, 382, 419, 422, 427–428, 436, 447
Rayburn, Sam, 72, 98, 168, 169, 235, 286–287, 353, 517; as vice presidential nominee, 530, 532
Reagan, Ronald, 180
Recession (1937–1938), 221, 240, 247, 249–257, 332; advisory committee, 253–254; anti-Semitism and, 296; background/causes, 250–251, 252; as factor in 1938 elections, 287; farm prices, 430; FDR's solution for, 253–256; spending cuts as cause, 252
Reconstruction Finance Corporation (RFC), 89, 90, 95, 121, 123, 127, 133, 256, 546, 568; Jones and, 353, 427, 575
Red Army, 449, 477, 483, 506, 548, 600
Red Cross, 37, 268, 325, 367, 471
"Red scare," 206
Reed, John, 173
Reed, Stanley, 160, 228, 239

Reform politics, 3, 8, 13, 16, 94. *See also* New Deal
Refugees from Nazism: FDR and, 295, 296–298, 325; Jewish, fate of, 593–594; League of Nations program for, 297; scientists as, 348–349
Reichstag, 113, 314, 408, 438
Reilly, Michael F., 607
Relief programs, 61–62, 73, 123, 130, 132, 133, 134, 138, 149, 314, 325; cuts in, 248–249, 251; families on (1937), 248; financing, 123, 222, 249, 251, 287, 294; rearmament and, 310; surpluses for needy, 131–132. *See also* New Deal; Work relief program
"Rendezvous with destiny" speech, 202–203
Reno, Milo, 131, 133, 134
Reorganization Act of 1939, 278, 281. *See also* Administrative reform
Repeal amendment, 97
Report on Economic Conditions of the South, 283
Republic Steel Company, 243
Republican Club, Harvard, 11
Republican party, 54, 55, 87, 135, 146, 155, 156, 168, 186, 187, 207, 227, 244, 375, 418, 475, 561; agriculture and, 13, 86, 141; bipartisan foreign policy and, 495; black issues and, 356; business and, 97, 144; campaign funds, vs. Democrats, 203, 204; conservatives in, 144, 169, 198, 518; depression and, 63, 65, 75, 78; Fala rumor, 543, 558; FDR and, 24, 59, 74–75, 139, 152, 200, 276, 286, 322, 355, 557–558; as FDR's critics, 25, 63–64, 75, 98, 127, 140, 191, 193, 206, 353, 355, 425–426, 494, 498, 539, 543–544, 558; FDR support in, 65, 74, 76, 128, 144, 352; internationalism and, 518, 522, 556, 560; isolationists, 335, 354, 366, 518, 522, 560; judicial reform and, 231, 232; liberals in, 363, 437; New Deal and, 103, 121, 122, 132, 140, 167, 188, 248, 323, 498; in New York, 18, 22, 25, 50, 54, 57, 58; 1912 election, 12; 1920 election, 38, 39–40; 1924 election, 52; 1928 election, 54, 55; 1930 election, 63–64; 1932 election, 75; 1936 election, 40, 169, 185, 191, 193, 195, 196, 197, 198, 200, 203, 206–207, 270, 306, 342; 1938 election, 285, 287; 1940 election, 327, 335, 338, 342, 343, 344, 346, 353, 354–356; 1944 election, 494, 516, 517–518, 522, 529, 536, 545, 551, 556, 557, 559, 560, 565, 566, 567–568; Old Guard, 18, 557; post–World War I investigation of Democrats, 37, 41; progressives in, 18, 81, 83, 98, 144, 154, 155, 196, 199, 345; prosperity/1920s and, 51, 52, 53, 55, 63, 75, 85, 94, 99; right wing in, 144, 198, 206; Tammany Hall, 21; TR as, 11, 17–18; World War II and, 323, 393, 407. *See also* Bull Moose party; Congress: Republicans in; Senate: Republicans in
Resistance movements, 383, 385; French, in Algiers, 455
Retirement. *See* Old-age insurance/benefits; Roosevelt, Franklin Delano: Career, retirement and; Social security program
Reuben James (destroyer), 394
Reuther, Walter, 243
Revenue Act of 1935, 167
Revenue Act of 1942, 434
Reynaud, Paul, 331, 337
Rhine frontier, 184, 311, 580, 583
Rhodes, 483, 490, 491, 548
Ribbentrop, Joachim von, 407–408
Richardson, James O., 378
Richberg, Donald R., 137, 228
Riefler, Winfield W., 125–126
Rigdon, William F., 484, 544
Right wing, 161, 170, 198, 238, 345, 347, 461, 503, 569; FDR's gestures toward/shift to, 142, 154, 345, 347, 498; as FDR's opponents, 141, 142, 143, 144, 147, 148, 152, 158, 161, 164, 201, 223, 230, 233, 492, 497
Rio de Janeiro, 216
Rise of Silas Lapham, The (Howells), 15
River Rouge plant, 243
Riviera, French, 504
Rivington Street Settlement House, 12
Roanoke Island, North Carolina, speech, 240–241
Robbins, Raymond, 223
Robbins, Warren Delano, 35
Roberts, Owen J., 191–192, 234
Robin Moor, 372
Robinson, Corinne Roosevelt, 12
Robinson, Joseph, 153, 182, 196, 198, 224, 231, 235, 236, 237; judicial reform and, 230, 235, 237
Rochester, New York, 54, 62
Rockefeller, Nelson, 219, 351
Rockey, Edna, 44, 45
Rogers, Will, 53, 165
Romania, 112, 408, 589
Rome, 31, 184, 299, 302, 470, 485, 504, 505, 526
Rommel, Erwin, 368, 450, 456
Roosevelt, Anna (daughter), 14, 77, 416, 497, 544, 545, 551, 572, 599, 604; ER and, 510, 511; FDR and, 34, 41, 53, 508, 511, 512, 527, 557, 558, 598, 599, 605; King Farouk and, 593; Yalta conference, 578–579, 584, 595, 596
Roosevelt, Betsy Cushing (daughter-in-law), 77
Roosevelt, Eleanor (wife), 12–14, 24, 33–37,

59, 116, 277, 298, 317, 353, 458, 475, 529, 538, 551, 539, 546, 570, 575, 592; ancestry/relation to FDR, 4, 12, 198; black issues and, 123, 245, 246, 283, 356, 508–509, 520; career, 12, 36–37, 46, 49–50, 123; on Churchill, 416; criticism of, 325–326, 426, 543–544; elections, campaigns, inaugurations, 53, 54, 73, 226, 343, 356, 564, 565; engagement and marriage, 12–13; family and children, 12, 14, 36–37, 508, 510, 526, 536, 572; on FDR, 3, 11, 193, 218, 224, 405, 441, 527, 606; FDR on, 94, 509; -FDR relationship, 12–13, 33–36, 117, 216, 508–512, 564; FDR's affair with Lucy Mercer, 33–34, 35–36, 509, 511; FDR's death, 606, 607; FDR's health and, 41, 42, 43, 44, 45, 46, 49, 512, 513–514, 529, 598, 604; as FDR's political adviser, 12, 35, 36, 42, 43, 46, 49–50, 55, 123, 124, 125, 197, 247, 283, 423, 509, 545; friendship with Joseph Lash, 509, 510–511, 526; high-mindedness, 12, 34, 35, 94, 427; Hoover and, 82; issues concerning, 3, 12, 13, 14, 31, 50, 93, 122, 123, 228, 282–283, 325, 426, 509; personality/outlook, 34–35, 36, 43, 44, 49; Sara Roosevelt and, 13–14; sex/physical affection and, 34, 509–510; speechmaking, for FDR, 49; travels, 27, 31, 189, 475, 536, 509, 510, 599; United Nations and, 416; upbringing, 12, 34, 36, 112; war/war involvement issues and, 265, 271, 402, 426–427, 429, 578; during World War I, 37

Roosevelt, Elliott (ER's father), 12

Roosevelt, Elliott (son), 14, 53, 73, 353, 385, 544, 572

Roosevelt, Franklin Delano

BACKGROUND AND UPBRINGING, 3–15; ancestors/forebears, 3–5, 566–567; ancestors' employment/occupation, 4, 5, 8, 109, 442; anti-Semitism of social class, 112; Belgian ancestry, 330; birth date, 6; childhood, 6–8, 211, 584, 599, 607; Delanos, 3, 5, 109, 566; Dutch ancestry, 4, 5, 249, 330, 525, 528; English ancestry, 5; mother, relationship with, 6, 7, 10, 11, 13–14, 34, 42, 43, 45, 216; name change, from Van Rosenvelt, 4; parents and, 3, 6–7, 9, 10; racial attitudes in, 244–245; Roosevelts, 3–5; as sheltered/isolated, 6–7, 8; socioeconomic status, 4, 5–6, 7, 34, 36, 129; statue of, at Hyde Park, 14

CAREER: as assistant secretary of navy, 16, 23–24, 25, 26–32, 28–331, 37–38, 73, 82, 109, 377, 409, 421; business enterprises, 15, 40; *Colliers* job offer, 328; as governor of New York, 17–23, 33, 38, 54–62, 63–65, 90, 99, 123, 150; as lawyer, 14–15, 17, 40; money/finances, 5–6, 34, 44, 53–54, 328, 435; navy as, desire for, 10, 402; newspaper, plan to start, 599; offers, 23; parents and, 3, 10; political education, 17, 23, 31, 66, 78; political goals, 49, 52, 59; politics, switch to, 15; presidency, early predictions of, 15, 16, 22, 33, 52, 54, 55, 60; renown/public relations and publicity, 18, 19, 22, 23, 27, 29, 31, 40, 41, 47, 49, 51, 52, 54, 59, 60, 107, 542; retirement and, 327, 328, 599; "Roosevelt" name and, 18, 19, 55; Senate nomination attempts, 38, 40, 52; as state senator from New York, 17–23, 25; vice presidential nomination, 38–40; as vice president of Fidelity and Deposit, 40

CRITICISM OF, 209; as anti-Catholic, 51; as dictator/tyrant, 97–98, 152, 193, 206, 207, 216, 232, 239, 241, 261, 273, 276, 277, 315, 343, 352, 366, 437, 438, 519, 531; in the future, for battle of the Atlantic, 393; in the future, for Pearl Harbor, 401, 402, 403, 406; Hitler comparisons, 178–179, 261, 277, 343, 366, 438, 519; by media, 125, 154, 158, 163, 201; as radical, Communist/socialist sympathizer, 70, 81, 123, 140, 165, 196, 206–207, 239, 346; response to, 145, 206, 207, 273; response to, as sensitive, 18, 20, 41, 125, 144, 263, 273, 343, 353, 457; rumors, 543–544, 558; as selfish, 344; as snob, 18, 20; of sons' commissions in armed forces, 353, 355; as superficial, 33; "Three Blind Mice" parody, 198–199 ?form; as untrustworthy/unreliable, 294, 308, 322, 325, 354; of working style, 106, 108–109, 152, 438–439

EDUCATION, 8–11; academics, 9, 10–11; at Columbia University Law School, 11, 14; German class at Bad Nauheim, 7; at Groton, 8–10, 11, 12, 16, 19, 20, 23, 216, 537; at Harvard, 8, 10–11, 12, 15, 107, 180; at Harvard, reunion, 59

HEALTH, 327–328, 358, 372, 493, 499, 501; angina attack, during Puget Sound speech, 545; blood pressure, 328, 512, 513, 514, 516, 556, 572, 587, 595, 603, 604; cancer, 515; in childhood/youth, 7, 10; Churchill on, 595; death, 605–607; decline of, 504, 507, 512–517, 572–573, 573–574, 579, 580–581, 587, 593, 595–596, 597, 598, 600–601, 603–604, 605–606; and disability, as political issue, 54, 55, 64, 76, 82, 516, 544, 545, 557, 562; doctors' negligence, 512, 513, 606; FDR on, 513, 516; gallbladder attacks, 514; heart/digitalis, 512, 513, 514, 516; illness at Tehran, 484; minor illnesses and complaints, 33, 370, 373, 422, 493, 501, 515,

Roosevelt, Franklin Delano (*cont.*)
551, 562, 579; during 1944 campaign, 529, 530, 531, 534, 536, 537, 538, 544, 545, 551, 552, 557, 562, 564, 565, 566; during 1944 Pacific trip, 541, 543, 544–545; physical disability, Hyde Park statue and, 14; physical disability, working with, 47, 49, 51–52, 53, 124, 190, 202, 218, 327–328, 343, 384, 389, 410, 458, 482, 542, 544, 545, 573, 579, 594, 597, 605; polio, 14, 40–48, 244–245, 513, 514, 516; pulmonary disorders, 507; rumors on, 64, 515, 557; self-diagnosis/-treatment, 507, 513, 515; smoking and, 512, 514, 562; stress/tension and, 512, 513; typhoid fever, 22; weight and diet, 512, 514, 515, 552, 572, 603

HONORS AND MEMBERSHIPS: Common Counsel Club, 24; at Groton School, Latin prize, 9; at Harvard, 11; Harvard Republican Club, 11; honorary degrees, 59; marine species named after, 298; Missionary Society, 9; Phi Beta Kappa, 59; Porcellian Club, failure to win, 11; from Yale University, 606. *See also* Democratic party

INFLUENCES AND IDEOLOGY, 3–4, 24, 98; as centrist/left of center, 143, 571, 575; in childhood, 7, 8, 16, 98; Churchill, 413; Cleveland, 16; common man/working class, 15, 50, 70, 140, 224–225, 247, 356, 423–424; conservative, 3, 498; Daniels (Josephus), 244; ER, 12, 13, 123, 124, 125, 197, 246, 247, 283; father, 18; "good neighborliness"/Golden Rule, 211; Groton School, and Peabody, 8, 10, 23, 574; Harvard, 10–11, 15; Hopkins, 363, 498; Howe, 197; humanitarianism, 61, 143, 200, 255 (*see also* Underprivileged: FDR's concern with); Jefferson, 85, 98, 121; Leahy, 508; morality in government/economy, 94, 126, 127, 134; public opinion/polls, 242, 243, 244, 358, 370, 376, 412, 422–424, 428; religion/Christianity, 8, 9–10, 16, 34, 41, 90, 202, 573; Roosevelts, 3–5; social responsibility, of well-born, 3–4, 8, 9, 10, 16; TR, 10, 11, 12, 15, 16–17, 19, 23, 24, 27, 30, 108, 142, 164, 196, 244, 251, 254, 577–578; Victorianism/Tory England, 3, 8, 16; Wilson, 16, 23, 29, 31, 33, 108, 142, 244, 385, 578; World War I, 16. *See also* Progressives

INTERESTS AND RECREATION, 224, 359, 402; adventure, 10; armed services, desire to enter, 30; automobiles, 18, 48, 190, 317, 564, 565, 568, 603, 604; bird collection, 7, 14; ceremony and protocol, 317; conservation, 6, 20, 21, 125, 192; fishing, 45, 158, 216, 235, 240, 286, 298, 318, 359, 371, 543; foreign affairs, 108; languages, French and German, 6, 7, 461, 527, 599; politics and political campaigns, 40, 54, 76, 196–197; reading habits, 7, 9, 10, 17, 50, 125; ships and sailing, 27, 30, 45–46, 113, 115, 216, 371, 402, 404, 578–579; social life, 8, 9, 10–11, 12, 14, 24, 31–32, 34, 35, 46, 47, 359, 598, 605; solitaire, 346; stamp collecting, 7, 436, 466; swimming/water, 41, 45, 46, 48, 514, 563, 572; technology, 348; writing, 10, 11, 15, 51, 291, 328. *See also* Conservation; Navy, U.S.

PERSONALITY AND DESCRIPTION, 3–4, 10, 13, 14, 31, 33, 34, 35–36, 53, 55, 66, 74, 122–125, 200, 260, 261, 334, 342, 363, 441, 462, 466, 547, 600; anecdotes, 175, 422–423, 516, 521, 573, 581; anger, 7, 9, 163, 182, 201, 207, 223, 314, 346; art, views on, 188; attitude/mental state, 9, 117, 154, 185–186, 370, 441, 456, 501, 573, 581, 583–584, 595–596; boredom, 40, 46, 193, 224; calm/patience, 153, 206, 319, 434, 441, 572; charm/sociability of, 11, 22, 31–32, 77, 81, 83, 92, 99, 113, 125, 197, 216, 256, 260, 273, 342, 423–424, 427, 443, 449, 462, 466, 477, 484, 499, 512, 542, 564, 572–573, 584, 596, 600; confidence/poise, 4, 9, 87–88, 92, 152, 196, 202, 223, 230, 231, 300, 378, 406, 441, 537; courage, 29, 87–88, 389; as dramatic, 18, 92–93, 99, 201, 203, 217, 224, 225, 239, 384; energy/enthusiasm/high spirits, 17, 33, 41, 48, 54, 60, 74, 77, 85, 126, 197, 216, 224, 226, 233, 234, 255, 278, 354, 387, 409, 413, 415–416, 460, 464, 480, 490, 514, 516, 527, 529, 542, 543, 547, 567, 579, 584, 587; exaggerations/boastfulness, 7, 11, 15, 28, 29–30, 39, 213, 409, 417, 448, 445, 484, 532, 541, 573, 599; fatigue/exhaustion, 150, 318, 346, 358, 370, 512, 546, 555, 572, 574, 580, 584, 587, 592; as Georgia farmer, 51, 283; humor, joking and teasing, 34, 46, 55, 77, 205, 206, 319, 363, 372, 482, 485, 516, 517, 543, 558, 577, 605; imitations of TR and Daniels, 17, 24; independence, 7, 9, 223; innovative and imaginative, 4, 40, 45, 61, 73, 93, 95, 108, 120, 139, 147, 215, 328, 467, 521; intelligence, 9, 12, 66–67, 466; knowledge, 39, 66, 125, 187, 190, 213, 279, 307, 436–437, 481, 482; loyalty, 197, 223; mannerisms, smoking/cigarette holder, 66, 72, 207, 327, 380, 384, 448; militarism, 27–28, 29; optimism, 4, 41, 42, 43, 54, 79, 88, 92, 95, 223, 225, 265, 334, 339, 351, 409, 414, 473, 480, 507, 527, 534, 572, 574, 597, 600; pessimism, during war, 333, 334; physical appearance, 9, 45, 47, 55, 158, 482, 493, 512, 516, 557; physical appearance, as handsome, 22, 31, 33, 35; popularity, 65, 165, 166, 216, 217, 218, 220, 273, 280, 284, 287, 288, 419, 517, 558, 564, 565, 568, 574, 607; privacy, 7, 13, 239, 371, 551, 542, 596; as a "scrootch owl," by Huey Long, 165; sensitivity, 14, 292; shrewdness, 68, 74, 99, 263, 504, 556; as "soft," 422; sphinx caricature, 327; stubbornness, 5, 13, 525, 528

PERSONAL LIFE: affair and relationship with Lucy Mercer, 33–34, 35–36, 354, 509, 511, 606; assassination attempt, 87–88, 186; birthday, sixty-third, 579; children, desire for six, 12; children and family, 12, 14, 34, 42, 43, 77, 298, 402, 526, 572; death, 411, 605–607; grandchildren, 573, 574, 605; marriage/relationship with Eleanor, 12–14, 33–36, 117, 427, 508–512, 599; portrait of, 605; sex/physical affection and, 34, 509–510; will, 574; women and, 12, 34, 35–36, 49–50, 56, 64, 122, 510, 511, 605; writing, memoirs, 328

SPEECHES AND SPEAKING STYLE: accent, in youth, 8, 9; acceptance addresses, 64, 73–74, 201–203, 346, 347, 537–538; *Alice in Wonderland* parody, 74–75; "arsenal of democracy," 360; as assistant secretary of navy, 24; from automobile, 545; at Bremerton, Washington, 544–545, 557; at Buenos Aires conference, 216–217; campaign, 18, 39, 40, 54, 70, 77, 78, 195–196, 198, 202–203, 205, 206, 207, 354–355, 356, 545, 562, 557–558, 562, 564–565, 565–566, 566–567; campaign, first major (1932), 74–75; Cleveland speech on defense, as model, 356; at Commonwealth Club, 77; disability, and standing for, 544, 545; as educating public, 424; errors/verbal mishaps, 545–546; extemporaneous, 66, 84, 126, 162, 189, 382, 431, 541, 544, 564, 565–566, 598; first, at 1920 Dutchess County Democratic picnic, 17; in Gainesville, Georgia, 283, 284; generalities/vagueness in, 21, 364; as governor, 54, 56, 58, 59; at Gridiron Dinner, 59; at Harvard, 37, 206; "I hate war," 205, 259, 270; inaugural addresses, 90, 93–94, 98, 211, 224, 225, 364, 406, 574, 607; in Kingston, Ontario, 300; at Madison Square Garden, 207; messages to Congress, 152, 330, 360–361, 597; in Miami, and assassination attempt, 87; militancy of, 394; Navy Day address, 393–394; "new deal," 73–74; "only thing...to fear is fear itself," 93, 607; Pan-American Day address, 216–217, 314; in Pittsburgh, 206; preparation methods, 544; on quarantine, in Chicago, 263–264, 264–265, 268; "rendezvous with destiny," 202–203; at Roanoke Island, 240–241; at San Diego Exposition, 190–191; for Smith nomination, 38, 52, 53; Spanish Civil War statement, 205; "stab in the back," 336, 355; State of the Union messages, 195–196, 224, 573; style, 18, 40, 58, 203, 537, 538, 597–598; to Teamsters, 557–558, 562; themes of, 27; from train platform, 77, 566; unconditional surrender statement, 463; University of Virginia address, 336, 355; war message, 405, 406–407; on wartime inflation, 429; in Washington (1944), 555; whistle-stop, *see* from train platform; writers, 84, 562; writers, Berle as, 216; writers, Cohen as, 120; writers, Corcoran as, 120, 201; writers, High as, 201; writers, MacLeish as, 570; writers, Moley as, 59, 66, 120, 124, 201; writers, Rosenman as, 55, 73, 189, 201, 202, 223, 394, 437, 544, 596, 598; writers, Sherwood as, 370, 544, 558, 604; writers, Tugwell as, 120; writing methods, 201, 544, 537, 557, 604; Yalta report, 597–598; to Youth Congress Pilgrimage, 325. *See also* Brain trust; Fireside Chats

TRAVEL AND VACATIONS, 352; airplanes and, 73, 479–480, 580–581; as assistant secretary of navy, 27, 28, 30–31, 33; Atlantic crossing, 527; by automobile, 565; to Bahamas, 158; to Buenos Aires, 215–216; campaign tours, 76–77, 195, 198, 204, 564–566; to Caribbean, 11, 286, 359; during childhood, 6, 7; to Galapagos, 298; to Germany, 6, 7, 599; as governor, in upstate New York, 59; to Hawaii, 539; on houseboat, 45–46; to Labrador, 318, 319; to Morocco, 458; to military installations and bases, 350; New England yacht trip, 115; to Pacific, 138, 286, 298, 527, 539, 540–544, 563; to Port Everglades, 371; to South America, 222; to South Carolina, Baruch's plantation, 514–515; to Tehran, 476, 479–480, 493; by train, 6, 39, 76–77, 189–190, 479–480, 551, 565, 566; to western U.S./West Coast, 189–191, 263, 535, 537; to Yalta, 578–581. *See also* Warm Springs, Georgia

WORKING METHODS AND STYLE, 120–121, 124–125, 319, 370–371, 379–380, 412, 422; as administrator, 58, 93, 120–121, 123, 125, 279, 328, 417–418; advice, ignoring and keeping own counsel, 84–85, 86, 162, 173, 255, 383; advisers and specialists, 58–59, 60–61, 66, 76, 84–85, 86, 98, 100, 101, 109, 115, 120, 123, 124, 133, 150, 189, 223, 235, 236, 253, 275, 278, 279, 306, 310, 341, 347, 350,

Roosevelt, Franklin Delano (*cont.*)
371, 374, 378, 379, 383, 384, 394, 396, 397, 401, 407, 411–412, 413, 414, 437–438, 495, 499, 504, 508, 549, 578, 581, 588; advisers, increasing dependency on, 417, 465–466, 508, 600–601; advisers/staff, fostering rivalry among, 120–121, 124, 125, 154, 201, 253, 274, 417–418, 531, 532; bedroom meetings, 124, 306, 379, 439; caution, 20, 40, 68, 94, 95, 98, 109, 110, 123, 152, 218, 240, 245, 247, 250, 277, 278, 290, 292, 293, 299, 300, 303, 320, 332, 334, 354–355, 358, 374, 380, 383, 391, 392, 394, 485, 520, 576; change and compromise, 20, 31–32, 50–51, 67–68, 98, 105, 120–124, 143, 144, 167, 169, 170, 178, 182, 186, 201, 233, 235, 236, 237, 238, 239, 242, 255, 281, 294, 370, 422, 438, 528, 532; as chief of staff, 124; as commander in chief, 341, 350, 402, 404, 409, 412, 417, 438, 539, 540, 565; contradictory goals/approaches, 39, 78, 106, 107, 115, 186; controversy, 129; credit for accidental accomplishments, 26, 159, 348, 383, 438; decision making, 55, 57, 75, 108, 124, 125, 158, 170, 236, 251, 252, 265, 290, 327, 328, 334, 335, 338, 349, 358, 368, 370, 392, 394–395, 448, 527, 531, 571; delegation of power, 280, 507–508; as devil's advocate, 125; grudges, 221, 223, 310, 502; effectiveness, 477, 482; errors, 174, 193, 194, 277, 292, 378, 383, 403; generalizations/ambiguities, 21, 22, 63, 67–68, 70, 75, 77, 80, 122, 150, 177, 178, 265–266, 300, 364, 366, 371, 422, 449; as "imperial president," 467; inaction/postponing action, 156, 189, 204, 230, 231, 253, 503, 571, 575, 595; ingratiating/use of flattery, 7, 18, 37, 44, 153, 224, 481, 541, 583; involvement, 108–109, 155, 156, 158, 187, 190, 197, 200, 204, 280, 310, 420, 446, 455, 457, 459, 465–466, 525; leadership/authority and control, 11, 12, 17, 33, 57, 84–85, 92, 106, 116, 117, 124, 160, 166, 264, 341, 368, 406, 409, 416, 422, 424, 439, 494, 501; "learning by doing" philosophy/trial and error, 17, 106; manipulation/maneuvering, 19, 27, 99, 147, 190, 223, 224; media, use of, 79–80, 99; militant tone, in reform, 240; nonpartisan/coalition approach, 59, 65, 74, 75, 76, 85, 98, 121–122, 128, 139, 143, 144, 187, 196, 322, 325, 425, 547, 568, 571; patronage, use of, 99, 153, 166, 186, 187, 197, 222; personal diplomacy, 106, 108–109, 172, 173, 174, 385, 386; pleasing all/agreeing with all, 51, 67–68, 83, 113, 124, 196, 252, 274, 386–387, 531, 533, 535; political timing and instinct, 204, 343, 545; responsibilities/agenda, 436–437; schedule/routine, 512, 514, 547, 572, 573, 582, 598, 603; secrecy, 79–81, 83–84, 108, 113, 228, 230, 232, 238, 290, 292, 300, 309, 343, 349, 365, 366, 384, 409, 508, 531, 532, 556, 601–602; security measures and, 87–88; "word is bond"/gentleman's agreement, 174, 175, 176

Roosevelt, Franklin, Jr. (son), 14, 117, 336, 572

Roosevelt, G. Hall (ER's brother), 271–272, 509

Roosevelt, Isaac, 4–5

Roosevelt, Jacobus, 4

Roosevelt, James (father), 5–6, 7, 8, 18; death of, 13; relationship with FDR, 6, 7, 34

Roosevelt, James (son), 14, 271, 289, 298, 327, 509, 513; FDR's campaigns/inaugurations and, 77, 202, 364, 536, 538, 573–547

Roosevelt, James Roosevelt (half-brother), 3

Roosevelt, John (son), 14, 34, 73, 355, 536

Roosevelt, Kermit, 261

Roosevelt, Sara Delano (mother), 5, 12, 109, 317; death of, 393, 509, 596; -ER relationship, 13–14; -FDR relationship, 6, 7, 10, 11, 13–14, 34, 42, 43, 45, 216; FDR's affair with Lucy Mercer and, 33–34, 35–36; FDR's polio and, 42, 43, 45; grandchildren and, 6, 14

Roosevelt, Theodore, 8, 11, 23, 94, 146, 196, 241, 244, 277, 537; African trip, 298; ancestry of, 4, 5; as assistant secretary of navy, 23, 27; Bull Moose party, 199; ER and, 12, 13; FDR's imitation of, 17; FDR's senate nomination and, 17–18; influence on FDR, 10, 11, 12, 15, 16–17, 19, 23, 24, 27, 30, 108, 142, 164, 196, 244, 251, 254, 577–578; New Nationalism and, 104; as Progressive, 16–17, 23, 24; Rough Riders, 342; style of, 152, 153

Roosevelt, Theodore, Jr., 196

Roosevelt Library, 327, 328, 370, 511–512

Root, Elihu, 26

Roper polls, 338, 495

Rosenberg, Alfred, 113

Rosenberg, Anna, 369, 601

Rosenman, Samuel I., 189, 207, 226, 228, 243, 263, 296, 419, 436, 437, 491, 542, 544, 557, 604; brain trust selection, 66; elections and, 346, 355, 531, 532, 533; on FDR, 55; as FDR's speech-writer, 55, 73, 189, 201, 202, 223, 394, 437, 455, 596, 598; as legal adviser, 437–438; Yalta report, 596, 598

Rosten, Leo C., 145

Rough Riders, 342

Rovere, Richard H., 354
Rowe, James, 280, 348
Royal Air Force (RAF). *See* Air force, British
Royal Navy. *See* Navy, British
Rubber industry, 242; wartime shortage, 422, 427–428, 436
Rugby, 8
Ruhr, 550, 560–561, 580
Rumania, 569
Runciman, Lord, 260, 261
Rundstedt, Karl R. G. von, 572
Rural Electrification Administration, 286, 571, 576
"Rural toryism," 241
Russian Revolution. *See* Bolshevik Revolution
Russo-Finnish War, 324–325, 326, 327
Rutherford, Lucy Mercer, 509, 511, 535, 599, 604, 605; FDR's affair with, 33–34, 35–36, 354; FDR's death and, 606
Ryan, Father John A., 270

Saar, 550, 561
Sachs, Alexander, 349
St. James Episcopal Church, 90
St. Lawrence, Gulf of, 323
St. Lawrence River, 58, 350
St. Lawrence Seaway, 436
Saint-Lô, France, 539
St. Louis, 533
St. Lucia, 352
St. Pierre, 323, 453
Saipan, 540
Sakhalin Island, 590, 591
Saki airport, 581
Salerno, 470
Sales tax, 434
San Antonio, Texas, 198
Sanctions, economic, 184, 264, 267, 291, 292; against Japan, 109, 315–316; quarantine vs., 265, 266. *See also* Blockade; Embargo; Quarantine
San Francisco, 77, 378; United Nations conference, 587, 600, 602, 603, 604, 607
San Francisco Chronicle, 114
San Diego, 183, 537, 539; Exposition, FDR speech at, 190–191
San Jacinto, 198
Sartre, Jean-Paul, 600
Saturday Evening Post, 484, 522
Saudi Arabia, 505, 593; FDR's irrigation plan for, 594–595
Savo Island, 446
Scandinavia, 317, 329–330
Schechter decision, 159, 160–164
Schenectady, New York, 8
Schlesinger, Arthur, Jr., 467
Schmitt, Waldo L., 298
Schneiderman, Rose, 50
Schofield Barracks, 541
Schuschnigg, Kurt von, 295
Science: for defense, 348–349; German, 377. *See also* Atomic bomb
Scripps Howard newpapers, 238–239
Seabury, Samuel, 69, 76. *See also* New York City: corruption in
Sears, Roebuck, 362, 418
Seattle, 543
Secret Service, 87, 88, 202, 218, 224, 598, 607
Section 7–a, 137, 161. *See also* Collective bargaining
Securities, 73; FDR's legislation on, 100, 105; regulation of, 84, 139. *See also* Securities and Exchange Commission
Securities Act, 102–103
Securities and Exchange Commission (SEC), 103, 123, 139, 147, 169, 530
Security. *See* Collective security
Security Council, 586, 587
Segregation, 245, 246, 283
Seine River, 336
Selective Service Act, 347–348
Selective service, 346, 347–348, 504; draft extension, 391
Self-determination, 387, 456–457, 488, 587, 596, 597. *See also* Democracy; Imperialism/colonialism
Senate, 29, 86, 187, 474, 530, 534; administrative reform and, 276–277, 278; anti-lynching bill in, 148; Atlantic Charter and, 387; Democrats in, 65, 141, 231, 235, 237, 285, 502, 573, 582; economic reform, 96, 129; embargo, discretionary vs. mandatory, 182–183; FDR and, 52, 96, 97, 98, 100, 103, 108, 268, 280, 311, 425–426, 467, 496; FDR as potential candidate, 38, 40; foreign aid and foreign policy, 331, 338, 352, 522, 577; holding-company bill, 168–169; inflationary tactics, 101, 103; isolationists, 311, 331, 338, 361, 368, 521–522; Japan and, 110; judicial reform and, 229, 230–232, 234, 235, 236, 238; labor and, Wagner bill, 158, 164; League of Nations and, 107; lend-lease passage, 361, 362; liberals in, 153; Long and, 146, 165; neutrality legislation and, 182–183; New Deal passage, 105, 110, 153; 1938 elections, 287; NRA and, 159; price control bill and, 430; progressives in, 154; Republicans in, 81, 287, 439, 582; right wing in, 238; social security and, 156, 164, 170, 500; soldiers' vote bill, 503; southerners in, 430; Soviet Union and, 582; State Department nominees and, 569, 570–571; taxes and, 165–166, 501, 502; United Nations, 549, 598; Versailles Treaty and, 38; Wallace nomination, 574–575; Wilson and, 494; World Court resolution, 154, 182;

Senate (*cont.*)
Yalta report, 597, 598. *See also* Democratic party: FDR's purge of
Senate Finance Committee, 81, 153, 156, 157
Senate Foreign Relations Committee, 110, 115, 182, 315, 522, 570
Senate Judiciary Committee, 236, 238
Senate Military Affairs Committee, 311
Senate Naval Affairs Committee, 38
Senior citizens. *See* Old-age insurance/benefits; Social security program
Separation of powers, 232
Sequoia, 113, 166
Seventh Division, 541
Seventh International Conference of American States. *See* Montevideo conference
Shangri-la, 436, 445, 456
Shannon, Jasper, 287
Sharecroppers, 145
Share Our Wealth program, 146, 165
Shays, Daniel, 230
Sheehan, Billy, 19, 51
Sherman Anti-Trust Act, 137, 251
Sherwood, Robert, 285, 355, 370, 411, 415, 416, 451, 464, 544, 558, 569, 604
Shipman, Fred, 370
Ships, 468, 570; aircraft carriers, 111, 409, 411, 529; in Allied invasion of France, 491, 527; for British, 359; German, 320, 372; German threat to, 321, 323; Italian, 372; Japanese, 378; merchant, 29, 363, 372, 393, 429, 480; oil tankers, 427; at Pearl Harbor, 559; shortage of, 466, 467; Soviet Union and, 319, 480, 505, 590, 592; war production and, 420. *See also* Atlantic; Navy, U.S.; Pacific; Submarines
Short, Dewey, 276
Short, Walter, 397
Shoumatoff, Elizabeth, 605, 606
Shouse, Jouett, 71, 74, 140
Siberia, 381, 383, 482, 529
Sicily, 460, 469, 492; Allied invasion of, 467, 468, 469, 526
Siegfried line, 318
Sikorski, Wladyslaw, 471
Silver, Rabbi Abba Hillel, 531
Silver, 7, 101, 111, 139, 146
Simon, John, 114
Sims, William S., 37
Sinclair, Upton, 141
Sing Sing, 37
Singapore, 216, 292, 293, 382, 528, 414, 441
Sioux Falls, South Dakota, 39
Small, John D., 420
Smaller War Plants Corporation, 419
Smith, Alfred E., 20, 56, 71, 81, 323; FDR and, 26, 38, 51–52, 52–53, 53–54, 55, 56–57, 67, 68, 69, 70, 71, 76, 81, 82, 133, 196, 566; Liberty League and, 140, 141; Nazi protest by, 112; as New York governor, 26, 38, 51–52, 55, 58, 65, 66; presidential campaigns, 51–52, 52–53, 54, 55, 72, 73
Smith, Ellison D. ("Cotton Ed"), 286, 287, 496
Smith, Gerald L. K., 186
Smith, Harold D., 278–279, 402, 421, 498
Smith, Howard W., 286, 432
Smith, Merriman, 423–424
Smith, Truman, 323
Smith-Connally (War Labor Disputes) Act, 519
Smithsonian Institution, 298, 363
Smolensk, Soviet Union, 471
Social insurance, 140, 157
Socialism, 67, 136, 141, 145, 146, 164, 204; FDR criticized as promoting, 123, 206–207, 229
Social reform/social justice, 3, 12, 15, 16, 20, 21, 67, 78, 146, 196, 217; Supreme Court threat to, 239
Social security program, 140, 141, 142, 148, 150, 151, 162, 164, 167, 170, 194, 247, 251, 433, 500, 565; passage of, 154, 155–157, 158; Republican opposition to, 207
Social Welfare, Department of, 275
Society of St. Tammany Celebration, 26
Sohier, Alice, 12, 34
Soil Conservation Act, 192, 193
Soldiers' vote bill, 496, 503, 508, 557
Solomon Islands, 446, 447
Somoza, Anastazio, 214, 316
Soong, T. V., 416
South (United States), 7, 123, 132, 144, 166, 248, 281, 345, 496; agriculture in, 145, 430; black issues/civil rights, 123–124, 148, 173, 233, 244, 245, 246–247, 283, 284, 286, 356, 508–509, 520, 532; campaigns and elections in, 65, 76, 567–568; conservatives in, 241, 281; Democratic party purge in, 282–287; Democrats in, 494, 502, 517, 530, 531–532, 534; education in, 503; electric power and, 168; FDR and, 51, 145, 200, 201, 494; FDR's opposition in, 254, 282–287, 494, 517, 530, 532; FDR support in, 67, 70, 75, 154, 244, 280–281, 283–284; industry in, 244; judicial reform bill and, 233; labor issues/working conditions, 241, 249, 281; poverty in, 254, 282–283; social security program, 155; two-thirds rule and, 65. *See also* Democratic party: southern; States' rights; Tennessee Valley Authority
South America, 51, 222, 316, 350–351, 386. *See also* Good Neighbor policy; Latin America; *names of individual countries*
South Africa, 297

South Carolina, 237, 284, 286, 496, 532; FDR's vacation at Hobcaw, 514–515, 516, 519
South Dakota, 39
Southern Pines Association, 281
Southern Railway, 5
Souvestre, Marie, 12
Soviet Union, 217, 264, 408, 441, 449–450, 487, 491, 505, 551, 589, 593, 601; Atlantic Charter and, 388; atomic bomb and, 553, 554–555; Baltic states and, 324, 388, 449, 479, 480; boundary issues, 449–450, 488; Britain and, 373, 374, 375, 449, 483, 505; China and, 266, 475, 476; Churchill and, 547–548; debts, 172, 175, 176, 592; at Dumbarton Oaks conference, 548–549; economy of, 479; Europe and, 477, 479, 568, 596, 600; FDR and, 215, 548–549, 600, 601–603; FDR's views on, 324, 325, 374, 447, 450, 481, 482, 582; FDR/U.S. negotiations with, 1933, 174–177; Finland "winter war," 324–325, 326, 327; French invasion, 449, 490; German non-aggression pact with, 318, 319, 325, 330, 449; German relations with, 173, 174, 176, 177, 489, 584, 585–586; German war with, 370, 373–374, 368, 375, 377, 393, 395, 408, 412, 451, 449–450, 458, 468, 471, 472, 479, 526, 539, 580; Hitler and, 179, 368, 377, 381; Japan and, 172, 173, 176, 369, 377, 381, 383, 396, 397, 473, 476, 478, 482, 483, 491, 493, 582, 589–590, 591; military strength, 172, 307; Pacific war and, 473, 476; Poland and, 314, 319, 471, 479, 488, 506, 548, 587–588, 589, 600, 601; postwar world and, 450, 466, 475, 486, 488–489, 490, 523, 549–550, 590; religious issues, 172, 173, 174, 175, 374; Spanish Civil War and, 269, 270; strategy of, 324, 339; at Tehran conference, 477, 479–490; three-power conference and, 375; unconditional surrender and, 463–464; United Nations organization and, 486–487, 578, 582, 600, 602, 607; U.S. recognition of, 173, 174, 175, 176, 375; U.S. relations with, 171–177, 319, 373–376, 449–450, 465, 470–473, 480, 506, 508, 548–549, 582, 589–590, 591, 600; xenophobia, 176; Yalta conference and, 577, 581–582, 600. *See also* Aid, U.S.: to Soviet Union; Siberia; Stalin, Joseph
Spain, 367, 370, 412, 454. *See also* Spanish Civil War
Spanish-American War, 10, 23, 289, 290, 427
Spanish Civil War, 204–205, 268–272, 454
Spanish Embargo Act, 270
Special interest groups, 98, 100, 273, 274, 275, 278, 497, 501
Spectator, 9
Spellman, Archbiship Francis, 175, 479
Springfield, Massachusetts, 566
Stabilization Act, 439
"Stab in the back" speech, 336, 355
Stalin, Joseph, 260, 375, 487, 495, 549; Atlantic Charter, reaction to, 388; atomic bomb and, 554–555; Baltic states and, 324; Churchill and, 449, 568–569, 590; description as "good old Uncle Joe," 375; FDR and, 174, 177, 205, 375, 449–450, 471–472, 473, 504, 506, 508, 525, 549, 553, 548, 574, 578, 583, 584, 590, 593, 600, 601–603, 604; -FDR-Churchill relationship, 373, 458, 465, 472, 473, 475, 477, 479–490, 547, 568, 583, 589; FDR compared to, 343, 366; FDR's conversations with, 480, 483–484, 486, 487–488; FDR's death and, 607; Finland and, 324–325; French invasion and, 472, 477, 482–483, 484–485, 490; German surrender negotiations, 601–602; Hitler and, 325, 449, 472; Italian campaign and, 470, 472, 473; Italian fleet and, 505; Japan/Pacific war and, 478, 482, 478, 491, 493; Jews and, 594; Moscow conference and, 475, 476; occupation strategy of, 549; Poland and, 324, 471, 504, 514, 548, 587–588, 589, 600, 601; postwar world, 471, 472–473, 476, 584, 585, 590, 591; purge, 176, 325; secrecy of, 583; at Tehran conference, 477, 479–490; territorial claims/Soviet boundaries, 449–450; unconditional surrender and, 463, 464; United Nations proposal, 586–587, 602–603, 604, 607; U.S. and, 173, 174, 175, 176, 549; war strategy, 583; at Yalta conference and agreements, 577, 578, 582, 583, 584, 585, 586, 587, 588–589, 590–591, 592, 600, 601. *See also* Soviet Union
Stalingrad, 458, 465, 468
Standard of living, 135, 225, 246, 424, 433, 500, 597. *See also* Four Freedoms
Standard Oil, 15, 290
Stark, Harold ("Betty") L., 339, 365, 370, 372, 411; Atlantic conference, 384, 386; defense policy and, 342; Japan and, 383, 397, 400; Pearl Harbor, 382, 404; war involvement, 394
Stassen, Harold, 518
State Department, 99, 107–108, 115, 474, 493, 508, 546, 607; anti-Semitism issue and, 112; Atlantic Charter and, 388; British royal family visit, 317; British view of, 260; Brussels conference and, 267, 268; Czechoslovakian crisis and, 301, 302; Declaration on Liberated Europe, 589; FDR's working style and, 107, 108–109, 172, 212, 300, 384; foreign service and, 107;

State Department (*cont.*)
France and de Gaulle's government, 453, 528; Germany/Hitler and, 314, 320, 374; Inter-American Conference and, 216; Japan and, 110, 181, 266, 267, 268, 292, 294, 379, 382, 399, 402; Latin American policy and, 212; neutrality legislation and, 181, 182, 319; postwar world and, 522; refugees from Nazism and, 296; reorganization of, 569–571, 575; Soviet Union and, 374, 449, 470–471, 476, 508, 569, 590; Soviet Union, recognition by U.S., 172, 173, 174, 177; Spanish Civil War and, 270, 271; war involvement and, 301, 337; Yalta conference, 578
State Department European Affairs Division, 585
State of the Union messages: *1936*, 195–196; *1937*, 224, 228–229, 232; *1944*, 499–501, 529; *1945*, 573
State sales tax, 167
Statesman (Boise), 165
States' rights, 16, 24, 87, 98, 227, 285, 286, 496, 497
Steel industry, 119, 137, 147, 242, 243, 249, 250, 497; European, 552, 553; Little Steel companies/decision, 243, 431, 433, 437, 438, 496, 497; war production, 418, 419, 420, 424; workers, 431, 433
Stein, Herbert, 255–256
Steiwer, Frederick, 198
Stettinius, Edward R., Jr., 376, 475, 498, 505, 549, 551, 595; as secretary of state, 569, 570, 571, 572; United Nations organization and, 602, 604; Yalta conference, 577, 578, 579, 581, 583, 585, 586, 590
Stilwell, Joseph ("Vinegar Joe"), 442, 443, 469, 561–562
Stimson, Henry L., 18, 99, 125, 172, 384, 386, 411, 421, 422, 492, 520, 553, 560–561, 580, 605; at Arcadia conference, 412, 414; defense policy, 342, 347, 368, 369, 374, 392, 394, 447, 450, 451; on FDR's working methods, 448; Japan and, 109, 400, 401, 404; postwar Germany and, 550–551; as secretary of state under Hoover, 63, 64, 75, 83, 107, 212
Stimson doctrine, 83, 109, 368
Stock market, 105; New Deal and, 90; 1929 crash, 60, 126; 1933 collapse, 126; recession and, 248, 250, 254; recovery and, 119, 248; social security legislation and, 150
Stone, Harlan F., 161, 192, 574
"Stop Roosevelt" movement, 70, 71
Stresa conference, 183, 184
Strikes, 26, 240; coal, 370, 371; farm, 133–134; FDR as arbitrator, 138; general, 138; longshoremen's, 138; Memorial Day massacre, 243–244, 247; Montgomery Ward, 519–520; as NRA by-products, 137–138; post-WWI, 39; Pullman, 7; railroad (1944), 496–497; sit-down, 234, 242–243; textile, 145; violence and, 242–244; war production and, 370, 371, 431, 432, 438; wildcat, 432. *See also* Collective bargaining; Labor; Unions
Stuart, Gilbert, 4
Submarines, 420; FDR on, 393; German, 359, 368, 369, 372, 383, 384, 386–387, 392–394, 411, 427, 447, 459, 460, 466, 473; German, in World War I, 29, 30; Japanese, 405, 406; U.S., 350
Subsidies, 436, 438
Suckley, Margaret ("Daisy"), 511–512, 604, 605, 606
Sudetenland, 298, 299, 300, 301–304, 305
Suez Canal, 586, 593
Sullivan, "Big Tim," 21
Sumners, Hatton, 229, 230, 233, 246
Supreme Court, 161, 368, 430, 439, 535; AAA ruling, 191–192, 193; conservatives on, 225, 226, 227, 233, 235, 236; FDR and, 163, 193, 194, 200; FDR's appointments/"Roosevelt Court," 238–239; FDR's packing, 194; liberal minority on, 227, 231, 234; minimum wage ruling, 194, 234; National Labor Relations Act and, 234; New Deal and, 144, 157, 159, 160–164, 170, 191–192, 193, 194, 226, 227, 228, 229, 230, 232, 234–235, 236 239; as 1936 campaign issue, 193, 194, 199, 206; NRA rulings, 160–164, 170, 194, 226, 228; oil legislation ruling, 162; Railroad Retirement Act ruling, 157; *See also* Judicial reform
Surplus food program, 131–132
Surprise, 109
Sutherland, George, 239
Swanson, Claude, 262, 291
Sweden, 215, 543
Switzerland, 117, 265, 601
Szilard, Leo, 348

Taber, John, 276
Taconic Parkway, 56
Taft, Charles, 244
Taft, Robert A., 287, 315, 342, 359, 374, 425, 439, 523, 566; as FDR critic, 425–426; as presidential candidate, 327, 335,
Taft, William Howard, 10, 18, 23, 59, 152, 226, 342
Talmadge, Eugene, 245
Tammany Hall, 204, 284; criticism of FDR for, 63–64, 67, 69–70, 76; FDR's working relationship with, 25–26, 57, 63, 64; FDR vs., 18–19, 19–20, 21, 22, 25, 38,

51, 67, 75–76; reform legislation and, 20, 21; "surrender" of, 19
Tanks, 419, 427, 468, 473
Tariffs, 73, 83, 84, 105, 111, 115, 116, 160, 215; as campaign issue, 74, 78. *See also* Economy: nationalism vs. internationalism; Trade
Taussig, Charles, 252
Tax(es), 57, 77, 496, 501; capital gain, 253; corporate, 164, 167, 192; estate, 164, 165, 167; FDR and, 62, 253, 282, 501, 502, 530; FDR on, 60, 164; income, 19, 128, 164, 167, 435, 501; increases, 62, 79–80, 81, 88, 128, 331, 496, 500, 501–502; inheritance, 164, 165, 167; New Deal programs and, 130, 149; 1935 "soak the rich" bill, 164–166, 167, 169, 170, 192; 1944 bill, 496, 500, 501–502, 534; payroll, and unemployment insurance, 148; politics and, 433–434; poll, 284, 532; processing, 86, 130, 133, 191–192; profits, 192, 193; Republican critics of, 198; state sales, 167, 434; unemployment, 150; wartime, 419, 423, 424, 425, 430, 432, 433–435; wealth distribution and, 164, 167; withholding, 501. *See also* Social security program
Taylor, Edward T., 153, 169
Teamsters Union, 545, 562; FDR's speech to, 557–558, 562
Teapot Dome, 287
Technology. *See* Atomic bomb
Tee Harbor, Alaska, 543
Tehran conference (1943), 476, 477, 479–490, 491, 493–494, 495, 497, 522, 529, 549, 578, 581, 588; Declaration, 490; FDR at, 494, 495; FDR-Stalin relationship at, 583; Polish issues, 587, 591; Stalin/Soviets at, 506, 590; success of, 493; U.S.-Soviet agreement/position, 480, 481, 482
Television, FDR's views on, 306
Temporary Emergency Relief Administration (TERA), 61
Temporary National Economic Commission (TNEC), 257
Tennessee, 83, 153, 226, 521, 576
Tennessee River, 87
Tennessee Valley Authority (TVA), 87, 100, 105, 122, 254, 547, 576; Commonwealth and Southern Utility Company vs., 342; modifications to, 147, 148; Supreme Court ruling on, 193
Teschen, Czechoslovakia, 303
Texas, 68, 70, 121, 168, 169, 229, 280, 353, 497; anti-lynching legislation and, 247; Democratic party in, 517, 531–532; FDR supporters, 72, 73; FDR's visit to, 198; Garner and, 68, 70, 71; Johnson and, 235; oil, 428
Texas Regulars movement, 517
Textile industry, 119, 127, 145, 244
Thailand, 382, 395, 400
Theodore Roosevelt Memorial, 196
Third Reich, 111, 178, 179, 314. *See also* Germany
Third term issue, 322, 327–328, 236, 341, 343, 356; opposition to, 341, 345, 346. *See also* Elections: *1940*
This I Remember (ER), 475
Thomas, Elmer, 101
Thomas, Norman, 67, 145
Thomas Amendment, 101, 103, 133
Thompson, Dorothy, 295, 545
Thompson, Malvina ("Tommy"), 326
Tilden, Samuel J., 18
Time magazine, 495; FDR criticism in, 158; on FDR, 31, 523, 557; on FDR assassination attempt, 88; on FDR's health, 516, 598; on FDR's mental state, during war, 441; on FDR's reaction to Supreme Court ruling on New Deal, 163; on hemispheric defense and naval bases, 350; on Inter-American Conference, 217; on UN draft charter, 523–524; on Willkie's criticism of FDR, 432; on WPA patronage, 189
Tito, Josip Broz, 483, 505, 549, 604
Tobruk, British surrender at, 450
Today magazine, 201; on FDR's tax proposal, 165, 166
Todhunter School, 37, 46
Togo, Shigenori, 397
Tojo, Hideki, 396, 539
Tokyo, 291, 383, 396, 397, 398; U.S. bombing of, 444–445, 529
Toledo Bar Association, 194
Topeka, 77, 203
TORCH (code name), 451. *See also* Africa, French North: Allied invasion
Totalitarianism, 93, 276, 293; threat of, 209, 212, 215, 294
Townsend, Francis, 141, 145, 146, 156, 204
Townsend movement/plan, 145, 156, 157, 158
Trade, 84, 89, 104, 108, 111, 171–172, 217, 388; British, 260, 359, 363; European dictators and, 314; Japan and, 292–293, 397, 389, 399; reciprocal, 115, 260; reciprocal, with Latin America, 212, 214–215, 218, 220. *See also* Tariffs
Trade associations, 136, 157, 158
Treasury Department, 89, 95, 123, 166, 250, 256, 279, 310, 320, 363, 433, 501, 550; banking crisis and, 90; objection to public spending, 149; social security and, 150
Trevelyan, George Macaulay, 312
Triangle Shirtwaist factory, 20, 21
Trident conference, 468–469
Trinidad, 307, 350, 352

Tripartite Pact, 379–380, 397, 398, 408
Tripoli, 291
Trondheim, Norway, 526
Troubetzkoy, Prince Paul, 14
Troy, New York, 137
Truman, Harry S., 278, 546, 568, 574, 576, 591, 598; FDR's illness and death and, 598, 606; Pendergast machine and, 534, 537; as vice presidential nominee, 530, 533, 534, 535, 536–537
Truman Doctrine, 491
Trusts and antitrust action, 15, 19, 104, 251. *See also* Sherman Anti-Trust Act
TUBE ALLOYS (atomic bomb code name), 555
Tubman, President, 520
Tugwell, Rexford G., 109, 121, 148; agriculture and, 66, 86, 103; brain trust and, 223; economic planning and, 84, 252, 253; as FDR speechwriter, 120; industrial reform and, 104
Tully, Grace, 202, 371, 404, 409, 512, 603
Tulsa, 559
Tunis, 492, 493
Tunisia, 458, 468
Turkey, 467, 482, 483, 491
Turner, Frederick Jackson, 11
Turner, Kelly, 383
Tuscaloosa, USS, 318
Tweedsmuir, Lord, 309
Tydings, Millard, 232, 282, 286, 287, 425

U-boats. *See* Submarines, German
Ukraine, 489, 586
Unconditional surrender, 453, 463–464, 469, 525; FDR's statement on, 463
Underground, French, 527
Underground, Polish, 548
Underprivileged, 61; agricultural surpluses for, 131–132; budget cuts and, 191, 248–249; economic bill of rights for, 573; FDR's concern for, 9, 15, 50, 61–62, 99, 128, 132, 142–143, 224–226, 248–249, 282–283; FDR's power to aid, vs. Supreme Court, 224–226, 232; FDR's tax programs and, 434; as FDR supporters, 356, 357; second New Deal programs for, 142–143; TR and, 17; "trickle down" theory of Hoover and, 127; worldwide, U.S. aid for, 530; wealthy vs., ER on, 429. *See also* Four Freedoms
Unemployment, 7, 79, 119, 131, 142, 143, 144, 192, 248, 250, 255, 500; Democratic popularity during, FDR on, 52; during depression, under Hoover, 65; Dewey on, 563; FDR's concern over, 99; FDR's early approach to, 60, 61; food distribution, 131–132; patronage and, 99; postwar, avoiding, 503, 573; private enterprise and, 249; recession and, 184; refugees and, 296; relief programs, 67, 100, 134–135, 138; rural planning and, 85; work week limits, 104, 127. *See also* Civilian Conservation Corps; Civil Works Administration; Public Works Administration; Works Progress Administration; Work relief program
Unemployment insurance, 61, 137, 148, 157
Union of Polish Patriots, 471
Union party, 204, 207
Unions, 148, 156, 158, 159, 426, 431–432, 534, 566; FDR's support, 158, 203–204; membership drives/growth of, 241–242; Montgomergy Ward and, 519–520; violence and, 242–244. *See also* Collective bargaining; Labor; Strikes
United Auto Workers (UAW), 138, 243
United Mine Workers, 167, 203, 204, 241, 243
United Nations, 219, 325, 449, 469, 473, 495, 578, 582, 586–587, 597, 600, 604; charter for, 523–524; FDR's ideas for international organization, 50, 466, 486, 582, 597; FDR's postwar goals and, 356, 418, 436, 450, 466–467, 486–487, 499, 500, 503, 504–505, 517–518, 521–524, 578; nonpartisan discussion on, 559–560; origin of, in goals of Atlantic Charter, 415–416; police role, 559–560; signing of manifesto, 416; support for, 598; voting procedure, 586–587, 602–603, 604; Yalta discussion on, 586–587, 586–587, 597, 602–603. *See also* Dumbarton Oaks conference; San Francisco: United Nations conference
United States: atomic bomb and, 553–555; Churchill/Grey on, 410; European war and, 321, 322, 323, 325, 329; fear of war in, 84, 177, 178, 204 (*see also* Isolationists); FDR's death and, 606; Hitler's view of, 179, 303; hysteria and rumors following Pearl Harbor, 407; imperialism of, 211, 213, 217; international role/leadership, 80, 94, 212, 290; morale of, FDR's effect on, 88, 92, 334, 413, 441; national interests, 106, 289, 314, 322, 323, 325, 363, 412; reaction to *Kristallnacht*, 313, 314; postwar world, 466, 475, 478, 552, 556; rearmament/war preparedness, 258, 259, 305, 306, 307, 310, 315, 318, 321, 329, 332, 334, 335, 339, 349–350, 347, 358, 359, 361, 364, 365, 366, 368, 370, 394, 395, 396, 397, 399, 441; refugee policy, 295, 296–298, 325, 593, 594; state of emergency declared, 371; war involvement and, 259, 261, 265, 343, 354–356. *See also* Aid, U.S.; Armed forces, U.S.; Army, U.S.; Economy; Foreign policy; Public opinion/polls; South (United States); United

Nations: FDR's postwar goals and; West (United States)
United States Employment Service (USES), 60
United States Steel, 243, 376, 475, 569
United Steel Workers, 437
Untermyer, Samuel, 19
Uranium committee, 348. *See also* Atomic bomb
U.S. Army in World War II (Watson), 310–311
Utilities. *See* Electric power; Holding companies; Public Utility Holding Act; Public utility holding companies; Tennessee Valley Authority

Van Devanter, Willis, 234, 236, 238
Van Rosenvelt, Claes Martenszen, 4
Van Rosenvelt, Nicholas, 4
Van Sweringen railroad interests, 71
Vandenberg, Arthur, 198, 232, 315, 316, 352, 362, 521, 522, 523, 582; on FDR, 425–426; as presidential candidate, 327, 335;
Vanderbilt, Cornelius, 5–6
Vargas, Getúlio, 216, 316
Vassar College, 20, 567
V-E day, 552
Venezuela, 218, 386, 572; as refugee destination, 298
Vera Cruz, Mexico, 28
Verdun, 453; Battle of, 337
Vermont, 207
Versailles conference, 31, 39, 218, 577
Versailles Treaty, 112, 173, 183, 233, 388, 474; Hitler and, 259; U.S. ratification of, 38
Veterans: benefits, 186, 192, 193, 251; benefits, and Bonus Army, 75; benefits, and FDR cuts/congressional restoration of, 96, 97, 105; FDR's plan for settlement in Alaska and Aleutians, 543; *See also* GI Bill of Rights; Soldiers' vote bill
Vichy government, 337, 367, 374, 382, 412, 456, 461; FDR's strategy for North African invasion, 453, 454–455, 457
Victory Program, 392
Victory Tax, 435
Vienna, 295, 547, 583
Vigilante citizen committees, 242
Villard, Oswald Garrison, 27
Vincennes, Indiana, 198
Vinson, Fred M., 496
Vinson-Trammell Act, 179
Virginia, 229, 232, 276, 286, 432, 517; University of, 336
Vistula, 548
Vladivostok, 176
Voice of America, 469
Voluntarism, 428
Voroshilov, Kliment E., 176, 481
Voting, 557; poll tax, 284, 532; registration drives, 557, 567; soldiers' bill for, 496, 503; woman suffrage, 20

Wadsworth, James W., 140
Wage(s), 138, 141, 157, 158, 248, 249, 253, 281; control/freezing, 93, 432, 433, 435, 439; cuts in, following NRA ruling, 161, 162; increases (1944), 496; legislation as hostage to court reform, 228; Little Steel decision, 431–432, 433, 437, 438, 496, 497; minimum, 104, 157, 194, 234, 281–282; National War Labor Board and, 431–432, 433; NRA and, 120, 126, 127, 137, 143, 160, 161, 162; prices vs., 429, 431; railroad union and, 496; urban vs. rural, 137; wartime, 425, 426, 429, 431–432, 433, 437, 438; for women, 20
Wagner, Robert F., 20, 26, 98, 104, 138, 148, 160, 153, 155, 157, 158, 159, 246, 248, 276, 344
Wagner Act, 158, 159, 160, 164, 241. *See also* National Labor Relations Act
Waikiki Beach, 541
Wake Island, 380, 406
Walker, Frank, 353
Walker, Jimmy, 69–70, 75–76, 536
Wall Street Journal, 90–91, 433
Wallace, Henry A., 115, 154, 194, 405, 502, 546, 574; agriculture and, 86, 103, 131, 154, 274; Chinese ambassador, 571; on FDR's mental clarity, 573; "guru letters," 353, 530; as Jones' replacement/secretary of commerce, 571, 575; New Deal planning, in agriculture, 86; supporters of, vs. FDR, 546–547; as vice presidential nominee, 345–346, 353, 529–530, 531, 533, 535, 536, 537, 546–547, 575, 603
Wallonia, 466
Wallowa Mountains, 535
Walsh, Bishop James Edward, 380
Walsh, David I., 355, 566
Walsh, Father Edmund A., 173
Walsh, Thomas J., 71, 76
War agencies, 417, 418, 425, 426, 439; World War I, 93, 178. *See also* War Production Board
War bonds, 424, 430, 432, 435
Warburg, James, 84, 101
War debts, 82, 83, 102, 105, 110–111, 171, 359; British-French-U.S. negotiations on, 110–111, 113, 115
War Department, U.S., 321, 326, 347
War Industries Board, 126, 418
War Labor Board, 431, 437, 439, 519, 520
War Labor Disputes Act, 519
Warm Springs, Georgia, 46–47, 48, 53–54,

Warm Springs, Georgia (*cont.*)
55, 56, 60, 110, 147, 192, 277, 283, 296, 456, 503, 570, 572, 603, 604, 605, 606; ER and, 46; FDR's contact with people of, 91 124, 423; FDR's funeral procession, 607; security at, 88; southern racism in, 244–245; underprivileged in, 283
Warm Springs Foundation, 47, 64, 166
War Office, British, 459
War Plans Division, 383, 411
War Powers Act, 436, 437–438, 439, 417
War production, 319, 349, 364, 372, 391–392, 409, 410, 417–422, 433, 455, 468, 473, 504; of aircraft, 303, 308, 309, 310, 311, 330, 339; civilian production vs., 415, 418, 419, 420, 421, 422–424, 496; construction and, 420; as deterrent to Hitler, 306, 307; FDR's plant visits, 423; FDR's power over, 417; German vs. U.S. capabilities, 308; goals/level of, 418, 422; of munitions and armaments, 3236–327, 495; reconversion, 495, 504; of ships, 420; small businesses vs. corporations, 419–420; strikes and, 370, 371, 432; U.S. potential, 308, 319, 410. *See also* Rationing; War Production Board (WPB)
War Production Board (WPB), 126, 418–422, 425, 428, 438, 499; army vs., 419, 421, 422; personnel, 420, 421–422; small business and, 419. *See also* War production
War referendum amendment. *See* Ludlow Amendment
Warren, Charles, 181
Warren, George F., 100, 101
Warren, Lindsay, 278
Warsaw, 318, 321; uprising, 548, 550
Washington, D.C., 75, 196, 475, 543, 544, 555, 557; Churchill in, 409–410; de Gaulle in, 527–528, 599; Dumbarton Oaks conference in, 549; FDR's return to, after 1944 election, 568, 572; FDR's return to, after Tehran, 491; FDR's return to, after Yalta, 595, 597, 598; as headquarters for Combined Chiefs of Staff/joint war effort, 415; war recruitment in, 407. *See also* Trident conference
Washington Navy Yard, 493
Washington Star, 186
Washington State, 298
Watson, Edwin M. ("Pa"), 326, 474, 595, 596
Watson, Mark, 310–311
Wave of the Future, The (Anne Lindbergh), 364
Wavell, Archibald, 414
Weapons and arms. *See* Atomic bomb; Disarmament; War production
Wedemeyer, Albert, 459
"Weekly Index of Business Activity" (*New York Times*), 75
Welfare, Department of, 276, 278
Welles, Sumner, 8 212–213, 291, 306, 466, 470, 553; at Arcadia conference, 412; Atlantic conference and, 384, 387; Brussels conference/nine-power conference and, 266; as Cuban ambassador, 212–213; European peace mission (1940), 329; as foreign policy expert, 51; Hull and Bullitt vs., 108, 212, 474–475; Japan and, 380; prewar activities (1939), 307, 316, 318; on quarantine plans, 263; Soviet Union and, 374, 474
Weona II, 45
West Indies, 4, 39
West Indies, French, 337
West Point, 364
West (United States), 168; coast area, fear of attack, 407, 445; FDR and, 51, 67, 70, 75, 76, 138, 189–191, 282; inflationary forces in, 101, 103
West Virginia, 123, 283, 565–566
Weygand, Maxime, 367, 454
Wharton, Edith, 8, 12
Wharton School, 66
Wheeler, Burton K., 139, 146, 168, 344, 362, 384, 523; judicial reform and, 231, 232–233, 234, 235, 238
White, Walter, 123
White, William Allen, 199, 204, 210, 214, 246, 279, 352
White House: FDR's funeral service in, 607; New Year's Eve, 1942, at, 458; 1945 inaugural at, 573–574; security, following Pearl Harbor, 405; wartime cutbacks, 435
White Russia, 586
White supremacy, in South, 233, 244, 246, 283, 520, 532
Whose Constitution? (Wallace), 194
Wickard, Claude, 436
Wilhelmina, Queen of the Netherlands, 330, 599
Williams, Aubrey, 255, 284, 571, 576
Willkie, Wendell, 345, 375, 418, 432, 444, 518, 522, 530, 560; as Commonwealth and Southern president, 166, 169; as presidential candidate, 342–343, 346, 347, 350, 352–353, 354, 355, 357, 562
Wilmington, Delaware, 566
Wilson, Ambassador, 314
Wilson, Charles E., 420, 421, 422
Wilson, Edmund, 79
Wilson, M. L., 103
Wilson, Woodrow, 18, 26, 28–29, 38–39, 84, 123, 144, 152–153, 177, 181, 210, 211, 218, 224, 227, 240, 244, 294, 345, 406, 408, 449, 494, 521; end of administration, 38, 568, 577, 606; FDR and, 39, 51, 65, 82; foreign affairs, 28, 172, 214; Fourteen Points, 360, 464; influence on FDR, 16, 23, 31, 33, 98, 108, 142, 385, 578; League of Nations and, 31, 38, 38,

68–69, 107, 556; New Freedom, 24–25, 104, 251; as president, 22–23, 29; progressivism, 51, 71, 240, 241; self-determination and, 388; Versailles, 39, 173, 233, 259, 474; World War I and, 28, 29, 30, 31, 93, 195, 299, 322, 329, 358, 372, 409, 418, 425
Wilson Conference, New York State, 22
Wilson Dam, 87
Winant, John G., 363, 364, 533
Windsor, Duke of, 351
Wisconsin, 231, 518; University of, 150
Wise, Rabbi Stephen S., 69, 112, 531
Withholding tax, 501
Witte, Edwin E., 150, 157
Wolff, Karl, 601
Woman suffrage, 20
Women, 64; antilynching legislation and, 246; in the depression, 79, 122; equal pay for, FDR and, 20; ER's work for causes of, 12; FDR and, 12; New Deal appointments and, 122; politics and, 49–50, 56; voting rights, 20; working conditions, 12, 225, 234; work protection, 20
Women's Trade Union League, 50
Wood, Robert E., 362
Woodin, William, 90, 95, 133
Woodring, Harry H., 310, 326
Woolley, Mary, 210
Worcester, Massachusetts, 566
Work relief program, 148, 149, 150–151, 154, 155, 170, 186, 187–190; budget cuts in, 191; funding, 168, 284, 285; politics/patronage and, 187, 188, 189; public works vs., 186. *See also* Relief programs
Work hours/work week, 104, 141, 249, 253, 431, 432; FDR on, 249; FDR's protection of, 157, 158; increase in, following NRA ruling, 160, 161; labor's view of, 158; legislation, 228, 281; NRA and, 126, 127, 143, 160, 161; wartime control, 426
Workman's compensation, 20, 137, 158
Work program. *See* Civil Works Administration (CWA)
Works Progress Administration (WPA), 142, 158, 186, 187–189, 192, 222, 248, 250, 284, 285, 310, 425, 550; arts and, 187–188; blacks in, 245, 365; criticism/opponents of, 188, 287; FDR on, 189; patronage and, 189; as political liability/asset, 186, 189; projects of, 187–188, 232
World Court, 68, 154, 182, 523
World War I, 28–31, 70, 123, 125, 126, 337, 341, 380, 410, 426, 462, 505; British/Churchill and, 332, 385; defense legislation of, 322; economic controls during, 93; equipment, 180, 331, 336, 350, 359, 541; FDR during, as assistant secretary of navy, 16, 23–24, 25, 26–32, 28–31, 37–38, 73, 82, 109, 377, 409, 421; Hoover and, 325; legislation, 322, 417; Liberty Loan drives, 136; profit investigation, 181, 182; shortages and rationing, 427; statutes. 341; Truman in, 534; U.S. economic gains in, 363; U.S. troop allotment, 386; veterans of, 75; war bond drives during, 435; war agencies, 178, 418. *See also* War debts
World War II, 316–317, 529, 593; British entry, 321; civilians, effect on, 422–424, 426–427; FDR on, from Lincoln's Second Inaugural, 538; FDR's conviction that U.S. entry unavoidable, 365, 394; FDR's nonpartisan approach to, 425; FDR's powerlessness and, 289–290, 300; FDR's strategy of aid/protection, 321–322, 323, 334, 337, 339–340, 341, 347, 349–351, 356, 358, 359, 361, 364, 365, 366, 368; FDR's strategy to avoid, 106, 107, 109, 114, 171, 172, 177, 178, 179, 181, 183–184, 191, 195, 215–216, 258–260, 289, 290, 299–300, 301, 302–303, 303–304, 305–306, 307, 314–315, 318, 319–320, 343, 350, 354–356, 358, 486–487; FDR's strategy to avoid, conference plan, 184, 205, 215, 216, 218, 259, 265, 294, 302, 314; French entry, 321; military planning, 334, 338, 339–340, 350–351; onset, in Polish Corridor, 111, 321; as "phony war," 329; "politics of comfort" in, 426; postwar world, *see* United Nations; reparations, 585–586, 604; shortages and rationing, 382, 424, 427–428; threat of/as imminent, 154, 190–191, 195, 215, 216, 218, 250, 294, 299–300, 305, 311, 313, 314, 317, 318; U.S. entry and FDR's war message, 404, 405, 406–407; U.S. goals, 384, 385, 418 (*see also* Four Freedoms); U.S. organization/agencies and personnel, 319, 341–342, 347, 349, 410–411; U.S. public opinion on, 422–423, 424; U.S. war resolutions, 407, 408. *See also* Aid, U.S.; Arcadia conference; Atlantic; Cairo conferences; Churchill, Winston; Czechoslovakia: Sudetenland crisis; France; Germany; Great Britain; Hitler, Adolf; Italy; Japan; Pacific; Pearl Harbor; Poland: Germany and; Selective service; Soviet Union; Stalin, Joseph; Tehran conference; Unconditional surrender; United States: rearmament/war preparedness; War production; Yalta conference
Wotje, 261
Writers, WPA and, 187–188
Wyman, David, 298
Wyzanski, Charles, Jr., 121, 226

Yale University, 210, 606
Yalta conference, 537, 555, 577, 578–592, 597, 600, 604; atmosphere of, 589; atomic bomb and, 554; facilities, 581–582; FDR's journey to, 578–579, 580–581; FDR's

Yalta conference (*cont.*)
mental state at, 580–581, 583–584, 598; FDR's report on, 595, 596, 597–598, 600, 601, 602; France, discussions on, 584–585; Germany's future, 584–586; in Malta, 579–580; negotiations/agenda, 582–592; Poland, discussions on, 587–589; secrecy of, 577, 602–603; Soviet requests/agreements, 589–590, 591, 600, 601, 602–603; U.S. advisers attending, 578; United Nations discussions, 586–587, 597, 602–603; war reparations, 585–586
Yamamoto, Isoroku, 381, 445
Yangtze, 262, 290
Yarnell, Harry E., 268, 291
Yenan, 561
Yorktown (carrier), 445, 446
Yorkvill, New York, 54
Young, Owen D., 106, 253
Youth Congress. *See* American Youth Congress
Yugoslavia, 368, 483, 505, 547, 569, 604
Yunnan, 469

Zangara, Joseph, 87–88
Zeros, 446
Zionists, FDR and, 594
Zita, Empress of Austria, 509, 553